THE MESSAGE OF THE PSALTER

By the same author

The Songs of Ascents:
Psalms 120 to 134 in the Worship of Jerusalem's Temples

Messiah ben Joseph

Jesus: The Incarnation of the Word

The Message of the Psalter

An Eschatological Programme in the Book of Psalms

DAVID C. MITCHELL

CAMPBELL
PUBLISHERS
GLASGOW SCOTLAND

CAMPBELL
PUBLISHERS

CampbellPublishers.com

Copyright © 2003 David C. Mitchell

First published in 1997 by Sheffield Academic Press in the Journal for the Study
of the Old Testament Supplement Series 252 (ISBN 1-85075-689-9)

Second edition: Campbell Publishers 2023

The author has asserted his moral right under the
Copyright, Designs and Patents Act, 1988, to be identified
as the author of this work

Hard cover ISBN: 978-1-916619-00-5

BrightMorningStar.org

Preface to the Second Edition

In 2003, Continuum bought Sheffield Academic Press and remaindered this book, whereupon the copyright reverted to myself. Therefore, since it has been difficult to obtain for some years – copies were selling on Amazon for $2,999 – I re-issue here the original text of the 1997 book, complete except for the advertisement for JSOT titles which ended the original book.

I am grateful to all who have read and cited this book over the last twenty-five years, and for its enduring impact on Psalms studies. My basic hypothesis, that the Book of Psalms was redacted as messianic prophecy, has not changed. Some said I was reading Christian pre-suppositions into the Psalms. But it should have been clear to anyone who read the book that the messianic programme which I outline in the Psalms was foreshadowed in the Baal Cycle, runs through the prophets, and continues into rabbinic literature. It is not an exclusively Christian programme.

Supplementary to this book, I wrote an addendum on the Psalms of the Sons of Korah: '"God Will Redeem My Soul from Sheol": The Psalms of the Sons of Korah' in *JSOT* 30.3 (2006) pp. 365–84. Also, in response to an article by G.H. Wilson, I published a general defence of my hypothesis, called 'Lord, Remember David: G.H. Wilson and The Message of the Psalter' in *Vetus Testamentum* 56 (2006) pp. 526–48.

Readers may also benefit from my *Songs of Ascents* (2015) which treats that group of psalms in detail. They may also like my *Messiah ben Joseph* (2016) for the fourth chapter ('Messiah ben Joseph in the Psalms') and the eleventh (revised translations of the midrashim found here in Appendix I).

Although my basic hypothesis has not changed, I now reject any idea that Psalm 110 was written by anyone other than David (p. 258). In the fourth and fifth chapters of my *Jesus: The Incarnation of the Word* (2021), I show that he could only have written it in a revelation of the Holy Spirit, just as Jesus says in Matthew 22.43.

Because this is a reprint of the original book, original typographic errors remain. In particular, the Talmud citation on page 14 should read:

כל הנביאים כולן לא נתנבאו אלא לימות המשיח
All the prophets prophesied only concerning the days of Messiah

David C. Mitchell
Brussels
May 2023

CONTENTS

ACKNOWLEDGMENTS

This book developed out of my doctoral research conducted at New College, Edinburgh, from 1992 to 1995. It is my pleasant duty to thank New College Senate, who kindly provided grants to assist in my research, and Edinburgh University Accommodation Services, who supported me free of charge throughout most of my period of study, first as an Assistant Warden and later on a scholarship. I acknowledge their kindness with deep gratitude.

My thanks are due also to the staff of New College for their unstinting assistance. My principal supervisor, Dr I.W. Provan, provided me with sound advice on every aspect of my work, and combined a generally easy-going approach with rigorous criticism as occasion required. Dr A.P. Hayman, my second supervisor for the last two and a quarter years, gave meticulously detailed advice on every aspect of rabbinics and Hebrew translation. He too was not unwilling to wield the critical knife when occasion demanded, a characteristic for which I am most grateful. My thanks go also to Professor J.C.L. Gibson, my second supervisor in the first year of my research. His suggestion that I concentrate on imagery rather than language led me to discover the seeds of this hypothesis.

A work of this scope also required specialist knowledge in several fields, and other New College tutors generously provided this, despite their busy timetables. Mr D. Wright checked my work on patristics. Professor J.C. O'Neill reviewed the New Testament section. Dr T. Lim read and commented on the Qumran material. Dr N. Wyatt advised me on the Ugaritic texts. To them and to other New College tutors, such as Professor A.G. Auld and Dr K. Vanhoozer, who taught me languages and interpretation respectively, I am most grateful. My thanks are due also to New College's ever-willing Library staff for their congenial help.

The reader will notice that I employ basic Hebrew terms in English transliteration: *bet* (house, dynasty), *malkut* (kingdom, empire, sovereignty), *mashiah* (anointed divine king; I sometimes use this term to avoid the full eschatological implications of English 'Messiah') and *shalom* (well-being, harmony, peace). They do not translate easily into English and I assume that the majority of readers will understand them.

Finally, I thank my parents for their support and assistance in many ways over many years. It was they who first taught me the Bible. To them this thesis is gratefully and respectfully dedicated.

ABBREVIATIONS

AB	Anchor Bible
ANET	J.B. Pritchard (ed.), *Ancient Near Eastern Texts*
BDB	F. Brown, S.R. Driver and C.A. Briggs, *Hebrew and English Lexicon of the Old Testament*
BETL	Bibliotheca ephemeridum theologicarum lovaniensium
BHM	Jellinek (ed.), *Bet ha-Midrash*
Bib	*Biblica*
B K	*Bibel und Kirche*
BTB	*Biblical Theology Bulletin*
BTFT	*Bijdragen: Tijdschrift voor Filosofie en Theologie*
BZAW	Beihefte zur ZAW
CBQ	*Catholic Biblical Quarterly*
CCSG	Corpus Christianorum series Graeca
CCSL	Corpus Christianorum series Latina
CH	*Church History*
CNEBC	Cambridge New English Bible Commentary
ConBOT	Coniectanea biblica, Old Testament
CPG	Geerard (ed.), *Clavis Patrum Graecorum*
CPL	Dekkers (ed.), *Clavis Patrum Latinorum*
CRAIBL	*Comptes rendus de l'Académie des inscriptions et belles-lettres*
DJD	Discoveries in the Judaean Desert
DNEB	Die Neue Echter Bibel
EncJud	*Encyclopaedia Judaica*
ETL	*Ephemerides theologicae lovanienses*
ExpTim	*Expository Times*
GCS	Griechische christliche Schriftsteller
HAR	*Hebrew Annual Review*
HAT	Handbuch zum Alten Testament
HBS	Herders biblische Studien
HDR	Harvard Dissertations in Religion
HSM	Harvard Semitic Monographs
HTKNT	Herders theologischer Kommentar zum Neuen Testament
HTR	*Harvard Theological Review*
HUCA	*Hebrew Union College Annual*
ICC	International Critical Commentary
IEJ	*Israel Exploration Journal*
Int	*Interpretation*
ITQ	*Irish Theological Quarterly*
JBL	*Journal of Biblical Literature*

JBQ	*Jewish Bible Quarterly*
JCS	*Journal of Cuneiform Studies*
JETS	*Journal of the Evangelical Theological Society*
JJS	*Journal of Jewish Studies*
JNES	*Journal of Near Eastern Studies*
JQR	*Jewish Quarterly Review*
JSNT	*Journal for the Study of the New Testament*
JSNTSup	*Journal for the Study of the New Testament*, Supplement Series
JSOT	*Journal for the Study of the Old Testament*
JSOTSup	*Journal for the Study of the Old Testament*, Supplement Series
JSP	*Journal for the Study of the Pseudepigrapha*
JSS	*Journal of Semitic Studies*
JTS	*Journal of Theological Studies*
KAT	Kommentar zum Alten Testament
KTU	M. Dietrich, O. Loretz and J. Sanmartin (eds.), *Keilalphabetischen Texte aus Ugarit*
LCL	Loeb Classical Library
LSJ	Liddell–Scott–Jones, *Greek–English Lexicon*
NCB	New Century Bible
NCE	McDonald (ed.), *New Catholic Encyclopaedia*
NEB	New English Bible
NovT	*Novum Testamentum*
NTS	*New Testament Studies*
ODCC	*Oxford Dictionary of the Christian Church*
OTE	*Old Testament Essays*
OTG	Old Testament Guides
OTL	Old Testament Library
OTS	*Oudtestamentische Studiën*
PG	J. Migne (ed.), *Patrologia graeca*
PL	J. Migne (ed.), *Patrologia Latina*
RB	*Revue biblique*
RevExp	*Review and Expositor*
RevQ	*Revue de Qumran*
RS	Ras Shamra Text
SBL	Society of Biblical Literature
SBLDS	SBL Dissertation Series
SBLMS	SBL Monograph Series
SBLRBS	SBL Resources for Biblical Study
SBLSCS	SBL Septuagint and Cognate Studies
Sem	*Semitica*
SJOT	*Scandinavian Journal of the Old Testament*
SPB	Studia postbiblica
SR	*Studies in Religion/Sciences religieuses*
STL	Studia Theologica Ludensia
TDNT	G. Kittel and G. Friedrich (eds.), *Theological Dictionary of the New Testament*

TDOT	G.J. Botterweck and H. Ringgren (eds.), *Theological Dictionary of the Old Testament*
ThB	*Theologische Beiträge*
TK	*Theologie und Kirche*
TZ	*Theologische Zeitschrift*
VT	*Vetus Testamentum*
VTSup	*Vetus Testamentum*, Supplements
WBC	Word Biblical Commentary
WMANT	Wissenschaftliche Monographien zum Alten und Neuen Testament
WUNT	Wissenschaftliche Untersuchungen zum Neuen Testament
ZAW	*Zeitschrift für die alttestamentliche Wissenschaft*
ZRGG	*Zeitschrift für Religions- und Geistesgeschichte*

Works Translated in Appendixes

Ag. M.	*Aggadat Mashiah*
As. M.	*'Asereth Melakhim*
NRSbY	*Nistarot Rav Shim'on ben Yohai*
Otot	*Otot ha-Mashiah*
Pir. M.	*Pirqê Mashiah*
Sef. Z.	*Sefer Zerubbabel*

Ordo psalmorum, qui mihi magni sacramenti videtur
continere secretum, nondum mihi fuerit revelatus.

Augustine,
Enarrationes in Psalmos 150.i

כל הנביאים כשלן לא נתנבאו אלא לימות המשיח:

b. Ber. 34b; *b. San.* 99a

Chapter 1

A REVIEW OF PSALMS INTERPRETATION

This book is a contribution to the contemporary debate on the purpose and message of the Psalter. It maintains that the Hebrew Psalter was designed by its redactors as a purposefully ordered arrangement of lyrics with an eschatological message. This message, as in many other Jewish documents of second temple times, consists of a predicted sequence of eschatological events. These include Israel in exile, the appearing of a messianic superhero, the ingathering of Israel, the attack of the nations, the hero's suffering, the scattering of Israel in the wilderness, their ingathering and further imperilment, the appearance of a superhero from the heavens to rescue them, the establishment of his *malkut* from Zion, the prosperity of Israel and the homage of the nations.

However, before discussing this proposed event-sequence in the Psalter, the general plausibility of regarding the Psalter as an eschatologico-predictive book must be demonstrated. This involves two distinct but related issues: arrangement and purpose. The Psalter may be regarded as a book, rather than an *ad hoc* collection, if it bears evidence of careful arrangement. It may be regarded as intentionally attempting to predict future events, if the book appears to have been designed by its redactors to refer to such events. In order to demonstrate these two points it is necessary to examine the evidence for redactional structuring and eschatological orientation in the Psalter. This shall be done in two stages. First, in this chapter, I shall review the history of Psalms interpretation with particular reference to the Psalter's purpose and arrangement, including the significance of the psalm-headings and doxological book divisions that form its clearest structural markers. Thereafter, in the next chapter, I shall investigate the Psalter itself to see what evidence it displays to prove or disprove the interpreters' opinions.

This chapter, then, is a historical retrospective of Psalms interpretation. Yet the point at which to begin such a retrospective is hard to know, for the distinction between text and interpetation is not absolute. Psalm headings might be considered interpretation rather than text, for, although ancient, each one dates at some remove from the time of its psalm's composition. Those headings, for instance, that claim their psalms were composed by David in a particular situation, clearly come from a later hand than their lyrics, for they refer to the psalmist in the third person. Similarly, the doxological subscripts that separate the five books of the Psalter seem, with the possible exception of 106.48, to have been added to their preceding lyrics by a later redactor.[1] However, as my intention is to investigate the final form of the Masoretic Psalter, I shall regard its headings and subscripts as text rather than interpretation and begin the retrospective proper with the ancient translations.

1. *The Ancient Translations*

The ancient translations all endorse the same sequence of lyrics as the Hebrew Psalter. The LXX Psalter, dating probably from the early second century BCE,[2] contains the 150 psalms of the Masoretic Text (MT), in the same sequence, together with an appended Psalm 151. Of course, there are differences in the division of the lyrics. MT Psalms 9–10 are one psalm in LXX, as are MT 114–15, while MT 116 and 147

---

1.   Mowinckel (1962: II, 196) suggests, on the basis of 1 Chron. 16.36, that this doxology was already attached to Ps. 106 when in use in temple service and may be 'original'.

2.   The prologue to Ben Sira relates that when the author's grandson came to Egypt in the 38th year of Euergetes (132 BCE), not only the Law and the Prophets, but also 'the rest of the books' were already translated into Greek. This surely included the Psalms, whether they were subsumed under 'the rest of the books', meaning, as Sarna maintains, the Hagiographa (1971: 1311), or within the Prophets, as Barton (1986: 47-48) would have it. Thus Haran (1993: 194) states that the LXX Psalter dates from 'no later than the first half of the second century BCE'. However, the LXX Psalter may be older still. Sarna suggests that 'the known fact that this version was made in response to the needs of the synagogue worship makes it virtually certain that the Psalms were turned into the vernacular in Alexandria even before much of the prophets' (1971: 1311). Likewise their acknowledged importance as a group in their own right beside the Law and Prophets may have ensured early translation (See 2 Macc. 2.13; Philo, *Vit. Cont.* 25; Lk. 24.44).

each become two. This leads to divergence in enumeration.[3] But still LXX reflects a Hebrew *Vorlage* with the same sequence of psalms as MT. As Haran comments, '…despite the slight differences between the Masoretic Text and the LXX when it comes to the conjunction of chapters, the two versions are essentially the same in their arrangement of the actual material.'[4] LXX also contains the first statement that this sequence is in some sense definitive, for the heading to its Psalm 151 describes this lyric as supernumerary (ἔξωθεν τοῦ ἀριθμοῦ), suggesting that the translators regarded it as extraneous to the foregoing 150 psalms. The Targum, which may date from before the turn of the era,[5] has the same number, sequence and enumeration of lyrics as the MT. The Peshitta Psalter is a fairly free translation that seems to be dependent not only on MT but also on LXX and Targum.[6] It has the same sequence of lyrics as MT, but, like LXX, has additional psalms suffixed to the standard sequence. These are usually five in number, beginning with a Syriac version of LXX Psalm 151. Like LXX, the Peshitta comprises MT 114 and 115 in one psalm, and MT 147 in two, giving an enumeration one behind MT throughout the intervening psalms.

The ancient translations endorse virtually all the internal structural markers, that is, the headings and doxologies, of the Hebrew Psalter. The LXX headings contain everything in their MT counterparts, except the לדוד ascriptions in Psalms 122 and 124. LXX sometimes supplements MT headings: 13 LXX psalms have Davidic ascriptions absent in

---

3.   Enumeration is concurrent until Ps. 9, where LXX Ps. 9 comprises MT Pss. 9 and 10. Thereafter LXX enumeration is one behind MT until LXX Ps. 113, which comprises MT Pss. 114 and 115. Then MT Ps. 116 comprises LXX Pss. 114 and 115. Thereafter LXX enumeration is again one behind MT until MT Ps. 147, which comprises LXX Pss. 146 and 147. Pss. 148–50 concur.

4.   Haran 1993: 194.

5.   As regards dating, Grossfeld (1984) comments, 'Another common feature of these two Targums (Job and Psalms) is the fact that between them they contain about a hundred variants in vowels and even consonants from MT, a feature not found with such frequency in the other Targums. Since a number of these same variants also occur in the Peshitta and Septuagint, they offer adequate proof of an early date of composition for these two Targums… A Targum to Job was among the many finds discovered among the Dead Sea Scrolls in 1947.' Grossfeld notes further evidence for the early date of *T. Pss.* in its partly allegorical and partly literal nature, the allegorical parts appearing to have been added to an older more literal targum. Delitzsch (1887: I, 52) also notes that the more literal character of *T. Pss.* suggests its composition prior to other targums, which tend to be more allegorical.

6.   Weitzman 1982: 283-84; 1985: 354.

MT and 22 of the 24 psalms that have no heading in MT gain one in
LXX, leaving only Psalms 1 and 2 untitled.[7] But these are additions,
not alterations. The headings are essentially those of the Hebrew. The
doxological subscripts equal those of MT, with two expansions (LXX
71.19; 105.48). The second of these emends MT's single אמן to γένοιτο
γένοιτο. Whether LXX is an expansion, or MT a contraction, of an
earlier *Vorlage* is unclear. But the greater resemblance of the four
subscripts in LXX suggests that they were regarded as functionally
similar structural markers early on, and that this is not an idea that
developed in rabbinic times. The Targum headings and subscripts
follow MT very closely: 'The Targum has a superscription only at
those psalms at which the Masoretic Text also has one. The 34 psalms
which have no superscription in the Masoretic Text are without superscription in the Targum also.'[8]

The Peshitta, like LXX, expands the headings found in the MT. Its
headings are often particularly expansive where MT has none, and
commonly provide a short message to the reader as well as a historical
statement about the psalm.[9] Nonetheless, although it adds to the
Hebrew headings, it omits little. Thus the ancient translations generally render MT's structural markers in full, a fact that is even more
striking than their adopting unaltered the Hebrew sequence of psalms.
For later redactors might well have wished to reunite psalms that
share common headings—the psalms of David, Asaph and Korah—
and are divided in the MT Psalter. Yet despite good reason to change
the received sequence, either by altering the headings or rearranging
the lyrics, they adhered to the MT-type sequence with all its pecu-
liarities. They apparently regarded this arrangement as more than
fortuitous.

The ancient translations also bear evidence that their translators
regarded the Psalms as future-predictive. LXX has rightly been called

---

7.   Pss. 1, 2, 10, 33, 43, 71, 91, 93, 94, 95, 96, 97, 99, 104, 105, 107, 114,
115, 116, 117, 118, 119, 136 and 137 are unheaded in MT, if the הללו־יה of Pss.
106, 111, 112 113, 135, 146, 147, 148, 149 and 150 is regarded as a heading. If it
is not, then the unheaded psalms are 34 in number, as Preuss tallies them below.

8.   Author's translation. 'Das Targum hat nur bei den Psalmen eine Überschrift, bei denen der Masoretische Text (M) ebenfalls eine bietet. Die 34 Psalmen,
welche in M ohne überschrift sind, werden auch in Targum (T) nicht damit versehen'
(Preuss 1959: 44).

9.   See Vosté 1944: 210-35. He lists variant headings on pp. 215-19.

the 'the first monument of Jewish exegesis', for, although it contains no commentary as such, it exhibits interpretation predating the earliest commentaries.[10] Its tendency to eschatological interpretation is widely recognized. Barton comments, 'The thrust of the whole collection is strongly eschatological.'[11] In the LXX Psalter, this tendency is most readily discernible in its interpretation of headings. The best example is the rendering of the Hebrew term למנצח.[12] The simplest understanding of this term is as a piel participle of נצח, *to shine, excel, be preeminent.* Thus it refers to a pre-eminent individual, a leader. The only use of that piel verb in the Bible is at 1 Chron. 15.21, where it describes the work of those leading cultic worship. Therefore the participle מנצח could indicate a chief musician, precentor, or *hazzan.* But it could be understood in other ways. The *leader* could mean Messiah, especially in the post-exilic period, when נצח is attested as having the meaning *conquer.*[13] Yet another possible meaning might be *For eternity.*[14] Now, although the cultic meaning is the one best supported by the internal evidence of the MT, LXX adopts a phrase that disregards it, but captures something of the two latter meanings: Εἰς τὸ τέλος. This might be taken as meaning *For the ruler*[15] or *For the end* or *consummation [of the cosmos].* Thus LXX, when faced with a choice between cultic or eschatological interpretation, adopts the latter, suggesting its translators interpreted Psalms eschatologically.[16]

LXX interprets other psalm headings in an eschatological vein. For instance, על־ששנים (MT 45, 69), על־ששנים עדות (MT 80), and על־שושן עדות (MT 60) become ὑπὲρ τῶν ἀλλοιωθησομένων (LXX 44, 68, 79) and τοῖς ἀλλοιωθησομένοις ἔτι (LXX 59). At first glance this seems to be no translation at all. But there is an underlying idea that links

10. S. Daniel 1971: 855.
11. Barton 1986: 22.
12. The term occurs in 55 MT psalm headings.
13. BDB: 663. See the LXX rendering of Hab. 3.19, where למנצח becomes τοῦ νικῆσαι, *Concerning conquering.*
14. That is, taking the term as לְמִנְצָה, a substantive of נֶצַח, which commonly signifies *eternity* in BH (BDB: 664).
15. Possible meanings of the term include *the highest station, the possession of full power, magistracy* (LSJ: 697).
16. Schwartz also notes that Εἰς τὸ τέλος 'allows for an eschatological explanation' (Schwartz 1993: 320 n.).

lilies[17] and *the transformation (of the year)*—the idea of springtime, when lilies bloom. So this may be an interpretation rather than a departure from the Hebrew. And there may be eschatological implications. For the idea of the transformation of the earth in spring connotes the image-complex of Passover, new creation and resurrection, for which lilies are an ancient symbol. Another example is the rendering of the heading על־הגתית (MT 8, 81, 84) as ὑπὲρ τῶν ληνῶν, *Concerning the winepresses* (LXX 8, 80, 83). The translators might presumably have chosen other interpretations of this term, like the Targum, which takes it as a kind of *Gath-harp* that David brought from that city. But they chose *winepresses*. The context of these psalm headings, following Psalms 7, 80, and 83, which refer to the judgment of the earth, suggests that the LXX translators wished to evoke the winepress of God's wrath, as in the eschatological judgment of Isa. 63.1-6. Another example might be the rendering of על־עלמות (MT 46). Whatever the original meaning of the Hebrew,[18] the LXX takes it as deriving from the root עלם and renders it ὑπὲρ τῶν κρυφίων, *Concerning the things concealed* (LXX Ps. 45.1).

Likewise the Targum interprets the Psalms as future-predictive. It generally does this by inserting interpretive comments in the headings, rather than by using terms with eschatological overtones, as does LXX. It regards David as a prophet: 'In the spirit of prophecy, by David' (14.1); 'By David, a prophetic word' (103.1). Certain Davidic psalms are interpreted messianically: 'For on account of the miracle and redemption that you have wrought for your Messiah...all the peoples, nations, and tongues shall praise' (18.32); 'King Messiah shall rejoice in your strength, O Lord' (21.2); 'For King Messiah trusts in the Lord' (21.8); 'You will prolong the days of King Messiah... Therefore I will glorify your name for ever in the day of the redemption of Israel, and in the day that King Messiah is anointed to rule' (61.7, 9). Non-Davidic psalms are likewise interpreted as future-predictive: 'As was said in prophecy by the hand of the sons of Korah... Your beauty, King Messiah, is superior to that of the sons of men' (45.1, 3); 'By the hand of the sons of Korah, in the spirit of prophecy at the time their father had hidden them; they were delivered and spoke the

17. See Feliks 1971: 1364-68 (esp. 1367) for the probable identification of שׁשׁנים with the white lily, *lilium candidum*.
18. The generally accepted view is that it designated women's voices or, more generally, high voices or a high pitch (Craigie 1983b: 342; Delitzsch 1846: II, 109).

canticle' (46.1); 'By the hands of Solomon it was said in prophecy, "O God, give King Messiah the precepts of your judgments"' (72.1; cf. also v. 17); 'And upon the King Messiah whom you made strong for yourself' (80.16); 'With which they have scoffed at the delay of the footsteps of your Messiah, O Lord' (89.52); 'Prophetic psalm' (98.1).

Likewise the Peshitta interprets Psalms eschatologically, particularly in its renderings of the headings. A few examples will suffice. Psalm 22: 'Spoken by David when his pursuers were taunting him, and a prophecy of all the suffering of the Messiah.'[19] Psalm 45: 'Prophesied about Messiah our Lord: and about the raising up of the church.'[20] Psalm 72: 'A Psalm of David, when he had made Solomon king, and a prophecy concerning the advent of the Messiah and the calling of the Gentiles.'[21] Psalm 110: 'Prophesied about the dispensing of the deliverances of the Messiah: and knowledge for us also about the separation of nature.'[22] Some of these interpretations are of Christian origin; others are probably pre-Christian Jewish; it is impossible to say more, as virtually every assertion regarding the authorship and origin of the Peshitta is a matter of controversy, and the widely varying textual traditions show that later scribes felt free to expand and alter as they wished.[23] Nonetheless, the Peshitta adds its testimony to that of LXX and Targum to show that eschatological interpretation of the Psalms was widespread wherever they were known in the ancient world.

2. *The Dead Sea Scrolls*

The writers of the Dead Sea Scrolls would probably have regarded the canonical Psalter as a purposefully shaped collection. This is evident not so much from their endorsing the MT-type sequence, although they probably did, but also, conversely, from their practice of producing alternative purposefully shaped psalms collections. This suggests that they, and presumably their contemporaries, did not compile psalms

19.   *'mr ldwid kd mmyqyn hww bh rdwpwhy wnbywt' kl ḥš' dmšyḥ'.*
20.   *mtnb' 'l mšyḥ' mrn : w'l qwym' d'dt'.*
21.   Cited by Kirkpatrick 1902: 416.
22.   *mtnb' 'l mdbrnwth dprwqn mšyḥ' : wmwd' ln 'p 'l pwršn' dkyn'.*
23.   For an outline of the various positions regarding the origin and development of the Peshitta see the anonymous article, 'Bible: Syriac: Peshitta and other Versions', *EncJud*: IV, 858-60.

collections in an *ad hoc* manner. They produced, and expected others to produce, purposefully ordered collections. And this may suggest that the earlier MT-type Psalter was produced with similar expectations in mind.

There seem to have been several different collections or part-collections of biblical Psalms in existence at Qumran.

First, there is 11QPs[a]. This, the best known of the Qumran Psalms manuscripts, is dated on palaeographic and archaeological grounds to the second half of the first century CE.[24] It contains a number of biblical psalms in a different sequence from MT, and also contains non-biblical material. Its contents are as follows:

> Psalm 101 → 102 → 103; 118 → 104 → 147 → 105 → 146 → 148 (+ 120) + 121 → 122 → 123 → 124 → 125 → 126 → 127 → 128 → 129 → 130 → 131 → 132 → 119 → 135 → 136 → Catena → 145; 154 + Plea for Deliverance → 139 → 137 → 138 → Sirach 51.13-30 → Apostrophe to Zion → Psalm 93 → 141 → 133 → 144 → 155 → 142 → 143 → 149 → 150 → Hymn to the Creator → David's Last Words (2 Sam. 23.[1]-7) → David's Compositions → Psalm 140 → 134 → 151A, B → blank column [end of scroll].[25]

J. van der Ploeg has demonstrated that 11QPs[b] appears to show the same sequence, as can be seen from its containing the 'Plea for Deliverance' and the sequence Pss. 141 → 133 → 144.[26] Flint suggests the same may be true of 4QPs[e].[27] Thus several copies of this arrangement may have existed at Qumran.

Secondly, the MT-type arrangement was almost certainly known at Qumran. According to Skehan, some 17 fragments agree with MT, and demonstrate the sectarians' familiarity with it.[28] Haran agrees, commenting, 'in the Qumran scrolls, the chapters of Psalms generally follow the order of the Masoretic Text and LXX', and 'all these scrolls are dependent on the canonical book of Psalms'.[29] Flint, on the other

---

24.   Sanders 1966: 6-10; Flint 1994: 33.

25.   From Flint 1994: 52. The sigla are Flint's. An arrow indicates that a passage is continuous with the one listed before it. The plus sign indicates that a passage follows the one listed before it, even though some of the relevant text is no longer extant.

26.   Van der Ploeg 1967: 408-12.

27.   Flint 1994: 40, 43, 47.

28.   Skehan 1978: 165-69, esp. 167.

29.   Haran 1993: 193, 194.

hand, states that there is no manuscript from Qumran 'whose arrange-ment *unambiguously* supports the Received Psalter against the 11QPs[a] arrangement'.[30] This position derives from his adopting Sanders's hypothesis that the missing first two-thirds of 11QPs[a] were similar to MT. As a result he does not recognize the many manuscripts that agree with the first two-thirds of MT, but do not *disagree* with 11QPs[a], as they feature psalms, in particular Psalms 1–100, absent from 11QPs[a]. If Sanders's theory is accepted, Flint would be correct in saying that there is no unambiguous evidence for the MT at Qumran. But the theory is speculative, and even if it were not, it would still be unwise to conclude that the MT arrangement was not recognized at Qumran. For it was the chosen version for synagogue worship as far afield as Alexandria some 250 years before 11QPs[a]. It was also known at nearby Masada at about the time when 11QPs[a] was written: MasPs[b] features Ps. 150.1-6 followed by a blank column, an arrangement known only in MT and disagreeing with 11QPs[a].

Thirdly, 4QPs[a] and 4QPs[q] feature Psalm 31 followed by Psalm 33. If this is not an earlier section of the sequence partly preserved in 11QPs[a], which it might or might not be, then it would appear to be the remains of another non-MT psalms collection that existed in more than one copy at Qumran.

Fourthly, 4QPs[f] contains Psalms 107–109 followed by 'Apostrophe to Zion' and two otherwise unknown lyrics, 'Eschatological Hymn' and 'Apostrophe to Judah'. As 'Apostrophe to Zion' is therefore in quite a different context from the one it has in 11QPs[a], Flint suggests that 4QPs[f] is part of yet another psalms collection divergent from both 11QPs[a] and MT.[31]

Fifthly, van der Ploeg has plausibly suggested that 11QPsAp[a] is yet another purposefully designed collection, possibly intended for exor-cism and to be identified with the 'psalms for making music over the stricken' mentioned in 11QPs[a] col. xxvii.[32]

Finally, other minor fragments contain sequences that disagree with all the above. 4QPs[d] contains Pss. 106(?) → 147 → 104. 4QPs[k] con-tains Pss. 135.6-16 and 99.1-5. 4QPs[n] contains Ps. 135.6-12 followed by Ps. 136.22.

30.   Flint 1994: 41; Flint's italics.
31.   Flint 1994: 45-47.
32.   Van der Ploeg 1971. This suggestion has been widely received. See e.g. Puech 1990.

All this suggests that a number of psalm arrangements were in circulation at Qumran. Moreover, some of the non-MT arrangements appear to have been arranged for specific purposes, or there was little reason for their existing in several copies. This suggests that psalters were not arbitrarily arranged in second temple times, and supports the likelihood of the MT-type Psalter having been purposefully arranged by its own redactors.

The Qumran interpreters further endorse the MT-type Psalter by their adherence to its literary structural markers, the headings and doxologies. 11QPs[a] has eleven legible psalm headings. Eleven of these are identical to MT;[33] three others lack minor parts of the MT heading;[34] four more show variants without any omission.[35] Only one, Psalm 144 without לדוד ascription, lacks any indication of the MT heading. In general, then, the headings of 11QPs[a] are closer to MT than even those of LXX. Given the general wide divergence of 11QPs[a] from MT, the similarity is striking, and seems to suggest that the lyrics in 11QPs[a] had their source in something like the MT Psalter. It is also noteworthy that the Qumran interpreters regarded the heading as an intrinsic part of a psalm, worthy of commentary like the body of the lyric, as in the *pesher* 4Q171.

> *For the leader: according to [lili]es. [Of the sons of Korah. Maskil. A love song.* Th]ey are the seven divisions of the penitents of Is[rael . . .][36]

Some Qumran interpreters may also have regarded the four doxologies as dividing the Psalter into five 'books', as can be seen from the fragment 1Q30.2-6:

33.   The headings are identical to MT in Pss. 121, 122, 126, 127 (partially legible), 129 (partially legible), 130, 133, 137 (i.e. no heading like MT), 138, 140, and 143.

34.   Pss. 148 and 150 lack the הללריה heading of MT. The significance of this is lessened by the preceding psalms, 146 and 149 respectively, which end with הללריה as in MT. This may be due to scribal error or to a notion that only one occurrence of the phrase was sufficient, as in LXX, which never has more than one occurrence of the phrase between two consecutive psalms.

35.   Ps. 93 is preceded by הללריה. Ps. 123 bears the addition לדויד and, like MT Ps. 121, has למעלות instead of המעלות. Ps. 145 reads תפלה לדויד instead of תהלה לדויד. The three opening phrases of Ps. 135, including the הללריה heading, are in retrograde order from that of MT.

36.   למנצח על [שוש]נים [לבני קרח משכיל שיר ידידת...ה]נ[מה שבע מחלקוח שבי יש[ראל... (DJD: V, 45).

מ[שיח הקדוש]
ב[שלישית את כול]
ס[פרים חומשים]
[ויותר על ארבעה]
[37] ופשריהם לפי [ ]

The term (חומש(ים, designating fivefold divisions, commonly refers in
a later period to the five books of the Pentateuch, Psalms, or
Megillot.[38] The editors suggest that in this case the reference is to the
Psalms, although they give no reason for the suggestion.[39] It may be
due to the fact that the Psalms appear to have been more popular at
Qumran than any other biblical book.[40] Or it may be because the
fragment's reference to *Messiah* makes most sense in relation to the
Psalms, which, as shall be seen below, were interpreted messianically
at Qumran.

The authors of the Qumran literature seem to have regarded the
Psalms as future-predictive. The prose insert in 11QPs[a] describes all
David's psalms, presumably including the immediately preceding
psalm from 2 Sam. 23.1-7, as composed by means of a divine prophetic endowment.

> And David ben Jesse was wise... and he wrote 3,600 psalms... and all
> the songs that he composed were 446, and songs for making music over
> the stricken, four. And the total was 4,050. All these he composed
> through prophecy which was given him before the Most High.[41]

The Qumran scribes juxtapose biblical psalms with eschatological
texts. The 'Apostrophe to Zion', in 11QPs[a] and 4QPs[f], claims itself
to be prophetic (v. 17), refers to the eschatological glory of Zion,
and foretells the coming of its longed-for deliverance (v. 2). 4QPs[f]

37.   'Holy [Me]ssiah... [in] third all the... [... b]ooks of the Pentateuch/
Psalter... and the rest on/at four... and their interpretations according to...' (DJD: I,
32).

38.   See Jastrow 1950: I, 436. חומשים designates the Pentateuch at *Soṭ.* 36b;
Hag. 14a; *y. Meg.* 3.1 (74a top). It designates the Psalter at *Kid.* 33a (...שני חומשים
בספר תהלים) and *Midr. Pss.* 1.2 (cited later in this chapter). At *y. Meg.* 2.4 (72a
bottom) it refers to the five *megillot*.

39.   'Si la lecture ספרים est exacte il s'agirait des livres חומשים, c.-à-d. du
Pentateuque ou plutôt du Psautier' (DJD: I, 133).

40.   Sanders comments, 'There were undoubtedly more copies of Psalms in the
Qumran library than of any other biblical writings' (1974: 9).

41.   11QPs[a], col. 27, lines 1-11. The text is at Sanders 1974: 136.

contains biblical psalms juxtaposed with the lyrics 'Eschatological Hymn' and 'Apostrophe to Judah', the former speaking of Yhwh's coming in judgment, the destruction of the wicked and the end-time fertility of the earth, and the latter of the rejoicing of Judah after the eschatological destruction of her enemies. Other texts interpret biblical psalms eschatologically. 11QMelch. refers Psalm 82 to the superhero Melchizedek and the battle with Belial and his hosts.[42] 4Q174.1 (Florilegium) interprets Psalm 2 as applying to the kings of the nations who shall rage against Israel in the last days.[43] 4Q171 interprets Psalms 37 and 45 eschatologically, as does 4Q173 for Psalm 128.[44]

3. *The New Testament*

The New Testament seems to regard the MT-type Psalter as definitive. The reference in Acts 1.20 to ὁ βίβλος ψαλμῶν suggests the writer of Acts, in the first century, regarded one particular collection as '*the* Book of Psalms'. Several things suggest that this βίβλος ψαλμῶν featured the MT-type arrangement of lyrics. First, the known prominence of that arrangement, as demonstrated in its being selected as the basis for all the translations, would make it likely. Secondly, the majority of New Testament quotes from Psalms come verbatim from LXX, which, of course, has the MT-type sequence. Thirdly, all New Testament citations from 'psalms' are found in the MT-type Psalter; the term is not used of non-biblical lyrics, such as those in 11QPs^a. Fourthly, Acts 13.33 cites from Psalm 2 and refers to its being written ἐν τῷ ψαλμῷ...τῷ δευτέρῳ. The only known arrangement of psalms that has this particular second psalm is the standard Psalter. Fifthly, no other arrangement of Psalms has passed into Christian tradition. This suggests that for the writer of Acts, and probably for the early Christian community at large, the collection regarded as '*the* Book of Psalms' was an MT-type Psalter.

---

42. The text is in Woude 1965; Jonge and Woude 1966; Milik 1972. There is an English translation in Jonge and Woude 1966: 303.

43. The text is in DJD: V, 53-57. There is an English translation in Vermes 1987: 293-94.

44. The text is in DJD: V, 42-53. There is an English translation in Vermes 1987: 290-92.

The New Testament writers also regard the Psalms as future-predictive. David is described as a prophet, through whom the Holy Spirit spoke (Mt. 22.43; Mk 12.36; Acts 2.30; 4.25). Those psalms ascribed to him are reckoned to foretell messianic events after their date of composition (Mt. 22.43-45; Acts 2.25, 31; 4.11). The New Testament as a whole cites passages from the Psalms more than 70 times, more than any other Old Testament book, to endorse Christian messianic claims. A few examples may be given from the gospels alone. Ps. 91.11-12 is taken as referring to Messiah's deliverance from evil (Mt. 4.6; Lk. 4.11). Ps. 118.22, 23 is regarded as foretelling his rejection by the leaders of Israel (Mt. 21.42; Mk 12.10; Lk. 20.17), while 118.25, 26 is associated with his entry to Jerusalem (Mt. 21.9; 23.39; Mk 11.9; Lk. 13.35; 19.38; Jn 12.13). Ps. 22.1, 18 is held to foretell his suffering (Mt. 27.35 [some MSS]; 27.46; Mk 15.34; Jn 19.24). Psalm 110 is referred to him as well, presumably in his role as conquering king (Mt. 22.41-46; Mk 12.36; Lk. 20.42-43).

It is worth noting, in passing, that the New Testament's Psalms hermeneutic seems little different from that of their contemporaries in first-century Israel.

(1) There are distinct similarities between the New Testament and Qumran. The New Testament view that David's utterances are predictive is not recognizably different from that of the prose insert describing David's compositions in 11QPs[a], col. 27, cited above. Similarly the New Testament's eschatological interpretation of Psalms is similar to that of 11QMelch.[45] Moreover, the New Testament shows the same general fascination with Psalms as do the Qumran writers. Just as the New Testament cites Psalms more than any other Old Testament book, so, at Qumran, manuscripts of the biblical Psalms outnumber those of any other book.[46]

(2) The New Testament itself represents other Jewish parties sharing its hermeneutic. At Mt. 22.41-46, Mk 12.36 and Lk. 20.42-43 the Pharisees are depicted as tacitly accepting the Davidic authorship of Psalm 110, even though Davidic authorship is the very point on which the Christian *apologia* depends. Diaspora Hebrews in Jerusalem, and others at Pisidian Antioch, are depicted as doing exactly the same thing in regard to Psalms 16 and 110 (Acts 2.25, 29, 34; 13.33-36).

45. The link between the eschatological vision of 11QMelch and Ps. 110 is discussed in Chapter 8.

46. Sanders 1974: 9.

Another passage shows the early Hebrew Christian community citing Psalm 118 as a messianic proof-text in dialogue with the Sanhedrin (Acts 4.10). That the New Testament community did in fact use the Psalms in just this way is confirmed by those New Testament books that are written to convince Jewish readers of Christian messianic claims. The epistle to the Hebrews, in particular, repeatedly cites from the Psalms.[47] So too does John's Gospel,[48] which recent commentators have described as a *Missionsschrift* to Israel.[49] And even if the intended readership of all New Testament books were exclusively Christian, these books must still represent the actual apologetic methods of the early church. For what would their writers gain by instructing their readership in apologetics not practised by the Christian community? So if, then, early Christian Israelites employed Psalms as messianic proof-texts, it follows that their opponents must have acknowledged the messianic referent of these same texts.

(3) Rabbinic traditions further confirm that the New Testament Psalms hermeneutic was essentially the same as that of other first-century Israelites. For the rabbinic movement was the chief heir of the hermeneutic traditions of the Pharisees and Sadducees after 70 CE. These traditions, as shall be seen below, interpret messianically many of the same psalms as the New Testament, including Psalms 22, 110, and 118.

4. *Rabbinic Literature*

Jewish Psalms manuscripts and incunabula endorse the definitiveness of the MT-type arrangement by their conformity to it. They have the same psalms as MT in the same order, apart from accidental omissions due to homoeoteleuton.[50] However, the number and enumeration of

47.   Ten different psalms (2, 8, 22, 40, 45, 95, 102, 104, 110, 118) are cited directly (Heb. 1.5, 7, 8-9, 10-12, 13; 2.6-8, 12; 3.7-11, 15; 4.3, 5, 7; 5.5, 6; 7.17-21; 10.5-7; 13.6). There are also allusions to particular psalms. Some of these are noted in the discussion on Ps. 110 in Chapter 8.

48.   There are direct citations at Jn 2.17 (Ps. 69.9); Jn 6.31 (Ps. 78.24); Jn 10.34 (Ps. 82.6); Jn 12.13 (Ps. 118.25-26); Jn 13.18 (Ps. 41.9); Jn 15.25 (Ps. 35.19; 69.4); Jn 19.24 (Ps. 22.18).

49.   Bornhaüser 1928; Robinson 1960: 117-31; Brooke 1988: 102-12; Carson 1987: 639-51.

50.   For a discussion of homoeoteleuton in Hebrew Psalter manuscripts see Ginsburg 1897: 171-82.

lyrics varies as a result of joining or dividing psalms. A Psalter of 147 chapters is mentioned in Amoraic times (*y. Šab.* 16.1, 15c; cf. 16.11; *Midr. Pss.* to 22.4) and exists in manuscripts[51] and in the first edition of the *Yal. Shimoni.*[52] The Leningrad Codex B and the Brescia (1494) and Naples (1491–94) Bibles are all divided into 149 psalms, an arrangement known also to Mishael b. Uzziel and Shmuel ha-Nagid, and present in some manuscripts.[53] Other Psalters feature divisions of 148, 151, 159 and even 170 psalms.[54] Commonly joined together are MT Psalms, 1–2, 9–10, 42–43, 53–54, 70–71, 93–94, 104–105, 114–15, 116–17, 117–118.1-4.[55] Psalms 115, 116, 118 and 119 are sometimes divided.[56] However, in every case the variation is not in the content of these Psalters, but only in the division and combination of psalm units. They uniformly display the MT sequence.

There is evidence that the rabbis regarded the Psalter's sequence of lyrics as purposefully arranged. A talmudic *baraitha* (*Ber.* 10a) establishes the validity of contextual interpretation of psalms and comments on the significance of the juxtaposition of Psalms 2 and 3.

> A certain *min* said to R. Abbahu: It is written, *A Psalm of David when he fled from Absalom his son* (Ps. 3.1). And it is also written, *A mikhtam of David when he fled from Saul in the cave* (Ps. 57.1). Which event happened first? Did not the event of Saul happen first? Then let him write it first? He replied to him: For you who do not derive interpretations from juxtaposition, there is a difficulty, but for us who do derive interpretations from juxtaposition there is no difficulty. For R. Yohanan said: How do we know from the Torah that juxtaposition counts? Because it says, *They are joined for ever and ever, they are done in truth and uprightness* (Ps. 111.8). Why is the chapter of Absalom juxtaposed to the chapter of Gog and Magog? So that if one should say to you, 'Is it possible that a slave should rebel against his master?', you can reply to him, 'Is it possible that a son should rebel against his father? Yet this happened, and so this too [will happen].'

Midr. Pss. 3.2 expresses the same view of the purposeful arrangement of the Psalms with a similar teaching about Psalms 2 and 3.[57]

51. Ginsburg 1897: 18, 777.
52. Salonica, 1521-26; cf. also Jacob b. Asher, *Ba'al ha-Turim*, Gen. 47.28.
53. Sarna 1971: 1306.
54. Ginsburg 1897: 536-37, 584, 725; Sarna 1971: 1306.
55. Ginsburg 1897: 18, 536, 725, 777, 853, 873. At *t. Peš.* 117a it is said, in reference to Ps. 117, that a two-versed psalm is preposterous.
56. Ginsburg 1897: 536-37, 584, 725-26.
57. 'R. Jacob said in the name of R. Aha: Why is the psalm on Gog and Magog

Thereafter follows the tale of how R. Joshua ben Levi sought to rearrange the Psalms, when a *bat kol* commanded, 'Arouse not the slumberer!' This appears to teach that the present order of Psalms is to be left alone, because it is significant. Similarly *Midr. Pss.* 111.1 refers back to Psalm 110 for an understanding of the context of Psalm 111. Kimhi also remarks on the arrangement of Psalms 1, 2 and 3, noting that, while the arrangement of Psalms cannot be explained according to historical order, yet they were thus arranged by David. Similarly, he notes that Psalm 53 is placed as it is to show that David was threatened by Doeg (52.1) and the Ziphites (54.1), but God made his kingdom stand firm.[58]

Rabbinic commentators also endorse the structural markers, the headings and subscripts, of the MT arrangement, and regard them as important for interpretation. A few examples illustrate this. The Talmud maintains that לדוד מזמור means the *shekhinah* rested on David and then he uttered a song, while מזמור לדוד means he uttered that song and then the *shekhinah* rested upon him (*Pes.* 117a). Midrash Tehillim discusses how the *sons of Korah* psalms relate to the figures of Num. 26.10, and states that the term ששנים (Ps. 45.1) refers to the sons of Korah, who were lilies gathered from among thorns that they might not be consumed. *Midr. Pss.* 84, like LXX, takes על־הגתית as *Concerning the Winepresses,* and relates it to the crushing of the eschatological foe. The mediaeval rabbis also comment at length on headings. Ibn Ezra discusses who Ethan the Ezrahi of Psalm 89 might be.[59] Rashi supposes the Korah psalms to have been composed by the sons of the Korah of the desert rebellion, a supposition central to his interpretation of the psalm.[60] Kimhi thinks likewise, and adds that they then came into David's possession and 'David collected these psalms by the Holy Spirit and gave them to the sons of the sons of Korah, who were singers in his time, to sing them.'[61]

The doxological subscripts were understood as section divisions in talmudic times. The Bavli refers explicitly to the חומשים, or five

---

(Ps. 2) placed next to the psalm on Absalom (Ps. 3)? To tell you that a wicked son works greater cruelty upon his father than will the wars of Gog and Magog.'

58.   Kimhi 1883: 53.
59.   Kimhi 1883: 89.1.
60.   Rashi 1934.
61.   כי דוד חבר אלה המזמורים ברוח הקדש ונתנם לבני בני קרח המשוררים הנמצאים בזמנו לשורר אותם (Commentary on Ps. 42).

divisions, of the book of Psalms (*Kid.* 33a). This dates from about 200
CE, if its attribution to the time of R. Hiyya and the young R. Simeon
b. Judah ha-Nasi is correct. The fivefold book division is also men-
tioned in *Midr. Pss.* 1.2, where it is compared with the five books of
the Pentateuch: 'As Moses gave five books of *Torah* to Israel, so
David gave five books of psalms to Israel: *Blessed is the man* (Ps. 1),
Blessed is the maskil (cf. Ps. 42.1), *A Psalm of Asaph* (Ps. 73), *A
Prayer of Moses* (Ps. 90), and *Let the Redeemed of the Lord say* (Ps.
106).'[62] No date is given for this saying, but its marked similarity to
Hippolytus' statement below suggests the existence of this idea early in
the first millennium.

Early Jewish and rabbinic writers commonly regard the Psalms as
future-predictive. The daily *Amidah,* dating from the second temple
period,[63] views David as an eschatological prophet. Referring probably to 1 Sam. 23.1-7, it states: 'Fulfil in our time the words of your
servant David, so that men are again ruled in justice and in the fear of
God. Let light dawn in the world in our days, for we wait and work
for your salvation.'[64] Josephus regards David as a prophet: καὶ ὁ
προφητεύειν ἤρξατο τοῦ θείου πνεύματος εἰς αὐτὸν μετοικισα-
μένου.[65] Aquila renders למנצח as τῷ νικοποιῷ, *For the conqueror,* a
phrase that appears to have messianic overtones. The Talmud frequently cites Psalms as referring to messianic and eschatological
events. For instance, Ps. 72.17: 'The School of R. Yannai said: His
name is Yinnon, for it is written, *His name shall endure for ever:
before the sun was, his name is Yinnon'* (San 98b). Numerous other
passages might be cited.[66] The Midrash regards Psalms writers, David
and the sons of Korah, as prophets (*Midr. Pss.* 2.2; 44.1; 45.4), and
interprets many psalms eschatologically. For instance, on Ps. 2.2: 'In

---

62. משה נתן חמשה חומשי תורה לישראל ודוד נתן חמשה ספרים שבתהלים לישראל
אשרי האיש ואשרי משכיל מזמור לאסף תפלה למשה יאמרו גאולי השם (*Midr. Pss.* 1.2).

63. See Heinemann 1971: 838-45. He notes, 'It is almost certain that by the
end of the temple period the eighteen benedictions of the weekday *Amidah* had
become the general custom' (p. 840). It is referred to in the Mishnah at *Ber.* 4.1-5.7
and *Ta'an.* 2.2.

64. *Forms of Prayer,* 236-37.

65. 'And he began to prophesy when the divine spirit removed [from Saul] to
dwell upon him' (*Ant.* 6.166).

66. See also *Ber.* 7b (Ps. 2 of Gog); *Ber.* 10a (Ps. 2 of Messiah); *Peṣ.* 118b
(Ps. 68 of Messiah); *Meg.* 18a (Ps. 50.23 of Messiah); *'Arak.* 13b (Pss. 12, 92 of
Messiah); *Sanh.* 97a (Ps. 89.52 of Messiah); 99a (Ps. 72.5 of Messiah).

the time to come, Gog and Magog will set themselves against the Lord
and his Messiah, only to fall down. David, foreseeing this said: *"Why
do the nations rage?"'* (*Midr. Pss.* 2.2). It understands למנצח messianically: 'In the days of the Messiah, however, there will be eight strings
to the psaltery, for it is said: *For the leader. Upon the Eighth*' (Ps.
12.1; *Midr. Pss.* 81.3). It interprets other psalms of messiah (2.3, 4, 9,
10; 16.4; 21.2, 4; 60.3; 72.3-6; 87.6), the eschatological conflict (2.2,
4; 11.5; 31.5), and God's *malkut* (2.4). Other *midrashim* interpret
similarly.[67] Those psalms commonly interpreted messianically or
eschatologically in the New Testament, receive similar treatment in
the *midrashim*: Psalm 22 (*Pes. R.* 36.2; 37.1); Psalm 110 (*Otot* 8.4);
Psalm 118 (*Pes. K.* 27.5; cf. also 22.2).

The mediaeval rabbis took a similar line. Kimhi proposes theoreti-
cal grounds for the prophetic nature of the Psalter, in which he discusses the distinction between the higher order of prophecy, that of
the *nevi'im*, and utterance in the Holy Spirit, as manifested in the
ketuvim. Both, he says, foretell the future, but have different characteristics. Utterance in the Holy Spirit is as follows.

> And he [the human author] speaks what is spoken after the manner of
> men, except that a higher spirit moves him and reveals the words upon his
> tongue, words of praise and thanksgiving to his God, or words of
> wisdom and instruction. He also speaks concerning the future, with the
> divine assistance in addition to the power of the speaker—with all the
> powers of those who speak. And in this power the Book of Psalms was
> uttered.[68]

In accord with this Kimhi interprets the majority of Psalms as speaking prophetically of the future. For instance, Psalms 2, 45, 53, 72 and
89 refer to Messiah, Psalms 46 and 53 to the battle of Gog and
Magog, Psalm 47 of the post-conflict messianic reign, Psalm 67 of the
eschatological fertility of the latter-day rain; the Songs of Ascents are
so named because they will be sung at the final ingathering of Israel,
and the true meaning (הנכון) of Psalm 22 is that *ayyelet ha-shahar*
refers to Israel in their present exile in which they cry out, *My God,
my God, why have you abandoned me?*[69] Ibn Ezra seems more aware

---

67.   See, for instance, the messianic interpretations at *Eccl. R.* 1.9.1 (Ps. 72),
Gen. R. 97 (Ps. 89); *Song R.* 2.13.4 (Ps. 89); *Pes. K.* 5.10 (Ps. 89).

68.   Commentary on the Psalms, Introduction to Book I.

69.   For Ps. 89, see the comment on Ps. 53; for the Songs of Ascents, see the
comment on Ps. 120; for the rest, see the comments on the respective psalms.

than Kimhi of historical context. Yet he too interprets Psalms prophetically, often giving both historical and eschatological interpretation together. Psalm 2: 'If this is about Messiah, the reference here is to Gog and Magog; if it is about David, the reference is to the nations around Jerusalem who fought against him, like the Arameans, Edom, Philistines, and Amalek.'[70] Psalm 45: 'And this psalm is spoken about David or about the Messiah his son, may his name prosper.' Psalm 72: 'A prophecy of David or one of the [temple] singers about Solomon or about Messiah.' Rashi tends to interpret historically rather than prophetically. However, he acknowledges that messianic interpretation is the established tradition among earlier commentators, and states that his own reason for avoiding it is to discountenance Christian interpreters.[71]

5. *Patristic to Reformation Christian Literature*

The New Testament suggests the Christian community inherited their hermeneutic from Israel through the early Israelite church and its leaders. It is therefore unsurprizing that patristic writers share by and large the same hermeneutical principles as the rabbis with regard to the Psalter.

Early Christian Psalters endorse the MT arrangement. The enumeration of some, like the Vulgate, follows LXX, while others, like Jerome's *Psalterium juxta hebraeos,* have the same enumeration as MT. But all of them evince the same sequence found in the MT. Explicit statements regarding the significance of the Psalter's arrangement are rarer in Christian than rabbinic literature, probably as a result of the New Testament's silence on the subject. (R. Abbahu's view, cited above, that *minim* do not derive interpretations from juxtaposition, may have been correct.) However a few comments on the subject are found. Origen observes that the order of the Psalms cannot be explained chronologically, and notes Jewish traditions that recognize a narrative sequence in the Songs of Ascents and which attribute to Psalms 91–100 the למשה heading of Psalm 90.[72] Augustine believes

---

70.   From the recently discovered fragmentary first commentary of Ibn Ezra on the Psalms. The text is in Simon 1991: 324-25.

71.   רבותינו פתרוהו על מלך המשיח ונכון הדבר לפותרו עוד על דוד עצמו לתשובת המאנים (Rashi 1934).

72.   Origen, *Selecta in Psalmos* (Lommatzsch 1831–48: XI, 370-71; XI,

the sequence of the Psalms is highly significant, yet confesses that he does not understand it: '...the sequence of the Psalms, which seems to me to contain the secret of a mighty mystery, has not yet been revealed to me.'[73] However he recognizes a progression to perfection in the whole arrangement.

> For it seems to me not without significance, that the fiftieth is of penitence, the hundredth of mercy and judgment, the hundred and fiftieth of the praise of God in his saints. For thus do we advance to an everlasting life of happiness, first by condemning our own sins, then by living aright, that having condemned our ill life, and lived a good life, we may attain to everlasting life[74]

In the same place he discusses, as does Origen elsewhere,[75] the symbolism of the different Psalms according to their number in the LXX sequence, a mode of interpretation that, whatever its shortcomings, indicates high regard for the received arrangement of Psalms. Gregory of Nyssa maintains the five books exhibit an upward progression to moral perfection: ἀεὶ πρὸς τὸ ὑψηλότερον τὴν ψυχὴν ὑπερτιθείς, ἕως ἂν ἐπὶ τὸ ἀκρότατον ἀφίκηται τῶν ἀγαθῶν.[76]

Patristic writers, like the rabbis, endorse the structurally important headings and subscripts by discussing their interpretative significance. Hippolytus and Origen comment at length on the titles and authors of the Psalms.[77] Gregory of Nyssa has two lengthy essays on Psalms' headings, Εἰς τὰς Ἐπίγραφας τῶν ψαλμῶν, in which he suggests they play an important part in the overall moral and mystical purpose of the Psalter.[78] Athanasius too, according to Jerome, wrote a commentary,

352-54; XIII, 107). The commentary on the Moses Psalms is cited in Chapter 9, and the one on the Songs of Ascents in Chapter 4, of this book.

73.   '...ordo psalmorum, qui mihi magni sacramenti videtur continere secretum, nondum mihi fuerit revelatus' (*Enarrationes* on Ps. 150 §1).

74.   'Non enim frustra mihi videtur quinquagesimus esse de paenitentia, centesimus de misericordia et iudicio, centesimus quinquagesimus de laude Dei in sanctis eius. Sic enim ad aeternam beatamque tendimus vitam, primitus peccata nostra damnando, deinde bene vivendo, ut post condemnatam vitam malam gestamque bonam, mereamur aeternam' (*Enarrationes* on Ps. 150 §3).

75.   Origen, *Selecta in Psalmos* (Lommatzsch: XI, 370-71).

76.   'It always tends toward the utmost height of the soul, until it comes to the pinnacle of good' (*In Inscriptiones Psalmorum* I.ix.).

77.   So Quasten 1950–86: II, 175. Parts of the introduction to Hippolytus' commentary are in Pitra 1884: II, 418-27. For Origen, see *CPG*: I, 149-50.

78.   Quasten 1950–86: III, 265.

now lost, *De psalmorum titulis*.[79] Jerome himself commented on Psalms headings: 'David symbolizes the victory of the believers; Asaph relates to the gathering together with the Lord, and the sons of Core [Korah] pertain to Calvary.'[80] Augustine regards the headings as containing profound truth: 'The scriptures of the Psalms usually place mysteries in the title and adorn the beginning of the psalm with the sublimity of a sacrament', and, 'In the title...mysteries are heaped together.'[81] Apparently the only early Christian writer who did not accept the traditions in the headings was Theodore of Mopsuestia, who asserted that David wrote all the Psalms, those that describe later events being written prophetically by him.[82]

Hippolytus gives the earliest written statement of the idea, later recorded in Midrash Tehillim, that the doxological subscripts were intended to divide the Psalter into five books. He states, Καὶ τοῦτο δέ σε μὴ παρέλθοι...ὅτι καὶ τὸ ψαλτήριον εἰς πέντε διεῖλον βιβλία οἱ Ἑβραῖοι, ὥστε εἶναι καὶ αὐτὸ ἄλλον πεντάτευχον,[83] and cites the psalms contained in each book according to the LXX numbering.[84] If this idea was known to a Roman bishop as a Hebrew idea in the late second or early third century, then it probably existed in Israel some

79.   Jerome, *De viris illustribus* 87. This Athanasian work is not the same as *De titulis psalmorum*, with which it is sometimes confused, which is thought to be by Hesychius of Jerusalem (Quasten 1950–86: III, 38).

80.   *Comm. on Ps.* 8.1 (CCSL: LXXII, 191).

81.   'Solet scriptura Psalmorum mysteria in titulis ponere et frontem Psalmi sublimitate sacramenti decorare' (*Enarrationes* on Ps. 58); 'In titulum...congesta mysteria' (*Enarrationes* on Ps. 80).

82.   Quasten 1950–86: III, 404-405; Ackroyd and Evans 1970: 497-501.

83.   Let it not escape your notice,...that the Hebrews divided the Psalter also into five books, so that it too might be another Pentateuch.

84.   The text can be found at Lagarde 1858b: 193; *PG*: X, 720B. Migne regards it as spurious, but it is not for that reason to be rejected. The Syriac form of Hippolytus' introduction to the Psalms (Lagarde 1858a: 86) is regarded as genuine (Quasten 1950–86: II, 175; Smith 1892: 194 n.). It speaks of the Psalter being divided into five parts or sections (*menawâthê*). Moreover, Eusebius of Caesarea (263–c. 340) and Epiphanius of Salamis (315–403) attribute such a statement to Hippolytus, using language similar to the above passage (Achelis 1897: 131, 143); cf. Eusebius (*PG*: XXIII, 66C); Epiphanius, *De mensuris et ponderibus* c. 5 (*PG*: XLIII, 244D–245A). Epiphanius is generally regarded as an important source for the reconstruction of Hippolytus' works (Quasten 1950–86: III, 384-85). There is therefore good ground to believe that the Greek reflects an authentic statement of Hippolytus.

time before. Moreover its similarity to the above-cited passage from *Midr. Pss.* 1.2, both in comparing Psalms and Pentateuch and in listing the Psalms in each book, confirms the antiquity of the rabbinic tradition. Jerome also knew of the five-book division: 'The third section comprises the Hagiographa. The first begins at Job. The second [book begins] at David, which is comprised in five divisions and in a single volume of Psalms.'[85] It is mentioned also by Augustine and other early Christian writers.[86]

The view that the Psalter was future-predictive was widely held in the early church. However, the fathers often interpret the Psalms as referring to the life of Jesus, rather than to the future redemption of the earth, for they regarded the messianic age as in some sense already come. Yet the basic hermeneutical supposition in each case was the same: the Psalter foretells messianic times. Unfortunately the commentaries that might best have preserved early Jewish exegesis, those of the Hebraists Origen and Jerome, are largely lost. But commentaries by other Christian writers are plentiful. Theodotion, like Aquila, renders למנצח messianically: εἰς τὸ νῖκος, *For the victory*. Hippolytus regards David as an eschatological prophet: καὶ Δαβὶδ προμηνύων τὴν κρίσιν καὶ τὴν ἐπιφάνειαν τοῦ κυρίου φησὶν ἀπ' ἄκρου τοῦ οὐρανοῦ ἡ ἔξοδος αὐτοῦ, etc. (LXX Ps. 18.7).[87] Justin cites Psalms 2, 3, 19, 22, 24, 68, 72 and 110 as messianic proof-texts.[88] Augustine finds messianic prophecy throughout the Psalter: Psalm 1: 'This is to be understood of our Lord Jesus Christ';[89] Psalm 2: 'This is spoken of our Lord's persecutors, of whom mention is made also in the Acts of the Apostles';[90] Psalm 3: 'The words, *I slept, and took rest, and rose for the Lord will wake me up,* lead us to believe that this psalm is to

85.   'Tertius ordo Hagiographa possidet. Et primus liber incipit a Job. Secundus a David, quem quinque incisionibus et uno Psalmorum volumine comprehendunt', *Prologus Galeatus.*

86.   Augustine, *Enarrationes* on Ps. 150 § 2. Kirkpatrick notes, 'The division is referred to by most of the Fathers' (Kirkpatrick 1902: xviii).

87.   'And David foretold the Judgment and the appearing of the Lord, saying, *From the summit of heaven is his going out,*' etc. (Lagarde 1858b: 34).

88.   *Dialogue with Trypho,* § 19, 32-34, 69, 88, 97-105, 121-22, 127.

89.   '...de Domino nostro Iesu Christo... accipiendum est' (*Enarrationes* on Ps. 1 §1).

90.   'Dicitur hoc enim de persecutoribus Domini, qui et in Actibus Apostolorum commemorantur' (*Enarrationes* on Ps. 2 §1).

be understood as in the Person of Christ';[91] and so on. Athanasius deals with the messianic character of the Psalms in his Psalms commentary and in his *Epistula ad Marcellinum de interpretatione Psalmorum*.[92] Jerome, as noted above, regards the Asaph Psalms as relating to an eschatological gathering, probably of souls, to the Lord, and the Korah Psalms as foretelling Calvary.[93] Similarly, like Theodotion, he makes no attempt to interpret למנצח cultically, but renders it 'Victori', *For the conqueror*.[94] Tertullian regards the immediate sense [praesentis rei sensum] of Psalm 1 as referring to Joseph of Arimathea, and its 'assembly of the wicked' to the Sanhedrin.[95] Even the 'historical-critical' Theodore of Mopsuestia held to the prophetic nature of the Psalter, albeit with a heterodox hermeneutic. He regarded David as a prophet who wrote all the Psalms, but generally limited his prophetic horizon to the Maccabean period. Yet he allows that four psalms, LXX Psalms 2, 8, 44 (MT 45) and 109 (MT 110), see beyond this period and were written prophetically in the character of Christ.[96] Commentaries by Ambrose, Basil, Chrysostom, Theodoret and others also survive, all of whom regard the Psalms as prophetic. Similar views prevailed for centuries to come. Venantius Fortunatus, bishop of Poitiers in the late sixth century, asserts David's prophetic foreknowledge.

> Impleta sunt quae concinit
> David fideli carmine,
> Dicendo in nationibus
> Regnavit a ligno Deus.[97]

91.   'Hunc psalmum ex persona Christi accipiendum persuadet quod dictum est: Ego dormiui, et somnum cepi, et exsurrexi, quoniam Dominus suscipiet me' (*Enarrationes* on Ps. 3 §1).

92.   Quasten 1950–86: III, 37-38.

93.   Comm. on Ps. 8.1 (*CCSL*: LXXII, 191).

94.   Jerome's varying approaches to this word are particularly interesting. In his Gallican Psalter (Vulgate), based largely on LXX (Berardino and Quasten 1950–86: IV, 223-25), he renders it, 'In finem', *For the end*. This corresponds to the foremost meaning of LXX's Εἰς τὸ τέλος. However, in his later Hebrew Psalter, written after he acquired greater familiarity with the Hebrew text and its traditions (Berardino and Quasten 1950–86: IV, 224-26), he gives instead 'Victori'. Thus, of the two possible eschatological meanings, he regards the more messianic one as correct.

95.   *De Spectaculis* 3 (Tertullian, *Writings* 1.11; *Opera* 1.5).

96.   Quasten 1950–86: III, 404-405; Ackroyd and Evans 1970: 497-501. The Syriac text of his headings is given in Baethgen 1885: 67-70.

97.   From 'Vexilla regis prodeunt' by Venantius Fortunatus (d. 609). Neale and

Likewise, the thirteenth-century author of *Dies irae* regarded David as a prophet like the highly eschatological Sybils.[98]

> Dies irae, dies illa,
> Solvet sæclum in favilla
> Teste David cum Sybilla.[99]

Indeed, the medieval church's emphasis on the prophetic nature of Psalms became such that Abarbanel,[100] in the fifteenth century, objected to their classifying David among the prophets.[101]

The same hermeneutic prevailed in Psalms interpretation throughout the Reformation period. Allegorizing speculations aside, the following words of Luther indicate that he recognized the Psalms' headings as an intrinsic part of the Psalter text, valid for interpretation, and that he regarded the psalmists as future-predictive prophets.

> Filii Chore spiritum propheticum fere semper ad incarnationem Christi habent magis quam ad passionem. Cuius mysteria clarius David in suo spiritu pronunciat. Ita quilibet prophetarum ad unam magis materiam quam ad aliam videtur spiritum habere. Unde raro filii Core de passione, sed fere semper de incarnatione et nuptiis Christi et Ecclesie loquuntur in gaudio: quod et psalmi eorum sunt iucundi et hilaritate pleni. David autem

Littledale (1874) translate it as, 'Fulfilled is now what David told, In true prophetic song of old; Among the nations, Lo, says he, Our God is reigning from the tree' ('The Royal Banners Forward Go'). The reference to God reigning from the tree is from the Old Latin Version of Ps. 96.10, as preserved in the Psalterium Romanum. It contains the reading 'Dominus regnavit a ligno', which is quoted by many Latin writers from Tertullian on as a prophecy of Christ's triumph through death. The only Greek authority for the tradition is Justin Martyr, who regards it as a prophecy of Christ's reign after his crucifixion (*Apol.* 1.41) and charges the Jews with having erased it from the text (*Dialogue with Trypho* 100.73). The charge is probably unjustified. The words are found in only two LXX MSS and in each case have probably been introduced from the Old Latin (Kirkpatrick 1902: 577-78).

98. 'Its author is almost certainly a 13th century Franciscan' ('Dies irae', *ODCC*: 398).

99. 'The day of wrath, that day, shall reduce the world to ashes, as David testifies together with the Sybils.'

100. Leiman 1968: 49 n., argues for the pronunciation 'Abarbanel' rather than the more common 'Abrabanel' or 'Abravanel'.

101. Rosenthal 1937: 36. Leiman 1968: 49-61, notes Abarbanel's general familiarity with Christian interpretation. It is hard to know how widespread Abarbanel's view on this matter might have been among Jews of the period. Certainly, the Talmud (*b. Soṭ.* 48b) classes David among the 'former prophets', although that does not necessarily imply ability to predict the future.

magis de passione et resurrectione et iis, que in virili etate gessit dominus. Asaph autem potissimum de discretione malorum a consortio piorum, de perditione impiorum et desructione synagoge, ut patet per psalmos eius. Et id forte nominum ratio postulat. Quia filii Chore plures sunt: significantes populum fidei novellum, qui de virgine natus sicut Christus, spiritualiter, ex aqua et spiritu sancto. Hec enim est mystica incarnatio Christi, quod nascitur in illis spiritualiter: immo ipsi ex eo nascuntur. Ideo de ista duplici nativitate, scilicet Christi capitis et corporis eius Ecclesie, omnis eorum psalmus resonat. At David 'manu fortis'[102] iam operantem virtutes et crucem sustinentem indicat: ideo et de illis fere semper loquuntur psalmi eius. Asaph tandem 'congregatio' significat,[103] discretum populum et congregatum ex illis, qui relinquuntur et non congregantur.[104]

In his introduction to the Psalter, Luther emphasizes its future-predictive nature: 'And for this reason alone the Psalter should be precious and beloved: because it promises Christ's death and resurrection so clearly and depicts his kingdom and the entire condition and nature of Christendom.'[105]

102. Jerome translates *David* as, 'fortis manu sive desiderabilis' (Opp. Paris [1579], III, p. 474).

103. Jerome translates *Asaph* as, 'congregans' (Opp. Paris [1579], III, p. 480).

104. 'The sons of Korah have the prophetic spirit almost always for Christ's incarnation rather than for his passion. David in his spirit speaks of the mysteries of the passion more clearly. Thus any one prophet seems to have the Spirit more for one matter than for another. Hence the sons of Korah rarely speak about the Passion, but almost always speak with joy about Christ's incarnation and his marriage with the church, so that also their psalms are joyful and full of mirth. David, on the contrary, deals more with the Passion and the Resurrection and the things the Lord did in his maturity. Asaph, in turn, talks mostly about the separation of the wicked from the fellowship of the godly, about the destruction of the ungodly and of the synagogue, as is clear from his psalms. And this is perhaps what the significance of the names calls for. The sons of Korah are many, denoting the new people of faith who were born spiritually of water and the Holy Spirit, as Christ was born of the Virgin. This is the mystical incarnation of Christ, that he is born in them spiritually, indeed that they are born of him. Therefore every one of their psalms echoes this twofold birth, namely of Christ the Head and of the church, his body. But David, 'strong of hand', shows Christ now doing miracles and bearing the cross, and therefore his psalms almost always speak about these things. Finally, Asaph means 'gathering,' the people separated and gathered from those who remain and are not gathered' (Luther 1883–1987: IV, 3-4).

105. 'Und allein deshalb sollte der Psalter teuer und lieb sein, weil er von Christi Sterben und Auferstehen so klar verheißt und sein Reich und der ganzen Christenheit Stand und Wesen verbildet'; from the introduction to the Psalter of 1528 and 1545 (Luther 1965: I, 3).

Of the other reformers, Bucer produced the first full commentary on the Psalter, *In Librum Psalmorum Interpretatio* (1524).[106] A capable Hebraist, he was well-acquainted with the commentaries of Rashi, Ibn Ezra and Kimhi, and refers to their opinions on virtually every page. He regards the headings, especially those containing historical information, as relevant to correct interpretation. He gives priority to the historical setting of psalms texts, yet believes they are to be understood typologically as predicting the true David, the Christ. Calvin, aware of the abuses of mystical interpretation, regards authorial intention and historical context as essential to correct interpretation, and dismisses, sometimes too readily, what is not immediately apparent.[107] Nonetheless, he too cautiously espouses the same broad principles observable in his predecessors. As regards arrangement, he comments that the redactor seems to have placed Psalm 1 at the beginning as a preface.[108] He regards the headings as valid for interpretation and thus an intrinsic part of the Psalms text. For instance, he takes לבני־קרח and לאסף to mean that David composed these psalms and gave them to these levitical musicians, and takes account of historical information in the heading when interpreting.[109] As regards eschatological prophecy, he is cautious, but allows that some psalms, such as 2, 21, 22, 45, 67, 72, 110, contain messianic prophecy, often typologically contained in the events of David's life. Coverdale, alone of all the reformers, changed the received text of the Psalter by omitting its headings in his Bible, but his successors did not hesitate to rectify the omission. Subsequent English reformers rectified the omission. Thus, among sixteenth-century Christians, the general hermeneutic of Psalms interpretation differed little from that of the previous two millennia, in the essentials of recognizing the Psalter's literary integrity and future-predictive purpose, although in specifics, such as Luther's 'destructione synagoge', it varies from rabbinic literature. Similar views prevailed until the early nineteenth century.

---

106. It is discussed by Hobbs 1994: 161-78. See also Hobbs 1971 and Hobbs 1984.

107. See, for instance, his comment on שׁשׁן of Ps. 45.1: 'Ego, ut de re non magni momenti, suspendo sententiam' (As this is a matter of no great consequence, I suspend judgment).

108. Comment on Ps. 1.

109. Comments on Pss. 42, 73 and, e.g., Ps. 51.

6. *The Nineteenth Century*

With the intellectual revolution of the Enlightenment, biblical interpretation in the universities of western Europe was loosed from the
authority of church and synagogue. This gave rise to forms of interpretation radically different from all that went before, as a result of
which biblical interpretation in the nineteenth century was divided
between revisionist and conservative viewpoints. Few, of course, sub-
scribed exclusively to one position, but still there was a dividing of
tendencies. It therefore becomes necessary from now on to consider
conflicting schools of interpretation.

The revisionist approach came to regard psalm headings as additions of such a late date as to contain no significant information about
their respective lyrics. In particular, they denied any link between
individuals named in ascriptions and the ensuing psalms. Thus De
Wette, von Lengerke, Olshausen, Hupfeld, Graetz, Kuenen, Reuss,
Stade, Cheyne and Duhm are unwilling to connect any psalms with the
individuals named.[110] Ewald and Hitzig are more generous, the
former allowing one psalm to David, the latter about thirteen.[111]
Cheyne omits all the headings from the text, while others render them
in some form or another extraneous.[112] Two points were adduced to
support this dismissal of the headings. First, the text of some psalms
was said to date from long after the time of the person named in the
heading. For instance, the temple seems to be mentioned in some לדוד
psalms, and some לדוד and לאסף psalms appear post-exilic (27, 69, 79,
83). It was therefore assumed that these, and all other headings as
well, are later pseudepigraphal ascriptions. Olshausen summarizes it
thus:

110. De Wette 1811: 12-14; Olshausen 1853: 4-5; Graetz 1882: 16; Cheyne
1888: xvi; Duhm 1899: xvi-xviii. Hupfeld does not discuss them in his introduction,
places them in parentheses in his translation, and disputes them in his commentary.
The opinion of von Lengerke is noted by Delitzsch (1887: 83). The opinions of
Kuenen, Reuss and Stade are noted by Briggs and Briggs (1906–1907: lvii).

111. Ewald 1899: 1-2; Hitzig 1863–65: xv.

112. See Cheyne's first Psalms commentary (1888). Hitzig and Hupfeld put the
headings in brackets, while Wellhausen prints them in red and the rest of the psalm in
black. Olshausen and Duhm do not cite the headings in their summaries and brief
quotes of the psalm text.

However, by a more exact and somewhat unprejudiced examination the conclusion has long been unavoidable that this tradition, despite its age, is not credible in the great majority of cases, because by far the greater part of these 90 Pss.,[113] according to their content, could not possibly have originated in the time indicated by the tradition. But thereby is their [the headings'] evidential value not merely weakened, but totally and completely invalid, and their statements worthless for criticism, even in those psalms whose composition in the time indicated cannot be ruled out, and which are partially understandable according to the circumstances of that time.[114]

Secondly, LXX additions to the Hebrew headings were thought to indicate an increasing tendency in scribal circles to create headings at all costs. Hence it was surmised that the whole tradition of the headings was itself of late origin. Baethgen summarized it thus:

At those psalms which have the לדוד superscription, it is chiefly to be noted that at many of these this לדוד is not text-critically established...; it is missing in three cases in the Jerusalem Targum, in one case in the Vulgate and in one case in Aquila Sexta. On the other hand, the fact that the LXX, at a greater number of Psalms, names authors, especially David, where they are absent in the Hebrew text, shows that there is a predominant tendency to give an author also to the nameless Psalms. The lack of לדוד in these five cases is only explainable by saying that these particular five psalms were yet untitled by the Hebrews in the translator's time. But if the statements about the authors are as late as this, then it follows that in these cases they have no critical value. From that conclusion follows further the obligation to investigate also those psalms whose author-ascription is already witnessed by LXX, in order to see whether or not in these cases also the לדוד etc. rests upon the notion of a later reader, or originally had another sense altogether.[115]

---

113. That is, those having proper names in the heading.

114. 'Einer genaueren, einigermassen vorurtheilsfreien Betrachtung hat es jedoch schon längst nicht entgehn können, dass diese Ueberlieferung, ihres Alters ungeachtet, in den allermeisten Fällen nicht für glaubwürdig gehalten werden darf, indem der bei weitem grösste Theil jener 90 Pss. seinem Inhalte nach unmöglich in den Zeiten entstanden sein kann, auf welche die Ueberlieferung hindeutet. Damit wird aber deren Beweiskraft überhaupt nicht bloss geschwächt, sondern ganz und gar hinfällig und ihre Angaben auch bei solchen Pss. für die Kritik werthlos, deren Abfassung in der bezeichneten Zeit nicht gerade unmöglich genannt werden kann und sich aus den damaligen Verhältnissen einigermassen begreifen liesse' (Olshausen 1853: 4-5).

115. Author's translation of 'Bei den Psalmen, welche die Überschrift לדוד haben, ist zunächst anzumerken, daß bei mehreren derselben dies לדוד textkritisch

The idea that the Psalter was purposefully arranged was also disputed. Indeed, after the headings fell, it was defenceless, for the headings and doxologies, demarcating groups of psalms, had always been the best evidence for internal structure. The Psalter came to be regarded instead as 'only the remains of the lyric poetry of the Israelites' and to suggest they were 'an anthology of lyrics' was 'misleading in the highest degree'.[116] Thus many commentators of the period make no remark on the existence of concatenation or upon the characteristics of heading-defined internal collections, such as the Asaph or Korah Psalms.[117] Ewald rearranged the psalms into what he considered their chronological order (1839).[118] Instead of being purposefully redacted, the Psalter was said to have grown into its present form by a process of accretion whereby groups of psalms were successively suffixed to one another. The rubric at the end of Book II was appealed to as evidence for this, it being said that since Davidic psalms appeared after that point, the statement that the prayers of David were ended must mark the end of an earlier collection.[119] Jahn states it thus:

> In the five books of the Psalms we have before us just as many collections
> of psalms as were made, and they are arranged in the order in which they
> followed one another. The first compiler wanted to pass on only songs of
> David; the second joined his collection to the first, and wanted to give a

nicht feststeht...; es fehlt in drei Fällen bei Hier. Targ., in einem Fall bei Hier. und in einem Fall bei Aq. Sexta. Andrerseits zeigt der Umstand, daß die LXX bei einer grösseren Anzahl von Psalmen Verfasser, besonders David, nennen, wo sie im hebräischen Text fehlen, daß die Tendenz herrschte, auch den namenlosen Psalmen einen Verfasser zu geben. Das fehlen von לדוד in jenen fünf Fällen läßt sich daher nur so erklären, daß die betreffenden fünf Psalmen zur Zeit der Übersetzer noch ἀνεπίγραφοι παρ' Ἑβραίους waren. Sind aber die Angaben über die Verfasser so spät, so haben sie zunächst in diesen Fällen keinen kritischen Wert. Daraus folgt dann aber weiter die Pflicht, auch bei den Psalmen, bei welchen die Angabe des Verfassers bereits von LXX bezeugt wird, zu untersuchen, ob nicht etwa auch bei ihnen das לדוד u.s.w. auf einer Vermuthung späterer Leser beruht oder ursprünglich einen anderen Sinn hat' (Baethgen 1897: vi).

116. Author's translation of 'nur die Überreste der lyrischen Poesie der Israeliten... eine lyrische Anthologie... in höchstem Masse irreleitend' (Baethgen 1897: xxxiv). In spite of this, Baethgen comments on the same page on concatenation.

117. See e.g. Olshausen or Baethgen.

118. This is referred to by later commentators; e.g. Cheyne 1904: xvi. I have unfortunately been unable to find a copy of it.

119. See de Wette 1811: 17; Ewald 1866: I, 13; Baethgen 1897: xxix-xxxiv.

supplement to the Davidic lyrics; yet he did not hesitate to include some other songs as well. The compiler of the third book was no longer concerned at all with the songs of David; and because he wanted to join his collection to the previous one, he placed after Ps. 72 the closural phrase about the end of the songs of David. The fourth compiler confined himself to nameless songs, and therefore he transmitted only one psalm of Moses and two psalms of David. The fifth finally put together all the remaining uncollected sacred songs which were to be found.[120]

The traditional assumption that the Psalms foretold eschatological events was likewise rejected by the revisionist movement. Two factors probably contributed to this. The first was the obfuscation of the Psalter's internal structure following the dismissal of the headings. The second was the prevailing naturalism that led to a denial not only of future-prediction in the Bible, but also of any attempt by biblical writers to foretell the future. Instead a new purpose was proposed for the existence of the Psalter, as Olshausen wrote, the original purpose of the whole collection can have been none other than to serve *the Israelite community as a spiritual songbook.*[121]

Of course, the rejection of the traditional view of the headings also influenced opinion on the dating of the Psalms. Having dispensed with any connection with figures like David or the levitical Korahites and Asaphites, there was no necessary link with the pre-exilic period. Olshausen found it unthinkable that some psalms could still originate

120.   'In den fünf Büchern der Psalmen haben wir eben so viele Sammlungen der Psalmen vor uns, die nach der Ordnung, in welcher sie aufeinander folgen, gemacht worden. Der erste Sammler wollte bloss Lieder Davids liefern; der zweite fügte seine Sammlung der ersten an, und wollte eine Nachlese der davidischen Lieder geben; doch scheute er sich nicht, auch einige andere Gesänge aufzunehmen. Der Sammler des dritten Buchs hatte seine Absicht gar nicht mehr auf die Lieder Davids gerichtet; und da er seine Sammlung der vorigen anschliessen wollte, so setzte er nach dem 72. Ps. die Schlussformel von dem Ende der Lieder Davids hinzu. Der vierte Sammler beschränkte sich auf namenlose Lieder, daher er nun einen Psalm Mose's und zwei Psalmen Davids liefert. Der fünfte endlich nahm alles zusammen, was noch von heiligen Liedern zu finden war' (Jahn [*Einleitung,* II, 718-19] cited by de Wette 1811: 17).

121.   Author's translation of 'die ursprüngliche Bestimmung der ganzen Sammlung keine andre gewesen sein kann, als die, *der israelitischen Gemeinde zum geistlichen Gesangbuche* zu dienen' (Olshausen 1853: 4 [Olshausen's emphasis]). The same idea occurs widely in this period. See Baethgen 1897: xxxv.

from the time of the pre-exilic kings.[122] Instead, the way was clear to date the entire corpus in the Maccabean period.

> If a large number of psalms in all parts of the collection belong to the times of the Syrian oppression and the Maccabean wars, as seems to be the case from the events mentioned, then it is to be expected that also many other songs, which are mixed among them, derive from the same time, even though they do not clearly demonstrate any direct relation to the state of the community.[123]

And books IV and V were dated yet later still, to the time of John Hyrcanus.[124] The denial of the traditional dating, although not directly relevant to the interpretation of the Psalter, yet affected the new view of it that was to be proposed.

Thus this period saw the overthrow of all the traditional tenets of Psalms interpretation regarding the headings, the arrangement of lyrics and the eschatologico-predictive nature of the collection. Instead of being predictive scripture, compiled largely from lyrics of Israel's golden age, it had become a haphazard collection of texts dating from post-exilic times and conglomerated piecemeal in the late Maccabean period to be a second temple hymnbook.

However, although the above views were predominant throughout the nineteenth century, a significant minority of commentators continued to maintain traditional tenets of Psalms interpretation. Hengstenberg (1848) maintains that לדוד and some other ascriptions indicate authorship.[125] He discusses the headings and book divisions at length, and finds the Psalter 'has in no respect the character of a work done piecemeal'.[126] He also finds messianic prophecy in individual psalms.[127] Alexander, who owes much to Hengstenberg, shares his view of the

---

122. Author's translation of 'unbedenklich, daß einige Pss. noch aus der vorexilischen Königszeit herrühren' (Olshausen 1853: 8).

123. Author's translation of 'Wenn eine große Zahl von Psalmen in allen Theilen der Sammlung den Zeiten der syrischen Unterdrückung und der maccabäischen Kämpfe angehört, wie es nach den erwähnten Umständen der Fall zu sein scheint, so lässt sich erwarten, daß auch manche andere Gesänge, die mitten unter jene gemischt sind, ohne daß eine unmittelbare Beziehung auf die Lage der Gemeinde deutlich hervorträte, aus derselben Zeit herstammen...' (Olshausen 1853: 7-8).

124. Olshausen 1853: 8.

125. Hengstenberg 1845–48: Appendix, xvii-xxii.

126. Hengstenberg 1845–48: Appendix, xxxii-liv, xxxix.

127. Hengstenberg 1845–48: Appendix, lxxviii-lxxxi.

headings and discusses the order of lyrics and concatenation.[128] He observes that trilogies and even more extensive systems of individual psalms can be traced, each 'independent of the rest, and yet together forming beautiful and striking combinations, particularly when the nucleus or the basis of the series is an ancient psalm...to which others have been added'.[129] He too holds that some psalms are intentionally predictive.[130] Delitzsch, also influenced by Hengstenberg,[131] achieves perhaps the best balance between criticism and tradition of all nineteenth-century commentators. He generally supports the validity of the headings. He therefore allows 'many' psalms to be by David and suggests that the initial collections behind Psalms 3–72 date from Solomon's time, and that Psalm 90 is by Moses.[132] He notes that the order of the lyrics cannot be explained purely on the basis of chronological evolution, and indicates evidence of editorial activity in the Psalter, noting concatenation in particular.[133] In the light of this he detects 'the impress of one ordering spirit', a compiler whose arrangement displays, on the lesser level, 'the principle of homogeneity',[134] and on the larger level, the same sort of upward progression remarked upon by Gregory of Nyssa: 'The beginning of the Psalter celebrates the blessedness of those who walk in conformity with the redeeming will of God...the end of the Psalter soars to the blessed height of the consummation of all things.'[135] Delitzsch also maintains that a central theme is discernible in the collection, that is, concern with the Davidic covenant and its ultimate fulfilment in a future Messiah.[136] He perceives this eschatological hope not only in the redactor's mind, but also in the mind of individual psalmists. Of Psalm 2 he remarks, 'The poet is transported into the future in which all the nations of the world will rebel against Yahveh and his Christ' (משׁיח).[137]

128.   Alexander 1850: vii-xiv.
129.   Alexander 1850: ix-x.
130.   Alexander 1850: 8.
131.   Delitzsch 1887: 84.
132.   Delitzsch 1887: 10, 20, 22-23.
133.   Delitzsch 1887: 18-28, esp. 25-26. He discusses concatenation at greater length in the treatise Delitzsch 1846.
134.   Delitzsch 1887: 24, 26.
135.   Delitzsch 1887: 24-25.
136.   Delitzsch 1887: 88-95.
137.   Author's translation of 'Der Dichter ist in die Zukunft versetzt, wo die

Other commentators of this period deal with the arrangement and purpose of the Psalter. One approach was that of de Lagarde (1880). Building on the temple hymnbook theory, he proposed that the five divisions of the Psalter were intended for five different portions of public worship, the requirements of which explained internal repetitions in the collection.[138] This approach was taken up and developed by a number of subsequent commentators. More neglected, yet more original, was the work of Forbes, Professor of Oriental Languages at Aberdeen, whose *Studies in the Book of Psalms* (1888) anticipates much recent scholarship. He realized more clearly than any of his contemporaries that the final arrangement of the Psalter is greater than its parts.

> But whatever may be thought of the original purport of these Psalms, when we look at the place which has been assigned them in the Psalter as now constituted (arranged certainly in its present form a considerable time before the Septuagint version), and to the order and connection in which they stand, it becomes impossible with any fairness to deny that they were intended to excite in the Jewish worshippers an expectation of the Messiah...[139]

His justification for this approach was twofold. First, the retention of the royal psalms after the extinction of the monarchy is explicable only on the grounds of 'an unshaken expectation, still continuing, of a greater king yet to come than either a David or a Solomon'; secondly, the prominent position accorded to these royal psalms in the Psalter shows a high significance was attached to them.[140] And if the remainder of Forbes's theory is less enduring, these introductory remarks anticipate the premisses of recent scholarship on the canonical form of the Psalter. Another original thinker was Bishop King. In the third volume of his commentary on Psalms (1898–1905), he proposes that the Psalter was designed to be read with the triennial lectionary cycle of Torah in the synagogue, and demonstrates striking correspondences between them.[141] Later commentators, who originated similar theories,

---

gesamte Völkerwelt sich wieder Jahve und seinen Christus (מְשִׁיחוֹ) erheben wird' (Delitzsch 1890: 107).
138. De Lagarde 1879–80: II, 13-15.
139. Forbes 1888: 3.
140. Forbes 1888: 4.
141. King 1898–1905: III, v-xiv.

apparently independently of King, may be the poorer for not knowing
his work.

7. *The Twentieth Century*

The Psalms interpretation of the twentieth century appears, in retro-
spect, like a process of slow reappraisal of the scepticism of the nineteenth. It can be regarded under four heads: a synthesizing period and
three schools. The first of these, the synthesizing period, dominating
the first quarter of the century, lacks any dominant disciplines or
schools of thought. Its significant commentaries aim for a middle
ground somewhere between the traditional and revisionist views. If
none is as conservative as Hengstenberg, neither is any as sceptical as
Olshausen. The first major commentary of the century is that of
Kirkpatrick (1902), which displays a broad mastery of the ancient literature. As regards the arrangement of the Psalter, he notes concatenation and suggests that the temple hymnbook theory is insufficient.
He recognizes eschatological and messianic themes, but does not
regard them as organizational principles in the compilation of the
collection, concluding that the compilers worked with a number of
ends in view, both liturgical and devotional.[142] As regards headings,
he states:

> While however the titles cannot be accepted as giving trustworthy infor-
> mation in regard to the authorship of the Psalms, they are not to be
> regarded as entirely worthless... It seems probable that, in many cases at
> least, they indicate the source from which the Psalms were derived rather
> than the opinion of the collector as to their authorship.[143]

His view of the five-book division is typically cautious: '...the division
of the books in part corresponds to older collections out of which the
Psalter was formed, in part is purely artificial, and probably had its
origin in the wish to compare the Psalter with the Pentateuch.'[144]
Cheyne, unlike Kirkpatrick, was unfettered by circumspection. In his
second commentary (1904), he makes bizarre changes without ground
or defence to the entire Psalter. The entire heading of Psalm 51, for
instance, is 'corrected' to *Deposited. Marked: of 'Arab-ethan. For the*

142. Kirkpatrick 1902: l-li, lxxvi.
143. Kirkpatrick 1902: xxxii-xxxiii.
144. Kirkpatrick 1902: xviii.

Sabbath. Briggs (1906) believes the Psalter was redacted at the end of the second century to be a hymn book suitable for use in both temple and synagogue.[145] He regards the headings as almost entirely spurious and dates the composition of most psalms in the late Persian to Maccabean periods, although he allows that some may be pre-exilic.[146] He seems to regard some psalms (2, 110) as intentionally messianic, and others as perhaps less intentionally so (22, 40, 69, and 'the royal psalms').[147]

Probably the most original thinker of the first quarter of the century was J.P. Peters, whose concern to ascertain the cultic life-setting of the Psalms anticipated the work of Mowinckel.[148] He emphasized the historical setting of psalms collections, rather than individual lyrics; indeed, so important to him were these collections that he rearranged the Psalter to reunite divided collections, such as the Korah Psalms. He made the interesting suggestion that the Elohistic Psalter originated in the Northern Kingdom—the Korah Psalms coming from the Dan cult and the Asaph Psalms from a Josephite shrine.[149] He also published a separate study on the Songs of Ascents.[150] He proposed that the distinctive headings of these collections indicated the cultic traditions from which they came, and gives considerable attention to headings in general.[151] Occasionally he suggests that parts of the Psalter were redacted on literary principles with eschatological aims.

> It [Ps. 72] is not a liturgy for a sacrifice, but an ode, like Ps. 2, to depict the glories of the kingdom of the ideal king of David's line, the Messiah or Christ that was to be, and appears to have been designed for the conclusion of the collection of the Psalms of David, as Ps. 2, a much more militant treatment of the same theme, was for the commencement of that volume.[152]

However, this thought-provoking work appears to have gone largely unnoticed until Goulder developed some of Peters's ideas more than six decades later.

145. Briggs and Briggs 1906–1907: xc-xcii.
146. Briggs and Briggs 1906–1907: lviii, xc-xci.
147. Briggs and Briggs 1906–1907: xcvii.
148. Peters 1922.
149. Peters 1922: 9-10, 273-75.
150. Peters 1894.
151. Peters 1922: 32-50.
152. Peters 1922: 270.

The first two of the three schools of twentieth-century Psalms scholarship were the form critical approaches developed by H. Gunkel and S. Mowinckel respectively. Gunkel, the pioneer of form criticism, attempted to define psalms according to categories of literary genres (*Gattungen*), and to discover the original life-setting (*Sitz im Leben*) of a *Gattung* and its psalms. These *Gattungen* were formulated partly by comparison with the literary forms of other recently discovered ancient oriental literature, but also took into account theme and content, and were therefore useful tools of broad categorization. Gunkel defined several major *Gattungen*: hymns, communal laments, royal psalms, individual laments (and psalms of trust), and individual thanksgiving psalms. He also indicated minor *Gattungen*: communal thanksgiving psalms, pilgrimage psalms and liturgies.[153] This approach, recognizing as it did the Psalms' resemblance to other ancient literature, helped re-establish a more realistic dating. Gunkel allowed that some psalms might have originated in the pre-exilic period. As regards the arrangement of the Psalter, he adopts a middle ground. At the beginning of his last work, *Einleitung in Die Psalmen*, he calls for investigation into inter-psalm links:

> Now it is an inviolable principle of scholarship that nothing can be understood without its context. Accordingly, *it will be the specific task of Psalms research to rediscover the connections between the individual songs.*[154]

However, while acknowledging Delitzsch's work on concatenation, he disagrees with his view that there is an overarching purpose in the Psalter,[155] believing it originated by a process of gradual evolution:

> The discovery that no unifying principle for the received sequence can be found, although various viewpoints can be detected in the juxtaposition of individual psalms... compels the conclusion that the Psalter owes its present condition to an intricate process of development.[156]

---

153. Gunkel 1926: 1-33. Successive chapters deal with the *Gattungen* individually.

154. Author's translation of 'Nun ist es aber ein unverbrüchliche Grundsatz der Wissenschaft, daß nichts ohne seine Zusammenhang verstanden werden kann. Es wird demnach *die eigentliche Aufgabe der Psalmenforschung sein, die Verbindungen zwischen die einzelnen Liedern wiederauszufinden*' (Gunkel 1926: 4; Gunkel's emphasis).

155. Gunkel 1926: 435.

156. Author's translation of 'Die Ergebnis, daß sich kein einheitliches Prinzip

He virtually ignores headings and subscripts. *Einleitung in die Psalmen* has no more than a short supplement on the musical terms, written by his student, Begrich, after Gunkel's death.[157] Yet while he recognizes no overarching purpose in the Psalter, he notes that certain psalms are in a form that shows them to be intentionally eschatological prophecy (9, 46, 47, 48, 68, 76, 93, 96, 97, 98, 99, 149).[158]

Mowinckel, Gunkel's student, built upon his teacher's *Gattungs-geschichte,* but emphasized the need to understand the Psalms in relation to their cultic function in Israel. For, although Gunkel had already recognized that some psalms were of cultic origin, he thought the majority were spiritualized imitations of earlier psalms, deriving from conventicles of pious laymen.[159] Mowinckel however recognized that the numerous cultic allusions in the Psalms require that the majority of them originated in the cult. In his *Psalmenstudien* (1921–24), he sought not only to define their *Sitz im Leben,* but also to reconstruct the festivals in which they originated. In the second *Psalmenstudien* monograph, *Das Thronbesteigungsfest Jahwäs und der Ursprung der Eschatologie* (1920), he proposed, by analogy with the annual 'enthronement of Marduk' ritual, or *bit akitu,* of the Babylonian autumn new year festival, that ancient Israel had an annual 'enthronement of Yhwh' festival. This celebrated Yhwh's victory, like that of Marduk or Baal, over the creation negating forces of chaos. He proposed that about 40 psalms were connected with this festival.

As regards the editorial purpose behind the Psalter, he rejects the hymnbook idea, considering historical preservation of ancient texts as the redactional impulse behind the collection.[160] He discusses psalm headings at some length.[161] He allows that some Davidic psalms are very ancient, dating even from David's time, but their ascriptions do

für die überlieferte Aufeinanderfolge erkennen läßt, wohl aber verschiedene Gesichtspunkte bei der Zusammenstellung einzelner Psalmen nachweisbar sind... drängt zu dem Schlusse, daß das Psalmbuch seinen gegenwärtigen Zustand einem verwickelten Entstehungsvorgang verdankt...' (Gunkel and Begrich 1933: 436).

157. Gunkel 1926: 455-58.

158. Gunkel and Begrich 1933: 329-81.

159. Cf. also Briggs and Briggs 1906–1907: xcv: 'Many of the Pss. in their original form were composed as an expression of private devotion.'

160. Mowinckel 1962: II, 204.

161. The fourth monograph, *Die Technischen Termini in den Psalmenüber-schriften,* investigates the musical and cultic terms in the headings. The sixth monograph, *Die Psalmdichter,* deals with personal names in the headings.

not indicate authorship.[162] Rather, some Psalms of David and Solomon may have been written for the use of these people, 'in whose name was a good omen', and these ascriptions were mistakenly thought by later generations to indicate authorship. From this arose the biblical tradition that David was a musician and a poet.[163] Other ascriptions, such as Asaph, Heman, Ethan and the Sons of Korah, indicate not authorship, but the names of guilds who made these collections.[164] He regards the five-book division as accidental, developing from the doxologies that were carried into the Psalter along with their preceding psalms.[165] He recognizes the prophetic tone of many psalms, and suggests they originated as cultic oracles in answer to contemporary requirements of divine guidance and exhortation.[166] However, he denies there is any intentionally eschatological or messianic reference in the Psalter.[167]

Other commentaries of the time tend to be overshadowed by the work of Gunkel and Mowinckel. Barnes (1931) is moderately conservative. He says little regarding the place of the headings in interpretation, but does not dismiss them, coming 'to the study of the Psalter prepared to find some Davidic compositions there'.[168] He appears to subscribe tacitly to the view that the Psalter is the second temple hymnbook. He regards some psalms (2, 72, 85, 89) as messianic in the sense that they long for the return of Israel's Golden Age under a righteous king. But Psalms 2 and 110 barely make it; apparently they are too warlike to refer to his conception of messiah.[169] Oesterley (1939) states that the headings 'formed no part of the text in its original form' but 'many of them indicate the collection to which the psalm in question belonged before being incorporated in the Psalter'.[170] He

162. Mowinckel 1921–24: VI, 72, 76. Elsewhere Mowinckel states that only a minority of psalms date from the 'late Jewish period' (Preface to *Psalms in Israel's Worship* [1962]).

163. Author's translation of '...in dessen Namen ein gutes Omen lag' (Mowinckel 1921-24: VI, 75, 72-81).

164. Mowinckel 1921–24: VI, 69-71.

165. Mowinckel 1962: II, 197.

166. See *Kultprophetie und prophetische Psalmen,* the third monograph of *Psalmenstudien.* Also Mowinckel 1962: II, 53-73.

167. Mowinckel 1962: I, 48-49.

168. Barnes 1931: xxviii.

169. Barnes 1931: xlii-xliv.

170. Oesterley 1939: 9.

says little about the date of composition of the lyrics, but rejects
Maccabean theories and suggests that some psalms may have originated in ancient dramatic epics like those associated with the cults of
Babylon and Ugarit.[171] He finds it likely that the Psalter was compiled
for use in the cult and seems to endorse the view that it was compiled
piecemeal over a period of time, but does not exclude the possibility
of purposeful final redaction.[172] He is emphatic that there is deliberate
eschatological prophecy in the Psalter, and comes close to suggesting
that the purpose of this redaction may have been to outline an eschatological drama: 'That for the whole picture of the Eschatological
Drama as presented in the Psalter the psalmists were indebted to the
prophets is as clear as anything could be; the thoughts expressed and
the very words used are in almost every detail taken from the
prophetical writings.'[173] Yet, strangely, he concludes, 'there is no reference to the Messiah; but this, too, is in accordance with the predominant teaching of the prophets'.[174]

Given the virtually universal acceptance of the temple hymnbook
theory, it was natural that other attempts, after de Lagarde and King,
should be made to connect the sequence of Psalms with synagogue
lectionary cycles. J. Dahse (1927) and N.H. Snaith (1933) suggested
that the 150 Psalms correspond to the sabbaths of a three-year period,
in line with the triennial lectionary cycle of Torah in the synagogue, a
practice current in Palestine in talmudic times (*B. Meg.* 29b).[175] Thus
the five books of Psalms would have been read with *sedarim* from the
Pentateuch. L. Rabinowitz claimed to find support for this idea in the
pentateuchal passages cited in Midrash Tehillim.[176] C.T. Niemeyer
countered that the triennial Torah reading was a late development
(1950).[177] However A. Guilding (1952) and A. Arens (1961–62) continued to support the hypothesis, the latter providing definite evidence
for a three-year Torah cycle in ancient synagogue worship.[178] Much

171. Oesterley 1939: 67-73, 2.
172. Oesterley 1939: 1-4.
173. Oesterley 1939: 93.
174. Oesterley 1939: 93.
175. Dahse, *Das Rätsel des Psalters gelöst*; Snaith 1898.
176. Rabinowitz 1936: 349ff.
177. C.T. Niemeyer, *Het Problem van de rangshikking der Psalmen*.
178. Guilding 1952: 41-55; Arens 1961; 1962: 107-32. Arens cites evidence from Elbogen (1931: 159ff.) for the antiquity of the triennial reading.

in these hypotheses remains cogent, in spite of disclaimers.[179]

The third quarter of the twentieth century continued to be dominated by the form critical approaches developed by Gunkel and
Mowinckel. Kissane (1953), Kraus (1978), Westermann (ET 1966) and
Jacquet (1976–78) tend to follow Gunkel in classifying psalms according to literary form. Johnson (1955, 1979), Weiser (1959) and Eaton
(1967, 1976) follow Mowinckel in their concern with reconstructing
the place of the Psalms in ancient Israel's cultus. In general, they make
no radical steps out of the form critical moulds established by Gunkel
and Mowinckel. They generally discuss psalm headings in detail, yet
conclude that they are later additions. Views vary on how much later
these additions might be, and on their usefulness for determining
origin and interpretation. Kraus is most sceptical:

> לדוד is not a reliable reference to the writer of a psalm. This critical judg-
> ment applies also for those psalms which according to the information in
> the title are to be credited to Solomon, Moses, Asaph, the Korahites,
> Heman, or Ethan. Originally all of the psalm poetry was transmitted
> anonymously.[180]

He has nothing to say about the arrangement of the lyrics. Others,
however, tend to regard personal ascriptions as denoting the collection
from which a particular psalm was taken.[181] There is a general consensus that many psalms originated in pre-exilic times.[182] Most agree
in dismissing the Maccabean hypothesis. All subscribe to the view that
the Psalter's redaction was piecemeal, that the arrangement of its
lyrics reflects only the order in which the various collections were
added to one another,[183] and that it was used as a hymnbook for
temple or synagogue worship.[184] But opinions vary on how intentional
this redaction was. Some think the final collection was deliberately
redacted for temple and synagogue worship. Others think there was
no actual purpose behind the final collection, but that it resulted only

179. Heinemann 1968; Porter 1963; Day 1990: 110.

180. Kraus 1978: I, 65. Weiser also thinks 'the psalms were originally anonymous and probably remained so for a long time' (1978: 95).

181. Kissane 1953–54: xxii-xxvii; Weiser 1962: 94-95.

182. Eaton 1967: 1; Kissane 1953–54: xi, xxxi-xxxii; Weiser 1962: 91ff.

183. Kraus 1978: I, 18-20; Eaton 1967: 18-19; Kissane 1953–54: ix-x; Weiser
1962: 99.

184. Kraus 1978: I, 18-20; Eaton 1967: 18-19; Kissane 1953–54: ix-x; Weiser
1962: 21.

from a conglomerative tendency inherent in collections of psalms.[185] The dominant theory tends to be that it was formed from three earlier collections: the first Yahwistic collection (3–41), the Elohistic collection (42–83 + 84–89), and the later Yahwistic collection (90–150).[186] Views vary on which collection was earliest.[187]

Views on messianism and eschatology vary. Kraus, in his lengthy section on the theology of the Psalms, makes no comment on eschatological or messianic content in the Psalter, and dismisses such passages as 'against Yhwh and against his messiah' as secondary additions.[188] Eaton likewise has no comment on intentional messianism or eschatology, but does note that Christians have understood the Psalms as referring to Christ.[189] Weiser does not refer specifically to eschatology, although he notes that these ideas existed in Israel at an early period and cannot therefore be used as evidence against the early dating of these psalms.[190] Kissane, however, regards some psalms as intentionally messianic. Their authors, he says, are 'dealing with the ideal king of the future, who reigns for ever and whose kingdom embraces all mankind'.[191] Among such psalms he includes 2, 20, 21, 72 and 110, and, to a lesser extent, 89, 132 and 45. He also calls some psalms, such as 87, 93, 97, 99, messianic, presumably in the sense of eschatological. He does note that some psalms that are applied to Jesus in the New Testament, such as 22 and 31, did not refer in their original context to Messiah. But he apparently does not consider the significance of their later context in the Psalter, or the possibility of an overriding theme in the collection.[192] Form critical approaches have persisted into the last quarter of the twentieth century. A fifth and revised edition of Kraus's commentary was published (1978; ET, 1988), most other modern commentaries contain some discussion of form critical issues, and M.D. Goulder's work, discussed below, is form critical in its suppositions.

185. Kraus 1978: I, 20.
186. Kraus 1978: I, 18-20; Kissane 1953–54: x.
187. For instance, Kraus (1978: I, 18-20) seems to suggest the Elohistic collection was earliest; Kissane (1953–54: xi) thinks the first Yahwistic collection was earliest.
188. Kraus 1978: I, 68-81, 123-24.
189. Eaton 1967: 26-28.
190. Weiser 1962: 92.
191. Kissane 1953–54: xx.
192. Kissane 1953–54; xx, xx-xxii.

The third school of twentieth-century Psalms scholarship focused its attention on the final redacted form of the Psalter, rather than on the origin, literary genre or cultic function of individual psalms. Several forces led to the development of this discipline. One was the general rise of interest, in the 1970s and 1980s, in the literary approach to biblical texts. Another was the related discipline of canon criticism developed at the same time by B.S. Childs, who, more than any other, became responsible for the development of 'final form' studies. However, interest in the purposeful arrangement of psalms was already developing some decades before. During the heyday of form criticism, several Jewish scholars, A. Cohen, S.R. Hirsch and U. Cassuto, noted concatenation, with its attendant implication of purposeful construction of the Psalter. Cassuto comments:

> One of the methods of arrangement that plays an important part in the Bible (in several books it even enjoys precedence) is that of association— not just association of ideas but also, and primarily, association of words and expressions, a technique whose initial purpose was possibly to aid the memory. The importance of this method in comprehending the arrangement of the Biblical books has not yet been adequately recognized in the study of the Scriptures. Although Delitzsch in his day sensed its existence to a certain extent in the Book of Psalms, yet in the course of time his observations on the subject in his commentary on the Psalter were forgotten, and today hardly anyone pays attention to them.[193]

W. Zimmerli also investigated concatenation. In his discussion of what he terms *Zwillingspsalmen* (1972), he identifies 20 psalm-pairs and allows there may be more.[194] Much of this had been recognized before, but Zimmerli's work was valuable in collecting it and bringing it to the fore. However, ten of Zimmerli's pairs overlap to form connected groups of three (73–75, 79–81) or four psalms (30–33, 38–41), and such triplets and quadruplets ought probably to be recognized in their own right. C. Barth also made a study of concatenation in the first book of Psalms, in which he lists 17 principles of concatenation, including exact recurrences of forms, recurrences of roots, recurrences of word-pairs and three- and four-word sequences.[195] Other

193. Cassuto 1973: 1-2. See also Cohen 1945; Hirsch 1960.
194. Zimmerli (1972) identifies as pairs Pss. 1–2; 3–4; 9–10; 30–31; 31–32; 32–33; 38–39; 39–40; 40–41; 43–44; 69–70; 73–74; 74–75; 77–78; 79–80; 80–81; 105–106; 111–12; 127–28.
195. Barth 1976: 30-40.

valuable studies on concatenation have since been made by L.C. Allen, P. Auffret, J.K. Kuntz, and J.L. Mays.[196]

While other commentators were studying the arrangement of small psalm-groups, C. Westermann, in the 1960s and 1970s published studies of the larger literary structure of the Psalter.[197] These owe much to the literary genres of form criticism. Indeed his observations began not with literary aims, but with yet another attempt to describe the diachronic process of the Psalter's compilation. He noted that Psalms 1–90 comprise chiefly laments and Psalms 91–150 chiefly *hodayoth*, or psalms of praise, and suggested that the Psalter was compiled from two collections of different form critical *Gattungen*. He then observed that the Psalter displays an overall pattern of progress from lament to praise, that praise psalms have a closural function in internal collections, and that the royal psalms form part of the framework of the Psalter.[198] These observations, a giant step for a form critic, led from the literary classification of individual psalms to studying their arrangement in the collection.

J.P. Brennan (1976) suggested that a link could be found between the micro and macro structures of the Psalter by allowing internal groups to show the way to the larger literary structure of the whole: '...the Psalter has not developed in a haphazard and arbitrary way, but has been carefully woven together in such a manner that previously independent compositions, or smaller collections of such compositions, now comment upon or respond to one another.'[199] For this reason, he concludes, a proper understanding of the Psalter requires that its parts be studied in relation to one another, 'since all of them together convey more than they do if looked at separately.'[200] In a later article (1980), Brennan moves tentatively toward the question of redactor-intent in the Psalter.[201] He notes the unifying and linking function of the wisdom motif throughout. Psalm 1 sets out two ways, presenting the subsequent collection as a book of wisdom commenting on the struggle between good and evil. Psalm 2 defines the opponents

196. Allen 1986; Auffret 1986; Kuntz 1986; Mays 1987.
197. The earliest article on this theme is 'Zur Sammlung des Psalters'; later work is summarized in Westermann 1981.
198. Westermann 1981: 250-58.
199. Brennan 1976: 126.
200. Brennan 1976: 127.
201. Brennan 1980: 25-29.

as Yhwh's anointed and the heathen. Therefore, although the historical origins of individual psalms were the Jerusalem cult, the Psalter in its final form is a book of wisdom rather than cultic material. Brennan concludes that 'such a reading of the Psalter opens the way to an eschatological and messianic interpretation of many texts which had originally only a limited national and historical setting'.[202]

Childs had already made similar observations (1979), arguing that there is a distinct eschatological thrust in the canonical shaping of the Psalter.[203] He notes that Psalms 1 and 2 form an introduction, creating an eschatological framework for the ensuing collection, and so impose a messianic interpretation even on originally non-messianic psalms.[204] This is confirmed by their being the only untitled psalms in LXX. In the period when the Psalter was redacted, a contemporary understanding of Psalm 2 would have referred it to the coming judgment and kingship of God. For, at that time, when the monarchy had been long destroyed, the term *mashiah* would have been understood only of the eschatological deliverer.[205] In addition, other royal psalms are scattered throughout the Psalter, and, unlike pilgrimage songs, and community and individual complaints, they do not appear as groups. Childs infers from this arrangement that their original *Sitz im Leben* has been disregarded by the redactor, and that they now represent the presence of the messianic hope pervading the whole collection.[206] He remarks,

> ...although the royal psalms arose originally in a peculiar historical setting of ancient Israel which had received its form from a common mythopoetic milieu, they were treasured in the Psalter for a different reason, namely as a witness to the messianic hope which looked for the consummation of God's kingship through his Anointed One.[207]

This eschatological reinterpretation applies not only to the royal psalms, but to the entire Psalter:

> However one explains it, the final form of the Psalter is highly eschatological in nature. It looks toward to [sic] the future and passionately yearns for its arrival. Even when the psalmist turns briefly to reflect on the

202. Brennan 1980: 29.
203. Childs 1979: 511-18.
204. Childs 1979: 511-13.
205. Childs 1979: 516.
206. Childs 1979: 515-16.
207. Childs 1979: 517.

past in praise of the 'great things Yahweh has done', invariably the movement shifts and again the hope of salvation is projected into the future (Ps. 126.6). The perspective of Israel's worship in the Psalter is eschatologically oriented. As a result, the Psalter in its canonical form, far from being different in kind from the prophetic message, joins with the prophets in announcing God's coming kingship. When the New Testament heard in the Psalms eschatological notes, its writers were standing in the context of the Jewish canon in which the community of faith worshipped and waited.[208]

J. Reindl (1981) regards the editors of the Psalter as belonging to the wisdom tradition, and sees Psalm 1 as a *prœmium* for the reader, setting out two ways. The finished Psalter is thus a wisdom document, in which the words *in his Torah he meditates day and night* may be applied to the Psalter itself. For this reason the original cultic *Sitz im Leben* of individual psalms becomes insignificant in the face of the new *Sitz im Leben* that the Psalter has received.[209]

The publication of several studies dealing specifically with literary aspects of heading-defined psalm groups, such as the Asaph, Korah or Ascents collections, also highlighted the question of the Psalter's literary structure. In one sense such studies had long been around.[210] However, the dominance of antipathetic hermeneutics throughout the previous 150 years, which denied any interpretational value to the headings, had limited their influence. As Mannati noted, these groups of psalms required to be treated in their own right, free from the dominance of theories that virtually denied their existence.

> To admit the existence within the biblical Psalter of a genre, 'Songs of Ascents', provides a principle of analysis for those which remain unclear without it... and increases the intelligibility of others... The case of the Ascents obliges us to relax Gunkel's theory about psalm genres. For the Ascents, it is not the structure of each text which is the specific element, but the curve, very clear and chronologically rigorous (the order cannot be modified, even if the phases are lacking).[211]

208. Childs 1979: 518.
209. Reindl 1981: 340.
210. See Armfield 1874; Kopfstein 1881; Cox 1885; King 1890; Kessler 1889; Peters 1894; Watts 1965; Wanke 1966; Keet 1969. Note the hiatus between 1894 and the mid-1960s, when scepticism as to the purposeful character of the Psalms collection was at its peak.
211. Author's translation of 'Admettre l'existence à l'intérieur du psautier biblique du genre « psaumes graduels » donne un principe d'explication pour ceux

M.D. Goulder tried to ascertain the original cultic *Sitz im Leben* of certain psalm-groups before their redaction into the Psalter. In 'The Fourth Book of the Psalter' (1975) he detects repetition of material among odd and even numbered psalms in Book IV, and suggests this reflects a pattern of morning and evening prayer connected with the Feast of Tabernacles; he then proposes a detailed liturgy based on these psalms. In *The Psalms of the Sons of Korah* (1982) he proposes that the Korah collection originally formed the liturgy for the Feast of Tabernacles at the Dan shrine, and entered the Psalter through the Jerusalem cult, which received it from the Dan priests, probably after the loss of Dan and Naphtali in 730 BCE.[212] In *The Prayers of David* (1990) Goulder proposes that Psalms 51–72 were written by 'a court poet, a priest, probably one of David's sons, "for David"', and that they 'were chanted liturgically in a procession one day in the autumn festival at Jerusalem'.[213] K.-J. Illman (1976) and H.P. Nasuti (1988) seek to identify the particular tradition-groups which lie behind the Asaph Psalms, and, in so doing, provide valuable literary analysis of this collection.[214] Y. Bazak (1990–91) has produced literary analyses of the Hallel Psalms.[215] K. Seybold (1978–79), E. Beaucamp (1979), M. Mannati (1979) and D. Grossberg (1989) have published studies of the Songs of Ascents containing various degrees of literary analysis.[216] P. Auffret (1982) offers detailed literary-structural studies of three psalm collections (Pss. 15–24, 120–34, 135–38).

This scholarship of the 1970s and early 1980s was seminal work. Several principles emerged from it to guide subsequent investigation. First, a literary rationale is responsible for the final form of the Psalter. Secondly, this rationale reflects a non-liturgical *Sitz im Leben*. Thirdly, wisdom motifs play some part in the scheme.[217] Others, building on this foundational work, have tried to ascertain the details

des psaumes qui sans lui restaient peu clairs, et augmente l'intelligibilité des autres... Le cas des graduels oblige à assouplir la théorie gunkélienne des genres des psaumes. Pour eux, ce n'est pas la structure de chaque texte qui est l'élément spécifique, mais la courbe, très nette et chronologiquement rigoureuse (l'ordre ne peut être modifié, même si des phases manquent)' (Mannati 1979: 99).

212. Goulder 1982: 16-19.
213. Goulder 1990: 24, 28.
214. Illman 1976; Nasuti 1988.
215. Bazak 1990, 1991.
216. Seybold 1978; Seybold 1979; Mannati 1975; Grossberg 1989.
217. These points are noted by Howard 1989: 61-62, in McCann 1993: 52-70.

of the Psalter's redactional agenda more precisely. The most influential is G.H. Wilson, a student of Childs. In *The Editing of the Hebrew Psalter* (1985) his twofold purpose is to demonstrate that purposeful editorial activity lies behind the Psalter, and to identify the agenda that guided the redaction. As regards the first of these, he does a thorough job. Having examined the use of headings and colophons in other ancient Near Eastern collections of hymnic lyrics, the Sumerian Temple Hymns, the Mesopotamian Hymnic Incipits, and the Qumran Psalms manuscripts, he notes that purposeful redaction is evident in all these texts. He then examines internal evidence for editorial activity in the Psalter and identifies both 'explicit' indicators, such as psalm headings and Ps. 72.20, and 'tacit' indicators, such as the grouping of *hallelu-yah* psalms (104–106, 111–17, 135, 146–50) at the end of segments.[218] He concludes:

> I have been able to show (1) that the 'book' divisions of the Psalter are real, editorially induced divisions and not accidentally introduced; (2) the 'separating' and 'binding' functions of author and genre groupings; (3) the lack of a s/s [superscription] as an indication of a tradition of combination; (4) the use of *hllwyh* pss to indicate the conclusion of segments; (5) the use of *hwdw* pss to introduce segments; (6) the existence of thematic correspondences between the beginning and ending pss in some books. All of these findings demonstrate the presence of editorial activity at work in the arrangement of the pss.[219]

As regards his second objective, to identify the editorial agenda behind the Psalter's redaction, Wilson notes that royal psalms are found at a number of 'seams' in Books I–III (i.e. Pss. 2, 72, 89).[220] He suggests these show 'an interesting progression in thought regarding kingship and the Davidic covenant'.[221] On the basis of this perceived progression he suggests that the purpose of the Psalter is to address the apparent failure of the Davidic covenant in the light of the exile and diaspora. Book I represents the institution of the covenant with David (Ps. 2). Book II represents its transmission to his descendants

218. Wilson 1985a: 9-10, 182-97.
219. Wilson 1985a: 199.
220. Wilson 1985a: 209-214. He initially suggested that Ps. 41 may also have been a royal psalm (1985a: 209-210). But later appears to abandon the idea, suggesting that Books I and II form a unit and therefore no royal psalm is required at the end of Book I [s].
221. Wilson 1985a: 209.

(Ps. 72). Book III represents its failure (Ps. 89).[222] Book IV, he suggests, is the editorial crux of the collection, responding to the failure of the covenant as represented in Psalm 89. Its message is that Yhwh was Israel's king in the past and will be in the future, and that those who trust him are blessed.[223] It ends with a plea for restoration from exile (106.47).[224] Book V shows that this plea will be answered if the people trust in God alone (Ps. 107), just as David did (Pss. 108–10), by obedience to his law (Ps. 119), and by recognizing him as the only king worthy of human trust.[225] Thus, for Wilson, the Psalter is a historical retrospective (Books I–III) followed by an exhortation directing Israel's future hope to theocracy unmediated by a Davidic king. The redactor's narrative standpoint is somewhere in the middle of Book IV.

J.H. Walton, building to some extent on Wilson's work, also seeks the editorial agenda behind the Psalter's arrangement, but bases his analysis more on psalm content than title or genre. He suggests the Psalter is a 'cantata' about the Davidic covenant.[226] Book I represents David's conflict with Saul; Book II represents David's reign; Book III represents the Assyrian crisis; Book IV is a post-exilic introspection on the destruction of the temple and the exile; Book V is praise for the return of the exiles.[227] Thus, for Walton, the Psalter is a post-exilic retrospective of Israel's history, the redactor's narrative standpoint being somewhere after the close of Book V.

Other commentators have remarked on the broad structure of the Psalter in terms that are in keeping with these principles. T. Collins suggests the Psalter is an integrated system in which the final work 'has something to say quite independent of the intention of the authors of individual psalms, the collectors of groups of psalms or the editors of the psalter'.[228] He sees in it the story of every just person, progressing through trials to triumph, and even recognizes its distinct eschatological drift. However his scepticism about author and even redactor intent sets his work apart from the majority of contemporary

222. Wilson 1985a: 213.
223. Wilson 1985a: 214-15.
224. Wilson 1985a: 219.
225. Wilson 1985a: 227-28
226. Walton 1991: 23.
227. Walton 1991: 24.
228. Collins 1987: 41.

commentators. W. Brueggemann notes the spiritual progression in the Psalter from simple obedience, through the trial of faith, to selfless praise. Psalm 1 calls the believer to a life of obedience with rewards of blessing; Psalm 73, the Psalter's theological centre, faces the crisis of belief when God's חסד is thrown in doubt; Psalm 150 represents faith's triumph, where God is praised not for his rewards, but for his being.[229]

In recent years increasing interest in the arrangement of Psalms has produced a substantial volume of literature. M.E. Tate's commentary on Psalms 51–100 deals in detail with issues of Psalms arrangement, noting overarching themes in the collection, and also inter-psalm links (1990a). A.R. Ceresko (1990) has published a survey of the sage in the Psalms, noting three aspects: first, the Psalms represent the sage as one who observes Torah; second, the sages wrote several psalms; third, the formation of the Psalter itself is a product of wisdom circles. He deals with this last point at length, emphasizing that there was a deliberate authorial activity in the redaction process that produced 'a unity intentionally greater than its parts'.[230] J.L. Mays (1991) notes that in the hermeneutical context of the Psalter several of the royal and Davidic psalms should be interpreted messianically.[231] The 1992 issue of *Interpretation* is devoted to Psalms studies, and contains three essays, by Wilson, J.C. McCann and G.T. Sheppard, on the subject of editorial activity in the Psalter.[232] A recent JSOT volume is devoted exclusively to the issue of the arrangement of the Psalms, and contains nine essays on the subject.[233] The first four are by Mays, R.E. Murphy, Brueggemann and Wilson, who agree, with various caveats, that contextual interpretation is a valuable discipline for understanding the Psalms.[234] The fifth essay is an update of D.M. Howard's review of the recent development of interest in editorial activity in the Psalter.[235] Two more essays, by Wilson and McCann, deal with the larger

---

229. Brueggemann 1991.
230. Ceresko 1990: 230.
231. Mays 1991. He considers Pss. 1–3, 18, 72, 89, 110, 132.
232. Wilson 1992; McCann 1993; Sheppard 1992.
233. McCann 1993.
234. The essays are: Mays 1993: 14-20; Murphy 1993: 21-28; Brueggemann 1993: 29-41; Wilson 1993: 42-51.
235. Howard 1989: 52-71. The earlier version of this article appeared in *Word and World* 9 (1989): 274-85.

shaping of the Psalter.[236] And two more, by P.D. Miller and Howard, deal with lesser scale inter-psalm links.[237] Other recent articles elsewhere comment on concatenation[238] and messianism[239] in the Psalter.

8. *Summary*

Several facts emerge from the preceding investigation. First, the great majority of interpreters, historically speaking, endorse the MT-type arrangement of Psalms, either tacitly, by transmitting it, or explicitly, by explaining or defending it. They recognize its rubrics, the headings and doxologies, as an intrinsic part of the text. The headings are regarded as having a bearing on interpretation, and the doxologies as indicating a fivefold 'book' division. Secondly, the great majority of interpreters, historically speaking, regard the Psalms as foretelling eschatological events, interpreting them of Messiah, eschatological war, the ingathering of Israel, and so on. The great exception to the general dominance of these two views is the period c. 1820–1970, when a number of influential commentators advanced quite opposite views. They denied that any purposeful redaction lay behind the MT-type arrangement, making it out to be essentially an *ad hoc* collection that had evolved piecemeal, either a temple hymnbook or simply a collection of cultic remains. The headings and doxologies were said to have been added sporadically to this already disordered collection at a later date, producing a finished product that was the result of evolutionary chance rather than purposeful redaction. The possibility of there being intentionally eschatological prophecy in the collection was tacitly denied by silence on the subject. Or it was mentioned, to be dismissed on the ground that eschatological belief was a late development. These views dominated the consensus of scholarly opinion for a century and a half, despite notable voices of dissent.

Such views continue to the present time. However, in the last two decades, some commentators, operating on the hermeneutical basis of

236. Wilson 1993: 72-82; McCann 1993: 93-107.

237. Miller 1993: 83-92; Howard 1993: 108-23.

238. Lohfink (1992a; 1992b; 1992c) suggests one editorial purpose of concatenation was to facilitate memorization. Vermeylen (1992) notes links between Pss. 50 and 51.

239. Füglister (1992) points out that the Psalter was regarded as messianic prophecy in the time of Jesus. Mosis (1992) and Wahl (1992) find eschatological implications in Pss. 51 and 67 respectively.

redactor intention, have returned to views not dissimilar to the pre-nineteenth-century one. They recognize purposeful redaction in the MT Psalter, with the headings and doxologies as structural markers. Some recognize eschatological concerns in the collection, either in particular psalms, or in the redactional agenda that lies behind the finished Psalter, or both. A few have tried to identify what the details of the redactor's message might be, yet so far no consensus has been reached.

Thus a historical perspective at the end of the twentieth century seems to suggest that western scholarship from c. 1820–1970 is, in some respects, a hiatus in Psalms interpretation, during which scholarly opinion diverged sharply from what must be considered, historically speaking, the dominant views. These traditional interpretational norms deserve reconsideration for several reasons. First, they are ancient, occurring in LXX and the Dead Sea Scrolls. Such antiquity carries the recommendation that its writers lived soon enough after the Psalter's completion to be in receipt of traditions regarding its redactional agenda. And even if they received no actual traditions, still they lived in a time and culture not distant from the final redaction, and might be expected to have understood better than a modern reader what ideas influenced the redactors. Moreover, these interpretational norms persisted virtually unchallenged until the nineteenth century. No doubt every age thinks itself wiser than its predecessors, but, in this case, the sheer consensus of opinion behind the traditional views invites enquiry as to whether there were not grounds for these beliefs, and whether clues to the Psalter's agenda might not be gleaned from those who did not share post-Enlightenment presuppositions. It is therefore appropriate to enquire whether the traditional view that the Psalter is a purposeful arrangement with an eschatological orientation might not be confirmed by internal evidence in the Hebrew Psalter itself. This shall be done in the following chapter.

Chapter 2

THE HEBREW PSALTER

I turn now to examine the Hebrew Psalter itself, in order to ascertain what internal evidence it may yield regarding its arrangement and the redactional agenda which determined it.

1. *The Arrangement of the Psalter*

a. *Does Psalm 72.20 Necessarily Indicate a Process of Accretion?*
From c. 1800–1970 the dominant view was that the Psalter came into being by a process of gradual accretion, rather than purposeful redaction. The principal piece of evidence initially cited for this view, in the eighteenth and early nineteenth centuries, was the fact that the end of Book II (Ps. 72.20) bears the legend כלו תפלות דוד בן־ישי, yet other Davidic psalms appear thereafter. This was taken as evidence that this statement had once marked the end of an earlier Davidic collection, and that subsequent sections of the Psalter featuring Davidic psalms were later additions.[1]

By the early nineteenth century, however, this view, that Ps. 72.20 marks the end of an earlier collection, was increasingly regarded as untenable. The principal objection to it was that none of the proffered scenarios of the redaction process can be reconciled with the existence of the Elohistic Psalter, that is, the group of Psalms 42–83, in which

1. According to de Wette: 'Schon *Carpzov* [presumably Jo. Gottlob, the Hebraist (fl. 1725–50, Leipzig), rather than Jo. Benedictus, the ecclesiastical theologian (fl. 1675–1710, Leipzig)] aber (a. O.S. 106ff. [I am unable to trace the reference.]) nimmt an, dass vor der letzten grossen Hauptsammlung, schon zu Hiskia's Zeit, eine kleinere Sammlung vorhanden gewesen, welche die ersten zwei und siebenzig Psalmen enthalten, und mit dem Schlusse: Ende der Psalmen Davids, den wir noch am Ende des 72. Ps. finden, versehen gewesen sei' (de Wette 1811: 16). The same view, according to de Wette, was shared by Eichhorn (fl. 1790–1825) (de Wette 1811: 17).

the divine name *elohim* predominates, in contrast to the rest of the Psalms, in which *Yhwh* predominates.[2] This feature distinguishes Psalms 42–83 as a literary unit in its own right, and therefore Psalms 1–72, as they now stand, could not have formed an initial collection, because the supposedly closural subscript to Psalm 72 falls in the midst of the Elohistic Psalter.

Therefore, faced with the glaring fact of the Elohistic Psalter, which had apparently gone hitherto virtually unnoticed, many nineteenth century interpreters were unable to agree on any theory about the Psalter's redaction, except to affirm that the process was piecemeal and disordered.[3] De Wette, for instance, states, 'In any case, we must accept a piecemeal development of the Psalms collection, in which disorder prevails.'[4] How this conclusion was reached is not clear. It generally seems to have been simply assumed.[5] But certainly, it does not follow from the existence of Ps. 72.20, which was still routinely cited as the remnant of an earlier collection.

It is worth noting, in passing, that the presence of Ps. 72.20 can be explained in a number of ways, without recourse to the theory that it is the unedited remnant of an earlier collection. The first thing that should be noted about this view is that it is a relative newcomer on the scene, not occurring before the eighteenth century. This is surprising, for both Jewish and Christian commentators were aware that the

2. The Elohistic Psalter (Pss. 42–83) is distinguished by the preponderance of the term *elohim,* which occurs 210 times in the absolute state, whereas *Yhwh* occurs only 44 times. This contrasts with the rest of the Psalter in which *Yhwh* predominates. In Pss. 1–41 *Yhwh* occurs 278 times and *elohim* 15 in absolute form; in Pss. 84–89 *Yhwh* occurs 31 times and *elohim* 7 in absolute form; and in Pss. 90–150 *Yhwh* occurs 339 times and *elohim* 6 in absolute form, discounting references to foreign gods (Figures from Kirkpatrick 1902: lv).

3. The alternative, that a later redactor affixed further psalms to an initial collection ending in Ps. 72.20, then carefully *elohim*-redacted part of that initial collection, together with his own additions, but left part of it unredacted, and left the closural suffix in the midst of his Elohistic Psalter, was not widely considered, although Hengstenberg and Delitzsch, who believed the collection was purposefully redacted, must have had some sort of schema in mind.

4. 'Auf jeden Fall müssen wir eine allmählige Entstehung der Psalmensammlung annehmen. Es herrscht Unordnung in derselben', De Wette 1811: 17.

5. I am inclined to think that this view of the Psalter's redaction may be just another manifestation of the evolutionary paradigm that dominated so much nineteenth-century thought. It finds its full flower in Marx, Darwin and Wagner, of course, but can be found earlier in, for instance, Keats's 'Hyperion'.

Psalter was redacted from diverse sources.[6] They were also aware of
the subscript to Psalm 72 and gave a number of opinions on it, but the
idea that it marked the end of an earlier collection was not one of them.

Kimhi interprets it as a comment on the messianic *malkut* depicted
in Psalm 72.

> And if it is [interpreted] concerning the King Messiah, Ibn Ezra interprets
> it as follows. When all these consolations will be completed, then
> *Fulfilled are the prayers of David ben Jesse*. It does not say 'Fulfilled are
> the songs' or 'Fulfilled are the hymns,' but *Fulfilled are the prayers of
> David,* in relation to atonement and deliverance. For when everything is
> completed, that Israel go forth from the exile and are in their land, and the
> King Messiah ben David rules over them, nothing will be lacking, neither
> atonement, nor deliverance, nor prosperity, for everything will be theirs.
> And then *Fulfilled are the prayers of David ben Jesse.*[7]

The same interpretation is noted also by Rashi and, as Kimhi says,
Ibn Ezra.[8] Rashi proffers another opinion of his own, that the subscript indicates that Psalm 72 was the last of David's psalms, written
when he nominated Solomon his successor. The view of *Midr. Pss.*
72.6 seems at first sight to be quite different again:

> *Fulfilled are the prayers of David ben Jesse.* And are not the remaining
> prayers also prayers of David ben Jesse? *Kalu,* however is to be read *kol
> 'ellu.* And hence the verse means that all of these [*kol 'ellu*] were the
> prayers David uttered concerning his son Solomon and concerning the
> King Messiah.

Rashi notes this opinion and takes it as indicating that all the psalms
are by David; he disagrees, saying that some psalms bear the names of
other individuals. But it is possible that the *kol 'ellu* of the midrash
refers only to the Davidic psalms. If so, the basis, at least, of this
saying may be not unlike Kimhi's view in emphasizing that the psalms
are David's prayers for the messiah. Christian commentators have
held similar views. Calvin, midway between Rashi and Kimhi, suggests the phrase shows that this psalm records the last of David's

---

6.   2 Macc. 2.13 states that Nehemiah collected the writings of David. *b. B. Bat.*
14b–15a states the Psalms were written by ten men and collected by David. *Song R.*
4.19 says Ezra participated in writing it. The idea that Ezra collected and redacted the
Psalms was known among patristic writers, including Athanasius and possibly
Hippolytus (Achelis 1897: 132).

7.   Kimhi 1883: 72.20.

8.   Ibn Ezra, Commentary on Ps. 72.20; Rashi, Commentary on Ps. 72.20.

prayers, made shortly before his death, concerning Solomon and the messianic kingdom.[9] Forbes, possibly aware of rabbinic tradition, gives a view similar to Kimhi's:

> The obvious meaning of these words, in the position they hold, is that David's highest aspirations—what formed 'all his salvation and all his desire' (2 Sam. xxiii.5)—will be answered when the consummation, anticipated in the immediately preceding Psalm, arrives. This necessitates us to regard Ps. lxxii. as *primarily*, in the idea of the author, a prayer for the coming of that perfect kingdom of 'righteousness and peace,' the expectation of which had been awakened by the promises made by God to David, with the tacitly implied petition, no doubt secondarily, that Solomon's reign (whether the Psalm was written *by* him or *for* him) might, in its imperfect measure foreshadow it.[10]

Hengstenberg suggested that Ps. 72.20 'must have been designed to separate the free and the bound, the scattered and the serial Psalms of David', as Job 31.40 separates the first formal collection of Job's speeches from his latter ones in chs. 40 and 42.[11] All these commentators offer plausible explanations of Ps. 72.20 without suggesting that it marked the end of an earlier collection. (Presumably they assumed the redactor would not have accidentally left vestigial remains of earlier collections in the midst of his composition.) This suggests that the nineteenth-century idea, that Ps. 72.20 marks the end of an earlier collection, is not as inevitable as it proponents imagine.

b. *Evidence for the Redaction Process in the Elohistic Psalter*
Other theories were formulated. These regarded the Elohistic Psalter (EP) as the initial collection. The subscript to Psalm 72 marked the end only of the לדוד psalms within that collection, and it was these psalms that 72.20 referred to as 'the prayers of David'.[12] Other parts of the Psalter, an extensive preface (Pss. 1–41), the EP's Yhwhistic coda (Pss. 84–89), and Books IV and V (Pss. 90–150), were added by later redactors. Doxologies marking the book divisions were added later still. However this hypothesis is also fraught with difficulties. The first is the question of why *elohim* predominates in Psalms 42–83 at all. Some suggest that an elohistic redactor took originally Yhwhistic

---

9.   Calvin 1557 (Anderson's translation): III, 99.
10.   Forbes 1888: 6.
11.   Hengstenberg 1845–48: li. This is also the view of de Wette 1811: 17.
12.   Gunkel and Begrich 1933: 447; Kirkpatrick 1902: 424; Kraus 1978: I, 18-20; Kissane 1953–54: x.

lyrics and changed them.[13] In support of this they point to such locutions as *God, my God* (43.4); *God, your God* (45.8 [7]; 50.7); *God, our God* (67.7 [6]). In all of these the double *elohim* appears awkward, and a phrase like *Yhwh your God* would seem more natural. Moreover parallel passages to these elsewhere in the Psalter and the Bible feature *Yhwh*.[14] The motive for this recension, it is suggested, may have been reverence for the tetragrammaton, a feature of late second temple times. As Craigie notes, 'Later in the history of Judaism, it was not used at all during normal worship and could only be pronounced by the high priest at a key moment in the observance of the Day of Atonement.'[15]

But the whole idea of an elohistic redactor is not that simple. The EP was redacted before reverence for the tetragrammaton was widespread, as the Psalter itself shows. For, if the elohistic redactor changed *Yhwh* out of tetragrammaton reverence, then presumably he did not get his hands on the Yhwhistic collections that flank the EP, otherwise they too would have undergone *elohim*-redaction. Therefore the EP and the Yhwhistic collections existed independently before their collation by a later redactor. This later redactor apparently did not share the views of the elohistic redactor or else he would have elohim-redacted the entire Psalter. Therefore, if the later redactor could use the tetragrammaton so freely, then it would seem the tetragrammaton was still in common use when the entire Psalter was redacted, which was obviously after the EP's redaction. Moreover, it was probably in common use earlier still, when Book V was redacted, as Psalm 108 demonstrates. Compounded of Ps. 57.8-12 [7-11] and 60.7-14 [5-12], it contains six of the seven occurrences of *elohim* in absolute form in Book V, which suggests it was compounded from Psalms 57 and 60 in the form in which they occur in the EP. In that case, Book V is later than the EP, though probably earlier than the final redaction of the Psalter. Yet it uses the tetragrammaton freely throughout.

It might be concluded then that the elohistic redactor came from a minority group of proto-tetragrammaton-reverencers. But even that is

13. Gunkel and Begrich 1933: 447-51; Kraus: 1978: 17-18; Day 1990: 113-14; Craigie 1983b: 29-30.
14. *Yhwh* in Ps. 14.2, 4, 7 becomes *elohim* in Ps. 53.3, 5, 7 [2, 4, 6]; likewise in Ps. 40.14a, 17 [13a-16] and Ps. 70.2a, 5 [1a, 4]. Cf. also Ps. 68.2, 8, 9 [1, 7, 8] with Num. 10.35 and Judg. 5.4,5; and theophanic Ps. 50.7 with Exod. 20.2.
15. Craigie 1983b: 29-30.

unlikely, for further evidence suggests that even the redactor of the EP did not suffer consistently from tetragrammaton-reverence. He allowed 44 occurrences of Yhwh to exist in the EP, and, when reproducing Ps. 40.14-18 [13-17] in Ps. 70.2-6 [1-5], he not only changed *Yhwh* to *elohim* twice (40.14a, 17 [13a, 16]; 70.2a, 5 [1a, 4]), but left it unchanged once (40.14 [13]; 70.6 [5]), and even changed *elohim* to *Yhwh* (40.18 [17]; 70.6 [5])! He also changes the inoffensive *adonai* (אדני) to *elohim* on one occasion (40.18 [17]; 70.6 [5]). The mystery deepens when the EP is viewed in relation to the literary structure of Books II and III (Pss. 42–89). It can be seen that the Korah and Asaph Psalms form a chiastic inclusio round the central David collection.

A:	Korah Pss. 42–49	
B:	Asaph Ps. 50	Elohistic
C:	David Pss. 51–65, 68–70	Psalter
B´:	Asaph Pss. 73–83	
A´:	Korah Pss. 84–85, 87, 88, (89)	

It appears from this that the real literary unit is Psalms 42–89, and not Psalms 42–83, which would form an incomplete chiasm in themselves. The book divisions confirm this. Whoever inserted them regarded Psalm 42 as a beginning and Psalm 89, not 83, as an end. This suggests that Psalms 84–89 are not a later addition to the EP, but part of a single literary unit with it from their first redaction. So it seems that the elohistic redactor added a Yhwhistic conclusion to his collection. Nor is this surprising, given his occasional use of *Yhwh* in Psalms 42–83. Such apparently deliberate use of Yhwh throughout Books II and III points to the conclusion that the EP's redactor was no mere knee-jerk elohist, but a literary craftsman who employed different divine appellations for different literary or theological purposes. His activity appears purposeful, even if his purpose is elusive. Therefore, the complex phenomenon of the EP is more readily explicable in terms of deliberate literary activity than in terms of simple prejudice for certain divine appellations. It follows that the same hand that employed different divine titles for different purposes in Psalms 42–89 was capable of redacting other parts of the Psalter, using other divine names for other purposes. Thus there really is no sharp dividing line between the EP and the rest of the Psalter, and so the case for the precedence of the EP, and the redaction hypothesis dependent on it, is undermined.

A further consideration of the literary structure of Books II and III stirs up more problems with the EP-precedence hypothesis. There is the issue of the Asaph Psalms. Why are they arranged with Psalm 50 standing alone and the others in sequence (Pss. 73–83)? Kraus answers: 'Very likely this psalm [50] assumed its present place at or after the completion of the entire Psalter.'[16] But he offers no explanation why this later redactor did not place Psalm 50 together with the other Asaph Psalms. If an answer were to be given it would need to concede that this later redactor thought Psalm 50 suited that particular place better for literary or theological reasons. Such reasons are not hard to find. There are substantial thematic and lexical links between Psalms 50 and 51.[17] But once it is admitted that a literary rationale lay behind this arrangement, such an impulse must be allowed for much else in the Psalter as well. And if that is the case, there is every likelihood that it was the redactor of the EP or of the entire Psalter who produced the distinctive arrangement of the Asaph Psalms. The same sort of problem arises with Psalm 86. Why did not the hand that added Psalms 84–89 to the EP, whether the elohistic redactor or another, place this David psalm before the subscript at Ps. 72.20? If these redactors are to be credited with any reason, it must be concluded that they had reasons for wanting Psalm 86 in that position, and that the subscript to Psalm 72 was not understood as suggesting that no further David Psalms are to follow.

So a careful examination of the structure of Books I–III shows that they are bound together in such a way as to appear the product of one process of literary composition. Books II and III, comprised of the EP with its Yhwhistic coda, form a chiasm that marks them as a literary unit. At the same time, Books I and II contain two large collections of לדוד psalms (Pss. 3–41, 51–71) that seem to have the effect of associating these two books together. These two overlapping psalm groups, the לדוד Psalms and the EP, seem to bind the first three books of psalms into one interlocking literary unit.

Book I	*Book II*	*Book III*
לדוד	לדוד	
	אלהים	אלהים

---

16. Kraus 1978: I, 18.
17. See Vermeylen 1992: 257-83.

These three books also have in common those headings generally classed as musical directions, particularly למנצח, but also בנגינות, על־ששנים, על־השמינית, and others. Such headings are absent from Books IV and V. Thus Books I–III seem to display an essential unity, as some commentators recognize.[18]

c. *Further Internal Evidence for Purposeful Arrangement*
The above evidence for purposeful arrangement is confirmed by the concurrence between the Psalter's major structural divisions and the content of the psalms found at these junctures. First of all, the Psalter begins, as many commentators note, with an introduction consisting of Psalms 1 and 2.[19] These two psalms display thematic and linguistic links that suggest they belong in some sense together.[20]

1.1	אשרי	2.12	אשרי
1.2	תורה	2.7	חוק
1.2	יהגה	2.1	יהגו
1.6	דרך...תאבד	2.12	תאבדו דרך

Ancient texts confirm both the introductory function and the close relation of these two psalms. In LXX they stand apart from the rest of the Psalter by being the only untitled psalms. Some western manuscripts of Acts 13.33 cite Ps. 2.7 and refers to its being written ἐν τῷ ψαλμῷ...τῷ πρώτῳ. The same idea may be reflected in 4QFlorilegium (4Q174), which proffers a 'Midrash of *Happy is the man that walks not in the counsel of the wicked*' (Ps. 1.1), follows with a brief *pešer*, and proceeds, without further introduction, to cite the opening lines of Psalm 2 followed by their *pešer*.[21] Talmudic sources attest that Psalms 1 and 2 were often conjoined (*Ber.* 9b-10a; *y. Ber.* 4.3, 8a; *y. Ta'an.* 2.2, 65c). The idea was known to Kimhi also.[22] Such

---

18. Westermann 1981: 252; Wilson 1993a: 73-74.

19. Hupfeld 1855: 2-3; Hitzig 1863–65: 1; Cheyne 1888: 1; Willis 1979: 381-401; Childs 1979: 511-16; Sheppard 1980: 142; Reindl 1981: 340; Brennan 1980: 29; Auffret 1986; Mays 1991: 2-3; McCann 1992: 118-23; Miller 1993; Walton 1991: 23-24. Wilson (1985a: 204-206; Wilson 1993a: 75, 78, 80; Wilson 1993b: 44) thinks Ps. 1 is introductory to the Psalter, while Ps. 2 is introductory to Book I. Others recognise that Ps. 1 is introductory but reserve judgment on Ps. 2: Calvin, Comm. on Ps. 1; Barnes 1931; Oesterley 1939: 119; Brueggemann 1993: 37.

20. From Sarna 1971: 1311.

21. 4Q174, col.1, lines 14-19. Text in DJD: V, 53-54.

22. Comm. on Ps. 2.1. He notes that others hold this view, though he himself seems sceptical about it.

widespread recognition of the close links between these psalms suggests the resemblance is not fanciful, but real and deliberate. They were placed, and possibly composed in part, together to form an introduction to the entire Psalter, which is to be read in the light of them.

The Psalter also has a conclusion, the great acclamation of Psalms 146–50. This is the only sequence of psalms in which each psalm features a double *Halleluyah,* one at the beginning and one at the end.[23] The jubilant outburst conveyed by this feature surpasses anything else in the Psalter, possibly in the Bible. It appears too that, as Wilson suggests, this follows in response to the last words of the previous psalm (145.21): *My mouth will speak the praise of Yhwh, and let all flesh bless his holy name for ever and ever;* and that this wish is fulfilled in Ps. 150.6, when *everything that breathes* is exhorted to join in praise (150.6).[24] The force and success and literary design of this closural arrangement again argue for the Psalter's being carefully and purposefully redacted.

The book divisions, demarcated by doxologies, also show evidence of purposeful planning, by the way in which they concur with thematic and genre changes in the psalms. The first doxology (41.14 [13]) separates the first David group, Psalms 3–41, from the first Korah group, which follows it. There are also lexical links between Psalms 1 and 41, which form an inclusio demarcating the boundaries of Book I of the Psalter.[25]

1.1	אשרי	41.2	אשרי
1.2	חפצו	41.12	חפצת
1.5	לא־יקמו	41.9	לא־יוסיף לקום
1.6	תאבד	41.6	אבד

The correspondence between royal psalms and strategic points of the Psalter was noted long ago by Forbes, and more recently has been central to Wilson's work.[26] The second doxology (72.18-20) is preceded by the Solomonic royal psalm, which stands between the end of the second David collection and the beginning of the Asaph group, Psalms 73–83. The third doxology (89.52 [53]) is preceded by royal

---

23. The same feature is shared by non-sequential Pss. 113 and 135, and also by Ps. 106, if the *Halleluyah* following the doxology at the end of Book IV (106.48) is included.

24. Wilson 1993b: 74.

25. Noted by Sarna 1971: 1311.

26. Forbes 1888: 4; Wilson 1985a: 207-208.

Psalm 89, which stands between the second Korah collection and Moses Psalms 90–100.[27] The fourth doxology (106.48) marks a thematic rather than a structural or genre division. Psalm 106 closes with a plea for ingathering from the nations, while Psalm 107 opens with thanksgiving for the *fait accompli* (107.1-3). The doxologies are therefore not arbitrarily positioned. Rather they demarcate changes of psalm-group and theme within the arrangement of the Psalter. Similarly, the beginning of the Elohistic Psalter coincides with the beginning of Book II and the Korah Psalms (Ps. 42), while its close coincides with the end of the Asaph group (Ps. 83). Such concurrences suggest that these junctures are the result of design.

The method by which the two halves of the Psalter, Books I–III and Books IV–V, are joined likewise suggests purposeful redaction. Psalm 90 is the turning point of the collection.[28] As a lament psalm, it continues the tone of the preceding sequence of psalms. Its vision of Israel wandering in the desert under God's wrath seems a fitting sequel to Psalm 89, which laments the negation of *bet*-David. On the other hand, it also relates to what comes after it. Modern commentators note its linguistic and thematic links to subsequent psalms, and ancient commentators regard Psalms 90–100 as one group.[29] The Psalter's redactor may have had similar ideas, for the doxology placed after Psalm 89 locks Psalm 90 into context with its following psalms. Thus the two halves of the Psalter, which might otherwise seem disconnected, are neatly joined together by this 'Janus-faced' psalm, which, to mix metaphors, binds the whole into a seamless garment. The psalm's fitness to its context suggests that the two major sections of the Psalter were conjoined with consummate and purposeful artistry, and are not simply the result of haphazard pairing.

The concurrence of book divisions and thematic content also suggests, of course, that the book divisions derive from the main

27. The idea that Pss. 90–100 are all to be subsumed under the למשה heading is ancient. It is mentioned by Origen (*Selecta in Psalmos*, Lommatzsch 1831–48: XI, 352-54), who received it from Jewish sources, and in *Midr. Pss.* 90.3; 91.1. Wilson has noted connections with Exodus and Mosaic themes in 90–92, 94, 102, 105, 106 (Wilson 1993a: 75-76).

28. This is noted by Westermann 1991: 257; Wilson 1985a: 214-15; Howard 1993: 109-10; Wilson 1993a: 75-76; Origen, *Selecta in Psalmos* (Lommatzsch 1831–48: XI, 352-54); Jerome, *Ep.* 140 *ad Cyprianum*; *Midr. Pss.* 90.3.

29. Howard 1993: 110-11.

redaction process that produced the final form of the Psalter, and are not a later and artificial addition, as some have maintained.[30] Other considerations confirm this. The first and fourth doxologies both contain *Blessed be Yhwh, the God of Israel, from everlasting to everlasting*. This may be an inclusio tying the first and last doxologies together. In addition, the phrase אָמֵן וְאָמֵן occurs nowhere in MT except in the first three doxologies.[31] This invites comparison between them and suggests they have a similar function. The objection that the fourth doxology has only a single אָמֵן is lessened by its LXX form, where γένοιτο γένοιτο is identical to the preceding three doxologies. Whether this is an LXX alteration or whether MT has diverged from an earlier Hebrew *Vorlage* (possibly in order to parallel 1 Chron. 16.36) is unclear. The similarity of MT, with its single *Amen*, to 1 Chron. 16.36, its only other biblical parallel, may suggest LXX's double *Amen* is a later addition, to strengthen the fourth doxology's resemblance to the preceding three. But whichever way, it confirms that the four doxologies were already regarded as having a similar function before LXX times. The fact is that by the second century BCE the four doxologies had been given a form that deliberately equated them. This suggests they were regarded as having a similar function.

Finally, the phenomenon of concatenistic links between adjacent psalms, noted by many commentators ancient and modern,[32] provides evidence that the Psalter was carefully arranged on the small scale as well as the large. The redactor was apparently concerned to represent minor structures and themes in his collection, as well as major ones.

d. *External Evidence for Purposeful Arrangement*
In addition to these internal evidences, several other points suggest purposeful shaping.

(1) There was insufficient time for the extended redaction process that some commentators propose. Peters, for instance, suggests the fourth doxology was added by a later redactor who wanted the same number of psalms in Book IV as in Book III, and so unwittingly divided the closely linked Psalms 106 and 107.[33] However, the presence of

---

30. Kraus 1978: I, 17; Kirkpatrick 1902: xviii; Peters 1922: 5; Gese 1974: 159-67.

31. It occurs without ו-connective at Num. 5.22 and Neh. 8.6.

32. This is discussed in the preceding chapter.

33. Peters 1922: 5.

post-exilic psalms suggests the main redaction took place after the exile; and LXX shows that it was already widely known, and in some sense authoritative, at least for the Alexandrian synagogues, by the early second century BCE.[34] It is unlikely that, within such a relatively short time, later redactors could have become so ignorant of the principles and procedure of their predecessors as accidentally to split psalms that even a modern reader can recognize as related.

(2) Other ancient Near Eastern collections of hymnic and liturgical material bear evidence of purposeful arrangement. Wilson's investigation of the Sumerian Temple Hymns Collection and Catalogues of Hymnic Incipits demonstrates the existence of definite editorial techniques in these collections. Some of these techniques are identical to those in the Psalter. One collection of Sumerian temple hymns ends with a concluding doxological hymn; a collection from Abu Salabikh contains 68 compositions, each concluding with a doxology.[35] This suggests that doxologies were regarded as having a closural function in much ancient Near Eastern literature, and supports Wilson's regarding them as closural in the Psalter. His investigation of the Qumran Psalms manuscripts leads to a similar conclusion. The similarity in cultural milieu of these texts and the Psalter suggests it is reasonable to expect that the latter should have been purposefully redacted.

e. *Summary*

There are a number of inconsistencies with traditional attempts to explain the form of the Psalter as the result of a process of piecemeal evolution. Ps. 72.20 does not necessarily indicate the existence of an earlier Davidic collection, as some have maintained. Books I–III seem to be designed as a consistent whole. So too, to a lesser extent, do Books IV and V. And while certain factors may suggest that these two groups developed independently, clearly their final joining, by means of Psalm 90, was purposefully done. Moreover, there is positive evidence for purposeful redaction. Internally, there is the chiastic

34. The dating of the LXX Psalter is discussed in Chapter 1, Section 1.

35. Wilson 1992: 130-31. His texts are from A. Sjöberg and E. Bergmann, *The Collection of Sumerian Temple Hymns* (Texts from Cuneiform Sources, 3; Locust Valley, New York: J.J. Augustin, 1960), and R.D. Briggs, *Inscriptions from Tell Abu Salabikh* (University of Chicago Oriental Institute Publications, 99; Chicago: University of Chicago, 1974): 45-56.

structure of the psalm-groups of Books II and III, the concurrence of
psalm content with the structural boundaries of the collection and concatenation. Externally, there is the relatively short timescale of the
redaction, which would not allow for a great diversity of redactional
agendas, and there is the evidence of purposeful arrangement in other
psalmic collections from the ancient Near East. I am not suggesting
that the Psalter fell from the sky. It was redacted, apparently from
earlier collections of lyrics. Nor am I suggesting that there were not
earlier partial redactions. There almost certainly were. But its final
form appears to be the result not of chance but design, resulting from
the single redactional impulse of a literary craftsman or craftsmen.
Moreover, certain factors, such as the use of divine names in Books II
and III, suggest there was a deliberate purpose or agenda behind the
redaction.

2. Current Theories on the Redactional Agenda behind the Psalter

Some modern scholars who recognize the Psalter's purposeful
arrangement have attempted to define its message. The most influential
of these is Wilson. Much must be said in praise of his work. More
than any other he has demonstrated the case for the Psalter's purposeful redaction, emphasizing the structural importance of different
headings and psalm-types, and showing that the fivefold book division
is intrinsic to its composition. He has also made important observations about redactional agenda, recognizing the centrality of Davidic
kingship and covenant, and the fact that Psalm 89 seems to indicate its
cessation. However his conclusion, that the Psalter's purpose is to
address the apparent failure of the Davidic covenant in the light of the
exile and its aftermath, and that Yhwh will be Israel's king in future,
as in the premonarchic past,[36] does not quite fit all the facts.

First, Wilson suggests that Books IV and V represent the message
that God will be Israel's king now that the 'Davidic covenant introduced in Ps. 2 has come to nothing'.[37] But if that is so, why does the
name of David appear in sixteen headings and several psalms in Books
IV and V. (For Wilson himself suggests that the לדוד psalms describe
the fortunes of David.) His answer seems to be that David is set up as
a model of the wise man who trusts in Yhwh, and so points the way

36. Wilson 1985a: 213-14.
37. Wilson 1985a: 213.

for Israel's future obedience.[38] But this seems an insufficient explanation for the intensity of the Davidic material in Books IV and V. Can Psalm 110, for instance, be regarded merely as pointing to David as a paradigm of trust in Yhwh's ability to protect from detractors?[39] Yhwh does indeed appear to be king in Book IV, as Wilson suggests, but it seems that, by Book V, David is unmistakeably back on the throne. Psalms 110, 132 and 144 depict a Davidic king. Moreover, if the house of David has come to nothing at the end of Book III, why do these later Davidic psalms represent him not conquered, but conquering. Is it all simply paradigmatic for Israel's trust in Yhwh? If the לדוד ascription has the same significance in Books IV–V as Wilson reckons it has in Books I–III—and he does not state otherwise—then David is forgiven, healed, redeemed and rejuvenated (103.3-5). He wakens the dawn with praise, and receives a divine oracle promising success in battle (108). He curses his enemy (109). He will rule from Zion, crushing the head of the wide earth and filling it with corpses (110). The name of Solomon is associated with the building of a 'house' (Ps. 127.1). The old Davidic and Zion theology is reasserted in the strongest terms (122; 125; 128.5-6; 132.11-18). David is rescued from the sword and sings a new song to God (144.9-10). The David of Books IV and V may not be doing as badly as Wilson suggests.

Secondly, if the purpose of the Psalter is to encourage Israel to trust in God alone in future, as Wilson suggests, then why do passages in Books I–III emphasize God's failure to keep his covenant promises? This is done explicitly, as in the following passage:

I will not defile my covenant, and the utterance of my lips I will not revise.
Once I have sworn by my holiness, 'If I should lie to David!'
His seed will be forever, and his throne like the sun before me;
Like the moon established forever, and the faithful witness in the sky.
    Selah.
But you yourself have rejected and spurned;
your wrath has overflowed against your mashiah. (Ps. 89.35-39 [34-38]).

A similar effect is achieved by the juxtaposition of the Davidic covenant language at the end of Psalm 78 and the harsh denial of Zion theology in Psalm 79.[40] The same thing is implied throughout Books

---

38. Wilson 1985a: 221; cf. also 217-18.
39. Wilson 1985a: 221.
40. This is pointed out by McCann 1993: 99.

II and III by restating Davidic and Zion theology (Pss. 46, 48, 76, 84, 87) in the context of their impending destruction at Psalm 89. Moreover, the end of Book III seems full of hopes for a new beginning. Ps. 82.8 calls on God to judge the earth. Psalm 83 shows the judgment imminent and implies the coming victory (10-19 [9-18]). Psalm 84 speaks of the blessedness of Zion, and requests God's favour on his *mashiah*. Psalm 85 promises the restoration of the land. Psalm 87 celebrates Zion. And then follows the horror of Psalms 88 and 89. The answer of McCann, who espouses Wilson's hypothesis, is that by this mixture of hope and lament 'Books I–III address the problem of exile and dispersion with the affirmation that hope is still possible'.[41] But what kind of hope is this? For if the house of David 'has come to nothing', then the divine promises are worthless. Yet the redactor seems deliberately to emphasize their failure, and God's falsehood, in vividly representing the disappointment of their hopes. Is it for this celebration of divine disloyalty and incompetence that jubilant halleluyahs close the Psalter? Such an approach would hardly encourage future trust in God alone, as Wilson suggests.

Thirdly, Wilson's theory does not accord with what is known of Israel's attitude to *bet*-David at any time when the Psalter might have been redacted. When did Israel say, as Wilson would have it said in the Psalter, that the Davidic house is simply finished and they must trust in Yhwh alone as in premonarchic times? I am not aware of this idea anywhere in literature of the period. On the contrary, although *bet*-David was eclipsed before Alexander, there was a continuing expectation, throughout second temple times and beyond, that it would be restored by a future son of David.[42] Thus there does not seem to be any period when the redactional agenda suggested by Wilson might have existed. Of course, one may posit the existence of a small school of heterodox belief who disowned any hope in the restoration of the house of David. But it is hard to imagine how such a group could produce a Psalms arrangement that came to be so widely accepted in Israel that, in its LXX form, it was already the standard for synagogue worship as far away as Alexandria in 200 BCE. Wilson himself seems to favour a late date for the final redaction and maintains, following

---

41. McCann 1993: 105.

42. Jer. 33.12-26; Ezek. 37.24-28; Zech. 12.7-9; *T. Sim.* 7; *T. Jud.* 24.1-6; *T. Nap.* 5.1-3; 8.2-3; *Pss. Sol.* 17; 4QPBless. 3; 4Q285.7.3-4; Mt. 1.1-17; 22.41-42; Mk 12.35-36; Lk. 1.32-33; 20.41-44; Rev. 22.16.

Sanders, that the Qumran Psalms manuscripts show that Books IV and V were still in a state of flux in 50 CE. But the final redaction would have to have been much later still, somewhere after Bar Kokhba, when Israel's messianic expectations were so greatly disappointed for the Psalter to reflect a belief that *bet*-David was finally finished. All such late datings are controverted by LXX, which shows an MT-type Psalter was widely accepted in 200 BCE.

J.H. Walton's work has the strength that, unlike Wilson, he emphasizes the content of particular lyrics in relation to his suggested schema. However he overcorrects, for he virtually disregards the headings, stating 'there may be little correlation between the Psalm titles, which convey information about an earlier *Sitz im Leben,* and the incidents to which the Psalms are applied in their cantata context'.[43] Such an approach allows Walton to make very tenuous links between psalm and event. For instance, Korah Psalm 44 'almost certainly' reflects the victory of the Philistines over the Israelites at the battle of Mount Gilboa, and 'Psalms 23 and 24...could very easily reflect a correlation to the incident with Nabal and Abigail reported in 1 Sam. 25'.[44] A major weakness of Walton's hypothesis that derives from this approach is his interpretation of Book III. Details such as the mention of Assyria and the rejection of Ephraim (Pss. 83.9 [8]; 78.67), lead him to state that Book III refers to the Assyrian crisis.[45] He reckons that Psalm 83 represents the Assyrian threat, Psalms 84–87 represent the southern kingdom's escape from the destruction in the north, Psalm 88 represents Hezekiah's illness and Psalm 89 the 'imminent rejection' implied in Sennacherib's attack on Jerusalem.[46] Walton admits that this 'leaves some gaps' between Sennacherib's invasion and Book IV, which he reckons to represent exilic times.[47] It does indeed. It would be a poor redactor, compiling a retrospective of Israel's history, who would omit more than a century of momentous events, including the Babylonian destruction and the fall of the house of David, whose establishment was his particular theme, according to Walton, throughout Books I and II. Finally, Walton offers no explanation for the Davidic psalms in Book V, although their presence is an

43. Walton 1991: 24.
44. Walton 1991: 25-26.
45. Walton 1991: 27.
46. Walton 1991: 27-28.
47. Walton 1991: 28.

embarrassment to his theory, as much as to Wilson's.

Neither of these current attempts to identify the agenda behind the Psalter's redaction can be judged entirely successful. But it is notable that they have in common a largely historical orientation. The narrative standpoint of Wilson's redactor is somewhere in Book IV, everything before being historical review, and Book V offering only encouragement to future trust. The narrative standpoint of Walton's redactor is after Book V, for to him the entire Psalter is historical review. No current theory develops the idea that an *eschatological* agenda lay behind the final redaction. This is surprising, for ancient interpretation of the Psalms might hint at an eschatological agenda in the redaction and recent commentators, not least Wilson's own teacher, Childs, have suggested as much.[48] However, none but Forbes, at the end of last century, has attempted to work out the details of the Psalter's arrangement. Now clearly, if an eschatological agenda were behind the Psalter's redaction, any attempt at understanding that failed to take account of this would be unlikely to succeed. Yet I am not aware of any statements among the historicist theories explaining why they have sought a historical rather than an eschatological agenda. In Wilson's case, certainly, it cannot be simply a belief in the late development of eschatology, for he dates the final redaction of the MT Psalter in the Christian period when eschatology was by all accounts well developed.[49]

3. *An Eschatological Orientation in the Psalter*

Several points suggest that the final form of the Psalter may indeed have been redacted in accord with an eschatological agenda. First, it originated within an eschatologically conscious milieu. The period of its redaction was apparently sometime between the end of the Babylonian exile, as the post-exilic psalms attest, and the translation of the LXX. Biblical literature written during this period, when Israel was in subjection and *bet*-David in decline, tends to look for a sudden dramatic divine intervention in history that will restore the nation's fallen fortunes.[50] Thus Ezekiel and Zechariah, in the early post-exilic

---

48. Delitzsch 1887: 88-95; Forbes 1888: 3; Childs 1979: 511-18; Brennan 1980: 29.

49. Wilson 1985a: 121.

50. Hanson notes: '...the stubborn insistence of the classical prophets in

period,[51] both anticipate a coming golden age of prosperity and dominion for Israel, under a Davidic king.[52] The discovery at Qumran of portions of *1 En.* 1–36 and 72–82 on manuscripts dating from the third century BCE further suggests that apocalyptic literature with eschatological themes existed in the early post-exilic period.[53] Even sober Tobit ends with prediction of future events, while the Testaments of the Twelve Patriarchs, the Sybilline Oracles and much of the Qumran literature have a predominantly eschatological message.[54] It therefore seems fair to regard the second temple period as a time of growing eschatological hope. As this was the context of the Psalter's redaction, it seems not unreasonable to suggest that its redactor shared the eschatological concerns of his contemporaries and that an eschatological agenda underlies his work, as it did theirs.

Second, the figures to whom the Psalms are attributed were regarded as future-predictive prophets even in biblical times. David is represented in 2 Sam. 23.2-4 foreseeing the reign of a just king, presumably the son predicted in 2 Sam. 7.11-16.

> Oracle of David ben Jesse, and oracle of the hero raised on high,
> *Mashiah* of the God of Jacob, and singer of the sweet songs of Israel.
> The Spirit of Yhwh spoke by me, and his word upon my tongue.
> The God of Israel spoke; to me said the Rock of Israel:

translating their vision of Yahweh's acts into the terms of politics and plain history was increasingly abandoned by the visionaries of the post-exilic period. The divine act stands in a much looser relation to historical processes' (1975: 291).

51. Most modern commentators would date the final form of these books in the earlier rather than later post-exilic period. Wevers considers that Ezekiel was redacted into substantially its present form before the end of the sixth century (1969: 29). Greenberg suggests 'the dates of the book are in line with the contents of its oracles' (1983: 17). Kirkpatrick comments: 'The Book of Ezekiel. . . comes to us in all probability direct from the prophet himself. He speaks throughout in the first person' (1892: 336). As regards Zechariah, R. Smith (1984: 170) and Stuhlmueller (1988: 117) think Zech. 9–14 originated at the end of the sixth or beginning of the fifth century BCE. Person believes it originated in the Persian period (1993: 205). Lamarche considers that it may have been written anytime between 500 and 200 BCE (1961: 22-23). Such views are in contrast, of course, to the dominant views of the nineteenth and early twentieth centuries. Duhm (1875; Duhm 1902: 75, 82), for instance, attributed passages such as Isa. 7 and 11 to the time of Alexander Jannaeus.

52. Eschatological prophecies from Ezek. 34–48, Zech. 9–14 and other biblical prophetic books will be discussed in Chapter 5.

53. Milik 1976: 7-11.

54. Eschatological literature from these collections will be discussed in Chapter 7.

'A ruler of mankind, a just one, a ruler in the fear of God,
Like the light of morning at sunrise, a morning cloudless,
From the brightness after the rain, grass from the earth.'[55]

Likewise, Asaph, Jeduthun and Heman are designated 'seers' (2 Chron. 29.30; 35.15; 1 Chron. 25.5). The term (חזה) signifies one who beholds visions and was used in biblical times to denote one who fore-knew future events (1 Sam. 9.15-17). Moses too was regarded as a prophet with predictive powers (Deut. 18.15; 31.19-22; 34.10). Since David, Asaph, Heman, Jeduthun and Moses were regarded in this way, it is not unreasonable to suspect that psalms bearing their names would be considered future-predictive.[56] And since such psalms constitute almost two-thirds of the Psalter, they might be expected to lend an eschatological aura to the whole. The fact that some of these psalms appear to refer only to historical events need not contradict this. The essence of Israel's view of prophecy was that historic events prefigure future ones. In later times this became a fixed hermeneutical idea:

> *That which has been is that which shall be* (Eccl. 1.9)...R. Berekiah said in the name of R. Isaac: As the first redeemer was, so shall the latter redeemer be. What is stated of the former redeemer? *And Moses took his wife and his sons, and set them upon an ass* (Exod. 4.20). Similarly will it be with the latter redeemer, as it is said, *Lowly and riding upon an ass* (Zech. 9.9). As the former redeemer caused manna to descend, as it is

---

55. The messianic significance of this text is demonstrated well by Delitzsch (1890: 67-68 n.): 'Die Erklärung: Wenn einer über die Menschen herrscht in Gottesfurcht, so ists gleichwie u.s.w. (so daß das Gesagte ein dem David vor-gehaltenes Musterbild ist, wie es von Raschi u.a. gefaßt wird), hat syntaktisch dies gegen sich, daß v.4 (mit וכאור beginnend) sich nicht als Nachsatz eines Bedingungsatzes kennzeichnet. Alles von 3b-4 ist complexes Subjekt, ein von Gott David vor Augen gestelltes Zukunftsbild, zu welchem ein Futurum (ein solcher wird erstehen und es wird sein wie u.s.w.) sich hinzudenkt. Sonderbarer Weise verteilt das Targum die benennungen 3b auf Gott und den Künftigen: „Der über die Menschenkinder herrscht als rechter Richter, hat gesagt (verheißen) mir einen König zu setzen, den Messias, welcher dereinst erstehen und herrschen wird in der Furcht des HErrn."' (*sic*).

56. It is likely that לדוד and other personal ascriptions in psalm headings were regarded as indicating authorship in early second temple times, as they were later in the Dead Sea Scrolls (e.g. 11QPsᵃ, col. 27, lines 1-11; cited on p. 25) and New Testament (e.g. Mt. 22.41-46; Mk 12.36; Lk. 20.42-43). Certainly the headings of Pss. 7, 18, 56, 57, 59, 60, 63 explicitly claim Davidic authorship. But even if authorship was not inferred from all such headings in ancient times, the connection with the name of the seer would give a psalm future-predictive status.

said, *Behold I will cause to rain bread from heaven for you* (Exod. 16.4), so will the latter redeemer cause manna to descend, as it is said, *May he be as a rich cornfield in the land* (Ps. 72.16). As the former redeemer made a well to rise, so will the latter redeemer bring up water, as it is said, *And a fountain shall come forth out of the house of the Lord, and shall water the valley of Shittim* (Joel 4.18).[57]

A similar idea occurs at *Midr. Pss.* 118.12.

> *All nations compassed me about; but in the name of Yhwh will I cut them off* (Ps. 118.10). Gog and Magog will come three times against Israel and ascend three times against Jerusalem, even as Sennacherib ascended three times against the land of Israel, and as Nebuchadnezzar ascended three times against Jerusalem.

It is with such a hermeneutic that Kimhi, for instance, interprets historical Ps. 52 messianically, by regarding David's adversities as typological of messiah's.

Thirdly, certain psalms seems to be of an intrinsically 'ultimate' character, that is, they describe a person or event in such glowing terms that the language far exceeds the reality of any historical king or battle. For instance, Psalms 2, 72 and 110 anticipate worldwide conquest by Israel's king. Psalms 21, 45 and 110 describe his invincibility in battle. Psalms 21 and 72 accord him endless life. Psalm 47 envisages the homage of the world's rulers in Jerusalem. Psalm 98 celebrates God's coming judgment and Israel's vindication. Psalms 82 and 83 describe the judgment of the tutelary deities of the nations and their corresponding peoples, followed by ultimate war and the inauguration of God's *malkut*.[58] Other examples, such as Psalms 24, 51, 67, 93, 97 might be given.[59] Such psalms therefore describe a superhero king and the golden age of his *malkut*, with all its blessings of just government, security and honour for Israel, the homage of the nations, the fecundity of the earth, and so on. The psalmists apparently wrote these lyrics in hyperbolous praise of contemporary people and events.[60] How far they believed these things would be fulfilled in the

57. *Eccl. R.* to 1.9.

58. The interpretation of Pss. 82 and 83 will be more fully discussed in the following chapter, and Pss. 2, 45, 72 and 110 in Chapter 8.

59. On Ps. 24 see Smart 1933: 175-80; on Ps. 51 see Mosis 1992: 201-15; on Ps. 67 see Wahl 1992: 240-47; on Ps. 93 see Gunkel 1926: 410-12; Welch 1926: 31-36; on Ps. 97 see Welch 1926: 36-42.

60. Mowinckel notes that 'these psalms refer not to a future king, the "Messiah",

contemporary king and how far it was simply flattery cannot be said. But the point is that if their hyperbole delineates a cosmic superhero king, then such a figure must have been part of the culture's intellectual furniture. And if a psalm depicts ultimate war followed by God's *malkut,* then that idea must have been current at the time of writing. The psalms reflect these ideas as they were conceived in ancient Israel, and when the historical kings went their way, the psalms remained as testimony to Israel's future hope, containing in themselves a truly eschatological vision of a superhero king and his *malkut.*

Fourthly, the very inclusion of the royal psalms in the Psalter suggests that the redactor understood them to refer to a future *mashiah*-king. For otherwise their presence in a collection for use in second temple times, when the house of David was in eclipse, would have made little sense.[61] They would either recall the failure of the divine promises celebrated by the Davidic bards or be simply redundant. This puzzled Olshausen:

> There are... some songs, which almost of necessity must derive from an older pre-exilic time, particularly some so-called royal psalms, such as Pss. 2, 20, 21 (compare also Pss. 28, 61, 63). Exactly why these songs found acceptance here is extremely unclear, as they could hardly have been used in services of worship at a time when there were no Israelite kings.[62]

but to the reigning king, who is a contemporary of the poet' (1962: I, 48). 'The kernel of truth in the Messianic interpretation is... that it is ultimately the same common oriental mythologically conceived superhuman king-ideal, which underlies both the psalm-poets' descriptions of the present king in David's city, and the prophets' description of the future king... The poets thought that the ideal was realized, or hoped that it would be realized, in the earthly king seated before them on the throne. The prophets were not satisfied with anything which the present reality could offer, and looked hopefully forward to a new king, whom God would send "in his own good time", and who would be the realization of the ideal which the present kings did not appear to fulfil, because it was beyond human power' (1962: I, 49].

61. This point has been made by Forbes 1888: 4; Childs 1979: 516.

62. 'Es finden sich... einige Lieder, die fast nothwendig aus einer älteren vorexilischen Zeit herrühren müssen, besonders einige sog. Königspsalmen, wie Ps. II. XX. XXI. vgl. auch Ps. XXVIII. LXI. LXIII. Weshalb gerade diese Gesänge hier Aufnahme gefunden, ist sehr unklar, da sie in einer Zeit, wo es keine israelitische Könige gab, kaum beim Gottesdienste gebraucht werden konnten' (Olshausen 1853: 31).

Indeed, Olshausen is stating only half the case. For he does not mention Psalms 110 and 132, which occur in Books IV and V, these books being, according to Olshausen, the latest to have been added to the Psalter. After the extinction of the kingdom psalms referring to the king or *mashiah* would have been understood as referring only to the anticipated future deliverer. The redactor's deliberate incorporation of these psalms into the Psalter therefore suggests that eschatological concerns were part, at least, of the editorial purpose. Of course, these psalms do not necessarily allow the whole Psalter to be read eschatologically. However they would have a tendency to 'infect' everything in their context with their vision, and the redactors may have intended as much.

That the redactors may indeed have wished the messianic psalms to 'infect' the interpretation of the whole Psalter is suggested by the positions in which they have been placed.[63] There is good ground, as was noted above, for regarding Psalm 2, together with Psalm 1, as functioning as an introduction to the Psalter. As such, it sets the tone and determines the interpretation of what is to follow. That means the ensuing collection is to be about ultimate war between Yhwh's *mashiah* and his foes, his triumph and the establishment of his universal dominion, centred on Zion. The combined effect of Psalms 1 and 2 together may be that Psalm 1 foretells the triumph of the righteous divine king who meditates on Yhwh's Torah, and Psalm 2 shows him going forth to battle with its predicted outcome.[64] Or Psalm 1 delineates the person who will share in the king's triumph, possibly as a warrior, and Psalm 2 pronounces that one's blessedness. The two psalms together announce that the ensuing collection is a handbook for the eschatological wars of the Lord, describing the coming events and the Yhwh-allegiance required of those who would triumph. Other messianic psalms occur in significant positions. Psalm 72 forms the conclusion to Book II; Psalm 89 to Book III. Psalm 110 precedes the jubilant *Halleluyah* group Psalms 111–17. This suggests the messianic theme is central to the purpose of the collection.

---

63. The point is made by Forbes (1888: 4): 'The remarkable and prominent position of these Psalms shows the high significance attached to them.'

64. The idea that Ps. 1 describes the divine king himself is made by Sheppard (1980: 142).

4. *Summary*

Detailed investigation of the MT Psalter reveals internal evidence that suggests it is more than a collection of songs for use as a temple or synagogue hymnbook.[65] Instead it seems to be a purposefully crafted 'scripture' with some kind of inbuilt message about the Davidic *malkut*. It bears evidence of this at both small- and large- scale levels. Thematic and linguistic links exist between adjacent psalms. Larger psalms-groups appear to have been deliberately placed. Books I–III are a carefully crafted sub-unit, skilfully linked to Books IV and V. Royal psalms occur at structurally significant points. The five-book division is intrinsic to the final shaping.

However, if attempts to prove purposeful redaction can be judged very successful, attempts to define the redactional agenda must be judged only partially so. Although current theories have major strengths, rightly noting the centrality of Davidic kingship and the importance of Ps. 89, they also fail to fit the evidence in a number of details. What these theories have in common is that they propose that the sequence of Psalms principally reflects historical events. However, there is internal evidence, particularly in the placing of royal and eschatological psalms, that the Psalter was designed to refer to escha-tological events. Such a view is supported by the historical context of the Psalter's redaction, which was dominated by eschatological con-cerns, and by virtually all ancient commentators, and some moderns. Such a conclusion seems not implausible, in light of the historical context of the Psalter's redaction, and the nature of certain psalms and their redactional placing. Yet, in spite of this no attempt has been made recently to explain the details of the Psalter's redaction in terms of an eschatological agenda. Those who seek the significance of the Psalter's arrangement, Wilson, Walton and McCann, assume a histori-cally oriented redactional agenda, while those who recognize an escha-tological agenda, Childs and Brennan, have not sought to work out its implications for the Psalter's arrangement. In the following chapters I shall combine these two approaches, investigating the Psalter's

65. Hossfeld and Zenger rightly comment: 'Aus der Bezeichnung »Buch der Preisungen« bzw. »Buch der Hymnen« darf freilich *nicht* geschlossen werden, das Psalmenbuch sei als *»Gesangbuch des Zweiten Tempels«* entstanden oder im Judentum der Zeit Jesu verwendet worden' (1993: 6).

arrangement in terms of an eschatologically oriented editorial agenda. In so doing, I hope to sketch the outline of a programme of eschatological events in the Psalter that makes sense of both heading and content of individual psalms, the sequence of psalms, the arrangement of internal collections and the five-book arrangement.

Chapter 3

THE PSALMS OF ASAPH

In the foregoing chapters I suggested that the Psalter may have been redacted as a literary unit with an intentionally eschatological reference. I shall now try to show that this is indeed a plausible way to read it, and in particular that this redaction takes the form of a programme of eschatological events. In this and the next chapter I shall investigate the Psalms of Asaph and the Songs of Ascents and conclude that each of these groups of psalms contains a sequence of events that can be read as depicting an eschatological ingathering. Then, in Chapter 5, I shall investigate the nature of eschatological programmes in the biblical prophets. Thereafter, in Chapter 6, I shall compare the motifs and themes of the two psalm-cycles to the principal motifs of the prophetic eschatological programme.

Twelve psalms (50, 73–83) contain in their heading the ascription לאסף, *Of Asaph*. I shall investigate them as an independent literary category, a self-contained psalm-cycle, somewhat like Schubert's *Liederkreise*. This is justified for at least three reasons. First, their common heading indicates that the Psalter's redactor regarded them all as belonging in some sense to an Asaphite tradition. Secondly, the unity imposed on them by the heading is confirmed by the consecutive placing of Psalms 73–83 in the Psalter. Psalm 50 is, of course, an exception. But I have already suggested that Psalms 50 and 73 were separated for literary and structural purposes, and shall suggest later that the same phenomenon also has an explanation in the Psalter's eschatological event-sequence. Thirdly, these psalms display a number of common linguistic and stylistic characteristics. Examples might include the *dis legomena* משואות/משאות at Pss. 73.18 and 74.3 and שדי זיז at Pss. 50.11 and 80.14 [13].[1] In addition to these twelve Asaph

---

1. Further thematic and linguistic characteristics of these psalms will be noted in Chapter 6.

Psalms, three further psalms (96, 105, 106) are connected with Asaph and his associates by the Chronicler (1 Chron. 16.7-36). As shall be seen, these 'deutero-Asaph' psalms share some characteristics of the Asaph group, and therefore shall also be considered in this investigation.[2]

1. *Heading and Tradition*

The simplest interpretation of the לאסף heading connects these psalms with the biblical figure Asaph and his descendants. The biblical tradition concerning them, mostly from Chronicles, is as follows.[3] Asaph was a Levite from the Korahite clan (1 Chron. 26.1). He was one of three heads of levitical families appointed by King David and the chief Levites to *be in charge of song in the house of Yhwh* (1 Chron. 6.31-39; cf. 15.16-17; 2 Chron. 5.12) and to *prophesy* [נבא] *with lyres, harps, and cymbals* (1 Chron. 25.1).[4] The prophetic nature of their ministry is elsewhere alluded to in that each is described as חזה or חוזה, *a seer* (1 Chron. 25.5; 2 Chron. 29.30; 35.15). These head Levites were under the supervision of King David, while the sons of each family served in the temple under their fathers' direction (1 Chron. 25.6). Asaph is identified as a composer of cultic songs, psalms *of Asaph and David* being sung in Solomon's temple (2 Chron. 29.30; 35.15). His descendants are accorded an illustrious role in Israel's cult. His son Joseph was head of the first of the twenty-four courses of Levites (1 Chron. 25.9). The Asaphites, with the Hemanites and the Jeduthunites, sang at the dedication of Solomon's temple (2 Chron. 5.12). An Asaphite in Jehoshaphat's time, Jahaziel, prophesied divine intervention in battle against foreign invaders (2 Chron. 20.14-17). Joah ben Asaph, the *mazkîr*, was part of the small delegation appointed to meet Sennacherib's threat (2 Kgs 18.18, 37; Isa. 36.3, 22). Asaph-ites, with Hemanites and Jeduthunites, took part in Hezekiah's reform,

---

2.   The phrase 'deutero-Asaph' is from Nasuti 1988: 80, 91, 190, *et passim*.

3.   As it is the motifs of these traditions which are my present concern, I shall avoid discussion of the historicity of the Chronicler's account. As regards the development of cultic prophecy in Israel, see Auld 1983: 3-23, 41-44; Murray 1982: 200-216.

4.   The three companies of singers are named as either Asaph, Heman and Ethan (1 Chron. 15.17-19), or Asaph, Heman and Jeduthun (1 Chron. 25.1, 6; 2 Chron. 5.12). The cognate names Ethan and Jeduthun may denote the same company.

purifying the temple, and possibly serving as musicians (2 Chron. 29.13; cf. vv. 25-30). By the time of Josiah's reform, only the Asaphites are mentioned as temple singers, although the historical role of Heman and Jeduthun is acknowledged (2 Chron. 35.15). In the records of the post-exilic return, apart from one Jeduthunite (Neh. 11.17), the only levitical singers to return were Asaphites, who formed more than a third of the returning Levites (Ezra 2.41, 65; Neh. 7.44, 67).[5] These sang and played at the foundation of the second temple, and the dedication of the wall (Ezra 3.10-11; Neh. 12.27-43). One of their number was chief Levite in the city (Neh. 11. 22).

a. *Prophet-Musicians*
One thing that is notable about this tradition is that the Asaphites are depicted as prophet-musicians. There are references not only to their musical and prophetic gifts, but to the conjunction of these gifts in a temple ministry of prophetic song.[6] These two gifts were often regarded by biblical writers as related. Miriam and Deborah are each called נביאה and connected with cultic song (Exod. 15.20-21; Judg. 4.4; 5.1). Prophets in Saul's time prophesied to music (1 Sam. 10.5). David's harp eased Saul's affliction from spirit oppression (1 Sam. 16.23). Elisha called for a harpist before prophesying (2 Kgs 3.15-16). Ezekiel was to his contemporaries 'like one who sings love songs with a beautiful voice and plays well on an instrument' (Ezek. 33.32). Likewise, the mediaeval Islamic mystic al-Ghazali wrote that music brings forth religious states in which there are 'revelations and sweet intimacies indescribable, ineffable'.[7] Such states are sought through music and dancing by Muslim and Sufi mystics. Thus it appears likely that ancient Hebrew writers regarded the psalms ascribed to the Asaphite musicians as future-predictive. Indeed, as Nasuti points out, some features of the Asaph Psalms themselves suggest that they originated in a community that regarded itself as having prophetic powers.[8] The occurrence of divine oracles in the Asaph Psalms is more than

5.   There seems to be a discrepancy between Ezra 2.41, which mentions 128 Asaphites, and Neh. 7.44, which has 148.

6.   The prophetic role is ascribed to the Asaphites in later Jewish literature. Josephus calls Jahaziel ben Asaph (2 Chron. 20) a *prophet* (*Ant.* 9.1.2), and the role of prophet is ascribed to Asaph in the Talmud.

7.   Guillaume 1938: 312-4.

8.   Nasuti 1988: 158.

three times greater than in the rest of the Psalter,[9] and Asaph Pss. 82.8 and 83.18 look forward to the future rule of Yhwh over all the earth.

b. *The* Mazkîr *and the* Zikhron *rite*

A second characteristic of the Asaphite tradition is the office of *mazkîr* and the apparently related *zikhron* ritual. The nature of the *mazkîr*'s role may have been improperly understood. Joah ben Asaph, it is said, was המזכיר (2 Kgs 18.18, 37; Isa. 36.3, 22), the definite article emphasizing the singularity of his position. RSV and NIV render the term as *the recorder*, presumably implying a scribal role. But this hiphil participle of זכר would be better rendered 'remembrancer', as would its Greek renditions, ἀναμιμνῄσκων (LXX) and ὁ ἐπὶ τῶν ὑπομνημάτων (Josephus).[10] A look at the biblical passages referring to this post may help clarify the nature of it.

(1) It appears in lists of court officials in the historical books (2 Sam. 8.16; 20.24; 1 Kgs 4.3; 1 Chron. 18.15). This suggests it was an important office. But in all these lists, as in the narratives about Joah, the *mazkîr* is a different person from the scribe. Their roles were apparently distinct. Joah the *mazkîr* is sent together with Shevna the scribe to meet the Assyrian commander (2 Kgs 18.18, 37; Isa. 36.3, 22). One scribe might be sent to record the Assyrian's words. Two would be unnecessary.

(2) Isa. 62.6-7 may further clarify the nature of the *mazkîr*'s role: *Mazkîrim of Yhwh* [מזכירים את־יהוה], *do not be silent, and give him no silence, until he establishes and until he makes Jerusalem a praise in the earth.* This suggests the *mazkîr*'s function is to ensure Yhwh's remembrance of his people's plight, so that he takes action on their behalf.

(3) It is unclear in 2 Kgs 18.18, 37 and Isa. 36.3, 22 whether *mazkîr* refers to Joah or Asaph. The ambiguity may be significant. Asaph himself was a *mazkîr* in function, if not in name, for he was

---

9. The main Asaph group, which comprises only 8 per cent of the Psalter, contains four divine oracles (50, 75, 81, 82). Elsewhere in the Psalter there are 12 more (2, 12, 46, 60, 62, 68, 87, 89, 91, 95, 110, 132), and one of these is deutero-Asaphic (95). (I classify as divine oracles only those psalms that describe particular speech as of divine origin, and not those psalms merely of oracular tone, such as Ps. 95.7d-11, which Gunkel, for instance, regards as an oracle [1926: 419].)

10. *Ant.* 9.1.2.

appointed to *make remembrance* (להזכיר) before Yhwh (1 Chron.
16.4). The natural designation for such a functionary would be
'*mazkîr*'. And if a reason is sought why the actual title is not applied
to Asaph, then it may be that the office was less developed in earlier
times. Now the tradition regards Asaph as a cultic prophet, not a
scribe. It is therefore likely that the *mazkîr's* role was prophetic and
cultic. Apparently, it was also associated with levitical music and the
sounding of priestly חצצרות, *hazozerot,* or trumpets (1 Chron. 16.5-6).

Thus the *mazkîr* or remembrancer seems to have been a cultic
official whose role was to bring Yhwh to remembrance of his people's
plight in order that he might deliver them. If that is so, then he may
have been a functionary in the cultic rite, referred to in Num. 10.8-
10, of making a *zikhron* (זכרון) or 'remembrance' before Yhwh.[11]
This rite consisted of priests blowing *hazozerot* before Yhwh in times
of foreign invasion to bring him to remembrance of Israel's plight
and obtain his deliverance. This is endorsed by other biblical passages,
where the *hazozerot* appear in unambiguously martial contexts (Num.
10.2, 9, 10; 31.6; Hos. 5.8; 2 Chron. 13.12, 14; 20.28).[12] They are
also blown *before the ark of Yhwh* (1 Chron. 15.24 [23]; 16.6), a
phrase probably having military associations, given the place of
the ark in Israel's warfare (Num. 10.35; Jos. 3-8; 1 Sam. 4.3-5; *et
passim*). In addition, the Numbers passage states that the *hazozerot* are
for gathering the people and breaking camp in the wilderness
marches, and for gathering the people to Yhwh's dwelling at the
tabernacle and to the appointed feasts and New Moon festivals (Num.
10.2-10).[13] Thus the trumpets of *zikhron* were for bringing Yhwh to

---

11. The connection between the *remembrancer* of the historical books and Num.
10 was suggested by King almost a century ago (1890: II, ix-x). I am not aware of
any discussion of it since.

12. In Ps. 98.6 they are mentioned in the context of Yhwh's coming to judge the
earth (v. 9). At 2 Kgs 11.14 and 2 Chron. 23.13 they are used for praise and rejoicing at the anointing of Joash, which was also the occasion of the destruction of
Athaliah and the priests of Baal. Elsewhere they are used in the general context of
praise (2 Kgs 11.14; 1 Chron. 13.8; 15.28; 16.42; 2 Chron. 5.12, 13; 15.14; 29.26,
27, 28; Ezra 3.10; Neh. 12.35-41). Yet even these cases are often contexts of
national reform, where cult and nation are, or had been, under threat. At 2 Kgs 12.14
[13] their function is unspecified.

13. The New Moon festival appears to have been a time for clan gatherings
(1 Sam. 20.5-6), as the Sabbath was for family groups, and the appointed feasts for
the whole nation.

remembrance of his people's situation, in particular in times of national gathering and foreign invasion.[14]

The persistence in Israel of the Holy War rites outlined in Num. 10 can be seen from the Qumran War Rule (1QM), which depicts *hazozerot* being blown by priests to make *zikhron* before Yhwh in a context of ultimate war. Every detail is consistent with the rite outlined in the Numbers. Indeed, the War Scroll requires that Num. 10.9 be proclaimed by the High Priest at the time of the battle.

> And it is you who said by the hand of Moses: *When the battle comes to pass in your land against the enemy who oppresses you, you shall sound the trumpets; and you shall be remembered before your God and shall be saved from your enemies* (1QM 10.6-8).

Other passages in this document show how the *hazozerot* were to be used for gathering the people and for war.

> [...the trumpets] of battle formations; and the trumpets of summons when the gates of battle are opened that the foot-soldiers may go out; and the trumpets of sounding of slaughter; and the trumpets of ambush; and the trumpets of pursuit when the enemy is overthrown; and the trumpets of ingathering (אסף) when the fighting men return (3.1-2).

> On the trumpets summoning the foot-soldiers to advance toward the enemy formations when the gates of war are opened they shall write, '*Zikhron* of Vengeance in God's appointed Time' (3.7-8).

> And when they return from battle to the formation, they shall write on the trumpets of return, 'God has ingathered' (אסף אל) (3.10).

> 'The priests shall blow [the *hazozer*]*ot* of the *zikhron* and all the battle formations shall gather [אסף] to them and shall divide against all the l[ines of the Kitt]im to destroy them utterly' (18.4-5).

> 'The priests, the sons of Aaron, shall stand before [the] formations and shall blow the *hazozerot* of *zikhron*. After this, they shall open the gates for the foot-soldiers (4Q493).

14. Ever since Barr's *Semantics* (1961), deriving the meanings of words from their roots has rightly been regarded with suspicion. Nevertheless, the verb חצצר, *to blow a hazozerah* (2 Chron. 5.13), even if partly onomatopoeic, may relate to the root חצר, which signifies *surround* or *enclose* in Arabic and Ethiopic (Gesenius 1978: 299), and which lies behind the Hebrew noun חצר, *a court* or *enclosure*. If such an etymology is allowed, it may confirm that the *hazozerot* are for gathering and protection.

Thus the ideas associated with making a *zikhron* with *hazozerot* alluded to in Numbers 10, were not forgotten in the post-biblical period. On the contrary, they have a prominent place in traditions about the latter-day ultimate Holy War.

There are clearly similarities between the descriptions of the *zikhron* rite and the office of the *mazkîr*. Both words derive from the root זכר, and the natural designation for one who makes *zikhron* would be the hiphil participle, *mazkîr*. Both are associated with bringing Yhwh to remembrance of Israel's plight so that he may deliver them. Both are associated with foreign invasion. Both are associated with the *hazozerot*. I would therefore suggest that the *mazkîr* was a functionary in the cultic rite of remembrancing Yhwh, a rite that was central to Israel's Holy War traditions. Exactly what part the *mazkîr* played is not clear. If the Chronicler's distinction between Levites and priests is accepted, then the role of the non-priestly Asaphites was probably not that of sounding the *hazozerot*.[15] Instead, as levitical prophet-musicians, their role may have been to chant petitions and prophetic oracles appropriate to the occasion, as did Jahaziel in Jehoshaphat's time,[16] or to sound the *shofar*.[17] But whatever the exact nature of the *mazkîr's* role, tradition records that it had long been associated the Asaphites. Asaph was a *mazkîr* in function, if not in name. Jahaziel fulfilled a *mazkîr* role. Joah in his day held the important position of 'the' *mazkîr*, possibly signifying that he was chief official in charge of this rite, responsible for ensuring Yhwh's assistance in time of war.

In the light of this, another glance at the Asaphite tradition yields further evidence that seems to confirm the Asaphites continuing association with this role.

(1) Joah the *mazkîr* was one of three men selected to meet the commander of the Assyrian invasion. These three men would hardly

15. It goes beyond my present purpose to discuss the complex question of the nature and the process of development of the priestly and levitical offices in Israel. Nonetheless, it is probably safe to assume that holy war traditions existed in pre-exilic times, and were associated with cultic personnel.

16. Humbert notes that the holy war rite, which he calls the *'teru'a'*, had both a vocal and instrumental component (1946: 22-28).

17. Hos. 5.8 suggests that the *shofar* and *hazozerah* were functionally similar, at least for purposes of sounding alarm. In the early period there may not have been a consistent distinction between the two instruments (Oesterley 1937: 113; Bockmuehl 1991: 201).

have been selected accidentally. They must have held positions entitling them to be intimately involved in such a matter. Elyakim, אֲשֶׁר עַל־הַבַּיִת, seems to have been the Chief Vizier or Home Secretary (2 Kgs 19.2; Isa. 37.2).[18] Shevna the scribe's task may have been to record the Assyrian's words. Joah too presumably held a position entitling him to be present. Such a position might be if he were the official in charge of the supernatural aspect of national security.

(2) At the point in these narratives when Elyakim and Shevna go to Isaiah to report the situation, Joah is unmentioned (2 Kgs 19.2; Isa. 37.2). His absence from this later delegation at such a time of national crisis is unusual. It is admittedly an argument from silence, but it is possible that he was absent because he was active elsewhere in matters connected with his office as *mazkîr*. Prayer for deliverance had already begun in the temple (2 Kgs 19.1; Isa. 37.1). Is it not possible that Joah was there, fulfilling his role as *mazkîr* in the cultic rite of remembrancing Yhwh for the nation, and that the prophetic oracle received by Isaiah may be intended as the divine response to the cultic act (2 Kgs 19; Isa. 37.6-7)?

(3) An Asaphite, Jahaziel, foretold divine intervention in battle against foreign enemies in Jehoshapat's time (2 Chron. 20.14-17). The singing and praises of levitical musicians are represented as instrumental in the ensuing victory.

(4) There are several references in the Asaph Psalms to foreign invasion. The LXX headings of MT Psalms 76 and 80 contain the ascriptions ᾠδὴ πρὸς τὸν Ἀσσύριον and ψαλμὸς ὑπὲρ τὸν Ἀσσύριον (LXX Ps. 75.1; 79.1), indicating a connection with Sennacherib's siege of 2 Kgs 18–19 and Isa. 36–37 and Joah the *mazkîr*. Ps. 79.1-3 refers to a situation where a foe has invaded the land of Israel and poured out blood around Jerusalem. Asaph Psalm 83 is a prophetic oracle about deliverance from an encircling ten-nation confederacy. Psalms such as 79 and 83 may be examples of just the kind of cultic liturgy chanted by the *mazkîr* in the cultic rite of remembrancing Yhwh.

(5) The root זכר, *remember*, occurs 16 times in Asaphite psalms, 13 times in the main group and 3 times more in deutero-Asaph Psalms

---

18. See Layton, who concludes that this governmental role developed from the early monarchic period until 'eventually the royal steward became a senior administrator, one of the highest officials in the state' (1990: 649). This accords with Josephus (*Ant.* 10.1.2.), for whom Elyakim was not simply the palace administrator, but ὁ τῆς βασιλείας ἐπίτροπος.

105 and 106.[19] Elsewhere in the Psalter it occurs only 38 times. Therefore the Asaph and deutero-Asaph Psalms, which comprise together about 10 per cent of the Psalter, contain almost a third of its occurrences of this verb. This disproportionate emphasis suggests that it was an important idea to the Asaphite community.

(6) The Asaphite interest in remembrancing is confirmed by the feature of historical review, which is pursued almost obsessively in the Asaph and deutero-Asaph Psalms.[20] The purpose of this is apparently to put God in remembrance of his former acts on Israel's behalf, and on that basis to request future deliverance. Such a purpose is particularly evident in such passages as Pss. 74.12-23 and 77.8-13 [7-12]. But it is discernible elsewhere, as in Psalm 80's repeated juxtaposition of historical reminiscence and pleas for mercy.

(7) Ps. 50.15 promises that when the faithful call upon God in the *day of hostility* (צרה) he will deliver them. In Ps. 77.2-3 [1-2] the psalmist calls to God to hear him in his *day of hostility* (צרה). Similarly, Ps. 81.8 [7] recalls that when Israel previously called to God in the Egyptian *hostility* (צרה), he delivered them. This idea of crying out to God for deliverance when threatened by hostile enemies reflects the role of the *mazkîr.*

(8) Asaph Psalm 81 mentions the sounding of the trumpet, the *shofar,* and sets out terms of deliverance from enemies (vv. 4, 14-17).

(9) The phrase על־הגיתית occurs in Ps. 81.1 and following Psalm 83 (84.1). Several translations of this word are possible.[21] However, LXX, apparently reading it as גיתות, chooses *concerning the wine-presses*: ὑπὲρ τῶν ληνῶν. Likewise, the majority of rabbinic and patristic interpreters, the former uninfluenced by LXX, 'unanimously

---

19. 74.2, 18, 22; 77.4, 7, 12, 12 [3, 6, 11, 11]; 78.35, 39, 42; 79.8; 105.5; 106.4, 45. If the deutero-Asaph Psalms are omitted, the main Asaph group, which comprises 8 per cent of the Psalter, has almost a quarter, 13 out of 41, of its occurrences of this verb.

20. 74.2-10; 76.3-9; 77.6-21 [5-20]; 78.4-72; 79.1-4; 80.6, 7, 9-17 [5, 6, 8-16]; 81.6-12 [5-11]; 83.10-13 [9-12]; 105.1-45; 106.2, 6-46.

21. The Targum suggests that it was a kind of harp from Gath. Rashi (1934) also notes this view. Kimhi (1883) states that it is a type of song, and also notes the notion that David was in Gath when he composed it, and that it was somehow connected with Obed-Edom the Gittite of 2 Sam. 6.11-12. Ibn Ezra and Sa'adya also note the last of these opinions (Ibn Ezra 1988; Sa'adya [c. 933] *Psalms... of the Gaon Rabbenu Saadiah* 20).

associated the word with the *gat* or wine press'.[22] The winepress image is frequently connected in biblical thought with the ultimate destruction of God's enemies in war (Isa. 63.2-3; Joel 4[3].13; Rev. 14.19, 20). This was also how it was understood by early Rabbis and Church Fathers.[23]

(10) Several individual Asaphites bear names suggesting a concern with remembrancing: Zikhri (1 Chron. 9.15), Zaccur (1 Chron. 25.2) and Zechariah (1 Chron. 26.1-2; cf. 9.21; 26.14; 2 Chron. 20.14; 29.13; Neh. 12.35).

c. *The Ingathering Theme*

Another characteristic of the Asaphite tradition is the motif of ingathering. As noted above, gathering is one of the functions of the *hazozerot* associated with the remembrancing rite. But there are a number of other gathering motifs in the Asaphite tradition. These not only confirm the Asaphite connection with the remembrancing rite, but also show that gathering was a significant theme for the Asaphites.

(1) First of all, the name Asaph means 'gather.' How this wordplay between name and motif arose is unknown. Possibly the eponymous founder of the Asaphite guild was early associated with this motif. But such a paronomasia in the psalm heading need not cause any surprise. Deliberate ambiguity is a recognized characteristic of biblical literature in general,[24] and of the Psalms in particular.[25] And punning upon proper names, later known as מדרשי שמות, was a staple of Hebrew interpretation from biblical times.[26] Garsiel suggests that a deliberate wordplay on the name Asaph and its meaning *ingather* is found at 2 Chron. 29.13-15.[27] Thus the very heading לאסף might be taken as meaning something like *For the Ingathering*. Such an interpretation was known to ancient Christian commentators.[28]

---

22. Schwartz 1993: I, 221. See also *Midr. Pss.* 8.1; 84.1.
23. Schwartz 1993: I, 221.
24. Glück 1970: 50-78.
25. Raabe 1991: 213-27 identifies intentional ambiguity in the Psalter at lexical, phonetic and grammatical levels. The לאסף heading would probably fall into his first category.
26. For the deliberate use of the technique by biblical writers, see Garsiel 1991b: 379-86.
27. Garsiel 1991a: 174.
28. Jerome renders Asaph as 'congregans' (Opp. Paris [1579] 3.480). See also Homily on Ps. 80 [MT 81], *Tractatus de Psalmo* 80.1 (CCSL 78: 76-78). *Comm. on*

(2) The first word of the first divine oracle of the first Asaph psalm is a command to ingather: אִסְפוּ־לִי חֲסִידָי, *Gather to me my faithful ones!* (50.5). The last psalm of the main Asaph group describes a ten-nation alliance gathered against God and Israel (83.2-9 [1-8]). Similar language occurs at the conclusion of the last Asaphite psalm in the Psalter, deutero-Asaph Psalm 106: *Save us Yhwh our God, and gather* [קַבְּץ] *us from among the nations* (v. 47). The prominent positions of these psalms, and of the references to gathering in them, suggests this is a significant concern in the Asaphite tradition.

(3) The Asaph Psalms show a particular interest in the person of Joseph.[29] The name occurs four times in the main group (77.16 [15]; 78.67; 80.2 [1]; 81.6 [5][30]) and also in deutero-Asaph Ps. 105.17, which features a short history of Joseph (vv. 17-22). It appears nowhere else in the Psalter. This name is cognate with Asaph.[31] It is dually etymologized in Genesis from the roots אסף and יסף with the

Ps. 8.1 (CCSL 72: 191). Augustine states that when Asaph is translated from Hebrew into Greek and then into Latin, it is interpreted 'synagogue' (*Comm. on Ps.* 72 [MT 73] § 4). Presumably the Greek verb has become the noun, otherwise the connection of Asaph with 'synagogue' is inexplicable. The idea was still current among Christian commentators 1000 years later. Luther states: 'Asaph means "gathering", the people separated and gathered from those who remain and are not gathered' (1883–1987: IV, 4). The absence of this idea in early Jewish literature is puzzling. One would expect at least a comment on the occurrences of אסף in the heading and v. 5 of Ps. 50. Could it be that the idea was so obvious as to require no comment, or that the prediction of ingathering to judgment was so distasteful as to avert comment?

29. A number of scholars have suggested that the Asaph Psalms' interest in Joseph may indicate that they derive from a group who regarded their home territory as being among the Joseph tribes in the north (Tate 1990a: 322-23). This accords with the Chronicler's tradition which appears to link the Levites of the Ephraimite tradition and the Asaphite singers (Anderson 1972: I, 45; Buss 1963: 382-92; Mowinckel 1962: II, 79-82; Nasuti 1988: 117; Tate 1990a: 228). Other details of the Asaph Psalms, such as the references to Assyria in the LXX headings (LXX Pss. 75.1; 79.1), would appear to confirm Ephraimitic connections.

30. There is a variant spelling of the name in this instance, יְהוֹסֵף. However, there is no suggestion in the ancient commentators that this signifies another Joseph. It is referred to the son of Jacob, although there is some discussion as to the significance of the variant (*Midr. Pss.* 81.7; *PRE* 54b). Boer considers that the spelling is intended to suggest *Yehudah* instead of *Joseph,* and is a scribal alteration indicating Judean opposition to those who hoped for the restoration of the House of Joseph (1984: 77).

31. This is noted by MacLaurin 1975: 27-29.

meanings *God has ingathered* and *Yhwh will add* (Gen. 30.23-24). The Genesis figure is also an arch-ingatherer, ingathering the tribes of Israel (Gen. 42.17 אסף; 45.19–46.27) and all the harvest of the earth (Gen. 41.48 קבץ). The Asaphite interest in Joseph is further shown in the fact that the name was borne by a son of Asaph (1 Chron. 25.2, 9), although it is not popular elsewhere in the Old Testament.[32]

(4) The Asaph Psalms show an interest in Jacob. Of the Psalter's 26 references to Jacob, seven, or more than a quarter, are found in the Asaph group, which forms only 8 per cent of the Psalter. This may relate to that patriarch's reputation as an ingatherer. For he is represented as commanding the gathering of the tribes of Israel in a context of prophetic utterance concerning the last days (Gen. 49.1-2; קבץ, אסף).

(5) Asaph Psalm 81 mentions the sounding of the *shofar* 'at the New Moon... and on the day of our Feast' (81.4 [3]).

Therefore the לאסף heading evokes a wide image-complex. This involves the Asaphite guild of cultic prophet-musicians, the cultic rite of remembrancing, performed by the *mazkîr* at times of invasion and siege by foreign armies, the sounding of trumpets and the gathering of the people. Many of these concerns are reflected in the Psalms of Asaph.

2. *Eschatological Orientation*

Several passages in the Asaph Psalms seem to refer intentionally to latter-day events. The most striking example is Psalm 83, whose pervasive quality of ultimacy would appear to date from its early composition rather than later redaction. It depicts an attack on Israel by a ten-nation alliance gathered from all points of the compass.[33] History records no such alliance as that described in the psalm. Gunkel suggests it may have happened in the 'fast ganzlich unbekannten Zeit von

---

32. Only one other Old Testament character bore it (Ezra 10.42), or two, if the testimony of Syriac and some LXX MSS is taken at Neh. 12.14.

33. The Edomites were from the south-east, the Ishmaelites from the south-west, the Moabites from east of the Dead Sea, the Hagrites from the north-east, Gebal from south of the Dead Sea (a district known to Pliny as Gebalene; not the Gebal near Tyre of Ezek. 27.9), the Ammonites from east of the Jordan, the Amalekites from the southern deserts, the Philistines from the west, Tyre from the north and Assyria from the north-east (Kirkpatrick 1902: 501).

Esra bis auf Alexander d. Gr.'.[34] But Assyria and Amalek (1 Chron. 4.42-43) had ceased to exist in pre-exilic times and are unlikely to have been represented as active half a millennium later. The only recorded event resembling that in the psalm is the invasion in Jehoshaphat's time (2 Chron. 20). This was an alliance of Moabites, Ammonites, Edomites and possibly Ishmaelites[35] (2 Chron. 20.1, 10, 22-23), four of the allies of Ps. 83.7-8 [6-7]. This invasion is further connected with Psalm 83 by the Asaphite prophecy of victory that preceded it (2 Chron. 20.14-17). It might therefore be a possible historical background to Psalm 83, and the psalm may represent a cultic prophecy of that period, predicting the establishment of Yahweh's universal *malkut* in the aftermath of the battle (Ps. 83.19-18 [18-17]). If so, the imperfect fulfilment of the prophecy in Jehoshaphat's time, and the reputation for predictive speech ascribed in Hebrew tradition to the Asaphites, may have led later interpreters, such as the Psalter's redactors, to see in this psalm a continuingly valid eschatological prophecy.

Moreover one consideration suggests that Psalm 83, in its present form, should be regarded as an intentionally eschatological prediction. The four nations of Jeshoshaphat's time have been augmented to ten. A historicist position might suggest that other nations had threatened to join the alliance, or had supported it surreptitiously. That is not impossible. But Assyria was of little significance in Jehoshaphat's time, and it is unlikely they would have taken part in a distant local quarrel, or that the psalmist would have recorded it if they had. This suggests that the psalm originated in the period after the rise of Assyria, and supports the view of those who think the psalm depicts an archetypal alliance of all Israel's ancient foes.[36] Two further factors support this and suggest that this archetypal alliance depicts eschatological war.

(1) The ten-nation confederacy against Israel (vv. 7-9 [6-8]) is a traditional motif of Hebrew eschatology, both in biblical and rabbinic

---

34. Gunkel 1926: 365.

35. LXX's *Ammonites with some Meunites* is preferable to MT's unlikely *sons of Ammon together with some Ammonites* (20.1). The Meunites, who are mentioned with Arabs at 2 Chron. 26.7, may have been of Ishmaelite stock. Josephus (*Ant.* 9.1.2) says that the Moabites and Ammonites took with them at this time a great body of Arabians.

36. This view is suggested by Kirkpatrick 1902: 499-500; Kraus 1978: II, 577.

literature.[37] The ten nations of Psalm 83 therefore suggest an eschatological conflict may be envisaged.

(2) Jehoshaphat's battle of 2 Chron. 20 was already regarded in
biblical times as prefiguring ultimate war (Joel 4.2 [3.2]; cf. 3.1–4.1
[2.28–3.1]), and was so regarded by later interpreters also (1QM 1.1-
2). Thus, since the list of nations in Psalm 83 seems intentionally to
evoke Jehoshaphat's battle, the psalm might well be alluding to such
eschatological traditions as are recorded in Joel. Yet the psalmist's
deliberate augmentation of the details of Jehoshaphat's battle suggests
he may have been trying to describe the antitype of which the historical conflict was the type.

Other Asaph Psalms have a feeling of ultimacy about them, which
suggests they envisage some sort of consummation of history. Psalm
50 depicts the advent of God, in tempest and blazing fire, to judge
between the righteous and the wicked (1-7, 16). Ps. 80.18-19 [17-18]
refers to a *man at your right hand, a son of man whom you have
raised up for yourself,* in whose time Israel will no longer turn from
God. It is unclear how far the psalmist envisaged an eschatological
figure. But the phrase would seem to indicate some kind of national
leader. And Israel's no longer turning from God would reflect eschatological hopes such as Jer. 31.31-34 and Mic. 7.16-20. Psalm 82
describes the final dispatch of all cosmic supernatural opponents of
God's *malkut*.[38] Anticipating the last verses of Psalm 83 it describes
all the nations as God's inheritance, that is, they are to become his
dominion.

Given the incipient eschatology of such passages, it is not surprising
that later interpreters take them as referring to eschatological events.
For instance, 4Q176 Tanhumim sees Psalm 79 as depicting an eschatological destruction of Jerusalem. The writer of 11QMelch cites Psalm
82 as a proof text for the superhero Melchizedek's destruction of
'Satan and the spirits of his lot [who] rebelled by turning away from
the precepts of God'. The Targum interprets the אמצתה לך בן, *son you
have strengthened for yourself,* of Ps. 80.16 [15] as מלכא
משיחא דחילתא לך, 'King Messiah whom you have strengthened for
yourself.' Moreover it is likely, in light of this, that the more explicitly human בן־אדם אמצת לך of 80.18 [17] might have been interpreted
as referring to an individual eschatological leader. Such a supposition

37. Dan. 7.7; Rev. 17.3, 12-16; *Sef. Z.* 40, 53-62; *PRE* 62b.
38. The intentional eschatology of Ps. 82 is recognized by Welch 1926: 42-44.

is supported by the wider context of the Psalter, where *the man at your right hand* (80.18 [17]) evokes the less ambiguously messianic figure of Ps. 110.1. *Num. R.* 14.1 interprets *Ephraim, Benjamin, and Manasseh* in Ps. 80.3[2] of messianic figures. *PRE* 62b names the enemies of Ps. 83.6-8, then comments, 'All of them are destined to die by the hand of the Son of David.' Kimhi states that Psalm 50 is about the gathering of the nations to the battle of Gog and Magog and the day of judgment.

Such passages, even if not unambiguously eschatological in intention, are likely to have been interpreted eschatologically by the Psalter's redactors, as they were by later interpreters.

The degree of intentional eschatology in these passages probably varies, but that did not prevent their being perceived as eschatological by later interpreters. It is therefore not unreasonable to suggest that the Psalter's redactors saw in these psalms hints, at least, of a latterday reference when they included them in the Psalter. And in that case, their eschatological tone may be taken into account in interpreting the Psalter.

3. *Narrative Sequence*

As shall be seen in the following chapter, several commentators have suggested that a sequence of events exists in the Songs of Ascents. Noone, however, as far as I am aware, has suggested the same for the Psalms of Asaph. Possibly this should make me wary. But the clear thematic links between the early and later Asaph Psalms encourage me tentatively to consider this possibility.

For instance, Psalm 50 contains all the major themes that occur in the collection, and seems to have an introductory function. Psalm 83 displays features which mark it as the conclusion of the main Asaph group, the theme of ultimate war and God's impending universal dominion, and several literary closural features.[39] In Ps. 50.2 God comes to judge his people in blazing fire. In Ps. 83.15 [14] his blazing fire of judgment is to be poured upon the nations. In Psalm 50 the first divine oracle of the collection commands: *Gather to me my faithful ones!* (50.5). In Psalm 83 an alliance of nations has gathered against Israel. In Ps. 50.4-7 Israel are gathered for imminent judgment,[40] and

---

39. These are discussed more fully below.
40. That is, taking the participle אסף not as a noun, but as a verb indicating

a court scene is envisaged, where God testifies against them. In Ps. 82.1 the *elohim,* the tutelary deities of the nations, are gathered in the divine council.[41] A court scene is envisaged where God rises to pronounce sentence on them (v. 1), and is then exhorted to judge the earth (v. 8).[42] Psalm 83 then depicts the eve of the enactment of this judgment. God is exhorted to destroy the nations gathered in alliance. In Ps. 50.15 God promises the righteous, *Call on me in the day of hostility and I will deliver you.* Psalm 83 represents the day of hostility, when Jerusalem is surrounded by armies, and the psalmist, the *mazkîr,* cries out to God for deliverance.

The collection also reflects the destruction of the temple (74.3-7). Likewise its repeated references to the Exodus, a motif elsewhere associated with redemption from exile (Isa. 43.16-21), suggests that exile is the background to the collection. Several commentators note that the collection depicts an exilic situation.[43] Therefore Psalm 50

impending action. Such a translation is favoured by Delitzsch (1887: II, 139, 146) and Kirkpatrick (1902: 80).

41. There is a school of interpretation which would equate *elohim* with human 'judges', making the psalm an appeal against civil injustice (e.g. Kirkpatrick: 1902: p. 494). This interpretation is unknown in ancient Jewish literature. The earliest known interpretation of Ps. 82, 11QMelch, understands *elohim* to indicate subordinate deities. The Masada Psalms fragment (MasPs[a]) seems to view the battle of Ps. 83 as the execution of the judgment passed in Ps. 82. Its only divergence from MT, at Ps. 83.7 [6], gives אדום אלהי, *the gods of Edom,* instead of MT's אדום אהלי, *the tents of Edom.* Many modern commentators also suggest that Ps. 82 should be interpreted as judgment upon the gods (Tsevat 1970: 123-37; Mullen 1980: 226-44; Morgenstern 1939: 29-126; O'Callaghan 1953: 311-14; Welch 1926: 42-43). Welch summarizes the case well: 'Appeal may be taken to Exod. 21.6 as offering some ground for the view that the name אלהים or gods was applied to judges in Israel, though even there this rendering stands so much in need of support that it is incapable of giving support. But there is no justification in Hebrew usage for calling judges "sons of the Most High" (v. 6). And if we are to accept the rendering "judges" in this verse, we must suppose Yahweh to be represented as saying "Ye are judges, and all of you sons of the Most High", a translation which seems to condemn itself' (1926: 43n.).

42. For the use of נצב with the sense 'to rise to pronounce a verdict or judgment' see Gen. 28.13; Num. 22.23, 31, 34; Amos 7.9; 9.1, all of which are consistent with uttering a verdict or enacting a judgment. The parallelism of Ps. 82.1 also supports such a translation. For further discussion, see Tsevat 1970: 127.

43. Kirkpatrick 1902: 427-30; Eaton 1976: 76; Illman 1976: 55-64; Beaucamp 1979a: II, 4.

depicts Yhwh commanding Israel's ingathering from exile, apparently
in order to judge among them (v. 4). The last psalm of the main
Asaph group (Ps. 83) depicts an ingathering of nations against Israel,
intent on destroying them (v. 5 [4]) and taking possession of their land
(v. 13 [12]). The end of the final deutero-Asaph Psalm refers explicitly to the ingathering of Israel from exile (106.47).

If I were to go further and tentatively suggest how the intervening
Asaph Psalms might fit into this overall progression of thought, I
might suggest something such as the following.

Psalm 50. Command to ingather Israel to judgment. God pronounces sentence. The righteous will be delivered in the day of hostility, the wicked torn in pieces.

Psalm 73. The wicked prosper. God will destroy them when he
arises.

Psalm 74. The nations destroyed the temple. They still mock God.
The *mazkîr* makes remembrance of their deeds before God, who is
exhorted to repay them.

Psalm 75. Praise. Divine oracle. God's judgment is near.

Psalm 76. A reminiscence of Yhwh's past deliverances. Such an
interpretation would make sense of the LXX heading, ᾠδὴ πρὸς τὸν
Ἀσσύριον (LXX Ps. 75.1) as recalling Jerusalem's deliverance from
Sennacherib.

Psalm 77. The psalmist-*mazkîr* cries to God in the day of hostility
(vv. 2-3 [1-2]). He calls God to remembrance, on the basis of his
former love to Israel, to act on Israel's behalf.

Psalm 78. Recollection of Israel's failures and God's mercies.

Psalm 79. The invasion of the nations. They have invaded God's
inheritance and destroyed Jacob's pasture (vv. 1, 7). They have killed
many Israelites and have surrounded Jerusalem, shedding much blood
(vv. 2-3). They have done this around Jerusalem, where they remain
and pour scorn on those within (vv. 3-4).

Psalm 80. The cry of the *mazkîr: Hear us!… Shine forth!…
Awaken your hero-might and come with deliverance to us!* (vv. 2-3
[1-2]). Plea for national restoration and divine enabling of the national
leader (v. 18 [17]). Promise of future obedience (v. 19 [18]).

Psalm 81. The music of the *mazkîr* before the battle (vv. 3-4).
Kraus notes that from v. 15 [14] 'we are to deduce that the people of
God are surrounded and threatened by enemies'.[44] An oracle

44. Kraus 1978: II, 152.

announces that the condition of deliverance is obedience (vv. 14-15 [13-14]).

Psalm 82. The first result of divine intervention in response to the remembrancing rite is the judgment of the tutelary deities of the nations.

Psalm 83. The day of hostility spoken of in Psalm 50. A ten-nation confederacy gathers for war against Israel. *PRE* 62b cites this psalm in connection with Sennacherib's attack, which it apparently regards as typological of the latter-day conflict, for it states that the ten nations are destined to fall by the hand of Messiah ben David.

4. *Summary*

An analysis of the Psalms of Asaph as a coherent group reveals several characteristics. They seem to be connected with the Asaphite guild of levitical prophet-musicians. This guild was apparently associated with the ancient holy war rite of remembrancing Yhwh by the *zikhron* ritual at times of foreign invasion. They also seem to have been associated with the theme of the gathering of Israel. Several aspects of the Asaph Psalms suggest that they have some degree of ultimate and cosmic reference. It is not unreasonable to assume that the Psalter's redactors might have understood them eschatologically, possibly altering them in places to strengthen such an understanding. A progression in thought is certainly discernible in the group, beginning with the gathering of Israel to judgment and ending with the gathering against them of a massive alliance of hostile nations. Thus this group of psalms can be read as representing an eschatological ingathering of Israel, culminating in battle. In Chapter 5, I shall present further evidence to support the likelihood of such eschatological conceptions existing in ancient Israel.

Chapter 4

THE SONGS OF ASCENTS

I turn now to investigate the Songs of Ascents, in order to see what situations and events they reflect, and how they might relate to second temple period eschatology. There are 15 psalms that bear the heading שיר ל/המעלות, *Song of Ascents* (120–34). Like the Psalms of Asaph, these may be investigated as an independent psalm-cycle, for several reasons. First, their common heading indicates that their final redactor, at least, regarded them in some sense as a group. Secondly, their consecutive placing in the Psalter further suggests that they were thought to belong together. Thirdly, as Hengstenberg notes, they display an elaborate structure of divine names that suggests they have been composed or redacted as a group.[1] On either side of the central Psalm 127 is a heptade of psalms, each containing the tetragrammaton 24 times. Each heptade is divisible into a tetrad and a triad, each containing the tetragrammaton 12 times. In addition, as Forbes notes, the third psalm of each heptade contains the name *Yah*.[2] Finally, the Songs of Ascents have in common a number of linguistic and stylistic devices that may suggest they derive from a common source.[3] These include step parallelism, verbatim repetition and other characteristics, which shall be discussed in this chapter and Chapter 6.

1. *Heading and Tradition*

The heading המעלות lends itself, like the Asaph heading, to several interpretations. First, it signifies *steps* at its every other occurrence in

---

1. Hengstenberg 1845–48: II, 410.
2. Forbes 1888: 190.
3. For linguistic and other elements suggesting the common origin of the Songs of Ascents, see Beaucamp 1979b: 73-90; Mannati 1979: 85-100; Viviers 1994: 275-89.

the Hebrew Bible.[4] This interpretation is supported by LXX, with its heading Ὠιδή τῶν ἀναβαθμῶν. For elsewhere LXX frequently uses the noun ἀναβαθμοί to denote *steps*.[5] Thus the heading readily lends itself to interpretation as a *Song of the Steps*. But of which steps are these songs? Two points suggest it may be the steps of the temple.

(1) The entire collection has a cultic and sacerdotal ethos that seems to indicate a close connection between these lyrics and temple worship. There are cultic formulae that appear originally to have formed responses in temple worship.[6] There are numerous formulaic blessings.[7] There is a close relationship, as Liebreich has noted, between the vocabulary of the Ascents and the Aaronic blessing.[8] And there are also references to Aaron (133.2) and to cultic acts (123.1; 132.8; 133.2; 134.1-3).

(2) The Mishnah makes a connection between the 15 Songs of Ascents and the 15 steps of the temple that led from the Court of Women to the Court of Israel.

> And countless Levites [played] on harps, lyres, cymbals, and trumpets, and instruments of music, on the fifteen steps leading down from the Court of the Israelites to the Court of the Women, corresponding to the

4. Steps of an altar: Exod. 20.26; of the throne: 1 Kgs 10.19-20; 2 Chron. 9.18-19; of the palace: 2 Kgs 20.9-11; Isa. 38.8; of the City of David: Neh. 3.15; 12.37; of ordinary buildings: 2 Kgs 9.13; of the temple: Ezek. 40.22, 26, 31, 34, 37, 49. It is also used of the steps of the temple at Otot 8.4 (Appendix 1).

5. LXX uses ἀναβαθμοί at 3 Kgs 10.19-20; 4 Kgs 9.13; 2 Par. 9.18-19; Isa. 38.8; Ezek. 40.49. Other terms are used at 4 Kgs 20.9-11; 2 Esd. 13.15; 22.37; Ezek. 40.22, 26, 31, 34, 37.

6. A characteristic of the Ascents is repeated phrases, such as *Who made the heavens and the earth* (121.2; 124.8; 134.3); *From now until eternity* (121.8; 125.2; 131.3); *Peace on Israel* (125.5; 128.6); *Yhwh bless you from Zion* (128.5; 134.3); *Hope, Israel, in Yhwh* (130.7; 131.3). That these are cultic formulae from temple worship is suggested by the fact that some of them disrupt the otherwise regular metre of their context. Those in 125.2, 5; 128.5; and 130.7, for instance, greatly extend the length of their lines beyond the usual 3 + 2 or 3 + 3 metre. Habel (1972: 321-37) reaches a similar conclusion. He suggests the phrase *Who made the heavens and the earth* is a cultic formula found in a blessing context

7. 121.8; 122.8; 124.8; 125.5; 126.5; 127.5; 128.1, 5; 129.8; 130.7; 132.15; 133.3; 134.3. The fact that 129.8 is a blessing *not* bestowed on the wicked does not discount its being a blessing formula, which might be spoken over the faithful.

8. Liebreich 1955.

fifteen Songs of Ascents in the Psalms; upon them the Levites used to stand with instruments of music and make melody.[9]

True, this does not actually connect the songs with the steps. It merely notes a correspondence of number. But Josephus, who was an eye-witness of the second temple, confirms that there were indeed 15 steps leading from the Court of Women to the great gate of Corinthian brass, the Nicanor Gate,[10] which opened on to the Inner Court.[11] So the correspondence in number was apparently a real and not an imaginative one. And the link between songs and steps is noted also by Hippolytus, writing about the same time as the redaction of the Mishnah. He states: '...there are certain Songs of Ascents, fifteen in number, the same number as the steps of the temple.'[12] That a Christian bishop as far away as Rome was aware of this idea by about the end of the second century suggests it was an established tradition in Israel at an earlier period, probably in temple times. The association of the Songs of Ascents and the temple steps in two such diverse early sources would seem to hint at a more than fortuitous numerological correspondence between them. Some real connection between them may have been perceived.[13]

---

9. *m. Suk.* 5.4. Compare *m. Mid.* 2.5, which adds that the steps 'were not four-square, but curved like the half of a round threshing-floor'. This led Armfield to suggest that the steps may have constituted the temple orchestra (Armfield 1874: 19).

10. As regards the identification of Josephus's gate of Corinthian brass with the Nicanor Gate and its position between the Court of Israel and the Court of Women on the east of the temple, see Busink 1970–80: II, 1080-82; Wiesenberg 1952: 14-15. For the Mishnaic references see *m. Mid.* 2.3, which states that all the inner gates of the temple were overlaid with gold except the Nicanor Gate, whose bronze shone like gold. As regards its position between the Court of Israel and the Court of Women, see *m. Šeq.* 6.3 and *m. Mid.* 2.6, which show it as an inner gate facing east; *m. Soṭ.* 1.5 shows it facing east at the inner side of the Court of Women, for the suspected adulteress was to be tried between it and the Eastern Gate opposite; *m. Mid.* 1.4 describes it as the eastern gate of the (inner) temple Court, next to the chamber of the keeper of the vestments. *m. Neg.* 14.8 says the leper to be cleansed must immerse himself in the Chamber of the Lepers, in the Court of Women (*m. Mid.* 2.5) before approaching and standing at the Nicanor Gate. As the temple had always been built facing east (Ezek. 8.16), the Nicanor Gate appears to have been the one between the Court of Women and the main approach to the temple through the Court of Israel.

11. *War* 5.3.

12. πάλιν τε αὐτοῦ εἰσι τινὲς τῶν ἀναβαθμῶν ᾠδαί, τὸν ἀριθμόν πεντεκαίδεκα, ὅσοι καὶ οἱ ἀναβθμοὶ τοῦ ναοῦ (de Lagarde 1858b: 190).

13. Even if the Ascents heading were pre-exilic in origin, this possibility would

Tosefta Sukkah seems to make such a connection explicit. It cites the mishnaic passage and states that the Songs of Ascents were actually sung at the time when the Levites stood upon the temple steps.

> *And Levites [played] on harps, lyres, cymbals, and all sorts of musical instruments [on the fifteen steps, etc.] (m. Suk. 5.4).* What did they sing? *A Song of Ascents. Come, bless Yhwh, all you servants of Yhwh, who stand by night in the house of Yhwh* (Ps. 134.1). Some of them would sing, *Lift up your hands to the holy place and bless Yhwh* (Ps. 134.2). And when they departed from one another, what did they say? *Yhwh bless you from Zion, who made the heavens and the earth* (Ps. 134.3).[14]

This idea was known also to Nicholas of Lyra and Jacob Leonitius.[15] Kimhi goes further, saying that the Levites sang one psalm on each of the 15 steps, possibly envisaging a sort of stylized pilgrimage up or down the steps toward the temple.[16] There may be some basis for this in the Mishnah, whose description of the singing of the Ascents, cited above, proceeds as follows:

> Two priests stood at the upper gate [the Nicanor Gate] which leads down from the Court of Israel to the Court of Women, with two trumpets in their hands. At cock-crow they blew a sustained, a quavering and another sustained blast. When they reached the tenth step they again blew a sustained, a quavering and another sustained blast. When they reached the Court [of Women] they again blew a sustained, a quavering and another sustained blast. They went on until they reached the gate that leads out to the east.[17]

What is described here seems to be a cultic and ritual procession down the 15 steps at dawn during the Feast of Sukkoth. The immediately preceding description of the singing of the Ascents on these steps suggests the two events were related. As shall be seen below, the Ascents themselves do seem to represent in literary terms an ascent and descent to the Feast. It is possible that the idea of singing successive psalms on each step is not without foundation. But whether or not the

not necessarily be precluded. For Ezekiel's ideal temple has 15 steps, even if not arranged as in the second temple (Ezek. 40.22, 24, 31, 37). This numerical coincidence with the second temple may suggest that the ideal of fifteen temple steps is an ancient one, possibly deriving from memories of the first temple.

14. *t. Suk.* 4.7-9.

15. Lyra, *Postille*; Leonitius in his Hebrew *Libellus effigiei templi Salomonis* (Amsterdam, 1650).

16. Comm. on Ps. 120 (Kimhi 1973: 3).

17. *m. Suk.* 5.4.

actual singing of the Ascents on the temple steps is only an imaginative expansion of the Mishnaic tradition, all these commentators show that Jewish tradition from early times perceived a link between the 15 'Songs of the Steps' and the 15 steps of the temple.

A second possible interpretation of המעלות is that which renders it *ascents* of pilgrimage to Jerusalem. The singular מעלה occurs in this sense at Ezra 7.9, and the verb עלה is used in this way both within the Ascents collection (122.4) and commonly elsewhere.[18] Apart from that עלה has a wide range of related meanings: ascent to the land of Israel,[19] to the temple,[20] and to God,[21] and offering of sacrifice.[22] All these usages seem to be aspects of the one great spatial metaphor of ascent that derives from the belief that supernatural beings dwell in supraterrestrial dimensions.[23] This led to natural elevations being chosen as sites for temples, and for shrines of all sorts.[24] This led in turn to the confirmation of the metaphor in the physical act of ascending to these shrines. Thus ascent to the land of Israel, Zion, the temple, and the offering of sacrifices could all be included under the מעלות heading, indicating one great movement of ascent to the divine presence. Indeed, in later Judaism, the term designates God's dwelling place.[25] It is this movement toward God's presence that is enacted by the pilgrim who goes to worship in Zion.

18. 1 Kgs 12.28; Ezra 1.3; 2.1, 59; 7.7; 8.1; Neh. 7.5, 6, 61; 12.1; Ps. 24.3; Isa. 2.3; Jer. 31.6; Mic. 4.2; Zech. 14.17-19; 2 Chron. 36.23. It is also commonly used for the approach of attacking armies to Jerusalem (2 Kgs 18.17, 25; 24.10; Isa. 7.1; 36.1, 10; 37.24; Jer. 4.13-14; Ezek. 38.9,16; 2 Chron. 12.2, 9; 24.23; 36.6). Such approaches are not pilgrimage. Nonetheless, the approach to Jerusalem is regarded as an *ascent.*

19. Gen. 46.4; Deut. 1.21; 9.23; Judg. 11.13, 16; 19.30; 1 Sam. 15.1, 6; 2 Sam. 2.1; 2 Kgs 18.13; 24.1; 2 Chron. 16.1; 21.17; Isa. 7.6; Ezek. 38.11; *et passim.* See too the *hiphil* form used in the common phrase *brought you up out of the land of Egypt* (Exod. 32.1, 4, 7, 8, 23 *et passim*).

20. 2 Kgs 19.14; 20.5, 8; 23.2; Isa. 37.14; 38.22; 2 Chron. 9.4; 29.20; 34.30.

21. Exod. 19.3, 24; 34.2.

22. Lev. 14.20; Judg. 6.26; 11.31; 1 Sam. 2.28; 2 Kgs 3.20; Isa. 57.7; 60.7; 1 Chron. 16.2, 40; 21.24; 23.31 *et passim.*

23. Exod. 2.23; 2 Kgs 19.28; Isa. 14.12-14; 37.29; 57.15; Amos 9.6; Ps. 103.19 *et passim.*

24. Deut. 17.8; 1 Sam. 1.3, 7, 22; 2.19; 9.14; Hos. 4.15.

25. See, for instance, the Memorial Prayer for the Dead, אל מלא רחמים, dating probably from the second temple period, which locates the dwelling of the *Shekhinah* במעלות קדושין וטהורים (*Forms of Prayer:* 300-303).

Thus the מעלות heading seems to connect the collection with temple worship. The lyrics of Psalm 122 provide more specific information about their cultic context. Ps. 122.3-4 says of Jerusalem, *There the tribes ascend* [עלו], *the tribes of Yah; [this is] a statute for Israel, to thank the name of Yhwh.* Such a description suggests the three appointed feasts, Passover, Weeks and Tabernacles or *Sukkoth*, legislated in the Pentateuch (Exod. 23.14-17; 34.18-24; Lev. 23.4-44; Deut. 16.1-17). The verb עלה is used of pilgrimage to the feasts at one of their earliest descriptions (Exod. 34.23).[26] *The tribes of Yah* would well describe those in attendance at the feasts, for every male Israelite was required to attend (Exod. 34.23; Deut. 16.16). Similarly, the statement that the ascent of the tribes is *a statute for Israel to thank the name of Yhwh* (122.4) would appear to suggest an association with the appointed feasts. For the Pentateuch represents them as divinely ordained statutes with the purpose of thanksgiving to Yhwh. Their Hebrew designation, מעדים *mo'edim,* is cognate with עדות *statute* in Ps. 122.4.

Several points suggest the Ascents were associated not only with the appointed feasts in general, but with the Feast of Sukkoth in particular:

(1) The Chronicler's description of the ark's entry to Solomon's temple contains a passage almost identical to Ascents Ps. 132.8-10 (2 Chron. 6.41-2). Presumably he is borrowing either from this ancient psalm or from an older tradition common to both.[27] As the ark's entry to the temple is said to have taken place at the festival of the seventh month, that is, the Feast of Sukkoth (1 Kgs 8.1-2; 2 Chron. 5.2-3), an association seems to have existed between this psalm and that feast. Since, as shall be seen below, the entire Ascents collection apparently depicts one festal period, the Sukkoth association would apply to the other Ascents lyrics as well.

26. Commentators generally regard Exod. 23.14-17 as the oldest biblical reference to the appointed feasts (de Vaux 1978: 470-74, 484-506; Kraus 1966: 26-70; Durham 1987: 332-33). However, Exod. 34.23 is likely to be of similar antiquity. Note that both passages describe the feast as 'the Ingathering' (אסיף), a name not used in later texts, which prefer 'Sukkoth'.

27. The antiquity of Ps. 132 is noted by a number of commentators. Dahood, for instance, remarks, 'this royal psalm appears to have been composed in the tenth century as part of the liturgy for the feast when the ark was carried in procession to Jerusalem' (1965–70: III, 241). The passage in question (Ps. 132.8-10) bears some similarity to the Song of the Ark (Num. 10.35-6), reckoned to be among the most ancient of Hebrew lyrics (Craigie 1983b: 25), and may have been influenced by it.

(2) The predominant imagery in the collection is of harvest, vintage, and general fertility (126.6; 127.3-5; 128.3; 129.6-7; 132.15). This is particularly appropriate to the harvest feast Sukkoth, also known as the Harvest Ingathering or *Asiph* (Exod. 34.22). Indeed, this would be the kind of imagery expected in a collection of songs for worship at harvest time.

(3) Zechariah 14 depicts all nations ascending to celebrate the Feast of Sukkoth in Jerusalem after the eschatological war. Its fivefold use of עלה (vv. 16, 17, 18, 18, 19) in connection with threefold reference to Sukkoth (16, 18, 19) shows a connection existed between the *ascent* motif and the feast in biblical times. If it originated with Zechariah 14, it would colour all subsequent traditions regarding the feast. In that case, the psalm heading would be a purposeful evocation of Sukkoth, and even Zechariah 14. On the other hand, if the heading predates Zechariah 14, the prophetic writer is employing an *ascent* motif already well-established in connection with the Feast.

(4) The passage *m. Suk.* 5.1-6 describes the celebration of the Feast in temple times, and indicates that the Songs of Ascents were sung in the temple then (*m. Suk.* 5.4). Likewise, Ps. 134.1 refers to a night service in the temple. The only such service referred to in rabbinic literature took place during Sukkoth (*m. Suk.* 5.2-4), and Psalm 134 is said to have been sung at that very time (*t. Suk.* 4.7).

Therefore the heading of the Songs of Ascents and internal factors in the collection seem to connect them with temple worship at the Feast of Sukkoth. This is confirmed by early rabbinic and Christian traditions. They may have been sung at the feast by Levites standing on the temple steps, as rabbinic traditions state. They may also have been sung by pilgrims going to and from the feast, who earlier heard them in the temple, as more recent commentators suggest.[28]

2. *Eschatological Orientation*

The Songs of Ascents, considered apart from their heading, contain no clear evidence that they are intentionally eschatological. Psalm 132 does refer to Yhwh's *mashiah* (vv. 10, 17), but there is no indication that this is necessarily an eschatological figure. However, a case might be made for suggesting that the *ma'alot* heading, whenever it may

---

28. Briggs and Briggs 1906–1907: lxxix; Seybold 1978: 73; Seybold 1990: 118, suggest the Ascents formed a *vade mecum* or a hymnal for pilgrims.

have been added, would encourage an eschatological reading of the whole group. I noted above that the term *ma'alot* appears to associate the Songs of Ascents with the Feast of Sukkoth. Now, the latter part of Zechariah 14 depicts all nations ascending to Jerusalem to celebrate Sukkoth in the latter days. The key word in this passage is the verb עלה, which occurs five times in four verses (14.16-19), a prominence unparalleled elsewhere in the Bible.

The eschatological tone of Zechariah 14 is striking. It opens by predicting יום...ליהוה (14.1) and the eschatological slogan ביום ההוא occurs throughout.[29] There is abundant use of future tenses, and the events described are of an ultimate nature. The Lord will appear from heaven with all the holy ones and strike the attacking nations with plague, so they decompose on their feet (14.3-5, 12-15). There will be great terrestrial and celestial upheaval (14.4-7). Jerusalem will be rebuilt, never again to be destroyed, and living water will flow from it (14.8-11). Yhwh's universal *malkut* will be established over all the earth, and all nations will worship him (14.9, 16-21). Jerusalem, like an Aaronic high-priest in the earth, will be קדש ליהוה in every part (14.20; cf. Exod. 39.30). The chapter's eschatological reference is confirmed by its being recognized by early interpreters. The apocalyptic texts *Enoch* 1.9 and 1QM 12.1-7 refer to the holy ones coming with the Lord, apparently alluding to Zech. 14.5, the only biblical passage where such language occurs. The supernatural מהומה that routs the nations at 1QM 1.5 and 4.7 seems to allude to Zech. 14.13. Acts 1.11 predicts the return of the Christian divine messiah to the Mount of Olives, an idea probably deriving from Zech. 14.4. 1 Thess. 3.13 predicts his return with the holy ones, apparently in reference to Zech. 14.5. The ὕδατος ζῶντος of Jn 7.38 and the ποταμὸν ὕδατος ζωῆς of Rev. 22.1 seem to connote Zech. 14.8's מים־חיים. And Jesus' driving the merchants from the temple seems to have been intended to assert that he was the fulfilment of the prediction in Zech. 14.21, based on the non-gentilic understanding of כנעני: *There will no longer be a trader in the house of Yhwh*.[30] The eschatological significance of the Mount of Olives in other early texts seems to derive from Zech. 14.4.[31] The Codex Reuchlinianus text of the Targum to Zechariah

---

29. Zech. 14.4, 6, 8, 13, 20, 21. Smith notes the eschatological import of this phrase (1984: 39).

30. Dodd 1953a: 300.

31. *T. Naph.* 5.1-2; Josephus, *War* 2.261-63; cf. *Ant.* 20.170.

inserts the resurrection of the dead at 14.4. Rabbinic texts frequently cite Zechariah 14 in messianic or eschatological contexts.[32] Modern commentators also remark upon the eschatological tone of this chapter, or of the whole of Zechariah 9–14.[33]

The writer of Zechariah 14 connects the Feast of Sukkoth with Yhwh's end time victory and *malkut*.[34] In so doing he established a connection between Sukkoth and the latter-day *malkut* that influenced later generations' ideas regarding the feast. Thus the Qumran fragments 4Q508.2 and 4Q509.3 connect Yom Kippur, preceding Sukkot, with the ingathering of Israel from exile. Rev. 7.9 depicts the redeemed of all the world holding palm branches, a custom associated with Sukkoth (Lev. 23.40; *m. Suk.* 3.1ff.). *Ta'an.* 2a contains a discussion on Sukkoth, rain and the resurrection of the dead. In *Midr. Pss.* 118.1 occurs the idea that judgment will take place on New Year's Day. Zechariah 14 may or may not have existed when the Ascents received their common heading, but it is likely to have been known by the Psalter's redactors. To them the *ma'alot* heading would connect the Ascents with the eschatological events of Zechariah. The mere predominance of the verb עלה in both texts, 17 times in the Ascents,[35] and 5 times in 4 verses in Zech. 14.16-19, would encourage comparisons between them, and the Sukkoth associations of both texts would confirm the connection. This association of the Ascents with the eschatological events of Zechariah 14 is confirmed by Kimhi, who notes that the *ma'alot* title refers to the ingathering of the exiles in the time to come, and cites Zechariah in that regard.[36]

---

32. For instance, Zech. 14.1 at *Eccl. R.* 5.7.1; Zech. 14.2 at *Song R.* 6.10.1; *Ruth R.* 5.6. Zech. 14.2-3 at *Midr. Pss.* 18.5; Zech. 14.3, 9 at *Lev. R.* 27.11 = *Est. R.* 7.23 (similar to *Mekhilta Amalek Beshallah* 2); Zech. 14.4 at *ARN* 34; Zech. 14.5 at *Ruth R.* 2; *Eccl. R.* 1.11.1; *Song R.* 4.11.1. Zech. 14.8 at *Gen. R.* 48.10. Zech. 14.9 at *Song R.* 2.13.4. Zech. 14.10 at *B. Bat.* 75b; *Song R.* 7.5.3.

33. Lamarche 1961: 152-57; Dodd 1953b: 64; Hanson 1975: 280ff.; Black 1991: 44, 57.

34. It is interesting to surmise whether this connection might not predate Zech. 14, and be an older, possibly Canaanite, idea, in which the end of harvest was typological of the end of the age. Note that the Canaanite (and old Hebrew) name for the seventh month, the month Tishri in later Hebrew, was Ethanim, that is, *perpetuity* (BDB: 450).

35. 122.4; 132.3; and in all 15 psalm headings.

36. *Comm.* on Ps. 120.

Other texts employ the verb עלה in reference to the gathering of all nations to Zion in the eschatological *malkut*. Most prominent is the passage from Isa. 2.1-5 and Mic. 4.1-5, where the nations declare, 'Come, let us ascend the mountain of Yhwh!' (Isa. 2.3; Mic. 4.2). Micah 2.13 also employs עלה in the context of ascent to Jerusalem at the latter-day ingathering.[37] It is cited as an eschatological prophecy in later Judaism. Such passages, together with Zechariah 14, would seem to indicate that the verb עלה came to be associated with an anticipated eschatological ascent to worship on Zion. If so, it seems not unreasonable to suggest that the מעלות heading which these psalms bear in the Psalter confers on them at least the possibility of being read as a description of the eschatological Feast of Sukkoth, described in Zech. 14.16-19. Certainly they were interpreted in this way by the ancient writers of the midrashim on Psalms 120 and 121 and, as mentioned above, Kimhi.

3. *Narrative Sequence*

If the מעלות heading allows these to be read as depicting an ascent to the eschatological Feast of Sukkoth, the contents of the collection are quite appropriate to such an interpretation. The existence of an event-sequence in the Ascents has been noted by a number of commentators.[38] There is no consensus about exactly what form this event-sequence takes, but all see it as in some way representing an ascent to worship in Jerusalem. I would suggest something like the following.

Psalm 120. The weariness of exile. The individual speaker, here as throughout the Ascents, should probably be taken as representing faithful Israel.[39] He laments his sad state, exiled in a violent and hostile environment, which he calls *Meshekh* and *Kedar* (v. 5), regions associated with death by archery. From Meshekh came the Scythians, bowmen whose cruelty was proverbial in Israel (2 Macc. 4.47; *3 Macc.* 7.5; *4 Macc.* 10.7).[40] The Ishmaelite warriors of Kedar were also

37. It is depicted as having an eschatological fulfilment at *NRSbY* 38.

38. Origen, *Selecta in Psalmos* (Lommatzsch 1831–48: XII, 107); Neale and Littledale 1874: 115; Forbes 1888: 190-92; Cox 1885: 308-309; Mannati 1979: 87.

39. Several commentators have noted that the 'I' of the Ascents ought to be interpreted communally. See e.g. Hengstenberg 1845–48: III, 404; Forbes 1888: 189.

40. 'During the first millennium BC groups of peoples known successively as Cimmerians, Scythians and Sarmatians...penetrated over the Caucasus and into north-eastern Anatolia' (Barraclough 1979: 60).

famed as archers (Isa. 21.17). As the psalmist could not have lived in both places simultaneously, the two nations are probably figurative for hostile neighbours in any place. The psalmist may also be using Meshekh and Kedar, Japhethites and Semites respectively, merismically, in order to indicate all nations in their hostility to scattered Israel. But whoever these hostile neighbours are, even their slander is like archery. Their tongue is רמיה, which can mean both *deceitful* or *shooting arrows*.[41] Their recompense will befit those whose mouths shoot destruction: Yhwh will give them *sharp-toothed* (שנונים) *arrows* (v. 4). The psalmist is weary of this hostile pagan environment. He is a sojourner there (גור, v. 5); it is not his home. His thoughts, turning to make the pilgrimage of ascent to Zion, are reflected in vv. 5-7 in the literary technique of step parallelism, in which a word from the last hemistich of one line is reiterated in the first hemistich of the next.

Woe is me that I sojourn in Meshekh	I *dwell* among the tents of Qedar
Too long has *dwelt* my soul	with the hater of *peace*
I *peace* do indeed speak[42]	they (speak) war

Psalm 121. The pilgrimage to Zion. The title is שיר למעלות, not המעלות, like the rest of the group. So this is a song not *of* the pilgrim-ascents, but a pilgrim song *for* the actual ascents. The pilgrim travelling upward through the Judean foothills raises his eyes to the mountains of Zion and affirms that his helper on pilgrimage is Yhwh (vv. 1-2). It is he who keeps from stumbling on the road, shades from burning sun and baleful moon, protects from all harm and guards coming and going (vv. 3-8). The sixfold repetition of שמר with Yhwh

---

41. This interpretation is from Grossberg (1989: 24), who notes that רמה bears the sense of *shooting arrows* at Jer. 4.29 and Ps. 78.9. There is a notable parallel between this passage and Jer. 9.7 (8) where the tongue is compared to an arrow that speaks with deceit (מרמה), and *each one speaks peace to his neighbour, but in his heart sets a trap for him.* Elsewhere in the Bible the tongue is compared to a bow that shoots arrows of falsehood (Jer. 9.2 [3]; Prov. 26.18ff.).

42. The translation is based on Peters's suggestion that MT displays 'a use of כי familiar in Assyrian' where the conjunction may place subject, object and prepositional phrase before itself and the verb; this would make אני and אדבר of v. 7 part of the same clause (1894: 31). Of course, the step parallelism of the Hebrew is not influenced one way or the other by a more traditional translation (e.g. *I am for peace, but when I speak...*).

as the object and the insistence on his wakefulness, emphasize the divine protective power. This psalm has the most pronounced step parallelism of all the Ascents, vividly representing in literary terms the pilgrim's weary upward trudge.

Psalm 122. The joyful arrival at Jerusalem. The pilgrim reflects on his gladness when first encouraged to go to Zion, and stands still in the gate savouring the moment of their arrival (vv. 1-2). With one deliberate step, represented by the step parallelism of the repeated *Jerusalem* (vv. 2-3), he enters the city. Gazing at its strong and wondrous buildings, he contemplates its significance. It is Yhwh's dwelling on earth, and the seat of the Davidic king who reigns and dispenses justice there. There the tribes of Yah, apparently politically unified, ascend to keep the appointed feast as commanded (vv. 3-5). The words *shalom* and *Yerushalayim* are prominent, suggesting that ירשלים is עיר שלום.[43] In v. 6 the two words produce a sequence of sibilant *sh* and *l* sounds, like the peaceful sounds used for pacifying young children. The psalm closes with the rhyming quatrain requesting peace and prosperity on the city (vv. 6-9).

Psalm 123. Prayer for national blessing. The pilgrim, possibly in the temple, now lifts his eyes directly *to you*, to Yhwh, and no longer to *the hills* as on his pilgrimage. The psalmist's impassioned prayer is that Yhwh will have mercy on them. What form this is to take is not specified, but the references in vv. 3-4 to their recent humiliation, presumably at foreign hands, suggest that national prosperity and restoration are envisaged. If the collection is treated sequentially, then this foreign oppression must have preceded the Davidic rule referred to in Psalm 122 (vv. 3-4). These songs are set in the immediate aftermath of the victory of *bet*-David, when the Davidic throne is secure but national restoration is not yet complete. There is no request for divine action against the oppressor, which suggests that, although the oppression has been sore, it has completely ceased.

Psalm 124. Thanksgiving for national deliverance. This psalm further describes the nature of Israel's recent troubles. *Men rose up* against them with hot anger, like voracious beasts and proud, overwhelming waters (vv. 2-5). The waters imagery probably signifies here, as elsewhere in Psalms, foreign nations (cf. Ps. 65.8 [7]). Aletti and Trublet recognize anti-creation motifs here, representing the

43. Schökel and Strus note the word-play on *Jerusalem* in this psalm (1980: 234-50).

nations as agents of chaos determined to overthrow God's creation, Israel, and thwart his *heilsgeschichtliche* purpose.[44] So overwhelming was this attack that Israel would have been completely consumed if Yhwh had not been with them to deliver them. There is no request for deliverance from continuing threat. Deliverance is complete and total. Nothing remains but to give thanks for their miraculous deliverance.

Psalm 125. An affirmation of Yhwh's protection of the faithful. The lack of prayer for deliverance from enemies and the peaceful confident tone suggest that this psalm, like the foregoing ones, regards Israel's deliverance as total and complete. In that case, יָנוּחַ (v. 3) should not be understood as an assertion that foreign rule will not *remain* in Israel (so NIV). Rather, it states a general principle, exemplified in the recent deliverance, that though evil may attack, its rule will not *rest* upon Israel (RSV, NRS). Yhwh will rescue Israel from all domination of evil, and will lead away with the evildoers any Israelite who turns to crooked ways (v. 5).

Psalm 126. Prayer for ongoing blessing. This psalm, like Psalm 123, suggests that, though Israel has been delivered, national restoration is incomplete. Its two strophes each begin with a *ketiv-qere* referring to Yhwh's *restoring our fortunes* or *bringing back our captivity* (vv. 1, 4). There probably is no way to determine which reading is preferable in each case, nor any need to. For the two are one, the return of the exiles being the chief feature of Israel's reversal of fortune. The voice of the ingathered people tells of their laughter and joy when Yhwh restored their fortunes (vv. 1-2). Even the nations recounted Yhwh's great deed on Israel's behalf (vv. 2-3). However, restoration is incomplete. Possibly some exiles have not yet returned. Possibly rebuilding is necessary. A plea is made that Yhwh turn all their fortunes to good (v. 4). The psalm ends with an affirmation that sorrows turn to joy: the labour of ingathering the exiles and national restoration, like the labour of harvest, brings glorious rewards (vv. 5-6).

Psalm 127. Building with Yhwh. This responds to Psalm 126's prayer for restoration by affirming that it is possible only with divine assistance. The psalm turns on the metaphorical relation between building cities and children, emphasized by the similar sounds of בָּנָה and בָּנִים.[45] Therefore the phrase *build the house* (v. 1) covers many

---

44. Aletti and Trublet 1983: 248-49.
45. This word play was familiar in Israel. It occurs also in the Talmud, which

enterprises. Miller lists them as: building Zion (Pss. 102.16; 147.2), or the sanctuary (Ps. 78.69), the palace (1 Kgs 7.1) or the temple (2 Sam. 7.13), the Davidic dynasty (2 Sam. 7.11-29), or any family by human procreation (Deut. 25.9; Ruth 4.11).[46] All these endeavours are good, for otherwise there were no possibility of Yhwh's assistance. And with his blessing the rebuilding will lead to national, cultic, civil and domestic prosperity and peace (vv. 3-5). The heading לשלמה points to that king in whose time Israel knew her greatest ever prosperity, and who built the first temple. If this psalm indicates one particular activity in the latterday period, it would surely be that of building the temple of the messianic time, referred to in Ezekiel 40–43.

Psalm 128. How to obtain Yhwh's blessing. Commentators note the similarity of this psalm to the preceding one.[47] Both mention progeny and fruitful labour. They share vocabulary: בית פרי, אשרי, גבר and בנים. Both begin with a general statement in the third person singular and move to specifics in the second person singular. Both have two strophes, the second beginning with הנה. Miller notes that the last two lines of each combine city and household.[48] But their similarity invites comparison of their differences. While Psalm 127 asserts that civic welfare is unattainable without Yhwh's blessing, Psalm 128 shows the way to obtaining this blessing. It is by individuals fearing Yhwh and walking in his ways, that is, avoiding what he forbids and doing what he commands. This will lead to fruitful and peaceful domestic life, which in turn will lead to security for city and nation (vv. 5-6). The psalm is not only an instruction, but a fertility blessing on the worshippers, appropriate to the Feast of Tabernacles (vv. 2-3).

Psalm 129. Thanksgiving for national deliverance. This resembles Psalm 124 in recalling divine deliverance from foreign oppression. The thematic similarity is reinforced by literary similarities, such as the phrase *let Israel now say,* which occurs only in the first verse of these two psalms. The principal difference between the two psalms seems to be one of distance from the deliverance. Psalm 124's emphasis on the scale of the threat and Israel's nigh destruction suggests the

comments on Isa. 54.13: 'Do not say, *your children,* but rather, *your builders' (Ber.* 64a).

46. Miller 1986: 132
47. Cohen 1945: 430; Keet 1969: 64; Mannati 1979: 96; Miller 1986: 136.
48. Miller 1986: 136.

psalmist is still stunned by the impression of a recent cataclysm. Psalm 129 takes a longer view. It says less of the recent threat, but contemplates Israel's sorrows from youth, and Yhwh's continual deliverances. There is a minimizing of affliction. The slave-drivers' lashes are furrows that the ploughmen have ploughed על־גבי *upon my hill* or *my back.* Such punning on past sorrows suggests temporal and psychological distance from them. There is a malediction on the haters of Zion. But it is mild, only a non-blessing. This is the malediction not of one presently or even recently crushed, but of one who has prospered and may regard past afflictions philosophically. This different approach to past sorrows suggests that the rebuilding is under way and that Zion is prospering.

Psalm 130. A reminiscence of deliverance. This psalm may be taken as a thanksgiving for deliverance, if קראתיך (v. 1) is taken as past tense, and v. 2 as the psalmist's citation of the words spoken in distress.

> Out of the depths I cried to you, Yhwh: 'My Lord, hear my voice!
> Let your ears be attentive to the sound of my supplications!'

The quote may finish at v. 2, or, alternatively, continue to the end of v. 4. This interpretation of v. 2 as a citation of past speech is supported by several points. First, LXX renders קראתיך as aorist ἐκέκραξά σε. Secondly, citation of significant past speech is a stylistic feature elsewhere in the Ascents.[49] Third, the cry is from מעמקים, *the depths,* precisely the opposite place to the present location, המעלות, *the ascents/heights.* Presumably then, the cry does not originate from the present situation, but is a reminiscence from a former one. Thus this psalm, like Psalms 124 and 129, could recall the deliverance from the attack of the hostile nations, when Israel cried from the depths of dismay in overwhelming peril. Or it could recall the former exile as represented in Psalm 120. Or it might represent all Israel's former troubles. The point is that Yhwh has redeemed. Thus the יפדה of the final line does not indicate only a future hope. It is a general statement

---

49. This feature is evident at 122.2; 126.2; 132.2-4, 11-12. A similar feature is the eliciting of citations or responses, as at 121.1, 2; 122.6-9; 124.1-2; 129.1-2, possibly 132.6-9, and in all the formulaic dicta. The aorist ἐκέραξα of LXX Ps. 119.1 (MT Ps. 120) suggests the opening lines of Ps. 120 should be interpreted in the same way as those of Ps. 130, making Ps. 120.1-2 another example of significant past speech in the Ascents.

of a truth experienced in the recent deliverance and in the ongoing reconstruction: *It is he who redeems Israel out of all his sins.* For Israel, now forgiven and living in the light of Yhwh's favour, is ascending from all the calamities that he sent upon them in judgment.

Psalm 131. Humble trust in Yhwh. The psalmist, likening himself to a child contented upon its mother,[50] renounces pride and haughtiness in favour of humble trust in Yhwh. 'The faithful human creature, like a small baby has no inclination for autonomy.'[51] This psalm and its predecessor are linked by the phrase, *Trust, Israel, in Yhwh.* The linkage is appropriate, just as humble trust should naturally follow redemption from sin and judgment. If interpreted as referring to the community, it suggests that Israel's experience of forgiveness, in Psalm 130, has led to a spiritual state of tranquillity and humble contentment.

Psalm 132. Yhwh's entry to the latter-day temple and a Davidic mashiah. There are two ten-line strophes, each beginning *verb + Yhwh + David* (vv. 1, 11). The first tells of David's labour for Yhwh's house; the second pronounces Yhwh's irrevocable promise to David and his descendants. This evokes 2 Sam. 7, where David's wish to build Yhwh a house is answered by Yhwh's promise to build a house, that is, a dynasty, for David. The narrative, if not the historical, context of the psalm is the ark's entry to the temple (v. 8).[52] In response to a petition (vv. 9-10), a divine oracle announces Yhwh's desire to dwell there for ever and to bless people, priests and Davidic king (vv. 15-18). In the context of the eschatological interpretation of the Songs of Ascents I am suggesting, this might refer to Yhwh's entry to the latter-day temple, whose construction was referred to in

---

50. There has been controversy over the significance of גמל, *a weaned child*, in v. 2. Delitzsch (1887: 303) and Weiser (1962: 777) suggest that as a weaned child seeks the mother not for milk, but for her own sake, so the psalmist seeks God not for his blessings, but for himself. Van Gemeren (1982: 56-57) thinks such views pedantically literal. He maintains that too much has been made of the distinction between suckling and weaned child. The word may denote an older child or a satisfied suckling or infant. It is an affective simile intended to produce feelings of quietness and would be better rendered *a contented child*.

51. Brueggemann 1984: 49.

52. Dahood notes that 'the language of the psalm is extremely archaic' (1965–70: III, 242). He regards it as 'composed in the tenth century as part of the liturgy for the feast when the ark was carried in procession to Jerusalem' (p. 241).

Psalm 127. The blessing upon the Davidic *mashiah* would be understood as referring to the latter-day Davidic hero-king spoken of by the
prophets.

Psalm 133. Reunited Israel goes down from the Feast. Allen notes
that the phrase, שבת אחים גם־יחד refers to the custom of the extended
family where brothers dwelt on the undivided patrimony after marriage.[53] Berlin draws out the implications of the metaphor:

> The image is not one of a quarrel free family snuggling round the hearth,
> but of undivided land holdings. This is a metaphor for an undivided king-
> dom. The psalm expresses a hope for the reunification of the north and the
> south with Jerusalem as the capital of a united kingdom.[54]

Such a view is supported by the image of *the dew of Hermon which
comes down on the mountains of Zion,* which might suggest the
people of the northern kingdom coming to Jerusalem. The imagery of
the psalm is characterized by a threefold use of ירד describing fra-
grant oil descending on the beard and clothes of the father of the
Aaronic priesthood. The imagery would appear to indicate Yhwh's
blessing descending upon the priesthood, the cult and the nation. As
the Israelites anticipate going down from the feast, Yhwh's blessing
will go before them. Like the high priest, reunited Israel has received
the divine anointing at the feast, enabling them to go down and fulfil
their ordained role of being a nation of priests to the world (Exod.
19.6). Note that the descent imagery of this, the penultimate Ascents
psalm, corresponds to the ascent imagery of the second Ascent psalm.

Psalm 134. A parting benediction from people to priests. The verb
עבד often specifies priestly temple service. Similarly, עמד has a recognized usage as *standing to perform priestly service* (Deut. 10.8;
18.7; 1 Chron. 23.30). Thus, as Cohen notes, the phrases כל־עבדי יהוה
and העמדים בבית־יהוה denote priestly ministry in the temple.[55] The
psalm concludes with a blessing (v. 3), which, given its cultic language, would appear to be from priests to people. (Blessing the
Israelites was a priestly function [Num. 6.22-27], and there are two
formulaic phrases in this one verse.[56]) Thus it would be reasonable to

53. Allen 1983: 212.
54. Berlin 1987: 141.
55. Cohen 1945: 440.
56. יברכך יהוה מציון, also found at 128.5, and עשה שמים וארץ, also at 121.2 and
124.8. It was noted above that these, and other similar formulaic phrases, are a characteristic literary feature of the Ascents, suggesting their use in temple worship.

regard vv. 1 and 2 as an exhortation to the priests to bless Yhwh, and v. 3 as the priestly blessing on the people. This is a fitting closure to this benedictive collection. The departing worshippers exhort the priests to ongoing temple worship to secure Yhwh's blessing on Israel. In return they receive Yhwh's blessing from the priests.

There might be some disagreement about the details of the above sequence, but it shows the ease with which the Songs of Ascents can be read as a narrative sequence of latter-day events. I would suggest that this is more than accidental. The hand that arranged these psalms in this order surely intended some kind of narrative progression in the final sequence.

Before leaving the question of the narrative sequence of the Ascents, it is worth considering the view of Origen. He envisages something rather different from the above. It is worth quoting in full.

> The first Song of Ascents [Ps. 120] was recited among the people whenever the enemy was expected:
> The second [Ps. 121] when they were making preparations and needing allies:
> The third [Ps. 122] after they had fought with the enemy and got the better of them:
> The fourth [Ps. 123] when they were hoping for victory at the end:
> The fifth [Ps. 124] after success:
> The sixth [Ps. 125] when they were returning:
> The seventh [Ps. 126] when they had returned:
> The eighth [Ps. 127] while they were constructing the temple:
> The ninth [Ps. 128] after they had attained peace, giving a description of the happy man, because they had received back their friends and were happy with them:
> The tenth [Ps. 129] as they were enjoying deep peace. They say that they had been many times at war, but that the enemy had never overpowered them:
> The eleventh [Ps. 130] when they had now leisure for the things of God and comprehended their depths:
> The twelfth [Ps. 131] as not being elated by their knowledge:
> The thirteenth [Ps. 132] as a prayer for the restoration of the Anointed:
> The fourteenth [Ps. 133] for the restoration of the church:
> The fifteenth [Ps. 134] on their duty of hastening to the house of God, standing therein, and blessing him, raising their hands to the sanctuary, that they also may be blessed of the Lord.[57]

---

57. Origen, *Selecta in Psalmos* (Lommatzsch 1831–48: XIII, 107). English translation based on Tollinton 1929: 99-101.

What is truly striking about Origen's sequence is that he interprets
Psalms 120–25 as concerning war against Israel by foreign invaders.
This is the more remarkable as his comments appear to bear little
relation to the content of these six psalms. Where, for instance, in
Psalm 121 is there any reference to preparation for war and needing
allies? Or why should Origen connect Psalm 122 with triumphing
over the enemy in the battlefield (for, in his schema, the return to the
city is not until Psalm 125), when the narrative context of the psalm
seems to be Jerusalem (v. 2)? Is there any explanation for this peculiar
interpretation of the Songs of Ascents? Origen, according to his own
testimony, studied Hebrew from his youth before writing even his
earliest books.[58] He often listened to Jewish exegetes and sometimes
discussed interpretations current in rabbinic circles with a convert
from Judaism.[59] Could it be that Origen was aware that Jewish interpretation associated the Songs of Ascents with the aftermath of a foreign invasion, and, under the influence of this idea, but unaware of its
details, constructed this unlikely narrative sequence? It is possible.
But, even if the full explanation is lost, it should be noted that this
ancient commentator, acquainted with Jewish exegesis, sets the beginning of the Songs of Ascents in the context of an attack of foreign
nations against Jerusalem. In so doing, he appears to endorse my own
suggestions above, that certain Songs of Ascents describe deliverance
from an overwhelming attack of foreign nations.

4. *Summary*

A group analysis of the Songs of Ascents reveals several characteristics. First, they seem to be connected with worship at the Feast of
Sukkoth. This is confirmed by rabbinic tradition. Secondly, when the
ma'alot heading is considered in the context of the prophetic writings,
the group appears to depict an ascent to Sukkoth, not in historical, but
in eschatological time, in the latter-day *malkut*. Thirdly, a narrative
sequence is discernible in the group. This indicates that Israel is
dwelling in peace following recent divine deliverance from a massive
foreign attack. Thus the Songs of Ascents resemble the Psalms of
Asaph in that both can be read as representing an eschatological

58. *De Prin.* 4.3.14 (GCS, Origen 5.346).
59. *In Jer. Hom.* 20.2 (GCS, Origen 13.178); *Epis. Afric.* 7, 8.

ingathering to Jerusalem. But they differ in that the Asaph group depicts a distressed ingathering to judgment and war, while the Ascents depict a joyful ascent to the Feast of Sukkoth in the aftermath of war. In Chapter 6, I shall make a more direct comparison of corresponding aspects of the two psalm groups that will further highlight these characteristics.

Chapter 5

THE INGATHERING OF GOD[1]

I have suggested that the Psalms of Asaph can be read as showing a sequence that progresses from the ingathering of Israel to ultimate war, while the Songs of Ascents can be read as describing an ascent to a latter-day Feast of Sukkoth in the aftermath of war. I shall now investigate the biblical prophets, to see whether their eschatologies display any motifs similar to those of the Asaph and Ascents collections. I shall suggest that some of them display a threefold sequence of ingatherings that forms a simple eschatological programme. In the following chapter, I shall relate these findings to the motifs and themes of the two psalm-cycles.

The motif of eschatological ingathering has been somewhat neglected by modern scholarship.[2] Why this should be is unclear, for it is a central motif of biblical and Jewish eschatology.[3] Maybe Widengren is right in suggesting that recent Old Testament research,

---

1.   The title is from the inscription אסף אל on the trumpets of return in 1QM. 3.10

2.   The best work I am aware of on the subject has been done by Black 1991. This detailed examination of Zech. 9–14, to which I shall refer in this chapter and Chapter 7, notes the existence of the ingathering theme within an eschatological programme. Gowan emphasizes the centrality of Jerusalem in Old Testament eschatology, and has useful sections on 'Restoration to the Promised Land' and 'The Nations' (Gowan 1986: 32, 21-32, 42-58), but does not note the sequential recurrence of the ingathering motif. Widengren compares biblical references to the ingathering of Israel to ancient Near Eastern parallels, but does not comment on their place in Hebrew eschatology (1977: 227-45).

3.   'Nevertheless the ingathering of the exiles is one of the principal tropes of Jewish belief. It is requested every day in the Shmoneh 'Esreh [the eighteen benedictions of Jewish daily prayer], of which it forms the subject of the tenth benediction' (Heinemann 1971: 841). Likewise, Oesterley regards the ingathering of the exiles as 'one of the great episodes of the Messianic Drama' (1910: 97).

in its preoccupation with form criticism and literary *Gattungen*, has been unable to see a theme that appears in diverse genres.[4] Or it might equally be, as Gowan suggests, that preoccupation with Messiah has marginalized other eschatological motifs.[5] But even modern Jewish scholarship, which might be expected to be less concerned with messianism and literary *Gattungen* is weak on the subject. The *Encyclopaedia Judaica* article 'Ingathering' is unusual in having no bibliography whatsoever, presumably reflecting the dearth of literature on the subject.[6]

If the ingathering motif has been neglected, the whole idea of an eschatological programme or sequence of events has been, I think, avoided. This may be a partially justified reaction to the excesses of certain popular works that have stressed the programmatic element of biblical prophecy.[7] But *abusus non tollit usum*. Some Old Testament writers, as shall be seen, apparently did envisage some sort of programme of eschatological events, as did their earliest interpreters.[8]

Therefore the ingathering motif and the whole idea of an eschatological programme seem to have lain relatively uninvestigated. If these ideas are central to Israelite eschatology, then it may be that their neglect is partly to blame for the present incomprehension regarding the shaping of the Psalter. Their re-examination might provide a key to the understanding its shaping that other motifs, such as Messiah, have failed to provide. In this chapter I shall investigate these themes. First, I shall establish the wider context of the Israelite beliefs by looking at similar ideas elsewhere in the ancient Near East, particularly in the Baal Cycle and Mesopotamian texts. Thereafter I shall look at the Bible's clearest ingathering programmes, in the books of Ezekiel, Zechariah and Joel. Thereafter I shall look at similar ideas in other prophetic books, which may confirm the motif-sequence observed in Ezekiel, Zechariah and Joel. Then, in the following chapter, I shall see how the ingathering motifs of these eschatological

4.   Widengren 1977: 228.
5.   Gowan 1986: 32.
6.   Rabinowitz 1971b: VIII, 1373-75.
7.   See, for instance, Lindsey and Carlson 1970.
8.   There are a number of apocalyptic midrashim, dating from the early first millennium CE onwards, that feature eschatological programmes substantially based upon those of the biblical prophets. Six of these are given in Appendix 1. They shall be discussed in Chapter 7.

programmes accord with the themes of the Asaph Psalms and the Songs of Ascents.

1. *Ingathering Motifs in the Ancient Near East*

a. *The Baal Cycle*

The tablets of the Baal Cycle date from the latter half of the second millennium BCE, and tell how Baal establishes and maintains his kingship, despite challenges, particularly from Yam-Sea and Mot-Death. There is some dispute about the sequence in which they should be read. Tablets II and III (*KTU* 1.1, 2) are generally regarded as sequential. So too are Baal V and VI (*KTU* 1.5; 1.6), the latter continuing immediately the goddess Anat's mourning for Baal described in the last column of tablet 5.[9] The positioning of Baal I and IV and other fragments is less certain. But while there may be some dispute about the sequence in which the tablets should be read, the several different attempts at ordering them witness to the widespread conviction that they do indeed constitute a sequence or sequences of events and are not simply unrelated tales.[10]

There are several principal motifs in the Baal Cycle. The fragment *KTU* 1.101, *obv.,* depicts Baal reigning unopposed in Sapunu, his holy mountain. De Moor suggests that this ought to be regarded as the first motif of the entire cycle.[11] But whether this actual fragment should be placed at the beginning or not, the fact that this is a cyclic myth celebrating Baal's triumph suggests that the opening motif should be the same as the final one, that is, Baal reigning unopposed.

Other motifs occur in Baal II and III (*KTU* 1.1; 1.2).[12] These contain Baal's struggle with Yam-Sea, and are generally regarded as sequential. Their sequence of events is somewhat as follows. El instructs Kothar-wa-Khasis, the divine artificer, to build a mansion (Baal II.iii.). Shortly thereafter Baal appears to have fallen into

---

9.   Clifford 1979: 137.

10.   Clifford proposes that Baal I–VI 'contain two variants of the same basic myth of the victory of the storm god rather than, as is often assumed, of a single connected story of a conflict with Sea followed by a conflict with Death' (Clifford 1979: 138).

11.   de Moor 1987: 1.

12.   Some commentators regard Baal II as the beginning of the myth, making the first event of the cycle the building of a palace for Yam (e.g. Gibson: 1978: 38).

disgrace. Someone, possibly Athirat, complains against him, saying that El should appoint Yam in his place. El does so, but suggests that Baal will ultimately triumph (Baal II.iv). Baal and Yam then quarrel over the latter's right to possess Baal's property and to rule. Yam sends messengers to the divine assembly to demand they surrender Baal to him. Baal threatens and opposes them. After a break in the text, Kothar-wa-Khasis is to build a palace for Yam. Then Baal describes his woeful situation to Kothar-wa-Khasis. The latter encourages him to fight Yam, and prophesies his ultimate triumph.

> Truly I say to you, Highness Baal,
> I repeat, Cloudrider,
> Now, Baal, your enemies—
>> now you should slay your enemies,
>> now you should silence your foes!
> Take your eternal kingship,
>> your everlasting dominion! (*Baal* III.iv.7-10).[13]

He then arms Baal with magic weapons, with which Baal slays Yam and regains control of Sapunu (III.iv).

Baal IV represents Baal victorious. He is on his mount and is told a palace will be built for him (Baal IV.v.i). He commands tribute to be brought, presumably by his worshippers and defeated enemies, for the building of his palace.

> '... Call a caravan to your mansion,
>> merchandise into your palace!
> Let the mountains bring you silver in plenty,
>> the hills the choicest of gold.
> Then build a mansion of silver and gold,
>> a mansion of purest lapis!'
> Baal the Almighty rejoiced.
> He called a caravan to his mansion,
>> merchandise into his palace!
> The mountains brought him silver in plenty,
>> the hills the choicest of gold,
>>> the slopes brought him nuggets (Baal IV.v.30-40).[14]

A palace is built for him (Baal IV.v.i; IV.vi.15-35). A feast follows (IV.vi.40-55). Baal gives forth his voice and the earth shakes (IV.vii.31-33).

13. de Moor 1987: 39.
14. de Moor 1987: 56.

A final group of motifs occurs in Baal V and VI (*KTU* 1.5; 1.6), which are almost certainly sequential.[15] Baal's lordship is again contested, this time by Mot-Death, the voracious king of death and the underworld. Baal enters into conflict with him and is pierced and dies, and descends to the underworld (V.vi). Later however he revives (VI.iii). He battles again with Mot, who is defeated and proclaims Baal the king (VI.vi).

The motifs in the Baal Cycle can therefore be represented as follows.

KTU *1.101*	*Baal II*	*Baal III*	*Baal IV*	*Baal V*	*Baal VI*
Baal reigns unopposed in Sapunu	Baal ousted from Sapunu by Yam. Returns to confront him	Baal's conflict with Yam-Sea. Yam is slain	Palace built for triumphant Baal on holy mount. Worshippers bring tribute	Baal pierced by Mot. Baal dies. Exiled from Sapunu in underworld	Baal revives. Defeats Mot. Baal proclaimed king

The full significance of this sequence will be considered in Chapter 7. For the purposes of the present chapter, it is enough simply to note three motifs:

Baal II	*Baal III*	*Baal IV*
Baal ousted. Returns to Sapunu	Baal's conflict with Yam-Sea. Yam is slain	Worshippers gather to Sapunu with tribute

Although the complete arrangement of these motifs may now be lost, it would seem fair to say that the Baal Cycle embodies what may be described as a programme of events, which features some 'gathering' and 'return' motifs. Of course, it is not eschatological in the sense that the later biblical prophets are, but it cannot be dismissed as a mere agricultural myth, any more than it is possible to dismiss Yhwhism, with its harvest festivals and metaphors, as such. It is a cosmogonic myth for the construction and reconstruction of the world. As it is a repeating and repeated myth, it is reasonable to imagine that it might have been viewed as having some ultimate reference to a re-creation of the cosmos into a new age. And that, of course, is where eschatology begins.

15.   Gibson 1978: 14.

b. *Mesopotamian Texts*

Turning from Ugarit to Mesopotamia, Widengren cites several texts that refer to ingathering of the scattered.[16] His purpose is to ascertain the date of ingathering sayings in Hebrew literature, and he concludes that the motif 'is so well attested in an early period that no decisive arguments speak against its authenticity among pre-exilic prophets'.[17] However, the texts he cites are of interest simply in showing that the gathering of the scattered was a standard motif of ancient Near Eastern statecraft. It was seen as a merciful function of a magnanimous lord. In the prologue of Hammurabi (c. 1790 BCE), the king styles himself *mupaḫḫir niši sapḫati ša Isin^{ki}*, 'the gatherer of the scattered people of Isin' (II 49f.).[18] Thus the theme goes back to remote times in Mesopotamian thought. Yet it occurs little changed a millennium later. In an inscription of Assurbanipal, the king describes his own actions towards Babylon:

nišašu sapḫati upaḫḫirama	Its scattered people I gathered
uter ašrušin.	and restored to their place.[19]

A seventh-century building inscription of Esarhaddon, Assurbanipal's father, proclaims his charitable deeds toward the Babylonians:

> For the citizens of Babylon the oppressed,
> I established anew as privileged their freedom,
> Under the protection of Anu and Enlil.
> They who were bought and brought to slavery,
> who had been put into chains and fetters,
> I gathered and counted as Babylonians.
>
> Their plundered property I restored.
> The destitute I clothed in clothes
> and caused their feet to take the way to Babylon.
> To settle down in the city, to build temples,
> to plant orchards, to dig canals
> I gave them confidence.
>
> Their privileged status, made vain, which had disappeared,
> I restored to its place.

16. Widengren 1977: 227-45.
17. Widengren 1977: 241; cf. 227.
18. Widengren 1977: 235.
19. Widengren 1977: 235; from Langdon 1912: 174.31-32.

The tablets of their freedom from taxes I wrote anew.
Into the four winds I opened their way,
in order that they might direct their intention
to have intercourse with the totality of countries.[20]

More particularly to the present investigation, ingathering was also a function of the propitiate deity.

ša saphi t[upaḫḫara ga]nunšu	The house of the scattered thou gatherest.[21]
[illat] niši^{meš} sapiḫti tuštešeri ḫarrana	For the scattered clan of the people thou guidest its way.[22]

Widengren also cites a prayer to the deity to gather the scattered clan: *illatu: sapiḫtu illati lipḫur.*[23] Sometimes the action of the deity is to be undertaken in the future. Widengren states, 'A future action is probably indicated in a series of so-called "apocalyptic" prophecies where one reads the following prophecy of salvation (CT XIII 50.7-9).'

mi-šá-ru iš-šak-kan	An act of justice will be promulgated,
e-šá-tu uš-te-še-ra	the confusion will be set aright,
dal-ḫa-a-tum i-zak-ka-a	the troubles will clear up,
sa-a[p-ḫu-tum i-paḫ-ḫu-ra]	those who have been scat[tered will be gathered],
na-as-ḫu-tum KI.MIN	those who have been uprooted DITTO,
ki-na-a-tum uk-tan-na-ma	the righteous will be re-established.[24]

Widengren concludes his discussion of the ingathering motif in relation to the deity: 'The promises clearly contain the aspect of futurity, and I am definitely of the opinion that our theme has been used

20. Widengren 1977: 234; from Borger 1956: 12ff.
21. Widengren 1977: 236; from Ebeling 1953: 44.53. Widengren (1977: 236) notes: 'Thanks to VAT 13681 it has been possible to restore a gap in King's publication.'
22. Widengren 1977: 236; from Ebeling 1953: 122.12.
23. Widengren 1977: 244; from Weir 1934: 296 s.v. *sapḫu.*
24. Widengren 1977: 237; from Biggs 1967: 121. Widengren states: 'To judge from the entire context, there can be little doubt about the restoration of the small gap in the fourth line quoted' (237). He notes (244) that later duplicates, added by Grayson and Lambert 1964: 7-30, have greatly facilitated the comprehension of this text.

"eschatologically" in Mesopotamia.'[25] Thus the broader ancient Near Eastern literature suggests that, in Ugarit, ingathering themes were basic to the cosmogonic sequence of the Baal cycle, and in Mesopotamia eschatological ingathering and scattering were standard motifs of royal benevolence or displeasure, and ingathering was one of the functions of the benign deity.

2. *Old Testament Eschatological Programmes*

Three Old Testament passages appear to display entire programmes of eschatological events. These passages are Ezekiel 34–48, Zechariah 9–14, and Joel 3–4. I shall investigate them individually.

a. *Ezekiel 34–48*

The prophecies in Ezekiel 34–48 seem unambiguously eschatological, referring as they repeatedly do to events that were patently not part of the writer's present experience.[26] Israel are to be revived and reunified and to return from exile (37.1-28). After this event, which, from the narrative standpoint of Ezekiel, is itself in the future, they are to suffer a massive attack by an alliance of nations led by a prince Gog from צָפוֹן יַרְכְּתֵי, *the utter north* (38.14, 15), the ancient mythological source, in Israelite thought, of chaos and the sinister. This is said to be the day spoken of by previous prophets, presumably the Day of Yhwh (38.17; 39.8). The aftermath will be a utopian

---

25. Widengren 1977: 237.

26. It is unlikely that this passage is a codified reference to the Babylonian destruction, as has been suggested. That event is referred to in Ezek. 33.21, following numerous premonitions (e.g. Ezek. 24.25-26), but no attempt is made anywhere within the book of Ezekiel to identify it with Gog's attack. On the contrary, Gog's attack takes place after the return from the Babylonian exile, an event which, from the narrative standpoint of the book, is still future. Likewise, Gog's area of origin, Rosh, Meshekh and Tubal, precludes his representing a Mesopotamian conqueror. These origins might bear some resemblance to those of the Scythian invaders. (Certainly, Josephus identifies Gog's land of Magog with Scythia [*Ant.* 1.6.1.].) But Gog's attack is clearly on a grander scale and has a more definitive defeat. However, the Scythian invasions, and a trans-Caucasian leader (King Gugu [Gyges] of Lydia [*fl.* 676–30 BCE]?), might well be the typological background to what the prophet envisages. As Eichrodt notes: 'the name of Gog is derived from legendary accounts of campaigns by northern nations and may in some way unknown to us have come to be the name given to their commander-in-chief' (1970: II, 522).

Jerusalem in which a life-giving stream flows from the rebuilt temple, making healing trees bear fruit every month and sweetening the waters of the Dead Sea (47.1-12). Phrases such as באחרית השנים (38.8), באחרית הימים (38.16) and ביום ההוא (38.10, 14, 18; 39.11) define the time of these events as in the far future.[27] Ancient interpreters recognize the eschatological referent of these chapters. For instance, the LXX translator, for whom the kingdom of Amalek was no more (1 Chron. 4.42-43), reinterpreted Balaam's prophecy at Num. 24.7 to apply not to *Agag,* Amalek's king, but to *Gog,* presumably recognizing a still future enemy in the figure of Ezekiel 38 and 39. Likewise, 4Q385 (Second Ezekiel[a]) interprets these chapters eschatologically.[28] So too does the Targum.[29] The New Testament envisages Gog's attack taking place one thousand years after the inauguration of the messianic reign (Rev. 20.8). Rabbinic literature regards Ezekiel 37 as a prediction of the end-time resurrection of the dead and repeatedly refers to Gog and Magog in eschatological contexts.[30] The Koran also regards Gog and Magog (Yajjuj and Majjuj) as eschatological figures, relating how they were confined behind a wall of brass by

27.   Steudel notes that the Qumran sectarians used the phrase אחרית הימים to refer to 'the final period of history' (Steudel 1993: 231). Ibn Ezra, although confessing he is sometimes unsure about which period a prophetic passage refers to (cf. e.g. Comm. on Hos. 2.25), accepts that whenever the phrase אחרית הימים occurs the prophecy refers to the age to come (cf. comms. on Gen. 49.1; Isa. 2.1; Mic. 4.1; also *Ibn Ezra* 1988: 45). Smith notes the eschatological import of ביום ההוא (Smith 1984: 39).

28.   For the text see Strugnell and Dimant 1988: 45-58. They comment, 'One of the surprises in the work is that the vision of the Dry Bones appears to be interpreted as predicting historical (that is, historical from the pseudepigraphic writer's viewpoint, but future from the narrator's) or eschatological events, in the same symbolic way as other visions were interpreted in other apocalyptic writings' (48).

29.   The Targum consistently interprets these chapters eschatologically but not messianically. Given the opportunities for messianic interpretation in the references to the eschatological Davidic king in 34.23-24, 37.24-25, this is remarkable. Levey observes that 'the Targumist or Targumists originally responsible for the Targum to Ezekiel did not find Messianism as imperative an issue as some of the others', and suggests they had an eschatological, non-messianic outlook (Levey 1974: 86-87).

30.   Only a few of the numerous references in talmudim and midrashim may be cited. Ezek.iel 37 is taken as referring to the resurrection of the dead at *Šab.* 152b; *Ta'an.* 2b; *Sanh.* 92b. Gog and Magog are mentioned in eschatological contexts at *Ag. M.* 2.4; *Pir. M.* 5.58; *As. M.* 4.14, *Ber.* 7b; *y. Meg.* 71b; *y. Yom.* 10a; *Midr. Tan.* (Korach, end); *Midr. Pss.* 2.2.

Alexander, to be held there until their release preceding the time of resurrection and judgment (Suwar 18 and 21). Modern interpreters too recognize that the passage refers to events in the far future.[31]

Ezekiel 34–48 also seem to contain a deliberate sequence of events, rather than just a catalogue of unrelated prophecies about the future. Ezekiel 38 and 39 is unmistakably a narrative, as modern commentators recognize. For instance, Blenkinsopp observes that 'the Gog passage tells a fairly clear and consistent story' and Cooke notes its 'loosely strung sequence of ideas'.[32] However, they are hesitant of recognizing a sequence of events in the wider context of Ezekiel 34–48. Blenkinsopp regards the present position of Ezekiel 38–39 as problematic.

> The logical sequence would seem to require that chapters 38–39 precede the section that deals with restoration in chapters 34–37, as in fact they do in one late LXX attestation (the J.H. Scheide papyri, second to fourth century A.D.). The finale of the Gog passage, 39.25-29, would serve very well as a prologue to the more detailed account of the restoration of Israel in chapters 34–37, the fate of the slain enemy's remains would make a fitting contrast with the resuscitation of the dry bones, and the promise concerning the sanctuary with which chapters 34–37 ends would lead smoothly into the vision of the new temple in chapters 40–48.[33]

On the other hand, Blenkinsopp himself seems uneasy with this, stressing that 'the abundant material preserved from Ezekiel's preaching and the editorial comment on it have been arranged according to a meaningful structure'.[34] He therefore suggests that 'since the Gog narrative presupposes return to the land but does not speak of a rebuilt temple, this was thought to be the most appropriate point at which to fit it in'.[35] Indeed, it could not be otherwise, for, although

31. Davidson: 'The time is indefinite, it is far into the years to come' (1906: 274). Fisch observes that these events are set in the messianic time (1950: 233, 252-53). Carley suggests Ezekiel 38 and 39 represent 'God's triumph over the world' (Carley 1974: 254).

32. Blenkinsopp 1990: 179; Cooke 1936: 407.

33. Blenkinsopp 1990: 180.

34. Blenkinsopp 1990: 180. Earlier he notes, 'On a first reading of the book, one gets an impression of continuity, structure, and order and of its being a well thought out whole to a much greater extent than other prophetic books' (3). The view of Kirkpatrick is similar: 'The Book of Ezekiel bears the marks of careful plan and arrangement' (1892: 336).

35. Blenkinsopp 1990: 180.

the narrative standpoint of Ezekiel is consistently exilic, Gog's attack is against the land of Israel, and therefore Israel's return and restoration is the necessary prerequisite to Gog's attack. The Gog narrative itself makes this clear (38.8-14). Thus the entire section of chs. 34–39 functions convincingly as a sequence and could not easily be arranged otherwise. As the ensuing chs. 40–48 also make sense in their present position, depicting the utopian Jerusalem in the aftermath of Gog's defeat, the entire passage Ezekiel 34–48 also functions well as a sequence. Therefore, since the rest of Ezekiel is carefully structured, as Blenkinsopp notes, it may tentatively be assumed that there is an intentional sequence of eschatological events throughout Ezekiel 34–48, and not in chs. 38 and 39 alone.

The details of this eschatological sequence or programme are as follows. Yhwh will gather his scattered flock back to their land (34.11-24), a theme repeated from earlier in Ezekiel (11.17; 20.34-41; 28.25). He will set David over them as shepherd, נשיא, and king (34.23-24; 37.24-25). The desolate land will become fruitful (34.26-29). There follows a prophecy against Edom and the nations who desolated Israel (35.1–36.7), then the theme of restoration is again taken up: the people will be gathered, forgiven and faithful; the land will be fruitful, populous and rebuilt (36.8-38). Then follow further prophecies of national restoration. Yhwh will revive כל־בית ישראל as from death (37.11-12). Commentators generally take the phrase as designating Josephites and Judahites together.[36] However, in v. 16 the same phrase denotes the Josephites in contrast to the Judahites, who are called בני ישראל, so there may be some emphasis on the resurgence of the Josephites in particular. Those revived, whether Josephites or all Israel, will be gathered to their land, and reunited (37.15-23), and their king and prince will be 'David' (37.24-25).[37] Then comes the attack of Gog and his vast alliance (38.1–39.16). This attack, which is divinely initiated (38.4-6, 16-17; 39.2), is to take place when the preceding prophecies have been fulfilled, and Israel is settled and prosperous in their land (38.8-12). Gog and his horde will

36.   See e.g. Cooke 1936: 397.

37.   It is unclear whether David *redivivus* is envisaged, or merely David represented in a descendant. There is some evidence for belief in a David *redivivus* in rabbinic times (Levey 1974: 86), though not before. The Targum casts no light upon this verse, but at Ezek. 17.22 it expects 'a child (יניק) from the kingdom of the house of David'.

be defeated by divine intervention and fall on the mountains of Israel, where beasts will eat them (38.18–39.20). At Gog's defeat the nations will know Yhwh and see his glory (38.16; 39.21). They will recognize his relationship to Israel and his sanctuary in Jerusalem; they will understand his former punishment of his people (39.23-24; cf. 37.28). Israel will acknowledge Yhwh as their God, and he will pour out his spirit upon them (39.22, 25-29). Then follows an extended description of the temple and Israel in the latter days (chs. 40–48). They will be ruled by their נשיא (44.3; 46.16-18), presumably of *bet*-David, like the one of 34.23-24; 36.25. The appointed feasts (45.21-25; 46.9-11) and the cult (45.13-46.24) will be restored. The 12 tribes will be reunited in their land around the temple (ch. 48), and foreigners will settle and be accepted among them (47.22-23).

Therefore, omitting for the moment the references to the Davidic king, Ezekiel seems to envisage the following eschatological schema.

Gathering of Israel, both Josephites and Judahites. Possible emphasis on Josephites	Gathering of hostile nations against Jerusalem	Israel live and worship in their land. The nations acknowledge Yhwh

The exact period of the Davidic reign is unclear. His description as *shepherd* in the context of Israel's ingathering probably implies that he will instigate, inspire or superintend it (34.23). He will dwell among the people in the utopian post-conflict period (44.3; 46.16-18), which should therefore probably be identified as an eschatological Davidic *malkut*. He is not mentioned among the events of the conflict or its immediate aftermath, but his appointment as Israel's *prince for ever* (37.25) suggests that his presence should possibly be inferred throughout the entire programme.

b. *Zechariah 9–14*

Zechariah 9–14 is eschatological in tone. This was noted earlier in regard to Zechariah 14.[38] But it is equally true of the preceding chs. 9–13. Zech. 9.10 depicts a king who will rule in universal peace. In chs. 12 and 13 the eschatological slogan ביום ההוא occurs repeatedly (12.3, 4, 6, 8, 9, 11; 13.1, 2, 4).[39] The eschatological reference of these chapters is confirmed by its being recognized by early

---

38. See Chapter 4, pp. 115-16.
39. Smith notes the eschatological import of this phrase (Smith 1984: 39).

interpreters. *1 En.* 71.14-15 describes a 'son of man' who shall 'proclaim peace to you', a phrase most resembling the description of the future king in Zech. 9.10. *Sib. Or.* 8.324 interprets Zech. 9.9 messianically: 'Rejoice, holy daughter Zion... Your king comes in, mounted on a foal, appearing gentle...he is son of God.'[40] New Testament writers saw these chapters as predicting messianic events, which they regarded as fulfilled in their own time.[41] The Targum interprets Zech. 10.4 messianically: 'Out of him [Judah] comes his king, out of him comes his Messiah.' The Talmud and Midrash Rabbah interpret several passages messianically or eschatologically.[42] Modern commentators also recognize intentional eschatological prediction throughout Zechariah 9–14.[43] Black, for instance, comments that 'these chapters...are wholly forward-looking and eschatological'.[44]

Zechariah 9–14 also seems to contain a deliberate sequence or sequences of events, rather than just unrelated prophecies. C.H. Dodd observes that chs. 9–14 of Zechariah have 'the character of an apocalypse, and while its component visions are not easy to bring into a consistent scheme, it can be understood as setting forth a whole eschatological programme'.[45] R.L. Smith refers to the passage's 'eschatological timetable'.[46] And Black, in his detailed study of the messianism of these chapters, notes,

> While it is obvious that no reading of Zech. 9–14 is capable of discover-
> ing a clear and well-ordered sequence of events beginning with chapter 9

40.	The passage is widely regarded as a Christian interpolation (on which see Collins 1987: 446-48). However that does not affect its significance as evidence of early messianic interpretation of this passage.

41.	See Zech. 9.9 at Mt. 21.5 and Jn 12.15; Zech. 11.12-13 at Mt. 27.9-10; Zech. 12.3 at Lk. 21.24; 12.10 at Jn 19.37 and Rev. 1.7; Zech. 13.7 at Mt. 26.31 and Mk 14.27.

42.	See, for instance, Zech. 9.9 at *Sanh.* 99a; Zech. 11.12 at *Gen. R.* 98.9; Zech. 12.10-12 at *Suk.* 52a. See too *Meg.* 3a, where it is said the land quaked at the Aramaic translation of the Prophets, but not of the Pentateuch, because the translation of the Prophets reveals hidden mysteries. The instance given of such a mystery is Zech. 12.11.

43.	Lamarche 1961: 152-57; Dodd 1953b: 64; Hanson 1975: 280ff.; Black 1991: 44, 57.

44.	Black 1991: 44.

45.	Dodd 1953b: 64.

46.	Smith 1984: 271.

and ending with chapter 14, it is not difficult to discover within Zech. 9–
14 an implied, though loosely organized sort of eschatological schema.[47]

Thus Zechariah 9–14, like Ezekiel 34–48, seems to depict a sequence
of anticipated latter-day events or, in Dodd's phrase, 'a whole eschatological programme'.

The characteristics of this programme can be unravelled somewhat
as follows. The first sequence of eschatological events occurs in Zech.
9.9-17, which seems to encompass in miniature the entire sequence
that later reoccurs in Zech. 10.1–14.21. To Jerusalem comes a king
(Zech. 9.9) whose Davidic lineage is implied in his Solomonic characteristics. He will impose peace, speak *shalom* to the nations and have
universal dominion, described in v. 10 in terms of the messianic motto
that occurs also in Solomonic Ps. 72.8. The description of his peaceful
reign further confirms his Solomonic qualities. Thereafter the ingathering of Israel is described (9.11). While it is not stated that the king
instigates this event, the narrative progression from his coming to
their gathering probably implies as much. Israel shall be liberated
(שׁלח) from the בור אין מים בו, *waterless pit* (v. 11). This phrase designates, first, a place of death, like the grave, or an underground dungeon.[48] But there seems also to be an allusion to the pit-captivity of
Joseph in Gen. 37.24, which features both the verb שׁלח and a description of the בור as אין בו מים.[49] This might suggest that the captives liberated are the Josephites, the exiled northern tribes, a supposition
supported by their appearing as Yhwh's weapon together with Judah
in v. 13, and by the more explicit reference to their return in Zech.
10.6-12, discussed below. The freed captives return to their בצרון,
fortress (v. 12), denoting Zion, as does בצר at Isa. 22.10, or possibly
just the land of Israel. Then comes holy war language (vv. 13-16).
The situation envisaged is an attack on Jerusalem by foreigners rather
than an Israelite military offensive. This can be seen from the statement that Yhwh will *defend* (יגן) them (v. 15), the verb גנן denoting at
its every other occurrence in the Bible, including Zechariah, the
defence or protection of Jerusalem at time of siege.[50] It is also implied

47. Black 1991: 52-53.
48. For the widespread metaphorical link between pit, imprisonment, and death
in the ancient Near East, see Keel 1978: 62-78.
49. Stuhlmueller (1988: 126) notes the 'almost verbatim' resemblance to Gen.
37.24.
50. Isa. 31.5; 37.35; 38.6; 2 Kgs 19.34; 20.6; Zech. 12.8.

in Yhwh's *delivering* or *rescuing* Israel (הושׁיעם; v. 16). It may also be
indicated in the rather opaque reference to the victorious Israelites
trampling the slingstones (v. 15), which might suggest a previous
attack by siege machines.[51] At this national crisis, Yhwh will fight on
Israel's behalf and save them. The restored Ephraimites and Judahites,
reunited Israel, shall be his weapons of attack. Thereafter the triumphant Israelites shall sparkle and rejoice in their land (v. 16).

A more complex version of the same sequence seems to be
described in Zech. 10.1–14.21. A number of features identify the present form of this passage as a literary unit, whatever its original
sources may have been. The difference in tone between the utopian
vision of 9.17 and the prophetic admonition of 10.1 marks it as a new
section. Its opening theme is that Yhwh alone is the rain-giver (10.1-
2) and the repetition of this theme in 14.17-19 forms an inclusio
marking the boundaries of the whole section. The prominence of the
shepherd theme (10.2-3; 11.3-17; 13.7), absent from the earlier part
of the book, supports the same conclusion.

As regards its sequence of events, it opens with a brief admonition
to look to Yhwh, not idols, for the blessing of rain (vv. 1-2). Then
follows a prediction of Israel's restoration (vv. 3-12). Judah will be
strengthened (vv. 3-6) and, in language allusive of Gen. 49.10, the
future kingship of Israel is accorded them (v. 4). Smith notes of v. 4,
'These metaphorical references are all to a new leader who is to come
out of Judah.'[52] The Targum, as noted above, agrees. The Judahites
dwelling in the land will be strengthened, and the Josephites will be
gathered from distant lands and repatriated in Gilead and Lebanon
(vv. 6-12). (In this Zechariah 9–14 differs from Ezekiel 37, which
envisages the ingathering of both Ephraim and Judah. This is consistent with the prophecies in Zechariah 9–14 having originated in post-
exilic times, when a community of Judahites had returned to the land.)

---

51.   R.L. Smith renders the phrase אבני־קלע as (*they will... tread down*) *the
sling stones* (Smith 1984: 258, 260). He does not state whether he envisages siege
machines or hand slings. But the former would be more likely in a siege situation,
and the closest parallel to this phrase, אבני קלעים at 2 Chron. 26.14-15, denotes
projectiles of siege machines.

52.   Smith 1984: 265. He notes that cornerstone (פנה) denotes leadership at Ps.
118.22 and Isa. 19.13, and tent-peg (יתד) at Isa. 22.23-24 [264-65]. Battle-bow is
not used elsewhere in the Bible to denote a king, but was a common royal designation in the Near East (Mason 1977: 100).

Then it is predicted that Jerusalem will be besieged by foreign armies (12.2-3). Yhwh will rescue Israel and destroy the attacking nations (12.9; 14.3-15). In the conflict the house of David will make glorious battle, going before Israel like אלהים and the מלאך אלהים (12.8-9). Thereafter the survivors of the nations will ascend to Zion to worship at the Feast of Sukkoth (Zech. 14.16-21). The worship of Israel with the nations at the latterday Feast of Sukkoth is not stated, but is implied simply by its location on Zion, as well as by the wider Zecharian context (8.20-23).

Although the golden age depicted in Zechariah 14 is emphatically a kingdom of God, with its threefold emphasis on Yhwh as universal king (vv. 9, 16, 17), that does not exclude the possibility that the writer envisaged an eschatological scion of the house of David ruling as Yhwh's representative. Indeed, though a human king is not mentioned *per se,* a number of points suggest that one should be viewed as present. First, Zech. 9.10 predicts that the coming king will have ultimate universal dominion. This can be fulfilled, in the context of Zechariah 9–14, only if he is regarded as ruling in the time when hostile nations have been finally subdued, that is, *after* the eschatological conflict in Zechariah 14. Secondly, references to *bet*-David's military prowess in the eschatological conflict (Zech. 12.8-9) suggest that they will triumph and rule in Zion thereafter. Thirdly, other prophets depict the eschatological kingdom as having a restored house of David.[53] The Zecharian writer, as shall be seen in the following section, was aware of the writings of at least some of his predecessors. It is therefore unlikely that he would have imagined a golden age for Israel with a vacant throne of David. Certainly, ancient commentators appear to have reasoned along these lines, when they represent Zechariah 14 as a Davidic *malkut.*[54] As Black notes, 'Although there

53. Isa. 11.1-9; Jer. 3.17; 23.3-6; Ezek. 37.21-25; 44.3; 46.16-18; Hos. 3.4-5; Mic. 4.8-5.1 [2]; Amos 9.11-14.

54. *Otot* 8.4 depicts Zech. 14.3 occurring in ben David's reign. *Sef. Z.* 50 describes ben David coming at the time when the Lord descends upon the Mount of Olives (Zech. 14.4). *Pir. M.* 5.65-6 sets Zech. 14.3, and probably 14.4, in the time of ben David (cf. *Pir. M.* 5.45). Sa'adya depicts the disintegration of the invaders (Zech. 14.12) and the nations' ascent to procure rain (Zech. 14.16ff.) as taking place in the time of the Messiah (*Kitab al-'Amanat,* VIII.vi; Rosenblatt 1948: 306-308). Ibn Tibbon adds to Sa'adya's text the words, 'the son of David will decree it upon them [the conquered nations] that they come every year to celebrate the feast of tabernacles' (*Kitab al-'Amanat,* VIII.vi; Rosenblatt 1948: 307). Black (1991: 152) notes

is no mention of any human agent in the MT of Zech. 14, this chapter is interpreted in a messianic context in a large number of rabbinic references.'[55]

Of course, the above-outlined Zecharian event-sequences omit most of Zechariah 11–13, with its shepherds rejecting and rejected, its mysterious pierced figure, its desolated Jerusalem and exiled people. These themes shall be considered in Chapter 7. But, disregarding them for the present, there is a broad similarity between the eschatological programmes of Zech. 9.9-17 and 10.1–14.21. These may be represented as follows.

Zech. 9.9-17	Gathering of Israel (Josephites)	Jerusalem attacked by hostile nations. Deliverance.	Triumphant Israel rejoice in their land
Zech. 10.1–14.21	Gathering of Israel (Josephites)	Gathering of hostile nations against Jerusalem. Attack. Deliverance	Israel worship Yhwh at Feast of Sukkoth with the nations

Black too recognizes a somewhat similar sequence in these chapters.

> While there is no single narrative which begins in chapter 9 and ends in chapter 14, there seem to be recurring narrative sequences, nearly all of which relate the events of the eschaton. The most obvious and frequently-recurring one envisions Yahweh gathering his people from the nations, leading them in battle, defeating the nations, establishing the blissful kingdom, and gathering the nations at Jerusalem. This sequence (or portions of it) is found in 9.1-8, 9.11-17, 10.3b-11.3, 12.1-9, and 14.1-21.[56]

c. *Joel 3–4 [2.28–3.21]*

The tone of the passage is eschatological. There occur phrases such as יום יהוה (3.4 [2.31]), בימים ההמה ובעת ההיא (4.1 [3.1]) and ביום ההוא (4.18 [3.18]), and the themes include the outpouring of the divine *ruach* upon all flesh (3.1 [2.28]), massive disruption of the heavenly bodies (3.1-2; 4.15-16 [2.30-31; 3.15-16]), Israel's final vindication

---

Song R. 2.13.4, which interprets Zech. 14.9, *The Lord shall be king over the whole earth,* in the time of the Messiah. He also notes various other passages which suggest a messianic interpretation of Zech. 14.3-4 (Black 1991: 142-57). Some of these shall be discussed in Chapter 7.

55. Black 1991: 156.
56. Black 1991: 54.

and Jerusalem's peace, forgiveness and divine indwelling for ever (4.1-21 [3.1-21]). The passage also seems to be consciously presenting a programme of events. One commentator describes it as an 'Apocalypse'.[57]

The sequence of events is as follows. Yhwh will gather all nations to the Valley of Jehoshaphat, where he will judge and recompense them for having previously scattered Israel (Joel 4[3].2-21). The location intended is probably the Valley of Berakhah beside Jerusalem,[58] where Jehoshaphat celebrated the supernatural rout of the Moabite and Ammonite alliance (2 Chron. 20).[59] Thus the scenario is one of ingathered Israel threatened at the gates of Jerusalem by a foreign invasion, while the location evokes the conceptual framework of 2 Chronicles 20, with its Asaphite holy war *zikhron*, victory and triumphant celebration. Yhwh addresses the nations directly, apparently in non-eschatological time, warning them of coming judgment and foretelling Israel's resurgence (4.4-8 [3.4-8]). Then the eschatological vision reoccurs. The nations are summoned to the valley. Yhwh will roar from Zion and they will be reaped like corn and trampled in the winepress (4.9-16 [3.9-16]). Then Israel will be blessed with abundant

57. Smith 1898: 431.

58. In 2 Chron. 20.26 the Israelites assemble in the Valley of Berakhah to praise Yhwh on the fourth day after their victory. As this is the only valley mentioned in connection with Jehoshaphat it is the likeliest candidate for the reference in Joel 4.2. (The battle itself is not said to have taken place in a valley.) Since the fourth century CE, the Valley of Berakhah has been identified with the Kidron valley between Jerusalem and the Mount of Olives (Myers 1960: 91). No earlier evidence for the identification is available, but the environs of Jerusalem would seem an appropriate spot for a victory celebration. The battle itself is said to have taken place in the direction of the Desert of Tekoa, south of Jerusalem (2 Chron. 20.20). However there is no indication that the Valley of Berakhah was in the same vicinity. Rather it was the place they assembled after the work of gathering booty was complete.

59. There seems insufficient ground for saying that, because Jehoshaphat simply means 'Yhwh judges', Joel's עמק יהושפט therefore refers only to Yhwh's judgment and not to the events of 2 Chron. 20 (*pace* Smith 1898: II, 432). As noted previously (p. 99), word-play upon proper names is a common technique in Hebrew literature from biblical times on. Indeed, given the divine judgment described in 2 Chron. 20, the very name 'Jehoshaphat' might be regarded as a wordplay in 2 Chron. 20 itself. Certainly, Ibn Ezra does not hesitate to identify the 'Valley of Jehoshaphat' with the Valley of Berakhah in 2 Chron. 20 (Comm. on Joel 4.2).

security and fertility, and a stream will flow from the Lord's house
and water the land (4.17-18). Israel's latter-day worship is not explicitly mentioned, but is implied in their reconciliation with Yhwh,
when *Jerusalem will be holy,* and the people's blood guilt pardoned
(4.17, 21 [3.17, 21]). After such a cataclysmic judgment, the nations
will presumably acknowledge Yhwh's supremacy and his dwelling in
Jerusalem. Thus the eschatological programme of this passage seems
to be as follows:

Ingathering of Israel	Ingathering of nations against Jerusalem. Divine deliverance	Israel blessed; recon- ciled with Yhwh; vindi- cated before the nations

Joel 3–4 contains no explicit reference to a latter-day *bet*-David.
However, the comparison of the latter-day conflict with that of
Jehoshaphat suggests that a Davidic king like Jehoshaphat is to lead
Israel at that time (4.2).

d. *One Eschatological Programme in Ezekiel 34–48, Zechariah 9–14
and Joel 3–4?*
These three prophetic passages therefore present remarkably similar
eschatological programmes. This similarity may be more than accidental. There is evidence of substantial literary relationship between
the three programmes, which suggests that the later ones may be
dependent on the earlier ones and be intentionally describing the same
anticipated events.

Several commentators observe that Zechariah 9–14 frequently
appropriates and reuses earlier biblical writings.[60] As Black notes,
'Perhaps more than any other Old Testament prophetic work, Zechariah 9–14 is the reinterpretation of earlier prophecy, some of which
has been expanded, some reinterpreted, and some even reversed.'[61]
This is evident in isolated allusions, such as those to Gen. 37.24,
49.10, Amos 8.10, and Ps. 72.8, at Zech. 10.4, 9.11, 12.11 and 9.10,
respectively. More significantly, there is extensive dependence on
blocks of earlier material, particularly from Isaiah, Jeremiah and
Ezekiel.[62] Black observes that, of all these, the most influential block

60.   Mason 1973; Delcor 1952: 385-411; Mitchell, Smith and Bewer 1912: 236-
39; Stuhlmueller 1988: 115.
61.   Black 1991: 48-49.
62.   Suggested influences of Jeremiah on Zech. 9–14 are listed by Black 1991:
50-51. For Ezekiel and Isaiah see below.

of scripture for Zechariah 9–14 is Ezekiel 30–48 (especially chs. 34, 36, 37 and 38).[63] Some of the more striking resemblances are as follows.

Ezekiel		Zechariah	
34.3	=	11.5, 16	Bad shepherds slaughter and eat the flock
34.4	=	11.16	Bad shepherds neglect the weak and sick sheep
34.10	=	10.3; 11.7-8.	Yhwh is *against* bad shepherds and rejects them
34.11-20	=	10.3.	Yhwh himself will care for his flock
34.26	=	10.1; 14.17ff.	Yhwh is the giver of rain in season
36.17, 25	=	13.1	Israel cleansed from impurity with clean water
36.26-33; 39.29	=	12.10	Spiritual renewal of Israelites
36.8; 37.23-7	=	13.9	Reiteration of covenant formula
37.15-22	=	11.7-14	Staffs/sticks signifying the unity of Israel
37.23	=	13.2	Israel cleansed of idolatry
38.15	=	10.5	Invading army mounted on horses
38.16; 39.2	=	14.2	Yhwh instigates the nations' attack
38.16	=	14.16-19	Nations know Yhwh after the invasion's defeat
38.19-20	=	14.4,10	Great geological upheaval
38.21	=	14.13	Attacking armies kill one another
38.22	=	14.12-15	Plague on the invading armies
39.10	=	14.14	The defeated armies will be plundered
47.1-12	=	14.8	A river will flow from Jerusalem

This suggests that Zechariah 9–14 is indeed dependent on Ezekiel 34–48, or, at least, upon the traditions behind it. Moreover, not only does Zechariah 9–14 repeatedly allude to Ezekiel 34–48, but there is some similarity of sequence in the allusions, as Black points out, 'Zech. 11 draws heavily on Ezek. 34 and 37; Ezek. 36 is a major source for Zech. 13; and Ezek. 38 provides much of the conceptual framework of Zech. 14.'[64]

The internal evidence for Zechariah 9–14's dependence on Ezekiel 34–48 is confirmed by early interpretation that regards the two texts

63.   Black 1991: 50.
64.   Black 1991: 50.

as foretelling the same events. The earliest indication of such a view may be LXX Ezek. 37.16-20, which renders Hebrew עץ, *stick*, as ῥάβδος, *staff*, possibly in order to agree with מקל, *staff*, at Zech. 11.7 (also rendered ῥάβδος in LXX). Better evidence is found in eschatological midrashim of the first millennium CE, which repeatedly describe the attack of Gog, who appears in the Bible only in Ezekiel, with citations from Zechariah 12 and 14.[65] Thus *Aggadat Mashiah* (26–30), dating probably from before 300 CE, describes Gog's attack with quotations from Zech. 12.12, 14.3 and 14.5. *'Asereth Melakhim* (4.14-15), dating probably from the mid-eighth century, describes it with quotes from Zech. 12.10 and 14.2, 4, 12. *Pirqe Mashiah* (5.58-67), dating from the early Islamic period, cites Zech. 14.1-2 and 14.3 in reference to Gog and Magog, together with Ezek. 39.17. Sa'adya Gaon cites numerous passages from Ezekiel and Zechariah in reference to the one sequence of eschatological events, which includes the attack of Gog and Magog.[66] *ARN* 34 refers to the war of Gog and Magog with a quote from Zech. 14.4.[67]

Other evidence that these texts were early regarded as referring to the same eschatological events may be found in rabbinic traditions that conflate the resurrection of the dead and the splitting of the Mount of Olives, the former event being described, metaphorically or otherwise, at Ezek. 37.12 but not in Zechariah, and the latter in Zechariah but nowhere else. The Codex Reuchlinianus text of *T. Zech.* 14.4 adds, preceding the splitting of the Mount of Olives, the words, 'At that time the Lord will take in his hand the great trumpet and will blow ten blasts upon it to revive the dead.' The north wall of the mid-third-century synagogue at Dura-Europos contains, in the 'Ezekiel Cycle', a painting of a mountain split in the middle that has dead bodies within it. In the following picture the dead are raised by angels.[68] These would appear to be early versions of the idea that occurs later in *t. Song* 8.5:

---

65.   The text of these midrashim, with remarks regarding their dating, is given in Appendix 1.

66.   Sa'adya, *Kitab al-'Amanat*, VIII.v-vi (Rosenblatt 1948: 302-312).

67.   'Ten descents did the *shekhinah* make into the world:... And one will take place in the future, in the days of Gog and Magog, as it is said, *And his feet shall stand that day upon the Mount of Olives*' (Zech. 14.4).

68.   Black 1991: 149-50.

> When the dead rise, the Mount of Olives will be cleft, and all Israel's dead
> will come up out of it. Also the righteous who have died in captivity, they
> will come by way of a subterranean passage and will emerge from beneath
> the Mount of Olives.

Thus ancient interpretation recognizes the dependence, or at least the similarity, between the two texts. Rashi seems to be summing up such traditions when he says at his comment on Ezek. 38.17, 'Zechariah also prophesied concerning the wars of Gog and Magog: *And I will gather all the nations,* etc.'[69] (Zech. 14.2); and, at his comment on Zech. 14.2, where he names Gog as the leader of that invasion.

Thus both internal parallels and ancient tradition suggest that Ezekiel's schema, or something very like it, underlies Zechariah 9–14. This seems to suggest that the writer or compiler of Zechariah 9–14 is deliberately setting out to re-describe the events of the eschatological programme in Ezekiel. That is not to say that he does not insert additional material or reinterpret events. He does.[70] He employs Ezekiel's 'stick' imagery to represent Israel's coming disunity, rather than unity, as in Ezekiel (Ezek. 37.15-22; Zech. 11.14). He adds a further exile following the future ingathering (Zech. 13.8–14.2). He also adds the death of a latter-day shepherd-king, whose description seems substantially dependent on Isaiah 40–55 and the 'servant songs' in particular (Zech. 11.17; 12.10; 13.7).[71] These issues shall be discussed in Chapter 7. But additions aside, the underlying schema of Zechariah 9–14 seems similar to that of Ezekiel 34–48, and to be modelled on it.

Joel, like Zechariah, shows substantial dependence on earlier writings, as a number of commentators note.[72] Ogden comments,

> One of the most intriguing features of Joel is its extensive quotation of
> other prophetic writings. We may generally state that where such parallels
> exist it is Joel who has done the borrowing... The reason for this con-
> clusion is that Joel places those materials within his own particular

---

69.   וזכריה שאף הוא נתנבא על מלחמות גוג ומגוג ואספתי את כל גוים

70.   Smith 1984: 271; Hanson 1975: 344; Black 1991: 75-76, all note that the writer of Zechariah 9–14 has reversed and supplemented the themes of Ezekiel 34–48.

71.   This has been argued by a number of scholars, including Rudolph 1976; Lamarche 1961: 124-30; Mason 1977: 88; Ackroyd 1962: 654; Mitchell, Smith and Bewer 1912: 331; Black 1991: 51, 86ff.; Wolff 1942: 40.

72.   Smith 1898: II, 384; Ogden and Deutsch 1987: 12; Wolff 1977: 5, 10. Other commentators note particular examples of borrowing (Prinsloo 1985: 58; Myers 1960: 95).

expressions. For example, Joel incorporates 2.13-14, which echo thoughts from Jonah 3.9 and 4.2, into a section carrying his basic 'before and after' theme. Sometimes Joel turns the borrowed statement around— 2.3b reverses Isa. 51.3; 2.21 similarly treats Ps. 126.3; 3.10 reverses Isa. 2.4. Virtually all of Joel's quotations come from other prophets, and the list is quite extensive.[73]

G.A. Smith, offering different grounds for Joel's dependence, reaches a similar conclusion.

> The literary parallels between Joel and other writers are unusually many for so small a book. They number at least twenty in seventy-two verses. The other books of the Old Testament in which they occur are about twelve. Where one writer has parallels with many, we do not necessarily conclude that he is the borrower, unless we find that some of the phrases common to both are characteristic of the other writers, or that, in his text of them, there are differences from theirs which may reasonably be reckoned to be of a later origin. But that both of these conditions are found in the parallels between Joel and other prophets has been shown by Prof. Driver and Mr G.B. Gray. 'Several of the parallels—either in their entirety or by virtue of certain words which they contain—have their affinities solely or chiefly in the later writings...'[74]

Joel does indeed cite directly from other Old Testament writers in a host of passages. One verse alone, Joel 1.15, has the following close linguistic parallels to other books.[75]

Joel		Other	
1.15	=	Ezek. 30.2	אֲ[הָ]הּ לַיּוֹם
1.15	=	Ezek. 30.3; Obad. 15; Zeph. 1.7; Isa. 13.6	כִּי קָרוֹב יוֹם [לַ]יהוה
1.15	=	Isa. 13.6	כְּשֹׁד מִשַּׁדַּי יָבוֹא

In addition to close linguistic parallels, Joel's eschatological motifs and themes also share many points of resemblance with other writers. Ogden suggests that the background to the outpouring of divine *ruach* in 2.28-29 seems to be Ezek. 39.25-29.[76] The earthquake at the time of the attack (4[3].16) occurs elsewhere only in the eschatological programmes of Ezek. 38.19 and Zech. 14.4-5. The slaughter is to be in a valley (4[3].14), as at Ezek. 39.11. Water flowing from the latter-day temple (4[3].18) occurs elsewhere in the Old Testament only at

73. Ogden 1987: 12.
74. Smith 1898: II, 384.
75. A detailed list of Joel citations from and close linguistic parallels to other prophetic texts is given by Ogden (1987: 56-57).
76. Ogden 1987: 37.

Ezekiel 47 and Zech. 14.8.[77] The similarity between the language of Joel 4[3].2a and Zech. 14.2a is striking. The language describing the divinely initiated alliance of many nations against Jerusalem is similar in each case (Joel 4[3].11-12; Ezek. 38.15-16; Zech. 14.2), as is its purpose in requiting the nations for their maltreatment of Israel (Joel 4[3].2-8, 19; Ezek. 36.5). The pronunciation of שממה, *desolation*, upon Egypt and Edom (Joel 4 [3].19) recalls Ezekiel, for whom the word is a key-term,[78] and in particular Ezek. 29.9-12, 32.15 and 35.3-15, which pronounce desolation against Egypt and Edom. All this suggests that Joel 3–4 [2.28–3.21] intentionally describes the same programme of eschatological events as Ezekiel 34–48 and Zechariah 9–14. This conclusion is supported by rabbinic tradition. Kimhi, who equates the programmes of Ezekiel and Zechariah, says also of Joel 4[3].2 that the nations it describes will come with Gog and Magog, and that this is the same event as is described in Ezek. 39.2.[79]

e. *Summary*
Ezekiel 34–48, Zechariah 9–14 and Joel 3–4 seem to present eschatological programmes that are similar in their broad outlines. This similarity apparently derives from the dependence of Zechariah and Joel upon Ezekiel. There may also be some influence between Zechariah and Joel. These eschatological programmes comprise a sequence of gatherings to Zion. First, scattered Israel, with an emphasis on the Josephites, gather from exile. Secondly, hostile nations gather against them. Thirdly, following Israel's deliverance, they and the survivors of all the nations will worship Yhwh at the appointed feasts in Jerusalem (Ezek. 45.13–46.24; Zech. 14.16-21). Thus the envisaged sequence of gatherings is as follows.

Ingathering of scattered Israel from exile (particularly Josephites)	Ingathering of nations against Jerusalem	Ingathering of Israel and nations to worship on Zion

That a distinct programme such as this formed part of the conceptual furniture of ancient Israel is confirmed by a similarity between it and

77. Myers may be correct in observing that the common background to this idea, from which all three writers borrowed, is Isa. 8.6 and its probable reference to the waters of Siloam (cf. Neh. 3.15).

78. Ezek. 6.14; 7.27; 12.20; 14.15, 16; 15.8; 23.33; 29.9, 10, 12 (× 2); 32.15; 33.28, 29; 35.3, 4, 7, 9, 12, 14, 15 (× 2); 36.34.

79. Kimhi, *Comm. on Joel* 4.2.

the motifs of the Baal Cycle, when analogy is drawn between Baal and Yhwh on one hand and Yam-Sea and the nations on the other. The connection between Baal and Yhwh is clear enough. Each was their nation's representative deity, each the dweller on the holy hill, each the cloudrider (Baal III.iv.8; cited above, p. 131; Ps. 68.5 [4]). A connection between the restless, surging nations and the sea is made by a number of commentators. C. Kloos maintains that the biblical theme of Yhwh's combat with the Sea, in Exodus 15, Psalm 29 and elsewhere, is largely derived from Canaanite mythology.[80] Jeremias suggests that Yhwh's triumph at Yam Suph has been placed in the framework of mythological battle with the sea.[81] Day maintains that the biblical theme of conflict with the nations is a historicization of Yhwh's conflict with the Sea.[82] Bentzen says that the revolt of the kings of the earth is 'an historification of the mythical powers of the Chaos'.[83] Certainly, the themes of Yhwh's war with the sea and its dragon, on the one hand, and with the nations, on the other, are equated in a number of biblical passages.[84] Bearing these parallels in mind, the following similarity in the Canaanite and Israelite sequences is discernible. The divine lord rules on his holy hill. Surging forces mount an attack against him, displace him and drive him away. (For Yhwh, along with his people, leaves Zion when it is overwhelmed by the nations [Ezek. 10.4-22; 11.22-23]). There follows a conflict between the divine lord and the usurper in which the latter is slain. Thereafter the divine lord returns to his mount, receives tribute, rebuilds his palace, and rules there, receiving tribute to himself.

Baal II	*Baal III*	*Baal IV*
Baal ousted. Returns to Sapunu	Baal's conflict with Yam-Sea. Yam is slain	Worshippers gather to Sapunu with tribute
Ingathering of scattered Israel from exile (particularly Josephites)	Ingathering of nations against Jerusalem	Ingathering of Israel and nations to worship on Zion

---

80.	Kloos 1986: 213-14.
81.	Jeremias 1965: 96.
82.	Day 1985: 139.
83.	Bentzen 1955: 20.
84.	Exod. 15.1-18; Isa. 8.5-8; 17.12-14; 30.7; 51.9-11; Jer. 51.34; Ezek. 29.3-5; 32.2-9; Hab 3; Ps. 18.5-18 [4-17]; 65.8 [7]; 68.23 [22]; 77.17-21 [16-20]; 87.4; 144.7-8 [18-19]. Most of these texts are discussed by Day (1985: 88-140).

There are, of course, differences between even the biblical programmes. Different narrative standpoints, for instance, lead to different perspectives on the ingathering. Ezekiel regards both Judah and Ephraim as absent from the land and in need of gathering (37.11-21); Zechariah regards only Ephraim as absent and in need of gathering, while Judah is present, but in need of strengthening (10.6). But, such differences apart, there are broad similarities between the motifs of these programmes. It is surely plausible to suggest that by early second temple times, some Israelites, at least, regarded such eschatological programmes as defining their expectation of future events.

3. *Further Ingathering Programmes in the Biblical Prophets*

Ezekiel maintains that its predicted eschatological conflict is not self-originated, but an established tradition among Israel's prophets (38.17; 39.8). As Davidson notes,

> The prophet is not the author of the idea of this invasion. It has been predicted of old by the prophets of Israel, prophesying over long periods (xxxviii.17, xxxix. 8). Neither is it probable that the idea was one read out of certain prophecies merely by Ezekiel. More likely it was an idea widely entertained.[85]

Zechariah 9–14 and Joel 3–4, by their heavy reliance on earlier prophets, imply that they too are consciously retelling earlier traditions. The writer of Jeremiah also regarded impending massive war as a recurrent theme among his predecessors (Jer. 26.17-23; 28.8). It is therefore worthwhile to consider briefly other prophetic books in order to see what motifs they may contain and what programmes of future events may be implied in them. It is worth noting at the outset that the following passages are not all as consistently eschatological as Ezekiel and Zechariah, whose anticipated events are set in the distant future. They tend to mix distant eschatology with 'near eschatology' and history. Nor is the motif sequence always as complete as in Ezekiel and Zechariah. Nonetheless, the same tripartite motif-sequence is discernible. As in Ezekiel and Zechariah, the narrative standpoint leads to different views of the anticipated programme of events.

---

85. Davidson 1906: 273-74.

a. *Zephaniah*

An eschatological tone is discernible throughout Zephaniah. There are references to יוֹם־יהוה (1.14), יוֹם אַף־יהוה (2.2), בַּיּוֹם הַהוּא (3.16) and בָּעֵת הַהִיא (3.19, 20). The book opens with a description of Yhwh's day of wrath as a fearful judgment on the earth in general (1.2-3), and Jerusalem in particular (1.4-18). Then Israel are exhorted to *gather together* and seek Yhwh before the day of wrath (2.1-2). Given the book's narrative standpoint in Josiah's time[86] this would seem to be an exhortation to all Israel, and particularly to those Ephraimites remaining in the north, to gather to Jerusalem for Josiah's passover, one aspect of which appears to have been an attempt to gather the remnant of Ephraim (2 Chron. 34.9; 35.18; 3 Ezra 1.21; *b. Meg.* 14b; *b. Arak.* 33a).[87] Then follows a series of prophecies against individual nations: Philistia, Moab, Ammon, Cush and Assyria (2.4-15). They will be destroyed by Yhwh (2.4-15), by Israel's hand (2.9), in recompense for their malevolence to Israel (2.10). There follows a brief message of judgment against Israel (3.1-7). Then it is said that Yhwh will gather all nations to pour out his wrath upon them (3.8). The survivors be purified and will worship and serve him, both in their own lands and in bringing tribute to him in Jerusalem (2.11; 3.9-10). Israel will be faithful to Yhwh and honoured among the nations (3.11-13;

---

86. The dating at Zech. 1.1 and the absence of any reference to the staggering event of Josiah's death suggests the prophecies that form Zephaniah were written during Josiah's lifetime. However, if those commentators who assign a later date to the final form of the book are right (see Hyatt [1962: 642] and Williams [1963: 83-85], who propose a date in Jehoiakim's time, and Smith and Lacheman [1950: 137-42], who assign the book's final form to 200 BCE, reckoning only 1.4-13 as authentic Zephaniah), then the absence of any reference to Josiah's death must still be taken as indicating a deliberate adoption of a narrative standpoint in Josiah's time.

87. I am not aware of this idea in other commentators. Gaster suggests the oracle was delivered at the autumn Feast of Sukkoth, because the description of the desolation of the earth in 1.2-3 suggests 'descriptions of the languishing earth in myths connected with the 'vanishing and returning' (or 'dying and reviving') deities of fertility' (Gaster 1969: 679). However the historical books make no mention of Josiah's keeping Sukkoth, whereas much is made of his celebration of Passover (2 Kgs 23.21-23; 2 Chron. 35.1-19; 3 Ezra 1.1-20). If Zephaniah is of post-Josianic origin, then 2.1 may be a veiled exhortation to later groups of scattered Israelites to gather together. Such groups might be Ephraimites after the Babylonian destruction (cf. Jer. 41.5) or Babylonian Jews after Cyrus's decree. Nonetheless, the narrative viewpoint of the text remains Josianic (1.1), and so the primary referent of 2.1 should be sought in the events of Josiah's time.

19-20). Finally, it appears that at the time the enemy is turned back a
further ingathering of Israel is to take place (3.15, 19-20). This is to
consist of those who have been scattered, which, given the date, or
ostensible date, of the prophecy in the reign of Josiah (1.1), would
seem to indicate the ten tribes. This would suggest that the prior gathering of Israel in 2.2 was partial. The motif-sequence is similar to that
in Zechariah and Ezekiel.

Gathering of Israel.	Gathering of nations.	Gathering of ten tribes.
Given the narrative	Attack and deliverance	Nations worship Yhwh
standpoint, particularly		in Jerusalem, together
Ephraim		with Israel

b. *Micah.*
A similar sequence of motifs is discernable in Micah 4. The passage
4.1-8 is, as Smith notes, 'freighted with eschatological overtones',
indicated especially by such phrases as באחרית הימים (4.1) and ביום
ההוא.[88] It contains two oracles of hope.[89] The first depicts the eschatological vision of all nations ascending to worship in Jerusalem (4.1-5).
The second relates that in that day Israel will be regathered and *the
former kingship,* presumably the splendid extent of the united Davidic
monarchy, will return to Daughter Zion (4.6-8). Following this future
vision, 4.9–5.3[4] features three salvation oracles, each beginning
(ו)עתה, which look from Israel's present predicament to their ultimate
deliverance. The first oracle (4.9-10) represents Daughter Zion crying
out in terror, as in the pangs of childbirth. The reason is apparently
that her immediate destiny is capture and exile in Babylon. However,
like the pangs of childbirth, Israel's sorrows will ultimately lead to
new life. Yhwh will redeem them from Babylon. The second oracle
(4.11-13) seems to present quite a different picture: *many nations are
gathered* against Zion to destroy her and gloat over her. But this time
they are gathered for destruction by Yhwh himself, who brings them
as *sheaves to the threshing-floor,* a phrase depicting Moriah's eschatological role in terms of its ancient one (1 Chron. 21.18–22.1). Israel
will thresh the nations and devote their wealth to Yhwh (4.13). The
third oracle (4.14-5.3 [4]) tells how Zion's besieging enemies humili-
ate Israel's judge (4.14). The writer looks forward to the appearance

---

88.   Smith 1984: 36, 39.
89.   The division of Mic. 4.1-5.3 [4] into a sequence of oracles, two of hope,
three of salvation, is suggested by Smith 1984: 37, 39, 40, 41, 43.

of a Bethlehemite *moshel,* a future David, whose worldwide greatness will secure peace for Israel (5.1-3 [2-4]). Until the time of birth (of this child?), Israel is to be forsaken by Yhwh. But when the *moshel* appears the rest of his brothers will return to the children of Israel (5.2 [3]), a phrase suggesting the gathering of a group of exiled Israelites. Given the pre-exilic standpoint of the text, and the Judahite lineage of the *moshel,* a reference to the return of the exiled Ephraimite ten tribes seems likely.

In these five oracles the distinctive motifs of the eschatological programmes repeatedly occur: ingathering of Israel, especially Ephraim; attack by hostile nations; deliverance; golden age; and future Davidic *malkut.* However, it is unclear whether any kind of purposeful programme is implied in the way this material is presented. Particularly puzzling is the discrepancy between the first two salvation oracles (4.9-13). The first indicates attack followed by exile; the second attack followed by deliverance. An attempt to reconcile these might produce a sequence of attack, exile, gathering, attack and deliverance.[90] Taken together with the other oracles, this would produce a programme like the tripartite sequence noted above, with an extra 'attack and exile' motif prefixed.

| Gathering of nations against Jerusalem. Exile in Babylon | Ingathering of Israel | Gathering of nations against Jerusalem. Deliverance | Gathering of Israel and nations to worship on Zion. Davidic *malkut.* Return of ten tribes |

Such a programme might seem hopelessly contrived, if it were not for the fact that Zechariah 9–14 also seems to depict two attacks, the first followed by exile, the second by deliverance. Could it be that this writer, like the Zecharian one, was influenced by the ancient Baal Cycle?[91] Or could this passage from Micah have been another of the many influences on Zechariah 9–14? It cannot be said for sure. But certainly these oracles contain all the motifs of the programmes of Ezekiel and Joel, and even of the full Zecharian programme. However their pre-exilic narrative standpoint sees these events beginning with

---

90. The use of עתה at 4.11 need not contradict this. The term is often used to draw attention to an imminent or ideal future time (BDB: 774), as at Mic. 5.3 [4].

91. The full programme of Zech. 9-14 and the influence of the Baal Cycle on its writer are discussed in Chapter 7.

the Babylonian attack and exile, while the post-exilic Zecharian writer continued to regard them as future events even in his day.

c. *Isaiah*

Portions of Isaiah indicate similar motifs, although none contains the entire sequence found in the above texts. Isaiah 27 is eschatological in tone, the slogan ביום ההוא occurring throughout (27.1, 2, 12, 13).[92] There are hints of an eschatological programme in Isa. 27.12-13. It describes a vast threshing, the gathering of the Israelites one by one, and the coming of the Israelites in Assyria and Egypt to worship in Zion. This *threshing* may indicate an eschatological rout of the nations. This is seen from analogy with other passages that employ threshing imagery similarly (Mic. 4.12-13; Ps. 83.14 [13]), and from the context, which previously foretells the destruction of Leviathan, the tieromorphized forces of chaos (27.1). At that time the Israelites will be *gathered one by one*, a phrase signifying the completeness of the gathering, which Slotki paraphrases, 'Not a single exile will be left behind.'[93] Whether they are gathered before, during or after the conflict is not stated, although the text's simple order of events might suggest the last of these. Those lost in Assyria who are to return are the scattered tribes of the northern kingdom (2 Kgs 15.29; 17.6).[94] Who those in Egypt are is not so clear. If the text is post-exilic it might refer to such groups as those mentioned in Jeremiah 42–43.[95] But there seem to have been Israelite groups in Egypt before that time (Hos. 11.11; Zech. 10.10), possibly taken there as captives (1 Kgs 14.25-26; 2 Chron. 12.2), and a reference to other earlier Israelites in Egypt cannot be excluded. What can probably be said of this passage is that it seems to predict the return of the ten tribes and their worship in Zion at, or after, the eschatological conflict. There may or may not be a reference to the exiled southern kingdom.

The final chapters of Isaiah are also notably eschatological, fore-telling the creation of new heavens and earth, and a utopian age of

92. Widyapranawa describes Isa. 24–27 as a 'long series of apocalyptic-eschatological prophecies' (1990: 163).

93. Slotki 1949: 125.

94. For an examination of the biblical accounts of the Assyrian captivity in the light of Assyrian records, see Becking 1992: 61-93. He concludes that Assyrian texts confirm the historicity of the biblical accounts (92-93).

95. So Widyapranawa 1990: 163. See also Bruce 1963: 112-13 n. 89.

longevity, happiness and reconciliation with brute creation (65.17-25). In this context appears again the familiar programme of events. First, an ingathering of Israel is the implied background to the chapter, for the return is a major theme in the preceding chapters.[96] After this ingathering, Yhwh will gather all nations *to see my glory* (66.18). The phrase apparently indicates a theophanic conquest in war, for afterwards the *survivors* will testify to Yhwh's *glory* among the nations, and the corpses of those who rebelled will remain visible as an object lesson (66.19, 24). Then the nations, who have now heard of Yhwh's glory, will bear the Israelites *from all the nations* to Jerusalem (66.20). This would include the ten tribes, as Deutero-Isaiah mentions only Babylon as the place of Judah's exile (48.20). The nations will worship before Yhwh, some even being selected as priests and Levites (66.21). The Israelites' *name will stand,* that is, they will be honoured (66.22). All mankind will come regularly to Jerusalem to worship there (66.23).

Isa. 27.12-13	—	War and deliverance	Gathering of ten tribes. Israel worship on Zion
Isa. 66.18-24	Implied ingathering of Israel from exile	Gathering of nations against Jerusalem. Divine deliverance	Gathering of all Israel. Worship of Israel and all nations on Zion

The absence of an initial ingathering of Israel in Isaiah 27 may be because of its dating from before the Judaean exile. Or the sequence may simply be incomplete. There was no obligation always to cite it in full. However both Isaiah 27 and 66 provide the last two motifs of the sequence in order, together with the concomitant ideas of a post-conflict gathering of the ten tribes, and the worship of Israel and the nations on Zion.

d. *Jeremiah*

The book of Jeremiah contains two passages that confirm the tripartite sequence and some of its concomitant sub-motifs. Jer. 3.6-18 can probably be regarded as a single pericope, opening with the time the prophet received the message and ending with an abrupt change of theme and language following v. 18, where prose becomes poetry and utopian vision reverts to recital of Israel's misdeeds. This passage

---

96.   Isa. 11.12; 40.11; 49.5; 49.17,18; 52.11-12; 54.7; 56.8; 58.8.

begins by telling allegorically how Yhwh exiled Israel, that is, the northern kingdom, for unfaithfulness, and proceeds to speak of Judah's unfaithfulness (3.6-10). Judah's exile, though not mentioned at this point, is implied in the later reference to their ingathering from a northern land (3.18). Israel, the northern kingdom, are to return— *one from a town and two from a clan*—to Zion (3.12-14). Then they will have rulers after Yhwh's heart and will multiply in the land (3.16). Jerusalem will be known internationally as Yhwh's seat. All nations will gather there to honour him and no longer follow evil (3.17). Judah and Israel will dwell together in the land, presumably worshipping and serving Yhwh faithfully, for these utopian events could hardly be imagined if Israel were still faithless (3.18). The motif of the nations' attack does not occur. But their homage at Jerusalem would imply that some kind of great international theophany and vindication of Israel has occurred. However, the absence of the eschatological attack motif does not signify ignorance of it, at least at the editorial level. For it occurs in the following chapter again in the context of a partial programme of future events. A *shofar* is to be blown throughout the land and the people exhorted to gather to Zion for safety (4.5-6), for a *destroyer of nations* is coming to lay waste the land and besiege Jerusalem (4.7, 16-17). The utopian aftermath does not follow here, as in the preceding chapter. But a utopian conclusion can probably be imagined, not only because of the preceding chapter, but also because of the insistence elsewhere in Jeremiah on Israel's ultimately happy end (e.g. Jer. 33.6-26).

A similar sequence of motifs can be discerned in the pericope Jer. 23.1-8. Yhwh will gather his flock *from the north country and from all the lands* (23.8), a phrase denoting the Josephites in particular who were exiled in Assyria in the north (2 Kgs 17.6; 1 Chron. 5.26), rather than in southern Babylonia, where the Judahites were taken. He will raise up for them a righteous Davidic king (23.5). *In his days Judah will be saved* (ישׁוע), *and Israel will live in safety*, an expression that would appear to denote deliverance and victory at a time of military threat and an ensuing peaceful *malkut* for the reunited 12 tribes (23.6). Then they will worship Yhwh, confessing that their latter deliverance surpasses the former Egyptian deliverance (23.7-8). The king's title, יהוה צדקנו, *Yhwh our Vindication,* suggests that Israel's vindication is internationally acknowledged (23.6). The motif sequences in these passages are as follows:

Jer. 3.6-18	Partial ingather-ing of 'northern kingdom'	(Implied theophany and vindication of Israel)	Reunited Israel worship and serve Yhwh together with the nations
Jer. 4.5–6.30	Gather to Zion	Attack of nations	
Jer. 23.1-8	Ingathering of Israel, particu-larly Josephites	Judah will be saved in the time of the righteous Davidic king	Reunited Israel worship Yhwh. They are vindi-cated before the nations

The separate stages of the eschatological programme occur else-where in Jeremiah. Chs. 30–33 are the largest sustained treatment in the Bible of the future ingathering of Israel, with a particular empha-sis on the restoration and gathering of Ephraim in 31.[97] The theme of massive future war also occurs elsewhere in Jeremiah (Jer. 28.8), where it is regarded as an ancient idea (26.18).

4. *Frequent Motifs of the Eschatological Programmes*

Some important motifs, which occur repeatedly in these eschatological programmes, require to be briefly discussed individually.

a. *The House of David*
The eschatological programmes depict latter-day Israel ruled by *bet*-David. It seems to be implied that a Davidic king will be present at the time of the ingathering, and possibly instigate or inspire it (Ezek. 35.23; Zech. 9.9-11; Mic. 5.2 [3]). *Bet*-David will fight in the eschato-logical conflict (Zech. 13.8-9; Joel 4.2) and afterwards rule reunited Israel and the whole earth from Zion (Ezek. 44.3; 46.16-18; Jer. 3.17; 23.3-6; Mic. 4.8-5.1 [2]; Zech. 9.9-10). This is in keeping with ideas about the eschatological role of the house of David elsewhere in the prophets. Isaiah 11 describes a Davidic king who will gather and reunite Israel (vv. 12-13), destroy all opposition (vv. 4, 14-16), and

97. The reference to the redemption of the Joseph tribes is noted by Davidson 1983–85: II, 83. Jer. 31 begins with the announcement that Yhwh will be the God of *all the clans of Israel* (v. 1). Thereafter the repentance and return of the northern tribes occupies the first part of the chapter exclusively (cf. vv. 5, 8, 9, 15, 18-20). Then the return of Judah is predicted in the last verses of the vision (vv. 23-26). The next section of the chapter refers to the return and revival of Israel and Judah together (vv. 27, 31, 36-37).

rule the nations righteously in a utopian age (vv. 1-10). Jer. 30.6 and
33.26 indicate a latter-day Davidic kingdom. Hos. 3.4-5 has latter-day
Israel gather to a restored Davidic *malkut*. Mic. 5.1-3 [2-4] speaks
about a future Bethlehemite ruler, presumably a second David, to
whom his dispersed brothers shall gather. Amos 9.11-14 anticipates
the restoration of *bet*-David, followed by Israel's conquest of the
nations and a utopian age. Other texts refer to an undefined future
leader supervising the gathering (Hos. 2.2 [1.11]; Mic. 2.12-13).

b. *The Gathering of the Josephites*
Another important motif of the eschatological programmes is the
resurgence of the Josephites. Ezek. 37.11 predicts a resurgence of
כל־בית ישראל, which in the context of v. 16 seems either to refer to
Joseph alone, or to give him particular emphasis.[98] Ezek. 37.19-22
predicts the gathering of Joseph along with Judah and the reunification
of both in the land. Joseph is given prominence by being placed first
(v. 19). Zech. 9.11 seems to predict the return of the Josephites from
captivity. Zech. 10.6-12 certainly does. It deals at greater length with
Joseph than with Judah and their coming king (10.3-6a), and describes
in detail their gathering, strengthening and repatriation. Zeph. 2.1-2,
given its narrative standpoint in Josiah's time, appears to be an appeal
for the gathering of the Ephraimites. Mic. 5.3 [4] looks forward to a
group of probably Ephraimitic exiles returning to the nation of Israel.
Isa. 27.13 predicts the return of 'those lost in Assyria' to worship on
Zion. Jer. 23.1-8 predicts a future Davidic *malkut* in which Israel and
Judah will be reunited in the land, the Josephites returning from their
exile in the 'north country', Assyria (Jer. 16.15; 23.8).

It is not entirely clear at which point in the programme this event is
to happen. It seems sometimes to occur in connection with the initial
pre-conflict gathering, and sometimes with the post-conflict gathering.
Ezek. 37.19-22 gives Joseph prominence over Judah, which might
indicate that they will be gathered first. Zechariah 9–14 places the
gathering of Ephraim before the conflict in each of its two versions of
the programme, which may suggest they will be gathered before the
conflict. Zeph. 2.1-2 calls for the nation, including Ephraim, to gather
before the conflict. On the other hand, Isa. 27.13 and Isa. 66.20
appear to place this event after the conflict, while Mic. 5.3 [4] simply

98.   See the discussion of the phrase כל־בית ישראל (Ezek. 37.11) on p. 138 of
this chapter.

indicates that it will take place during the time of the anticipated Davidic ruler. These may represent variant ideas on the theme, possibly influenced by the authors' historical standpoint. Or they might be complementary, if it were allowed that the initial ingathering is partial and that the full gathering will take place only after Israel's vindication. In that case, perhaps a distinction should be made between the remnant of Ephraim living in the north of the land and the ten tribes exiled in Assyria.[99]

The prominence in the eschatological programme of the theme of Josephite resurgence is in keeping with its frequency elsewhere in the prophets. Sometimes their resurgence is described in conjunction with Judah (Isa. 11.12; Jer. 30.3; 31.1; 32.30-37; 50.18-20; Ezek. 16.53-55; 20.40-41; Obad. 20[100]) and sometimes alone (Isa. 9.1-2; Jer. 31.5-20; 49.20;[101] Amos 9.14-15, cf. 1.1; Mic. 5.2 [3][102]). But even when

---

99. Some such harmonization seems to have envisaged by rabbinic writers. See, for instance, the eschatological midrashim in Appendix 1. In *Aggadat Mashiah*, Israel gather in Galilee under a Josephite Messiah before the conflict (19), and 'the exiles' gather to Jerusalem after the conflict (41-43). In *Otot ha-Mashiah*, there is a pre-conflict gathering of Josephites under the Josephite Messiah (6.5) followed by a post-conflict gathering of the tribes (10.1-3). In *'Asereth Melakhim*, Israel gather in Galilee under a Josephite Messiah before the conflict (13) and the nine and a half tribes gather after the conflict (16). In *Nistarot Rav Shimon ben Yohai*, Israel gathers under an Ephraimite Messiah before the conflict (22), and 'all Israel' gathers after the conflict (30). See also Sa'adya, who has the Josephites gather in Galilee under their Josephite Messiah before the conflict (VIII.v; Rosenblatt 1948: 301) and, citing Isa. 66.20, all the remnant of Israel gather after the conflict (VIII.vi; Rosenblatt 1948: 308).

100. This verse is problematic. What is גלת החל־הזה לבני ישראל אשר כנענים? LXX has καὶ τῆς μετοικεσίας ἡ ἀρχὴ αὕτη τοις υἱοῖς Ισραηλ γῆ τῶν Χαναναίων, *And this prince of the captivity (will give?) to the sons of Israel the land of the Canaanites.* I have adopted here the suggestion of RSV, that החל־הזה is a corruption of 'Halah,' one of the places where the exiles of the northern kingdom were scattered (2 Kgs 17.6; 1 Chron. 5.26). But whether this is correct or not, the verse proceeds to speak of Jerusalem exiles repossessing the southern part of the land, and of another group repossessing the north. This other group probably comprises northerners.

101. Unlike modern English translations (RSV, NIV), which make צעירי הצון the object of the sentence, rabbinic tradition (*Gen. R.* 73.7; 75.5-6; 97 [NV in Soncino edn]; 99.2; Sa'adya, *Kitab al-'Amanat,* VIII.v [Rosenblatt 1948: 302]) and AV make it the subject: *Surely the young of the flock* [the children of Rachel] *shall drag them* [the Edomites] *away.* This is by no means an unlikely interpretation, for several reasons. (1) The question, *Who is the chosen one I shall appoint for this... Who is the*

the resurgence is in conjunction with Judah, the Josephites seem to receive particular prominence. Those passages that mention both groups place Joseph first (Isa. 11.12; Jer. 30.3; 32.30, 32; 50.20; Obad. 20). And in describing the repatriation of the whole nation, Jer. 50.18-20 refers to areas only in Josephite territory. The resurgence of the Josephites is a frequent theme in post-biblical literature also.[103] The only known dissenter was Akiva, whose view is said to have been publicly censured (*b. Sanh.* 110b).

c. *The* Shofar
Every mention but one of the *shofar* in prophetic literature occurs in the broad context of an eschatological programme.[104] In the programme of Zech. 9.9-17, it seems to signify coming victory in the ultimate holy war: *Lord Yhwh sounds the shofar and marches in the storms of the south* (9.14). In the brief programme of Isa. 27.12-13, a great *shofar* will be blown at the time of the conflict and the scattered Israelites will gather to Zion (v. 13). In other passages it signifies jeopardy rather than salvation. Preceding the programme of Joel, the sounding of the *shofar* on Zion appears to be a ritual at time of national threat, in order to gather the people together (2.15) and possibly to put Yhwh in remembrance of their plight (2.1). Following the programme of Jer. 3.6-18, the *shofar* is to be sounded throughout the land in order to gather the people to Zion before disaster comes from the north (4.5). At Zeph. 1.16 the day of the Lord is a day of *shofar* and *teru'ah,* suggesting anguished plea, by means of the *zikhron* ritual,

---

shepherd will stand against me? (Jer. 49.19) goes unanswered if the *young of the flock* is not the subject of v. 20. (2) The *young of the flock* is an apt designation for the children of Rachel (רחל, *ewe*), the shepherdess (Gen. 29.9), who is herself referred to as הצעירה, *the young one,* at Gen. 29.26. (3) As noted above, the resurgence of Joseph is a frequent theme throughout Jeremiah, and also in the nearer context of 49.20 (50.18-20).

102. It refers to a time of 'gestation' after which the brothers of the Bethlehemite *moshel* (v.1 [2]) *will return to the sons of Israel.* This would appear to represent one group of Israelites resident in the land and the rest (יתר, 'remnant') in exile (Smith 1984: 44). A reference to the return of the northern kingdom's exiles is therefore likely.

103. Tob. 13.13; *1 En.* 57.1-2; 90.33; *Sib. Or.* 2.170-73; *1 Bar.* 78.1-7; 84.2-10; *4 Ezra* 13.12, 39-47; *m. Sanh.* 10.3; *Otot* 10.1; *As. M.* 4.16.

104. The exception is Amos 3.6, where the reference is to the divine origin of a threatened military disaster.

for divine assistance. In each of these passages, whether the context is deliverance or disaster, the *shofar* is blown either before or at the time of the impending conflict. There is no clear reference to its being blown in the post-conflict *malkut*. This is consistent with the Asaphite tradition's depiction of *hazozerah* and *shofar* being used for gathering and *zikhron* in time of war.

5. The Language of the Ingathering Programme

A comparison of all the biblical texts referring to the ingatherings of the prophetic eschatological programme suggests that there may have been a tendency to use particular verbs for its particular aspects.[105] In texts referring to the gathering of Israel, the predominant verb is קבץ, with some thirty occurrences to ten of אסף. In reference to the gathering to war, אסף predominates, with eight occurrences to six of קבץ. In regard to the gathering to worship, עלה predominates, with seven occurrences to six of קבץ and two of אסף.[106] The programme in Zechariah 9–14 seems to be, in this as in other things, a paradigm or crystallization of earlier tendencies. It uses קבץ in regard to the gathering of the exiled Josephites (Zech. 10.8, 10), אסף for the subsequent gathering of the nations against Jerusalem (Zech. 12.3; 14.2), and עלה for the gathering to worship at Sukkoth on Zion (14.16-19). Other verbs used include the infrequent התקשש, קוה, לקט and כנס, and also בוא, השיב and הוציא, which occur more regularly, but whose frequency throughout the Bible renders their particular use undistinctive. Thus the key verbs employed for the different ingathering stages of the prophets' eschatological programme are somewhat as follows.

Gathering of Israel from exile	Gathering of hostile nations	Ascent to worship on Zion
קבץ (also אסף)	אסף (also קבץ)	עלה (also קבץ and אסף)

6. Summary

A number of biblical texts feature what may fairly be described as programmes of eschatological events. The best examples are Ezekiel 34–48, Zechariah 9–14 and Joel 3–4, which contain detailed

---

105. These texts are cited in Appendix 2.

106. A further occurrence of עלה may refer to the ascent to worship, if its ironic use at Ezek. 38.9 is included, where Gog ascends to Jerusalem to be a sacrificial offering at Yhwh's festive feast for the wild beasts and birds (39.17-20).

programmes, apparently dependent on similar ancient traditions. Zechariah and Joel seem also to be dependent on Ezekiel, and to be attempting to describe the same events. Although they differ in detail, there is substantial agreement in their broad picture. Yhwh will gather scattered Israel to the land promised to their forefathers. Thereafter an alliance of hostile nations will gather to attack them. Yhwh will destroy the invaders and save Israel. Then Israel will worship Yhwh on Zion, together with the survivors of the nations. The same programme, either in eschatological or generally future time, is discernible also in Zephaniah, Micah, Isaiah and Jeremiah. If to these texts is added Daniel, where a similar programme is also found,[107] and other texts that seem to contain particular aspects of it,[108] then it seems plausible to suggest that some sort of eschatological programme, with motifs similar to those identified above, was widely recognized in biblical times and is an important aspect of Old Testament eschatology. Moreover a similar sequence of motifs occurs in the Ugaritic Baal Cycle, and there is evidence that ingathering was regarded as an eschatological divine action in Mesopotamia. This suggests that the Israelite motifs and sequences were neither particularly Israelite nor a particularly late development, although the more consistently eschatological form of the programme may have been unique to Israel.

107. The eschatological programme of Dan. 9.24-27 resembles the full form of the programme in Zechariah 9–14. It shall therefore be discussed in Chapter 7, following the discussion of the Zecharian programme.

108. The individual motifs of the eschatological programme, ingathering of Israel, ingathering of hostile nations, and ingathering to worship, occur in Deuteronomy, Nehemiah, Hosea, Amos, Obadiah and 2 Chronicles. The relevant passages are cited in Appendix 2. A case could probably be made for finding implied motif-sequences in some of these texts, such as 2 Chron. 36.23. But that is beyond the scope of this work.

Chapter 6

ESCHATOLOGICAL PROGRAMMES AND THE PSALTER

It is now time to ingather the various themes I have investigated so far. I have suggested that the Psalms of Asaph and the Songs of Ascents might plausibly be read as representing quite individual and distinct sequences of eschatological ingathering. The Asaph Psalms could be taken as depicting a sequence of latter-day events beginning with the ingathering of Israel to judgment in a time of national distress and desolation, and culminating in the gathering of a ten-nation alliance against them. The Ascents could be read as representing Israel being gathered for festive thanksgiving at the latter-day Feast of Sukkoth in the aftermath of deliverance from enemies who arose overwhelmingly against them.

I also investigated eschatological programmes in the prophetic books and found that ingathering was one of their principal themes. A number of ingathering motifs usually occur in the same sequence. The most important ones are, first, an ingathering of Israel from exile, secondly, an ingathering of hostile nations against Israel, and thirdly, an ingathering of Israel and the surviving nations to worship on Zion.

On the basis of this research I now wish to make my central proposition, which is that a resemblance can be discerned between the event-sequences of the psalm-cycles on the one hand, and the eschatological programmes of the prophetic literature, particularly Zechariah 9–14, on the other. Specifically, I would suggest that the themes and events of the Psalms of Asaph correspond to the early, pre-deliverance stages of the eschatological programme, from the ingathering of Israel to the conflict, while the themes and events of the Songs of Ascents correspond to the post-conflict ascent to worship at Sukkoth, as described in Zechariah 14. This may be demonstrated as follows:

The Asaph Psalms	(Pss. 50, 73–83)	The Ascents (Pss. 120–34)
Ingathering of scattered Israel from exile	Ingathering of hostile nations against Jerusalem	Gathering of Israel and nations to celebrate Sukkoth on Zion

In this chapter I shall try to demonstrate the plausibility of this hypothesis by comparing and contrasting the two psalm-cycles directly, the better to see their characteristic features, and relating their characteristics to the motifs of the eschatological programme in Zechariah 9–14 and the other prophetic books. These comparisons shall be made under seven heads: psalm heading and tradition, event-sequence, view of God, condition of Israel, prominent figures, imagery and other characteristics.

1. *Psalm Heading and Tradition*

The key word for the Psalms of Asaph is אסף. It occurs in the heading of all 12 psalms and is the first word of the first divine oracle in the first psalm of the group (Ps. 50.5). This word, as noted earlier, connotes the Levite Asaph, his guild of prophet-musicians, and the themes of ingathering and *mazkir* prophecy connected with Israel's holy war traditions at times of foreign invasion. The key word for the Songs of Ascents, on the other hand, is עלה. It occurs in the heading of all 15 psalms and in the lyrics of Pss. 122.4 and 132.3. It connotes a complex of traditions connected with pilgrimage to and worship at the appointed feasts, particularly the Feast of Sukkoth.

I noted in the previous chapter that the distinctive linguistic elements for each ingathering stage of the prophetic programme are as follows:

Gathering of Israel from exile	Gathering of hostile nations	Ascent to worship on Zion
קבץ (also אסף)	אסף (also קבץ)	עלה (also קבץ and אסף)

The root אסף occurs frequently in regard to the first two gathering stages of the eschatological programme. This would suggest a correspondence between the Psalms of Asaph and the pre-deliverance ingatherings of the prophetic programme. In addition, the *mazkir* and holy war traditions connected with these psalms, in which Yhwh is reminded of Israel's plight by prophetic song and music at times of foreign invasion, are quite appropriate to the prophetic picture of the eschatological onslaught of the nations. The root עלה, on the other hand, is the predominant word in regard to the post-deliverance ascent to worship on Zion. This would suggest a correspondence between the Psalms of Asaph and the later post-deliverance ingathering of the prophetic programme.

It might be objected that the predominance of קבץ in prophetic texts referring to the ingathering of Israel militates against אסף being representative for that stage of the prophetic programme. However a number of considerations suggest that אסף might indeed have been regarded as a representative term for both the pre-deliverance ingatherings.

(1) Both קבץ and אסף are often used interchangeably for both pre-deliverance ingatherings. אסף refers to the ingathering of Israel ten times, קבץ to the gathering of the nations six times. Both terms appear in parallel five times for the gathering of Israel (Isa. 11.12; Ezek. 11.17; Mic. 2.12 *bis*; 4.6) and twice for the gathering of the nations (Mic. 4.11-12; Zeph. 3.8). Clearly both terms were understood as applicable to both ingathering stages.

(2) As shall be seen more clearly in the examination of Zechariah 11–13 in Chapter 7, the attack of the hostile nations is, in a sense, the real culmination of Israel's initial latter-day ingathering. Thus the verb אסף, as particularly denoting the climactic attack, would serve well as a key word for the entire pre-deliverance period.

(3) The verb אסף, connoting Asaph and the *mazkir* tradition, binds together the ideas of Israel's gathering for defence in a time of attack, Yhwh's being petitioned on their behalf, and Israel's holy war rituals. Thus this verb connects the idea of Israel invaded by the nations in a way that קבץ does not.

(4) In biblical times the verb אסף had a wide range of meanings of an ultimate and final nature. It was used of human death, of harvest, of the death of the year and presumably, by implication, of the death of an epoch. This root would therefore be ideal to describe the events of the end of the era preceding the inauguration of God's *malkut*. The root קבץ, which does not share this wide range of teleological meanings, would not serve this purpose as well.

(5) There is some evidence that, in intertestamental times, when the Psalter probably underwent its final redaction, אסף was already beginning to replace קבץ as the key word for both pre-deliverance ingatherings.

In both LXX and the Greek apocrypha and pseudepigrapha the principal verb for ingathering is συνάγω.[1] In LXX it commonly renders all the Hebrew 'gathering' verbs: קבץ, אסף, לקט, קוה, התקשש, and כנס. However there are exceptions, and they are instructive. In every case but one אסף is rendered by forms of συνάγω, the exception being Isa. 58.8, where the translator, apparently wanting to stress the idea of *enfolding*, has used περιστέλλω. קבץ is also regularly rendered συνάγω, but not as consistently as אסף. In several instances it is rendered by other verbs of virtually identical meaning, forms of δέχομαι, for no apparent reason (Jer. 23.3; Ezek. 20.34; Zeph. 3.19, 20). But most instructive of all are those cases in which the two Hebrew verbs occur in parallel, and two distinct Greek verbs would be expected in the translation. The Isaiah translator renders both Hebrew verbs with συνάγω in the two instances where they occur in parallel (Isa. 11.12; 43.9). This merely confirms the predominance of συνάγω as the key term for ingathering. However, in every other case where the Hebrew verbs occur in parallel (Ezek. 11.17; Mic. 2.12; 4.6; Zeph. 3.8), the translators render אסף by συνάγω, and קבץ by forms of δέχομαι. Likewise, the rendering of קבץ by forms of δέχομαι at Zech. 10.8, 10 seems intentionally to point up the distinctive use of the Hebrew verbs in this passage, as was noted in the preceding paragraph. It therefore seems that whenever אסף and קבץ are in competition for the Greek key-word συνάγω, there is a bias toward אסף. However, the increasing dominance of אסף does not seem to have any influence on those texts featuring עלה, which is rendered by Greek verbs other than συνάγω.

This tendency may possibly be discernible in the Dead Sea Scrolls as well.[2] They employ אסף both for the gathering of Israel (1QSa 1.1) and for the gathering of nations against Israel (1QM 14.5). However, קבץ is never, as far as I am aware, employed in eschatological contexts.[3] עלה may be used of the latter-day post-deliverance ascent to Jerusalem in 1QM 1.3. But the text is tantalizingly incomplete. Vermes renders it: '. . . when the exiled sons of light return from the Desert of the Peoples to camp in the Desert of Jerusalem; and after the battle they shall go up [יעלו] from there t[o Jerusalem?].'[4] The reading 'Jerusalem' seems likely. These opening verses of the scroll would appear to summarize its subsequent events, and, while the end of the scroll is missing, the victory song of 1QM 19 suggests that triumphal procession to Zion is in view: *Zion, rejoice greatly! Rejoice, all cities of Judah!* (19.5). Moreover this exhortation to Zion to rejoice, מאדה, seems to allude to Zech. 9.9, and so the consummation of the Zecharianic vision, progress to Jerusalem, might be expected here also. Certainly other suggested readings seem less likely. עלה would hardly be used of progress to Egypt, as Lohse suggests.[5] Egypt from biblical perspective is

---

1.   Apocryphal and pseudepigraphal texts referring to ingathering are cited in Appendix 2.
2.   The eschatological programme implicit in Qumran texts will be discussed in Chapter 7.
3.   At 1QpHab 8.11; 9.5 and 4QpNah 11 it is used in reference to the acquisition of wealth.
4.   Vermes 1987: 105.
5.   Lohse 1964: 181.

down, geographically and otherwise, and never up (cf. ירד at Isa. 30.2; 31.1). It is equally unlikely that it is the nations who will go up after the battle, as Dupont-Sommer suggests.[6] The whole theme of 1QM is the total destruction of the nations (1.5-6). The only possible alternative to 'Jerusalem' would be that in 1QM 14.2, where the ascent is from *the slain* to *the camp*. But that is unlikely to have been considered the ultimate destination of the victorious armies. Thus Vermes's suggestion, that the ascent is to Jerusalem, seems likely, in which case עלה has the same overtones in 1QM's eschatological programme as it has in Zechariah's.

A few facts appear from this. First, the key Greek verb for latter-day ingathering was συνάγω. This is suggested by its overall predominance, even to the extent of the Isaiah translator's rendering parallel occurrences of the two Hebrew verbs by this one word. Secondly, a tendency to link אסף with συνάγω at the expense of קבץ is discernible in LXX. Moreover אסף is the only verb used for latter-day ingathering in the Qumran literature. This suggests that in early second temple times, אסף may have been displacing קבץ for at least the first two aspects of the ingathering programme, the pre-deliverance gatherings of Israel and of the nations against Jerusalem. However, the post-conflict ascent to worship is usually rendered by Greek terms quite distinct from συνάγω, and עלה may be used of this aspect of the ingathering programme in the Qumran literature. There is therefore no reason to think that עלה ceased to be the key-word for the post-deliverance gathering to Zion. I would therefore tentatively suggest that in Hebrew usage of second temple times the key-words associated with the different aspects of eschatological ingathering may have been as follows:

אסף		עלה
Gathering of Israel from exile	Gathering of nations to war	Ascent to worship on Zion

Thus it would appear that there is some ground for regarding אסף as the key-word for the gatherings of the pre-deliverance period and עלה as the key-word for the post-deliverance ascent to worship on Zion. This supports a connection between the לאסף Psalms and the prophetic programme's pre-deliverance period and the מעלות psalms and the post-deliverance period.

As regards the traditions associated with the headings, I noted, in Chapter 3, that the Asaph Psalms seem to be connected with Israel's holy war traditions and in particular with the Asaphites, who apparently were associated with the rituals of sounding the trumpet for gathering and *zikhron* in time of war. I also suggested, in the preceding chapter, that the sounding of the *shofar* occurs frequently in the pre-deliverance period of the eschatological programmes of the prophets, and that its uses there accord with those of Asaphite tradition.

6. Dupont-Sommer 1961: 170.

This similarity of motifs further supports a connection between the Asaph Psalms and the pre-deliverance period of the prophetic eschatological programmes.

I noted, in Chapter 4, that the Songs of Ascents seem to be connected with traditions of temple worship at the Feast of Sukkoth. I also suggested, in the preceding chapter, that Zech. 14.16-19 depicts the post-deliverance *malkut* as being distinguished by observance of this feast, and that Ezekiel sees the celebration of Sukkoth and the other appointed feasts as a characteristic of the eschatological age (45.21-25; 46.9-11). The Songs of Ascents would therefore correspond well to the celebration of Sukkoth in the post-deliverance *malkut* of the prophetic eschatological programmes.

2. *Event-Sequence*

The event-sequence of the Psalms of Asaph begins with an ingathering of Israel to the presence of God (50.5), during which time they are led by a divinely appointed ruler (80.16-18 [15-17]), and ends with a massive attack of allied nations against Jerusalem (83.2-9 [1-8]). This is exactly the sequence of events which characterizes the first stages of the eschatological programme in the prophets.

The Songs of Ascents seem to depict a faithful Israelite living among the nations who forsakes his erstwhile home and makes pilgrimage to worship at the feast in Zion, arriving joyfully and worshipping at the feast there and departing from it in fullness of *shalom*. Such a sequence of events would correspond to the prophetic picture of the remnant of Israel gathering from the lands in the aftermath of the divine deliverance.

3. *View of God*

a. *The Psalms of Asaph: Divine Judgment of the Wicked*
The distinctive theological characteristic of the Asaph Psalms is divine judgment of the wicked.[7] The root שפט occurs 14 times in the Asaph and deutero-Asaph Psalms (50.6; 75.3, 8 [2, 7]; 76.10 [9]; 81.5 [4];

---

7.   This has also been noted by Illman, who points out that conflict, or punishment, or judgment is a theme in every Asaph Psalm. He notes that judgment is sometimes directed at Israel and sometimes at the nations (1976: 30-38, 42-43). It is also noted by McCann 1993: 98.

82.1, 2, 3, 8; 96.13, 13; 105.5, 7; 106.3), and דין thrice (50.4; 76.9
[8]; 96.10). In a few cases this judgment is directed against the
unspecified wicked in general (50.16-21; 73.3-9, 18-20, 27; 75.8-9 [7-
8]). More often it is directed against Israel or against the nations.

Judgment on Israel is a frequent theme. At Psalm 50 *El Elohim
Yhwh speaks and summons earth from sunrise to sunset... He calls to
the heavens above, and to the earth, to judge* [דין] *his people...for
Elohim, is about to judge* [שפט] (vv. 1, 4, 6). Elsewhere in the collection he has judged them by rejecting them (74.1; 77.8-11 [7-10];
78.59), by subjugating them and destroying the temple by the hand of
the nations (74.1-8; 78.59-64; 79.1-9; 80.4-8, 13-14 [3-7, 12-13]), by
ceasing communication with them (74.9), and by putting them to death
in the wilderness (78.31-34). The reason for this judgment is their
disbelief and disloyalty to the covenant (78.21-22, 32, 37, 56-58; 79.8;
81.12-13 [11-12]).

However, the nations, God's instrument of wrath on Israel, also
suffer judgment, as does the whole earth. The nations figure prominently in the Asaph Psalms. The noun [ם]גוי occurs eight times, and
most occurrences of שפט and דין refer to the nations. At Psalm 75 the
powers of east and west will be impotent when God executes judgment
at his appointed time (v. 3 [2] שפט, v. 8 [7] שפט) against the wicked of
the earth (v. 9 [8]). At Psalm 76 God is terrible to the kings of earth
(v. 13 [12]). He uttered דין and arose to establish משפט (9-10 [8-9])
and the enemy were devastated (vv. 4-7 [3-6]). Psalm 82 differs in an
interesting way. God judges the *elohim*, the representative deities of
the nations, rather than the nations themselves. He rises amidst the
divine assembly to pronounce judgment, apparently death, upon them
for their maladministration of the earth (vv. 1, 7). The root שפט
occurs four times, the first and last referring to God's judgment of the
elohim (vv. 1, 7), and the second and third being his indictment of
their failure in judgment (vv. 2, 3).

Six, or possibly seven, further Asaph Psalms contain the idea of
judgment of the earth, although שפט and דין do not occur. In Psalm 74
God, the creator of earth and destroyer of cosmic chaos (vv. 15-17),
is exhorted to arise and no longer withhold his hand from those who
have destroyed his sanctuary (vv. 11, 22, 3-8). Psalm 77 recalls the
exodus, when God displayed his strength among the peoples and
redeemed Israel with his arm (vv. 15-19 [14-18]). Psalm 78 recalls
the judgments on Egypt with references to God's anger, wrath and

indignation (vv. 43-50), when he put his adversaries to *rout* and to *everlasting shame* (vv. 43-50). At Psalm 79 God is exhorted to pour out his anger on the nations that do not know him, to avenge his servants and recompense sevenfold the destruction of Jerusalem (vv. 1-7, 10, 12). Ps. 80.17 [16] is ambiguous, but may contain a wish that the destroyers of Israel perish at the rebuke of God's countenance (v. 17 [16]).[8] At Psalm 81 God will subdue Israel's enemies if they obey him (vv. 14-16 [13-15]). Psalm 83 is a fitting consummation to the theme of judgment of the nations, exhorting God to destroy all the nations that oppose him and his people, as he has destroyed other nations in the past (vv. 2-13 [1-12]). The psalm concludes with a list of fearful destructions and humiliations that will cause them to acknowledge Yhwh's sovereignty over *all the earth* (vv. 14-19 [13-18]).

Only two psalms with the Asaph heading (50, 73) do not refer to the judgment of the nations. However Psalm 50 makes a distinction between those addressed as *my people* and *the wicked* (vv. 7, 16), who presumably are not Yhwh's people. Thus, whether *the wicked* are biological Israelites or *goyim*, they are effectively heathen and under Yhwh's judgment. Likewise Psalm 73 does not mention the nations, but speaks in no uncertain terms about the destruction of the wicked in general (vv. 3, 18-20, 27). This probably applies both to foreigners and Israelites, those who are *far away* from Yhwh and those who are *unfaithful* (v. 27). It appears then that the judgment of the nations is explicit in ten Asaph psalms and implicit in two. This is a significantly higher occurrence than in the Psalter as a whole, where the theme occurs explicitly in only six other psalms (2.1-12; 7.9; 9.6-9, 19-20; 94.10; 96.13; 98.9). Moreover, every one of the four divine oracles in the Asaph group has divine judgment as its theme (50.5-23; 75.3-6 [2-5]; 81.7-17 [6-16]; 82.2-7). This must therefore be regarded as a prominent characteristic of the Asaph Psalms.

8.   There is ambiguity as to whether Israel or her enemies perish in this verse: *It* [the vine] *is burned with fire, it is cut down; from the rebuke of your countenance they perish* or *let them perish* or *they will perish* (יֹאבֵדוּ). Briggs and Briggs argues that the subject is the enemies (1906–1907: II, 207); Tate agrees (1990a: 308). Delitzsch, however, rightly notes that the enemies are at no point named in the context and that the expression is quite consistent with the metaphor of the vine (1887: II, 445). LXX's future tense, ἀπολοῦνται, might more readily refer to the enemies, because Israel's devastation is present fact to the psalmist, not a future one. However, such a viewpoint could well be that of the LXX translator. It must probably be admitted that the Hebrew itself remains ambiguous.

Related to the theme of divine judgment is that of God's anger. There are eight occurrences of אף in the main Asaph collection (74.1; 76.8 [7]; 77.10 [9]; 78.21; 78.31; 78.38; 78.49; 78.50), and one more at deutero-Asaph 106.40. All refer to the anger of God. Elsewhere in the Psalter the term is used of God's anger fifteen times.[9] Thus the Asaph and deutero-Asaph Psalms, which comprise about 10 per cent of the Psalter, contain more than a third of its references to divine אף. Similarly, there are five occurrences of חמה in the Asaph and deutero-Asaph Psalms (76.10 [11] *twice;* 78.38; 79.6; 106.23). All are in some way connected with God's wrath.[10] Elsewhere in the Psalter it is used of God's wrath six times.[11] Therefore almost half the references to divine חמה are found in the Asaph 10 per cent of the Psalter. Again, three of the Psalter's four occurrences of *hithpael* עבר occur in Asaph Ps. 78.21, 59, 62. Other similar words occurring in the collection are the nouns עברה (78.49), one of five in the Psalter, זעם (78.49), one of four, חרון (78.49), one of six, קנאה (79.5), one of three; and the verb אנף (79.5), one of four. Wrath is expressed in other terms. At God's advent as judge *a tempest rages around him,* the same verb, שער, as is used of military wrath at Dan. 11.40. In addition, אש, *fire,* is a common metaphor for anger. It occurs 13 times in the Asaph and deutero-Asaph Psalms (50.3; 74.7; 78.14, 21, 63; 79.5; 80.17 [16]; 83.15 [14]; 89.47, 46; 105.32, 39; 106.18). This is almost half the total occurrences in the Psalter, where it occurs elsewhere 14 or 15 times.[12] Likewise, three of the Psalter's seven occurrences of בער (79.5; 83.15 [14]; 106.18) are found in these Psalms.

The outworking of divine anger is destruction or subjugation. Such terminology abounds in the Asaph Psalms. God will *tear to pieces* the

9. I have discounted the use of the word in describing God as *slow to anger,* for this indicates not his active anger, but his patience (86.15; 103.8; 145.8). The term is also used of human anger (37.8; 55.4 [3]; 124.3; 138.7) and *nostrils* (10.4; 18.9, 16 [8, 15]; 115.6)

10. Ps. 76.10 [11] is an interpretational knot. Nonetheless, it is connected with God's wrath in that he is to be thanked as a result of this wrath, and to gird himself with it. Moreover the context of the entire psalm is God's slaughter of an enemy host.

11. It signifies snake venom at 58.5 [4] *(twice)* and 140.4 [3], and human anger at 37.8.

12. It occurs in some MT MSS at Ps. 18.14 [13]. This however may be dittography. It is absent from other MSS, and these are supported by LXX and 2 Sam. 22.14.

wicked (50.22). He is *glorious, mighty from the mountains of prey* [i.e. the defeated enemy] (76.4-5). God *slew* the Israelites (78.34). Asaph Ps. 75.1 is one of the four psalm headings containing the plea אל־תשחת, *Do not destroy.* This phrase seems to be a plea that God would not destroy Israel. At least, that is what it means at its only other occurrence in the Bible, Deut. 9.26. The midrash on Psalms interprets both phrases similarly.

> *For the leader: Al-tashheth.* These words are to be considered in the light of what Scripture says elsewhere: *For the Lord your God is a merciful God; He will not fail you, nor destroy you* (Deut. 4.31), and also, *And I prayed unto the Lord, and said: 'O Lord God, destroy not your people'* (Deut. 9.26). The Holy One, blessed be he, answered Moses: I will not destroy, as it is said, *And the Lord hearkened to me that time also; the Lord would not destroy you* (Deut. 10.10). Asaph also said to the Holy One, blessed be he: Master of the Universe, even as you listened to Moses, so listen to us.[13]

Thus Psalm 75 seems to reckon that Israel is in imminent peril of destruction by the wrath of God. Other terms of destruction in the Asaph Psalms are אבד (73.27; 80.17 [16]; 83.18 [17]), שבר (74.13; 76.4 [3]; 105.16, 33), חרף (78.66; 79.4, 9), and בהל (83.16, 18 [15, 17]). Sometimes these verbs denote God destroying the nations, and sometimes the nations destroying Israel. But either way, they describe God's judgment, for the Asaph Psalms regard the nations as agents of divine judgment on Israel (78.56-64; 79.5-9).

The reason for God's judgment on the wicked, whether Israel or the nations, is because of their guilt and sin. Such terminology is frequent in the Asaph Psalms. The collection begins with God's arraignment of those who hate his laws, spurn his instruction, break the eighth, seventh and ninth commandments, and forget him (50.16-22). Similarly, Psalm 73 describes the wicked as proud, violent, callous, malicious, arrogant, oppressive, blaspheming heaven and dominating earth (73.6-10). Verbal forms of חטא occur three times in Asaph and deutero-Asaph Psalms (78.17, 32; 106.6). These all refer to Israel's sin, a usage unique to this group in the Psalter.[14] Likewise, one of the Psalter's two uses of חטאת for Israel's sin is at Asaph Ps. 79.9. Three of the Psalter's half dozen or so references to Israel's עון occur in

13. *Midr. Pss.* 75.1.
14. Six more verbal forms of this root occur elsewhere in the Psalms (4.5 [4]; 39.2 [1]; 41.5 [4]; 51.6, 9 [4, 7]; 119.11). All refer to individual sin.

Asaph and deutero-Asaph Psalms (78.38; 79.8; 106.43).[15]

Finally, although the Asaph Psalms perceive God as active in judgment, they perceive him as inactive on Israel's behalf. Particular attention is given to the theme of his arising from inactivity, קום being used three times (74.22; 76.10 [9]; 82.8), עור three times (73.20; 78.38; 80.3 [2]) and קיץ twice (73.20; 78.65) of his arising from sleep. Similarly, the cry *How long?* (74.10; 79.5; 80.5 [4]) denotes God's inactivity, as does *God, be not silent, be not quiet, do not sleep!* (83.2 [1]), and other expressions (74.11; 77.8-10 [7-9]; 79.10). Taken in order these describe what will happen when God arises (73.20), exhort him to arise (74.10, 22), reminisce about his former not arising in mercy and his former arising in judgment (76.10 [9]; 78.38, 65), exhort him to arise (80.3, 5 [2, 4]), describe his arising against the *elohim* (82.1, 8), and exhort him to arise against the nations (83.2 [1]). Yet God is not said to be presently arising on their behalf. In their time of trouble he is inactive.

b. *The Songs of Ascents: Divine Blessing of the Faithful*
In contrast, the Songs of Ascents appear unconcerned with judgment, whether of the nations or of anyone else. דין is absent as are verbal forms of שפט. The noun משפט occurs at 122.5, but only in the sense of civil justice. The nations, rather than suffering judgment, recount Yhwh's great deeds to Israel (126.2). Even the punishment of the wicked is only once mentioned in passing (129.5-8).

The theological characteristic of the Ascents is divine blessing of the faithful. The root ברך occurs 11 times, and אשרי 3. Blessing dicta using other vocabulary also occur (121.8; 122.6-8; 125.5; 128.6). The concept is expressed in other ways as well. For instance, Psalm 121's sixfold repetition of שמר emphasizes the divine protection surrounding the faithful pilgrim; Psalm 125 speaks of Yhwh surrounding the righteous; Ps. 127 highlights divine protection of state and family. Altogether 13 of the 15 Songs of Ascents conclude with some kind of greeting or blessing formula (121.8; 122.8; 124.8; 125.5; 126.5 127.5; 128.6; 129.8; 130.7; 131.3; 132.14-18; 133.3; 134.3). Moreover, the only divine oracle in the collection has as its theme blessing on the house of David, on Zion, and on her citizens (132.14-18).

---

15. Elsewhere it occurs at Pss. 85.3 [2]; 90.8; 130.8. Ps. 103.10 probably refers to Israel. Ps. 130.3 refers to Yhwh's general willingness to forgive, but the context concerns Israel (v. 8).

Those who are blessed are the faithful. Faithful trust is variously expressed: בטח (125.1), קוה (130.5 twice), יחל (130.5, 7; 131.3), ירא (128.1, 4). The formulaic dicta acknowledging Yhwh as helper (121.2; 124.8) also express trust, as does the lifting of eyes in Ps. 123.1. The blessing the faithful enjoy, not found outside Yhwh's land (120.6-7), is שלום, a word occurring seven times in the Ascents.

The theme of divine anger is absent from the Songs of Ascents. Indeed, anger itself is virtually absent. No term describing anger occurs in the collection except אף, once at 124.3, where it refers to the anger of human foes. Israel were delivered from this enmity by Yhwh, and so the term indicates his salvation rather than his wrath. Nor is there any reference to fire. The threat of past enmity at Psalm 124 is likened to water, a less urgent image, suggesting not rage, but unruly cosmic forces. There is no indication in the Ascents of present wrath or destruction, divine or human, against Israel. Ps. 129.5 asks that *all who hate Zion be put to shame and turned back.* But in the context, a reminiscence of former deliverance, this seems to be a general statement that all enmity to Zion is doomed to failure. The theme of present destruction and subjugation is likewise absent from the Ascents. The roots אבד, חרף and בהל do not occur. In Ps. 124.7 שבר occurs once, but describes only the breaking of the fowler's snare that the nations set for Israel. Enmity certainly is referred to in Pss. 123.4; 124.1-8; 129.1-8, but it is in the past, and is now recounted calmly without the violent and destructive language and imagery of the Asaph Psalms. It is beautified in imagery of the natural world and, in Psalm 127, even whimsified in a pun (Pss. 124.7; 129.3-4). This calm about past enmity confirms that Israel has been completely delivered from danger. One is reminded of the words of R. Nachum Yanchiker at the German slaughter of Jews on the invasion of Poland.

> And when the world returns again to stability and quiet, never become weary of teaching the glories, the wisdom, the Torah and the *Musar* of Lithuania, the beautiful and ethical life which Jews lived here. Do not become embittered by wailing and tears. Speak of these matters with calmness and serenity, as did our holy sages in the Midrash *Lamentations Rabbati.*[16]

The theme of sin is also not prominent in the Ascents. There are no arraignments of the wicked, nor descriptions of their deeds. The root

---

16. *Forms of Prayer:* 257.

חמא and its derived forms do not occur. עון does occur twice (130.3, 8), but the context is not iniquity's guilt or punishment, but its סליחה, *forgiveness* (v. 4), the only occurrence of this term in the Psalter. The urgent crying for redemption, noticed in the Asaph Psalms, is absent here. As noted above, *my cry for mercy* (130.2) is probably a citation of the psalmist's past words, and not a present cry. Instead the mood is one of quiet waiting on God (vv. 5-6). There is no sense that this forgiveness is incomplete. On the contrary, the psalmist stresses Yhwh's abundant redemption (v. 7). To be consistent with this, יפדה should probably be viewed as present tense: *It is he who redeems Israel out of all his sins* (v. 8).

The Asaphic theme of God's inactivity or slumber or failure to arise in Israel's defence does not figure in the Ascents. Instead Yhwh is the *guardian of Israel who neither slumbers nor sleeps* (121.4). The only use of קום is at 132.8, where Yhwh is besought to return to his dwelling in the temple: *Arise, Yhwh, and go to your dwelling place, you and the ark of your power.* The similarity of the language to Num. 10.36, where the context is bringing the ark back from war, suggests that the aftermath of victorious battle may be in mind in Psalm 132. Elsewhere in the Ascents Yhwh is not exhorted to arise and deliver Israel; he has already delivered them and so thanksgiving is more appropriate (124.1-8; 126.1-3; 129.1-3). He is also perceived as continuing active among Israel, blessing and keeping the faithful.

In contrast, divine blessing of the faithful does not figure in the Asaph Psalms. ברך and אשרי do not occur, nor is the idea much apparent. Faithful trust does not figure largely either. יחל, ירא and קוה do not occur, and בטח describes only unfaithful Israelites who *did not trust* (78.22). Likewise אמן refers four times to the unbelieving (78.8, 22, 32, 37). Neither do the faithful find שלום. At the term's one occurrence in the Asaph Psalms it is the wicked who enjoy it (73.3).

Thus the two different psalm-cycles have quite different theological flavours. The Asaph Psalms emphasize divine judgment on Israel and the nations arising from divine anger over human misdeeds and resulting in destruction and subjugation. This judgment is directed against Israel for their sins of disloyalty to Yhwh, and against the nations for their malice against Israel. Such a viewpoint would correspond well with the pre-deliverance ingatherings of the prophets' eschatological programmes, which seem to imply God's anger and judgment on Israel in bringing invasion against them. For in the theology of the prophetic programmes disaster comes upon Israel only by divine decree and in deserved recompense for unfaithfulness.[17] God's wrath and anger with the nations for their maltreatment of Israel is also an avowed purpose of his gathering them to destruction at Jerusalem (Ezek. 38.16–39.6; Joel 4 [3].2-8,19).

The Ascents, on the other hand, emphasize divine blessing, arising from reconciliation and forgiveness, and resulting in Israel's prosperity and pre-eminence. Such a viewpoint would correspond well with the prophets' depiction of the period of the post-deliverance ascent to Zion. They emphasize Israel's latter-day purity of devotion and freedom from guilt (Ezek. 39.26; Joel 4[3].21; Zech. 13.2-6) and Yhwh's presence making Jerusalem a place of supernatural splendour and international pre-eminence (Isa. 2.2-4; Ezek. 47.7-12; 22–23; 48.35; Joel 4[3].17-21; Mic. 4.1-3; Zech. 14.8, 9, 16-21).

c. *Divine Names*

A tendency can be discerned in the Bible to use the name *Yhwh* in contexts referring to God's mercy and steadfast love (Exod. 33.19; 34.6), and the term *elohim* in contexts referring to his judgment or universal sovereignty (Exod. 22.7, 8 [8, 9]). This was recognized by rabbinic interpreters, for whom it was a fixed interpretational principle. As Hayman remarks,

> The doctrine of the two divine attributes, Justice and Mercy, runs like a thread through all the rabbinic writings. It is the basis of a fundamental exegetical rule, namely that the divine name *Yahweh* denotes the attribute of Mercy, the name *Elohim*, the attribute of Justice.[18]

An early example is found in Sifre Deuteronomy, redacted not later than the early third century from tannaitic and pre-tannaitic sources.[19]

---

17. At Ezek. 39.23 the Israelites are said to have gone into exile for sin. At Zech. 11.8–12.3 wrath and judgment come on Israel for rejecting Yhwh in his representative. At Joel 2.12-14, repentance may avert the coming disaster; at 4 [3].21 one of the blessings of the golden age will be the pardoning of Israel's unforgiven bloodguilt. For the prophets in general, national disaster was always of divine origin (Amos 3.6). The root of such theology may have been the ancient Song of Moses, which predicted exile as one of the results of disloyalty to Yhwh (Deut. 32.21-25). Even Job, whose treatment of the issue of individual suffering is more theologically complex, does not deny that all human suffering is of divine origin.

18. Hayman 1976: 465.

19. Hammer 1986: 8.

It states,

> *The Lord* (Deut. 3.24): Whenever Scripture says *the Lord*, it refers to his quality of mercy, as in the verse, *The Lord, the Lord, a God merciful and gracious* (Exod. 34.6). Wherever it says *elohim*, it refers to his quality of justice, as in the verses, *The cause of both parties shall come before* elohim (Exod. 22.8 [9]), and *You shall not revile* elohim *(nor curse a ruler)* (Exod. 22.27).[20]

Numerous other passages in rabbinic literature contain a similar teaching, and in every case cite biblical passages to support it, apparently believing that the usage was of biblical origin.[21]

Excursus. A. Marmorstein has suggested that the rabbinic tradition is actually the reverse of the ancient practice, in which *elohim* represented mercy and *Yhwh* judgment.[22] His evidence is a passage from Philo, to which he alludes as follows: 'Philo taught just the reverse; the term θεός = אלהים means εὐεργέτης, the good, the God of love and benevolence; κύριος = אדני expresses God's Lordship, Rulership, Judgement.'[23] Although accepted by Wolfson,[24] this theory has otherwise found little support. Before Marmorstein, Frankel had already suggested that Philo's view was due to his ignorance of Hebrew. More recently, Urbach has plausibly suggested that 'It is the Greek translation that caused Philo to reverse the Palestinian tradition. The rendering of *Y.* by κύριος... gave this word the meaning of lordship and dominion. Whilst in the original text the readers saw the Specific Name as it was spelt... the Hellenistic reader was confronted by the word κύριος in its accepted sense.'[25] Another suggestion might be that Philo intended by κύριος, not the tetragrammaton, but Hebrew אדני, which would be consistent with 'Lordship, Rulership, Judgement', without derogating from the tradition that *Yhwh* signifies mercy. Segal, although considering both Philo and the rabbinic tradition to be responses to a 'two powers' heresy, suggests that the connection of *elohim* with judgment exists earlier than Marmorstein allows, among the first-century *tannaim*, and possibly even in the

---

20. *Sifre*, Piska 27.

21. See Rabinowitz 1971a: 684; *Pes. K.* 149a (Supplement 6 in edn of Braude and Kapstein) cites Exod. 34.6 (Yhwh) and Exod. 22.27 (*elohim*); *Midr. Pss.* 47.2 cites Exod. 34.6 (Yhwh); Zohar on Exodus 173b/174a; Cohen 1945: 156; Buber 1985: 213 (Glossary). See also Kirkpatrick 1902: 277.

22. Marmorstein 1927: I, 43-53.

23. Marmorstein 1927: I, 43. Marmorstein neither cites the Philo passage nor gives any reference. This is a peculiar omission, as he generally gives detailed references. Urbach suggests the passages are *De Plantatione* 86; *De Abrahamo* 124-25 (Urbach 1975: II, 888, fn. to I, 452).

24. Wolfson 1948: I, 224-25.

25. Urbach 1975: I, 453.

book of Jonah.[26] Segal notes that 'Marmorstein has been severely criticized and largely dismissed' for his view.[27] Certainly, his theory that the rabbinic interpretational principle was fundamentally wrong and at variance with all tradition must be regarded as unproven. Subsequent Jewish interpretation has recognized this in continuing to regard the rabbinic principle as valid for biblical interpretation.[28] Moreover, one salient point emerges from this: the association of different divine names with particular manifestations of God's character was established in Philo's time at least. This increases the likelihood of such ideas having existed at a time when they might have influenced the redaction of the Psalter, including the Elohistic Psalter and the Psalms of Asaph.

In view of this, it is certainly interesting that in the Asaph Psalms, where God has in anger scattered his people, is estranged from them, and is judging Israel and the nations, *elohim* is the most frequent divine epithet.[29] It occurs 53 times to denote Israel's God, and 3 times more with reference to other deities (77.14 [13]; 82.1, 6). The singular form *el*, recalling the remote patriarch of the Canaanite pantheon, occurs 19 times, of which 16 or 17 refer to Israel's God.[30] *Elyon,* the term of divine transcendence *sans pareil,* occurs eight times. *Adonai* occurs six times (73.20, 28; 77.3, 8 [2, 7]; 78.65; 79.12). Another feature of the collection is the conglomerating of divine names to emphasize God's majesty and greatness.[31] The first words of the collection are *El Elohim Yhwh* (50.1), 'a majestic heaping together of the Divine names, as if a herald were proclaiming the style and titles

26. Segal 1977: 45 n., where he notes, 'In Jonah 3.8 and 4.3, God's change of mind in regard to the punishment of Nineveh is interpreted by means of God's interpretation of his name to Moses in Exod. 34.6: "YHWH, YHWH is a God merciful and gracious, longsuffering and abundant in goodness and truth."' See also 44-46, 173-80.

27. Segal 1977: 46.

28. See Buber 1985: 213; Cohen 1945: 156.

29. Of course, *elohim* is the most frequent divine epithet throughout Pss. 42-83. But that does not detract from the fact of the phenomenon itself. Moreover, the Asaph Psalms may have been more originally *elohistic* than other psalms in the Elohistic Psalter. They contain only one of the locutions thought to indicate later redaction: *God, your God* (50.7).

30. *The cedars of God* (80.11 [10]) is ambiguous; it can refer to numinous majesty or to Israel's God, or both.

31. This literary technique is used even in modern times to eulogise potentates. Compare the legend which in the 1980s adorned public pictures of a certain African leader: 'His Excellency, the Right Honourable Reverend Comrade Canaan S. Banana, the President of Zimbabwe.'

of a mighty king at the opening of a solemn assize'.[32] Similarly, a sense of intensification of the psalmist's plea is achieved by the increasing divine titles in the refrain of Psalm 80: *Elohim* (v. 4 [3]), *Elohim Tsebaoth* (v. 8 [7]) and *Yhwh Elohim Tsebaoth* (v. 20 [19], also 5 [4]). Similar constructions are *Yhwh Elohim* (76.12 [11]; 81.11 [10]) and *Adonai Yhwh* (73.28). Although *Yhwh* is included in the conglomerated divine titles it is comparatively rare on its own, occurring only eight times.[33] Other divine titles include *God of Jacob* (76.7 [6]; 81.2 [1]), *Holy One of Israel* (78.41), and *Shepherd of Israel* (80.2 [1]). Thus a total of 13 different divine titles or combinations of them occur in the Asaph Psalms. This suggests importunate prayer, like the prayer of a *mazkir,* using all God's names to stir him to action by remembrance of his attributes. The relative absence of *Yhwh* suggests that God's mercy is not strongly perceived.

It is likewise appropriate that Yhwh, denoting mercy and compassion, is predominant in the Ascents, occurring 53 times. The related term *Yah* also occurs twice (122.4; 130.3). Elohim occurs only twice, both times in apposition with Yhwh (122.9; 123.2). Adonai occurs three times (130.2, 3, 6). This small range of names suggests a simple and peaceful faith that does not need to exhaust the range of divine appellatives to attract the deity's attention. Similarly, if the name Yhwh indicates God's favour, mercy, intimacy and nearness, then its nearly exclusive use in this collection suggests that it views him in such a light. Such a viewpoint is appropriate to the Ascents where God has restored fortunes (Ps. 126), and where he protects (Pss. 121; 125), blesses (128.1-6; 132.15-18; 133.3; 134.3), forgives (Ps. 130), maintains covenant (132.11-18), and dwells on Zion (128.5; 132.13-14; 134.3).

Thus the Asaph Psalms predominantly use divine titles, particularly *elohim,* denoting God's judgment and remote transcendent power. The Ascents, on the other hand, use titles denoting his mercy and favour, particularly *Yhwh.* These different emphases are appropriate to the corresponding stages of the prophets' eschatological programme. God's judgment, as noted above, is a feature of the pre-deliverance gatherings of Israel and the nations. His mercy, particularly to Israel, but also to the nations gathering to worship in Zion, is a feature of the post-deliverance *malkut.*

32. MacLaren 1893–1904: II, 117.
33. Pss. 74.18; 75.9 [8]; 78.4, 21; 79.5; 81.16 [15]; 83.17, 19 [16, 18].

Likewise, the terms used to describe Zion and the temple highlight these different perceptions of God. For the Asaph Psalms Zion is the place from which *elohim* blazes forth in judgment (50.2-3; 76.3-10 [2-9]; 80.2-4 [1-3]). Their preferred terms for the temple are קדש (74.3) and מקדש (73.17; 74.7; 78.69). Both terms, deriving from the root קדש, emphasize God's holiness, his numinous otherness, as does היכל קדשך (79.1). The root קדש also appears elsewhere in the group (77.14 [13]; 78.54). This is the holiness that, in the experience of the Asaph Psalms, smote Israel, and estranges them from God. In addition, מועד occurs twice in Psalm 74, once describing the temple (v. 4) and once provincial religious meeting places (v. 8).[34] But these places are now destroyed and, although God will come to judge from Zion (50.2-4), present fellowship with him *in* Zion has ceased (74.3-9).[35] For the Ascents, Zion is the place from which Yhwh blesses (128.5; 132.13-18; 133.3; 134.3).They employ קדש once, apparently to designate the Holy Place in the temple, where hands are raised in prayer before the incense altar (134.2). But generally the preferred term is בית־יהוה suggesting Yhwh's present dwelling in the midst of the city. This term is, significantly, absent from the Asaph Psalms. In every mention of the temple in the Ascents it is envisaged as standing and functioning as a centre of worship.

4. *Israel's Condition*

The condition of Israel is differently represented in each group. In the Asaph Psalms their condition is lamentable. The people have been

34. Gelston (1984: 82-87), and Tate following him (1990a: 249-50), note several possible interpretations of this term. They conclude that it refers to 'non-sacrificial Yahwistic cult centers in Judah, and, as such, precursors of the synagogue' (Gelston 1990a: 85). 1 Macc 3.46 may refer to such a place in its reference to a former 'place of prayer' at Mizpah. Of course, if the Asaph Psalms derive originally from a north Israelite context, as some scholars suggest (cf. Chapter 3, p. 100 n. 29), the reference may equally well be to Yahwistic cult centres, non-sacrificial or otherwise, in Ephraim.

35. Ps. 73.17 might seem to contradict this. But the phrase מקדשי־אל is unusual, the only parallel elsewhere in the Bible being נורא אלהים ממקדשיך of Ps. 68.36 [35], where the precise meaning is again doubtful. Tate notes several possible meanings for the term, including 'the ruined temple site' (1990a: 229). It might equally designate provincial meeting-places, as in Ps. 74.8. Or it may be that, in the canonical sequence of the Psalter, the destruction of the temple is not envisaged until Ps. 74. For Ps. 68.25-32[24-31] represent it as standing.

slain (79.2-3) or scattered abroad in need of gathering (50.5). They
are mocked by the heathen (74.18; 79.4; 80.7 [6]), and feel alienated
from God (74.9), believing their condition to be his judgment on their
disobedience (79.8; 81.12-17 [11-16]) and themselves under his active
displeasure (74.1; 77.7-11 [6-10]; 79.5, 8, 9; 80.5 [4]). City and
temple have been destroyed (74.4-8; 79.1) and remain ruined (74.3;
80.13-14 [12-13]). This was done by foreigners (79.1, 6, 7) who
remain scornful and hostile (74.18, 22; 79.4; 80.13 [14]). Israel
request of God restoration and protection (74.22-23; 79.8). Instead,
they are invaded again by hostile foreign nations, and cry out for
forgiveness and deliverance (79.1, 8; 83). There is no reference to the
present existence of the Davidic monarchy, although David is once
mentioned briefly and the legitimacy of his royal house endorsed
(78.70). Yhwh is asked to remember them (74.18-21; 80.15-19 [14-
18]), forgive them (79.8-9), deliver them (80.18 [17]), and requite
their destroyers (74.22-23; 79.6-12; 80.17 [16]).

In the Songs of Ascents Israel is represented as prosperous after
having come through sore trial. They apparently suffered a devastat-
ing attack by foreign adversaries intent on destroying the whole
nation, but were rescued by Yhwh (Pss. 124; 129.1-4). Now their
captives have returned, and their fortunes have been restored (126.1),
even if the restoration is not yet complete (126.4; 127.1).[36] All the
tribes of Israel are reunited in their land (133.1), and so great is their
change of fortunes that the nations speak of Yhwh's great deeds on
their behalf (126.2). Jerusalem is a city built up and very much
inhabited, where faithful pilgrims of Israel's tribes come and go
(122.1-4). The temple is standing and the appointed feasts have been
restored (122.4, 9; 134.1-2). Zion is like a great spiritual power station from which divine blessing flows to all the land, bringing *shalom*
wherever it goes (Pss. 128, 133, 134). Yhwh protects the city (125.2).
The people feel forgiven and reconciled to Yhwh (130.4). Kingship
has been restored to the house of David; the Lord's *mashiah* exercizes
justice there (122.5; 132.10-17). It appears monarchic stability and
state security exist, for their continuance, rather than their initiation,
is requested, and the tone of the requests, unlike the agonized cries of
the Asaph Psalms, is quiet and confident (132.10; 122.6; 127.1). An

36. 125.3 also indicates incomplete redemption if יָנוּחַ is taken as a future. But if it
is taken as an English present tense denoting a general principle, *the sceptre of the
wicked does not rest*, it need not.

oracle promises the *mashiah* glorious dominion (132.17-18).

Such different presentations of Israel's condition are appropriate to the different stages of the eschatological programme. When Israel initially return from exile to the land their condition is clearly one of adversity. The people, land, city and temple have been desolated and must be rebuilt (Ezek. 38.12; Zech. 14.11; Joel 4[3].2-5, 20). They are surrounded by hostile nations, as the vast alliance soon to gather against them testifies (Ezek. 38.4-16; Zech. 9.13-16; 12.3; 14.2; Joel 4[3].2, 11-14). And, in the Zecharian programme at least, the actual period of the attack is one of acute distress (Zech. 14.1-2). Thus the prophetic depiction of Israel in the latter-day period from their initial ingathering to the nations' attack corresponds with their condition as represented in the Asaph Psalms.

Similarly the prophetic depiction of Israel's latterday *malkut* after the divine deliverance corresponds with their situation as represented in the Ascents. Israel will be prosperous and exalted (Zech. 14.14-21; Ezek. 39.25-29; Joel 4[3].17-21). The tribes will be reunited (Ezek. 37.15-22). They would remember the attack of the nations, but their own ultimate victory and vindication would free the memories of rancour. The nations will confess Yhwh's greatness and his love for Israel (Ezek. 39.21-24). The Davidic king will rule from Zion (Ezek. 34.23-24; 37.24-25; 44.3; 46.16-18; Jer. 3.17; 23.3-6; Mic. 4.8-5.1 [2]; Zech. 9.9-10). Yhwh will dwell there (Ezek. 48.35; Joel 4[3].21; Zech. 14.16-21). The cult and appointed feasts will be re-established, and Israel will worship Yhwh, together with the nations (Ezek. 45.13–46.24; Zech. 14.16-21).

5. *Prominent Figures*

A concern with Joseph is discernible in the Asaph Psalms.[37] The name occurs four times (77.16 [15]; 78.67; 80.2 [1]; 81.6 [5]). It also occurs in deutero-Asaphic Ps. 105.17, which features a short history of Joseph. It does not appear elsewhere in the Psalter. Ephraim, the foremost of the two Joseph tribes, is mentioned at Asaph Pss. 78.9, 67 and

---

37. Many commentators have noted this feature of the collection, including King 1898–1905: II, iv-v; Delitzsch 1887: II, 142; MacLaren 1893–1904: II, 116; Kirkpatrick 1902: 430; Peters 1922: 295; Nasuti 1988: 80. But no consensus exists as to why this should be so. Delitzsch (1887; II, 438) asks, 'Was Asaph, the founder of this circle of songs, of a Levite city in the territory of Ephraim or Manasseh?'

80.3 [2]. Elsewhere in the Psalter the name occurs only in one duplicate passage (60.9 [7]=108.9 [8]). Ps. 80.3 [2] also mentions the other tribes associated with the Ephraim camp of the desert wanderings, Manasseh, and Joseph's full brother Benjamin (Num. 2.18-24). The concern with Joseph may also be reflected in an interest in Jacob, a name that some biblical writers use to indicate the northern tribes in distinction to Judah.[38] It occurs nine times in the collection (75.9; 76.6; 77.16 [15]; 78.5, 21, 71; 79.7; 81.1, 4), slightly less than a third of the 30 references to Jacob in Psalms.

By contrast, Joseph does not figure in the Songs of Ascents, and Jacob occurs only twice, in the epithet *Mighty One of Jacob* (132.2, 5). The dominant figure of the Ascents is David, whose name occurs eight times (122.1, 5; 124.1; 131.1; 132.1, 10, 11, 17).[39] Four lyrics are inscribed or ascribed to him and one to his son Solomon (127.1). The emphasis is on the house of David as a continuing institution, particularly in Psalms 122 and 132, which depict it in full possession of regal authority. There is no request for the restoration of the Davidic monarchy, as at Ps. 89.36-52 [35-51]. This would be expected in a collection so interested in David if the dynasty were in eclipse. In contrast the Asaph Psalms mention David only twice in one brief reference to the past inauguration of his kingdom (78.70-72).

This corresponds with the motifs of the eschatological programme. I noted that the Josephites were often prominent in the first stage of the ingathering (Ezek. 37.19-22; Zech. 9.11; 10.6-12) and that later interpreters held that these tribes would initiate the ingathering and possess Jerusalem before the eschatological conflict.[40]

---

38. *Jacob* can denote the northern kingdom alone (Isa. 17.3-4; Amos 7.2, 5; 9.8; cf. 1.1; 7.9; Mic. 3.1), or even the northern kingdom in distinction to Judah (Mic. 1.5). Of course, like *Israel*, it can also indicate the 12 tribes (e.g. Jos. 7.16). The source of the identification is probably the same as that of the identification of the allonym *Israel* with the northern tribes in distinction to Judah (e.g. Jer. 30.3; 31.27; Hos. 1.4; Amos 1.1; 9.9; *et passim*). Amos 9.7 seems to employ both uses of *Israel* in one verse: v. 7a addresses the *people of Israel*, who, in the context of Amos 1.1, are probably the northern kingdom (cf. 9.9); v. 7b says Yhwh brought *Israel* out of Egypt, which, in the light of surviving exodus traditions, would appear to include the Judahites (cf. e.g. Num. 1.26; 13.6).

39. The fact that several of these references occur in headings does not detract from their significance. There existed a connection between David and the Songs of Ascents in the mind of the Psalter's redactor, even if nowhere else.

40. In addition to the passages cited, see also *Ag. M.* 20; *Otot* 8.6 (cited with a

When the Holy One, blessed be he, in the future will gather Israel from
the four corners of the world, the first whom he will gather will be the
half-tribe of Manasseh, as it is said, *Gilead is mine, and Manasseh is mine*
(Ps. 60.9 [7]). After that, Ephraim, as it is said, *Ephraim is the defence of
my head* (Ps. 60.9 [7]). After that, Judah, as it is said, *Judah is my
sceptre* (Ps. 60.9 [7]).[41]

By whose hand will the Kingdom of Edom fall? By the hand of the War
Messiah, who will be descended from Joseph. R. Phinehas said in the
name of R. Shmuel b. Nahman: We have a tradition that Esau will fall
only by the hand of Rachel's descendants, as it is said, *Surely the young
of the flock shall drag them away* (Jer. 49.20). Why does he call them
'the young of the flock?' Because they are the youngest of the tribes.[42]

Thus the Asaph Psalms' interest in Joseph would support the theory
that they represent the initial ingathering of Israel.

I noted also that in the eschatological programme of the prophets
the third stage of the ingathering was to be identified with a latter-day
Davidic *malkut* (Ezek. 44.3; 46.16-18; Jer. 3.17; 23.3-6; Mic. 4.8–5.1
[2]; Zech. 9.9-10). This would correspond with the Ascents' interest in
David and with the hypothesis that they represent the ascent to worship at the latter-day Feast of Sukkoth in the Davidic *malkut*. Such a
balance in the Psalter between an initial ingathering of Josephites and
a post-conflict Davidic *malkut* would even explain why the Asaph
Psalms recount Yhwh's rejection of Joseph's leadership in favour of
Judah's (78.67-72). For the Psalter's redactor followed the same
eschatological programmes that give Joseph prominence in the initial
ingathering, yet regard the kingship as Judah's.

discussion of their dating in App. I); *B. Bat.* 123b; *PRE* 19b; 22a; *Gen. R.* 73.7;
75.5-6; 97 (NV in Soncino edn.); 99.2; Sa'adya, *Kitab 'al Amanat*, VIII.v
(Rosenblatt 1948: 301-304). The same thing is also implied by those texts which
understand the Messiah ben Joseph to be the initiator of the latter-day ingathering, for
a gathering led by an Ephraimite messiah would be regarded as an Ephraimite movement. (Messiah ben Joseph [ben Ephraim] is an Ephraimitic eschatological king who
dies in battle. He figures in the apocalyptic midrashim which comprise Appendix 1,
and will be more fully discussed in subsequent chapters.) It is implied also in those
texts which regard Messiah ben Joseph as a descendant of Joshua (*Targ. Ps.-Jon.* to
Exod. 40.11; Sa'adya, *Kitab al 'Amanat*, VIII.v [Rosenblatt 1948: 301-304]). For a
Joshuanic antitype would fulfil the function of his ancestor in bringing the people out
of exile into the land.

41. *PRE* 19b.

42. *Gen. R.* 99.2.

6. *Imagery*

Shepherd imagery figures prominently in the Psalms of Asaph, occur-ring eight times in six psalms. In Psalm 74 Israel are *the sheep of your pasture* (v. 1). In Psalm 77 God led his people like a *flock* (v. 21 [20]). In Psalm 78 he led them from Egypt like sheep and through the wilderness like a flock, and then committed them to the shepherd care of David (vv. 52, 70-72). In Ps. 79.13 there reoccurs the phrase *the sheep of your pasture,* also found at 74.1, and, at 79.7, a reference to Israel as a *pasture.*[43] At Ps. 80.2 [1] the *Shepherd of Israel* leads Joseph like *a flock.* At Ps. 83.13 [12] Israel is אלהים נאות *the pastures of God.* In deutero-Asaph Ps. 95.7 Israel are the people of God's pasture and the flock of his hand. There are therefore a number of explicit examples of shepherd imagery in eight Asaph and one deutero-Asaph psalms. Elsewhere in the Psalter it occurs explicitly at only three places (23.1-4; 100.3; 119.176), and implicitly at two (28.9; 44.12 [11]). Further shepherd imagery is discernible in the Asaphite predilection for נהג, a verb usually denoting the *leading* of beasts. Three of the four occurrences of this verb in the Psalter are in the Asaph Psalms (78.26, 52; 80.2 [1]), the subject being Yhwh in every case.

In addition, the Asaph Psalms' concern with shepherd imagery may be reflected in their interest in Jacob. Of the 30 references to Jacob in the Psalter, 9 are found in the Asaph group, which forms only 8 per cent of the Psalter. Such a proportion indicates that Jacob was a significant figure in the Asaphite tradition. Jacob was the shepherd-patriarch *par excellence.* He was the first biblical character to apply the Shepherd metaphor to God (Gen. 48.15; 49.24). He, more than any other biblical character, is described as overseeing in detail the manifold activities of sheep (Gen. 29.1-10; 30.25-43). And his favourite wife, and the mother of the Josephite tribes, was רחל, *ewe,* the shepherdess (Gen 29.9).

Some commentators have noted that there is a close connection

43. Given the pastoral emphasis of the Asaph Psalms, נוה is best translated *pas-ture.* Many translations seem to miss this, rendering it *dwelling place* (AV), *habitation* (RSV), *homesteads* (NEB) and *homeland* (NIV). This is in spite of the fact that most Old Testament occurrences of נוה require in their context the translation *pasture* or *fold* (Job 5.24; Isa. 65.10; Jer. 23.3; 33.12; 49.20; 50.19; Ezek. 25.5), and that these English versions translate it so in most of these cases.

between shepherd and exodus imagery.[44] This connection is evident in the Asaph Psalms, six of which appear to contain the exodus motif. Ps. 74.2 suggests the redemption from Egypt; the words קנית and גאלת being taken directly from the Song of the Sea (Exod. 15.16, 13), where they are used in a similar context. The same event is evoked in 74.13: *You it was who split the sea by your power.* Likewise v. 14 evokes the crushing of Pharaoh the *Leviathan,* and v. 15 the water from the rock and the Jordan crossing. The phrase at Ps. 76.7 [6], *Cast down are rider and horse,* appears to connote the Song of the Sea (Exod. 15.1). Ps. 77.15-21 [14-20] refers to God displaying his power among the peoples when he redeemed his people, when the waters writhed and his path led through the sea. Ps. 78.12-55 is an extended description of the Exodus, the wilderness wanderings and the entry into Canaan. Ps. 80.9[8] refers to God bringing a vine *out of Egypt.* Psalm 81 refers to the judgments on Egypt to Israel's redemption from Egypt, and to the testing at Meribah (vv. 6-11 [5-10]). Exodus language also occurs in deutero-Asaphic Pss. 105.23-45 and 106.7-33. Elsewhere in the Psalter the Exodus is mentioned only three times (114.1-3; 135.8-12; 136.10-22).

Finally, two later psalms in the Asaph group contain imagery depicting the violent aspects of harvest, threshing and trampling. Israel is depicted as Yhwh's vine, ravaged, burned with fire, and plucked by passers-by (80.9). The last psalm in the group, depicting Zion surrounded by a coalition of hostile nations, wishes Israel's enemies to be like *chaff before the wind* (83.14 [13]). Psalm 81 bears the viticultural heading על־הגיתית, *concerning the winepresses,* which, as was noted earlier, seems to be connected with the idea of the crushing of Israel's eschatological foes. The same heading also occurs in Psalm 84. Although this is not an Asaph psalm, it follows an Asaph psalm about universal military judgment, as the two other על־הגיתית headings (8.1; 80.1) also follow psalms about judgment, Ps. 7.8-9 [7-8] calling for the judgment of the nations, and Psalm 80 describing Israel's punishment and calling for retribution (v. 17 [16]).[45] It seems

44. Freedman 1976: 139-66; Milne 1975: 237-47.

45. There is, as noted in p. 173 of this chapter, some ambiguity about whether Israel or their enemies are referred to here. I concluded that the latter was more likely. However, even without this verse, the cry, *Awaken your might* (v. 3 [2]) and the repeated calls for deliverance (vv. 3, 4, 8, 20 [2, 3, 7, 19]), suggest that the psalmist hopes for Israel's vindication and, hence, for judgment of their oppressors.

therefore not unreasonable to regard the harvest imagery of Ps. 84.1 as part of the context of Psalm 83.[46]

The Songs of Ascents, in contrast, display no shepherd imagery, nor do they mention Exodus or Egypt. They do feature harvest imagery, but the emphasis is wholly upon the bountiful harvest-home, and not the period of threshing and trampling that precedes it. Ps. 126.5-6 tells how the labour of sowing results in the joy of reaping. Ps. 129.5-8 pronounces an unblessing to the effect that the haters of Zion be like withered corn not worth the reaping. Presumably, the implication is that Zion's friends will be like a good harvest. These two psalms, referring to agricultural harvest, form an inclusio around Psalms 127 and 128, which refer to domestic abundance, human fertility and the fruit of the womb. Ps. 127.2-5 states that food and prosperity come to Yhwh's beloved, and that children are his blessing for the upbuilding of home and state. Ps. 128.2-3 is gravid with rich harvest and fertility imagery: *you will eat what you have laboured for, your wife will be like a fruitful vine in the thighs of your house, your children like olive shoots around your table.* The divine oracle of Ps. 132 pronounces abundant provisions (צידה) and bread to the inhabitants of Zion (v. 15). Psalm 133.2 depicts abundance of good olive oil. Pilgrimage imagery is also prominent in the Ascents. Psalms 120–23 represent a pilgrimage to Zion.[47] Psalm 120 depicts the pilgrim leaving his pagan surroundings to journey to Zion. Psalm 121 pronounces protection on the traveller journeying through the hills to Jerusalem, the step parallelism embodying his upward trudge. Psalm 122 represents him standing in the gate, entering the city and admiring it. In Psalm 123, he lifts up his eyes in prayer. The Psalms of Asaph, on the other hand, appear to contain neither harvest-home nor pilgrimage imagery.

These two distinct bodies of imagery correspond to the different stages of the eschatological programme I associate with each psalm-

---

46. Indeed, if Thirtle's theory (1904), that some psalm-headings contain displaced subscripts, is correct, then the three occurrences of על־הגנית (Pss. 8.1; 81.1; 84.1) may be displaced subscripts of Pss. 7, 80 and 83. There is an evident harmony between the ominous phrase *For the winepresses* and the explicit theme of judgment of the nations in Pss. 7, 80 and 83. In contrast, Pss. 8, 81 and 84 appear to have little in common.

47. Such a narrative structure has been noted by a number of commentators. See Cox 1885: 308-309; Neale and Littledale 1874: 115; Mannati 1979: 87. The issue of narrative structure in the Asaph and Ascents collections is considered more fully below.

cycle. The predominant imagery used of the gathering of scattered Israel in the prophetic writings is that of the *divine shepherd and his flock*. It occurs in the context of predictions of Israel's gathering at Isa. 40.11; Jer. 3.14-15; 23.3, 4; 31.10, 23; 50.4-7, 17, 19; Ezek. 34.11-14; Mic. 2.12; Zech. 10.2, 3, 8, 9. It is also implied at Mic. 4.6-7 and Zeph. 3.19, where the feminine particle הצלעה, *the lame*, probably indicates flocks, particularly given the reference to *the flock* in Mic. 4.8. The close connection between shepherd and exodus imagery was noted earlier, Yhwh being the shepherd who leads his flock through the desert and into the green pastures of the promised land. It is consistent with this that exodus language and imagery are also associated with the latter-day gathering of Israel, thus linking the past and future exodus figuratively together: Isa. 51.10-11; Jer. 16.14-15; 23.7-8; Ezek. 20.34-38; Zech. 10.10-11. Apart from Shepherd–Exodus imagery, no other image complex appears to be used consistently in connection with the ingathering of Israel.

The predominant imagery used of the gathering of the nations against Jerusalem is that of threshing, sifting, winnowing and trampling. This might be described as *the threshing of the nations*. This imagery is employed several times in the eschatological programmes considered above. Joel 4[3].12-13 presents the gathering and judgment of the nations in terms of cutting corn and trampling grapes. Mic. 4.12-13 represents the nations gathered to the *threshing floor,* an ancient designation and function of the temple hill (2 Sam. 24.18-25; 2 Chron. 3.1). Isa. 27.12-13 depicts Yhwh threshing the entire fertile crescent at the time of Israel's gathering. Jer. 12.9-12 describes the nations' attack and says Judah is receiving the due bad harvest for their sins (v. 13). Elsewhere in the Bible, even where an eschatological programme is less evident, the destruction of the nations in ultimate or future war is presented in threshing imagery. Isa. 63.1-6 and Jer. 25.30 represent the conflict as Yhwh's treading the winepress. Hab. 3.12 depicts the conflict as Yhwh's threshing the nations. Zeph. 1.14-2.1 describes the day of the war as overflowing like *chaff* (2.1). More generally, similar imagery elsewhere describes the destruction of the wicked in general, including unfaithful Israel, often in eschatological contexts (Isa. 17.13; 29.5-8; 30.28; Jer. 9.22; 25.30-31; 51.33; Amos 8.2; 9.9; Mic. 4.13; Pss. 1.4; 35.5; Job 21.18; Lam. 1.15; Dan. 2.35). The imagery fits the event. Threshing and trampling suggest violence. Pressing grapes depicts bloodshed. Separation of grain from chaff and juice from grapeskin indicates separation of the good and desirable from the bad and worthless. This widespread and probably ancient connection in Hebrew thought between harvest and future judgment may explain why the verb אסף, which had harvest overtones from early times (Exod. 34.22), later ousted קבץ as the key verb for the pre-deliverance gatherings of the eschatological programme.

The predominant imagery used for the gathering to worship on Zion in the prophetic eschatological programme is that of garnering harvest after the threshing of the grain, *the harvest of the earth.* Widyapranawa notes, 'In both the Old and New Testament, apocalyptic employs the picture of "harvest home" for the last judgment.'[48] Zech. 9.17 speaks of post-conflict Israel thriving on an abundant harvest of grain and new wine. Zech. 14.16-19 depicts all nations making pilgrimage to celebrate the Feast of Sukkoth, the harvest festival (Exod. 34.22), at Jerusalem. Joel 4.18 describes the abundant agricultural fertility of earth in the post-conflict period. Isa. 27.12 describes how, after the threshing of the nations, the Israelites will be gathered like grain. Isa. 66.20 depicts the nations bearing the Israelites to Jerusalem, *as the Israelites bring their grain offerings to the house of Yhwh in pure vessels.* Thus there would appear to be a close correspondence between the imagery of the ingathering stages of the eschatological programme and of the psalm-cycles, as follows:

Psalms of Asaph (Pss. 50, 73–83)		*Songs of Ascents (Pss. 120–34)*
Ingathering of Israel	Ingathering of hostile nations	Ingathering to worship
Imagery: shepherd–exodus	Imagery: threshing and trampling	Imagery: harvest-home

7. Literary Characteristics

The literary characteristics of the two collections express well the ethos of each. The literary devices of the Asaph Psalms produce a sense of weak internal cohesion, or 'centrifugality', which in turn conveys feelings of alienation, decentralization and *angst.* The literary devices of the Songs of Ascents produce a high degree of internal cohesion, or 'centripetality', that conveys a feeling of harmony, wholeness and *shalom.*[49]

---

48. Widyapranawa 1990: 163.

49. The terms 'centripetal' and 'centrifugal' in relation to poetic cohesion derive from Stankiewicz 1982.

a. *Time and History*

The attitude to time and history in the two psalms groups produces different levels of cohesion. Historical review is almost an obsession in the Asaph and deutero-Asaph Psalms (74.2-10; 76.3-9; 77.6-21 [5-20]; 78.4-72; 79.1-4; 80.9-17 [8-16]; 81.6-12 [5-11]; 83.10-13 [9-12]; 96.3; 105.1-2, 5, 8-45; 106.6-46).[50] They also look repeatedly to the future, praying for God's coming in judgment and deliverance, and for the inauguration of his *malkut* (50.2-6; 73.18-20; 74.10-11, 22-23; 75.8-11 [7-10]; 79.5-13; 80.2-20 [1-19]; 82.8; 83.19 [18]; 96.10-13; 106.47).[51] This intent gazing at past and future gives the Asaph Psalms a high degree of non-cohesion, which conveys a sense of the psalmist's discontent, restlessness and alienation from his present situation.

The Ascents are much more at home in the present tense. Historical reviews are not absent (123.3-4; 124.1-5; 126.1-3; 129.1-4; 132.1-7), but are fewer and briefer, and have a different quality. While those of the Asaph group call attention to the pitiful state of Israel, and request deliverance on the basis of God's past covenant and deeds, those of the Ascents give thanks for past deliverance, or, in Psalm 132, recall the covenant with David to request, not deliverance from adversity, but continuance of present blessings. This greater emphasis on the present moment, rather than the past and future, gives the Ascents a high degree of cohesion, which conveys a sense of the psalmist's being content and at peace in his present situation.

b. *Proper Names*

Another literary characteristic that produces different levels of cohesion is the use of proper names. They proliferate in the Asaph Psalms. Omitting names that also feature in the Ascents, Israel, Jerusalem, Zion, David, Jacob and Aaron, the following 37 proper names occur in the Asaph Psalms: Asaph, Leviathan, Judah, Tanninim, Salem, Jeduthun, Joseph/Jehoseph, Moses, Ephraim, Egypt, Zoan, Ham, Shiloh, Benjamin, Manasseh, the River (Euphrates), Meribah, Edom, Ishmaelites, Moab, Hagrites, Gebal, Ammon, Amalek, Philistia, Tyre, Assyria, Lot, Midian, Sisera, Jabin, Kishon, Endor, Oreb, Zeeb, Zebah and Zalmunna. One might possibly add to this Hot Anger,

50. Illman notes the use of historical rehearsal in several Asaph Psalms (1976: 19-29, 42).

51. The imperfect tenses in Pss. 73 and 75, rendered as present tense in most English Bibles, may, of course, be rendered as futures.

Wrath, Indignation and Hostility, personified as *a band of evil mal'akhim* at Ps. 78.49. In addition, there are 13 names for God, as noted above. And if deutero-Asaph Psalms 105 and 106 are taken into account, then there must be added Abraham, Isaac, Canaan, Yam Suph, Dathan, Abiram, Baal of Peor and Phinehas. This kaleidoscope of proper names is largely a natural by-product of the historical reviews, which necessarily name places and people. But it produces its own literary effect, a complex cast of characters and scenery, which produces a highly non-cohesive texture. In addition, the fact that over 20 of these names and places are non-Israelite conveys well the plight of Israel surrounded by the nations. The greater profusion of names in Psalm 83 has a closural function in regard to the entire Asaph cycle. It highlights the encyclopaedic scale of the judgment of the nations, and serves as a *tutti* finale to the entire collection.

The Ascents are moderate in their use of proper names. Apart from those common to both groups, they feature only Meshech, Kedar, Negeb, Solomon, Ephratah and Hermon. They are, of course, half the length of the Asaph Psalms. But even double this number of names gives only 12, as opposed to 37. In contrast to the names in the Asaph Psalms, most of which are connected with foreign nations, the Ascents mention only two foreign peoples in the first psalm, and the pilgrim immediately departs from their midst.[52]

c. *Repetition*

Another literary device that gives different levels of cohesion to the two psalm-groups is repetition. It is widely employed throughout the Ascents. There are the formulaic phrases, mentioned above, which appear to have been cultic responses. Some of these occur twice and others three times in the collection.[53] There are the literary techniques of step repetition (120.5-7; 121.1-2, 3-5, 7-8; 122.2-3, 4a-b, 5a-b; 123.2-4; 124.4-5, 7a-b; 126.2b-3; 133.2a-b) and verbatim repetition (124.1-2; 126.2b-3; 127.1-2; 129.1-2; 130.6; 131.2b). Grossberg comments on the use of repetition in biblical poetry: 'Repetition in its various forms is the most frequent cohesive device. The reiterated

---

52. See my discussions on the narrative sequence of the Ascents above, pp. 117, 171.

53. *Who made the heavens and the earth* (121.2; 124.8; 134.3); *From now until eternity* (121.8; 125.2; 131.3); *Peace on Israel* (125.5; 128.6); *Yhwh bless you from Zion* (128.5; 134.3); *Hope, Israel, in Yhwh* (130.7; 131.3).

unit is recalled and *ipso facto* related.'[54] Thus the Ascents repetitions produce strong inner cohesion. This conveys feelings of familiarity, simplicity and *shalom*. The Asaph Psalms, on the other hand, do not feature repetition. They contain no repeated formulaic phrases, no step repetition, no verbatim repetition. This produces weak cohesion, and the occurrence of what is always new and unrecognized produces feelings of alienation, unfamiliarity, complexity and restlessness.

Thus the Asaph Psalms regularly employ poetic techniques conveying anxiousness and distress, while the Songs of Ascents employ those conveying peace and contentment. These different poetic moods correspond well with the different stages of the prophets' eschatological programme. The troubled and unhappy mood of the Asaph Psalms would well represent the distressed condition of Israel gathering from exile in a time of hostility that culminates in massive foreign invasion. The peaceful and happy mood of the Songs of Ascents, on the other hand, would well represent Israel's condition in the latter-day *malkut*.

8. *Summary*

The following contrasts and comparisons have been noted between the Psalms of Asaph and the Songs of Ascents.

The Psalms of Asaph	*The Songs of Ascents*
Heading and Tradition: אסף. Asaphite guild; *mazkir* prophet musicians; holy war	עלה. Pilgrim ascent and worship at the Feast of Tabernacles
Event-sequence: From divine command to ingather Israel (Ps. 50.5) to overwhelming foreign invasion (Ps. 83)	From pilgrimage to worship at Sukkoth on Zion (Ps. 120) to joyful descent from Zion in fullness of blessing (Ps. 134). Takes place in aftermath of divine deliverance
View of God: Divine judgment of the wicked, both Israel and nations. Divine wrath on human sin, resulting in destruction. Divine title: *elohim*—expresses *middah* of judgment	Divine blessing of the faithful. Divine mercy and forgiveness, resulting in shalom. Divine title: Yhwh—expresses *middah* of mercy

54. Grossberg 1989: 9.

The Psalms of Asaph	The Songs of Ascents
Israel's condition: Distress and trouble. Jerusalem ruined; people scattered; alienated from elohim; awareness of national guilt; requesting national restoration and judgment on the nations	Prosperity, shalom. Saved from foreign invasion. Jerusalem and temple built, inhabited, functioning as cult centre; people gathering; reconciled to Yhwh; forgiven; *bet*-David restored
Prominent figure: Joseph	David
Imagery: Shepherd–Exodus. Threshing imagery in Psalms 80 and 83 appropriate to the coming judgment	Harvest–fertility and pilgrimage. This is appropriate to the harvest festival Sukkot
Other: Temporal complexity, numerous proper names, and little repetition give non-cohesive texture leading to a sense of discontent and *angst*	Temporal simplicity, few proper names, and much repetition give a cohesive texture leading to a sense of contentment and *shalom*

The correspondences between the Psalms of Asaph and the initial ingatherings of the prophetic programme may be summarized as follows.

The Psalms of Asaph	The Pre-Deliverance Ingatherings
Heading and Tradition: אסף. Asaphite guild; *mazkir* prophet musicians; holy war	(a) Predominant verb: אסף (b) Holy war
Event-sequence: From divine command to ingather Israel (Ps. 50.5) to overwhelming foreign invasion (Ps. 83)	Begins with gathering of Israel that is succeeded by a gathering of hostile nations against Jerusalem
View of God: Divine judgment of the wicked, both Israel and nations. Divine wrath on human sin, resulting in destruction. Divine title: *elohim*— expresses *middah* of judgment	The purpose of the pre-deliverance ingatherings is to judge Israel and the nations
Israel's condition: Distress and trouble. Jerusalem ruined; people scattered; alienated from *elohim*; awareness of national guilt; requesting national restoration and judgment on the nations	Israel's condition when gathered to a ruined city in a time of continuing national threat would necessarily be one of distress and trouble, in which they request restoration
Prominent figures: Joseph	Josephites are first to be gathered in Zechariah 9–10

The Psalms of Asaph	The Pre-Deliverance Ingatherings
Imagery: Shepherd and Exodus. Threshing imagery in Psalms 80 and 83 appropriate to the coming judgment	Prophetic texts employ Shepherd and Exodus imagery for the gathering of Israel and imagery of threshing and trampling for the judgment of the nations
Other: Temporal complexity, numerous proper names and little repetition give non-cohesive texture leading to a sense of discontent and angst	Discontent and *angst* are appropriate to Israel's distressed and threatened situation

The correspondences between the Songs of Ascents and the final ingathering of the prophetic programme may be summarized as follows:

The Songs of Ascents	The Post-Deliverance Ascent to Zion
Heading and tradition: עלה. Pilgrim ascent and worship at the Feast of Sukkoth	(a) Predominant verbs: עלה. (b) The latter-day Feast of Sukkoth (Zech. 14)
Event-sequence: From pilgrimage to worship at Sukkoth on Zion (Ps. 120) to joyful descent from Zion in fullness of blessing (Ps. 134). Takes place in aftermath of divine deliverance	The post-deliverance period will be characterized by celebration of Sukkoth on Zion in the aftermath of the deliverance (Zech. 14)
View of God: Divine blessing of the faithful. Divine mercy and forgiveness, resulting in shalom. Divine title: *Yhwh*—expresses *middah* of mercy	In the post-deliverance *malkut* Yhwh will dwell in Zion and there confer blessing and fertility (Zech. 14.16-19)
Israel's condition: Prosperity, shalom. Saved from foreign invasion. Jerusalem and temple built, inhabited, functioning as cult centre; people gathering; reconciled to Yhwh; forgiven; *bet*-David restored	Yhwh saves Israel from a foreign invasion, raises them to international preeminence, and restores *bet*-David. temple and city are rebuilt and people gather to appointed feasts
Prominent figure: David	The kingdom is restored to *bet*-David

The Psalms of Asaph	The Pre-Deliverance Ingatherings
Imagery: Harvest–fertility and pilgrimage. This is appropriate to the harvest festival Sukkot	Contentment and *shalom* appropriate to the happy age following the deliverance. Prophetic texts employ harvest–fertility imagery for the latter-day *malkut*. Zechariah 14 represents it as a pilgrimage to Sukkoth
Other: Temporal simplicity, few proper names, and much repetition give a cohesive texture leading to a sense of contentment and *shalom*	Contentment and *shalom* are appropriate to Israel's prosperous and happy situation in the post-deliverance *malkut* of *bet*-David

The collective force of the above suggests a distinct overall correspondence between the events and themes of the Psalms of Asaph and the pre-deliverance ingatherings of the prophetic programmes, and between the Songs of Ascents and the post-conflict ingathering. These two psalm-groups occur, of course, in the correct sequence to reflect the order of events in the eschatological programmes.

It therefore appears that the arrangement of these psalms in the Psalter produces a document that bears some similarity to the eschatological programmes of the prophets. This confirms my working hypothesis that the final form of the Psalter has been shaped, presumably by its redactor(s), as an eschatologico-predictive text. Presumably, they took two existing psalms collections and joined them, possibly making changes to both text and rubrics. To what extent these collections underwent reinterpretation by being set in this new context depends on their original function. If the Asaph Psalms were originally extracts from a levitical song book of cultic remembrancing rites, then their use in the Psalter may not be too far from their original function. The same would be so if the Songs of Ascents were originally lyrics for temple worship at Sukkoth. But whatever their original *Sitz,* their themes were probably sufficiently close to the redactor's eschatological themes as to make the significance of his document comprehensible to his contemporaries.

Chapter 7

A TIME OF TROUBLE FOR ISRAEL[1]

The preceding chapters explained my central argument, that a parallel
is discernible between the Asaph and Ascents psalm-cycles and the
stages of ingathering in the eschatological programmes of the prophets, and that this seems to confirm my working hypothesis that the
Psalter itself is shaped so as to depict an eschatological programme.
The remaining chapters serve to corroborate this hypothesis further.
First of all, in the present chapter, I shall investigate Zech. 11.4–13.9
and suggest that it adds two further motifs to the basic ingathering
programme: a stricken *mashiah* and an eschatological exile. I shall
then seek to identify the full eschatological programme of Zechariah
9–14, and confirm it by investigation of subsequent eschatological
writings. Then, in the following chapters, I shall suggest that the
motifs of the stricken messiah and the eschatological exile may be
discerned in the Psalter. In Chapter 8, I shall suggest that the Psalter's
royal psalms may be read as depicting the messianic motifs of the
eschatological programme. In Chapter 9, I shall suggest that Book IV
of the Psalms may be taken as representing the eschatological exile.

1. *The Motifs of Zechariah 11.4–13.9*

In the earlier investigation, in Chapter 5, of the eschatological programme in Zechariah 9–14, I omitted discussion of Zech. 11.4–13.9,
noting that the entire passage, framed as it is by the description of a
stricken shepherd (11.4-17; 13.7-9), represents an addition to the programmes of Ezekiel and Joel, consisting of a time of trouble that is to
precede the final deliverance. This passage and its motifs now warrant
investigation.

---

1.   The title עת צרה לישראל is from 1QM 15.1. (cf. Jer. 30.7; Dan. 12.1)

a. *The Stricken Shepherd*

Zech. 11.4-17 and 13.7-9 both feature a stricken shepherd and a suffering flock. In the absence of evidence to the contrary, it may probably be assumed that their similarity of imagery and theme indicate that the same figure is represented in each case.[2] The sequence of events is obscure, but something such as the following seems to be envisaged. The shepherd is appointed by Yhwh to pasture the flock (11.4-5). He does so, dismissing former shepherds who had oppressed them (11.7-8). Shepherd and flock then become weary of one another, and he rejects them (11.8-14). At Yhwh's command he personates a worthless shepherd (11.15-16). An oracle announces that he will be smitten by Yhwh, apparently for deserting the flock (11.17).[3] The narrative then proceeds through 11.18 to 13.6, until there is a return to the theme of the striking of the shepherd (13.7). The result of his death is that the flock are scattered. Two-thirds perish, and one-third are refined, tested, and restored to covenant with Yhwh (13.7-9).

The primary key to the identity of this figure is the shepherd metaphor itself. Shepherd is a widespread metaphor for kingship, both in the Bible and in other ancient Near Eastern literature.[4] Before 2000 BCE an Egyptian writer, Ipu-wer, described an ideal king who would be 'the herdsman of all men. Evil is not in his heart. Though his herds may be small, still he has spent the day caring for them.'[5] Hammurabi, in the prologue to his laws, identified himself as 'the Shepherd called

---

2.   Ewald felt the similarity so keenly that he suggested 13.7-9 should be placed following 11.17 (cf. Saebo 1969: 276; Driver 1906: 271). Mason (1977: 110) and Hanson (1975: 338-39) concur, as does NEB, which actually transfers 13.7-9 to the end of ch. 11. Black (1991: 70-71) notes that the two passages should be considered together.

3.   The identification of *my worthless shepherd* (רֹעִי הָאֱלִיל; v. 17) with the divinely appointed shepherd of v. 4 is supported by v. 15, where the shepherd of v. 4 is told to *take again the implements of a foolish shepherd* (רְעֵה אֱוִלִי). This shows that the shepherd of vv. 15-17 is the one of v. 4 adopting another persona, and moreover, as the עוֹד makes clear, he is also the one who rejects the flock in vv. 8-14. As Rudolph notes 'Daß er nicht sich selbst spielt ist aus v. 15ff. völlig klar und ist deshalb auch für v. 4ff. maßgebend' (1976: 205). The identification of the figure of v. 17 with that of v. 4 is further confirmed by his being Yhwh's shepherd (רֹעִי; v. 17).

4.   Davidson 1983–85: II, 24; Smith 1984: 264.

5.   *ANET*: 443.

by Enlil'.[6] In the Bible Yhwh is commonly compared to a shepherd, as are human leaders.[7] And the almost identical parallelism of the passage in hand makes it quite clear that the 'shepherd' is a royal figure: *I will cause men to fall each into the hand of his shepherd, and each into the hand of his king* (11.6).

So the shepherd of the passage would seem to be a king. But more than that, he would appear to be a Davidic king. This can be seen from the parallel between Zechariah 11 and Ezekiel 34 and 37.[8] Instead of two sticks being joined to represent the reunification of Israel (Ezek. 37.15-22), one stick is broken to represent their division (Zech. 11.14). Instead of a covenant of peace being established to banish the 'wild beasts' of the nations from the land (Ezek. 34.25, 28; 37.26), a covenant with the nations, presumably for the sake of Israel's peace (since its breaking is followed by desolations [Zech. 11.16]), is broken (Zech. 11.10). Instead of predictions of peace and harmony (34.26-29; 37.26-27), there are predictions of devastation (Zech. 11.16). And, particularly, instead of one divinely appointed shepherd, David, caring for the flock (Ezek. 34.23; 37.24), there is a divinely appointed shepherd who briefly cares for the flock, then consigns it to destruction (Zech. 11.4-9). These parallels suggest that the shepherd of Zechariah 11–13 should be regarded, like the one of Ezekiel 34 and 37, as a Davidic king. This supposition is confirmed by the shepherd's intimate relation to Yhwh. He is appointed by him (11.4), and Yhwh calls him *my shepherd* (רֹעִי: 11.17; 13.7), and *the man who is my compeer* (גֶּבֶר עֲמִיתִי: 13.7). There are few biblical kings of whom such language puts us in mind as readily as David. He was the shepherd-king *par excellence*, taken from the sheepfolds to be the shepherd of Israel (Ps. 78.70-72; 1 Chron. 11.2). And Old Testament tradition accepts no king, other than of *bet*-David, as divinely appointed ruler over Israel.[9] Thus Gese states,

> It seems certain that the mysterious title ['my shepherd, the man who stands next to me'], which hints at divine sonship, refers to the Davidic

6.   *ANET*: 164.
7.   Yhwh as shepherd: Gen. 49.24; Isa. 40.11; Ezek. 34.11-31; Pss. 23.1; 74.1; 78.52; 79.13; 80.2 [1]; 95.7; 100.3. Human kings as shepherd: Num. 27.17; Isa. 44.28; Jer. 6.3; 23.2-4; Ezek. 34.2-10, 23; 37.24; Mic. 5.3 [4].
8.   These reversed motifs are noted by Hanson 1975: 344; Smith 1984: 271.
9.   See e.g. 2 Sam. 7.16; 1 Kgs 8.16; Isa. 9.7; Ps. 89.5, 36-38 [4, 35-37]; 132.10-18.

> king, and this term of honor, together with the quite positive royal title
> 'my shepherd,' can only refer to a ruler who is acknowledged by God.[10]

Thus this passage would appear to feature an eschatological Davidic king—a messiah, in the later sense of the word—who is stricken by God. This view was certainly known in ancient interpretation. The New Testament applies Zech. 13.7 to its messiah (Mt. 26.31; Mk 14.27). *Gen. R.* 98.9 apparently identifies the one given the 30 silver pieces in Zech. 11.12 as the Messiah. Following a discussion on the messianic interpretation of Gen. 49.11 and Zech. 9.9, it says,

> For what purpose will the King Messiah come and what will he do? He
> will come to assemble the exiles of Israel and to give them [the Gentiles]
> thirty precepts, as it is said, *And I said to them, 'If you think it best, give
> me my hire; and if not, keep it.'* So they weighted for my hire thirty pieces
> of silver (Zech. 11.12).

Lam. R. 2.2.4 applies Zech. 11.17, *Woe to the worthless shepherd,* to Bar Kokhba, whom some considered a messianic figure for a time (*y. Ta'an* 4.8) and who is said to have claimed to be Messiah (*b. Sanh.* 93b). Several apocalyptic midrashim cite Zech. 13.9 and 14.2 in regard to the scattering of Israel that is to follow the death of Messiah ben Joseph.[11] Modern commentators also recognize the figure's messianic identity. As Ackroyd notes,

> The description of the shepherd as 'the man who stands next to me'—an
> associate of God, a suitable term for a royal figure—perhaps suggests a
> disaster to some messianic personage (should we compare 12.10?), so
> that the picture is one of messianic woes ushering in the final age.[12]

Rudolph sums up the issues as follows.

> In v. 10b he identifies himself with Yahweh (כרתי), in v. 13 Yahweh
> identifies with him (יקרח), and what he says and does is 'the word of
> Yahweh' (11b). He is therefore Yahweh's representative on earth and,
> because of the clear dependence of the vision on Ezek. 34, there can be no
> doubt that these details signify only the Messiah (Ezek. 34.23; 37.24).[13]

---

10.   Gese 1981: 151.

11.   Zech. 13.9 is cited, following the death of Messiah, at *Otot* 7.19 and *NRSbY* 24. (Both texts are cited in Appendix 1.) Sa'adya, *Kitab al-'Amanat,* VIII.5 cites Zech. 14.2.

12.   Ackroyd 1962: 654-55.

13.   Author's translation of 'In v. 10b identifiziert er sich mit Jahwe (כרתי), in v. 13 Jahwe mit ihm (יקרח), und was er redet und tut, ist 'Jahwes Wort' (11b). Er

b. *The Pierced One*

At the centre of the pericope bounded by the 'stricken shepherd' passages (11.4-17; 13.7-9) occurs another description of an afflicted hero, one who has been pierced, and upon whom Israel gaze and greatly mourn (12.10-14). Like the stricken shepherd, this figure seems to be Yhwh's representative and intimately connected with him. This is seen from the divine oracle that speaks as if Yhwh himself is pierced in this figure—*they will look upon me* (אלי) *whom they have pierced and mourn for him* (12.10)—the reading אלי being supported not only by the majority of Hebrew texts, but by LXX,[14] Targum,[15] Syriac and Vulgate. The following verse, which describes the mourning for this pierced one as *like the mourning for/of Hadad-Rimmon in the plain of Megiddo* (12.11), provides two further analogies, Baal and Josiah, which help identify this figure further.

One of the bynames of Baal attested in the Ugaritic texts is 'Hadad'.[16] Consequently, commentators have suggested that the writer 'is making direct reference to the standard ritual wailing for Baal-Hadad, the god of rainfall and fertility, who is ousted from the earth during the dry summer'.[17] Such ritual mourning might have resembled the mourning for the god in the geographically and conceptually

ist also Jahwes Stellvertreter auf Erden, und bei der starken Abhängigkeit der Vision von Ez 34 kann kein Zweifel sein, daß damit nur des Messias gemeint sein kann (Ez 34, 23; 37, 24)' (Rudolph 1976: 205).

14.   LXX softens the fate of the pierced one: καὶ ἐπιβλέψονται πρός με ἀνθ' ὧν κατωρχήσαντο καὶ κόψονται ἐπ' αὐτὸν, *they will look to me because they* [the enemies?] *have danced in triumph (over him), and they will mourn for him*, the verb κατορχέομαι meaning *dance in triumph*, or, figuratively, *treat despitefully* (LSJ: 424). But the reading *look to me* is nonetheless confirmed.

15.   The Targum also departs from the Hebrew. Instead of *they shall look upon me whom they have pierced*, it reads 'they shall entreat me because they were exiled' ויבעון מן קדמי על די איטלטלו. Note however that its קדמי confirms MT's אלי, Yhwh being the object of Israel's attention in each case.

16.   2.i.46; 4.vii.36; 12.i.41; Texts at Gibson 1978: 43, 65, 134.

17.   Gaster 1969: 687. Similar opinions are expressed by Bruce 1968: 113; Mason 1977: 119-20; Smith 1984: 278; Stuhlmueller 1988: 149-50; Lamarche 1961: 84. Lamarche cites many other commentators, from Hitzig to the mid-twentieth century, who endorse this viewpoint. Gaster suggests that much of the imagery of Zech. 9–14, particularly that of rain, rivers and fertility in 14.7-19, is conceived in terms of the background of pagan seasonal festivals (Gaster 1969: 686-87). One might also add the emphasis on Yhwh as raingiver in 10.1, and his storm-riding advent to deliver (9.14).

related Dumuzi (Tammuz) cult, described at Ezek. 8.14. The opinion of Jerome, that Hadad-Rimmon was a town, does not necessarily contradict this.[18] For any town named after Hadad, especially within the borders of Israel, is likely to have been a place where cultic worship of Hadad was established and where ritual mourning was made for the slain god. Three things may probably be inferred from this comparison. First, the writer of Zechariah 9–14 was aware of some kind of correspondence between his eschatological programme and some form of the ancient cosmogonic Baal Cycle. The fact that such a reference is likely to have shocked his contemporaries suggests it was consciously made. Secondly, he regarded the death of this figure as in some ways like the death of Baal, whose death brought life and fertility to earth and was followed by his resurgence. Thirdly, the comparison with 'Our King, Highness Baal' implies the exalted nature and royal status of the pierced one.[19]

The royal status of the pierced one is confirmed by another figure evoked by the metaphor of 12.11, that is, Josiah, killed at Megiddo by Pharaoh Neco (2 Kgs 23.29; 2 Chron. 35.25). This is how the Targum understands the verse:

> At that time the mourning in Jerusalem shall be as great as the mourning for Ahab bar Omri[20] whom Hadadrimmon bar Tabrimmon killed, and as the mourning for Josiah bar Amon whom Pharaoh the Lame killed in the valley of Megiddon.[21]

18.   He writes: '... urbs est juxta Jezraelem... et hodie vocatur Maximianopolis in campo Mageddon, in que Josias, rex justus, a Pharaone cognomento Nechao vulneratus est' (Comm. on Zech. 12.11, in *PL*: XXV, 1515.c).

19.   *mlkn. 'al'iyn. b'l.* Baal III.E.40. The text is in Gibson 1978: 54.

20.   The reference to Ahab is hard to understand. According to the biblical record he died not at Megiddo, but at Ramoth Gilead east of the Jordan, more than 80 km away (1 Kgs 22.29-37; 2 Chron. 18.28-34). Nor is there any record of mourning for him. Rather, it is said that dogs licked up his blood (1 Kgs 22.38), an end which, having been foretold by Elijah as a recompense for his crime, must be considered the opposite of a lamented death (1 Kgs 21.19). One explanation might be that it is an attempt to account for the term *Hadad-Rimmon* by one who either did not understand it, or disliked the comparison between Baal and Yhwh's representative, and so took the term as the name of the king of Aram, whose royal house favoured names with the theophoric element 'Hadad' (1 Kgs 20.1-34; 2 Sam. 8.3-12; 1 Kgs 11.23), and who ordered Ahab's death (1 Kgs 22.31; 2 Chron. 18.30).

21.   *T. Zech.* 12.11 is also cited in the Talmud at *b. Meg.* 3a; *b. Mek.* 28b; and is alluded to at *B. Kam.* 17a. However, the verse is cited in connection with Ahab, as the basis of an *a fortiori* argument that, if he was mourned, how much more

Like Zechariah's figure, Josiah was pierced in battle and his death was followed soon after by national exile (2 Kgs 22.14–25.21; Zech. 13.7–14.2). Megiddo was the place where he received his mortal wound, and possibly died.[22] After his death he was mourned greatly throughout Israel, and the mourning continued by decree year after year until at least the time of the writer of 3 Ezra (2 Chron. 35.24-25; 3 Ezra 1.32). Jerome, who was not unacquainted with rabbinic interpretation, recognizes a reference to the death of Josiah in this verse, as do some modern commentators.[23] Thus, if a reference to Josiah may legitimately be seen here, then the pierced one, by analogy, may be taken as an antitype of Josiah, that is, as an eschatological Davidic king. The Davidic lineage of the pierced one is confirmed by the fact that the *house of David* mourn for him (12.10, 12). The descendants of David would be expected to mourn a stricken king of their own number. But they, the representatives of what the Old Testament regards as the only legitimate ruling house of Jerusalem, would hardly be expected to mourn the passing of a king who was of another lineage, and therefore a usurper.

It seems therefore fair to suggest that the pierced one of 12.10-14, like the stricken shepherd, is an eschatological Davidic king, and therefore a messianic figure in a fairly full sense of the word. Certainly, this is how ancient interpretation understands it. The New Testament applies Zech. 12.10 to its messiah, Jesus (Jn 19.37; Rev. 1.7). A talmudic *baraitha,* attributed to the early tannaitic period, applies the same verse to the slain Messiah ben Joseph (*b. Suk.* 52a).

should others be. Josiah is not mentioned. But there may be a distant connection between Josiah and Zech. 12.10 at *b. Mek.* 25b, which cites Amos 10.8c in regard to the death of Josiah. This passage from Amos looks like yet another of deutero-Zechariah's sources, for it resembles Zech. 12.10 in its reference to mourning *like the mourning for an only son* (יחיד). If the talmudic tradition linking Amos 10.8 to Josiah was an old one, then the Zecharian writer's allusion to that verse may have been an allusion to the death of Josiah.

22.   2 Kgs 23.29 states that Josiah was killed at Megiddo, whereas 2 Chron. 35.25 and 3 Ezra 1.30-31 state that he was mortally wounded there, but died in Jerusalem. Kings may be regarding Josiah's death as proleptically actual in his mortal wound. Or, on the other hand, Chronicles, followed by 3 Ezra, may have relocated Josiah's death in Jerusalem, for reasons related to its Davidic and Jerusalem theology.

23.   Jerome, Comm. on Zech. 12.11 (*PL:* XXV, 1515.c); Kraus 1978: 203; Stuhlmueller 1988: 148-49.

The verse is applied to the same messianic figure, also known as ben/ bar Ephraim, in the marginal reading of the Codex Reuchlinianus Targum to Zech. 12.10, which Gordon regards as older than the standard targumic reading on this verse.[24]

> And I shall cause to rest upon the house of David and upon the inhabitants of Jerusalem the spirit of prophecy and true prayer. And afterwards the Messiah bar Ephraim will go out to do battle with Gog, and Gog will slay him in front of the gate of Jerusalem. And they shall look to me and shall inquire of me why the nations pierced Messiah bar Ephraim.

A host of later Jewish texts likewise interpret Zech. 12.10 of this figure.[25] Several modern interpreters too have suggested that there is intentional depiction of a messianic figure in this passage. Lamarche, for instance, suggests

> This conversion which seems sincere and definitive, the transformation of hearts brought about by Yahweh and the fountain of purifiaction, which recalls the pure water of Ezek. 36.23-28, the expression 'in that day', the importance of mourning, the fact that Yahweh is regarded as transpierced in his representative, all these invite us to see the Messiah in this figure.[26]

c. *One Afflicted Hero in Zechariah 9–14?*

The pierced one of Zech. 12.10-14 has a number of characteristics in common with the stricken shepherd of Zech. 11.4-17 and 13.7-9. Both

---

24.   Gordon suggests the omission of the piercing in the standard Targum (cited earlier) may be due to its being 'subjected to (incomplete) revision as a reaction to Christian citation of this verse as a messianic prooftext' (Cathcart and Gordon 1989: 220 n. 2). If this is so, then the above reading would represent an Aramaic version dating from before the split between church and synagogue in the last decades of the first century.

25.   Midrash Wayyosha' (*BHM*: I, pp. 55-57) §20 (p. 56); *As. M*. 4.14 (Appendix 1); *NRSbY* 24 (Appendix 1); Sa'adya, *Kitab al-'Amanat* VIII.5; Abravanel on Zech. 12.10; Alshekh, *Marot ha-Tsove'ot* on Zech. 12.10. Rashi and Kimhi (Comms. on Zech. 12.10) note the prevalence of the messianic interpretation of this verse among their predecessors, although they themselves proffer alternative interpretations. *Ag. M.* 27 (Appendix 1) applies Zech. 12.12, describing the mourning for the pierced one, to Messiah ben Joseph.

26.   Author's translation of 'Cette conversion qui semble sincère et définitive, la transformation des cœurs opérée par Yahweh et la source de purification, qui rappellent les eaux pures d'Ez 36, 23-28, les expressions « en ce jour-là », l'importance de deuil, le fait que Yahweh s'estime transpercé à travers son représentant, tout cela nous inviterait à voir dans ce personnage le Messie' (Lamarche 1961: 85). Similar views are expressed by Rudolph 1976: 224; Torrey 1947: 253-77.

are Yhwh's representative and intimately associated with him. Both
are eschatological kings, probably of the house of David. Both die a
violent death, one by the sword, the other pierced through by an inde-
terminate sharp instrument, presumably sword or spear. Such similarities, together with the inclusio structure that the stricken shepherd
passages form around the pierced one of 12.10-14, have led several
commentators to suggest that the two figures should be equated.[27] This
conclusion is also supported by ancient interpreters, who equate both
the stricken shepherd and the pierced one with slain Messiah ben
Joseph. The midrash *Nistarot Rav Shimon ben Yohai* cites Zech. 12.10
in regard to Messiah ben Joseph, and proceeds to describe the consequent exile with Zech. 13.9, which describes the events following the
death of the stricken shepherd.[28]

Indeed, Lamarche has suggested that both these suffering figures
should be equated with the coming king of Zech. 9.9, thus making one
king figure central to the whole eschatological programme of Zechariah
9–14.[29] Several points would seem to support this. First, as noted in
Chapter 5, the figure of Zech. 9.9, like the afflicted hero(s) of Zechariah
11–13, is an eschatological Davidic king. Secondly, this figure, like
those of Zechariah 11–13, is afflicted (עני: 9.9). Indeed, a number of
recent commentators have suggested that the conception of all these
royal figures, as well as other details of Zechariah 9–14, seems to
be substantially based upon the depiction of the afflicted עבד יהוה
of deutero-Isaiah, and especially upon the account of his death in
Isa. 53.[30]

At the first appearance of the king in Zech. 9.9, he is צדיק, עני and
נושע by Yhwh, all characteristics of the Isaianic figure (53.11, 7; 50.7,

---

27.   Lamarche 1961: 150-52; Rudolph 1976: 223-4; Black 1991: 85; Ackroyd
1962: 654-55.

28.   *NRSbY* 24 (See Appendix 1).

29.   Lamarche (1961: 150-57) finds a messianic figure portrayed in the coming
king (9.9-10), the rejected shepherd (11.4-17), the pierced one (12.10-13.1) and the
smitten shepherd (13.7-9).

30.   Rudolph (1976: 213, 224); Lamarche 1961: 124-30; Mason 1977: 88, 119;
Ackroyd 1962: 654; Mitchell, Smith and Bewer 1912: 331; Wolff 1942: 40; Black
1991: 66-68; 83-88. The likelihood of Zecharian dependence on deutero-Isaiah is
confirmed by the recent work of Hanson, who argues that the visionary tradition that
produced Zech. 9–14 and Trito-Isaiah descended from the author of deutero-Isaiah
(Hanson 1975: 404-407).

9; 61.10).[31] Such language denotes, as Mason observes, 'one who, like the Servant of Second Isaiah, and perhaps the עני of some of the Psalms, has suffered wrongfully, and been deemed to be 'afflicted'; but who, in fact, is צדיק, and even more, the bearer of salvation to others'.[32]

Both figures are represented as humble and gentle in bearing (Zech. 9.9; Isa. 42.2). Both become an international cynosure, bringing blessing to the nations, peace or justice, light and salvation (Zech. 9.10; Isa. 42.1, 4, 6; 49.6). Both release captives from the pit or dungeon and the released captives receive a double portion (Zech. 9.11-12; Isa. 42.7; 61.1, 7). Both gather the scattered people of Israel (Zech. 9.12; Isa. 49.5-6). The resemblances between the afflicted hero(s) of Zechariah 11–13 and the Isaianic figure are just as marked. For instance, both are pierced. As Rudolph notes,

> This figure [the pierced one of Zech 12.10], because of [Zech.] 13.7 (q.v.), can be none other than the Messiah of [Zech.] 11.4ff., who at that passage became so disagreeable and unbearable that they sought his life (here also the prophet is influenced by Isa. 53, where in v. 5 the verbs חלל and דכא are synonymous with דקר, employed here).[33]

---

31. Of course, the identification of the עבד יהוה of the servant songs with the משיח רוח of Isa. 61.1ff. cannot be automatically assumed. The references to the latter figure are therefore included only as subsidiary evidence, the parallels between the Zecharian figure(s) and the servant being clear enough in themselves. Nonetheless, Beuken has argued for the identification of the herald of Isa. 52.7, the suffering servant of Isa. 53 and the anointed of Isa. 61 (Beuken 1989: 411-42). Lim has suggested that 11QMelch links the herald of Isa. 52 with the anointed of Isa. 61 and with the dying prince/messiah of Dan. 9 ('Appendix 1', in Vermes: 1992: 92). The last of these connections might also suggest a link between the anointed of Isa. 61 and the suffering servant. Such ideas are in keeping with recent rejection of the tendency, which originated with Duhm (1899), to view the 'servant songs' as a genre apart from their wider deutero-Isaianic context. Instead, there is an emphasis on viewing them within their context (Mettinger 1983: 89-107).

32. Mason 1973: 52. Mason seems to follow LXX Zech. 9.9, σῶζων, rather than MT's *niphal*, נושע. But the root ישׁע is used of the figures of Zech. 9.9 and Isa. 61.10 nonetheless.

33. Author's translation of 'Dieser kann wegen 13,7 (siehe dort) kein anderer sein als der Messias von 11,4ff., der demnach so mißfällig und untragbar geworden war, daß man ihm nach dem Leben trachtete (auch hier steht der Prophet unter dem Einfluß von Jes 53, wo in V.5 die Verba חלל und דכא mit dem hier gebrauchten דקר synonym sind)' (Rudolph 1976: 224).

Both are associated with shepherd imagery (Zech. 11.4-17; 13.7-9; Isa. 53.6-7) and suffer because of a scattered flock (Zech. 11.17; Isa. 53.6). Both believe they have laboured in vain (Zech. 11.4-9; Isa. 49.4). Both are rejected by the people (Zech. 11.8; Isa. 53.3). Both suffer in accordance with the will of Yhwh (Zech. 13.7; Isa. 53.6, 10). Both die in consequence of the sins of the people (11.8-17; 53.5-6). Both are mourned by the people (12.10; 53.4-12). Both provide some kind of atonement for the people by their death (12.10–13.1, 9; 53.5-12).[34] And, if the parallel with Hadad in Zech. 12.11 is followed to its conclusion, then the pierced one, like the Isaianic figure, will rise to dominion and power after his suffering and affliction (Isa. 53.10-12). In addition, a number of other linguistic links exist between the language of Zechariah 9–14 and deutero-Isaiah. Each has a divine oracle announcing to בת־ציון the coming of her deliverer or king (Zech. 9.9; Isa. 62.11). Each has divine oracles in the name of Yhwh, who stretches out the heavens, founds the earth and gives life to its people (Zech. 12.1; Isa. 42.5; 51.13). Each describes Israel's coming redemption in terms of passing through the sea, as at the exodus (Zech. 10.11; Isa. 63.11-12). And each envisages a consummation in which all nations will gather to worship Yhwh in Jerusalem (Zech. 14.16; Isa. 66.23).

Thus there is some basis for identifying the stricken king of Zechariah 11–13 with the coming king of Zech. 9.9, making one king figure central to Zechariah 9–14. As regards this figure, Black would appear to be justified when he comments, 'The unique picture which has emerged may well be the result of the combination of the future Davidic leader from Ezekiel (and elsewhere) with the servant of Isaiah.'[35]

---

34. That the events of 13.1 are consequent on those of 12.10-14 is seen from the fact that the fountain is opened to cleanse *the house of David and the inhabitants of Jerusalem* (13.1), precisely those who in 12.10 have had bestowed on them רוח חן ותחנונים, *a spirit of mercy and supplication,* which results in their mourning the pierced one (12.11-14). That the phrase *the house of David and inhabitants of Jerusalem* (12.10; 13.1) functions as an inclusio is noted by Lamarche (1961: 85-86), who argues that Zech. 12.10-13.1 is a literary unit with the structure ABB´A´, and by Rudolph (1976: 227); Smith (1984: 280) also notes its literary-structural significance.

35. Black 1991: 88.

d. *A Latter-day Exile in Zechariah 13.7–14.2*

According to Zech. 13.7-9, several events follow as a consequence of the king's being struck. First, *the sheep will be scattered*, a phrase suggesting Israel's exile from the land (13.7).[36] Then, among those left *in the land*, two-thirds will be slain, and one-third will remain (13.8). This surviving third will be refined and tested; they will call on Yhwh, who will answer them and, as the covenant formula implies (13.9c), restore them to covenant (13.8-9). According to Zech. 14.1-2, the nations' attack will result in half the population of Jerusalem being exiled, while the other half remain in the city. The two sections, 13.7-9 and 14.1-2, should probably be regarded as describing events of the same period. Not only does the one follow the other without intermission, but to regard them as describing different events would make it necessary to posit two eschatological exiles, which would certainly complicate the scenario. That the scattering should have two causes, the striking of the king and foreign invasion, is not a problem. Events obviously do have multiple causes, and the removal of a charismatic leader, in particular, might be expected to render the land defenceless against foreign invasion. Thus a composite picture of Zech. 13.7–14.2 envisages Israel desolated by the nations at about the time their king suffers. Two-thirds of the people will be slain (13.8), some will remain in the land, including half the inhabitants of Jerusalem (13.8; 14.2), and some will go into exile (13.7; 14.2).

This theme may also have been borrowed from Ezekiel. Although I noted that the eschatological programme of Ezekiel 34–48 lacks the events of Zechariah 11–13, nevertheless an earlier section, Ezek. 20.34-38, does seem to be aware of a period of trouble, which bears a number of similarities to Zech. 13.7–14.2, prior to the final deliverance. This period is to be an exile in the מדבר עמים (Ezek. 20.35). The writer draws a deliberate parallel with the desert wanderings of the exodus (20.35-36) as does the writer of Zech. 10.10-12.[37] The

36. The verb פוץ is frequently used in the Old Testament, particularly in Ezekiel and Jeremiah, to denote Israel's exile. BDB: 807 notes that this usage frequently occurs, as in Zech. 13.7, in the context of pastoral imagery. See e.g. Deut. 4.27; 28.64; 30.3; 32.26; Jer. 9.15 [16]; 10.21; 13.24; 18.17; 23.1-2; 30.11; Ezek. 11.16, 17; 12.15; 20.23, 34, 41; 22.15; 28.25; 34.5, 6, 21; 36.19; Neh. 1.8.

37. It should be noted that, although this passage refers chiefly to the initial ingathering, its vision seems to overshoot that event, and even those of Zech. 11–13, and look to Israel's ultimate restoration to covenant with Yhwh (Zech. 10.12), somewhat as in Zech. 13.9.

purpose of this eschatological exodus is to purify Israel (Ezek. 20.38; cf. Zech. 13.9). Thereafter they will dwell in their land, faithful to Yhwh and free of idolatry (Ezek. 20.39-44; cf. Zech. 13.2-9). The main difference between the two accounts is that Ezekiel's account seems to envisage the testing as taking place immediately preceding Israel's return to the land (20.38), whereas the Zecharian account seems to regard it as a result of the invasion which comes upon Israelites returned to the land (14.2). However, the idea which both accounts have in common is that a time of testing is to precede the final deliverance. Indeed, a synthesis between the two could be made, if it is allowed that the initial ingathering is partial, as Isa. 66.19-20 suggests. In that case the Zecharian account would refer to the dispersal of the partial number already gathered, while Ezekiel would refer to a testing of those not yet gathered. Some such harmonization was probably envisaged by later interpreters, who did regard the initial ingathering as partial, and equated Ezekiel's *desert of the nations* with the same period as the exile of Zech. 13.7–14.2.[38]

In this context, Hos. 2.16 [14] might also be considered. The passage is eschatological in tone.[39] It describes a time when Israel will be faithful, there will be a covenant with brute creation, war will be abolished from the land and earth will be fruitful (2.18-25 [16-23]). However, a desert exile must precede this golden age: *Therefore I am now going to allure her; I will lead her into the desert and speak tenderly to her* (v. 16 [14]). The idea may have arisen from cyclic views of history that, as in Ezek. 20.36, expected the latter redemption, like the former, to be preceded by a desert exile. Ancient interpreters certainly connect this verse with the eschatological exile preceding the messianic *malkut*.[40] Micah too envisages a time of trouble—the

38.   *Otot* 7.19 cites Zech. 13.9 and Ezek. 20.38 in regard to the exile following the death of ben Joseph. Sa'adya cites both Zech. 14.2 and Ezek. 20.35-38 in regard to the same event (VIII.5; Rosenblatt 1948: 302-303). Both regard the initial ingathering as partial (*Otot* 6.6; Sa'adya VIII.5 [Rosenblatt 1948: 302]). The writer of 1QM 1.3 regards the מדבר עמים of Ezek. 20.35 as the precursor to the final deliverance, an event he describes in language resembling Zech. 14. (See the discussion of this text later in this chapter.)

39.   So Braude, on commenting on the passage at *Pes. R.* I.320 n. As regards the wider context, Kuhnigk considers that עלה מן הארץ (Hos. 2.2 [1.11]) is resurrection language (1974: 8-10), an idea Stuart considers 'appealing' (1987: 36). Renaud also notes the eschatological tone of this passage (1983: 498).

40.   *Otot* 7.21; *Pes. R.* 15.10. The citation of Hos. 3.4 at CD II.16 suggests the

impending Babylonian exile (4.10)—between the attack and the final deliverance (4.1-8, 13). Although this lacks the fully eschatological viewpoint of Zechariah, it may also indicate a tradition that exile was to precede the latter redemption.

e. *A King Concealed in Zechariah 14*

I suggested in Chapter 5 that Zechariah 14 depicts a messianic *malkut* apparently without a messiah. I would now suggest further that a messianic figure may indeed be present in and with the person of Yhwh descending upon the Mount of Olives and coming with his holy ones (vv. 4-5). What initially prompts such a reading is that messianic interpretation of vv. 4-5 appears to have existed in ancient times. *T. Naph.* 5.1 describes the sun and moon standing still on the Mount of Olives, where they are seized by Levi and Judah. This suggests that the writer regards the Mount as a place of messianic activity, in terms of the typical messianism of *Test. XII Patr.*, which anticipates a priestly messiah from Levi and a royal messiah from Judah.[41] In second temple times the Mount was known as הַר הַמִּשְׁיחָה, *mount of anointing*.[42] The origin of the term is unknown. It may have something to do with the oil of the olive harvest. But, in the light of later traditions, a messianic reference, even a punning one, cannot be excluded. Josephus records how a self-styled prophet collected 30,000 followers and led them from the desert to the Mount of Olives, asserting that at his command Jerusalem's walls would fall and they would take the city from the Romans, an account that suggests that the Mount was regarded as at least significant by messianic claimants.[43] Acts 1.11

Qumran writer regarded the Hosean passage as eschatological prediction.

41.   As regards the messianism of *Test. XII Patr.*, see Kee 1983: 779.

42.   Braslavi and Avi-Yonah 1971: XII, 483. The mount is also called הַר־הַמַּשְׁחִית, *mount of corruption*, at 2 Kgs 23.13, the identification being clear not only from the geographical description of it as east of Jerusalem and north of the hill of Solomon's shrines, but also from the targum which calls it explicitly טוּר זיתיא. There would appear to be some kind of word-play between the two lexically similar but semantically different terms, a fact apparently recognized by both Rashi and Kimhi who each discuss both terms in the same context. (Rashi suggests that the מַשְׁחִית soubriquet derived from the worship of the stars and the zodiacal signs that took place in the vicinity of the hill.) Whether מַשְׁחִית preceded מַשְׁחָה or vice versa, and when the later name arose, is not clear, although, presumably, the Zecharian prophecy may have played a part in the mount's restitution.

43.   Josephus, *War* 2.261-63; *Ant.* 20.169-70.

anticipates the coming of Messiah to the Mount of Olives. 1 Thess.
3.13 alludes to the descent of Yhwh with his holy ones in Zech. 14.5,
but says that the one to come is *our Lord Jesus*. The midrash *Nistarot
Rav Shimon ben Yohai* has the same sequence of events as Zech. 13.7–
14.3, that is, death of Messiah, desert exile, and heavenly deliverer
(25-28).[44] The only difference is that the deliverer is the King
Messiah, described with a citation from Dan 7.13, rather than Yhwh.
Since this sequence of events occurs in the Bible only in Zechariah, it
seems that this writer's traditions considered the Messiah as included
in the reference to Yhwh in Zech. 14.3. The late midrash *Ma'aseh
Daniel* relates that, 'Messiah ben David, and Elijah, and Zerubbabel
will go to the top of the Mount of Olives, and the Messiah will command Elijah to sound the trumpet... And at the second blast of the
trumpet which Elijah will blow, the dead will live.'[45] Texts and traditions that associate the Mount of Olives with the resurrection of the
dead, even without mentioning Messiah, should also be considered,[46]
for the resurrection was commonly understood to be a messianic
function, or at least to take place during the messianic reign.[47]

What might have led these interpreters to regard the reference to
Yhwh's descent on the Mount in Zech. 14.4 as including the person of
the Messiah? It is hard to say, but two factors may have contributed to
it.

44.   The text is cited in Appendix 1.
45.   Jellinek 1853–77: V, 128.
46.   The Codex Reuchlinianus text of *T. Zech.* 14.4 adds, preceding the splitting of the Mount of Olives, the words, 'At that time the Lord will take in his hand
the great trumpet and will blow ten blasts upon it to revive the dead.' The north wall
of the mid-third-century synagogue at Dura-Europos contains, in the 'Ezekiel Cycle',
a painting of a mountain split in the middle that has dead bodies within it. In the following picture the dead are raised by angels (Black 1991: 149–50). This would
appear to be a representation of the dead rising from the split Mount of Olives of
Zech. 14.4. A similar idea is found in *T. Song* 8.5: 'When the dead rise, the Mount
of Olives will be cleft, and all Israel's dead will come up out of it. Also the righteous
who have died in captivity, they will come by way of a subterranean passage and will
emerge from beneath the Mount of Olives.' Finally, the Mount and the Kidron Valley
have been a favoured burial ground from first temple times until the present, when
virtually the entire area is covered in graves (Brasavi and Avi-Yonah 1971: 484).
This may suggest a longstanding association of the area with the resurrection.
47.   4Q521.1.2.12 (Vermes 1992: 303-304]; 1 Thess. 4.16-17; Rev. 20.4-5;
AgM 34-40; Otot 8.1-9.1; SefZ 49; PirM 5.45-49; 6.2-4; *Ma'aseh Daniel (BHM*:
117-30): 128.

(1) The high degree of anthropomorphism in Zech. 14.4 might have suggested a human figure. Biblical references to God's feet are generally found in supraterrestrial imagery (Exod. 24.10; 2 Sam. 22.10; Ps. 18.10 [9]; Nah. 1.3) or in passages that describe the temple as Yhwh's footstool (Isa. 60.13; 66.1; Ezek. 43.7; Lam 2.1; Pss. 99.5; 132.7; 1 Chron. 28.2), as opposed to his throne in heaven. Both these usages emphasize Yhwh's divine majesty and immensity, but do not necessarily suggest his physical contact with the earth. Another passage comes closer to doing so: *Before him will go plague, and pestilence will proceed with his feet* (Hab. 3.5). But even this depiction of Yhwh striding along between heaven and earth lacks the actuality of the present passage. For Zech. 14.4-5 not only predicts that Yhwh will come and make physical contact with the earth, but also names the exact geographical spot at which his feet will touch, the result which this will have on both the land and the population of Jerusalem, compares the whole event to an historical earthquake, and sets it within the context of an eschatological programme's future conflict. The physical and geographical dimensions of such a picture might easily have led interpreters to regard the *Yhwh* of v. 4 as representing Yhwh's human agent anointed with full divine power and authority.

(2) The conflation of Yhwh and the Davidic shepherd-king throughout Zechariah 9–14 would justify, even if it might not inspire, such an interpretation. The king describes Yhwh's covenant with the nations as his own (11.10). Yhwh reckons the price set upon Messiah as the price set upon him (11.12-13). The house of David is כאלהים (12.8). The piercing of the king is regarded by Yhwh as his own piercing (12.10). And Yhwh calls the shepherd-king גבר עמיתי, *my equal friend* (13.7).

Indeed, one might question why the writer has avoided any mention of the king in Zechariah 14. Could it be that the king is unmentioned simply because his presence is implied in the Lord descending on the Mount of Olives, and that Zech. 14.4 is the apogee of this writer's high messianism?

f. *The Entire Eschatological Programme of Zechariah 9–14*
A case can therefore be made for regarding the eschatological programme of Zechariah 9–14 as containing, in addition to the motifs identified earlier, the striking of an eschatological Davidic king and the consequent scattering of Israel. How these motifs cohere with the previously identified ones is not completely clear, but the following

points may be made. The references to Israel's gathering begin at 9.11, after the coming of the king, and conclude at 10.12, after which there are no further references to this theme. Following the taunt-song (11.1-3), which functions as a kind of bridge passage, the section Zech. 11.4–13.9 can be outlined as follows:

11.4-17	Striking of shepherd and scattering of flock
12.3	תאספו עליה כל גויי הארץ
12.10-14	They look upon the pierced one and mourn for him
13.7-9	Striking of shepherd and scattering of flock
14.2	ואספתי את־כל־הגוים אל־ירושלם

What emerges is that the affliction of the king takes place in the general context of the eschatological conflict. Moreover, 11.4-17 may be regarded as an anticipation of 12.10-14 and 13.7-9, as it only implies the flock's ultimate scattering, whereas 13.7-9 states it explicitly. In that case, the affliction of the king figure occurs between two references to eschatological attack (12.3–14.2). Does this indicate two separate attacks upon Jerusalem? It is hard to say. But it should be noted that the first reference to the nations' attack is followed by accounts of the striking of the king and the scattering of Israel (12.3–13.9), whereas the second is followed by an account of the divine rout of the attacking nations and the latter-day prominence, glory and dominion of Jerusalem. There is therefore a whole section of 'trouble for Israel' slotted in between the nations' attack and their final rout. This would be consistent with the general approach in Zechariah 11–13, whose themes, as noted above, appear to be a deliberate addition to the programme in Ezekiel 34–48, beginning with a conscious reversal of the motifs of Ezekiel 34. So it is possible to regard the death of the king and the subsequent scattering as taking place either between two separate attacks of the nations, or else following an attack, after which the nations remain in possession of Jerusalem. Either way it takes place between the first attack of the nations and the final divine deliverance, and Israel will apparently regather to Jerusalem at the end of the exile, for they are depicted as being there at the time of the final deliverance (14.2-5). Thus Zechariah 9–14 as a whole seems to display an eschatological programme somewhat as follows:

Ingathering of Israel under eschatological king (9.11–10.12)	Gathering of hostile nations against Jerusalem (12.3/14.1)	King dies. Israel exiled (12.10-14; 13.7-9; cf. 11.4-17)	Israel regather. Divine rout of nations (14.2-15)	Nations ascend to worship at Sukkoth in Jerusalem (14.16-21)

Black, in his investigation of these chapters, similarly concludes that they contain 'an implied larger schema'.[48] And while he cautions that 'it need not be precisely in this order', he still maintains that 'the formation of a general order is the natural consequence of interpreting the oracles of the eschatological period'.[49] He suggests that the order of events envisaged is as follows:

1. God gathers people from exile	9.11-12	10.6-12		
2. God sends shepherd/king	9.9	11.4ff.		
3. God condemns evil shepherds	10.1-3a	11.5	11.8	13.2-6
4. Shepherd/king is rejected	11.8ff.			
5. Shepherd/king is afflicted	9.9	11.17	13.7	12.10
6. God punishes people	11.6	11.15-16	14.1-2a	
7. God purifies and restores people	13.1	13.8-9	14.2b	
8. People mourn for shepherd	12.10ff.			
9. God fights against nations	9.1-6a	9.13-15	11.1-3	14.3-5, 12-15
10. God strengthens people in battle	10.3b-5	12.1-9		
11. God establishes peaceful kingdom	9.10	9.16-17		
12. God glorifies Jerusalem	14.6-11	14.20-21		
13. God gathers nations to Jerusalem	9.6b-8	14.16		
14. God punishes nations who fail to come		14.17-19		

Black's schema does differ in some details from mine. For instance, I would insert an initial foreign attack before the rejection and death of the king. But our proposed programmes are substantially the same, both in the motifs envisaged and in the order in which they occur. I am not suggesting that this is the only possible interpretation of Zechariah 9–14. The passage is too complex for that. Other readings might be valid. But this interpretation is a possible one.

g. The Eschatological Programme of Zechariah 9–14 in Context

This interpretation is confirmed when Zechariah 9–14 is viewed in the context of its historical precedents and antecedents. I noted above that the Zecharian writer makes deliberate reference to the Baal Cycle at Zech. 12.11 and was apparently influenced by the ancient Ugaritic myth. Therefore it should be no surprise if a similarity is discernible between his programme and the motifs of the Baal Cycle outlined in Chapter 5.[50] This can be seen in the following simple comparison of

48.   Black 1991: 57.
49.   Black 1991: 58. The table is from p. 57.
50.   Nor, of course, is there anything remarkable in the fact that a Ugaritic cosmogonic cycle has become eschatologized in Israelite hands. Scholars of Hebrew

their motifs. The tablet Baal IV, which displays no clear internal evidence of its sequential position, has been placed after Baal V and VI.

Baal II	*Baal III*	*Baal V*	*Baal VI*	*Baal IV*
Baal ousted, then returns to Sapunu	Yam-Sea attacks Baal on his holy hill	Baal pierced, dies. Exiled from Sapunu in underworld	Baal revives. Defeats Mot. Becomes king	Palace built for triumphant Baal on holy mount. Worshippers bring tribute

Zechariah 9–14

Israel exiled. Ingathered by eschatological king (9.11-10.12)	Gathering of hostile nations against Jerusalem (12.3/14.1)	King pierced, dies. Israel exiled (12.10-14; 13.7-9; cf. 11.4-17)	Israel regather. Hostile nations routed. *Malkut* inaugurated (14.2-15)	Nations ascend to worship at Sukkoth in Jerusalem (14.16-21)

This similarity would appear to confirm that the programme I have detected in Zechariah 9–14 is not entirely of my own invention. Moreover, the Zecharian programme is confirmed not only by its Ugaritic precedent, but also by its Israelite antecedents. For several post-Zecharian apocalyptic writers seem to anticipate a sequence of eschatological events similar to the above, and, in some cases, cite Zechariah 9–14 in regard to it. This shall be investigated in the remainder of this chapter.

2. *The Eschatological Programme of Zechariah 9–14 in Later Literature*

In this section I shall examine a number of post-Zecharian apocalyptic and eschatological texts in order to show that the eschatological programme identified in Zechariah 9–14 was indeed known to later writers.

a. *Daniel 9.24-27*
The sequence of events in this passage, whatever its historical significance, comes to us garbed in the language of eschatological prediction. As Goldingay notes,

eschatology have long recognized that the ideas of creation and consummation are closely related in the Hebrew mind, simply because the consummation is regarded as the beginning of a new creation (cf. e.g. Gunkel 1895; Gressmann 1905; Childs 1960: 73-84).

> ...the terms used to describe these troubles are theologically freighted.
> The crisis is an anticipatory embodiment of the last great battle, a historical
> embodiment of the first great battle between the forces of chaos and the
> forces of order. Porteous compares Ezek 38–39 and 1QM.[51]

The seer envisages a time of the end, after 70 sevens, when Israel's sin
and waywardness will be removed, when they will have everlasting
vindication (צדק עלמים), and when vision and prophecy will be 'sealed
up' (9.24, 27). The events preceding the end begin with the rebuilding
of Jerusalem in *a time of trouble* (ובצוק העתים). This implies a former
desolation of the city. Similarly, Israel's resurgence, implicit in the
rebuilding, implies their former exile or subjugation. A *mashiah*-
prince, an Israelite leader,[52] will come (9.25). This is followed by the
'cutting off' of a *mashiah* and the destruction of city and temple in the
context of a foreign invasion (v. 26). It is not clear whether the invasion precedes or follows the *mashiah's* cutting off, for נגיד הבא can be
taken either as the *prince who has come,* or the *prince to come.* If the
former interpretation is adopted, then the cutting off occurs between
the initial invasion and the final deliverance, a sequence similar to the
Zecharian one. If the latter interpretation is taken, the invasion might
be seen as the consequence of the 'cutting off'. Whichever way, the
foreign ruler will apparently control Jerusalem until *the decreed end
is poured out upon him* (v. 27). This again implies Israel's subjugation
and, given their former experiences at conquerors' hands, probably
also exile. The eventual 'outpouring of the decreed end' denotes divine
judgment upon the invaders of Jerusalem, and implies the city's deliverance, and the inauguration of Israel's future golden age, referred to
previously (v. 24). The implied programme in this short passage is
therefore somewhat as follows. The similarities to the Zecharian pattern should be recognizable.

Zechariah 9–14	Ingathering of Israel	Gathering of hostile nations	Death of king and Israel's exile	Divine rout of nations	Nations worship in Jerusalem
Daniel 9.24-27	Resurgence of Israel	Implied gather-ing of hostile nations	*Mashiah* cut-off. Desolation (v.26)	Judgment poured out upon invader	Era of Israel's sovereignty

51. Goldingay 1989: 261-62.
52. 'A non-Israelite ruler would more naturally be referred to here as מלך, as
commonly in Daniel. In the absence of indication to the contrary, then, 'an anointed,
a leader', is more likely an Israelite figure' (Goldingay 1989: 261).

b. *The Sibylline Oracles*
Sib. Or. 2.161-76 describes the events that will happen in 'the last generation' (l. 162), at the gathering of the harvest of articulate people (τὸ θέρος μερόπων ἀνθρώπων), that is, presumably, the god-fearing who fully possess the divine attribute of speech (l. 164). There will be an ultimate revelation of the forces of evil, for false prophets, and then Beliar himself, will do signs on earth (ll. 165-68). Subsequent events are reminiscent of the Zecharian programme:

> ... Then indeed there will be confusion of holy
> chosen and faithful men, and there will be a plundering
> 170 of these and of the Hebrews. A terrible wrath will come upon them
> when a people of ten tribes will come from the east
> to seek the people, which the shoot of Assyria destroyed,
> of their fellow Hebrews. Nations will perish after these things.
> Later will rule over them exceedingly mighty men,
> 175 faithful chosen Hebrews, having subjected
> them as of old, since power will never fail.[53]

The events envisaged seem to be that an ingathering of Israel, the return of the ten tribes to seek their fellow Hebrews, will be followed or accompanied by 'a plundering' and 'a terrible wrath' against the Hebrews, suggesting the desolation of Israel by foreign powers. At the same time there will be a 'confusion of holy, chosen and faithful men'. Such a phrase might be taken as indicating one or more Israelite messianic kings and their followers. For since they suffer the wrath against Israel, they are presumably in the same location as Israel identified with them. Thereafter the nations will perish, having been subjected by 'exceedingly mighty, faithful, chosen Hebrews', who will then rule over them. The fact that this subjugation comes from the divine 'power' that never fails (l. 176), suggests that these Israelite kings are again messianic figures. This passage is then followed by a further lengthy description of the judgment of the world, including the coming of Elijah (l. 187) and Messiah (l. 241), which is probably intended to be another description of the same events rather than a sequel to them.

A sequence of events similar to the above occurs also in *Sib. Or.* 3.652-723.

---

53.   Collins 1983: 349.

And then God will send a king from the sun
who will stop the entire earth from evil war,
killing some, imposing oaths of loyalty on others;
655   and he will not do all these things by his private plans
but in obedience to the noble teaching of the great God.
The Temple of the great God (will be) laden with very beautiful
      wealth,
gold, silver, and purple ornament,
and earth (will be) productive and sea full
660   of good things. And kings will begin
to be angry with each other, requiting evils with spirit.
Envy is not good for wretched mortals.
But again the kings of the peoples will launch an attack
together against this land, bringing doom upon themselves,
665   for they will want to destroy the Temple of the great God
and most excellent men when they enter the land.
The abominable kings, each one with his throne
and faithless people, will set them up around the city.
And God will speak, with a great voice,
670   to the entire ignorant empty-minded people, and
judgment will come upon them from the great God, and all will
perish
      at the hand of the Immortal ....
....
675   The all-bearing earth will be shaken in those days
by the hand of the Immortal ....
....
680   He will break the lofty summits of the mountains and the mounds of
giants
and the dark abyss will appear to all.
....
But the sons of the great God will all live
peacefully around the temple, rejoicing in these things
which the Creator, just judge and sole ruler, will give.
705   For he alone will shield them, standing by them magnificently
as if he had a wall of blazing fire round about.
They will be free from war in towns and country.
No hand of evil war, but rather the Immortal himself
and the hand of the Holy One will be fighting for them.
710   And then all islands and cities will say,
'How much the Immortal loves those men!
....
716   'Come let us fall on the ground and entreat
the immortal king, the great eternal God.

Let us send to the Temple, since he alone is sovereign
and let us all ponder the Law of the Most High God,
720 who is most righteous of all throughout the earth.
But we had wandered from the path of the Immortal.
With mindless spirit we revered things made by hand,
idols and statues of dead men.'[54]

God will send a king who will bring abundant peace to Jerusalem and the earth (ll. 663-60). It is not specifically said that this is an Israelite messiah, but his heavenly origin (l. 652), his peacemaking (l. 653), his obedience to the divine will (ll. 655-56), and his glorification of Jerusalem (ll. 657-58) suggest as much. Nor is an ingathering of Israel specifically mentioned. This relates, of course, to the problematic question of the dating of the parts of the *Sibylline Oracles*.[55] The silence on Israel's ingathering suggests the passage dates from before 68 CE, when Israel had some political control in their land. In that case the writer simply looks forward to a more glorious Jerusalem, possibly with a greater populace. If, however, the passage dates from after the destruction, then a future ingathering, although unstated, must be envisaged, if only to rebuild the temple. Either way, the glorious temple implies a Zion populous with ministering priests and worshipping people. Thereafter an alliance of kings will attack the land, intending to destroy the temple and *most excellent men,* including, surely, the king from the sun (ll. 660-68). They will apparently achieve some success in this, although the degree of destruction is not detailed, for they will subdue the land as far as Jerusalem, and set up their thrones around the city. Then God will destroy them and the earth will be shaken and convulsed (ll. 679-81). Thereafter God's sons will live peacefully in Zion (ll. 702-704). All the nations of the earth will repent of their idolatry and come to worship in Jerusalem (ll. 710-23; cf. also ll. 772ff.). Thus this passage, with its softer 'time of trouble', presents a sequence of events much like that of Ezekiel, but also compatible with the Zecharian programme.

Thus the sequence of events envisaged in books 2 and 3 of the *Sibylline Oracles* resemble the Zecharian pattern as follows.

54. Collins 1983: 376-78, in Charlesworth 1983–85: I, 317-472.
55. Collins dates the main corpus of book three in the period 163-45 BCE (1983: 355), but considers that other passages were added later, one even as late as post-70 CE ['The Sibylline Oracles,' 355-60, in Charlesworth 1983–85: I, 317-472].

Zech. 9–14	Ingathering of Israel	Gathering of hostile nations	Death of king and Israel's exile	Divine rout of nations	Nations gather to Jerusalem
Sib. Or. 2.161-76	Return of ten tribes	Plundering and wrath against Hebrews. Confusion of holy, chosen, faithful men		Nations will perish	Israelite hero-kings will rule the nations
Sib. Or. 3.652-68	King from sun will subdue earth, restore Jerusalem	Kings launch attack against Israel	Subjugation of Israel	Judgment from God on the invaders	Israel dwell in peace; nations worship God

c. *The Testaments of the Twelve Patriarchs*

There is much debate as to the dating of *Testaments of the Twelve Patriarchs*. However the view of Kee, that the bulk of the work dates from the mid-second century BCE, and that it also contains later interpolations from a Christian source, can probably be taken as representing prevailing opinion.[56] In *T. Jud.* 22–25 the narrator, Judah the patriarch, predicts the future of Israel. His starting point is the post-exilic period, as might be expected in a book written for post-exilic Israelites, and therefore the gathering from the Babylonian exile can be taken as the background to these predictions. Judah speaks of how his rule, that is the Judahite kingship of *bet*-David, shall be terminated by aliens until the salvation of Israel come, and all nations will enjoy tranquillity and peace under a restored Davidic kingship (22.2-3). But this happy conclusion is to be preceded by tribulation. Because of Israel's sins, the Lord will send famine, plague, besieging, scattering, slaughter of infants, plunder of sustenance, rape of wives, destruction of the sanctuary, desolation of the land and subjugation to Gentiles (23.1-4). The language, particularly the reference to rape, evokes Zech. 14.2 with its full-scale invasion of Jerusalem. Exile too is suggested by the desolate land and the subsequent *captivity*, from which repentant Israel will later be divinely liberated (23.3, 5). Thereafter Jerusalem will presumably be freed from heathen domination. A righteous Judahite king will arise and rule over the nations and judge among them (24.1-6). The curse of Babel will be revoked, for all mankind will speak one language. There shall be no spirit of error on the earth and the dead shall rise (25.1-4). Then, as previously said, all the nations shall dwell in tranquility (22.2).

56.   Kee 1983: 777-78.

T. Dan. depicts a similar sequence of events. Israel, because of their sins, will be led into captivity, until they turn back to the Lord. Then they will receive mercy and be released from captivity and he will lead them back to his holy place (5.1-9). Thereafter a messianic hero, 'The Salvation of the Lord', will arise to them. He will effect the final deliverance by making war against Beliar. He will turn the hearts of the disobedient to the Lord and grant eternal peace to those who call on him (5.10-11). Thereafter the New Jerusalem shall be established forever and Israel will suffer no more captivity, for the Lord will dwell among them and rule over them (5.12-13). God will assemble the righteous from among the nations (8.3). Although the narrator is the patriarch Dan, the events predicted should probably be taken as referring not to the Babylonian captivity, but to one future to the writer's time, as in Zechariah 9–14. For, like *T. Jud*. 22–25, this passage was written in and for second temple times.

The sequences of events envisaged in these passages resemble the Zecharian pattern as follows:

Zech. *9–14*	*Ingathering of Israel*	*Gathering of hostile nations*	*Death of king and Israel's exile*	*Divine rout of nations*	*Nations gather to Jerusalem*
T. Jud. 22–25	(Ingathering from Babylon)	Siege by enemies	*Bet*-David terminated. City desolated. Exile	The Lord will free them from captivity	Judahite king will rule the nations
T. Dan. 5, 8	(Ingathering from Babylon)	Implied attack by enemies	Israel led captive for their sins	Restoration to Jerusalem. Messianic king routs Beliar	New Jerusalem. Israel in peace. Nations worship there

d. *The Psalms of Solomon*

The Psalms of Solomon probably date from the mid-first century BCE.[57] The author therefore lives in the period when Israel dwelt in the land, following the partial gathering after Cyrus's decree. *Pss. Sol.* 17 describes how the throne of David was despoiled by sinful Israelites (17.5-6), and how thereafter a lawless foreigner laid waste the land, took Jerusalem, and set up idols there (17.7, 11-15). He also scattered the righteous, who became exiles in the desert (17.16-18). These and other details indicate Pompey's invasion of 63 BCE.[58] The writer looks forward to the coming of Messiah the son of David, who

57. For the dating see Wright 1985: 640-41.
58. So Wright 1985: 641; Gray: 1913: 629-30.

will destroy the foreign invaders with the word of his mouth (17.21-24). Then he will gather a holy people, the tribes made holy by God (17.26-27, 44). These are presumably the exiles in the wilderness and other righteous Jews among the ten tribes. He will distribute them in the land according to their tribes (17.28). Jerusalem will be resanctified (17.30). The nations will serve him, and will come from the ends of the earth to see his glory, bringing the Israelites with them as gifts (17.31-34). He will rule over Israel righteously for ever, and govern the nations (17.29, 34, 43).

Other passages confirm this sequence of events. *Pss. Sol.* 8 tells how the leaders of Jerusalem welcomed a foreign enemy, who came and desolated the city and killed and exiled its people (8.16-22). This is regarded as divine punishment for Jerusalem's multifarious sins (8.8-13, 21-22). God is requested to turn to them in mercy and ingather the dispersed of Israel (8.27-28). *Pss. Sol.* 11 bears the heading *In Anticipation,* and looks forward to a joyful ingathering of Israel. A trumpet shall sound in Zion and the Israelites shall gather from distant lands (11.1-3). Israel will be exalted and glorified by the Lord for evermore (11.7-9). Likewise, *Pss. Sol.* 10 anticipates the time when 'the gatherings of Israel shall glorify the name of the Lord' (10.8). *Pss. Sol.* 15 seems to look forward to the invaders' coming requital, when a flame of fire shall go out from the Lord's presence to destroy sinners (15.4-5). *Pss. Sol.* 18 celebrates the glories of Messiah's reign (18.6), when he will bless Israel, and all nations will be subject to his compassionate authority (18.3-5). This writer regards the coming of Messiah as at hand,[59] and therefore believes the events of his time to be end-time events. His eschatological programme compares with the Zecharian model as follows.

Zech. 9–14	Ingathering of Israel	Gathering of hostile nations	Death of king and Israel's exile	Divine rout of nations	Nations gather to Jerusalem
Pss. Sol. 17	(Ingathering from Babylon)	Foreign invasion	*Bet*-David despoiled. Desolation and exile	Ben David destroys invaders by divine power; gathers exiles	Ben David rules Israel and the nations

59.   So Wright 1985: 645; Gray 1913: 629.

e. *The Dead Sea Scrolls*

The Community Rule (1QS) is regarded as one of the oldest Qumran texts, dating probably from the early first century BCE.[60] It contains the following passage alluding to a retreat into the desert. The scribe represented the tetragrammaton by four dots.

> And everything that was concealed from Israel, but was discovered by the Man who Sought, do not conceal from these [community members] out of fear of the spirit of apostasy. And when these things take place in Israel at these appointed times they shall separate from amidst the habitation of ungodly men to go into the desert to prepare the way of Him; as it is written, *In the wilderness prepare the way of... Make straight in the desert a highway for our God* (1QS viii.12-14).

This passage, and ix.19-20, probably alludes to the founding period of the Qumran Community.[61] The picture emerges of the members of the sect departing from Jerusalem and settling in the desert because of a catastrophe brought about by 'ungodly men'. This event was regarded as the fulfilment of something 'concealed from Israel', but foreknown to the Community. Dupont-Sommer suggests this catastrophe was the invasion of Pompey in 63 BCE.[62] Vermes, on the other hand, maintains that the Community's origins date from a hundred years earlier, in the early Maccabaean period.[63] But whichever way, the founders of the Qumran Community appear to have left the city following a 'time of wrath' (CD i.5), and to have gone to live in the desert.[64] They believed that this departure was in fulfilment of biblical prediction. They believed too that they lived in the latter times[65] and that their purpose in the desert was to *prepare the way of the Lord.*

60.   Dupont-Sommer 1961: 71; Vermes 1987: 61.

61.   Dupont-Sommer 1961: 71.

62.   Dupont-Sommer 1961: 339-57, especially 357.

63.   Vermes 1987: 28.

64.   Golb envisages a Jerusalem origin for the Dead Sea Scrolls and suggests that the Community's use of Isa. 40.3 in 1QS viii.14 is only metaphorical and that they never actually dwelt in the desert (Golb: 1980: 1-24). However Brooke has recently reasserted the generally accepted view that they actually lived in the desert, arguing that Isa. 40.3 was understood by the Community, and others of their time, both metaphorically and literally (Brooke 1994: 132).

65.   The eschatological consciousness of the Qumran Community has been widely recognized. See, for instance, Steudel (1993: 231), who notes that the Community regarded themselves as living in the אחרית הימים, a phrase designating, in the Qumran literature, 'the final period of history.'

Given the general eschatological tenor of Qumran belief, and the interpretation of Isa. 40.3 current among contemporaries who were probably influenced by the Qumran community (Mt. 3.1-3; Mk 1.2-4; Lk. 3.2-6),[66] this expression would suggest that they expected the imminent appearance of the messianic *malkut*.

The War Rule (1QM) also attests to the fact that the Community regarded their abode in the desert as a precursor to the end-time deliverance.

> [The Rule of] War on the commencement of the attack of the sons of light against the company of the sons of darkness, the army of Belial: against the band of Edom, Moab, and the sons of Ammon, and the ar[my of...]
> the Philistines, and against the bands of the Kittim of Assyria and their allies the ungodly of the covenant. The sons of Levi, Judah, and Benjamin, the exiles in the desert, shall battle against them in...all their bands when the exiled sons of light return from the desert of the peoples to camp in the desert of Jerusalem; and after the battle they shall go up from there t[o Jerusalem...] (1QM i.1-3).

The sectarians, the sons of light, regard themselves as dwelling in the מדבר עמים, *the desert of the peoples*. The phrase, which occurs in the Bible only in reference to the eschatological exile of Ezek. 20.35, suggests that the writer regarded the community's desert exile as the precursor to the final deliverance. The sectarians shall return from the desert of the peoples to the desert of Jerusalem, and after the battle ascend (עלה) to celebrate the inauguration of the messianic *malkut*. Their ascent is to Jerusalem, as can be seen not only from the general geography of i.3, but also from iii.11 and xii.13-14. The battle itself and the deliverance apparently take place in the 'desert of Jerusalem'. Thus the very opening words of this document are a classical statement of the Old Testament picture of the ingathering to war and the

---

66.	A number of commentators (Allegro 1956a: 163-65; Scobie 1964: 32-48; Betz and Riesner 1994: 145) consider that John the Baptist originally came from an Essene background. Certainly his residence in the desert, his priestly descent, his expectation of an imminent messianic appearance, his poverty and asceticism, his diet, and his emphasis on repentance followed by baptism may suggest that he was linked with the Community. On the other hand, his un-Essene association with the common people would probably require that at least his formal links with the Community had been severed by the time he began the work attributed to him in the gospels. But whatever form his links with the Community took, it would be most unlikely, given his residence in the Judean desert, that he was uninfluenced by their teachings and biblical interpretation.

ascent to worship in its aftermath. Nothing is mentioned of the period prior to the departure from the Desert of the Peoples. However the earlier invasion of Jerusalem, mentioned in CD and 1QS, is alluded to in the description of the enemy as those who oppress Israel in their land, and are in possession of Jerusalem (x.7; xii.14).

The scenario presented in 1QM is uncompromisingly supernatural and eschatological. The enemies are the hosts of Belial (i.1), or else-where Gog and his assembly gathered about him (xi.16). Their alliance includes Edom, Moab and Ammon (i.1), the aggressors in Jehoshaphat's battle (2 Chron. 20), which was already regarded as typological of ultimate war in biblical times (Joel 4.2 [3.2]; cf. 3.1ff. [2.28ff.]), and the aggressors also in the eschatological war psalm, Psalm 83, in which they form an alliance with Philistia and Assyria, also mentioned here (i.2).[67] The other nations mentioned in Psalm 83 may have occurred in the break in the text before 'the Philistines'. This is the conflict that has been predicted and appointed from ancient times (i.10; xi.11; xiii.14), and is עת צרה for Israel (xv.1). The sons of light are to be joined in the battle by the Holy Ones and angels and gods (xii.4; xv.14). The messianic figure of the 'Prince of the Congregation' is present in the conflict, probably as leader (v.1). Other superheros are mentioned: the Great Angel of the kingdom of Michael, who is to bring eternal succour in the war (xvii.6), and the Prince of Light (xiii.10) who also appears in CD A.v.18 and 1QS iii.20. With them the elect of heaven will fight in the battle, and pos-sibly also the risen dead.[68] God himself will fight with them from heaven (xi.17). The result of the war is the total destruction of the attacking nations (xiv.5), and thereafter the authority of Michael will be raised up in the midst of the gods, and the dominion of Israel will be over all flesh (xvii.7-8). The riches of the nations will be brought

67.   The *Kittim* invariably designates the Romans in 1QM, if not in all the Qumran literature (Dupont-Sommer 1961: 166-69). The Kittim of Assyria therefore designates the Roman forces of Syria. (Pompey annexed Syria in 64 BCE.)

68.   The phrase קמי ארץ is as likely to signify the *risen of the earth* (as Vermes renders it in his translation of Dupont-Sommer 1961: 187) as *the rebels of the earth* (as Vermes renders it elsewhere [1987: 117]) or *die Gegner des Landes* (Lohse 1964: 207). However the parallelism of the passage would seem to support the former translation: *the risen of the earth in the multiplicity of your judgments // with the elect of heaven in [your] blessing[s]*. That the Qumran sectarians may have held that the dead would rise at this time, is supported by 4Q174.2, which cites Dan 12.10, whose context refers explicitly to the resurrection (12.2).

into Jerusalem and the kings of the nations will serve her (xii.13-15; xix.5-6).

The Damascus Rule (CD) provides perhaps the clearest schema to show how the Community understood their place in the scheme of end time events. It begins by relating the origins of the community in a time of social upheaval, when power in Jerusalem has been usurped by the wicked (A.i.13–ii.1), the land has been desolated and the temple defiled (v.20-21; B.ii.23).[69]

> Because of their unfaithfulness with which they forsook him, he hid his face from Israel and its Sanctuary and delivered them up to the sword. But remembering the covenant of the patriarchs, he left a remnant to Israel and did not deliver them to destruction. And in the time of wrath, three hundred and ninety years after he had given them into the hand of Nebuchadnezzar king of Babylon, he visited them, and caused a plant root to spring from Israel and Aaron to possess his land and to grow fat on the bounty of his earth. And they perceived their iniquity and recognized that they were guilty men, yet for twenty years they were like blind men groping for the way. And God observed their deeds, that they sought him with a whole heart, and he raised for them a Teacher of Righteousness to guide them in the way of his heart (i.5-11).

There has been much speculation concerning the Teacher of Righteousness, or מורה צדק,[70] but a few facts about him seem to be clear in the Qumran corpus. He was a Zadokite priest whose death was particularly significant to the Community (B.ii.14). 1QpHab ii.2-8 suggests that he was remorselessly persecuted by the Jerusalem priesthood, who attacked him in his exile on the Day of Atonement, and may have killed him.[71] Whether, and in what sense, the Teacher was

---

69. The Cairo Genizah MS B is placed after col. viii by Vermes (1987: 90-91). Lohse gives the different MSS in order, with B.ii last (1964: 104-107).

70. The name seems to have been derived from Hos. 10.12.

71. 1QpHab xi.5, with the verb בלע, might be read as *swallow him,* or *confuse him,* or, by analogy with 2 Sam. 20.19-20 ,where the same verb occurs in parallel with השחית, *kill him.* But on the basis of the *pesher* on Ps. 37 (4Q171, cols. iii.14-16; iv.7-10; Vermes 1987: 291-92) a number of scholars accept that the Teacher died a violent death, possibly at the instigation of his enemy, the Wicked Priest (Allegro 1956a: 98ff.; Allegro 1956b: 89ff.; Rowley 1952: 62ff.; Dupont-Sommer 1961: 358-67; Stauffer 1956: 250-53; Stauffer 1957: 128-32; Goossens 1950: 336-53; Michel 1954: 271; O'Neill 1991a: 97-98). Note too that the apparent identification of the Teacher with the stricken shepherd of Zech. 13.7, whose death precipitates the eschatological exile, suggests that he died a violent death.

regarded as a messianic figure is hard to say.[72] But a number of points suggest that the sectarians may have associated him with the stricken shepherd of Zechariah 11 and 13.

(1) Zech. 13.7, *Awake, sword, against my shepherd, against my companion,* is cited at CD B.i.7-9. Rabin and van der Woude understand the citation to refer to the Teacher.[73] Two considerations support this. First, the following words describe those who heed the shepherd as *the poor of the flock* (Zech. 11.11) who will be saved at the time of Visitation (B.i.10). The *poor of the flock* appears to refer to the Community itself,[74] and it is therefore their shepherd (leader) who is struck. Second, the shepherd's designation as Yhwh's *companion* or *compeer* (גבר עמיתי) would be appropriate only to one, such as the Teacher, whom the writer considered a divinely appointed leader. It is unlikely to refer to the leader of the Community's enemies or the Hellenizing Jerusalem aristocracy,[75] or any others outside *the poor of the flock* (non-members of the Community). Even though the non-Community members will be struck by the sword, this will happen at the time of the Visitation, when the Community members will be saved (B.i.10).

(2) Like the Zecharian figure, his death was regarded as an epoch-making event in the schema of redemption, which was to be followed by a desert exile. B.ii.14-20 describes how a period of 40 years, a second Exodus, was to elapse from his death until the divine redemption, a period that was to be a time of wrath for Israel (B.ii.13-17). In regard to this period Hos. 3.14 is cited, a passage that occurs in the context of Hosea's future desert exile (Hos 2.14 [16]).

(3) Indeed, if the hymns of 1QH, or some of them, are by the Teacher, as a number of scholars allow,[76] then the Teacher may have regarded himself as the stricken figure of Isaiah 53 or Zechariah 11–13, or both. For the speaker of the hymns repeatedly refers to himself

---

72. That the 'Teacher of Righteousness' is a messianic figure has been argued in various forms by Davies (1983: 119-25; Davies 1988: 313-17) and Murphy-O'Connor (1985: 239-44). On the other hand, Knibb thinks the identification is unconvincing, although he does recognize that the יורה הצדק of CD A.vi.10, 11 is a messianic figure (Knibb 1990: 60, 58).

73. Rabin 1954: 31; Woude 1957: 38-39.

74. Dupont-Sommer 1961: 138 n.

75. *Pace* Betz 1960: 178-79; Rabinowitz 1954: 27-28.

76. Bruce 1966: 95; Vermes 1987: 32; Fitzmyer 1992: 56.

in language borrowed from the Isaianic servant songs,[77] and the Zecharian figure, as was noted earlier, is described in language apparently borrowed from the same source.[78]

(4) There may have been an expectation, following the Teacher's death, that he, or one like him, would reappear at the end of the age (A.vi.10, 11).[79] If this is so, the anticipated Teacher *redivivus* should possibly be identified with the Messiah of Aaron, whom the Community expected to participate in the eschatological banquet, or with the Interpreter of the Law,[80] whose appearance was also anticipated at the end-time, or with both of these figures.[81]

But whether or not the Teacher was in any sense a messianic figure who died a violent death, he was nonetheless a venerated religious leader to whom many looked for the restoration of Israel, and whose death was regarded by the Community as a key occurrence in the events leading to the end-time redemption (CD B.ii.14-20). He apparently led his followers into exile from Jerusalem to Damascus (A.vi.3-5; vii.14-15; B.ii.22), possibly a symbolical name for Qumran.[82]

---

77. Many of these borrowings are noted by Dupont-Sommer 1961: 361-65.

78. See the discussion of the dependence of the Zecharian figure on the servant songs earlier in this chapter.

79. עד עמד יורה הצדק באחרית הימים. The phrase יורה הצדק seems to indicate a messianic figure who is to appear in the end-time [Knibb,]. This is, of course, not the standard phrase used for the Teacher; that is, מורה צדק (cf. eg. CD A.i.11). Some commentators regard יורה צדק as a reference to the Teacher of Righteousness *redivivus* (Dupont-Sommer 1961: 131), others translate it so as to avoid any such implication (e.g. Vermes 1987: 87). Neither position can be conclusively established. But the writer would probably have been aware of the ambiguity of the former expression. That he did not avoid may suggests that he expected the reappearance of the Teacher or one like him. Note that even biblical literature indicates the reappearance of a departed hero of faith, Elijah, at the end-time (Mal. 3.23 [4.5]). Moreover, some later Jewish traditions identify Elijah with the Priest Messiah (Moore 1927: II, 358 n; cf. *PRE* 66b; *Sef. Z* 36), the messianic figure with whom the Teacher is most likely to have been identified (see below).

80. Allegro has suggested that the Teacher of Righteousness is to be identified with the Interpreter of the Law (1956b: 175-76).

81. Bruce (1966: 97) has little hesitation in equating the anticipated יורה הצדק of CD A.vi.11 with the Messiah Priest and the Interpreter of the Law, but says of this eschatological figure that 'there is nothing to warrant the statement that he would be the earlier Teacher of Righteousness, risen from the dead'.

82. Vermes 1987: 32.

There they entered a New Covenant with one another to walk according to the Law (A.vi.19; viii.21; B.ii.12), and anticipated retaking the land of Israel (A.viii.14-18; B.ii.34). This was expected to happen forty years after the Teacher's death (B.ii.13-15). Two messianic figures are mentioned as appearing at the time of the redemption (A.vii.18-19). The first is the Interpreter of the Law, who shall come to Damascus and, presumably, lead them back to Israel.[83] The second is the Prince of the Congregation who shall smite their enemies.[84] They shall return to the land, and 'prevail over all the sons of the earth' (B.ii.34). This may equal the move, referred to in 1QM i.3, from the Desert of the Peoples to the Desert of Jerusalem. At that time they will see the salvation of God (B.ii.34), a term encompassing victorious battle, the establishment of the messianic *malkut,* and possibly also the messianic deliverer(s), as at *T. Dan.* 5.10-11.

1QSa, a manuscript dating from the mid-first century BCE, is 'a Rule for a Community adapted to the requirements of the Messianic war against the nations', and foreshadows the War Rule (1QM) in its precepts and doctrines.[85] Its opening words suggest that the Community members regarded themselves as the guardians of the Zadokite priesthood and anticipated a time when others, the 'Congregation of Israel', would gather to them in the last days: 'And this is the rule for all the congregation of Israel in the last days, when they shall gather [אסף] [to the Community to wa]lk according to the law of the sons of Zadok, the Priests.'[86] This is in preparation for the 'war of the vanquishing of the nations' (1QSa i.21). There follows a description of a messianic banquet in the time when the messiah will

---

83. That the Interpreter of the Law is a messianic figure is recognized by Vermes 1987: 83. It is suggested also by the citation of the classic messianic text Num. 24.17 regarding him (7.19-20).

84. The whole question of messianism at Qumran is complicated further by the so-called 'Pierced Nasi' text (4Q285), which some suggest may describe the piercing of the Prince of the Congregation, identified with the Branch of David (Eisenmann and Wise 1992: 24-29). Others, however, oppose such an interpretation, maintaining that the Branch of David pierces the Prince of the Conregation, who is the leader of the foreign invasion (Vermes 1992a 85-94). Even taking into account all considerations of word-order and context, it seems that the available Hebrew text can be interpreted either way.

85. So Vermes 1987: 100.

86. (1.1). וזה הסרך לכול עדת ישראל באחרית הימים בה[א]סְפם

have been born, or will have descended, to them.[87] Two messiahs are present, a Priest-Messiah and a Messiah of Israel. 1QSb contains a blessing upon the 'Prince of the Congregation', a non-priestly messianic figure, mentioned in CD vii.20 and 1QM v.1. He is described in terms of the Isaianic oracle concerning the shoot from Jesse (Isa. 11.1-5) at v.24-26, and resembles the Davidic Messiah of *Pss. Sol.* 17.23-51 and 18.6-14. He shall devastate the earth, smiting it by the breath of his lips; he shall rule all nations, and all peoples shall serve him (v.24-28). He is possibly to be equated with the Messiah of Israel of 1QSa.[88]

4Q174 (Florilegium) anticipates the conflict at the end of days, citing Ps. 2.1 (1.18ff.). It refers to a Branch of David, that is, a Davidic Messiah, who will arise to save Israel and sit on the throne of Zion at the end of days (i.11-13), when the temple will be rebuilt (i.1-7). The 'Apostrophe to Zion' in 11QPs[a] xxii.1-15, describes the latter-day prosperity and blessedness of Zion.[89] This is to take place after all Zion's enemies are cut off round about, and her foes are scattered (xxii.13).

Thus the Dead Sea Scrolls seem to present a sequence of ingatherings similar to other literature of the period, although they appear to display a particular interest in the eschatological conflict and its aftermath. This was apparently because they thought their self-imposed exile to be the one predicted at Zech. 13.7–14.2, Ezek. 20.34-38, and possibly Hos. 2.16 [14], and therefore regarded themselves as living in the later stages of the Zecharian programme. The historical facts of the Babylonian return and the Community's departure from Jerusalem after its seizure by foreign or foreign-influenced usurpers may be assumed as the background even to those texts that do not directly refer to them. The sequence of events presented by these texts therefore compares with the Zecharian model as follows:

Zech. 9–14	Ingathering of Israel	Gathering of hostile nations	Death of king and Israel's exile	Divine rout of nations	Nations gather to Jerusalem
1QS	(Babylonian return)	Take-over by alien-influenced forces	Departure to desert	Anticipated messianic *malkut*. Consequent dominion and glory for Israel	

87.   The text's רֹ[..]יֹ can be read as either יוליד or יורד.
88.   Dupont-Sommer 1961: 112n.
89.   The text with translation is in Sanders 1967: 124-27.

Zech. 9–14	Ingathering of Israel	Gathering of hostile nations	Death of king and Israel's exile	Divine rout of nations	Nations gather to Jerusalem
1QM	(Babylonian return)	Take-over by alien-influenced forces	Residence in מדבר עמים	To Jerusalem desert; war against nations	Dominion and glory for Israel
CD	Babylonian return	Take-over by alien-influenced forces	Death of Teacher. 40-year exile	Return to Jerusalem	Salvation of God
1QSa/b	(Babylonian return)	(Take-over by alien-influenced forces)	(Residence in desert)	Israel gathers for war against the nations	Messianic *malkut*
4Q174 (Flor.)	(Babylonian return)	(Take-over by alien-influenced forces)	(Residence in desert)	Conflict and victory	Davidic *malkut*; new temple
Apos. Zion	(Babylonian return)	(Take-over by alien-influenced forces)	(Residence in desert)	Destruction of Zion's surrounding enemies	Zion blessed

f. *The New Testament*

The synoptic gospels, like the New Testament generally, differ from other second temple period literature in regarding the next stage of Israel's history, from their historical standpoint, to be not an ingathering, but another desolation and scattering in the aftermath of war, with no hope of divine deliverance (Mt. 21.33-45; 23.38; 24.2; Mk 12.1-12; Lk. 13.35; 19.41-44; 20.9-19; 21.20-24). The reason given for this is that Israel were unwilling to gather to Jesus (Mt. 23.37; Lk. 13.34; 21.24), but rejected him (Mt. 21.37-41; Mk 12.6-9; Lk. 19.41-44; 20.13-16; 23.27-31). At the time of this attack, the Israelites will be slain and taken into exile as prisoners, and Jerusalem will be 'trampled' by the nations until the appointed period of the nations is fulfilled (ἄξρι οὗ πληρωθῶσιν καιποὶ ἐθνῶν; Lk. 21.24). The latter phrase seems to suggest that the foreign domination is to last for a divinely ordained period and thereafter be revoked, after which, presumably, the exile will end and Israel will gather to repossess Jerusalem.[90] Such an interpretation seems to be confirmed by the parable about the budding of the fig tree, which occurs close by in the same narrative after a brief description of other end-time events (Lk. 21.29). The fig tree was established as a metaphor for Israel by

90.   See Tiede 1980: 89; Chance 1988: 133-34.

Jeremiah 24, and is employed as such in Lk. 13.6-9, apparently to indicate the impending destruction on the unrepentant nation (cf. Lk. 13.1-9).[91] So, if the fig tree represents Israel, the parable seems to suggest that their future budding and flourishing, that is, their national restoration, will indicate the coming of the end. This period will also see the appearance of Messiah from heaven (Lk. 21.27-36; cf. Mt. 24.30-37; Mk 13.26-35). In keeping with the distinctive pan-national theology of the New Testament, he will gather the righteous elect of all nations (Mt. 13.30; 22.8-10; 24.30-31; Mk 13.26-27).[92] They live thereafter in his *malkut,* and feast in the messianic banquet (Mt. 8.11-12; Lk. 13.29). Jerusalem's immediate destruction is to be brought about by armies (Lk. 21.20) and the temple is to be desecrated by the *abomination of desolation* in the Holy Place (Mt. 24.15), apparently a future event similar in kind to Antiochus Epiphanes's profanation of the temple.[93] However the synoptics make no specific mention of hostile forces at Messiah's return.

A similar prediction of desolation, exile and eventual restoration may be contained in Jn 2.19. Although the evangelist interprets the logion as referring to Jesus' body (v. 21), that does not preclude its referring also, even primarily, to the destruction and rebuilding of the temple, particularly given its setting in the temple courts.[94] Such a prediction would be quite in keeping with the prophetic climate of the

91.   Telford (1980: 264-66) notes that the cursed fig tree represents the temple and the cultus also in the Markan parallel (Mk 11.12-14, 20-21).

92.   Note how the distinctive Old Testament ingathering imagery, discussed in Chapter 6, pp. 188-92, reoccurs in the New Testament. Harvest imagery, both threshing and gathering, is employed for judgment and redemption (Mt. 3.12; 9.37; 13.30, 40-43; Lk. 3.17). But unrighteous Israelites are among those to be threshed (Mt. 3.12; Lk. 3.17), while righteous Samaritans are to be harvested (Jn 4.35). Such ideas are not without Old Testament precedent, as in the eschatological hymn Ps. 67 (cf. v. 7 [6]). Pastoral imagery also occurs. Faithful Israelites are a flock (e.g. Lk. 12.32), as are believing Gentiles (Jn 10.16); but some Israelites are shepherdless sheep (Mt. 9.36).

93.   The phrase βδέλυγμα τῆς ἐρημώσεως is from the Greek of Dan. 9.27; 11.31; 12.11, which most commentators regard as referring to Antiochus Epiphanes's profanation of the temple in 167 BCE (Lacocque 1976: 148; Davies 1985: 57-62; Goldingay 1989: 267-68).

94.   Bultmann regards the original source of Jn 2.19-21 as a prediction of the temple's destruction to which references to Jesus' body have been added subsequently (1971: 126).

time.[95] In that case Jn 2.19 seems to indicate a belief that the temple, and implicitly the entire national life of Israel, is to be destroyed and, after a specified time, restored. The intervening period between destruction and restoration is presumably one of national subjugation and exile. The rebuilding of the temple will take place *in three days,* an expression that, as it cannot be taken literally, should probably be regarded as symbolic of longer periods of time.[96]

The Epistle to the Hebrews appears to envisage a similar sequence of events. The writer, in common with the rest of the New Testament, believes that Messiah has died and ascended to heaven (cf., for example, 1.3; 2.9). He addresses second temple period[97] Israelite Christians whose faith in Jesus's messiahship is wavering (3.14), and reminds them of the fate of their unbelieving ancestors—their bodies fell in the desert (3.7-17). He warns them, 'See to it, brothers, that none of you has a sinful and unbelieving heart' (3.12), and implies that, if they have, they will suffer the same fate as their ancestors (4.1-11). Thus, like the synoptic writers, this writer seems to believe that Israel's rejection of Jesus would result in their exile. Indeed, his tacit assumption of the fact in writing to unconvinced Christians

95. Josephus speaks of prophetic warnings against Jerusalem in the period before the destruction (*War* 6.5.3-4). See also *y. Yom.* 43c. Bultmann notes: 'The *age* and perhaps also the *originality* of the saying are confirmed by its intelligibility within the context of the apocalyptic prophecies of Judaism. Just as the destruction of the temple had already been prophesied in Mic. 3.12, Jer. 26.(33) 6, 18, so it seems that similar voices were heard in Jesus' age...' (Bultmann 1971: 126 n.; Bultmann's italics). O'Neill argues that *5 Ezra* (2 Esdras) 1.33 is a Jewish writing of temple times predicting the destruction of the temple (1991b: 226-35).

96. As far as I am aware, ancient tradition, both Jewish and Christian, recognizes only one metaphorical referent for the expression 'one day,' that is, 1000 years, which is equal to the day of God. The idea was known in Old Testament times, either arising from Ps. 90.4 or already known to the psalm writer. It is referred to in 2 Pet. 3.8; *Ep. Barn.* 15; Justin Martyr, *Trypho* 81; Irenaeus, *Adv. Haer* V.28.3; *Num. R.* 14.12 and alluded to in traditions regarding the week of creation as lasting 7000 years (*2 En.* 33.1f.; *b. 'Abod. Zar.* 9a; *b. Sanh.* 97a), Adam dying within 1000 years according to Gen 2.17 (*Jubilees* 4.30; *Gen. R.* 19.8; *Num. R.* 14.12; *PRE* 22b), Daniel's four kingdoms lasting one day (*PRE* 33b), and an hour of God as lasting 84 or 83.5 years, that is, one-twelfth of a thousand (*PRE* 8b; 67b).

97. See Heb. 7.23-28; 8.3-5; 10.1-4, 11, all of which presuppose ongoing temple worship.

suggests that it was not a specifically Christian belief. Probably his contemporaries outside the Christian community were also aware of a tradition that Messiah's death would be followed by exile. As regards the rest of his eschatological programme, the writer ultimately anticipates a second appearance of Messiah, this time from heaven (9.28; 10.37), the subjugation of Messiah's enemies (10.13) and the inauguration of an unshakeable *malkut* (12.28).

The book of Revelation anticipates two attacks against Jerusalem in the distant future. The first attack is by ten confederated kings (Rev. 17.12-14) who are gathered to the land of Israel by demonic agents (16.14-16;[98] 14.14-20). Then Messiah, who has previously died (1.18; 5.6), appears with the armies of heaven and kills the invaders with the sword of his mouth (19.11-21). After this Messiah reigns 1000 years together with the resurrected righteous (19.21–20.7). At the end of that time Jerusalem will again be surrounded by enemies. These are Gog and Magog, deceived and gathered by Satan, with nations from the four corners of the earth. They will be destroyed by fire from heaven (20.7-9). Then earth's kings will bring tribute to Jerusalem (21.24-26). Israel's exile is not mentioned, but should probably be assumed before the first attack. For the book was probably written after the destruction of 70 CE, and therefore sees the exile as a historical fact that is to end in Israel's ingathering before the first future attack on Jerusalem. And, second, the first attack is to be met by the appearance of the heavenly deliverer, which would make it parallel to the deliverance following the exile in the synoptics.

2 Thess. 2.1-10 refers to a rebellion and to the revelation of a man of lawlessness, who will proclaim himself God in the Jerusalem temple and be destroyed by the breath of Jesus's mouth at his coming. Destruction by the breath of Messiah descending from heaven suggests this event is parallel to the first attack of the nations in Revelation 14–19, in which the allied kings meet a similar fate. How the lawless one's self-apotheosis in the temple is to be reconciled with events in the synoptics and Revelation depends on its date of writing and its writer's awareness of predictions about a coming destruction of Jerusalem. If it was written after the destruction of 70 CE, then the writer

---

98. Αρμαγεδών seems to represent (the hill of ?) Megiddo. This was a site of war in Judg. 5.19; 2 Kgs 23.29-30. The death of Josiah in the latter passage was regarded as typological of future events by the writer of Zech. 12.11.

presumably expects a future rebuilding of the temple to precede the apotheosis of the lawless one (2 Thess. 2.4). But, if it was written before the destruction,[99] it is still plausible that he expected a future destruction and rebuilding to precede the lawless one's appearance. For certainly a coming destruction and exile of Jerusalem was among the earliest of Christian traditions.[100] Synoptic references to the event are numerous and often attributed to Jesus.[101] They are also of an ingenuous and artless nature, appearing in parable (Mt. 21.33-45; Mk 12.1-12; Lk. 20.9-19) and even in a garbled form at Jesus' trial (Mt. 26.61; Mk 14.58), all of which suggests that they are not inventions of post-70 CE. The writer is therefore likely to have been aware of predictions about a coming desolation. Yet he could hardly have imagined the lawless one's apotheosis as taking place at the imminent invasion. For the invader is to be destroyed by messiah at his appearing, and it is unlikely that the writer envisaged the temple being destroyed after the appearance of the heavenly deliverer. Therefore he presumably anticipated (or had seen) a destruction and exile, but expected it to end with the rebuilding of the temple and the apotheosis of the lawless one.

In trying to identify an eschatological programme implicit in the New Testament, I am not, of course, suggesting that its writers had identical beliefs about every aspect of eschatology. But, if a programme similar to the Zecharian one dominated eschatological thinking of the time, then it might be expected that individual New Testament books would be in broad agreement with it. The eschatological ideas of the New Testament writers seem to compare with the Zecharian model as follows.

---

99. Many commentators, perhaps the majority, accept 2 Thessalonians as genuinely Pauline and hence, pre-70 CE. For a discussion of viewpoints on dating and provenance see Bruce 1982: xxxiv-xlvi.

100. This, as noted above, is the view of Bultmann, for instance, who regards 2.19 as an ancient Christian prophecy of the temple's destruction, to which other material has subsequently been added (1971: 126 n.).

101. Mt. 21.33-45; 23.38; 24.2; Mk 12.1-12; Lk. 13.35; 19.41-44; 20.9-19; 21.20-24. Acts 6.13-14 represents the impending destruction of Jerusalem as part of earliest Christian belief with its origin in the teaching of Jesus.

Zech. 9–14	Ingathering of Israel	Gathering of hostile nations	Death of king and Israel's exile	Divine rout of nations	Nations gather to Jerusalem
Synoptics	(Babylonian return)	(Roman invasion)	Death of Messiah. Israel destroyed by Rome and exiled	Israel gathered; temple rebuilt. Abomination of desolation. Messiah comes from heaven	Many from east and west at messianic banquet
Jn 2.19	(Babylonian return)	(Roman invasion)	Destruction of temple. (Exile)	Restoration	
Hebrews	(Babylonian return)	(Roman invasion)	Death of Messiah. Desert exile for his rejecters	Messiah comes from heaven. His enemies are subdued	*Malkut*
2 Thess.	(Babylonian return)	(Roman invasion)	(Death of Messiah. Exile)	Temple rebuilt. Lawless one comes. Destroyed at coming of Messiah	(*Malkut*)
Rev.	(Babylonian return)	(Roman invasion)	Death of Messiah. (Israel exiled)	(Israel gathered). Ten kings attack. Messiah appears from heaven and destroys them	1000 year malkut. Gog and Magog attack and are destroyed. Kings bring tribute

g. *Apocalyptic Midrashim of Post-Temple Times*

The destruction of the second temple did not destroy Israel's messianic hope. Eschatological texts, such as the *Sibylline Oracles*, the *Testaments of the Twelve Patriarchs* and *4 Ezra*, were redacted in subsequent decades. Fifty years later, Bar Kokhba's revolt commanded considerable support. It may plausibly be surmised that his contemporaries, some of whom regarded him as Messiah,[102] considered the years from the destruction of the temple as the pre-deliverance exile predicted by Zechariah 13–14. The event, however, proved otherwise, and the crushing of Bar Kokhba's uprising seems to have led to a temporary loss of faith in any eschatological hope among many Jews, as evidenced by the non-eschatological character of the Mishnah.

---

102. R. Akiva apparently maintained that Bar Kokhba was Messiah (*y. Ta'an.* 4.8; *Lam. R.* 2.2.4). This claim may have been made by Bar Kokhba himself, for *b. Sanh.* 93b says he was slain because he falsely claimed to be messiah.

However, the eschatological hope was dormant rather than dead, and reappeared after the mishnaic period in a genre of apocalyptic midrash, featuring eschatological programmes similar to Zechariah 9–14.[103]

In the early midrash *Aggadat Mashiah,* Israel gather in Galilee under Messiah ben Joseph, ascend to Jerusalem and subjugate the surrounding lands. They are then attacked by Gog and Magog and defeated. Messiah ben Joseph is slain, and Israel are scattered in the wilderness. Messiah ben David appears to them, and they plunder Rome and ascend to Jerusalem, displacing the invaders. Thereafter the remainder of exiled Israel gather to Jerusalem. It should be noted that, in spite of the statement that 'all Israel' will initially ascend to Jerusalem (v. 20), this does not include the 'exiles', possibly the lost ten tribes, who are gathered later (v. 41). The initial ingathering therefore seems to be partial.

In *Otot ha-Mashiah* Messiah ben Joseph conquers Edom (Rome) and goes to Jerusalem. Israel gather to him, and they subjugate all the surrounding nations (6.7-8). Then Armilus gathers forces to the valley Jehoshaphat (Joel 4.14). In the ensuing battle, Messiah ben Joseph is slain (7.12-13). Israel flee into the desert for 45 days, where they are purified (7.14-25). Then Messiah ben David appears, the Israelites gather to him, and they ascend to Jerusalem (8.2-4). Armilus again gathers to make war against Jerusalem, but the Holy One fights on behalf of ben David and destroys them (8.4-6). Then the scattered remnant of Israel are carried to Jerusalem on the shoulders of kings (9.1-2), and the ten tribes come from Trans-Euphrates (10.1), suggesting that the earlier gatherings are partial, in spite of 8.3-4.

In *Sefer Zerubbabel* Messiah ben Joseph gathers all Israel 'as one man' (40) and they live in Jerusalem 40 years. They are attacked by the Persians, but overcome them. Then Armilus attacks Jerusalem with ten kings. Ben Joseph is slain and Israel are exiled in the wilderness (43). Then, after other events, the dead of Israel are raised and, presumably, return to Jerusalem. Then the Lord and Messiah ben

103. Translations of six of these, together with a discussion of their dating, are given in Appendix 1: *Aggadat Mashiah, Otot ha-Mashiah, Sefer Zerubbabel, Pirqê Mashiah,* '*Asereth Melakhim,* and *Nistarot Rav Shim'on ben Yohai.* Similar midrashic material occurs in Sa'adya Gaon's *Kitab al-'Amanat* VIII (Rosenblatt 1948: 290-322). Rosenblatt dates it from 933 CE (xxvii).

David come and kill Armilus and his troops. Jerusalem is again restored and God's *malkut* is inaugurated (64).

In *'Asereth Melakhim* Messiah ben Joseph ascends to Jerusalem, builds the temple and offers sacrifices. A gathering of Israelites with him is not mentioned, nor is the conquest of the heathen inhabitants of Jerusalem, but both should probably be inferred, as he would hardly rebuild the temple alone in a deserted Jerusalem. Then Israel are attacked by Gog, who kills ben Joseph. Three-quarters of the Israelites go into exile and one-quarter remain in the city. The Holy One then fights the invaders and defeats them. He blows on a great *shofar* and gathers the exiles, including the nine and a half tribes. Then Messiah ben David rules for a thousand years.

In *Pirqê Mashiah* King Nehemiah the Messiah, a pseudonym for Messiah ben Joseph,[104] leads Israel. They conquer Rome and go up to Jerusalem. There, in warfare with the city's Arab overlords, Messiah is killed. Israel is exiled to the wilderness. There the King Messiah, that is, ben David, appears to them and incites all the nations to war with him. When they attack he slays them with the breath of his mouth.

In *Nistarot Rav Shim'on ben Yohai* Messiah ben Joseph ascends with Israel to Jerusalem. There they build the temple and offer sacrifices. Military success is implied not only in their taking the city, but also in the quote from Dan. 11.4 (*NRSbY* 21). Armilus attacks them. In the conflict Messiah ben Joseph is slain, and then Israel are exiled in the wilderness (24-25). After other events, Messiah ben David appears with the clouds of heaven (27). He kills Armilus with the breath of his lips and takes dominion (28). Then all Israel gather and go up to Jerusalem (29).

Sa'adya has Messiah ben Joseph gather individual Israelites in Galilee, and go up with them to Jerusalem. There they will be attacked by Armilus and in the conflict ben Joseph will be killed. Then Israel will be driven into the wilderness.[105] Messiah ben David will appear to them suddenly, kill the usurpers of Jerusalem, resettle and rebuild the city, and rule there, with Israel in prosperity.[106] Then Gog and Magog shall gather an army from sundry nations to attack him, but

---

104. Messiah ben Joseph is called Nehemiah ben Hoshiel at *Otot* 6.5; 7.11ff. and *Sef. Z.* 44.

105. *Kitab al-'Amanat* VIII.v (Rosenblatt 1948: 301-302).

106. *Kitab al-'Amanat* VIII.vi (Rosenblatt 1948: 304-305).

they shall be destroyed by divine intervention, and the survivors will submit to Israel and do menial service.[107] Messiah ben David will command that all nations make annual pilgrimage to the Feast of Sukkoth in Jerusalem, as in Zechariah 14, and those Israelites still remaining among the nations will be borne to Jerusalem, along with the wealth of all the nations.[108]

There is therefore a marked similarity in these midrashim. All anticipate a future gathering of Israel under a messianic king. This initial ingathering consists principally of Josephites or Ephraimites, a fact sometimes stated explicitly,[109] and elsewhere implied in the Josephite descent of their leader. This is followed by an attack on Jerusalem by a foreign alliance, who slay the Messiah and devastate the city. Israel are then driven into exile in the wilderness.[110] Later they return to Jerusalem, where the nations are routed by divine power, either directly, or by the mediation of Messiah ben David. The *malkut* of ben David is then inaugurated and the remainder of Israel scattered in the world, particularly the ten tribes, gather to Jerusalem. The similarity of these motifs to the Zecharian model should be noticeable.

---

107. *Kitab al-'Amanat* VIII.vi (Rosenblatt 1948: 304-307). Sa'adya seems to be aware of a tradition similar to that in Rev. 19.19 and 20.7-9, discussed above, in which Gog and Magog attack after the establishment of the Davidic *malkut*. Thus both these writers envisage three foreign invasions: one in which a Messiah dies, one in which a Davidic messiah triumphs, and a final one in which a Davidic Messiah finally crushes all opposition. Note too that *Midr. Pss.* 118 §12 and 119 §2 state that Gog and Magog will go up against Jerusalem three times. Possibly the variant traditions arose as a result of (1) divergent opinions as to how the programmes of Ezekiel and Zechariah should be harmonized and (2) lack of clarity about the number of attacks in the Zecharian programme.

108. *Kitab al-'Amanat* VIII.vi (Rosenblatt 1948: 307-12).

109. *Ag. M.* 13; *Otot* 8.6; Sa'adya VIII.v (Rosenblatt 1948: 302). See also *B. Bat.* 123b; *Gen. R.* 73.7; 75.5-6; 97 (NV in Soncino edn); 99.2.

110. The midrash writers apparently had no doubt of this theme being biblical in origin. *Otot* 7.19 and *NRSbY* 24 cite Zech. 13.8-9; *As. M.* 4.14 and Sa'adya VIII.v (Rosenblatt 1948: 302) cite Zech. 14.2; *Otot* 7.20 and Sa'adya VIII.v (Rosenblatt 1948: 303) cite Ezek. 20.34-38; *Otot* 7.20 also cites Dan. 12.10. *Otot* 7.21 and *Pes. R.* 15.10 cite Hos. 2.16 [14]. Sa'adya takes pains to emphasize that all these themes originate from Scripture (*Kitab al-'Amanat* VIII.v [Rosenblatt 1948: 302-304]).

Zech. 9–14	Ingathering of Israel	Gathering of hostile nations	Death of king and Israel's exile	Divine rout of nations	Nations gather to Jerusalem
Aggadat M.	*	*	*	*	*
Otot ha-M.	*	*	*	*	*
Sefer Zer.	*	*	*	*	
'Asereth M.	*	*	*	*	*
Pirqê M.	*	*	*	*	*
Nistarot	*	*	*	*	*
Sa'adya	*	*	*	*	*

h. *Summary*

Post-Zecharian apocalyptic programmes seem to display eschatological programmes similar to that of Zechariah 9–14, and regularly refer to these chapters. This suggests that the programme I identified in Zechariah 9–14 was also recognized by early interpreters, and is not simply a product of my own reading. Whether these interpreters derived it directly from Zechariah or from similar traditions now lost cannot be ascertained. But certainly, as the Zecharian programme is without parallel in the Bible for scale, scope and detail, it would seem to be the likeliest origin for these beliefs. It is plausible to suggest that such an eschatological programme could have been known to the redactor(s) of the Psalter and may have influenced the shaping of their collection. Assuming tentatively that this is the case, I shall try, in the following chapters, to identify the latter-day desert exile and messianic motifs in the Psalter.

Chapter 8

THE MESSIAHS OF THE LORD[1]

If the striking of the king and the latter-day exile take place, in the
Zecharian programme, between the initial attack on ingathered Israel
and their final deliverance, then, if these events are reflected in the
Psalter, they should appear somewhere between the Asaph Psalms
(Pss. 50, 73–83) and the Songs of Ascents (Pss. 120–34). I would suggest that Psalm 89 can be read as representing the stricken king and
Book IV (Pss. 90–106) as representing the ensuing exile. I would
further suggest that Psalm 45 represents the initial appearance of the
king to Israel, that Psalm 72 depicts his initial reign, and that Psalm
110 represents his appearing as the agent of divine deliverance. In this
chapter, therefore, I shall examine the royal psalms, and try to
demonstrate the plausibility of connecting them in this way with the
king figures of the Zecharian programme. Then, having surveyed the
peaks, I shall, in the next chapter, descend to the trackless wilderness
and investigate the parallels between Book IV and the latter-day exile.

1. The Royal Psalms

Following Gunkel, most scholars have recognized the group of psalms
that refer to Yhwh's king or *mashiah* as forming a separate literary
Gattung.[2] Usually included in this group are Psalms 2, 18, 20, 21, 45,
72, 89, 110 and 132. However the similarity between these psalms is
sufficiently clear for it to have been noted by earlier writers also. The
New Testament writer of Heb. 1.5-13 cites Psalms 2, 45 and 110 in
sequence, and alludes in v. 6 to Ps. 89.28 [27], in the context of a discussion about messianic belief. This suggests that these psalms were

---

1.   שנאמר ולציון יאמר איש ואיש ילד בה אלו משיחי ה' משיח בן דוד ומשיח בן אפרים
(*Midr. Pss.* 87.6 [5]).

2.   Gunkel and Begrich 1933: 140-71.

understood as a related group with a messianic message even in temple times. Ibn Ezra also noted the similarities among these psalms:

> The right interpretation of this psalm [110] in our opinion is that one of the singers composed it about David, like the psalm, *The Lord answer you in the day of trouble* (Ps. 20.2 [1]), *Lord, in your strength the king rejoices* (Ps. 21.2 [1]), and, *For Solomon. God give the king your judgments* [Ps. 72.1]. And this psalm was composed when David's men swore an oath, saying, 'You shall not go out with us to battle.' And this is the beginning of the singer's words: *The Lord said to my lord*, that is, David.[3]

In recognizing the royal psalms as a group, these ancient writers seem to be simply noting what is already implicit in the Psalter. For as Forbes, Childs, Wilson and others have noted, the royal psalms have been positioned in such a way as to make them appear significant.[4] Many of them occur in positions that mark them as being particular highpoints in the collection. Psalm 2 functions together with Psalm 1 as an introduction to the entire collection. Psalm 72 occurs at the end of a large group of David psalms and closes Book II, Psalm 89 occurs at the end of the Korah Psalms and closes Book III, and Psalm 110 is the last of a short group of Davidic psalms that precedes the Hallel group (Pss. 111–18). Other royal psalms, such as 20, 21, 45 and 132 may not be as immediately prominent, but their kingship theme links them with the more prominent royal psalms.

Commentators have also noted that these psalms appear to have been interpreted messianically by the redactor.[5] For their very inclusion in the Psalter, at a time when the house of David was in eclipse, suggests that the redactor was looking forward to its resurgence under a future Davidic king. And if they are to be interpreted messianically, then their prominence within the collection suggests that the messianic theme is central to the message of the Psalter. I shall briefly examine Psalms 2, 45, 72, 110 and 132 to identify their major themes and consider what similarities they might have to the Zecharian eschatological programme.

---

3. Ibn Ezra, Comm. on Ps. 110.
4. Forbes 1888: 4; Childs 1979: 515-17; Wilson 1985a: 209-214.
5. Forbes 1888: 4; Westermann 1981: 258; Childs 1979: 515-17; Allen 1983: 5.

2. *Psalm 2: Victory Announced*

This psalm has already been reviewed in Chapter 2, and it is unnecessary to repeat the comments made there. However it is worthwhile to re-emphasize that this psalm appears to have been set together with Psalm 1 as an introduction to the entire Psalter. As a result the theme of how Yhwh's *mashiah* will conquer all opposition and rule the world from Zion must be considered as one of the broad, overarching themes of the Psalms, in whose light all the ensuing lyrics, including the royal psalms, should be interpreted.

J.T. Willis has suggested that the psalm's literary *Gattung* is that of a 'Cry of Defiance' before the onset of battle.[6] He indicates ancient Near Eastern parallels, including Mot's pre-battle rhetoric of defiance before he enters single combat with Baal and is defeated (Baal I AB V.8-23), and the mutual defiances of Goliath and David (1 Sam. 17.41-47). He notes that such cries of defiance tend to have three characteristics also shared by this psalm: first, a threat of impending conflict; secondly, an affirmation that the speaker's forces will prevail; thirdly, warnings of impending defeat to the enemy and offers of clemency if they capitulate.[7] If this suggestion is accepted, then Psalm 2's introductory role in regard to the Psalter is strengthened. It defies all the opponents of the inauguration of God's messianic rule, *the kings of the earth* (v. 2) and announces that, like Baal, Messiah will ultimately triumph and reign secure on his holy mountain.

3. *Psalm 45: The Bridegroom King Comes to Daughter Zion*

This psalm is a royal epithalamion, almost certainly from Israel's monarchic period.[8] The bard addresses himself to the praises of the royal bridegroom (v. 2 [1]). He eulogizes his beauty, kind and gracious speech, divine favour and appointment, military prowess, righteous justice, elegant habitation and the status of his consorts (vv. 1-10 [1-9]). He then addresses the bride, calling her בת, *daughter,* because of her youthful beauty and innocence (vv. 11-13 [10-12]). She is to

6.   Willis 1990a: 33-50.
7.   Willis 1990a: 46.
8.   Craigie rightly comments, 'All that can be affirmed with reasonable certainty is that the psalm originated at some point in the history of the Hebrew monarchy' (1983b: 338).

forget her former family allegiances and give herself wholly to her new lord. Thus shall she be beloved by him and honoured with rich gifts by the wealthy and influential. He proceeds to describe the bride's glorious apparel in the inner chambers, and the bridal procession's progress to the king's palace (vv. 14-16 [13-15]). The psalm closes with a blessing on the king—may the fruit of the coming union be royal descendants who shall carry his name in all generations (17-18 [16-17]).

The notorious crux of the psalm is v. 7 [6]: כסאך אלהים עולם ועד. Several interpretations exist from ancient times on. Ibn Ezra renders it as כסאך כסא אלהים, *Your throne is a throne of God,* a suggestion in line with 1 Chron. 29.23.[9] Both he and Kimhi record Sa'adya's interpretation: כסאך יכין אלהים, *God establishes your throne.*[10] In modern times a host of alternatives has been suggested.[11] However, the obvious interpretation of the Hebrew is to take *elohim* as a vocative addressed to the king, as do AV, RV, and NIV. That this interpretation is likeliest is admitted even by those who maintain that the context cannot support it.[12] And the arguments in its favour are such that a number of commentators, following detailed linguistic analysis of the verse, conclude that no alternative is as viable.[13] Ancient writers know of no other interpretation, LXX, Targum,[14] New Testament (Heb. 1.8), Aquila, Symmachus, Peshitta and Vulgate all assuming the vocative. Moreover there is evidence elsewhere in the Old Testament to

9. Ibn Ezra, Comm. on Ps. 45.7.

10. Ibn Ezra, Comm on Ps. 45.7; Kimhi, Comm. on Ps. 45.7.

11. Dahood revocalizes כסאך as the Piel of a denominative verb 'enthrone', giving, *The eternal and everlasting God has enthroned you* (1965–70: 273). NEB proposes, *Your throne is like God's throne, eternal* (cf. Emerton 1968: 338-40). RSV has *Your divine throne.* But, as Craigie notes, none of these suggestions seems linguistically convincing, all either requiring alterations to MT, or contravening Hebrew grammatical conventions (Craigie 1983b: 337).

12. Craigie 1983b: 337; Cohen 1945: 141. See too Porter who, after providing support for an alternative suggestion of Driver's, concludes that it is better to continue to take *elohim* as a vocative (1961: 53).

13. Delitzsch 1887: II, 95-98; Porter 1961: 51-53; Kraus 1978: 452; and Couroyer (1971) who cites Egyptian analogies in support of the vocative. Craigie, although he adopts Dahood's revocalization, notes that the vocative 'is the most likely interpretation' (1983b: 337).

14. The Targum is paraphrastic: כורסי יקרך יי קיים לעלמי עלמין, *Your glorious throne, O Lord, endures for ever and ever.* But note that it confirms the vocative address to the deity.

support such a form of royal address. Elsewhere in the Psalter the king is called the son of God and said to be divinely begotten (2.7,12; 89.27 [26]), language that probably reflects similar ideas preserved in 2 Sam. 7.14 and 1 Chron. 17.13. That which is divinely begotten surely merits divine appellation. Porter also parries the objection that *elohim* cannot refer to the king:

> ...in three passages of the Old Testament, 2 Sam. xiv.17, 20, xix.28, King David is described as כמלאך אלהים. Judges xiii strongly suggests that 'the Angel of God' was indistinguishable from God himself. Further, at 2 Sam. xiv.17, David is called the Angel of God because he is able לשמע הטוב והרע: this recalls Gen. iii.22 לדעת טוב ורע, and it was precisely this knowledge which placed Adam among the אלהים. Thus it is hardly correct that an address to the king as God finds no close parallel elsewhere in the Old Testament.[15]

The same is more emphatically true of the prophets' future David. The Isaianic Davidide is called אל גבור (Isa. 9.5-6 [6-7]). The Zecharian one is identified with Yhwh (12.10), who is his social equal (13.7), and said to be כאלהים and כמלאך אלהים (12.8), the mysterious being who bears Yhwh's name (Exod. 23.20-23).

The likeliest interpretation of v. 7 [6] would therefore seem to be that the king is indeed addressed as *elohim*. Now Kraus remarks, 'In the ancient Near Eastern cult of kings that is certainly a common phenomenon, but without parallel in the Old Testament.' But if Old Testament parallels, such as those above, can be found, should it not perhaps be considered that Israel's ideology of kingship resembled those of their neighbours more than is commonly accepted? Israel may have rejected the more extreme Egyptian form of divine kingship ideology, in which the king was intriniscally divine.[16] But the biblical passages cited above suggest that something like the more moderate Babylonian form, in which the king became the son of God by adoption, was also held in Israel.[17] Such an ideology would differentiate

---

15. Porter 1961: 51.

16. See, for instance, the early third millennium pyramid text: 'Recitation by Nut, the greatly beneficent: The King is my eldest son who split open my womb; he is my beloved, with whom I am well pleased' (Faulkner 1969: 1).

17. Such a difference between the Egyptian and Babylonian divine kingship ideologies is noted by Mowinckel 1962: I, 50-51. See also Engnell (1943) who gives an overview of the divine kingship ideologies of Egypt, Sumeria, Akkadia, Babylon, the Hittites and Ugarit. Given the ubiquity of the idea, it is unlikely that Israel had no such conception.

between Yhwh, as the transcendent deity, and the king upon whom he bestowed divine nature, just as the psalm in question distinguishes between the *elohim*-king and his *elohim* who anoints him with the oil of joy, an action that may have symbolized the anointing of the divine spirit (Ps. 45.8 [7]). The idea of adoption and regeneration to divine sonship was current in Israel as late as the first century CE, when the New Testament speaks of mortals obtaining divine sonship by divine generation (Jn 1.12-13) and partaking in the divine nature (φύσις; 2 Pet. 1.4). If such an ideology of kingship did indeed prevail in monarchic Israel, then the divinely anointed (משׁח; v. 8 [7]) *elohim* of this psalm is a משׁיח indeed, though a historical and not an eschatological one.

However, after the downfall of *bet*-David, the continuing belief in its future resurgence would have led to the psalm's being regarded as referring to a future Davidic king. Subsequent commentators certainly interpret it messianically. The Targum renders v. 3 [2] as, 'Your beauty, King Messiah, surpasses that of the sons of men.'[18] Another early interpretation is Heb. 1.8, whose author applies v. 7 [6] to the Christian messiah. The mediaeval rabbis thought likewise. Ibn Ezra: 'This psalm was spoken about the David or about the Messiah his son, may his name endure! [Of whom it is said] *And David my servant shall be their prince for ever*' [Ezek. 37.25].'[19] Kimhi: 'This psalm was spoken about the King, the Messiah. It is called *A love song* [Ps. 45.1], which is to say, the love of the Lord for his Messiah.'[20] Mezudat David: 'This song is about the King Messiah.'[21] More recent commentators also suggest that this psalm was intended to have a messianic reference within the context of the Psalter,[22] or at least that it is readily amenable to messianic interpretation.[23] Thus the bridegroom figure of this psalm was regarded from early times as representing the anticipated future Davidic hero-king, and this

---

18. שׁופרך מלכא משׁיחא עדיף מבני נשׁא

19. זה המזמור נאמר על דוד או על המשׁיח בנו שׁכן שׁמו ודוד עבדי נשׁיא להם לעולם

20. זה המזמור נאמר על המלך המשׁיח. תקרא שׁיר ידידות כלומר אהבת ה׳ למשׁיחו

21. השׁיר הזה הוא על מלך משׁיח

22. Baethgen: 'Dazu hat es den Anschein, dass schon der Sammler des Psalters unter dem Könige nicht einen irdischen sondern den himmlischen, den Messias verstand' (Baethgen 1897: 34). Delitzsch notes that the admission of this psalm into the canon is 'inexplicable' unless it was interpreted messianically (Delitzsch 1887: II, 85).

23. Kirkpatrick 1902: 244-45; Craigie 1983b: 340-41.

interpretation, as was noted earlier, is a likely explanation for its preservation in the Psalter.

If then, the Psalter's redactor might have regarded this as a messianic text, what significance might he have intended for it in the broader context of the collection and its eschatological programme? A number of similarities exists between the picture of the king in this psalm and in Zech. 9.9. These are so marked as to suggest, like other previously noted similarities, some kind of influence one way or the other between the Psalter and the Zecharian programme. First, the king in both cases is a representative of the house of David, intimately associated with Yhwh, and exalted, even divine, in being. Moreover, both figures display Solomonic characteristics.[24] The psalm's king dispenses justice (v. 8 [7]), marries a foreign princess, and has a harem (v. 10 [9]); the Zecharian figure speaks *shalom* to the nations, and is described with the motto that also occurs in Solomonic Ps. 72.8 (Zech. 9.10). Secondly, like the figure of the psalm, the Zecharian king is a bridegroom. He comes to Jerusalem as to a young maiden, *Daughter Zion,* who rejoices in eager anticipation at his approach. The bride in each case is addressed as בת (Ps. 45.11 [10]; Zech. 9.9).[25] Thirdly, in both texts the king is represented riding, the verb רכב being used in each case (Ps. 45.5 [4]; Zech. 9.9). Delitzsch maintains that the psalmic figure is going to war and therefore should not be envisaged as mounted on an ass.[26] This is no doubt true. But there is nothing in the psalm to contradict explicitly the חמור of Zech. 9.9, and possibly this should be regarded as another of the prophet's reversals of earlier traditions, like those noted in the preceding chapter. Fourthly, the characteristics of each figure are justice and humility. The one rides forth on behalf of ענוה־צדק (Ps. 45.5 [4]); the other is צדיק and עני (Zech. 9.9). True, the Zecharian figure is actually humble or humbled

---

24. Both Kirkpatrick and Delitzsch reject the suggestion, based on Ahab's ivory palace and Tyrian bride (v. 9 [8]; cf. 1 Kgs 16.31; 22.39), that the figure of the psalm might represent Ahab, noting that the language of the psalm is based upon the messianic predictions to *bet*-David (Kirkpatrick 1902: 223-24; Delitzsch 1887: II, 86-88). Delitzsch allows that it could have been written for either Solomon or Jehoram, but thinks the latter likelier. Kirkpatrick, on the other hand, considers that Solomon is the likelier, noting, in my opinion rightly, that the Yhwhistic poet would not have regarded an alliance with the idolatrous house of Ahab with such satisfaction.

25. Note the similarity to the eschatological programme of Mic. 4–5, where the former kingship comes to and enters בת־ציון (Mic. 4.8).

26. Delitzsch 1887: II, 93.

(עֲנִי), while his counterpart merely contends on behalf of 'just humility'. But the identification with the humble cause is the same, though greater in degree, and the use of the same verbal roots in each case is striking.

Such similarities seem more than fortuitous, and suggest some kind of link between the ideas of the psalm and Zech. 9.9. The prophetic writer may have borrowed from the psalm, already arranged into some kind of programmatic proto-Psalter. Or the psalm's place in the Psalter may have been inspired by the Zecharian reference to it. Or other alternatives might be proposed. But this much is clear: in the eschatological programmes of Zechariah 9–14 and the Psalter, the latter-day Davidic king is represented as a bridegroom coming to Israel, mounted, and identified with the concepts עֲנָה and צֶדֶק.

Such an interpretation of Psalm 45 makes sense of the surrounding lyrics. Psalms 42 and 43 represent Israel in exile, separated from the temple (42.3-5 [2-4]), taunted by the heathen, crying to God for redemption, and anticipating its coming (42.10-11 [9-10]; 43.1-5). Psalm 44 rehearses the events of the exodus (vv. 2-4 [1-3]), celebrates God's saving power (5-9 [4-8]), laments Israel's sorrows that God has brought upon them (10-23 [9-22]), and culminates with a plea that God redeem them (vv. 24-27 [23-26]), presumably just as he formerly did at the exodus, by leading them out of heathen oppression to the promised land. Psalm 45 therefore becomes the answer to this prayer, revealing the redeemer, the bridegroom-king, who will turn Israel's sorrow to joy. Psalms 46–48 then celebrate the ultimate triumph of God's cause (46), kingdom (47) and city (48), before the divine command to gather Israel is issued at Asaph Ps. 50.5.

4. *Psalm 72: A Kingdom Established*

This psalm is a prayer and blessing for a king whose just empire shall encompass the whole earth. LXX and many subsequent interpreters regard the לִשְׁלֹמֹה heading as meaning *for Solomon* rather than *by Solomon*.[27] Certainly, the heading suggests that the one addressed is a

---

27. LXX has εἰς Σαλωμών. The Syriac heading is, 'A Psalm of David, when he had made Solomon king.' The Padua edition of Midrash Tehillim (Warsaw, 1865) says, *David said of Solomon* (72.2). Although Buber's edn (1881) has at the same place the variant, *Solomon also said,* both editions regard Solomon as the addressee of the psalm at their comment on v. 20: *All of these were the prayers David uttered*

king of the house of David, either Solomon or, by implication, a successor. The psalm begins with a prayer that God grant the king divine discernment (מִשְׁפָּטֶיךָ) and integrity (צִדְקָתֶךָ) so as rightly to maintain justice, as a result of which (the בְּ of בִּצְדָקָה indicating instrumentality[28]) the land will bear *shalom* to the people (vv. 1-4). The psalmist then speaks of the universal dominion of the king, in which all his enemies submit and all nations become tribute to him (vv. 8-11). There follows a further description of the beneficial effects of his reign to the poor and needy, whom he will rescue from oppression and violence (vv. 12-15). The psalmist then recapitulates all his themes, conferring on the king length of life, wealth, the prayers, blessing and esteem of his subjects, eternal honour and renown, and on the kingdom abundant provisions and populace (vv. 15-17). The psalm concludes with a benediction on Yhwh (vv. 18-19).

As with other royal psalms, the messianic interpretation implied by its inclusion in the Psalter is explicit in later interpreters. Ben Sira refers to v. 8 in the context of Israel's eschatological hope, saying that Abraham's seed will inherit from sea to sea, and from the River to the ends of the earth (44.21): The Targum renders v. 1 as 'God, give King Messiah the precepts of your judgments.'[29] *PRE* 14a and *Num. R.* 13.14 interpret the psalm of Messiah ben David. *Midr. Pss.* 72.6 regards it as referring to Solomon and to the Messiah. Ibn Ezra adopts the same dual interpretation, as does Kimhi, who notes that the messianic interpretation was widespread among his predecessors.[30] Early Christian interpreters likewise regard it as a messianic psalm.[31] Modern commentators also recognize in the psalm a degree of intentional messianism, in the sense that it refers to an ideal king. Peters, for instance, comments,

> It reminds one of such Psalms to divine kings as have come down to us from ancient Babylonian sources for the celebration of the royal birth feasts and the like, and may have been influenced by the existence of such

---

concerning his son Solomon and concerning the King Messiah (*Midr. Pss.* 72.6). The same opinion is held by Rashi, Ibn Ezra and Kimhi (Comms. on Ps. 72.1).

28. See the suggested translations of Delitzsch (1887: II, 342) and Kirkpatrick (1902: 419).

29. אֱלָהָא הִלְכוּת דִינָךְ לְמַלְכָּא מְשִׁיחָא.

30. Ibn Ezra, Comm. on Ps. 72.1. Kimhi, Comm. on Ps. 72.1 and 20.

31. See Justin Martyr, *Dial. with Trypho* 34. Further examples are noted by Carrière 1991: 49ff.

worship and such compositions, with their similar pictures of the king administering justice, caring for the needy, bringing prosperity and peace to his people and much more; but all these elements, it must be added, already existed in Hebrew literature, and are constantly referred to from an early period onward as the marks of a good king. The picture of the Messianic rule, which is specifically Hebrew, is very ancient in its origin, going back nearly if not quite to the reign of David...[32]

Kirkpatrick regards both eschatological and historical interpretations as valid:

> It is even possible that the Psalm does not refer to any particular king, but is a prayer for the establishment of the Messianic kingdom under a prince of David's line according to prophecy, the lyrical counterpart in fact of Zech. ix.9ff. At the same time it does appear to have a definite historical background, and to be a prayer for a king who is actually on the throne.[33]

However, the earliest messianic interpretation is the one that also connects it with the Zecharian eschatological programme, for v. 8 is cited almost verbatim at Zech. 9.10 in reference to the coming king. Moreover, in both the Psalter and Zechariah this prediction of universal dominion occurs in a similar position, following the advent of the messiah (Ps. 45; Zech. 9.9) and preceding the eschatological war (Ps. 83; Zech. 9.13-16). Therefore the significance of the psalm in terms of the Psalter's eschatological programme may be related to the significance of its citation in the programme of Zechariah 9–14. The possibilities of what the citation may represent are as follows.

(1) It may simply be a prediction of the king's ultimate dominion depicted in the homage of the nations in Zech. 14.16-19, where the king's presence is unstated but implied.

(2) On the other hand, it may indicate a temporary messianic rule preceding the latter-day war and the king's affliction. For, if he is to be a stricken king, and Israel are to control Jerusalem prior to the time of the conflict, then some kind of temporary messianic *malkut* must be envisaged before the time of trouble.

(3) Perhaps the most likely suggestion is that both the temporary and the final *malkut* are symbolized by this prediction of universal rule, the lesser initial kingdom being described in terms of the greater and ultimate one.

---

32. Peters 1922: 270-71.
33. Kirkpatrick 1902: 417.

As with Zech. 9.10, so with the eschatological programme of the Psalter. Psalm 72 could symbolize either a temporary messianic kingdom preceding the war in Psalm 83, or anticipate the final kingdom represented in Psalms 120–34, or a combination of both, the temporary kingdom being represented in terms of its ultimate triumph. I would tentatively adopt the last of these positions. In that case, Psalm 72 symbolizes the initial kingdom of the one who came to Daughter Zion like a bridegroom in Psalm 45, and represents it in terms of its ultimate extent in the final *malkut*, when all opposition shall be overcome. The intervening psalms would therefore represent the period between the king's coming and the inauguration of his kingdom. Psalms 46–49 look forward to Israel's ingathering. Asaph Psalm 50 represents the divine command to gather Israel. Psalm 51 might represent the king's repentance for the former crimes of *bet*-David and his prayer for the restoration of Jerusalem (v. 20 [18]). The subsequent David Psalms 52–70 might represent the king's hardships in establishing the kingdom. Their context is initially one of persecution in the desert, but they progress to a Jerusalem context and become increasingly triumphant. Psalm 67 proclaims the ultimate triumph of Yhwh's kingdom over all nations.[34] Psalm 68 is likewise a battle psalm, featuring a triumphal procession (vv. 25-32 [24-31]). These hardships and wars culminate in the *malkut* of Psalm 72, which is followed by the Jerusalem context of Asaph Psalms 73–83, culminating in the invasion of the ten-nation alliance in Psalm 83.

5. *Psalm 89: The King Cut Off*

Psalm 89 is an appeal to Yhwh regarding his apparent breach of covenant in the extinction of the Davidic line. It opens with a declaration of Yhwh's covenant faithfulness (חסדי יהוה), as if in defiance of the apparent breach of that faithfulness that is the psalmist's concern (vv. 2-3 [1-2]). This is followed by a citation of the terms of Yhwh's covenant with David, emphasizing the promise of the eternal endurance of his line (vv. 4-5 [3-4]). Then follows an extended hymnic passage of praise to Yhwh that develops the themes of vv. 2-3 (vv. 6-19

---

34. A later tradition illustrates the messianic conquest theme of Ps. 67. It relates that this psalm was inscribed on David's shield in the form of the *menorah*, and that 'when he went forth to battle, he would meditate on its mystery and conquer' (Scholem 1971: XI, 695).

[5-18]). It emphasizes Yhwh's אמונה (v. 9 [8]), צדק, משפט, חסד and אמת (v. 15 [14]), together with his sovereignty and power, which ensure the success of all his purposes (vv. 6-14 [5-13]). Then the themes of vv. 4-5 undergo further expansion in an extended exposition of the origin and terms of the Davidic covenant (vv. 20-38 [19-37]). Particular emphasis is placed on the eternal nature of the covenant. It is לעולם (vv. 29, 37 [28, 36]) and ועד (v. 30 [29]) and עולם ועד (v. 38 [37]), and its guarantee is said by Yhwh three times to be his own אמונה and חסד (vv. 25, 29, 34 [24, 28, 33]), leading to a covenant that will never be broken (v. 35 [34]), confirmed by an oath sworn by Yhwh's own holiness (v. 36 [35]). A more inviolable declaration can hardly be conceived. Then comes the crux of the psalm, to which this extended rehearsal of Yhwh's faithfulness, sovereignty and power has been leading. The dynasty, which the eternal, almighty, faithful God swore to preserve forever, has come to an end. God himself has rejected David and the covenant; he has destroyed David's city, exalted his foes, degraded his royal line and cut off the days of his youth, that is, prematurely terminated either David's line or its representative, or both (vv. 39-46 [38-45]). There seems to be a hint, in the phrase, *you have pierced/defiled* [חִלַּלְתָּ] *his crown to the earth,* that the Davidic king, like Josiah, has been pierced in battle. For, even given the well-attested secondary meaning of חלל as *defile,* the writer could not but have been aware of connoting its fundamental idea, *pierce.*[35] The use of this verb might be thought to connect the afflicted king of the psalm with the מחלל figure of Isa. 53.5, apparently so influential to the Zecharian writer, and perhaps with the afflicted one of Ps. 88.1 also.[36] Having stated the irresolvable problem, he can do no more than appeal to Yhwh, asking how long he will remain inactive and negligent of his חסד (vv. 47-50 [46-49]) and of the whole multitude of nations (כל־רבים עמים) that have scorned every step of his anointed king (vv. 51-53 [50-52]).

Commentators have varied in their approach to the psalm. Those who seek a historical context for its origin have found one in the death

---

35. Both meanings of חלל are attested in the *piel*. The meaning *pierce* is attested in both *qal* and *piel* (Ezek. 28.9) forms. The less common meaning, *defile,* is usually *piel,* and is not attested in *qal*. The latter may be derived from the former, possibly by the idea of defilement by (sexual?) piercing (cf. Lev. 19.29; 21.7) (BDB: 319-20).

36. See below for the possible derivation of מחלת לענות (Ps. 88.1) from חלל.

of Josiah at Megiddo[37] or the situation with King Jehoiachin after 597 BCE,[38] or elsewhere. Another school of thought, disregarding historical questions, maintains that the psalm originated as a liturgy for a ritual humiliation ceremony for the Israelite king. The two approaches, as Tate notes, are not necessarily antithetical.[39] What is significant, however, is that each of these approaches regards the psalm as referring to the apparent extinction of the Davidic line, possibly in the death of its representative. No other interpretive option seems to be available.

Like other royal psalms, Psalm 89's preservation in the Psalter after the eclipse of *bet*-David suggests it was understood as indicating an anticipated future Davidide. This is particularly likely with this psalm, whose references to Yhwh's משיח (vv. 39, 52 [38, 51]; cf. 21 [20]) would have been most readily understood in post-exilic times of a future figure. Its implicit messianic interpretation in the Psalter is confirmed by later interpreters. The Targum renders v. 52: 'With which your enemies have scoffed, O Lord, with which they have scoffed at the delay of the footsteps of your Messiah, O Lord.'[40] The addition of 'delay' conveys 'the idea that the enemies cannot scoff at the Messiah himself, since he has not yet come, but rather they scoff at the fact that the Jewish people is looking for him and he is delayed.'[41] So the *meturgeman* regarded the psalm as referrring to a messiah not yet come. The New Testament writer of Heb. 1.6 seems to allude to this psalm, in the context of a sequence of messianic proof-texts, when he calls the Messiah πρωτότοκον, *firstborn,* a term used of human leaders in the Old Testament only in this psalm (LXX 88.28) and Deut. 33.17, the latter also being widely regarded as a messianic text.[42]

---

37. Kraus 1978: II, 203; Bentzen 1955: 30; more tentatively, Goulder 1982: 213-19; Tate 1990a: 416. This view is also noted by Anderson 1972: II, 631.

38. This is the preferred opinion of Goulder (1982: 213-19) and Tate (1990a: 416). The view is also noted by Anderson 1972: II, 631.

39. Tate 1990a: 414.

40. די חסידו בעלי דבבך יי די די חסירו איחור רושמת רגלי משיחך יי

41. Levey 1974: 121.

42. *Gen. R.* 75.6; 99.2; *Num. R.* 14.1; *Midr. Tan.* 11.3; and *PRE* 22a all apply the text to Messiah ben Joseph. *Pes. R.* 53.2 applies it to messiah non-specifically. Possibly the earliest evidence for the messianic interpretation of Deut. 33.17 is the bull figure of *1 En.* 90, which commentators regard as a messianic symbol (Charles 1913: 258 n.; Isaac 1983: 5-89]: 5; Milik 1976: 45; Torrey 1945: 112; Torrey 1947: 266). The use of the term *firstborn* seems to connect the Davidic king of this psalm

Rev. 1.5 alludes to the same verse. Juel notes that much other New Testament messianic language appears to derive from this psalm.[43] Rabbinic literature also attests a well-established tradition of messianic exegesis of this psalm.[44] The following passage from *Gen. R.* on 49.8 cites Psalm 89, as Juel notes, among the familiar messianic oracles Gen. 49.8-12, Isa. 11.1-16 and 2 Sam. 7.10ff.[45] It also identifies the cut-off 'David' of the psalm as Messiah.

> Furthermore, the royal Messiah will be descended from the tribe of Judah, as it says, 'And it shall come to pass in that day, that the root of Jesse, that standeth for an ensign of the peoples, unto him shall the nations seek' (Isa. 11.10)... Judah was the fourth of the tribal ancestors to be born, just as the daleth is the fourth letter of the alphabet and is the fourth letter of his name. On the fourth day the luminaries were created, while of the Messiah it is written, 'And his throne [shall endure] as the sun before me' (Ps. 89.37)... and so it says, 'The sceptre shall not depart from Judah' (Gen 49.10); it is also written, 'And thy house and thy kingdom shall be made sure forever' (II Sam. 7.16); also, 'For ever will I keep him for My mercy' (Ps. 89.29).[46]

Likewise, *Exod. R.* on 13.1 identifies Messiah with the central figure of the psalm, particularly in regard to the mysterious designation 'firstborn', applied to slain Messiah ben Joseph in other literature of the period.

> R. Nathan said: The Holy One, blessed be He, told Moses: 'Just as I have made Jacob a firstborn, for it says: "Israel is My son, My firstborn" (Exod. 4.22), so I will make the King Messiah a firstborn, as it says: "I also will appoint him firstborn"'[47]

It is not difficult to imagine how this psalm would fit into a proposed eschatological programme of the Psalter. As in the Zecharian programme the Davidic king is stricken, pierced and mourned for (Zech. 11.17; 12.10; 13.7), so here also the Davidic line is extinguished in the cutting off (v. 46 [45]), and possibly the piercing (v. 40

---

with the Ephraimitic conqueror of Deut. 33.17. This shall be discussed more fully in the comment on Ps. 92 in Chapter 9.

43. Juel 1988: 107ff.

44. *b. Sanh.* 97a; *Gen. R.* on 49.8; *Exod. R.* on 13.1; *Song R.* 2.13; Ibn Ezra on Ps. 89.1, 53.

45. Juel 1988:105.

46. *Gen. R.* on 49.8. The translation is from Freedman and Simon 1939.

47. *Exod. R.* on 13.1. The translation is from Freedman and Simon 1939.

[39]), of its representative. Just as in Zechariah this event takes place at or during the foreign invasion (Zech. 12.3; 14.2), so in the Psalter it comes in the wake of the invasion represented in Psalm 83. The connection is strengthened by the Psalm's possible reference to Josiah, which accords with the reference to Megiddo in Zech. 12.11, and the Targum's understanding it of Josiah.

If this psalm represents the cutting off of the Messiah then the preceding psalms may be interpreted in light of it. Psalm 83, as noted, depicts the invasion of Israel by a ten-nation confederacy. Psalm 84 appears to be a prayer for divine assistance in establishing the *mashiah* (vv. 9-10 [8-9]), an interpretation also found in the Targum to v. 10 [9]: *See, O God, the righteousness of our fathers, and look upon the face of your Messiah.*[48] Such a prayer would suggest that king and kingdom are in jeopardy. The speaker is represented as a Korahite Levite (v. 1), returned from exile with others (vv. 6-8 [5-7]), to a Jerusalem in which the temple is now rebuilt (vv. 2-5, 11 [1-4, 10]). Psalm 85 gives thanks for the ingathering of the exiles (vv. 2-4 [1-3]), implores that God turn away his present *anger* (vv. 5, 6; כעס, אנף and אף), possibly a reference to the invasion of Psalm 83, and looks forward to deliverance (v. 10 [9]) and a happy aftermath (vv. 11-14 [10-13]). In the next psalm, Psalm 86, the לדוד superscription suggests that the plight of the king is now in view. The voice is that of an individual calling to Yhwh to save his life, for he is helpless and in dire straits (vv. 1-7). He is being attacked by a confederation of tyrants (עדת עריצים), a phrase that might well describe the protagonists of Ps. 83.6-9 [5-8], and whose reference to foreign nations is confirmed by vv. 8-9, which affirm that Yhwh is greater than foreign gods, and that all nations will some day pay him homage. Psalm 87, an encomium of Zion, seems strange in the context of Psalms 86 and 88. All that can be said is that it appears to anticipate the city's future glory, when all nations will confess her as the fount of the world's joy. However, if its particular applicability to the latter-day war is unclear, its general connection with exactly such a context was recognized by ancient interpreters: '*This man and that man* refer to the Messiahs of the Lord, to Messiah ben David and Messiah ben Ephraim.'[49] Such a connection with the dying Ephraim (Joseph) Messiah suggests that the psalm was connected with the period of his reign, which preceded the

48. זכות אבהתא חמי אלהים ואסתכל אנפי משיחך

49. *Midr. Pss.* 87.6.

conflict. Psalm 88 is the cry of a suffering individual who describes himself as descending into Sheol (vv. 4-7 [3-6]). The horrors of his situation are described in the 'deadly threat' imagery of darkness and overwhelming waves of divine wrath and judgment (vv. 8-9, 15-18 [7-8, 14-17]). Such a psalm might represent the death cry of the suffering Messiah. This interpretation would seem to be confirmed by the heading, על־מחלת לענות, which would appear to mean something like *Concerning the sickness of affliction* or *the afflicted one*. The root ענו would connect the figure of this psalm with the afflicted king of Zech. 9.9, a connection that would be strengthened if Goulder's derivation of מחלת from חלל is accepted,[50] giving the sense *For the piercing of the afflicted one*, thus providing a connection with the pierced king of Zech. 12.10. It should be noted too that the suffering figure of Isaiah 53 is also identified with the roots חלה (vv. 3, 4, 10), חלל (v. 5), and ענה (v. 7), a fact that strengthens the possibility, noted in the previous chapter, of links between the figures of Zechariah 11–13 and Isaiah 53, and connects both with this psalm. Certainly, ancient Christian interpretation applies the psalm to the death of messiah,[51] and the idea may be present in Lk. 23.49, where the γνωστοί of the dying messiah stand afar off, as in Ps. 88.9 [8] (LXX 87.9).

6. *Psalm 110: The Heavenly Conqueror*

The origins of this psalm are obscure. It may be, as some have suggested, an attempt to legitimate Jerusalem and the priestly prerogative of the Davidic line by appeal to Melchizedek's ancient royal priesthood in Jerusalem, described in Genesis 14.[52] A case has also been made for its being eschatological and messianic from the outset.[53] Such questions, however, must be omitted from the present investigation. Instead, an attempt shall be made simply to determine what the psalm is saying about the king figure it describes.

---

50. Goulder 1982: 202.

51. See Neale and Littledale, who cite a host of patristic and mediaeval writers who interpret this psalm in relation to the death of Jesus (1874: III, 90-106). Eusebius of Caesarea, for instance, says that the writer 'prophesies the death of Christ' (91). Jerome states that the entire sons of Korah collection pertains to Calvary (Commentary on Ps. 8.1 [CCSL, 72: 191]).

52. Ishida 1977: 137-40; Allen 1983: 81.

53. Kissane 1954: 106; Rehm 1968: 329-31; Kidner 1975: 392.

The psalm's central figure is a king. The tone is martial and pro-mises the king dominion from Zion over all nations, achieved by holy war waged by Yhwh's power. The psalm opens with his being offered the place at Yhwh's right hand. This may be metaphorical for the king being honoured by Yhwh. Or it may indicate the position of the royal palace on the south side of the temple.[54] Or it may relate to a corres-ponding ritual position at a cultic enthronement ceremony, or refer to a throne to one side of the Holy of Holies.[55] However, metaphor and interpretation aside, the words as they stand suggest that the king is being offered a place in Yhwh's heavenly throne room or divine council. Certainly, the psalm leaves itself open to such an interpreta-tion, and ancient texts and interpreters suggest that it was formerly so understood.

(1) Hay suggests that the vision of the divine throne room in Dan. 7.13-14, with its thrones, one for God and one apparently for a human figure, is based upon Ps. 110.1, the 'only scriptural text which explicitly speaks of someone enthroned beside God'.[56] Later interpre-tation of the Daniel passage appears to support Hay's suggestion: 'But how explain, *Till thrones were placed?* [Dan 7.9]—One [throne] was for himself and one for David. Even as it has been taught: One was for himself and one for David: this is R. Akiba's view' (*b. Sanh.* 38b).[57]

(2) The Melchizedek figure of 11QMelch, referred to as *elohim* and head of the sons of heaven, appears from above to preside 'over the final judgment and condemnation of his demonic counterpart, Belial/Satan, the Prince of Darkness'.[58] Such a figure appears to have been influenced by this psalm, the interpreter apparently understanding על־דברתי (v. 4) as *on my account* or *according to my promise*,[59] and *Melchizedek* as vocative: that is, *You are a priest forever according to my promise, Melchizedek.*[60] Certainly the heavenly conqueror

54. Kirkpatrick 1902: 666.
55. Kraus 1978: 348.
56. Hay 1973: 26.
57. For Jewish legends regarding a heavenly throne of David, see Mosca 1986: 35.
58. Vermes 1987: 300; van der Woude 1965: 354-73.
59. So Schreiner 1977: 217.
60. The simple understanding of על־דברתי would be that the *yodh* indicates a pronominal suffix, as at Job 5.18, where the same term occurs. The more unlikely translation, *according to the order of Melchizedek,* finds support in LXX's κατὰ τὴν τάξιν Μελχισεδεκ, which may have originated from the translator's unwillingness

Melchizedek envisaged in the Qumran text could hardly be dependent upon Genesis 14 alone. 11QMelch therefore seems to reflect an early understanding that the central figure of this psalm was to appear from the heavenly realms to wage cosmic war.

(3) The New Testament repeatedly understands Ps. 110.1 as referring to the heavenly throne room of God. It is cited at Acts 2.29-36, where the argument is that David was buried and did not ascend to heaven (vv. 29, 34), but he wrote of one who did (v. 34), and therefore he was speaking of the Messiah (vv. 31, 36). The writer of the Epistle to the Hebrews argues that the glorified Messiah has sat down 'at the right hand of the throne of the Majesty in heaven' (8.1; cf. 1.3; 10.12; 12.2) and there waits 'for his enemies to be made his footstool' (10.13). Many other New Testament references to this psalm can be understood only of a heavenly enthronement (Mt. 26.64; Mk 14.62; 16.19; Rom. 8.34; Eph. 1.20; Col. 3.1).

(4) *T. Job* 33.3 understands 'the right hand of God' as being in the heavenly throne room. Job says, 'My throne is in the heavenly world and its glory and splendour are at the right hand of God.' Moreover, this passage describes the vindication of a righteous sufferer, an idea akin to that of the king figure in the Psalter, who must be 'cut off' in Psalm 89 before attaining the sovereignty described in the present psalm and Psalm 132.

Thus a case can be made for seeing the king of this psalm initially enthroned at Yhwh's right hand in heaven, where he is promised dominion over his enemies (vv. 1-2). However, as the king's final position in the psalm is in earthly battle (v. 5), a descent from heaven to earth may be envisaged. Might רְדֵה of v. 2 at some time have been understood, possibly by ancient aural ambiguity, as רִדָה: *Descend among your enemies*? There is no textual evidence for it, although descent (ירד) upon the earth, albeit metaphorical, is attributed to the superhero-king of Ps. 72.6. However, even without such a reading, the psalm suggests that the king is descending from heaven to earth to make war.

Tournay has called v. 3 the most obscure verse in the Psalter.[61] However, some of it at least, enough to aid understanding, is comprehensible. Given the martial context, עמך נדבת ביום חילך (v. 3a) seems

to have the Davidic king addressed as Melchizedek. It is therefore significant that the Hebrew writer of 11QMelch delineates a figure who resembles the hero of Ps. 110, yet is not merely *in the order of Melchizedek,* but Melchizedek by name.

61. Tournay 1960: 11.

to indicate that the king's *people,* his army, will be, in Delitzsch's phrase, 'altogether cheerful willingness' upon his day of battle.[62] This is confirmed by Judg. 5.2, where in a holy war context the phrase בהתנדב עם denotes warriors' willingness for combat, as confirmed by LXX's rendering, ἐν προαιρέσει λαοῦ. If then v. 3a turns from the description of the king to depict his army assembled for the messianic conquest, either of the variant readings for the next part of the verse, the better-attested בהדרי קדש or the alternative בהררי קדש, makes sense. The latter would describe the scene of the battle, *the holy hills* of the land of Israel, upon which the eschatological war takes place (Ezek. 38.21; 39.17). The former reading would describe the army's attire. As soldiers of the priest-king (v. 4), they are clad in supernatural holy garments to carry out the great sacrifice of the messianic war (cf. Ezek. 39.17).

> הדרת קדש is the vestment of the priest when performing divine service (xcvi.9, xxix.2); in 'holy attire' the Levite singers go forth before the army (2 Chron. xx.21)—here, however, all the people, without distinction, wear holy festive garments. Thus they surround the divine King like dew born out of the womb of the morning. It is a priestly people whom he leads forth to holy battle, just as in Rev. xix.14 heavenly hosts upon white horses follow the Logos of God, ἐνδεδυμένοι βύσσινον λευκὸν καθαρόν—a new generation, wondrously born as it were out of heavenly light, numerous, fresh and vigorous like the pearly dew, the children of the dawn.[63]

The next phrase, מרחם משחר לך טל ילדתך, should be interpreted in the same general context of the description of the messianic army. Thus Allen notes, 'The military context suggests that the basically abstract ילדות is used concretely and collectively with the sense "young men."'[64] טל is a simile denoting the freshness and vigour of the troops. The latter part of the phrase might therefore be rendered *your young soldiers, like dew, will come to you.* The rich imagery of מרחם משחר evokes many associations. What can be most simply maintained is that it denotes the army's place of origin, a place both splendid and supernatural. It may be the place of the dawn. It may also suggest the dawning of a new age, described elsewhere in sunrise imagery (cf. Isa. 60.1; Mal. 3.20 [4.2]). It might even contain a reference to the

---

62. Delitzsch 1887: III, 168.
63. Delizsch 1887: III, 169.
64. Allen 1983: 81.

resurrection of the dead. For there is a striking parallel with the language of Isa. 26.18-19, probably the earliest unmistakable reference to resurrection in Hebrew literature, in the imagery of birth, dew and dawn: *For dew* [טל] *of the dawn* [אורת] *is your dew; the earth to the dead* [רפאים] *will give birth* [תפיל].[65] The idea that the faithful dead will rise at Messiah's appearing is, of course, well-attested in later Hebrew literature.[66]

Following v. 4, wherein the king is promised eternal sovereignty and priesthood by a divine oath, vv. 5 and 6 describe the messianic war as such. At this point it is necessary to note that the figures of the king and Yhwh become conflated. The application to Yhwh of the plural form of the title initially used of the king (v. 1; אֲדֹנִי) prepares the way for coming ambiguities. *The Lord,* presumably Yhwh, now goes forth on the king's right hand (v. 5). The reversal of positions from v. 1 changes the metaphor from one of honour to one of defence and strength. In battle, the left side of the body was covered by the shield, whereas the right was unprotected, and so the right-hand man gave secure protection in battle. Similarly, the deity at the right hand

65. Sawyer rightly says of this passage, 'This is a reference to the resurrection of the dead which no-one but a Sadduccee, ancient or modern, could possibly misconstrue' (1973: 234).

66. The possibility of a reference to resurrection in the Psalter probably depends as much on who is to be resurrected as upon when the concept of resurrection originated. Compare the development of the idea of the afterlife in Egypt, which was at first the prerogative only of royal figures, as in the following spell from a funerary text of the late fifth or early sixth dynasty (first half of third millennium BCE): 'Nu has commended the King to Atum, the Open-armed has commended the King to Shu, that he may cause yonder doors of the sky to be opened for the King, barring (ordinary) folk who have no name' (Faulkner 1969: 117). But later the lower classes were increasingly thought eligible for participation in the afterlife, as is evident throughout the *Book of the Dead* (Faulkner 1985). Sawyer recognizes a reference to a general resurrection of the dead in Isa. 26.19, but makes no comment on his view of its dating (Sawyer 1973: 234). 4Q521, which probably dates from the late third century BCE, refers to a Messiah in whose time the Lord will raise the dead (4Q521.1.2.12. The text is in Vermes 1992: 303-304. The dating is from Prof. Vermes in a personal letter of 7 March 1993). Again a general resurrection seems to be in view. This supports those scholars who have previously argued that the idea of resurrection predates the classic statement in Dan. 12.2 (Saracino 1982: 185-203; Stemberger 1972: 273-90). In that case, the idea of the favoured righteous rising at Messiah's coming may be older still, and might have been entertained by the redactor, or even the poet, of this psalm.

suggests the strengthening of the sword arm, and hence success in battle. The subject of v. 6, who executes judgment and *crushes head* in victorious world war, is presumably Yhwh again, since no other subject has intervened since the beginning of v. 5. But by the beginning of v. 7, although no other subject is stated, the subject appears to have become the king again. For the action of drinking from *a stream upon the way* is more readily comprehensible of a human king than of Yhwh himself. Thus there seems to be a conflation of Yhwh and the king, in a way not dissimilar to what was noted in Zech. 12.8, 10 and Ps. 45.7 [6]. This is presumably to stress their oneness of will and purpose. And while the stress is on Yhwh as warrior throughout (vv. 1, 2, 5, 6), the king cannot be omitted from the warfare, for it is probably he who drinks to refresh himself after the battle (v. 7a). Yet more than refreshment is in view; על־כן (v. 7b) emphasizes that the drink is the reason for the hero's lifting his head. It is a source of new strength. Some mythological river may be indicated, possibly the eschatological stream that the prophets envisage flowing from the latter-day house of Yhwh (Ezek. 47; Joel 4 [3] 2a; Zech. 14.8).[67]

The messianic interpretation of this psalm, implied in its preservation in the Psalter, is also found in early interpretation. In 11QMelch, the depiction of the heavenly warrior Melchizedek who executes cosmic judgment seems, as noted above, to be dependent on this psalm. The New Testament cites this psalm more than any other Old Testament text, invariably interpreting its king figure as the Messiah.[68] It also represents those outside the Christian community as interpreting it likewise.[69] This is a weighty argument for its being an accepted

---

67. The eschatological stream occurs in *Otot* 10.2 in conjunction with the same peculiar motif of drinking בדרך, *by the road*. If this were part of the established imagery of the eschatological stream, then it strengthens such an interpretation of Ps. 110.7. Although נחל is not used of the eschatological river in the Bible, it does occur in this connection in post-biblical Hebrew (cf. *Pir. M.* 6.9).

68. It is cited at Mt. 22.44; Mk 12.36; Lk. 20.42-43; 22.69; Acts 2.34-35; Heb. 1.13; 5.6; 7.17, 21. It is alluded to at Mt. 26.64; Mk 14.62; 16.19; Rom. 8.34; 1 Cor. 15.25; Eph. 1.20; Col. 3.1; Heb. 1.3; 5.10; 6.20; 7.3; 8.1; 10.12; 10.13; 12.2; and possibly Jn 12.34 (Ps. 110.4). Some of these suggest a future return of Messiah from heaven.

69. The Pharisees are represented as accepting the force of Jesus' argument based on the messianic interpretation of Ps. 110 at Mt. 22.43-46; the temple crowd do likewise at Mk 12.35-37. Similarly, the letter to the Hebrews, which argues the case for Jesus' messiahship to an Israelite readership, accepts the messianic

messianic text in the first century, for the apologetic aims of these documents suggest that their arguments were designed to interact with accepted contemporary exegesis. There is also explicit evidence from a slightly later period that Judaism regarded this psalm as messianic prophecy.[70]

> R. Yudan said in the name of R. Hama: In the time to come, when the Holy One, blessed be he, seats the Lord Messiah at his right hand, as it is said, *The Lord says to my Lord, 'Sit at my right hand'* [Ps. 110.1] (*Midr. Pss.* 18, sec.29).

(*Otot* 8.4; *Midr. Pss.* 18.29). Similarly, Christian tradition, following the lead of the New Testament, ubiquitously regards this psalm as a messianic prediction.[71]

In my proposed eschatological programme, this psalm would come at the time of Israel's deliverance, paralleled in the Zecharian programme by Zech. 14.3-8. A number of parallels between the psalm and the Zecharian programme make this likely.

(1) In each case the one who does the deliverance is Yhwh himself (Zech. 14.3-5; Ps. 110.5-6).[72] Yet in both the psalm and Zechariah 9–14 the actions of Yhwh and the king are conflated to such a degree that the two figures merge into one.[73] There is therefore little difficulty in regarding the deliverer in each case both as Yhwh's representative king and as Yhwh himself coming with his king. For it would be a high degree of anthropomorphism indeed to regard Yhwh as physically touching the earth with his feet so that it split (Zech. 14.4). I would suggest that the picture of a king fully endued with Yhwh's anointing fits both texts.

(2) In Zechariah, as in the psalm, the deliverer descends upon the earth from above. Yhwh's proper residence is the supraterrestrial

---

interpretation of Ps. 110 as a given throughout.

70. Apart from the messianic interpretation, the psalm is also interpreted historically as concerning Abraham (*b. Ned.* 32b; *b. Sanh.* 108b; *Midr. Pss.* 110, sec.4).

71. See, e.g., Justin Martyr, *Dialogue with Trypho* 32-33. Other uses of this psalm in Christian messianic interpretation are given by Briggs and Briggs 1906–1907: 132ff.

72. Schmidt (1971: 455-56) notes the emphasis on the war's being Yhwh's in vv. 2, 5-6.

73. In regard to Zech. 9–14, see Chapter 7 where it is noted that Yhwh and the Davidic shepherd-king are conflated in their actions (11.10), in the actions against them (11.12-13; 12.10) and in their being (12.8).

region. Thus, if at his appearing his feet are to touch the Mount of Olives (Zech. 14.4), a descent from heaven seems to be envisaged.

(3) In Zechariah, as in the psalm, the descending deliverer brings with him an army of glorious beings. In the psalm, they are the newborn of the sunrise. In Zech. 14.5 they are כל־קדשׁים. If, as I have suggested, the troops of the psalm are the resurrected righteous, then this would accord well with the traditional interpretation of Zech. 14.5. A Christian writer, in late second temple times, appears to envisage the resurrection of the dead at the appearance of the heavenly deliverer in Zech. 14.3-5. He alludes to the Zecharian coming of the Lord with his holy ones (1 Thess. 3.13), and says that the dead and living righteous will rise to meet Messiah in the air as he descends and they will return to earth in his victory procession (1 Thess. 4.16-17).[74] Rabbinic tradition interprets the *holy ones* of Zech. 14.5 as the prophets of old, that is, righteous mortals who have been raised from death.[75] Black notes that these rabbinic traditions suggest the description of the resurrection of the dead in the Codex Reuchlianus Targum to Zech. 14.4.[76] Certainly, the ancient traditions associating the resurrection with Zech. 14.4 might suggest that the קדשׁים of Zech. 14.5 are the resurrected righteous.

(4) The parallel between the two passages is confirmed by the apocalyptic midrash *Otot ha-Mashiah*, from the mid-first millennium, which cites Psalm 110 and Zech. 14.3 together in the context of the final deliverance of Jerusalem by the Lord and Messiah ben David:

> And the Holy One (blessed be he) needs nothing for the battle, but to say to him [Messiah ben David], *Sit at my right hand* [Ps. 110.1]. And he [Messiah ben David] will say to Israel, *Stand firm, and see the deliverance of the Lord which he will accomplish for you today* [Exod. 14.13]. Thereupon the Holy One (blessed be he) fights against them, as it is said,

74. The expression εἰς ἀπάντησιν followed by the genitive signifies, at its every other New Testament occurrence (Mt. 25.1, 6; Acts 28.15) and frequently in LXX (e.g. Judg. 4.18; 6.35; 11.31, 34), *to go out to meet someone and to escort them back*. There is no basis in 1 Thess. 4.16-17, nor anywhere else that I am aware of, for the modern popular rapture idea, which holds that Messiah will appear to remove his faithful from earth and take them elsewhere.

75. *Ruth R.* 2; *Eccl. R.* 1.11.1; *Song R.* 4.11.1.

76. Black 1991: 149. The traditional association of Zech. 14.4 with the resurrection is discussed in Chapter 5, pp. 148-49, where the Codex Reuchlinianus passage is also cited.

*And the Lord will go forth and fight against those nations as he fights on a
day of battle* [Zech. 12.3] (*Otot* 8.4).

Such an interpretation of Psalm 110 shows the way to understanding
its surrounding psalms in terms of the proposed eschatological timetable. Psalm 107 begins with thanksgiving for Israel's ingathering
from the latter-day exile subsequent to the messiah's 'cutting off'
(107.1-3). The remainder of the psalm describes sorrows that would
have attended exile (vv. 4-32), divine justice according to a nation's
deeds (vv. 33-38) and Yhwh's kindness in eventually redeeming them
(vv. 39-43). Psalm 108, a David psalm, might be the Messiah's petition and sword song. He praises Yhwh (vv. 2-6 [1-5]), requests his aid
in deliverance (v. 7 [6]), announces the divine oracle of victory over
enemies (vv. 8-10 [7-9]), beseeches aid once more, exclaiming that if
God, who previously rejected them, now goes with them, they shall
surely triumph (vv. 11-14 [10-13]). Psalm 109, another David psalm,
might be regarded as a pre-battle ritual curse on the evil leader of the
assembled nations, the ראש על־ארץ רבה (Ps. 110.6), much like the
pre-conflict curse on Satan and his lot at 1QM 13. The voice of the
curse would be that of Israel, or the Messiah, speaking on Israel's
behalf. The situation is that which precedes a battle: *words of hatred
surround me* (v. 3). The curse then follows, pronouncing against the
evil king of the invading nations a list of disasters blood-chilling in its
scope (vv. 6-15). This is succeeded by a list of unkindnesses that the
evil king and his people have perpetrated against Israel (vv. 16-20).
The petitioner then implores Yhwh's assistance for his distressed situation (vv. 21-26). He concludes that Yhwh will save him in a way
that all will acknowledge, and he will praise Yhwh for his deliverance
(27-31). Such an interpretation of Psalms 107–109 as precursory to
the final eschatological conflict is supported by 4QPs[f], which contains
Psalms 107–109, followed by three eschatological lyrics: 'Apostrophe
to Zion', which refers to Zion's enemies cut off on every side;
'Eschatological Hymn', which describes the destruction of the wicked
and earth's end-time fecundity; and 'Apostrophe to Judah', which
describes Judah's latter-day rejoicing.

After Psalm 110's description of the advent and conquest of the
heavenly David, the Hallel group (Pss. 111–18) might represent the

paeans of praise to the conqueror.[77] This is how they are interpreted in the Talmud:

> The prophets among them enacted that the Israelites should recite it [the Hallel] at every epoch and at every trouble—may it not come to them!—and when they are redeemed, they will recite it for their deliverance (*Pes.* 117a).[78]

The Hallel is followed by the massive acrostic Psalm 119, which is the prayer of a repentant who has strayed far from Yhwh, has been disciplined and now returns to him, by obedience to Torah (vv. 175-76). This might indicate the repentance of the tribes of Israel scattered in all the world, an idea supported by its shepherd imagery (v. 176), which, as was noted earlier, is the central image for scattered Israel. In spite of being scattered among hostile heathen (vv. 23, 87, 134, 161), the exiles have not forgotten Yhwh's Torah (v. 176). They therefore prepare to return to Zion when he seeks them. This theme continues into the Songs of Ascents (Pss. 120–34), which depict exiled Israel making pilgrimage to Zion (Pss. 120–21) to celebrate the Feast of Sukkoth in Jerusalem (Pss. 122–34), under the rule of the Davidic *mashiah* (Ps. 132).

7. *Psalm 132: The Messianic Reign*

This psalm has already been considered in Chapter 4. It is mentioned again at this point only to emphasize that its depiction of the Davidic king regnant, implied in the prayer at the end of the first strophe that Yhwh not reject his *mashiah* (v. 10), followed by the corresponding blessing at the end of the second strophe (vv. 17, 18), provides the natural conclusion to the foregoing messianic psalms, and sums up many of their themes. The king is reigning from Zion, his ultimate destination as foretold in Psalms 2.6-11; 45.7, 18 [6, 17]; 72.8-11;

---

77. The term 'Hallel' (or 'Egyptian Hallel', because Ps. 114 celebrates the Exodus) is properly applied to Pss. 113–18, most of which (but not Pss. 114 or 118) feature the term הללו־יה. Bazak has argued that these psalms (113–18) display considerable internal evidence that they have been redacted as a single literary unit (1990: 182-91; Bazak 1991: 91-93). Nonetheless, it is probably fair to regard Pss. 111 and 112 as introductory to the main Hallel collection. They also bear the הללו־יה heading, and Wilson suggests that MT Pss. 111–17 are structured as a coherent unit (1985a: 126-27).

78. Messianic interpretation of the Hallel appears also at *Pes. K.* 22.2; 27.5.

89.28 [27]; and 110.2. His hardships on Yhwh's behalf are overcome and remembered (132.1). Yhwh's covenant with David, which in Psalm 89 appeared to be abrogated, is reaffirmed (vv. 11, 12, 17, 18).

8. *Summary*

The messianic psalms seem to display a progression of theme that accords with the latter-day events of Zechariah 9–14 and fits in with my earlier suggestions concerning the Psalms of Asaph and the Songs of Ascents. Psalm 45 represents the king as a bridegroom coming to Daughter Zion. Psalm 72 represents his initial rule over all the earth. Psalm 89 represents the premature termination of his kingdom, or his rule, or his life, or all three. Psalm 110 represents his appearance, possibly from above, to destroy his enemies and conquer the earth. Psalm 132 depicts the victorious Davidic king regnant on Zion.

Psalms			*Psalms of Asaph*				*The Hallel*	*The Ascents*
	Ps. 45	Ps. 50	Ps. 72	Pss. 73-83	Ps. 89	Ps. 110	Pss. 111–18	Pss. 120–34 incl. Ps. 132
Zech. 9–14	Bride-groom-king comes to Daughter Zion	Gathering of scat-tered Israel to Jerusalem	Tempor-ary mes-sianic *malkut*	Hostile nations gather against Jer-usalem	The king cut off	Rescue by king messiah	Paeans of messianic victory; the hero's welcome	Ascent of Israel and all nations to Sukkoth on Zion in mes-sianic *malkut*

The feasibility of the Psalter's redactor envisaging such a pattern is confirmed by its similarity not only to the themes of Zechariah 9–14, but to similar patterns in other early Israelite messianic and apocalyptic texts. The New Testament represents Jesus as initially coming, gaining a widespread following in Galilee, being killed and ascending to heaven, after which Israel is exiled and then regathered before he returns from above to establish his unopposed reign in Jerusalem. The apocalyptic midrashim featured in Appendix 1 feature a similar pattern, except that, instead of one messiah's ascending and returning, two separate figures, ben Joseph and ben David, fulfil the initial and final messianic roles. If these two figures are regarded as essentially one, a possibility for which there is some evidence,[79] a picture

79. The personae of the Ephraimitic and Davidic Messiahs are conflated in a number of texts. John's Gospel twice refers to Jesus as 'son of Joseph' (1.45; 6.42), the first of these occurrences being in the context of a messianic confession. It

emerges that is yet more like the one proposed here. Messiah appears to Israel, sets up an initial kingdom, is slain, and then reappears to destroy the hostile nations and establish his *malkut* in Jerusalem.

Finally, it should be added that the idea of Messiah returning to

never refers to him as 'son of David', and its crowds disallow his messiahship because, unlike the synoptic crowds (Mt. 12.23; 15.22; 20.30-31; 21.9, 15; Mk 10.47; 11.10; cf. Mt. 1.1, 6, 17; Lk. 3.31), they doubt his Davidic ancestry (Jn 7.42). Thus this writer was clearly aware of traditions regarding a Davidic Messiah, and must have known of them also within Christian circles, yet, without denying them, he presents Jesus as a 'Joseph' Messiah, and the Ἰουδαῖοι, *the Judahites* as his deadly foes (5.16; 7.1). This may suggest that he regarded Jesus as both an Ephraimitic and Davidic Messiah in one, while his own sympathies were with the Ephraimitic tribes. (Some commentators have suggested that the Ephraimitic bias of John's Gospel indicates the author's Ephraimite or Samaritan origins [Buchanan 1968: 149-75; Bowman 1971: 45-47; Purvis 1975: 161-98.]). At *Pes. R.* 36 and 37 the Ephraim (ben Joseph) Messiah's sufferings are described with an allusion to Ps. 22.16 [15]: *because of their sins your tongue will cleave to your jaws.* Thereafter Ps. 22.16 [15] is applied to ben David and he is addressed as 'Ephraim'. The same midrash also gives to ben Joseph functions elsewhere attributed to ben David: he will destroy his enemies by the breath of his mouth (37.1), and have universal dominion (36.1). The distinction between the two figures is so blurred, and the conflation so blatant, that one feels the author intended to suggest that the two messiahs are actually one. Likewise *Pir. M.* 5.2-3 seems to depict a dying ben David, and later *Pir. M.* 5.41-5 has a dying King Nehemiah the Messiah, possibly a pseudonym of ben Joseph, as it is at *Otot* 7.7-11 and *Sef. Z.* 41. The same conflation occurs in the traditions regarding Ps. 92.11 [10]. All MSS of *PRE* 22a, except the Venice one, refer Ps. 92.11 [10] to Messiah ben Joseph. However, the Venice MS and *Midr. Pss.* 92.10 interpret it of Messiah ben David, but cite Deut. 33.17, the blessing on the Joseph tribes that predicts a coming Ephraimite hero. And the Venice edition of *PRE* 22a has the Davidic Messiah leading the Joseph tribes. In addition, the traditions about messiah's disappearance may also suggest an underlying monomessianism behind the figures of ben Joseph and ben David. *Pes. R.* 15.10; *Pes. K.* 5.8; *Song R.* 2.9.3; and Num. 11.2 all note that messiah will disappear for 45 days, during which time Israel will be exiled in the wilderness, the period being calculated in each case from Dan. 12.11-12. Other texts similarly refer to this 45-day wilderness period, calculating it from the same biblical text, but regard the period as that between the death of Messiah ben Joseph and the final coming of Messiah ben David (*Otot* 7.12–8.2; *Pir. M.* 5.45; cf. *Ag. M.* 27–34). The only discrepancy between the two forms of the tradition is the number of messiahs, which might suggest that an older monomessianic tradition, like that of Baal's disappearing in the underworld, has been expanded to feature two distinct messiahs, one suffering and one conquering. Indeed, we seem to return here to the fact, noted previously, that Israel's eschatology seems like a teleologized version of a cosmogony little different from that of Ugarit.

heaven is not essential to my proposed programme in the Psalter. Psalm 110 might be taken as simply representing earthly conquest without a descent from above. However, it should be noted that there is evidence of early Israelite belief that messiah would descend from heaven.[80] There are also texts that speak of his return to heaven[81] and his coming back again.[82] Similarly, there is evidence of the possibly

80. The idea is, of course, widespread in the New Testament (cf. e.g. Mt. 24.30; 26.64; Mk 14.62; Rev. 1.7). But see also *4 Ezra* 13.3; *b. Sanh.* 98a; *Pir. M.* 5.1; and *NRSbY* 27, which, like Rev. 1.7, apply Dan. 7.13 to messiah. Likewise, *Num. R.* 13.14 applies Dan. 7.14 to messiah. See also the texts cited in the second footnote following.

81. The idea is central to New Testament messianic belief (see eg. Jn 6.62; Acts 1.11, 22). But there is considerable evidence for the idea outside Christian literature. At *T. Naph.* 5.6-7, Joseph catches a great black bull and ascends into the heights. At *NRSbY* 25 Messiah ben David is rejected by Israel and returns to God. In addition, the passages cited in the following footnote, in which Messiah returns from heaven, imply his having previously gone there.

82. Again the idea is common in the New Testament (Jn 14.2-3; Acts 1.11), but also exists outside Christian literature. *Pss. Sol.* 18.5: καθαρίσαι ὁ θεος Ισραηλ...εἰς ἡμεραν ἐκλογῆς ἐν ἀναξει χριστοῦ αὐτοῦ. Gray (1913: 651 n.) comments, 'The term ἀναξις here used, if we might press the force of the Greek, would imply a "bringing again" or "bringing up" of a pre-existing Messiah.' The reference may be to the return of David or the restoration of his line, but the possibility of Messiah's departure and return can also be read in the phrase. At *2 Bar.* 30.1-3 Messiah is to return in glory when the time of his parousia is fulfilled, after which the dead will rise. Most commentators seem to regard this as indicating a return to, rather than from, heaven (Charles 1908: II, 498; Klijn 1983: 631; Brockington 1984. The latter makes it explicit with additions: 'And it shall come to pass after this, when the presence of the Messiah *on earth* has run its course, that he will return in glory *to the heavens*: then all who have died and set their hopes on him will rise' [857; Brockington's italics]). But it may equally be understood as a return to earth, a scenario that accords better with the subsequent resurrection of the dead. For the idea of the resurrection occurring at Messiah's departure is, as far as I am aware, unknown elsewhere, while much other literature envisages it occurring at Messiah's advent, or during his presence on earth (e.g. 4Q521.1.2.12 [Vermes 1992: 303-304]; 1 Thess. 4.16-17; Rev. 20.4-5; *Ag. M.* 34-40; *Otot* 8.1-9.1; *Sef. Z.* 49; *Pir. M.* 5.45-49; 6.2-4; *Ma'aseh Daniel* [*BHM*: 117-30], 128.). *Sib. Or.* 5.256-59 describes a second Joshua (ὃ ἠέλιόν ποτε στῆσεν φωνήσας ῥήσει τε καλῇ) who will come again from heaven to where he spread upon the fruitful wood his hands. Although the passage has been considered a Christian gloss, Kurfess (1951: 310) and O'Neill (1991a: 87-88) regard it as authentic. The latter cites several reasons why it cannot be Christian, among which is the fact that, although a typological parallel between Joshua and Jesus is known in patristic literature, an actual Ephraimitic messiah is unattested

related idea that he would initially be revealed to Israel and then hidden before effecting the final deliverance.[83]

anywhere in Christian writings (O'Neill 1991a: 87-92). If *Sib. Or.* 5.256-59 is not Christian, then there is less reason why the fragment at *Sib. Or.* 3.95 should be so: *All shall obey him who descends again into the world.* At *NRSbY* 25-27, Messiah ben David is revealed, is rejected by Israel, and withdraws, after which the 'King Messiah' appears suddenly to Israel. The two figures should probably be equated, as elsewhere in rabbinic literature, David being the royal paradigm *par excellence.* Justin represents the Jew Trypho admitting belief in two messianic advents (*Dial.* 49). More generally, Wis. Sol. 3.1-9 holds that the souls of all the righteous dead, including presumably a dead messiah, are in the hand of God until the time of their visitation (ἐν καιρῷ ἐπισκοπῆς αὐτῶν), when they shall judge and rule nations.

83. There is the above-mentioned tradition of the 45 days of Messiah's disappearance at *Pes. R.* 15.10; *Pes. K.* 5.8; *Song R.* 2.9; *Num. R.* 11. See also Targum Jonathan on Mic. 4.8: 'And you, Messiah of Israel, who have been hidden away from the sins of the congregation of Zion, the kingdom is destined to come to you' (Levey 1974: 92). A similar idea is probably encountered at *b. Sanh.* 98a where Messiah is sitting among the lepers of Rome, bandaging their sores until the time of his appearing, and at *Sef. Z.* 24, where he is bound in prison in Rome until the time of his appearing to Israel.

Chapter 9

THE WILDERNESS OF THE NATIONS[1]

Having investigated the isolated peaks formed by the royal psalms, I
complete the map of the broad terrain by identifying those psalms that
might represent the latter-day exile, depicted in Zech. 13.7–14.2. If
the king's affliction is represented by Psalm 89, and the divine deliverance by Psalm 110, then the parallel with the eschatological programme of Zechariah would suggest that the latter-day exile falls in
between. I would therefore suggest that the redactor may have represented the exile by Book IV of the Psalter (Pss. 90–106). In this
chapter the psalms of Book IV will be examined in sequence with this
hypothesis in mind. Particular attention will be given to themes of
wilderness exile and ingathering, and to issues of guilt and forgiveness, which would naturally occur in the context of national
punishment.

1. *The Book IV Psalms*

The Psalms of Book IV seem to be divisible into two large groups,
Psalms 90–100 and Psalms 101–106. The first of these is demarcated
by the למשה ascription that heads Psalm 90. As no other personal
ascription occurs until לדוד Psalm 101, this ascription might be
regarded as heading all Psalms 90–100. This is certainly how ancient
commentators regarded it. Origen claims to have learned this tradition
from Jewish sources:

> ... having my interest in some of the oracles aroused by Jullus, the patri-
> arch, and through one of those who were termed wise men among the
> Jews, I heard that through the whole book of the Psalms, beginning with
> the first and second, those Psalms which in the Hebrew have no title, or
> which have a title but not the name of the writer, belong to the author

1. Ezek. 20.35.

whose name stands at the head of the last preceding Psalm that has a title. Speaking on these matters he used at first to assert that thirteen Psalms belong to Moses. But, from what I heard[2]... their number is eleven. Later I enquired of one they account a wise man and was told that the number is eleven, of which the 89th [i.e. MT 90] begins, *Lord thou hast been our refuge from one generation to another.*[3]

He then proceeds to list all the psalms as far as Psalm 100. Similarly, Jerome, also acquainted with Jewish interpretation, held that Moses wrote Psalm 90–100, because anonymous psalms are to be attributed to the author last named.[4] Origen's claim that this is a Hebrew idea is confirmed by *Midr. Pss.* 90.3, which states, 'Moses composed eleven Psalms appropriate to eleven tribes.' It then connects Psalms 90–95 with Reuben, Levi, Judah, Benjamin, Gad, and Issachar, and concludes, 'from here on reckon them out for yourself'. Of course, Mosaic authorship of Psalms 90–100 is unlikely, if only because Psalm 95 consciously addresses a post-exodus generation and Psalm 99 refers to Samuel. But the point is that interpreters have long recognized that, first, Psalms 90–100 are a group with one heading, and, secondly, that Moses is a central figure in them. Modern scholarship endorses this. One principle that Wilson derives from his study of the headings of the Psalms and other ancient semitic literature is that lack of psalm-heading indicates a tradition of combination,[5] a principle that, for him, binds Psalms 90–99 together as one group.[6] Likewise, D.M. Howard regards Psalms 90–100 as a coherent group, which, by thematic and linguistic analysis, he further subdivides into Psalms 90–92 and 93–100. Based on what he calls 'close lexical correspondences' and the 'almost identical structure and content of 95.6b-7c and 100.3b-c', he concludes that Psalms 95 and 100 'form an inclusion around the Kingship group in 96–99'.[7] He then suggests that this group, Psalms 96–99, 'stands as the 'center' of Book IV, both positionally and thematically'.[8]

The Moses theme that occurs with the first word of Book IV is

2.   There is a lacuna in the MS here.
3.   English translation from Tollinton 1929: 96-97. The original text is in *Selecta in Psalmos* (Lommatzsch 1831–48: XI, 352-54).
4.   *Ep.140 ad Cyprianum.*
5.   Wilson 1985a: 199.
6.   Wilson 1985a: 177-79.
7.   Howard 1986: 207.
8.   Howard 1986: 217.

prominent throughout the whole book. As Tate notes, it 'seems to be the 'Moses Book' in the Psalter'.[9] He is mentioned by name seven times (90.1; 99.6; 103.7; 105.26; 106.16, 23, 32), including three times with Aaron (99.6; 105.26; 106.16), whereas elsewhere in the Psalter he appears only once, also with Aaron (77.21). Another closely related theme in this book is that of the wilderness wanderings or exile. Wilson calls the group Mosaic 'because of the title of Psalm 90, the use of the old divine names El Shadday and El Elyon, references to Moses and Aaron, the Exodus wanderings and other thematic correspondences'.[10] Book IV, as shall be seen below, also has many verbal allusions to the ancient Song of Moses, which also seems to refer to experiences of exile (Deut. 32.19, 26, 35, 39).[11] It has therefore been suggested by a number of commentators that, as Tate says, 'The Moses-wilderness themes in these psalms suggests very strongly that the collection reflects the "wilderness" of the exile and post-exilic periods.'[12] That a period later than the actual desert wanderings is indicated by these psalms is confirmed also by the headings at LXX Ps. 95.1 (MT 96): *When the house was being built after the captivity*; and LXX Ps. 96.1 (MT 97): *For David, when his land was being settled.*

Apparently then the redactors of Book IV were, by reference to the wilderness wanderings, indicating metaphorically a later exile. But could it have been not the Babylonian exile, but the latter-day exile of Ezek. 20.35-38, Zech. 13.7–14.2, and Hos. 2.16 [14]? Several points seem to support such a conclusion. First, the broader sequence of Psalms seems to depict already an earlier exile and ingathering in Books II and III. Likewise Ps. 85.2 [1] refers to the reversal of Jacob's captivity. Secondly, the pronounced ultimacy of preceding psalms, and of the whole finished Psalter, would make such an interpretation likely. For instance, the events of the Babylonian desolation, no matter how grievous, did not match the cosmic scale of the invasion depicted in Psalm 83. Thirdly, the frequent 'wilderness' language

---

9. Tate 1990a: 530.

10. Wilson 1993a: 75-76, in McCann 1993: 72-82.

11. For the antiquity of the Song and Blessing of Moses (Deut. 32 and 33), see Craigie 1983b: 25. Given Widengren's observance that scattering was an established motif of divine or royal displeasure in ancient Near Eastern thought, it is not necessary to regard the apparent references to threat of exile in Deut. 32 as later interpolations (Widengren 1977: 227-45).

12. Tate 1990a: 530.

in these psalms, although no doubt appropriate to any exile, would be particularly appropriate to the future one, which Ezek. 20.35 locates in the מדבר עמים.

The second main group of Book IV is Psalms 101–106. Wilson suggests that these have a 'repentance' theme:

> The Exile is the result...not of Yahweh's weakness but of Israel's sin and disobedience (90.7-8; 106.6-42). Like Isaiah in the temple, Israel in the presence of Yahweh is forced not only to acknowledge his holiness but must also confront the reality of its own guilt. Any hope of restoration must be based on Israel's admission of guilt and repentance before God. For this reason, the fourth book concludes with (1) a call to integrity in Psalm 101 ('I will study the way that is blameless. When shall I attain it?'); (2) a lament that acknowledges Yahweh's continuing kingly power and calls for mercy on his distressed people (Ps. 102); (3) a thanksgiving psalm that celebrates Yahweh's kingship and the outpouring of divine mercy in forgiveness of sin (Ps. 103.8-14); (4) praise for Yahweh's sustaining power (Ps. 104); (5) a history of Yahweh's gracious deeds in behalf of Israel (Ps. 105); and (6) a psalm that rehearses Israel's consistent failure to respond to Yahweh's gracious acts with loyalty and obedience, which is a confession of sin ('Both we and our ancestors have sinned; we have committed iniquity, have done wickedly,' 106.6).[13]

Such a theme is an appropriate finale to a group of psalms representing an exile. For, according to ancient biblical theology, there can be only one ground for Israel's banishment, disloyalty to Yhwh (Deut. 31.19-29; 32.15-25). It would be unthinkable that they could be shattered and exiled for no good reason. And therefore the necessary prerequisite to their restoration is repentance, after which they will be gathered again to their land (Deut. 30.1-5). The prelude to the ingathering is signified, typically, by two psalms that, by language and by the Chronicler's ascription, are connected with the Asaphites, the *mazkirim*-prophets of ingathering.[14] As a result, this group of psalms, which begins with a vivid depiction of wilderness-exile, closes with the characteristically Asaphite cry, *Save us, Yhwh our God, and*

---

13. Wilson 1992: 140-41.

14. See Chapter 3 for the linguistic elements which Pss. 105 and 106 share with the main Asaph collection. Pss. 105.1-15 and 106.1, 47-48 are substantially the same as the psalmic passages in 1 Chron. 16.8-22 and 16.35-36 respectively. Nasuti notes the resemblance between these and the main body of Asaph Psalms and calls them 'deutero-Asaphic' (1988: 80, 91, 190, *et passim*). Brooke also notes that they display evidence of Asaphite traditions (1989–90: 274).

gather us from the nations (Ps. 106.7). Each of these psalms will now be examined in turn.

2. *Psalm 90*

This psalm evokes the desert wanderings of the exodus, not only by the למשה heading that belongs to it particularly, but also by the language and imagery of the whole lyric. The reader senses that its author was surrounded by a generation dying in futility. At the command of God, אנוש, man in his frailty,[15] crumbles to powder (v. 3). God is eternal, man ephemeral, and the years of human life speed by in futility (vv. 4, 10). People are like grass that sprouts for a day and is mowed down (v. 5). Such a corporate sense of the brevity and futility of life seems to reflect a generation waiting to die. The second section of the psalm (vv. 7-12) explains this situation as resulting from the anger and punishment of God (vv. 7-12). He gazes upon the people's iniquities; their days pass away beneath his wrath (vv. 8, 9). The power of his anger is incomprehensible (v. 11), and his judgment is inescapable. All this is appropriate to the exodus generation, who were condemned by God to die in the wilderness because of unbelief (Num. 14.21-35). The psalm concludes by requesting that God return to favour them (v. 13) and repay them with good for the evil he has given, so that even these seemingly futile years might bring their own reward (vv. 14-17). One is reminded of Robinson Crusoe, who, at the end of his long exile for youthful disobedience, found his lands had accrued vast profit. Or maybe it is like a tree that, after a season of barrenness, puts forth new growth, not in spite of the barren period, but because of it.

Specific linguistic terms connote the desert wandering, bearing resemblances to the Song of Moses (Deut. 32), the blessing of Moses (Deut. 33), and other passages from Deuteronomy and the Pentateuch. The idea of God as man's מעון (v. 1) occurs elsewhere only in Deut. 33.27 (מעונה), in the following psalm (91.9), and in Ps. 71.3, the two former passages also emphasizing God's eternity. The term ימות occurs only in this psalm (v. 15) and in Deut. 32.7, in both instances in parallel with the poetic term שנות. The verb שבע occurs both in this psalm (v. 14) and Deut. 33.23 in the sense of being *filled* with God's blessing.

---

15. That is, deriving the term from אנש, *to be weakly, sick* (BDB: 60).

The appropriateness of the imagery and language of Psalm 90 to the desert wanderings has been recognized by commentators to such an extent that some have argued its Mosaic authorship. Delitzsch maintains:

> There is hardly a literary monument of antiquity, which can so brilliantly justify the traditional testimony to its origin as this Psalm. Not only in respect of its contents, but also in respect of its literary form, it is thoroughly appropriate to Moses.[16]

And even those who doubt Mosaic authorship willingly admit Mosaic characteristics:

> The Psalm is worthy of him, and at first sight its contemplation of the transitoriness of human life, its acknowledgement of suffering as the punishment of sin, and its prayer for the restoration of God's favour, seem appropriate enough to a time towards the close of the Wandering in the wilderness, and a natural utterance for the leader who had watched one generation of Israelites after another dying out for their faithless murmuring.[17]

So, whether it is Mosaic by authorship or only by ascription, it is not unreasonable to suppose that this psalm intentionally evokes the cry of the wilderness generation, dying in futility under God's curse for disbelief.

3. *Psalm 91*

Several features of Psalm 91 seem particularly appropriate to the exodus context established by the למשה heading and Psalm 90. For instance, the promise to the God-fearer that though all around him die, he will simply observe the punishment of the wicked (v. 7) might evoke the exodus generation dying in the desert. The promise of angelic protection, *lest you strike your foot against a stone* (v. 12), is appropriate to a prolonged sojourn in rough terrain. Likewise, the promise of protection from different types of lion (שחל; כפיר) suggests a wilderness environment (v. 13).

Several other points, less immediately obvious, strongly suggest a wilderness context for this psalm. First, like Psalm 90, it has linguistic

16. Delitzsch 1887: III, 2.
17. Kirkpatrick 1902: 547.

parallels with Deut. 32.[18] There is the use of the verb חסה (vv. 2, 4) with the idea of taking refuge in God or gods (Deut. 32.37). There is the striking use of אברתו and כנפיו in parallel at Ps. 91.4 and Deut. 32.11, a usage found nowhere else in the Bible. The description of angels bearing the believer in their hands (Ps. 91.12) resembles the picture of the eagle bearing its young on its pinions (Deut. 32.11), the verb in each case being a *qal* imperfect form of נשא. Ps. 91.6 promises the godly protection from pestilence (דבר) and plague (קטב), while Deut. 32.24 predicts fever (רשף) and plague (קטב) upon the rebellious. Ps. 91.8 employs שלם in the sense of God's recompense of the wicked, as do Deut. 32.35 and 41. Ps. 91.9 and Deut. 33.27 describes God as man's מעון, a usage occurring elsewhere only in the preceding psalm (90.1) and Ps. 71.3. Ps. 91.13 and Deut. 32.33 exhibit a parallel usage of תנין, *dragon*, and פתן, *venomous snake*, a word-pair occurring nowhere else in the Bible.

Secondly, this psalm is connected with a desert context by its theme of protection from demons. Gaster notes of vv. 5-6, 'the disasters which he lists are in fact specific demons believed to operate at specific hours. He commences with the "terror by night" because the Hebrew day began at the preceding nightfall.'[19] Gaster identifies the *terror of night* (פחד לילה) with the nightmare, which he describes as a universal figure in folklore, and cites its occurrence in a Mesopotamian magical text.[20] He identifies the *arrow that flies by day* (חץ יעוף יומם) with the 'faery arrow' of pestilence and disaster.[21] The phrase probably connotes the Canaanite god of pestilence, Resheph, who is described in an Ugaritic text as 'Resheph the archer'.[22] A fourth-century BCE Phoenician-Greek bilingual inscription from Cyprus calls him 'Resheph of the arrow' and equates him with 'far-darting Apollo',[23] who hurled darts of pestilence upon the Achaeans at Troy.[24] This reference to faery arrows suggests another link between this psalm and the Song of Moses, which mentions Resheph by name

---

18. These are noted by Kirkpatrick 1902: 554.
19. Gaster 1969: 770.
20. Gaster 1969: 770.
21. Gaster 1969: 770.
22. *b'l ḥz ršp*. RS 15.134; C. Virolleaud, in CRAIBL 1952: 30.
23. *ršp ḥz*. Cook 1905: no. 30.
24. *Iliad* 1.40.

(Deut. 32.24; also Hab. 3.5).[25] The *pestilence that stalks in darkness* (דבר באפל יהלך, v. 6; cf. also דבר הוות, v. 3) is, says Gaster, the demon *Deber*, whose name means 'Reverse, Catastrophe'.[26] And the *destruction that ravages at noon* (קטב ישוד צהרים) is sunstroke, the demon of noonday heat.[27] Such an interpretation is confirmed by LXX's, δαιμονίου μεσημβρινοῦ, *(from) the demon of noonday*. Similarly, *Num. R.* 12 states that קטב is a שד, *demon*. As direct influence from LXX to *Num. R.* is unlikely, it would appear that קטב was widely understood to be a demonic entity. Likewise, Aquila and Symmachus find references to demonic power indicated in the verbal form ישוד, which they apparently connect with שד. Finally, as if this nest of four demons in vv. 5-6 was not enough, v. 13, for the LXX translator, at least, features two more. He renders the פתן as βασιλίσκος, and the תנין as δράκοντα.

The demonological emphasis of the psalm is confirmed by its ancient uses in rites of exorcism. The Qumran text 11QPsAp[a] consists of three unknown psalms followed by Psalm 91. The text is badly damaged and the first three psalms are beyond reconstruction, but they seem to refer repeatedly to demonic subjects. The words תנין (Fr. A, line 4), והשדים (col. i.3) and לתהום רבה (col. iii.7) are legible, and Ploeg plausibly reconstructs [השד]ים (Fr. A, line 9), בשא[ו]ל תחתיה תחתיה (col. iv.9) and similar terms.[28] Ploeg therefore suggests that 11QPsAp[a] was designed for exorcism and protection against demons. So, if the Qumran sectarians regarded Psalm 91 as appropriate for inclusion in an exorcistic liturgy, it suggests that they thought it would protect from demonic malice. Later traditions bear out this conclusion. In certain rabbinic texts it is called שיר פגעים, *song of the demons*, or שיר פגועים, *song of demoniacs*,[29] and it has been used by Judaism as a means of defence against demons.[30] In Christian liturgy it

25. Gaster 1969: 671.
26. Gaster 1969: 771. He derives the name from Akkadian *dab/paru*, 'thrust back'.
27. Gaster 1969: 770.
28. Ploeg 1971: 130, 138.
29. See Jastrow 1950: 1135; Shebu 15b calls it שיר של פגעים, and some call it the song of plagues (נגעים)'; *y. Erub.* X 26c (bot) relates that they used to recite the שיר של פגעים in Jerusalem in the Temple when someone was threatened with insanity; *y. Šab.* VI 8b (top) calls it שיר פגועין; *Midr. Pss.* to Ps. 91.1 says Moses recited שיר של פגעים, which begins *He that dwells in the secret-place of the Most High*, when he ascended to the firmament.
30. Ploeg 1971: 128.

has long been part of the office of Compline, to request divine help against the perils of night, including demons.[31]

Psalm 91 should therefore be regarded as promising protection from demons and monsters. It would therefore be most necessary if one were in the vicinity of demons. This is where it connects with the desert theme of the preceding psalm, for Semitic thought regards the lifeless desert as the demons' chief abode. Gaster comments on Deut. 32.10 as follows:

> ... the description of the desert, in which the infant Israel was exposed as a *howling waste* reflects a common bedouin belief that the shrill winds and other eerie sounds which infest it are the shrieks of demons. Indeed, a popular Arabic designation of the wilderness is 'Howl-land'; and it is significant that the Ancient Aramaic Version (Targum) renders the expression in our text by the words, 'a place where demons and spirits howl.'[32]

Similar ideas may be detected in the Bible. In Isa. 34.13-14, Edom's cities in the Arabah wilderness are to be destroyed and populated with לילית, the *night-demon*, and תנים, properly *jackals,* but sometimes a variant of תנין, *dragon* (cf. Ezek. 29.3; 32.2), and rendered by LXX as σειρήνων, *sirens,* supernatural creatures that howl like jackals. Similarly, in the same passage LXX renders the obscure terms ציים and איים as δαιμόνια and ὀνοκένταυροι. Likewise, in the ceremony for the Day of Atonement, the goat chosen for Azazel is carried away into the wilderness to Azazel, a demon or fallen angel (Lev. 16.8, 10).[33]

The use of Psalm 91 in the New Testament's temptation narratives confirms and draws together all the themes of exodus, desert, Deuteronomy and demons. Jesus is led into the desert (Mt. 4.1; Mk 1.12; Lk. 4.1). All his words, save the Matthean, Ὕπαγε, Σατανᾶ (4.10), are from Deuteronomy 6–8, in which Moses recounts the desert wandering and its purpose of testing and refining Israel.[34] Therefore Jesus is represented as meditating upon the desert wanderings of the exodus. One might say that he is in the desert, and the desert is in him. Into this double desert, who should appear, attended

31. Ploeg 1971: 128.

32. Gaster 1969: 320.

33. BDB records it as the opinion of most commentators that עֲזָאזֵל is a spirit haunting the desert (p. 736).

34. Mt. 4.4 and Lk. 4.4 = Deut. 8.3; Mt. 4.7 and Lk. 4.12 = Deut. 6.16; Mt. 4.10 and Lk. 4.8 = Deut. 6.13.

by 'wild beasts', but the prince of שדים himself, quoting Ps. 91.11, 12, no less, and thereby assuring Jesus angelic protection from every evil that might result from obeying his instructions (Mk 1.13; Mt. 4.6; Lk. 4.10-11). Jesus, however, avails himself of the psalm's promised angelic assistance by withstanding rather than obliging the tempter (Mk 1.13). This complex New Testament passage amply illustrates the theme of this psalm: God will protect his faithful one banished in the desert from every demonic attack.

Thus Psalm 91 shares the wilderness atmosphere of its predecessor and could likewise have been designed by the redactor to represent the latter-day exile. But, unlike Psalm 90, which is a prayer for redemption, Psalm 91 is a promise of protection to the *dweller in the shadow of Shaddai* (91.1). Who, in the context of the end-time exile, might this represent? One answer might be that it represents any godly Israelite in exile. Another might be that it represents the nation as a whole, promising them protection even during the exile.[35] Another answer might be that it represents the stricken and pierced king of Psalm 89, who even in his afflicted state will receive divine protection from all evils. The New Testament's use of this psalm might suggest that such a messianic interpretation was not unknown in second temple times.

4. *Psalm 92*

This psalm contains one image, the simile of mankind being like grass (v. 8 [7]), which evokes the characteristic wilderness atmosphere of Book IV. The full form of this simile, which mentions both the flourishing and the perishing of the grass, occurs in the Psalms only in Book IV (90.5-6; 92.8 [7]; 103.15, 16). Reduced forms of it occur in one other Book IV psalm (102.5 [4], 12 [11]) and in Ps. 37.2 and 129.6-7. Elsewhere in the Old Testament it occurs only in desert

---

35. This is how Kirkpatrick understands it (1902: 553-54). Form critical scholars are divided over the issue of whether many Book IV psalms should be classified as individual or communal. This stems from their interest in a psalm's origin rather than its finished form, and their various views on when and how an individual psalm can have a metaphorical communal referent. Kirkpatrick, who lived before Gunkel, had no such problems. He simply points out that Israel is often addressed in the singular in the Bible, and that the metaphorical link between individual and community is a common one, both in ancient and modern literature (Kirkpatrick 1902: li-lii, 553 n.).

contexts (2 Kgs 19.26; Isa. 40.6-8; Job 14.2). It is, of course, a particularly appropriate image to such a context. For where does one see grass sprouting and withering so well as in a desert wilderness? In well-watered grasslands, the growth and death of plants is imperceptible among the perpetually luxuriant verdure. But in dry lands grass flourishes, possibly following a brief shower of rain, and perishes, unconcealed by the coverage of new growth.

In general the psalm has the tone of a victory song. But what and whose victory might it celebrate? The idea that it celebrates the resurgence of the stricken king finds some support in rabbinic literature, which interprets messianically v. 11 [10]: *You have exalted like a reëm my horn.*[36] *Midr. Pss.* 92.10 interprets it of Messiah ben David, as does the Venice edition of *PRE* 22a.[37] Other manuscripts of *PRE* interpret the passage of dying and rising Messiah ben Joseph:

> *But my horn hast thou exalted like that of a reëm*: Just as the horns of the reëm are taller than those of all beasts and animals, and it gores to its right and to its left, likewise with Menachem ben 'Ammiel ben Joseph, his horns are taller than those of all kings, and he will gore in the future towards the four corners of the heavens. And concerning him Moses said this verse, *His firstborn bullock, majesty is his, and his horns are the horns of the reëm. With them he shall gore the peoples all of them, even the ends of the earth* (Deut. 33.17). [With him are the ten thousands of Ephraim, and the thousands of Manasseh, as it is said: *And they are the ten thousands of Ephraim, and they are the thousands of Manasseh* (Deut. 33.17).[38]] All the kings will rise up against him to slay him, as it is said: *The kings of the earth set themselves, and the rulers [take counsel together]* (Ps. 2.2). And Israel who will be in the Land [will suffer] great trouble.[39]

Admittedly, these traditions are late.[40] But there is evidence that the image of the horns of the *reëm* was already connected with a coming Josephite hero in biblical times. Moses' blessing on the tribes describes

---

36. The Hebrew term ראם *reëm* designates the aurochs. The animal may possibly be extinct, though there have been reports that some may still exist in the highlands of Kurdistan (Bodenheimer 1960: 51, 102-104).

37. Friedlander, *PRE*, 131 n. For a fuller discussion of the MSS, see Friedlander, *PRE*, xiv-xv.

38. This passage occurs only in the Venice edition (Friedlander, *PRE*, 131 n. 7).

39. *PRE* 22a. Friedlander's translation is on p. 131.

40. Pirqê de Rabbi Eliezer was redacted in the second or third decade of the ninth century CE from considerably older material (Friedlander, *PRE*, liii-liv).

a coming Josephite conqueror, presumably Joshua, who is described as בכור שורו *his (Joseph's) firstborn bull* with קרני ראם *horns of a reëm* (Deut. 33.17).[41] The imagery not only denotes the conqueror's fierce vigour,[42] but also emphasizes his descent from Ephraim, who was reckoned as Joseph's firstborn (Gen. 48.13-20), and the general precedence of the Joseph tribes, who are said to have inherited the firstborn rights of Reuben and thereby to have had prominence even over Judah (1 Chron. 5.1-2). Such imagery, *the horns of the reëm* and the *firstborn bull,* is used in the Bible of no other group.[43] After Joshua's time, it appears to have passed into the military ideology of royal *bet*-Ephraim, if the iron horns that the prophet Zedekiah ben Kenaanah sported before King Ahab are any indication (1 Kgs 22.11; 2 Chron. 18.10).[44] It is surely plausible that the Ephraimites might have anticipated a coming Joshuanic antitype. Certainly, by the first century CE, the Samaritan remnants of Ephraim expected a messianic Joshua who was identified with resurrection and, presumably, death.[45] Later interpreters also speak of the Ephraimitic messiah with reference to the imagery of Deut. 33.17.[46] Is it improbable that this

41. The link between the two images, *firstborn bull* and *reëm,* may be more than mere contiguity in this verse. The Latin name for the aurochs or *reëm* is *bos primigenius* (Bodenheimer 1960: 102-104). This may indicate some ancient association of the aurochs with primogeniture, an association that may have been shared by, or derived from, the semitic cultures among which this animal lived.

42. The strength and untameableness of the aurochs is noted at Num. 23.22; Job 39.9-12. Bodenheimer 1960: 108, notes its ferocity.

43. All the tribes of Israel are described as a *reëm* at Num. 23.22, but the horns are absent, as is the *firstborn* terminology.

44. Note that Zedekiah's language, with its imagery of destruction of the nations and its use of the verb נגח, *gore,* suggests he is citing the tradition preserved in Deut. 33.17.

45. Crown notes a messianic Joshua and resurrection tradition among the Samaritans. If, as he suggests, such beliefs created schism among the Dositheans in the first century CE, they must have been in existence among the Samaritans for some time previously (1967–68: 85). O'Neill suggests that even in Judah the prevalence of the name 'Joshua' among high-priestly families in the later second temple period suggests that they anticipated a Joshuanic Messiah (O'Neill 1991a, *passim*).

46. *Gen. R.* 75.6; 99.2; *Num. R.* 14.1; *Midr. Tan.* 11.3 apply it to Messiah ben Joseph. *Pes. R.* 53.2 applies it to messiah non-specifically. Possibly the earliest evidence for the messianic interpretation of Deut. 33.17 is the bull figure of *1 En.* 90, which commentators regard as a messianic symbol (Charles 1913: 258 n.; Isaac 1983: 5; Milik 1976: 45; Torrey 1945: 112; Torrey 1947: 266).

Ephraimite imagery might have represented a dying and rising messiah at the time of the Psalter's redaction?[47] If so, the *horns of the reëm* imagery in this psalm, and the *horns* and *firstborn* of Ps. 89.25, 28 [24, 27], might indicate some early allusion to such a figure.

It might be objected that the Psalter cannot have both an Ephraim and a Davidic Messiah. But there is evidence that the two figures are regularly conflated from at least the time of John's Gospel; perhaps, if they arose from an originally monomessianic tradition, they always were.[48] Perhaps the hand that shaped these psalms employed Ephraimitic messianic imagery to express the dying and rising aspects of the king, and Davidic language to express his royal authority. But, however this imagery arose, the rabbinic tradition may well be close to the redactor's intention in decoding the *horns of the reëm* imagery to indicate a resurging messiah with Ephraimite characteristics. Such a figure, Davidic with Ephraimitic qualities, would well represent the Solomonic figure who earlier gathered the Josephites in Zech. 9.11-13; 10.6-12 and the Asaph Psalms (cf. Ps. 80.2-3 [1-2]).

5. Psalm 93

This psalm inaugurates a group ending with Psalm 100, which celebrates Yhwh's kingship.[49] There is no explicit mention of the exile or exodus theme in this psalm. However, as Tate notes, there is a link with exodus traditions in the characteristic phrase יהוה מלך, *the Lord reigns* (93.1; 96.10; 97.1; 99.1).[50] The first reference in biblical history to the kingship of Yhwh is in the Song of the Sea: יהוה ימלך לעלם ועד (Exod. 15.18), so the theme does appear to have exodus

47. It is interesting to surmise how this idea became associated with the Ephraimite Messiah. One suggestion might be that it arose from analogy with his eponymous tribes, who were slain by the Assyrians, but were expected by the prophets to revive (see Chapter 5, pp. 161-63).

48. See pp. 268-69 n. 79.

49. Howard (1986) has made an extensive structural and linguistic analysis of Pss. 93–100, and concludes that they form a logical, coherent unit within Book IV (216). He argues that Ps. 93 introduces the section, while Pss. 95 and 100 bracket the heart of the section in Pss. 96–99. Although Ps. 94 is thematically dissimilar to other psalms in the section, it still shows significant ties with them (Pss. 201-206). The close similarities between this group of psalms are widely noted by commentators (see i.e. Cohen 1945: 307; Tate 1990a: 474ff.)

50. Tate 1990a: 530.

connections, and would therefore be appropriate in a collection representing the latter-day exile.[51]

Now if Book IV of the Psalter is to be interpreted eschatologically, as I have suggested the wider context requires, then the repeated references to Yhwh's kingship and the worship of the nations within Psalms 93–100 (96.7-13; 96.10; 97.1; 98.2-3, 7-9; 99.1-3; 100.1) would suggest that they, excepting Psalm 94, represent God's eschatological *malkut*. This is how rabbinic tradition regards them.[52] Rashi, not generally given to eschatological interpretation, says on this psalm, '*The Lord reigns. It speaks of the future. The world is established.* In his kingdom the earth shall rejoice.'[53] As to why the *malkut* should be celebrated in the midst of Israel's latter-day exile, two reasons seem feasible. The group may be an anticipation of the eschatological kingdom of God, which actually appears later with the advent of the heavenly conqueror at Psalm 110. Such an anticipatory passage would be consistent with the genre of apocalyptic from Zechariah 9–14 on.[54] Or it may be that these psalms signify that knowledge of Israel's God, and possibly even the eschatological *malkut*, has begun among the nations during the period of Israel's latter-day exile.

6. *Psalm 94*

No explicit references to the wilderness occur in this psalm. But then the latter-day exile, like the Babylonian exile, is a wilderness only metaphorically. What is actually envisaged is an exile among hostile nations (Ezek. 20.35; Zech. 14.2), and this psalm is appropriate to such a setting. As commentators rightly note, it depicts Israel oppressed by foreigners.[55] The opening petition asks that the *Judge of the earth* requite the proud and wicked (vv. 1-3). The evildoers crush

---

51. Indeed, several modern commentators would date this psalm not long after the Song of the Sea. Howard regards it as dating from probably the tenth, but possibly as early as the twelfth, century BCE (Howard 1986: 48-55). Lipinski (1965: 163-72), Shenkel (1965: 401-402), Dahood (1965–70: II, 339) and Kraus (1978: II, 816) propose a tenth-century date.

52. Cohen 1945: 307.

53. ה' מלך. יאמרו לעתיד: אף תכון תבל. במלכו תשמח הארץ: (Rashi, Commentary on Ps. 91.1).

54. Anticipation and recapitulation are recognized features of apocalyptic literature. See Black 1991: 54; Collins 1976: 43ff.

55. Delitzsch 1887: III, 40; Kirkpatrick 1902: 566.

Yhwh's people and his inheritance, expressions denoting that 'it is the community as such (v. 5) and not one portion of it, which is oppressed.'[56] Likewise, the psalmist's statement that God disciplines nations implies that the evildoers referred to are not faithless Israelites, but hostile foreigners (vv. 7-10). Moreover, the situation described is one not of foreign invasion, but exile among foreigners. They pick off the weak and defenceless, the widow, the orphan and the wanderer, such as the exiled Israelite (v. 6). Their power derives from corrupt authority[57] and law, by means of which they kill the innocent, not in battle, but by legal process (vv. 20-21). The result of this is that Israelites, the only feasible referent for the עַם of v. 8,[58] are perplexed with the discrepancy between God's omniscience and justice and maintain that he has forsaken his people.

The statement that God disciplines nations implies that 'Israel, as well as the nations (v. 10) is being divinely educated'.[59] Thus their exile results from their misdeeds (v. 10). Indeed the גֶבֶר of v. 12 whom the Lord disciplines is probably Israel as much as the psalmist himself.[60] Both he and his nation have been disciplined by Yhwh. Both he and they came close to death at the hands of the oppressors, but called to Yhwh for help and were delivered (vv. 16-19). For this he blesses Yhwh, and states that all who are willing to be corrected by the Lord's teaching will be protected from the troubles of exile until such time as God requites the heathen nations for their mistreatment of Israel (vv. 12-13, 22-23). For the Lord will not forsake his people, but ultimately avenge them, and, since they are his

---

56. Kirkpatrick 1902: 566.

57. Delitzsch, 1887: III, 45, maintains that כִּסֵּא [v. 20] is here the judgment-seat, just as the Arabic *Kursi* directly denotes the tribunal of God (as distinguished from his royal throne).' This is certainly likely, though a reference also to the royal throne cannot be excluded. Corrupt judiciary and monarchy tend to go together, and the term may function metonymically for any seat of power.

58. So Delitzsch 1887: III, 41; Kirkpatrick 1902: 568.

59. Kirkpatrick 1902: 569.

60. Kirkpatrick 1902: 570. Albrektson (1963: 126-28) and Gottlieb (1987: 121-26) likewise suggest that that the גֶבֶר of Lam. 3.1 represents not an individual but Zion and her people as a collective. Provan, however, thinks it unlikely, in view of the feminine representation of Zion in Lam. 1–2 (1991: 80). But might not some kind of harmonization be possible, wherein the גֶבֶר represents the nation, the בְּנֵי יִשְׂרָאֵל, while the feminine Zion represents the city, desolate and widowed, bereft of husband and children (Lam. 1.1, 5, 15, 16, 18)?

inheritance, restore them to all they are entitled to by virtue of his covenant (vv. 14, 23).

7. *Psalm 95*

After an exhortation to praise Yhwh for his universal sovereignty and his care for Israel, the psalmist warns contemporary listeners against the sin of the desert generation. He recalls the events at Massah and Meribah (Exod. 17.7; Num. 20.13), and describes that generation's rebellion (vv. 8-10), which resulted in Yhwh's forbidding them entry to his rest (vv. 10-11). The psalmist's purpose in this reminiscence is to warn contemporary listeners against the error of their ancestors. For *today* they confront the same temptation as came to their ancestors, that is, to harden their hearts on hearing God's voice (v. 8). The psalmist warns against this, lest the same fate befall them as befell their ancestors. As Davies notes, 'the abrupt ending is to be interpreted as a threatening innuendo... Israel's behaviour in the desert met with a condign punishment, and the inference is that similar unbelief in the present will meet a corresponding fate.'[61] This psalm therefore regards its hearers, whatever their actual circumstances, as being like the Exodus generation, wandering in the desert and potentially in danger of rejecting God and being rejected by him.

The earliest surviving interpretation of this psalm, at Heb. 3.7–4.11, connects it with the latter-day exile of the eschatological programme in just the way I have suggested. The writer addresses Israelites whose faith in Jesus' messiahship is wavering (3.14) and reminds them that their ancestors failed to inherit God's rest and fell in the desert because of disbelief (vv. 17-19). He warns them that if they similarly disbelieve, the same fate, that is, perishing in the desert, will overtake them (3.12; 4.1-11). I noted earlier that the New Testament, in accord with the eschatological programme of Zechariah 9–14, expects a prolonged exile to follow the death of Jesus (Lk. 19.41-44; 21.20-24), just as exile is to follow the striking of the Zecharian latter-day king (Zech. 13.7–14.2).[62] The writer of Hebrews, in warning his contemporaries of their impending fate, seems to hold the same view. The proof text that he cites to warn them about the impending exile is this psalm, which warns Israelites of the post-wilderness generation not to

61. Davies 1973: 195.
62. See Chapter 7.

repeat their ancestors' mistake (3.7-11, 15; 4.3, 7). This suggests that at least some Israelites of the first century CE, including this writer and his readership, understood this psalm as referring to the latter-day exile.

8. *Psalm 96*

This psalm, which apparently originated in a cultic context (v. 8), contains no explicit references to exile or exodus. However it does contain the phrase יהוה מלך (v. 10), which was noted in Psalm 93 as occurring in the Song of the Sea and thus having exodus overtones. It also contains the phrase שירו ליהוה שיר חדש (vv. 1-2), which occurs only here and in Ps. 98.1. The expression שירו ליהוה makes its first appearance in the Song of the Sea (Exod. 15.21; cf. 15.1). It occupies a prominent position in both texts, forming a threefold invocation at the beginning of the psalm and an inclusio around the Song of the Sea (Exod. 15.1, 21). This suggests that the psalm intentionally evokes the events of the exodus. However, this time a *new song* is to be sung, suggesting a new order of redemption, comparable with the redemption from Egypt, but greater. The idea of redemption does not exclude the exile theme. For the Egyptian redemption was followed by a desert period to purge Israel of the faithless before their entry to the land. Other details might support the idea that this group of psalms represents a latter-day exile. The exhortation that Israel declare Yhwh's glory, wonders and kingship among the nations (vv. 3, 10) is appropriate to an exilic setting, as is the denunciation of foreign deities (vv. 4-5), as in exilic Isa. 46.1-2, and the exhortation to the 'clans of the nations' to ascribe glory and strength to Yhwh, worship in his temple, and tremble before him (vv. 7-9). The psalm closes with the affirmation that Yhwh will justly judge the earth and its peoples. This recalls the theme of Yhwh's requital of the nations' maltreatment of Israel that closes Psalm 94.

9. *Psalm 97*

Some characteristic Book IV themes occur in this psalm. There is the יהוה מלך proclamation. As at its previous occurrences, Yhwh's dominion over the entire earth is in view (vv. 1-9). As in Psalm 96, idols are declared worthless. In the light of the appearance of God's kingdom their worshippers feel foolish, and even the deities of the nations are to worship the Most High (vv. 7, 9). As in Psalm 93, such language may either anticipate the coming latter-day *malkut* or indicate that it has already begun to spread among the nations during Israel's latter-day exile. Divine protection and deliverance from the power of the wicked is promised to Yhwh's faithful (v. 10), a theme noted earlier in Psalms 94 and 96 as appropriate to the latter-day exile. The righteous of Israel anticipate the dawning of divine light upon them (vv. 11-12).

10. *Psalm 98*

Characteristic Book IV themes occur in this psalm also. There is the refrain, *Sing to Yhwh a new song*, which hints at a new order of redemption. This is intensified in v. 4: *Shout to Yhwh all the earth*. The theme of Yhwh's rule over the nations also reoccurs. He has revealed his ישועה and צדקה to all nations (vv. 2-3), and has revealed himself as the God of Israel (אלהינו; v. 3). Yet although Yhwh's rule and salvation have been revealed to the nations, a final manifestation is yet to come, for his future advent in judgment is still expected: *he comes to judge the earth, he will judge* [future: ישפט] *the world with justice* (v. 9). This hiatus between initial revelation and consummation might suggest, as in Psalms 93 and 97, that knowledge of God has begun to spread among the nations during the period of Israel's latter-day exile. The nations and all creation are exhorted to rejoice and praise him both for his self-revelation and for his coming judgment (vv. 5-8).

11. *Psalm 99*

The desert theme is alluded to also in Psalm 99. It begins with an acclamation of Yhwh as universal king and a call to praise the one who has done justice in Jacob, and bow before him (vv. 1-5). The latter part of the psalm centres on a reminiscence of the great prophets of Israel's early history.

> Moses and Aaron were among his priests, and Samuel among the callers
> on his name,
> they were callers to Yhwh and he answered them.
> In the pillar of cloud he spoke to them; they kept his testimonies and the
> decree he gave them.
> Yhwh, our God, you answered them; a forgiving God were you to them,
> but punishing their misdeeds (vv. 6-8).

The 'pillar of cloud' refers to the desert wandering, of course. It applies directly to Moses and Aaron. Samuel also heard Yhwh in the Shiloh sanctuary, but there is no mention of the pillar of cloud. It may be that, in Samuel's case, it refers to the *shekhinah* dwelling in the sanctuary, or, as Tate suggests, to the column of smoke from the altar. But probably there is no need to push the reference to such detail.

There has been some discussion over the interpretation of v. 8b. The problem is that an assertion of God's forgiveness seems out of place juxtaposed with a statement that he punished misdeeds. Thus Symmachus, Kimhi and more recently Whybray have taken the pronominal suffix of עלילותם as an objective genitive.[63] However, it seems better to retain the simple reading of the MT, as above, and take v. 8b as referring to the hard fact that God's forgiveness does not always include absolution from punishment. Forgiveness is given, to be sure, otherwise the relationship between God and believer would not be restored, but punishment is necessary so the misdoer learn the seriousness of his deed. This idea is familiar in the Bible. For instance, Nathan tells David that Yhwh has taken away his sin, yet predicts the sword against his house, the rape of his wives and the death of his son (2 Sam. 2.9-14). Or again, as Brueggemann points out in regard to this psalm, God is *the forgiver of wickedness, rebellion, and sin, yet not leaving the guilty unpunished* (Exod. 34.7).[64] The idea is expressed in general terms by the Christian who wrote, 'When we are judged by the Lord, we are being disciplined so that we will not be condemned with the world' (1 Cor. 11.32). So this psalm's reference to the desert generation seems to be similar to that of Psalm 95 in warning the psalmist's contemporaries that while God will ultimately forgive the nation, he will also punish their misdeeds, presumably in the desert exile.

12. *Psalm 100*

This psalm, the last lyric in this section of Book IV, forms a doxological conclusion to the theme of Yhwh's universal kingship that began with Psalm 93. 'Yahweh is assumed to be Lord of all the world and all lands and peoples should come before him with homage and praise... Yahweh is the great king over all the earth, although this psalm does

---

63. Kimhi, Comm. on Ps. 99; Whybray 1969: 237-39.
64. Brueggemann 1984: 149.

not directly say so.'[65] All peoples are exhorted, as in 98.4, to *Shout to Yhwh* (v. 1) and serve him as his worshippers. They are to acknowledge not only that he is the true God, but also that Israel are his people, his especial creation, and his flock (v. 3). This psalm therefore concludes the theme that knowledge of Israel's God has spread among the nations during their latter-day exile. There are no explicit references to the exile. However, as Tate notes, the image of the divine shepherd links this psalm to the Moses–Exodus–Wilderness features in Psalms 90–99.[66]

13. *Psalm 101*

With Psalm 101 begins what Wilson regards as the repentance section of Book IV.[67] Allen is surely right in noting that this psalm needs to be taken as a complaint if the question in v. 2 is to be given its full force.[68] The speaker, whom the לדוד heading might indicate to be a royal figure, beseeches Yhwh to delay no longer in coming to him (v. 2), for he has assiduously performed his covenant share of royal obligations to maintain justice and integrity in the state. He has kept his heart and deeds in line with Yhwh's way (vv. 2-3), he has promoted the righteous and purged the civil body of evildoers (vv. 4-8). The likely background to this fervent plea would seem to be, as Allen notes, one of distress.[69] What might be the relevance of such a psalm to the beginning of the repentance that leads to the end of the latter-day exile? Might it not indicate the voice of the latter-day representative of *bet*-David, possibly the same one as suffered in Psalm 89? He protests that he himself is innocent and that, by means of the exile, he has purged Israel of undesirable elements. Yhwh therefore need delay no longer in vindicating him and hastening his great plan for Israel and the world to its conclusion.

14. *Psalm 102*

If Psalm 101 might represent the Davidic king calling upon Yhwh to act swiftly, then this its successor might represent a similar plea by

65. Tate 1990a: 536.
66. Tate 1990a: 538.
67. Wilson 1992: 140-41.
68. Allen 1983: 4.
69. Allen 1983: 4.

Israel languishing in the wilderness-exile. The heading, תפלה לעני,
would suit such an application. Of course, it might also indicate the
king himself, as at Zech. 9.9. There need be no contradiction in this,
for the suffering king is the representative head of the suffering
nation. But the condition of the speaker, described in vv. 1-12 [1-11]
in terms appropriate to one perishing in the wilderness, would suggest
that the primary reference might be to Israel. He is like the smoke and
embers of sear and withered grass (vv. 4-5, 12 [3-4, 11]), a lonely
desert owl among the ruins (vv. 7-8 [6-7]), a lengthening shadow (v.
12 [11]). This situation comes from the anger of Yhwh (v. 11 [10]),
who, while the speaker is daily wasting away (vv. 5-6 [4-5]), is by
contrast forever enthroned (v. 13 [12]). The speaker exhorts Yhwh to
show them mercy and rebuild Zion for now the time has come (vv.
13-17a [12-16a]). Foreseeing the consummation of the eschatological
programme, he announces that Yhwh will reveal himself in his glory
and that peoples and kingdoms will gather in Zion to worship him
(vv. 16-23 [15-22]). He closes by stating that Yhwh has broken his,
that is, Israel's, strength halfway through his life and requests that this
be reversed and that their future generations will be established before
Yhwh (vv. 24-29 [23-28]).

15. *Psalm 103*

This psalm is an exhortation to praise Yhwh for his forgiving loyal
love, both to the speaker and to the exodus generation. As regards the
speaker, Yhwh has forgiven his sins, cured his sicknesses, redeemed
him from the disintegration of the grave (שחת), crowned, satisfied and
rejuvenated him (vv. 1-5). The exodus generation are recalled in vv.
6-7, with reference to the wilderness metaphor of humans perishing
like grass (vv. 15-16). Yhwh saved them from oppression (v. 6). He
revealed his nature to Moses, and even the mass of Israelites saw his
deeds of power (v. 7). This revelation displayed his essential characteristics of compassion, generosity, patience and loyalty (v. 8), the
theophany at Exod. 34.6-7 possibly being in mind. And even though
Israel merited wrath they did not receive what their deeds deserved
(vv. 9-10). Instead, his חסד prevailed (גבר, v. 11) over their rebellion,
and after punishing them he removed, like a father, his punishment
from them, פשעינו signifying probably the punishment or result of

rebellion and not the mere deed (v. 12).[70] His loyal love still continues with those who fear him (v. 17-18). Universal creation is therefore exhorted to praise him (vv. 19-22). As regards this psalm's significance in the context of the Psalter, the לדוד ascription may suggest that the speaker is the Davidic king. Verses 3-5 may be taken as his thanksgiving for Yhwh's forgiving the iniquities of *bet*-David, and redeeming it from the sickness and שחת represented in Psalms 88 and 89. Verses 6-18 may be his meditation upon not only Yhwh's mercy to the exodus generation, but also his impending mercy to the eschatological wilderness-exiles, whom he has not treated according to their iniquities, and whose punishment will soon be removed.

16. *Psalm 104*

Brooke suggests that Psalms 104–106 have been selected to form a conclusion to Book IV.[71] Certainly this psalm takes up quite a different theme from its predecessor, in celebrating Yhwh's creator benefits to his creatures. It begins by acknowledging his greatness: he established the heavens and they serve him (vv. 1-4). It then turns to his work on earth. He founded the earth and the seas, establishing their contours and boundaries. He sends fresh water to sustain animals, birds and vegetation (vv. 5-13). He provides food for man and beast and makes the sun and moon mark times and seasons (vv. 14-23). All the multitude of life comes from him and he sustains it moment by moment (vv. 24-30). The singer closes with ascription of praise to Yhwh: may his creation ever glorify and please him, and may elements that resist his will be destroyed (v. 31-35). The function of this paean of praise in its context in the Psalter is unclear. Wilson, who rightly notes the repentance theme of Psalms 101–106 seems unsure of it, merely commenting that it is 'praise for Yahweh's sustaining power'. Certainly it does not seem to relate directly to the repentance theme. But perhaps it may be taken as affirming Yhwh's universal sovereignty, which will enable him to deliver Israel from latter-day exile and give them life as from the dead. And, as Old Testament theology often connects the themes of creation and Yhwh's kingship,[72] it may be a final reference to the themes that dominated Psalms 93–100

70. So Allen 1983: 17.
71. Brooke 1989–90: 291.
72. Allen 1983: 28.

and an anticipation of the coming *malkut,* when all nations shall ascend to worship Yhwh lest he withhold his life-giving rain (Zech. 14.16-21).

17. *Psalm 105*

The desert theme and the related exodus theme reoccur in Psalm 105, which celebrates God's gift of a land to Israel and the deeds of power by which he gave it. After the opening call to give thanks to Yhwh and proclaim his deeds among the peoples (v. 1), there follows an exhortation to *remember his wonders* (v. 5), for *his judgments [have been evident] in all the earth* (vv. 5-7). Then follows a restatement of the *eternal covenant* to the patriarchs whereby Canaan was given them for their possession (vv. 8-11). Next the events of the exodus are described in detail (vv. 24-36), with emphasis on the divine acts of supernatural power that subdued the oppressing Egyptians. The next section deals with the desert period (vv. 37-45), again with an emphasis on the divine acts of power that redeemed and preserved Israel, which led to their possessing the lands of the nations (vv. 39-44). Finally, the psalmist concludes that the purpose for all this manifestation of divine favour and power was *so that* [בעבור] *they would keep his precepts and observe his instructions* (v. 45). God's purpose was to found a holy people and to that end he gave them their land by acts of divine power.

What might be the purpose of this affirmation? None is explicitly given other than that these things are a basis for thanksgiving and praise (vv. 1-3). But there are clues to another. This psalm's references to the desert wandering are quite unlike earlier treatments of the same theme in Book IV, in Psalms 90, 95 and 99, which emphasize Israel's sin and God's judgment. Psalm 105 makes no mention of these things, suggesting it is not designed to serve the same admonitory function. Its emphasis on Yhwh's power and success in the redemption of Israel might therefore have been framed with the intention to comfort and encourage. In the context of the latter-day exile this might serve to encourage Israel to expect that God will again look to his *eternal covenant* and take up his purpose for them, bringing them back from captivity by deeds of power so that they might indeed be a holy people before him, and not fail his purpose as before.

18. *Psalm 106*

This psalm, the Psalter's most comprehensive and sustained confession of Israel's national guilt, forms a fitting conclusion to the latter-day exile. Its representation of Israel's deep repentance opens the way for the appearing of God's ישועה. After a brief ascription of praise and a prayer for blessing on the speaker and all the faithful (vv. 1-5), it launches into a confession of Israel's sin, rebellion, forgetfulness, cravings, idolatries, grumblings, abominable sacrifices, and more, in Egypt, Yam Suph, Horeb, Meribah and the promised land itself (vv. 6-39). It acknowledges Yhwh's justice in afflicting them by war and exile, and recalls how, like the figures of Psalm 90 and 102, they wasted away (vv. 40-43). It relates how in former times Yhwh remained merciful in spite of their failings and rescued them from captivity when they cried to him (vv. 44-46). Following this sustained recollection, they call again to be delivered from among the nations, that they may fulfil the purpose of Israel's creation in thanking and praising him (vv. 47-48). This seems to signify the end of the latter-day wilderness-exile; Book V opens with thanksgiving for the accomplished fact of Israel's final ingathering from all the nations (Ps. 107.1-2) and for their redemption from many different troubles (vv. 4-32), and meditates on Yhwh's power to transform situations to the advantage of those whom he favours (vv. 33-43).

19. *Summary*

Book IV of the Psalms is distinguished by wilderness themes. It repeatedly refers or alludes to Moses and the wilderness wanderings. Some of its characteristic expressions, שירו ליהוה and יהוה מלך, recall the Song of the Sea (Exod. 15). Its imagery of baleful creatures and withering vegetation are likewise appropriate to a desert context. At the same time, there seems to be a progression of thought within the collection: from sin through repentance to forgiveness, from despair to expectation of a new world order, from exile to ingathering. Such a collection would readily lend itself to being read as depicting the eschatological exile referred to in Zech. 13.7-14.2. In that case, the eschatological programme in the Psalter would appear somewhat as follows:

| Psalms | Ps. 45 | Psalms of Asaph | | | Ps. 89 | Book IV | Ps. 110 | The Hallel | The Ascents |
		Ps. 50	Ps. 72	Pss. 73-83		Pss. 90-106		Pss. 111-18	Pss. 120-34
Zech. 9-14	Bridegroom-king comes to Daughter Zion	Gathering of scattered Israel to Jerusalem	Temporary messianic malkut	Hostile nations gather against Jerusalem	The king cut off	Israel exiled in desert. Gather and return to Zion	Rescue by heavenly king messiah	Paeans of messianic victory; the hero's welcome	Ascent of Israel and all nations to Sukkoth on Zion in messianic malkut. Includes royal Ps. 132

Chapter 10

CONCLUSION

I have attempted to demonstrate the plausibility of an eschatological programme underlying the Psalter. I suggested that the historical view of the Psalter as eschatologico-predictive is borne out by internal features of the Masoretic text. I then examined the Psalms of Asaph and the Songs of Ascents and suggested that they can be read as depicting two different kinds of gathering to Zion: the former depicts Israel gathering and threatened by gathering hostile foes; the latter depicts them gathering joyfully to an eschatological Feast of Sukkoth. I then examined passages in the prophets, particularly in Ezekiel, Joel and Zechariah, which may reasonably be described as eschatological programmes. These appear to depict just such a sequence of gatherings as that in the Psalms of Asaph and Songs of Ascents. Many parallels of language, theology and imagery support the connection.

The Asaph Psalms (Pss. 50, 73–83)		The Ascents (Pss. 120–34)
Ingathering of scattered Israel from exile	Ingathering of hostile nations against Jerusalem	Gathering of Israel and nations to celebrate Sukkoth on Zion

I then examined in detail the eschatological programme in Zechariah 9–14. It appears to contain two motifs absent, or at best hazy, in the other prophetic programmes: a smitten shepherd-king and an ensuing exile. This makes the following sequence of events:

Ingathering of Israel under eschatological king (9.11–10.12)	Gathering of hostile nations against Jerusalem (12.3/14.1)	King dies. Israel exiled (12.10-14; 13.7-9; cf. 11.4-17)	Israel regather. Divine rout of nations (14.2-15)	Nations ascend to worship at Sukkoth in Jerusalem (14.16-21)

An examination of post-Zecharian eschatological texts showed that some such programme was also envisaged by later writers. I then examined the royal psalms and suggested that Pss. 45, 72, 89, 110 and 132 could be read as depicting the various messianic motifs of this programme. I finally looked at Book IV of the Psalter and suggested it could be read as depicting Israel's eschatological exile. Thus the Psalter can be read as containing an eschatological programme similar to the Zecharian one, as follows.

Psalms		Psalms of Asaph				Book IV		The Hallel	The Ascents
	Ps. 45	*Ps. 50*	*Ps. 72*	*Pss. 73-83*	*Ps. 89*	*Pss. 90–106*	*Ps. 110*	*Pss. 111–18*	*Pss. 120–34*
Zech. 9–14	Bride-groom-king comes to Daughter Zion	Gather-ing of scat-tered Israel to Jeru-salem	Tempor-ary mes-sianic malkut	Hostile nations gather against Jer-usalem	The king cut off	Israel exiled in desert. Gather and return to Zion	Rescue by king mes-siah	Paeans of mes-sianic victory; the hero's welcome	Ascent of Israel and all nations to Sukkoth on Zion in mes-sianic mal-kut. Includes royal Ps. 132

This hypothesis concurs with much modern research on the Psalter. It agrees with Forbes, Delitzsch, Childs and Brennan in seeing an eschatological orientation in the final form of the Psalter. It agrees with the insights of Wilson, McCann and Sheppard in recognizing the structural importance of psalm-headings, the centrality of the Davidic covenant theme, and the 'covenant crisis' in Psalm 89. It also bears some resemblance to the work of the Uppsala school and Goulder in associating Psalms 88 and 89 with the humiliation and affliction of the king, but it locates these events in the anticipated eschaton rather than in historical ritual. Indeed, if it is allowed that these rituals might have been not only cosmogonic but recosmogonic, that is, tending towards eschatological, then the parallels between such form critical views and the present hypothesis become closer still.

This hypothesis also harmonizes with the ancient commentators, both Jewish and Christian. It accords with the general eschatological interpretation of the Psalms found in the ancient translations, in the Qumran literature, in the New Testament and in rabbinic and patristic literature. It also accords with their view that the Psalter is purpose-fully shaped. But it agrees with them not only in general matters, but also in particular interpretations of individual psalms. The suggestions I have made as to the place of certain psalms or psalm-groups in the eschatological programme, such as Psalms 2, 45, 69, 72, 82, 83, 87, 88, 89, 90, 91, 92, 95, 109, 110, the Hallel, and the Songs of Ascents, including Psalm 132, are supported by the ancient commentators' referring to them in connection with the same or similar events.

This is not insignificant. These commentators lived close to the time of the Psalter's redactor(s), and are likely to have been in receipt of traditions concerning the purpose of his work. And even if they were not, are they not likely to have been able to ascertain the purpose of the collection at least as well as we, who live some 2000 years later in an alien culture? Indeed, this hypothesis not only concurs with the ancient interpreters, but suggests that their interpretations were rational and consistent rather than merely spurious allegorizations. For instance, if Messiah is the redactor's intended referent of Psalm 110, then those who cite it in that regard are not allegorizing when they do so. Likewise, if the redactor intended Psalm 87 to represent the temporary kingdom of the Messiah before his cutting off, then *Midrash Tehillim* is right in interpreting it of Messiahs ben Joseph and ben David. Or similarly, if the redactor intended Psalms 69 and 109 to refer to Messiah's opponents, then citing them of Judas is less gratuitous than it appears (Acts 1.20).

Like the ancient commentators, this hypothesis also takes account of imagery, typology, and analogy in interpretation. These are the foundations of Israelite exegesis. As Maimonides wrote:

> Know that the key to the understanding of all that the prophets, peace be on them, have said, and to the knowledge of its truth, is an understanding of the analogies [משלים], of their import, and of the meaning of the words occurring in them.[1]

This hypothesis is therefore in accord with Israelite exegesis in regarding the Asaph Psalms, with their holy war traditions, as typologically indicating the end-time conflict. Likewise, it regards the royal psalms as typologically indicating the anticipated future Davidic king, and the Songs of Ascents, with their Sukkoth traditions, as typologically indicating that feast's eschatological counterpart. It also takes the psalm-group headings, לאסף, לדוד and שיר המעלות, as symbolic of all that each group represents.

This hypothesis also hints at a literary and theological explanation for the Elohistic Psalter (Pss. 42–83) in exactly its present scope and position. As in the Asaph Psalms, so in the rest of the Elohistic Psalter, the predominance of the term *elohim* might suggest that Israel

---

1. *Moreh Nevukhim* 6b (ET in Maimonides 1963: 10-11).

in the initial period up until the eschatological conflict are estranged from God and under his judgment and wrath. Similarly, the predominance of *Yhwh* after the Elohistic Psalter might suggest that he is favourable to them in the period after the death of the king. It might take some rationalization to explain how God might be favourable during the eschatological exile. But however the details are explained, the hypothesis that the Psalter contains an eschatological programme opens the way to interpreting its peculiar use of divine names in a literary and theological manner in accord with ancient rabbinic traditions on the interpretation of these names.

Finally, this hypothesis offers some support for the parallel, perceived by ancient commentators, between the five books of the Pentateuch and the five books of Psalms. If, as I have proposed, Book II of the Psalter represents an exodus from exile, then it accords well with the principal theme of the second book of the Pentateuch. Book III of the Psalms is levitical, consisting entirely of Asaph and Korah lyrics, and ends in the possibly sacrificial death of the king.[2] It therefore accords well with the levitical and sacrifical themes of Leviticus.

2.　The question of whether the Messiah's death is sacrificial is clearly disputable. But deutero-Isaiah's עבד יהוה dies sacrificially (Isa. 53.4-6, 10-12) and the writer of Zech. 9–14 seems to have based his stricken shepherd on this figure, as was noted in Chapter 7. Zimmerli suggests that the LXX may indicate a messianic understanding of Isa 53 (*TDNT*: V, 676-77), while Jeremias discerns messianic interpretation of the עבד in Ben Sira and *1 Enoch* (*TDNT*, V.686-77). More recently, Puech (1992: 449-501) and Brooke (1993: 83-100) have suggested that 4Q541 exhibits an individual and messianic interpretation of Isa. 52–53, dating from at least the second century BCE (Puech 1992: 500). See also *T. Ben.* 3.1-8 where the Josephite Lamb of God 'as spotless for the lawless... will be given up, and as sinless for the godless... will die'. The reference to a Josephite Messiah suggests it is not a Christian gloss ('Lamb of God', 2-30). Certainly *Pes. R.* 36 is not Christian, yet envisages Messiah's death as an atonement: 'The Holy One (blessed be he) made an agreement with him [Messiah ben Ephraim]. He said: Those whose sins are stored up with you will bring you into an iron yoke and make you like this calf whose eyes are dimmed [with pain]. They will force your spirit into a yoke, and because of their sins your *tongue will cleave to* your jaws (Ps 22).' A Christian gloss is even more unlikely in Alshekh's *Marot ha-Zove'ot* where the following comment on Zech. 12.10 occurs: 'They shall lift up their eyes unto me in perfect repentance, when they see him *whom they have pierced,* that is, Messiah ben Joseph. For our rabbis of blessed memory have said that he will take upon himself all the guilt [כל אשמות] of Israel, and shall then be slain in the war to make an atonement [לכפר], in such a manner that it shall be accounted as if Israel had pierced him.'

Book IV takes place 'in the desert', which accords well with *Bemmid-bar,* the fourth book of the Pentateuch. Book V of the Psalter represents the final ingathering to worship Yhwh at Sukkoth in Jerusalem, a theme that corresponds with that of Deuteronomy, in which Israel are about to possess the land and there serve and worship Yhwh at the appointed feasts (Deut. 11.31–16.16). I have hardly touched on the themes of Book I, but would suggest that it is in some sense foundational to the following four books, much as Genesis is foundational to the Pentateuch. Certainly, parallels of theme and imagery seem to exist between Book I and Genesis. Note, for instance, after introductory Psalms 1 and 2, the 'morning/evening' theme of Pss. 3.6 [5]; 4.5, 9 [4-8]; 5.4 [3]; and 6.7 [6] which resembles Genesis 1. Likewise, Psalm 8, which tells how the 'paragon of animals' rules all creation, might correspond to Gen. 1.26-29.

Clearly, further research is needed to substantiate this hypothesis. The following topics, in particular, invite investigation. First, there are lengthy sections of the Psalter that I have not discussed. In particular, it needs to be considered how the לדוד psalms might relate to this hypothesis. Their heading would seem to connect them with the house of David, which is how I have interpreted those few I have discussed (e.g. Psalms 101, 103, 108–110). They might therefore refer to the troubles and triumphs of that house and, in particular, of its eschatological son. This is how Kimhi regards them, as does Wilson later.[3] A detailed study is required of their headings, language, poetics, thematic development and imagery in relation to this hypothesis. Related to this is the place of Book I in the Psalter. I have no suggestions to make about this, other than the feeling that it is somehow foundational to all the Psalter's themes, including the messianic ones (Psalms 20–22). However, I would not exclude the possibility that it refers to past events, from the redactional standpoint, either historical, like the Babylonian exile, or mythical.

Nor have I touched in any depth upon the *Psalms of the Sons of Korah* and the significance of their heading. My feeling is that they have something to do with the redemption of the righteous from Sheol on the day when *the earth is changed and the mountains fall into the heart of the sea* (Ps. 46). This is supported by the only other Old Testament reference to these figures, Num. 26.11, which tells how the

---

3. See Kimhi's commentaries on, for instance, Pss. 52–54. Wilson's views on this issue are noted in Chapter 2.

sons of Korah did not go down alive to Sheol as did their father and his following. Thus they might represent redemption from Sheol, a conclusion consistent with the group's many references to the underworld and with midrashic interpretation. Redemption from Sheol might signify, in the Psalter, the resurrection of the dead, either as a metaphor for Israel's renewal, or, more literally, in reference to the cut-off king of Psalm 89 or to the end-time resurrection at the appearance of the heavenly conqueror.

The significance of the psalms following the Songs of Ascents should also be considered. Psalms 135–37 seem to be a kind of *codetta* to the Ascents,[4] while the Halleluyah Psalms 146–50 appear to be a grand *coda* to the entire collection.[5] But it is interesting to note that the intervening לדוד collection (Pss. 138–45) seems to feature yet another attack upon the messianic throne, in Psalms 140–44. Violent evildoers threaten the Davidic speaker: with military force (140.2-3[1-2]; cf. v. 8 [7]; 144.1, 10); they set a trap for him (140.6 [5]; 141.9; 142.4 [3]); they pursue him (142.7 [6]; 143.3). However Psalm 144 anticipates the rescue of the speaker, David (114.10), from the sword and the rout of these hostile foreigners (v. 7). And Psalm 145 appears to celebrate Yhwh's deliverance as a *fait accompli* (v. 19) and proclaims the eternity of his kingdom (vv. 12-13), for now, at last, all opposition has been permanently crushed. These psalms may suggest that the Psalter's redactor anticipated as many as three eschatological attacks upon Jerusalem, an idea not unknown to other early Israelite writers.[6]

The significance of the Elohistic Psalter (Pss. 42–83) requires further investigation. I have an intuition that it may have to do with Jacob's struggle with the Angel of Yhwh at the Jabbok. The name *Jacob* is predominant in this collection and is scarce elsewhere in the Psalter, while the reverse is true for the name *Israel*. The man Israel

---

4. This is the view of Seybold 1978: 74-75; and Wilson 1985a: 225. The latter notes the verbal and thematic correspondences between Pss. 134 and 135–37.

5. Wilson 1993a: 74.

6. Rev. 19.19 and 20.7-9 describe two future foreign attacks, in addition to the period of foreign domination in the author's time, in which his Messiah was killed. *Midr. Pss.* 118.12 and 119.2 say that Gog and Magog will go up against Jerusalem three times. Sa'adya also has three attacks (*Kitab al-'Amanat* VIII.vi. [Rosenblatt 1948: 305-307]). In the first, Messiah ben Joseph dies; in the second, Messiah ben David conquers; and the third is overwhelmingly crushed by ben David.

may be a figure for the nation, who, in the end-time, will struggle with God until God prevails (גבר, Pss. 103.11; 117.2) over them. Likewise, the parallel between the five books of Psalms and of the Pentateuch needs to be further investigated. That may lead in turn to a better understanding of Book I. Finally, the place of the *Hallel* (Pss. 111-18) in connection with this proposed eschatological programme invites further investigation.

Wilson has compared the Psalter, with its individual lyrics joined in purposeful sequence, to an oratorio.

> Rather than a hymnbook, the Psalter is a symphony with many movements, or better yet an oratorio in which a multitude of voices—singly and in concert—rise in a crescendo of praise. While each individual composition may stand on its own—as an aria from the *Elijah*—the whole has an integrity that cannot and must not be ignored.[7]

The metaphor is felicitous. But it reflects the very point on which, I feel, Wilson's hypothesis falls—that is, in viewing the Psalter historically rather than eschatologically. It would have been better compared not to Mendelssohn's *Elijah,* with its historical themes, but to Handel's eschatological *Messiah.*

---

7.   Wilson 1993a: 72-82, in McCann 1993: 82.

Appendix 1

APOCALYPTIC MIDRASHIM

1. *Introduction*

This appendix contains translations of six eschatological programmes from rabbinic texts dating from the early to late first millennium CE: *Aggadat Mashiah, Otot ha-Mashiah, Sefer Zerubbabel, 'Asereth Melakhîm, Pirqê Mashiah* and *Nistarot Rav Shimon ben Yohai* (the Hebrew appears pp. 335-50). My purpose in translating these documents was to provide evidence that ancient Israelite interpreters also recognized an eschatological programme like that in Zechariah 9–14. These do not pretend to be critical editions of texts like *Sefer Zerubbabel* and *Pirqê Mashiah*. That would be an undertaking beyond present requirements. Only the relevant sections of the two longest texts, *'Asereth Melakhîm* and *Pirqê Mashiah*, are translated. The other four texts are translated in full. As far as I am aware this is the first rendition of them in English. The other eschatological midrash I have cited, that of Sa'adya Gaon, in his Arabic treatise *Kitab al-'Amanat*, is available in English.[1]

In these texts, as in other haggadic literature, Edom is frequently identified with Rome. This usage is first attested in the period just after Bar Kokhba, if two attributions of it to R. Meir can be accepted.[2] Its origin is uncertain, although Baron notes the views that it derives from Herod, a descendant of Edomite proselytes, who was virtually a Roman vassal, or that it is connected with the tradition that the Edomites burned the First Temple (1 Esd. 4.45) as the Romans burned the second.[3] After the Amoraic period the name became synonymous with Christian Rome and thence with Christianity in general.

2. *Aggadat Mashiah*

This midrash is found in the commentary on Num. 24.17 in *Leqah Tob (Pesiqta' Zutarta)*, which was compiled by Tobiah b. Eliezer in 1097 and re-edited by him about a decade later.[4] The text I have used is from Buber's edition of *Leqah*

---

1.   Rosenblatt 1948; Altmann 1946 (abridged).

2.   At *y. Ta'an.* 1.1 (64a), R. Meir reads רמא משא for דמה משא of Isa. 21.11; at *Pes. K.* 7.11 he reads ראמים of Isa. 34.7 as Romans. Meir was a fourth generation (c. 140–65) *tanna* (Danby 1933: 800).

3.   Baron 1957–83: II, 152.

4.   So Strack and Stemberger 1982–92: 389–90.

Tob.[5] Jellinek and Horowitz also have this midrash. Their texts are also from *Leqah Tob*, though presumably not from Buber's edition, as they differ in having אומות העולם, *nations of the world*, where Buber has הכנענים *the Canaanites*.[6] Dalman is probably correct in rejecting the former variant.[7] For Messiah ben Joseph, when he initiates the ingathering of Israel, does not destroy all the *nations of the world*, but only the usurpers of Israel's land. On the other hand, the more likely term, *Canaanites*, would seem to signify an intentional analogy between Joshua's conquest of the land and its reconquest by his descendant, Messiah ben Joseph.[8] Apart from minor differences in spelling there are no other textual variants. I have used Jellinek's title, and enumerated the sentences of Buber's text.

Jellinek recognizes that *Aggadat Mashiah* is an older work incorporated into Tobiah's book.[9] Several points suggest that it is of considerable antiquity. First, the writer's evident desire for the destruction of Rome (2.17-19) suggests an origin before the fall of Rome in 455 CE. Secondly, it is simpler than other apocalyptic midrashim. For instance, it covers the same sequence of events as *Otot ha-Mashiah*, composed probably between 540 and 630 CE, but is less detailed. Jellinek suggests that this indicates its antiquity: 'Among the various messianic tales collected in this volume, this Hagada is the oldest, because it is the simplest.'[10] Thirdly, it mentions the biblical figure Gog, but not Armilus, the evil Roman emperor of later midrashim. While Gog frequently appears in pre-geonic texts, Armilus is rare. He does not occur in the Talmud, and of the two targumic references to him one is doubtful.[11] Monstrous Armilus is a star figure in apocalyptic texts of geonic times—he was too choice a character to omit—and his absence from this midrash may suggest that it originated early in the first millennium, before the figure of Armilus developed.

Account of the Messiah

A star goes forth from Jacob [Num. 24.17]. It was taught in the name of our rabbis: In the week in which ben David comes, the first year [will have] no food, all [will be] privation. 2. The second [year], half famine will be sent.[12] 3. The third [year, there will be] great famine. 4. In the fourth, neither famine nor plenty. 5. In the fifth, great plenty. 6. And a star will spring forth from the east, and it is the star of

---

5.   Buber's edition has been reissued in 2 volumes (Jerusalem, 1959). The original date and place of printing are not given, but this seems to be the Wilna edn of 1880, referred to by Dalman 1888: 10. The text of this midrash is found in vol. 2, pp. 258-59 (קבכ).

6.   Jellinek 1853–77: III, 141-43; Horowitz 1881: 56-58. Horowitz later edited *Leqah Tob* in full under the title *Siphre Zutta* (1917).

7.   Dalman 1888: 10.

8.   Messiah ben Joseph is said to be a descendant of Joshua at *Targ. Ps-Jn.* to Exod. 40.11; Sa'adya 1948: 8.5.

9.   *BHM*: III.xxviii.

10.   'Unter den verschiedenen, in diesem Bande mitgetheilten messianischen Sagen ist diese Hagada die älteste, weil einfachste', *BHM*: III, xxviii.

11.   The reference to Armilus at *Targ. Isa.* 11.4 is not found in the best editions (Chilton 1987: xxxi-ii, 28). The other reference to him is at *Targ. Jon.* to Deut. 34.3.

12.   Literally, *they will send*.

Messiah. And it remains in the east fifteen days, and if it lasts longer it [will be] for the benefit of Israel.[13] 7. The sixth [year, there will be] voices and rumours. 8. The seventh [year, there will be] wars. 9. And at the end of the seventh, it shines for Messiah. And the sons of the west will exalt themselves and they will go and seize kingship without a struggle and they will go as far as Egypt and take many captives.[14] 10. In those days a brazen-faced king will arise over an afflicted and needy people, and he will seize *kingship by trickery* [Dan. 11.21]. 11. Concerning that time Isaiah said, *Come, my people, enter your chambers*, etc. [Isa. 26.20]. 12. The sages said: Rabbi Hiyya commanded his generation, 'When you hear that a brazen-faced king has arisen do not remain there, for he will decree that everyone who says, 'The God of the Hebrews, he is one!' will be killed.' 13. And he will say, 'All of us will be one tongue and one people.' He will abolish times and appointed feasts and sabbaths and new moon feasts. He will abolish Torah from Israel, as it is said, *And he will think to change the times and the law; and they shall be given into his hand for a time, two times, and half a time* [Dan. 7.25]. 14. *A time* is one year. 15. *Two times* is two [years]. 16. *And half a time* is half a year. 17. They said to him, 'Master, where shall we go to be safe?' He said to them, 'To upper Galilee, as it is said, *For on Mount Zion and in Jerusalem there will be those who escape* [Joel 3.5 (2.32)]. 18. *And on Mount Zion there will be those who escape, and it shall be holy'* [Obad. 17].

19. *And he shatters the princes of Moab* [Num. 24.17]. 20. R. Huna says in the name of R. Levi: This teaches that Israel will be gathered in upper Galilee. There Messiah ben Joseph will apear to them from the midst of Galilee, and they will ascend from there, and all Israel with him, to Jerusalem, to fulfil what is written, *And the forceful men of your people will lift themselves up to fulfil the vision, but they shall fail* [Dan. 11.14]. 21. And he goes up and builds the sanctuary and offers sacrifices and fire falls from heaven. And he shatters all the Canaanites. 22. And he goes against the land of Moab and kills half of them and takes the remainder captive. They send him tribute and afterwards he makes peace with Moab, as it is said, *And I will restore the fortunes of Moab* [Jer. 48.47]. Then they [Israel] will dwell 40 years in safety, eating and drinking, *and the sons of foreigners will be your farm-labourers and vintners* [Isa. 60.5].

23. *And he shall break down all the sons of Sheth* [Num. 24.17]. 24. That is, he breaks down all the Canaanites who are called *Sheth*. 25. As it is said, *God has appointed* [shath] *for me another seed* [Gen. 4.25]. 26. After all this, Gog and Magog hear and go up against them, as it is said, *The kings of the earth set themselves, and the rulers take counsel together, against the Lord and against his Messiah* [Ps. 2.2]. 27. He [Gog] forces entry and kills him [Messiah ben Joseph] in the streets of Jerusalem, as it is said, *And there will be a time of trouble* [Dan. 12.1]. Israel sees this and says, 'Messiah is perished from us, and no other messiah will come.' And four families mourn for him, as it is said, *The land will mourn, each family by itself; the family of the house of David by itself* [Zech. 12.12]. 28. And the

---

13.   For the meaning *remain* for עשׂה, see Jastrow 1950: II, 1125.
14.   Literally, *and take captive all captivity*.

Holy One, blessed be he, goes forth and fights with them, as it is said, *Then the Lord will go forth and fight against those nations* [Zech. 14.3]. The mountains will melt and the hills totter and the Mount of Olives will split asunder. 29. And the Holy One, blessed be he, will descend upon it, and Israel flee and make their escape, as it is said, *And you will flee to the valley of my mountain* [Zech. 14.5]. 30. *And this shall be the plague* [*with which the Lord shall strike all the nations,* etc. (Zech. 14.12)]. 31. And after this Israel will be exiled to the wilderness of marshes to feed there for 45 days on sea-purslain and roots of broom. And clouds of glory surround them, and there Israel will be hidden. But whoever has evil thoughts in his heart about the Holy One, blessed be he, the clouds throw him out and the Canaanites kill him. 32. And many from Israel go over to the Canaanites, and they will have no portion with Israel in the age to come. However, to those who are prepared to fare meagrely on sea-purslain for 45 days, comes at the end of that time a heavenly voice, saying to them, 'Go down to Babylon!' As it is said, *And you will go down to Babylon; there you will be rescued* [Mic. 4.10]. 33. And a heavenly voice proclaims a second time, 'Go to Edom and execute there my vengeance!' As it is said, *And I will lay my vengeance upon Edom by the hand of my people Israel* [Ezek. 25.14]. And Israel goes to Rome. And a heavenly voice proclaims a third time, 'Do to her as Joshua did to Jericho!' And they surround the city and blow the trumpets, and the seventh time they raise a battle-cry: *'Hear Israel! The Lord our God, the Lord is one!'* [Deut. 6.4]. And the walls of the city fall, and they assemble within it and find her young men dead in her squares, as it is said, *Therefore her young men shall fall in her squares,* etc. [Jer. 49.26]. 34. And after this they gather all the spoil and Israel seeks their God and David their king. And thereupon the King Messiah is revealed to them. And he says to them, 'I am the King Messiah, for whom you have waited!' And he says to them, 'Take the silver and the gold.' And they take it and ascend [to Jerusalem], as it is written, *A multitude of camels will cover you* [Isa. 60.6]. 35. And a fourth heavenly voice proclaims and says, *'The voice of a crier in the wilderness!'* [Isa. 40.3]. 36. And a fifth heavenly voice says, *No lion shall be there* [Isa. 35.9]. And a sixth heavenly voice says, *I will put in the wilderness the cedar, the acacia, and the myrtle* [Isa. 41.19]. 37. And a seventh heavenly voice proclaims, *Comfort, comfort my people!* [Isa. 40.1]. And Elijah announces to Israel, *Your God has become king!* [Isa. 52.7]. 38. And an eighth heavenly voice proclaims and says, *Speak kindly to Jerusalem* [Isa. 40.2]. A ninth heavenly voice says, *Open the gates, that the righteous nation may enter in!* [Isa. 26.2]. 39. And a tenth heavenly voice says, *Lift up, O gates, your heads* [Ps. 24.7,9]. 40. And the dead will live, as it is said, *Your dead will live, my corpses will rise!* [Isa. 26.19]. 41. Then the exiles will gather together, as it is said, *And in that day a great trumpet will sound* [Isa. 27.13]. 42. Then is fulfilled [the word], *A star goes forth from Jacob* [Num. 24.17]. 43. Yes, may it be pleasing before our Father in heaven that the verse, *And he will raise an ensign for the nations, and will assemble the outcasts of Israel* [Isa. 11.12], be fulfilled in our days and in the days of all Israel.

The Account of the Messiah is Ended

3. *Otot ha-Mashiah*

This is a translation of אותות המשח from Jellinek's *Bet ha-Midrash*.[15] His text is
dependent on the collection אבקת רוכל.[16] Section and sentence enumeration have
been added to facilitate reference. These correspond to the paragraphs and sentences
of Jellinek's text.

Only an approximate date of composition can be given. The lack of reference to
Islam suggests it dates from before the Muslim capture of Jerusalem in 638 CE. The
writer clearly hoped for the demise of Roman power and, like the author of *Nistarot
Rav Shimon ben Yohai,* who saw the Islamic armies as the instrument of divine
vengeance on Rome, would have mentioned Rome's defeat by the Muslims if it had
already taken place.[17] He might also have depicted Jerusalem in Arab hands at the
time of the end, as does the writer of *Pirqê Mashiah*.[18] So the silence of this text
regarding Muslim power suggests it was written before Islam presented any threat
whatsoever to Roman power in Palestine, say before 630 CE. Indeed, Messiah ben
Joseph's plundering of the temple of Julianus Caesar (6.7) would suggest a date of
composition prior to the fall of Rome (455 CE), possibly as early as the time of Julian
(*r.* 361–63). One fact however qualifies an unquestioned assumption of such an early
origin, which is that the term *Gaon of Jacob* seems to be used in its specific sense as
a formal title of the heads of the large diaspora academies of Sura and Pumbedita
(1.2). Sherira mentions a tradition that Ravai of Pumbedita (c. 540–60) was known
as *gaon,*[19] however there is no evidence either for or against the specific use of the
term at an earlier date. If one can accept a specific use of *gaon* in Roman times, then
this midrash might well have been written pre-455 CE, and possibly as early as the
time of Julian. But if Sherira's comment demarcates the earliest specific use of the
term, then an origin sometime between the mid-sixth and early seventh centuries
would have to be proposed.

There is no evidence regarding authorship. Jellinek mentions an edition of the text
that purports to be from 'the *midrashim* of Rav Hai Gaon'.[20] None of the three
geonim Rav Hai could have been the author, given the early date of the text, but the
phrase may indicate that one of them included it in a collection of *midrashim*.[21]

---

15.   *BHM*: II, 58-63.

16.   Amsterdam edition, 2b. These are the only bibliographical details supplied by Jellinek.

17.   Jellinek 1853–77: III, 78-82. See p. 78. The text is given later in this appendix.

18.   Jellinek 1853–77: III, 68-78. See p. 71. The text is given later in this appendix.

19.   So Abramovitch and Brand 1971: VII, 315-24]: 315. Incidentally, the opinion of some
scholars, which is noted in passing by Abramovitch and Brand, that *gaon* only became a formal title
in the Islamic period, is disproved by the present text, which appears to be pre-Islamic and to use
gaon in the formal sense.

20.   'In cod. 17 der Leipziger Rathsbibliothek steht eine kurze Recension der *Zeichen des
Messias* mit der Ueberschrift: והעיקתי אותות ממשיח ממדרשי רב האי גאון ז'ל' (*BHM*: II, xxiii). I
am assuming הז'י equals האי.

21.   Hai ben Nahshon, *gaon* of Sura (885–96); Hai bar Rav David, *gaon* of Pumbedita (890–
98); Hai ben Sherira, *gaon* of Pumbedita (998–1038).

Signs of the Messiah

1. The First Sign. The Holy One, blessed be he, will raise up a triumvirate of kings, and they will deny reason, and lie, and present themselves to people as worshippers of the Holy One, blessed be he, but they will not be. And they lead astray and confuse all mankind, and on account of their laws the nations of the world will deny [the truth]. And even apostate Israelites, who have given up hope of the redemption, will deny the Holy One, blessed be he, and forsake the fear of him. And of this generation it is said, *And truth is lacking* [Isa. 59.15]. And what does *lacking* mean? It means the masters of truth become like flocks, and go and flee and hide themselves in caves and holes in the ground.[22] And all the great ones of the generation die, and honest men cease to exist. The gates of wisdom are hidden, and the world neglects study. And at that time [there will be] no king and no prince in Israel, as it is said, *For Israel shall dwell many days without king or prince, without sacrifice or pillar,* etc. [Hos. 3.4]. 2. And [there will be] no heads of academies of *gaon*[23] of Jacob, and no faithful shepherds or pious believers, and no wonder-workers. And the doors of heaven[24] are fastened, and the gates of provision and sustenance locked. 3. And when the Messiah is revealed in his might his generation [of that time] will be having the life squeezed out of it, because of the harsh laws and perplexities and terrors which these three kings decree. 4. Moreover, they will pass a decree banning the Holy Place, the Lord and the Torah. And the Holy One, blessed be he, has decreed that the evil kingship will hold sway for nine months, from one horizon to the other, as it is said, *Therefore he shall give them over until the time when she who is in travail gives birth* [Mic. 5.2 (3)], and they will have nothing except an oath, as it is said, *Therefore I swear to the house of Eli* [1 Sam. 3.14].[25] 5. They will decree harsh decrees and multiply tenfold the tribute imposed on Israel. Whoever was giving ten gives a hundred, and everyone who was giving eight gives eighty, and everyone who has nothing, they cut off his head. 6. And throughout all these nine months they promulgate decree after decree, each harsher than the one before. 7. And people will emerge from the ends of the earth who will be particularly ugly, and all who see them will die from fear of them. They do not need to make war, for merely from fear they will kill everyone. And each of them will have two heads and seven eyes, burning like fire and swift in motion as gazelles. 8. At that time Israel will cry out and say, 'Woe! Woe!' And the little ones of Israel will be terrified and will go

22.   There is a wordplay on *lacking* (נעדרת) and *flocks* (עדרים עדרים). Similar expressions occur at *Sanh.* 97a: 'What is meant by *truth is lacking*? The scholars of the school of Rab said, 'This teaches that it will split up into flocks [עדרים עדרים] and depart''; and at *Song R.* 2.13: 'Where does banished truth go? She goes and sits in flocks [עדרים עדרים] in the desert.'

23.   I have left *gaon* untranslated, as the term is being used in its specific sense with reference to the heads of the large academies of the diaspora.

24.   Or, *the doors of the mill.* There appears to be a wordplay upon the double sense of שחקים as *heaven, clouds,* and *grinding* (cf. Jastrow 1950: II, 1550-51).

25.   The allusion is unclear. It may imply that Israel will have only God's oath for reassurance. Or it may intend the latter part of the verse to refer to the three evil kings (*the iniquity of Eli's house shall not be expiated by sacrifice or offering for ever*).

and hide themselves, every one under [the garment of] his father and mother, and say, 'Woe! Woe, father! What is happening?'[26] And their fathers will answer them, 'Now we are drawing near to the redemption of Israel.'

2. The Second Sign. The Holy One, blessed be he, makes heat come on the world from the heat of the sun, together with wasting disease, fever, many malignant illnesses, and plague, and they kill a thousand thousands from the nations of the world every day (and all the wicked in Israel die), until the nations of the world will wail and cry out, 'Woe to us! Where shall we go? Where shall we flee?' And each one digs his own grave while alive, and they ask to die. 2. They conceal themselves in barren places, towers and thickets, in order to cool themselves, and go into caves and holes in the ground. 3. And if you say, 'How will the righteous be saved from the heat of the sun?' The Holy One, blessed be he, will make a means of healing in this heat, as it is said, *But for you who fear my name the sun of righteousness shall rise with healing in his wings* [Mal. 3.20 (4.2)]. 4. And concerning this wicked Balaam testified prophetically, *Woe! Who will live when God does this?* [Num. 24.23].

3. The Third Sign. The Holy One, blessed be he, will make a dew of blood descend, and the nations of the world will think it is water, and they will drink of it and die. And even the wicked of Israel, who have given up hope of the redemption, will drink of it and die. But the righteous, who hold to faith in the Holy One, blessed be he, are not injured at all, as it is said, *Those who are wise shall shine like the brightness of the firmament* [Dan. 12.3]. 2. And all the world shall become blood for a full three days, as it is said in Hosea, *And I will give portents in the heavens and on the earth, blood and fire and columns of smoke* [Joel 3.3 (2.30)].[27]

4. The Fourth Sign. The Holy One, blessed be he, makes a dew of healing descend to heal the blood, and the ordinary people[28] will drink of it and be cured of the diseases, as it is said, *I will be as the dew to Israel; he shall blossom as the lily, he shall strike root as Lebanon* [Hos. 14.6 (5)].

5. The Fifth Sign. The Holy One, blessed be he, turns the sun to darkness for three days, as it is said, *The will be turned to darkness and the moon to blood* [Joel 3.4 (2.31)]. 2. After three days the Holy One, blessed be he, restores it to its former state, as it is said, *They will be gathered together as prisoners in a pit; they will be shut up in prison, and after many days they will be released* [Isa. 24.22]. 3. And the nations of the world will be terrified and abashed, knowing that all these signs are because of Israel, and many of them become secret Jews, as it is said, *Those who adhere to vain idols will forsake their faithful love* [Jon. 2.9(8)].

26.   Or, *What shall we do?*

27.   It is not clear why the writer cites Joel as Hosea. He may regard Hosea, the first of the 12 prophets, as representative of them all. Or it may be an error.

28.   That is, those neither righteous nor wicked.

6. The Sixth Sign. The Holy One, blessed be he, makes evil Edom rule over all the world, as we said above. 2. And another king of the Romans will arise, who will rule over all the world for nine months and lay waste many countries. 3. And he will rage against Israel and impose heavy tribute on them. 4. And Israel will be in great distress at this time because of the number of decrees and perturbations proclaimed against them every day. And Israel will decrease and waste away at this time, and [there will be] no helper for Israel. And Isaiah prophesied of this time and said, *He saw there was no man and he was astounded,* etc. [Isa. 59.16]. 5. At the end of the nine months Messiah ben Joseph will appear, and his name is Nehemiah ben Hoshiel, and with him the tribe of Ephraim, Manasseh and Benjamin, and some of the sons of Gad. 6. And Israel hears in all the countries that the Messiah of the Lord has come, and a few from every province and city gather to him, as it is said in Jeremiah, *Return, rebellious sons, says the Lord, for I am your master, and I will take you, one from a city and two from a clan, and bring you to Zion* [Jer. 3.14]. 7. And Messiah ben Joseph will come and stir himself up for his war with the king of Edom. He will conquer Edom and kill heaps and heaps and heaps of them. And he will kill the king of Edom and destroy the country of the Romans and will bring out some of the vessels of the sanctuary of the sons of Israel, which are in the temple[29] of Julianus Caesar.[30] And he will go to Jerusalem, and Israel will hear and gather to him. 8. And the king of Egypt will make peace with him, and he will kill all the people of the countries around Jerusalem as far as Damascus and Ashkelon. And all the people of the world will hear and great terror will fall upon them.

7. The Seventh Sign. The Holy One, blessed be he, the master of wonders, performs a miracle in the world. 2. They say there is a stone in Rome which has the form of a shapely girl, and it[31] was not made by human hand, but the Holy One, blessed be he, made it thus by his power. 3. And the wicked nations of the world, the sons of Belial, abuse it and lie with it. And the Holy One, blessed be he, preserves their drops [of semen] in the stone and creates in it a being and forms in it a child. And it splits apart and out of it comes a human form. His name is Armilus the Satan. This is he whom the nations call Antichrist. And his height is 12 cubits and his width 12 cubits. There is a span between his two eyes and they are dark red. And the hair of his head is as if coloured gold. 4. The soles of his feet are green and he has two heads. 5. And he will go along to evil Edom and say to them, 'I am Messiah. I am your God.' Thereupon they believe in him and make him rule over them. All the sons of Esau are spellbound by him, and going with him march out and crush all the countries. And he says to the sons of Esau, 'Bring me my Torah, which I gave you.' 6. And they bring him their prayers.[32] And he says to them, 'This which I gave you

---

29.   Or *palace*.

30.   Flavius Claudius Julianus, known as Julian the Apostate (331–63 CE), Roman emperor from 361–63 CE.

31.   Or *she*, and so throughout 2 and 3.

32.   The term *prayers* seems unusual. The reason for its use may have been to introduce a deliberate wordplay between תְּפִלּוֹת, *prayers*, and תִּפְלוֹת, *triviality, obscenity*, referring, in the context, to the New Testament or other Christian writings.

is true.' And he says to the nations of the world, 'Trust in me, for I am your Messiah.' Thereupon they trust in him. 7. At that time he sends to Nehemiah ben Hoshiel and all Israel and says to them, 'Bring me your Torah and testify of me that I am your God.' Thereupon they are afraid and look anxiously at one another. 8. At that time Nehemiah ben Hoshiel will rise up with 30,000 warriors of the warriors of the sons of Ephraim. And they will take the book of Torah and read before him, *I am the Lord your God. You shall have no other gods before me* [Exod. 20.2-3; Deut. 5.6-7]. 9. And he will say to them, 'There is nothing in this Torah of yours. But come, testify of me that I am God in the same way that all the nations have done.' 10. Thereupon Nehemiah will withstand him, and he [Armilus] will say to his servants, 'Seize him and bind him!' 11. Thereupon Nehemiah ben Hoshiel will rise up, and the 30,000 who are with him, and do battle with him. And they will kill 20,000 of them. 12. Thereupon the fury of evil Armilus will burn, and he will gather all the forces of the world to the Valley of Judgment [Joel 4.14]. And he will do battle with Israel. And they [Israel] will kill heaps and heaps of them, but only a few will be smitten from Israel. But Messiah of the Lord will be killed. And ministering angels will come and carry him away and hide him with the eternal fathers.[33] 13. Thereupon the courage of Israel will melt and their strength will weaken. But evil Armilus will not know that Messiah is dead. For if he knew, he would leave neither survivor nor fugitive of Israel. 14. And at that time all the nations of the world drive Israel out of their countries and they do not let them live in their countries. And they say, 'You saw the people despised and humiliated, who rebelled against us and set up a king.'[34] And there will be distress for Israel, such as never was from ancient days to this time. 15. And at this time Michael will arise to purge the wicked from Israel, as it is said, *At that time Michael, the great prince who is appointed over the sons of your people, will arise. And there shall be distress such as never was*, etc. [Dan. 12.1]. 16. Thereupon all Israel will flee into the deserts, and every one whose mind is in doubt will return to the nations of the world and they will say, 'This redemption for which we wait is because the Messiah was killed.' 17. And all who are not waiting for the redemption will become ashamed of it and return to the nations of the world. 18. At that time the Holy One, blessed be he, tests Israel and refines them like silver and gold. 19. As it is said in Zechariah, *And I will bring a third of them through fire, and refine them as silver is refined* [Zech. 13.9]. And it is written in Ezekiel, *I will purge you of those who rebel against me*, etc. [Ezek. 20.38]. 20. And in Daniel it is written, *Many will be purified, made spotless and refined, but the wicked will continue to be wicked*, etc. [Dan. 12.10]. And all the remnant of Israel, the holy and ritually clean, will be in the desert of Judah 45 days and they will subsist by eating salt herbs and they will pluck leaves from shrubs. 21. And in them is fulfilled what is said in Hosea, *Therefore I am now going to allure her; I will lead her into the desert and speak tenderly to her* [Hos. 2.16 (14)]. 22. And the number of days is 45 because it is said, *From the time that the daily sacrifice is abolished and to the setting up of the abomination that makes desolate [there will be] 1290 [days]* [Dan. 12.11].

---

33.   That is, the heroes of the Old Testament. See the Hebrew of Sir. 44.1.

34.   Or possibly, *'Have you seen the people...?'*

23. And it is written, *Blessed is the one who waits for and reaches the end of 1335 [days]* [Dan. 12.12]. 24. Between these there are 45 days. 25. At this time all the wicked of Israel, who were not worthy to see the redemption, will perish. 26. And Armilus will go and make war against Egypt and capture it, as it is said, *And the land of Egypt will not escape* [Dan. 11.42]. And he will turn his face to Jerusalem to destroy it a second time, as it is said, *He will pitch his royal tents between the seas at the beautiful holy mountain. Yet he will come to his end and no one will help him* [Dan. 11.45].

8. The Eighth Sign. Michael will stand and blow three blasts upon the shofar, as it is said, *And in that day a great shofar will sound, and those perishing will come*, etc. [Isa. 27.13]. And it is written, *The Lord God will sound the shofar and march in the storms of the south* [Zech. 9.14]. 2. At the first blast Messiah ben David will reveal himself, and Elijah the prophet, to the purified righteous of Israel who fled to the desert of Judah. At the end of 45 days their courage will return and they will strengthen their feeble hands and make firm their weak knees. 3. And the remnant of Israel in all the world will hear the sound of the shofar and they will know that the Lord is mustering them and that the final redemption has come. And they will gather and come, as it is said, *And those perishing in the land of Assyria come*, etc. [Isa. 27.13]. And at this sound fear and trembling will fall on the nations of the world, and terrible diseases will fall on them. 4. And Israel will gird themselves for departure. And Messiah ben David will go, and Elijah the prophet, with the righteous ones who returned from the desert of Judah, and with all of gathered Israel, and he will go to Jerusalem. And he will ascend the steps[35] to the remains of the temple and take his seat there. And Armilus will hear that a king has arisen for Israel and he will say, 'How long will this contemptible little nation act like this?' Thereupon he will gather all the armies of the nations of the world and go to make war with the Messiah of the Lord. And then the Holy One, blessed be he, needs nothing for the battle, but to say to him [Messiah ben David], *Sit at my right hand* [Ps. 110.1]. And he [Messiah ben David] will say to Israel, *Stand firm and see the deliverance of the Lord which he will accomplish for you today* [Exod. 14.13]. Thereupon the Holy One, blessed be he, fights against them, as it is said, *And the Lord will go forth and fight against those nations as he fights on a day of battle* [Zech. 12.3]. 5. And the Holy One, blessed be he, makes fire and brimstone come down from the heavens, as it is said, *I will execute judgment upon him with plague and* hail, *and I will pour out torrential rain and hailstones*, etc. [Ezek. 38.22]. 6. Thereupon evil Armilus will die, he and all his army, and evil Edom, who laid waste the temple of our God and exiled us from our land. And at that time Israel will wreak on them a great vengeance, as it is said, *The house of Jacob will be a fire and the house of Joseph a flame, and the house of Esau will be stubble*, etc. [Obad. 18].

9. The Ninth Sign. Michael will blow a great blast [upon the shofar] and the catacombs of the dead in Jerusalem will break open and the Holy One, blessed be he,

35. Or, *ascents*.

will make them live. And Messiah ben David will proceed, and Elijah the prophet, and they will revive Messiah ben Joseph, who was gathered [in death] at the gates of Jerusalem. And they will send Messiah ben David for the remnant of Israel scattered in all the lands. 2. Thereupon all the kings of the nations of the world will lift them on their shoulders and bring them [to Jerusalem], etc.

10. The Tenth Sign. Michael blows a great blast [upon the shofar] and the Holy One, blessed be he, brings out all the tribes [of Israel] from the River Gozan, and Halah and Habor and the cities of Media.[36] And they will come with the sons of Moses without number. 2. *The land is like the Garden of Eden before them, and behind them a flame burns* [Joel 2.3], and they will not leave behind a [single] possession of the nations of the world.[37] When the tribes depart, clouds of glory will surround them, and the Holy One, blessed be he, will go before them, as it is said, *He who breaks through will go up before them* [Mic. 2.13]. And the Holy One, blessed be he, will open the springs of the tree of life to them and will make them drink by the road, as it is said in Isaiah, *I will open rivers on barren heights, and springs within the valleys; I will make the desert a pool of water, and the parched land into fountainheads of water* [Isa. 41.18]. 3. And it is written, *They shall not hunger or thirst, neither shall scorching wind nor sun smite them*, etc. [Isa. 49.10]. 4. The Holy One, blessed be he, make us worthy to see the redemption quickly, and make us worthy to see the shining temple.[38] 5. May he establish among us a convocation, as it is written, *Behold, I will restore the fortunes of the tents of Jacob, and have compassion on his dwellings; the city will be rebuilt on its ruins and the palace stand in its proper place* [Jer. 30.18]. May he establish for us all his consolations and promises, as it is said by his prophets, and it is written, *At that time I will bring you, and at that time when I have gathered you, I will surely give you honour and renown* [Zeph. 3.20].

The Signs of the Messiah Are Ended.

4. Sefer Zerubbabel

This does not pretend to be a critical edition of *Sefer Zerubbabel*. Those who wish to familiarize themselves with the extensive textual variants should compare the texts of Jellinek, Wertheimer, Eben-Shmuel and Eisenstein, together with the Cairo Genizah manuscripts.[39] The following is simply a translation of Jellinek's text, together with the variant readings that he includes. I have inserted these variants in the main text, as does Jellinek. The formula *v.r.* (*variant reading*) is employed to render Jellinek's נ״א

---

36.   These are the places, according to 2 Kgs 17.6 and 1 Chron. 5.26, to which the Assyrians carried the captives of Samaria.

37.   That is, they will plunder the nations as at the exodus from Egypt (Gen. 15.14; Exod. 11.1ff.; 12.35-36; Ps. 105.37).

38.   Or, *The Holy One, blessed be he, will make us worthy*, etc. And so through v. 5.

39.   Jellinek 1853–77: II, 54-57; Wertheimer 1952–55: 495-505; Eben-Shmuel 1954: 71-88, 379-79. The Genizah texts are in Hopkins 1978: 10, 15, 64-65, 72-73.

and מוסיף א"נ is rendered *v.r. adds.* The sentences of Jellinek's text have been enumerated.

Sefer Zerubbabel was a popular work. It exists in 'countless medieval manuscripts', deriving from all the main centres of mediaeval Judaism.[40] It was widely accepted by Jews of almost every ideology, the principal exception being Maimonides and his followers, who found it incompatible with their view that the Messiah was to be an earthly Davidic king who would die a natural death and be succeeded by his descendants.[41] This popularity led to a profusion of texts and, inevitably, textual variants, and the text is sometimes bewildering in its multiplicity of names and pseudonyms.

As regards dating, Baron suggests that some manuscripts indicate 638 CE as the year of redemption, which would indicate that these texts originated shortly before that time:

> By identifying the recurring name Sirois with a king of Persia by that name, Lévi reinterpreted the entire tract within the context of the final stages of the Perso-Byzantine war and the rise of Islam (629–36). His argument was accepted by Ibn Shemuel who added the observation that, in the version published by Lévi from a Bodleian manuscript, the date of 990 years could relate not to the fall of Jerusalem (a second passage mentions specifically 'Jerusalem's ruins'), but rather to the building of the Second Temple which, according to Jewish tradition, had lasted altogether 420 years. Subtracting these 420 years, the prediction aimed at the remaining 570 years after the fall of Jerusalem in 68 CE, that is at the year 638.[42]

The work's silence on Islam would also appear to indicate a date some years before the Muslim conquest of Jerusalem in 638 CE, for midrashim of the Islamic period, such as *Nistarot Rav Shimon ben Yohai* and *Pirqê Mashiah,* generally make reference to the Arabs.[43] A date sometime in the early seventh century would therefore appear likely.

The Book of Zerubbabel

1. The message which came to Zerubbabel ben Shealtiel, the Prince of Judah; (*v.r.* he showed me there) this vision. 2. I was praying before the Lord in a trance, the vision which I saw at the River Kebar, when I said (*v.r.* and saying), 'Blessed are you, Lord, who raises the dead.'

3. My heart murmured within me, saying, 'How will be the appearance of the eternal Temple?'

4. And he answered me from the doors of heaven, and said to me, 'Are you, Zerubbabel, Prince of Judah?'

5. And I said, 'I am your servant.'

---

40.   Dan 1971: XVI, 1002.

41.   Dan 1971: XVI, 1002; Hyman 1971:, XI, 776.

42.   Baron 1957–83: V, 354. Baron is referring to Lévi 1914–20, I: 129–60; 69 (1919) 108–21; 71 (1920) 57–65. This Persian king does not appear in Jellinek's text.

43.   These are included in this appendix. See *NRSbY* 3-7; *Pir. M.* 43.

6. And a voice came forth to me (*v.r.* and answered me) and spoke to me as a man speaks to his friend. 7. His voice I heard, but his form I did not see. 8. And I rose and prayed as before, and I said (*v.r.* and I concluded) my prayer and I returned to my house.

9. And on the eleventh day of Adar (*v.r.* of the month) he was speaking with me and he said to me, 'Come to me. Ask of me.'

10. And I said, 'What should I ask for? 11. Few (*v.r.* short) are the days [until] my end, and I am completing my days.'

12. And he said to me, 'I will revive you.' 13. And he said to me, 'Be revived.'

14. And a wind lifted me up between the heavens and the earth, and brought me to Nineveh the great city, and it is a city of blood. And I was in great distress. And I arose from distress to pray and entreat the face of the God of Israel. And I confessed my transgression and my sin, and said, 'I am the one who has sinned, transgressed and become guilty, which has led to my grief.[44] 15. You are he who is the God of Israel, who made everything by the breath of your mouth, and at your word the dead will live.'

16. And the Lord said to me, 'Go to the house of shame (*v.r.* house of pleasure), the place of desire.'[45] 17. And I went as he commanded me. 18. And he said to me, 'Turn and go further off.' 19. And I turned and it wearied me. And I saw a man despised and crushed.

20. The man who was crushed and despised said to me, 'Zerubbabel, what (*v.r.* business) are you doing here?'

21. And I answered and said, 'The Spirit of the Lord lifted me up, to where (*v.r.* to this city) I know not, and brought me to this place.'

22. And he said to me, 'Do not fear, because it was in order to be shown this that you were brought here.'

23. And when I heard his words I was reassured, and I asked him, 'What is the name of this place?'

24. And he said, 'This is great Rome in which I am bound in prison until my appointed time.'

(*v.r.* And I said to him, 'My Lord, who are you, and what do you want, and what are you doing here?'

And he said to me, 'I am the Messiah of the Lord, who am bound here until the time of the end.') 25. When I heard this, I hid my face for a moment before him, and again I looked at him, and again I hid [my face] because I was afraid. 26. And he told me, 'Do not fear and do not be dismayed. Why are you silent?'

27. And I said, 'I have heard of your fame, for you are the Messiah of my God.'

---

44. Or possibly, *led to my grievous offence.*

45. Or possibly, *the house of exchange (v.r. house of pleasure), the market place.* חורך was the binding passage in a legal document (Jastrow 1950: II, 1658). But חורפה and חורך also mean *decay, filth,* and the phrase מקום בית התורפה/תורך is attested as meaning *obscenity* or *genitalia* (Jastrow 1950: II, 1658). שוק can denote both *sexual desire* and *market* (Jastrow 1950: II, 1540-41). I have chosen the more lascivious interpretation as that seems to be the one favoured by the alternative reading בית הלצות. The double meaning may be intended, possibly indicating the kind of business transacted in certain quarters of the market.

28. And thereupon he seemed to me like a youth, the perfection of beauty and loveliness, a peerless young man. 29. And I said to him, 'When will the light of Israel shine?'

30. And as I was speaking to him, behold! a winged man came to me and he said to me, (*v.r. adds:* 'What more will you ask the Messiah of the Lord?

And I answered and said, 'When will the time of redemption come?'

And he told me) that he[46] was the commander of Israel's host who fought with Sennacherib and with the kings of Canaan, and he is destined to fight the war of the Lord with the Messiah of the Lord, and with the brazen-faced king, and Armilus ben Eben, who came out of the stone.[47]

31. And Metatron spoke again and he told me, 'I am the angel who led Abraham in all the land of Canaan, and I am he who preserved Isaac, and wrestled with Jacob at the fords of the Jabbok. I am he who led Israel in the wilderness for 40 years in the name of the Lord. I am he who appeared to Joshua at Gilgal. And I am he whose name is like the name of my master, and his name is in my inmost being. 32. And you, Zerubbabel, ask me and I will tell how he will call your people in the latter days.'

33. And he said to me, 'This is the Messiah of the Lord, who is hidden here until the time of the end.' (*v.r.* And he said to me, '[This is] Messiah of the Lord who will come at the time of the end, and his name is Menahem ben Ammiel, and he was born in the days of David, King of Israel, and a wind took him up and hid him here until the time of the end.')

And I asked Metatron, and he said to me, 'The blessed Lord will give a sceptre of deliverance to Hefzibah, the mother of Menahem, and a star will shine before her and she will go forth and kill two kings. The first is Noph from Teman, and the name of the second is Antioch (*v.r.* Asarnu from Antioch). And these signs will take place in the Feast of Weeks, and the message will come true (*v.r. adds:* when he is killed). And when the city is built 420 years it will be desolated a second time, and [there will be] 20 years of servitude (*v.r.* Roman oppression) to Rome. And they will make 70 kings rule in it. And when ten kings have been completed in it, the tenth will desolate the sanctuary, and cause the daily burnt offering to turn aside. And from that day 990 years will be reckoned to you, [and then] will be the salvation of the Lord. And he will remember his holy people, to redeem them, and take them, and carry them, and gather them. 34. And the staff that the Lord will give to Hefzibah, the mother of Menahem, is of almond (*v.r.* of [the wood of] almond trees), and it is hidden in Rakkat (*v.r. adds:* a town of Naphtali). 35. And it is the staff of Aaron, and Moses and David, king of Israel. 36. And it is the staff which sprouted in the Tent of Meeting, and gave forth flowers, and bore almonds, and Elijah ben Eleazar hid it in Rakkat, which is Tiberias. And there Messiah ben Ephraim hid it.'[48]

---

46. The latter part of the sentence suggests that the pronoun indicates the winged man, Metatron, rather than the Messiah.

47. For Armilus origin as the offspring of Satan and a statue, see *Sef. Z.* 40; *Otot* 7.2-3.

48. Moore 1927: II, 358 n., notes that some rabbinic literature identifies Elijah with Phineas (eg. *PRE* 66b). Such a belief would account for Elijah's patronymic here. Stranger still is the apparent

37. And Zerubbabel ben Shealtiel answered (*v.r.* and said to Michael) and said, 'Please, my Lord, when will the light of Israel come, and what will be after all this?'

38. And he said to me, 'Messiah ben Joseph will come five years after Hefzibah, and will gather all Israel as one man. And they will remain 40 years in Jerusalem and will offer sacrifice. And then the king of Persia will go up against Israel and there will be great distress in Israel. And Hefzibah, wife of Nathan the prophet, will go forth with the staff which the Lord will give her. And the Lord will give them [the Persian army] a spirit of dizziness and they will kill each other, and wickedness will die there.'

39. And when I heard his words I fell on my face and said to him, 'Tell me the truth concerning the holy nation.'

40. And he took me and showed me a stone in the shape of a woman, and he said to me, 'Satan will lie with this stone, [and it will become pregnant,] and Armilus will come out of it. And he will rule over all the world and no one will stand before him, and all who will not believe in him will die by his heavy sword. And he will enter the land of Israel with ten kings, [and they will go] to Jerusalem, and there they will kill Messiah ben Joseph and 16 righteous ones with him. And Israel will be exiled in the wilderness, but Hefzibah, the mother of Menahem, will remain there. That evil one will not enter (and that evil one will not see). And this war will be in the month of Ab. 41. And there and then there will be trouble for Israel such as never was like it ever in the world. And they will flee into towers, and caves in the wilderness. All the nations of the world will encamp behind this evil Satan[49] Armilus, except Israel. All Israel will mourn Nehemiah ben Hoshiel who was slain. His corpse will be thrown before the gate of Jerusalem, but the beasts and the birds will not touch it.'

42. When I heard his words it distressed me greatly (*v.r. adds:* about the slaying of ben Joseph and about all Israel). And I arose to pray before the Lord, and he heard and sent his angel to me, and I knew that he was the angel who had been speaking to me, and I fell prostrate before him.

43. And he said to me, 'What is wrong with you, Zerubbabel?'

44. And I said to him, 'A spirit terrified me.'

45. And Metatron stood and answered, and said, 'Zerubbabel, ask of me before I go away from you.'

46. And I asked him and said, 'When will the light of Israel come?'

47. And he answered me and said, 'As the Lord lives, who sent me, I will tell you the deed of the blessed Lord. For the holy voice sent me to tell you everything that you may ask.'

48. And Michael said to me, 'Draw near to me, and give heed to what I say to you, for the message is true, in the name of the living God.' 49. And he said to me, 'Menahem ben Ammiel will come suddenly in the month of Nisan and stand on the Valley of Arbel,[50] and all the sages of Israel will go out to him. And ben Ammiel will say to them, 'I am the Messiah, whom the Lord has sent to announce good news to

---

identification of Elijah with Messiah ben Ephraim, a belief that I am aware of nowhere else.

49.   Or *adversary.*

50.   In Galilee, near Zepphoris.

you, and to save you from the hand of your enemies.' But the sages will regard him and despise him, like you yourself despised him (*v.r. adds:* and did not believe in him). And his anger will burn in him, and he will put on garments of vengeance for clothing, and he will go to the gates of Jerusalem, and Elijah with him, and they will awaken and revive Nehemiah (*v.r.* ben Shealtiel,[51] who was slain). And they [the sages] will believe in him.

50. And so Metatron swore to me that for the completion of the desolation of Jerusalem [there will be] 990 years, [and then] will be the salvation of the Lord. Menahem ben Ammiel and Elijah will stand beside the Great Sea and read aloud from the prophets, and all the corpses of the Israelites who threw themselves into the sea because of their captivity will come out. And then the assembly of Korah will ascend, and they will come with Moses. And those who died in the wilderness will live, and gather to the host of the Korahites. And the blessed Lord will descend upon the Mount of Olives, and the Mount will split at his shout. And he will fight with those nations, and like a man of war he will stir up his zeal. Messiah ben David will come, and he will blow into the nostrils of Armilus, and they will kill him. All Israel will see the return of the Lord to Zion eye to eye, (*v.r. adds:* as it is said, *Eye to eye they will see the return of the Lord to Zion* [Isa. 52.8]), like a man of war, and a helmet of salvation upon his head, and clad in a breastplate. And he will make war with Armilus and with his troops, and all of them will fall down dead corpses in the Valley of Arbel. The survivors, 5,500 of them, will escape and assemble in Sela.[52] But 100,500 from Israel, clad in armour and with Nehemiah at their head, will kill them.

51. And after this Menahem ben Ammiel will come, and Nehemiah and Elijah, and they will ascend to Jerusalem. In the month of Ab they will restore[53] the ruins of Jerusalem and there will be great joy for Israel. They will present their offerings, and the sacrifice of Judah and Israel will be pleasing to the Lord as in the beginning. He will smell the odour of our sweet incense, and he will rejoice greatly in the splendour of the Temple superbly rebuilt, and he will increase its length and breadth. He will rule from the sunrise and from the Great Desert to the Western Sea and to the great river, River Euphrates.[54] Moreover the Temple will be built on (*v.r.* five) mountain-tops.

---

51.   Messiah ben Joseph bears the pseudonym Nehemiah ben Hoshiel, in this text (41) and elsewhere (*Otot* 6.5; 7.7-11). But Nehemiah ben *Shealtiel* would seem to be a reference to the biblical Nehemiah, whom some later traditions identify with biblical Zerubbabel (Dan 1971: XVI, 1002). The text may therefore be saying that the historical Zerubabel will reappear.

52.   That is, Petra of the Edomites (cf. Judg. 1.36; 2 Kgs 14.7; Isa. 16.1), continuing the identification of Rome and Edom.

53.   That is, taking ישבו as defective for ישיבו, the Hiphil of שוב, a variant attested at Deut. 1.22.

54.   The apocopated form, ירד, of ירדה is attested (*BDB*: 922) and I am assuming that such is the case here. The standard imperfect of ירד would be possible if the reference were to the boundary of the Temple *going down from the east* (cf. *BDB*: 433). But the enormous extent of the area and the similarity to the language of Ps. 72.8 suggests that the latter-day *malkut* and not the Temple boundary is in view.

52. And I asked him, 'What are their names?'

And he replied and said to me, 'Lebanon, Mount Moriah, Tabor, Carmel and Hermon.'

53. And these are the ten kings that will arise over the nations for seven years. The first: Seleucus from Spain.[55] 54. The second Armanius[56] (*v.r.* Artimus) from the province of the sea. 55. Three: Killus[57] (*v.r.* Tallis) from Geta. 56. Four: Paluus (*v.r.* Paulus) from Gallia.[58] 57. Five: Romatrius from Mauretania.[59] 58. Six: Meclinius from Zaltaia (*v.r.* Mercurius from Italia[60]). 59. Seven: he is Arctonius from Adamius (*v.r.* Actonius from Rodamia). 60. Eighth: Maspalisnium (*v.r.* Aphalistius) from Aram Naharaim. 61. Nine: Paros of the Persians (*v.r.* Shiron from Persia). 62. Ten: Armilus ben Shaphon. (*v.r. adds:* And this is the distinguishing mark of Armilus's appearance. The hair of his head is like gold and like straw, and his hands [reach] to his heels. This is [the appearance of] his eye. [There is] a span between one eye and the other, and his eyes are crooked. He has two heads, and all who see him are afraid of him. Ten kings, who will be created together with him, will arise over the nations.) 63. Immediately after him, the kingdom will be the Lord's. 64. Our eyes will see the long-awaited city, which, in the prolonged exile for our sins until today, has been our prolonged hope. (*v.r.* Thereupon the kingdom will be the Lord's. [May it be] soon, in our days.)

The End of the Book of Zerubbabel

5. *'Asereth Melakhîm*

The text of this midrash is from Eisenstein's *Ozar Midrashim*, 2.461-66. It concerns the ten kings who rule from one end of the earth to the other, a theme occurring also in *PRE* 81a, the Second Targum to Esther 1, and the Yalkut Shimoni on Kings 13. This particular form of the midrash names the ten omnipotentates as the Holy One, the first and last, with Nimrod, Joseph, Solomon, Ahab, Nebuchadnezzar, Cyrus, Alexander of Macedon and Messiah ben David, as the second to ninth kings. According to Eisenstein, the references to Islamic rulers in the midrash indicate a date of composition about the middle of the eighth century.[61] The following extract is the latter half of the fourth and final paragraph.[62] The sentences of Eisenstein's text have been enumerated.

55.   Assuming אספמיא is אספמיא, *Hispamia*.

56.   Assuming ארממיס is equivalent to ארמניס, which may derive from ארמיא, *Armania* (Romania).

57.   Killus was one of the generals who came against Jerusalem under Vespasian (*Lam. R.* to 1.5).

58.   *Gallia* may indicate either (1) Gaul in Europe (*Yeb.* 63a) or (2) Galatia in Asia Minor (*Roš Haš* 26a; *Ket.* 60a).

59.   Assuming מורטיא is defective for מורטניא.

60.   Assuming מורקולוס equals מרקוליס, which denotes the Roman deity Mercury at *m. Sanh.* 7.6; *Sanh.* 64a; *y. 'Abod. Zar.* 4.1 (50a); *t. 'Abod. Zar.* 6(7).13; *B. Maz.* 25b.

61.   Eisenstein 1915: II, 461.

62.   Eisenstein 1915: II, 466.

The Ten Kings

11. And after all this, if Israel are not pure, a brazen-faced king will arise, and he will kill the king of the sons of the east in the month of Ab. And he will decree decrees against Israel and abolish the appointed feasts and Sabbaths, as it is said, *And he will think to change the times and the law, and they shall be given into his hand for a time, times, and half a time* [Dan. 7.25]. *A time* [is] a year, *times* [is] two years, *and half a time* [is] half a year. 12. After this a king will arise, and his name is Moshiv, and he will restore[63] [to power] all who serve idols, as it is said, *And he will vent his fury against the holy covenant* [Dan. 11.30]. And he will rule nine months, as it is said, *Therefore he shall give them up until the time when she who is in labour has given birth* [Mic. 5.2(3)]. And what is the time for giving birth? Nine months.

13. And after all this Satan will descend and go into Rome to a stone statue, and will couple with it in a miraculous manner. And the stone will become pregnant and give birth to Armilus, and he will rule 40 days. And his hands are heavier than 40 seahs.[64] And he decrees evil decrees against Israel. And men of deed[65] cease and men of violence increase. If Israel are worthy, Messiah ben Joseph will spring forth in Upper Galilee. And he will ascend to Jerusalem, and build the Temple, and offer sacrifices. And fire will come down and consume his sacrifices. And all his days Israel will live in safety. 14. And the army of Gog will ascend and destroy Jerusalem and kill Messiah ben Joseph. This is that which is written: *The kings of the earth set themselves,* etc. [*and rulers take counsel together, against the Lord and against his messiah* (Ps. 2.2)]. And Israel mourn and lament messiah, as it is said, *And they shall look on him whom they have pierced, and mourn for him* [Zech. 12.10]. And they will divide into four groups; three of them will go into exile and one will remain, as it is said, *But the rest of the people shall not be cut off from the city* [Zech. 14.2]. 15. And after that the Holy One, blessed be he, will go forth to fight with them, as it is said, *And the Lord will go forth and fight against those nations, as he fights on a day of battle* [Zech. 14.2], as it is written in the same place, *And on that day his feet will stand on the Mount of Olives* [Zech. 14.4], and it says, *And this will be the plague,* etc. [*with which the Lord will smite all the nations that fight against Jerusalem* (Zech. 14.12)]. 16. And the Holy One, blessed be he, will blow on a great shofar, *and he will say to the north, 'Give them up!' and to the south, 'Do not withhold!'* [*Bring my sons from afar and my daughters from the end of the earth* (Isa. 43.6)]. And it says, *The redeemed of the Lord shall return* [Isa. 35.10]. And it says, *Saying to the captives, 'Come forth!' and to those in darkness, 'Be free!'* [Isa. 49.9]. *To the captives, 'Come forth!'*—these are those at the River Sambation,[66] who are in captivity. *And to those in darkness, 'Be free!'* [Isa. 49.9]—these are the nine and a half tribes, who are dwelling [beneath the Dark Mountains].[67] 17. And the

---

63. Hebrew: *meshiv.*

64. That is, about 300 kg. Armilus will rule heavy-handedly.

65. That is, *wonder-workers.*

66. סמבטיון or more often סבטיון, *Sabbation,* a legendary river said to rest on the seventh day. There was a tradition that the ten tribes were exiled within its confines (*Gen. R.* 73; *y. Sanh.* 10 [29c bot.]; *Targ. Y. Exod.* 34.10).

67. The phrase is bracketed in Eisenstein. The Dark Mountains were the mountain range

Holy One, blessed be he, will gather them, and they will ascend to Jerusalem, and he will comfort them with a double measure, as it is said, *I, I am he who comforts you* [Isa. 51.12].

18. Israel say in the presence of the Holy One, blessed be he, 'Lord of the Universe, we sinned before you upon the mountains.'

He says to them, 'I will remove them,' as it is said, *For the mountains will depart* [Isa. 54.10].[68]

19. And again they say, 'We have disgraced ourselves by [worshipping] the sun and moon.'

He says to them, 'I will remove them,' as it is said, *The moon will be abashed and the sun ashamed* [Isa. 24.23].

20. And the Holy One, blessed be he, will send Elijah, who will gladden the heart of Israel, as it is said, *Behold, I will send you Elijah the prophet* [Mal. 3.23 (4.5)]. And he proclaims to them tidings of peace and happiness, as it is said, *How lovely on the mountains are the feet of a herald of good news,* etc. [Isa. 52.7], until the kingdom returns to the house of David.

21. *The Ninth King.* This is Messiah ben David, who will rule from one end of the earth to the other, as it is said, *And he will rule from sea to sea and from the River to the ends of the earth* [Ps. 72.8]. And Israel will dwell in peace 1000 years, and they will eat Behemoth, Leviathan and Ziz of the fields.[69] And at the end of a thousand years they will be gathered for judgment, as it is said, *After two days he will revive us; on the third day he will restore us, that we may live before him* [Hos. 6.2]. This is the day of judgment. Blessed is the one who is acquitted upon it. [And then the Holy One, blessed be he, will reign, and he is the tenth king.[70]] 22. The Holy One, blessed be he, acquit us upon it, together with all Israel. Amen and Amen.

Blessed be the Merciful One who helps us.
Blessed be he who gives to the weary strength,
and increases the power of the powerless.

6. *Pirqê Mashiah*

The following is an extract from Jellinek's text of *Sefer Eliyahu u-Pirqê Mashiah we-Nistarot Rav Shimon ben Yohai* (*BHM*: III, 65-82), the title deriving from the sub-script to the third section of the manuscript: תם ספר אליהו ז׳׳ל ופרקי משיח ונסתרות ר׳ שמעון בן יוחי. This extract comprises paragraph five and part of paragraph six of the middle section, *Pirqê Mashiah* (*BHM*: III, 70-74). Jellinek, who reckons the work originated in Persia of the gaonic period, took his text from a collection

---

behind which the Amazons were said to dwell (*Lev. R.* s. 27; *b. Tam.* 32a). The mention of Carthage in these legends seems to point to a location in Africa.

68. Or possibly the direct speech should close after the biblical quotation in this and the following sentence.

69. A traditional interpretation of the phrase, זיז שדי, which occurs in Ps. 50.11, associates it with a fabulous bird, the *Ziz* (*Lev. R.* 22 [end]; *b. B. Bat.* 73b; *NRSbY* 33).

70. Eisenstein gives this variant reading in a footnote.

published in Thessalonica in 1743.[71] The text appears to be either somewhat corrupt or else marked by dialect elements.[72]

5. Now it is said in praise of King Messiah that he is going to come with the clouds of heaven and two seraphim, [one] at his right hand and [one] at his left, as it is said, *Behold, with the clouds of heaven, one like a son of man is coming* [Dan. 7.13]. 2. In the generation in which ben David comes, seraphim of fire will be sent to the Temple, and stars will seem like fire in every place, and [there will be] pestilence for three years in succession. This is sent by the Holy One, blessed be he, as it is said, *Before him goes pestilence and plague follows at his feet* [Hab. 3.5], as it is said, *Its plagues are plagues of fire* [Song 8.6]. 3. In the third year of pestilence atonement will be made for the exile, and at the end of the year the king will be slain.[73] And they [Israel] will flee into the deserts and the land will cry out from its place. And the disciples of the sages will die: *The treacherous betray, with treachery the treacherous betray* [Isa. 24.16]. And another passage strengthens the interpretation: *And though a tenth remains in the land it will again be laid waste* [Isa. 6.13]. 4. And the fifth year comes, and it transpires in all the kingdoms that all the kings will engage in battle one with another, the king of Persia with the king of Arabia, and they will destroy [one another], as it is said, *And they will fight each man with his fellow, etc., kingdom with kingdom* [Isa. 19.2]. 5. And at the time when Edom falls, heaven and earth will quake from the noise of its downfall, and half the world will be captured on account of it, as it is said, *The Lord will roar from on high, and from his holy habitation utter his voice* [Jer. 25.30]. 6. And the Holy One, blessed be he, will gather hordes and deliver them into the hand of Israel, as it is said, *And I will lay my vengeance upon Edom by the hand of my people Israel* [Ezek. 25.14].

7. And the Holy One, blessed be he, will bring the Prince of Edom and flog him, and the Prince of Edom will say, 'Where can I flee? If I go to Egypt, the *shekhinah* is there, as it is said, *Behold, the Lord is riding on a swift cloud and comes to Egypt* [Isa. 19.1]. 8. And if I flee to Edom, the *shekhinah* is there, as it is said, *Who is this coming from Edom?* [Isa. 63.1]. 9. If I flee to Babylon, the *shekhinah* is there, as it is said, *For your sake I will send to Babylon* [Isa. 43.14]. 10. If I go to Elam, the *shekhinah* is there, as it is said, *And I will set my throne in Elam* [Jer. 49.38].'

11. It is like [the parable of] the vixen to whom the lion said, 'Pay me a toll!' She got up and ran away, a distance of three days' journey. And again the lion grabbed her and said to her, 'Pay me a toll here as well!' She said to him, 'I ran away from you!' He said to her, 'You are still standing in my territory!' 12. Likewise the Holy One, blessed be he, will say to the Prince of Edom, 'Why are you trying to hide

---

71.   *BHM*: III, xviii-xix.

72.   Note for instance the ה-suffix on מחריבה following a masc. pl. subject (4), the changes of gender suffix to the verbs in the parable of the lion and the vixen (11), and the plural part. מכסים following a singular subject (67).

73.   *King* probably indicates messiah, because (1) no other king is mentioned in the context, and (2) Israel's flight into the desert is the sequel to Messiah's death both in this text and elsewhere (5.45; *Ag. M.* 2.12; *Otot* 7.14-16; *Sef. Z.* 40-41; *NRSbY* 24; Sa'adya 1948: VIII, 5).

yourself from my face?' And the Holy One, blessed be he, will give him into the hands of Israel.

13. And the Holy One, blessed be he, will put on garments of vengeance to exact vengeance on 70 nations, as it is said, *Mine is vengeance and recompense* [Deut. 32.35]. 14. And he will put on ten garments, corresponding to the ten times when Israel is called the bride of the Lord. And these are they: *I have come into my garden, my sister bride* [Song 5.1]; 15. *Come with me from Lebanon, bride* [Song 4.8]; 16. *A garden enclosed is my sister bride* [Song 4.12]; 17. *How delightful is your love, my sister bride* [Song 4.10]; 18. *Your lips drip honey, bride* [Song 4.11]; 19. *You have ravished my heart, my sister bride* [Song 4.9]; 20. *Voice of bride-groom and voice of bride* [Jer. 33.11]; 21. *You shall bind them on as a bride* [Isa. 49.18]; 22. *And the bridegroom rejoices over the bride* [Isa. 62.5]; 23. *And as a bride adorns herself with her jewels* [Isa. 61.10].

24. And these are the ten garments. *The Lord has become king, he is robed with majesty* [Ps. 93.1]. [This is] at the creation of the world. 25. *The Lord is robed, he is girded with strength* [Ps. 93.1]. [This is] on the day of the giving of the Torah. 26. *He will garb himself with righteousness as with a breastplate* [Isa. 59.17]. [This is] on the day when he hands over the peoples of the world to Israel. 27. *And he will garb himself in garments of vengeance for clothing* [Isa. 59.17]. [This is] on the day of the downfall of Edom. 28. *In crimsoned garments from Bozrah* [Isa. 63.1]. [This is] on the day when he does battle with the nations of the world. 29. *He that is glorious in his apparel* [Isa. 63.1]. [This is] on the day of Gog and Magog. 30. *Their lifeblood is spattered upon my garments* [Isa. 63.3]. [This is] in the Kingdom of Italia.[74] 31. And these are the two garments on the day of the resurrection of the dead, as it is said, *Bless the Lord, my soul! You are clothed with honour and majesty!* [Ps. 104.1]. 32. *Why is your apparel red?* [Isa. 60.2]. 33. [This is] on the day when the Holy One, blessed be he, grasps his sword and does battle, as it is said, *I will make my arrows drunk with blood, and my sword shall devour flesh* [Deut. 32.42]. 34. *And I will lay my vengeance upon Edom by the hand of my people Israel* [Ezek. 25.14].

35. Before Edom falls, ten places will be desolated and ten places will be destroyed, and ten shofars will sound, and ten voices will be heard, and fifteen countries will suffer massacre, and ten evils will befall, and ten evils will gush forth. And a brazen-faced king will arise and decree evil decrees in his kingdom. 36. And a great king will go forth and encamp against Alexandria. 37. And great evil will be in the world, and he will rule for three and a half years and behave lawlessly. 38. And the princes of Edom will fall, and there will be ten wars, and then Israel will be master over all the peoples. 39. *And I will lay my vengeance upon Edom* [Ezek. 25.14].

40. And ships from the land of Israel will go to Edom, and Israel will say, 'What have we to do with Edom?' as it is said, *Who will bring me to the fortified city? Who will lead me to Edom?* [Ps. 60.11 (9) = 108.11 (10)].

---

74.   *Italia* designates the southern part of the Italian peninsula, where Rome is located. Cf. *Meg.* 6b (some texts): איטליה של יון זה כרך גדול של רומי, *Greek Italia, that means the great city of Rome.*

41. And Israel will go and encamp upon a rock for 40 days, and at the end of 40 days they will arise at the time of recitation of *Shema* and say, *'Hear, Israel, the Lord our God, the Lord is one!'* [Deut. 6.4]. 42. And the walls of the city will fall, the city will surrender to them, and they will pass through into it. They will plunder all the silver and gold and whatever is left, and from there they will go to Rome. They will bring out the vessels of the sanctuary, and King Nehemiah the Messiah[75] will depart with them, and they will go to Jerusalem.

43. And Israel will say to the king of the Arabs, 'This is our Temple. Take silver and gold and leave the Temple alone.'

But the king of the Arabs will say, 'You have no claim at all in this Temple. But if you select for yourselves, as in former days, an offering, as you did of old, then we will also bring a sacrifice, and whoever's offering is accepted, we will all become one people [with them].'

44. And Israel will sacrifice and not be accepted, because Satan will denounce them before the Holy One, blessed be he. But the sons of Kedar will sacrifice and be accepted, as it is said, *All the flocks of Kedar will gather to you, [they will come up with acceptance upon my altar* (Isa. 60.7)].

45. And then the Arabs will say to Israel, 'Come and believe in our religion!'

Israel will reply to them, 'Even if we must fight to the death, none of us will deny the faith.'

At that time swords will be drawn and bows bent and arrows loosed, and the slain will fall from the Ephraim gate to the Corner Gate. And Nehemiah will be killed with them. And the survivors will flee to the desert of Moab and the land of the sons of Ammon, and there these fugitives of Israel will remain. And the Lord will do miracles for them there. A spring will come out of the deep for them, as it is said, *The dispersed of Moab will sojourn among you* [Isa. 16.4], and there they will eat roots of broom for 45 days. At the end of 45 days, Elijah and the king messiah will suddenly spring up for them.

Elijah will announce good news to them, saying, *'What are you doing here* [1 Kgs 19.9], Israel?'

And Israel will reply, saying, 'We have perished and are ruined!'

Elijah will say to them, 'Arise, for I am Elijah, and this is the King Messiah.' But none of them will believe him because Nehemiah came and was killed. And he will say to them, 'Perhaps you seek a sign, like Moses?'

And they say, 'Yes.'

46. Then he will do seven miracles. 47. The first miracle: He will bring to them Moses and his generation from the wilderness, as it is said, *Gather to me my faithful ones* [Ps. 50.5]. 48. The second miracle: He will bring up Korah and all his assembly to them, as it is said, *You will make me live again; from the depths of the earth you will bring me up again* [Ps. 71.20]. 49. The third miracle: He will resurrect for them Nehemiah who was slain. 50. The fourth miracle: He will reveal to them the

---

75. A pseudonym of the dying messiah (cf. 45). Messiah ben Joseph is called *Nehemiah ben Hoshiel* at *Otot* 6.5; 7.7-11 and *Sef. Z.* 41.

storeroom of the earth, and the jar of manna,[76] and the anointing oil. 51. The fifth miracle: The Holy One, blessed be he, will give a sceptre of power into his hand, as it is said, *Your strength, Israel,* etc.[77] 52. The sixth miracle: He will grind all the mountains of Israel like standing corn, as it is said, *I will lay waste mountains and hills* [Isa. 42.15]. 53. The seventh miracle: He will reveal to them the secret, as it is said, *This is the sign of the covenant* [Gen. 9.12].

54. As soon as they see these, they send and tell all the princes who are plundering Jerusalem to come and fight with them. They go forth, as invited, to pursue Israel.[78]

And Israel will say to the King Messiah, 'It is not good for us to rest? Why have you come to engage us in battle, as of old?'

And the King Messiah will say to them, *'Stand still and see the deliverance of the Lord!'* [Exod. 14.13]. And he will breathe on them [the enemies] with the breath of his mouth, and all of them will fall slain before him, as it is said, *And with the breath of his lips he shall slay the wicked* [Isa. 11.4]. 55. [And he says,] 'Go and learn from Sennacherib, as it is said, *And behold, they were all dead bodies!'* [2 Kgs 19.35; Isa. 37.36]. 56. At that time Elijah will fly into all the world and announce good news to Israel, as it is said, *Behold, I send you Elijah the prophet!* [Mal. 3.23 (4.5)]. 57. And that day [will be] a strict and wrathful day, making a division between two epochs. And the wicked will say, 'Aha for the day! For the day of the Lord is near!' And it says, *Woe to those who long for the day of the Lord* [Amos 5.18]. And Jerusalem will expand and overflow all that day, as it is said, *And that will be a unique day, known to the Lord,* etc. [Zech. 14.7].

58. Gog and Magog will go up on that day and encamp against Jerusalem for seven and a half days, and he will capture Jerusalem. And the community of Israel will say in the presence of the Holy One, blessed be he, 'Our Master of the World, I am too ashamed to return to every nation which has despoiled me and take what is mine from its hand.'

And the Holy One, blessed be he, will reply to her, 'I am bringing all of them into the midst of you, as it is said, *Behold, a day of the Lord is coming when your plunder will be divided in the midst of you. 59. And I will gather all the nations to Jerusalem for battle* [Zech. 14.1-2].'

And these are they:[79] Gomer, Agpaiah, Togarmah, Africa, Garmit, Garmamiah,[80] Cappadocia, Barbary, Italia, Cush, Andalusia, and Saba, Harmine,[81] and Dolim,

---

76.   The jar of manna preserved by Aaron (Exod. 16.33-34).

77.   The phrase עוז ישראל is not biblical. It may be a substitution for עוז ציון (Isa. 52.1). Or possibly, given the context of *sceptre* and messianic deliverance by ben David, it may be a corruption of [יהוה] עוז ישלח [מטה] (Ps. 110.2). Ps. 110.1 is cited regarding ben David at *Otot* 8.4.

78.   Or possibly, *They go forth, ready, to pursue Israel.*

79.   Many of the following place names are necessarily tentative.

80.   This term occurs in the Targum on Ezek 38.6 as equivalent to MT's *Gomer.* It may be equivalent to *Germania,* which occurs at *Targ. Ezek.* 38.2, and may represent Kerman in South Persia (Fisch 1950: 254).

81.   הרמן may be defective for הרמיני or הורמיני, *Harmine/Hurmine,* a province of Armenia. Or it might signify ארמון, *Armon,* a place mentioned in *b. Yeb.* 45a.

Aharsan, Sassania, Galicia, Gozzia, Lombardia,[82] Calabria, Pentapoli, Tripoli, Tyre, Macedonia, Anglia,[83] Monkakh, Sepphoris, Niro, Nozan, Daromea,[84] Asia,[85] Tiliki, Armannia,[86] Tarshish, Elam, and all the rest. 60. And the sons of their provinces go forth with spears and swords and bows, and every one of them fortifies the gate, held firm by a bolt, as it is said, *Each one helps his neighbour* [Isa. 41.6]. And they divide into three parties. 61. The first party drinks all the waters of [Lake] Tiberias. 62. The second drinks the sediment. 63. The third—they cross over on foot and say each to his neighbour, 'This place, whose is it?' And they will cut a pass through the rocks of the mountains of Israel on their horses. And Jerusalem will be given into their hand, and they will take the city captive, but they will not kill anyone, as it is said, *And the city shall be taken, and the houses plundered, and the women lain with.*[87] And, in the midst of the city, two women from two families shall be ravished.

64. Rabbi Yohanan said, '[*The women*] *shall be used as prostitutes*[88] is what is written. To what shall it be compared? To a king into whose palace thieves entered. The king said, 'If I catch them in my palace now, they will say, 'The king has no power except in his palace.' But I will be patient with them until they go outside [and then I shall catch them].' 65. Likewise the Holy One, blessed be he, will say, 'If I kill them in Jerusalem now, they will say, "He has no strength except in Jerusalem." But I will be patient with them until they go out to the Mount of Olives.' 66. And there the Holy One, blessed be he, will be revealed to them in his glory, and he will do battle with them until not one of them remains, as it is said, *And the Lord will go forth and fight against those nations as when he fights on a day of battle* [Zech. 14.3]. 67. And the Holy One, blessed be he, will summon all the beasts of the field and the birds to eat their flesh, as it is said, *Speak to the birds of every sort* [Ezek. 39.17]. 68. And for seven years Israel will burn the wood of their bows and shields and spears.

6. At that time the Holy One, blessed be he, will endue messiah with a crown, and put *a helmet of salvation upon his head* [Isa. 59.17], and bestow splendour and majesty upon him, and adorn him in glorious apparel, and set him upon a high mountain to announce victory to Israel. And he will proclaim, 'Deliverance has come.'

---

82. Assuming לומרדיאה is defective for לומברדיאה.

83. That seems the likeliest rendering of אנגליס.

84. דרוניה possibly equivalent to דרומיה. *Darom* was a town in the Negev area of southern Palestine (*b. Pes.* 70b; *b. Yeb.* 45a; *b. Zeb.* 22b). *Daromea* may indicate its surrounding area, that is, the country of the Edomites.

85. This seems the likeliest rendering of אוסיה. But it may represent the tribe אולסי referred to in *Targ. Ps.* 120.5.

86. אלמניה, *Almania*, probably equivalent to ארמניאה, *Armannia*, that is, Romania/New Rome/Constantinople.

87. The *Qere* of Zech. 14.2, תשכבנה, is used in preference to the more offensive *Ketiv*, תשגלנה.

88. That is, תשגלנה.

And Israel will say, 'Who are you?'

And he will say, 'It is I, Ephraim!'

And Israel will say, 'Are you he whom the Holy One, blessed be he, called *'Ephraim, my firstborn'* [Jer. 31.9]. *'Is not Ephraim my dear son'?'* [Jer. 31.20].

And he will say to them, 'Yes.'

And Israel will say to him, 'Go and announce the good news to the sleepers of Makhpelah, who will arise as of old.'[89]

2. At that time he will go up and announce the news to the sleepers of Makhpelah, and say to them, 'Abraham, Isaac and Jacob, arise! You have slumbered enough!'

They will reply and say, 'Who is this who removes the dust from above us?'

And he will say to them, 'I am the Lord's Messiah. Deliverance has come! The time has come!'

And they will reply, 'If that is really so, go and announce the good news to Adam, the first man, so that he may rise first.'

3. At that time they will say to Adam, the first man, 'You have slept enough!'

And he will reply, 'Who is this who chases sleep from my eyes?'

He will reply, 'I am the Lord's Messiah, one of your descendants.'

4. Thereupon Adam, the first man, will stand up, and all his generation, and Abraham, Isaac and Jacob, and all the righteous, and all the tribes,[90] and all the generations from one end of the earth to the other. And they will utter the sound of joy and song, as it is said, *How lovely upon the mountains are the feet of the Announcer-of-Good-News* [Isa. 52.7]. And why [does it say] *upon the mountains*? Only [to signify], *How lovely* are Moses and his generation coming from the desert.

5. Or another interpretation of *How lovely upon the mountains:* It is like a king who had two sons and one of them died. And all the people of the province dressed in black. The king said, 'You dressed in black when my first son died; I will clothe you in white at my second son's rejoicing.[91]' 6. Likewise, the Holy One, blessed be he, will say to the mountains, 'Because you wept over my sons[92] at the time they were exiled from their land, as it is said, *Upon the mountains I will take up weeping and wailing* [Jer. 9.9 (10)], so I will bring the rejoicing of my sons upon the mountains, as it is said, *How lovely upon the mountains'* [Isa. 52.7]. 7. King Messiah is lovely proclaiming victory to Israel, and the mountains will frolic like calves before him and the trees of the field will applaud together[93] at the deliverance of Israel, as it is said, *You shall go out in joy and in peace,* etc. [Isa. 55.12].

8. How lovely [will be] the mountains of Israel, flowing with milk and honey like cascading streams of water, and also rivers of wine, as it is said, *And it will be in that day that the mountains will drip new wine* [Joel 4.18 (3.18)]. And a fountain

89.   See *Song. R.* to 7.10 for the legend concerning the sleepers of Makhpelah.

90.   This probably denotes the tribes of Israel, rather than the tribes of all the earth. שבטים usually refers in the Bible to the *tribes* of Israel, and 'the tribes of all the earth' are probably represented by the following phrase, *all the generations from one end of the earth to the other*.

91.   That is, probably, *wedding day*.

92.   Or *son*. And similarly later in the sentence.

93.   The text, ועצי השדה יהיו מכין כף אל כף, differs quite markedly from Isa. 55.12, וכל־עצי השדה ימחאו־כף, to which it apparently refers.

shall go forth from the house of the Lord and water the valley of Shittim. 9. And what is the fountain like when it goes forth from the house of the Holy of Holies to the threshold of the Temple. At first it is like a thread of the warp. As far as the Temple it is like a thread of the woof. As far as the court it is like a ram's horn.[94] As far as the altar it is like the horns of locusts.[95] As far as the Temple enclosure it is like a small flask, as it is said, *Behold, waters flowing!* [Ezek. 47.2]. And from there they descend like a cascading stream and they purify from wrongdoing, uncleaness and sin.

7. *Nistarot Rav Shimon ben Yohai*

This is the third and final section of *Sefer Eliyahu u-Pirqê Mashiah we-Nistarot Rav Shimon ben Yohai*, details of which are given in the introduction to the preceding translation of *Pirqê Mashiah*. The text of this midrash appears in Jellinek (*BHM*: III, 78-82). It dates from some time well into the Islamic period. Jellinek reckons that the war between the sons of the East and the sons of the West (49) may be a reference to the early Crusades. If so, the final form of the work dates from the end of the first millennium.

The Mysteries of Rav Shimon ben Yohai

1. These are the mysteries that were revealed to Rav Shimon ben Yohai, when he was forced to hide in a cave from fear of Caesar, king of Edom. And he stood in prayer 40 days and 40 nights and finally he began thus: '*Lord God, how long will you smoke against the prayer of your* servant?' [Ps. 80.5 (4))]. 2. Thereupon secrets of the end and mysteries were revealed to him, and he began to sit and study. *And he saw the Kenite* (Num. 24.21). 3. As soon as he saw the kingdom of Ishmael, which was coming, he began to say, 'What the evil kingdom of Edom did to us, was it not enough for us? And [must we endure] the kingdom of Ishmael also?'

4. Thereupon Metatron, the Prince of the Presence, answered and said to him, 'Do not fear, son of man. The Lord, blessed be he, brings the kingdom of Ishmael only to deliver you from this evil. He appoints over them a prophet, according to his pleasure, and with them he will trample the land. And they come to restore it in great measure, and great fear will be between them and the sons of Esau.

5. And Rabbi Shimon answered him and said, 'And how will they be our salvation?'

And he said to him, 'And did not Isaiah the prophet speak thus: *And when he sees riders, horsemen in pairs,* etc. [Isa. 21.7]. Why does *A rider on an ass* precede *a rider on a camel* [Isa. 21.7]? He should not have said that, but rather, "A rider on a

---

94.　Literally, *it is like to horns and to rams,* ‏לקרנים וליובלא‏. The phrase may indicate, as does the latter word alone, the ram's horn *shofar* of the Jubilee (Jastrow 1950: 567). The point seems to be that it will be narrow at one end and wider at the other.

95.　‏קרני חנבים‏, that is locusts' antennae. This seems unusual, as it would suggest diminution from the previous *ram's horn*. The point may be that the stream's rate of expansion will decrease, just as locusts' antennae taper less rapidly than ram's horns.

camel, a rider on an ass." For when he comes he rides on a camel, and when his kingdom has flourished by his hand he rides on an ass.'

6. Another interpretation [of] *a rider on an ass* [is that] since he rides on an ass, we learn from this that they will provide deliverance for Israel like the deliverance of a rider on an ass.[96] 7. And again, Rabbi Shimon used to say that he heard from Rabbi Ishmael, as soon as he heard that the kingdom of Ishmael was coming, [that] the time will come when the land will be divided in lots, as it is said, *and he will distribute the* land *for a price* [Dan. 11.39].[97] 8. They will make cemeteries into pastures for flocks, and when one of their people dies they will bury him in any place that they find and then return and then plough over the grave again and sow it, as it is said, *Thus the sons of Israel will eat unclean bread* [Ezek. 4.13]. 9. For this reason no *Bet ha-P'ras*[98] will be observed. 10. A further interpretation [of] *And he saw the Kenite* (Num. 24.21). For what reason did that wicked man [Balaam] deliver his oracle? Only because he saw that his grandchildren would arise and subjugate Israel did he begin rejoicing and said, '*Enduring* [ethan] *is your seat!* [Num. 24.21]. I see sons of men, who eat only according to the commandments of Ethan the Ezrahite.'[99]

11. The second king who will arise from Ishmael will be favourable to Israel and will repair their breaches and the breaches in the Temple, and shape Mount Moriah and make it completely level, and build a mosque there upon the foundation stone, as it is said, *Your nest is set on the rock* [Num. 24.21]. He will make war with the sons of Esau and destroy their[100] forces and take a great number of them captive. And he will die in peace and in great honour. 12. And a great king will arise from Hazarmaveth,[101] and he will rule a few days. And the warriors of the sons of Kedar will rise against him and kill him, and set up another king, whose name is Mario. They will take him from following the flock and the she-asses and raise him to kingship. From him four powers will arise and they will wall off the Temple. After the reign of the four powers will arise another king, and he will reduce the *ephah* and the measures of length and weight. He will rule securely for three years but there will be discord in the world in his days. He will send great forces against the Edomites but he will die there of hunger. There will be plenty of provisions with them, but he will withhold them from them, giving them nothing. And the sons of Esau will arise against the sons of Ishmael and kill them. The sons of Ishmael will arise and burn the provisions and the survivors will flee and go away. 14. Thereafter a great king will arise and he will rule for nine years. 15. These are his reddish marks that will turn every eye: he has three blemishes, one on his forehead, one on his right hand

---

96.   That is, probably, like a messianic deliverance (cf. Zech. 9.9).

97.   The text has והארץ instead of Dan 11.39's ואדמה.

98.   A field of half a furrow's length square, declared unclean on account of bones carried into it from a ploughed grave.

99.   Possibly indicating Abraham, who is sometimes identified with Ethan the Ezrahite in rabbinic tradition (*b. B. Bat.* 15a; *Pes. K.* 4.3; *Pes. R.* 6.5. The same idea is alluded to at *b. Roš Haš.* 11a, which has the patriarchs born in the month Ethanim; and *Midr. Pss.* 1.6, where the list of ten psalm writers includes Abraham but not Ethan).

100.   Literally, *his*, referring presumably to Esau as representative head of his descendants.

101.   A Semitic clan, according to Gen. 10.26.

and one on his left arm. 16. He will plant saplings and build many cities. He will split open the deeps to bring up water to water his saplings so that his numerous great-grandchildren may eat. All who rise against him will be given into his hand. The land will be at rest in his days and he will die in peace. 17. Another king will arise and he will seek to dig the waters of the Jordan. He will bring aliens from foreign lands in order to dig and make a canal to raise the Jordan's waters to irrigate the land. But the earthworks will fall on them and kill them, and their princes will hear of this and rise against the king and kill him. 18. Another king will arise by force, a man of war, and [there will be] discord in the world in his days. And this will be the sign for you. When you see that Giron the western, which is in the west, has fallen, the mosque of the sons of Ishmael in Damascus, then his kingdom has fallen, and they will only [be able to] come and go by payment of tribute [to their conquerors]. And so the kingdom of Ishmael will fall. Regarding them it says, *The Lord has broken the sceptre of the wicked* [Isa. 14.5]. 19. And who carries out this tyranny of theirs? 20. Beside him are vigorous warriors of the sons of Kedar. But the north-eastern corner [of his kingdom] will rebel against him, and they will go up against him. Three great legions of them will fall at the River Tigris and in Persia. He will flee before them, but will be caught and killed and his sons will be hanged on the tree. 21. After this a brazen-faced king will arise for three months. Thereafter the evil kingdom will rule over Israel nine months, as it is said, *Therefore he will give them over until the time when she who is in travail gives birth* [Mic. 5.2 (3)]. 22. Messiah ben Joseph will spring forth for them and he will take them up to Jerusalem. He will build the Temple and offer sacrifices, and fire will come down from heaven and consume their sacrifices, as it is said, *The forceful men of your people will lift themselves up* [Dan. 11.4]. 23. If they are not pure, Messiah ben Ephraim[102] will come; and if they are pure, Messiah ben David will come.[103] An evil king will arise and his name is Armilus. He is bald, his eyes are small, and he has leprosy on his forehead. His right ear is closed over and the left is open. 24. If anyone speaks to him of virtue, he will incline to him the closed ear; and if anyone speaks to him of evil, he inclines to him the open ear. 25. He is the offspring of Satan and the stone.[104] He will ascend to Jerusalem and join battle with Messiah ben Ephraim at the East Gate, as it is said, *And they will look upon him whom they have pierced* [Zech. 12.10]. Israel will be exiled to the barren wilderness to feed on sea-purslane and roots of broom for 45 days. At that time they are tested and refined, as it is said, *And I will bring this third through the fire*, etc. [Zech. 13.9]. 26. And Messiah ben Ephraim will die there and Israel will mourn him.[105] Afterwards the Holy One, blessed be he,

---

102. That is, Messiah ben Joseph.

103. The idea that Messiah ben Joseph comes only if Israel are impure occurs also in *b. Sanh.* 98a, *y. Ta'an.* 1.1 (63d), and Sa'adya 1948: VIII, 2, 5, 6.

104. For the idea of Armilus as the offspring of Satan and a statue, see also *Sef. Z.* 40 and *Otot* 7.2, 3.

105. As in other midrashim, the place of Messiah ben Ephraim's slaying would seem to be Jerusalem, for it is there that he is pierced (25). The beginning of 26 therefore seems to be a recapitulation following an aside about the fate of Israel subsequent to his death. However it might

will reveal to them Messiah ben David. Israel will want to stone him, saying, 'You have lied![106] For the Messiah has already been killed and no other messiah is destined to arise.' And they will despise him, as it is said, *He was despised and rejected by men* [Isa. 53.3]. He will withdraw and be hidden from them, as it is said, *Like one from whom men hide their faces* [Isa. 53.3]. 27. In their distress Israel repent and cry out from hunger and thirst. Thereupon the Holy One, blessed be he, appears to them in his glory, as it is said, *And all flesh together will see* [Isa. 40.5]. 28. The King Messiah will spring up there, as it is said, *And behold, with the clouds of heaven* [Dan. 7.13]. And it is written afterwards, *And he was given dominion* [Dan. 7.14]. 29. And he will blow on that evil Armilus and will kill him, as it is said, *With the breath of his lips he will slay the wicked* [Isa. 11.4]. 30. And the Holy One, blessed be he, whistles and gathers all Israel, and he will take them up, as it is said, *I will whistle for them and gather them in* [Zech. 10.8]. Fire will come down from heaven and consume Jerusalem to a depth of three cubits, removing uncircumcised foreigners and the impure from the midst of her. Jerusalem will descend, built-up and shining, from the heavens. In her are are 72 pearls, whose glistening [is seen] from one end of the world to the other.[107] 31. All the nations come to her radiance, as it is said, *Nations will come to your light* [Isa. 60.3]. 32. And the Temple, which is prepared in the fourth heaven, which Moses, peace upon him, saw in the Holy Spirit,[108] will descend, built-up, from the heavens, as it is said, *You will bring them and plant them* [*on the mountain of your inheritance* (Exod. 15.7)]. 33. Israel will live in security 2000 years and eat Behemoth, Leviathan and Ziz. They slaughter Behemoth, and then Ziz tears Leviathan to pieces with his claws, and Moses will come and slaughter *Ziz of the fields* [Ps. 50.11; 80.14 (13)]. 34. At the end of 2000 years, the Holy One, blessed be he, sits on his judgment throne in the valley of Jehoshaphat. 35. Thereupon the heavens and earth gradually wear away, and the sun is abashed and the moon ashamed, and the mountains will be removed so that they do not remind Israel of their sins. On the third day the gates of Gehenna open in the Valley of Joshua and the gates of the Garden of Eden in the east, as it is said, *After two days he will make us live* [Hos. 6.2]: these are the days of the Messiah, which are 2,000 years.[109] 36. *On the third day* [Hos. 6.2]: this is the day of judgment. Woe to all who die on that day! The Holy One, blessed be he, makes every nation pass before him and says to them, 'You who worship gods of silver and gold, see if

conceivably be taken as meaning that messiah dies in the wilderness although he receives his death-wound at Jerusalem.

106. Presumably in claiming to be messiah.

107. A heavenly Jerusalem that would be revealed in the last times was a common conception in earlier Israelite literature: Gal. 4.26; Rev. 3.12; 21.2, 10; *2 Bar.* 4.2-6; *4 Ezra* 7.26; 8.52; 10.27-50; 13.36. Something similar is implied at a yet earlier date in *1 En.* 90.28-29.

108. For the idea that there are a heavenly Jerusalem, Temple, and altar in *Zebul*, the fourth heaven, see also Hag. 12b. Moses is said to have seen heavenly antitypes of cultic items at Exod. 25.9, 40; *2 Bar.* 4.5.

109. For the idea that the messianic period will be the last two millennia (days) of the six millennia of this age and be followed by the Day of Judgment and the Sabbath millennium, see *'Abod. Zar.* 9a; *Sanh.* 97a; *Ep. Barn.* 15.

they can save you.' 37. Thereupon they go away and are burned, as it is said, *The wicked depart to Sheol* [Ps. 9.18 (17)]. Israel comes after them, and the Holy One, blessed be he, says to them, 'Whom do you worship?'

They say, *'Surely you, our Father, though Abraham does not know us,'* etc. [Isa. 63.16].

38. The nations of the world say from the midst of Gehenna, 'Let us see if he will judge his people as he judged us.'

39. Thereupon the Holy One, blessed be he, passes through the middle of Gehenna with Israel and it becomes like cool waters before them, as it is said, *Their king will pass through before them* [Mic. 2.13]. And he says,[110] *'When you walk through the fire you will not be burned'* [Isa. 43.2]. 40. At that time the apostates of Israel are poured into Gehenna for 12 months and afterwards the Holy One, blessed be he, brings them up, and they live in the Garden of Eden, luxuriating in its fruits, as it is said, *And all your people shall be righteous* [Isa. 60.21].

41. Rabbi Shimon says: In future the Holy One, blessed be he, will whistle for bees which are in the distant streams of Egypt and they will come and make war in the midst of Egypt. 42. The first king, who will lead them and bring them out, he is a servant who rebelled against his master, as it is said, *Thus says the Lord...to the one despised and abominated by the nations* (the one abominated among the nations, these are the sons of Canaan), *the servant of rulers* [Isa. 49.7]. He will rebel against his master, and men will gather to him who have rebelled against their masters, and they will go forth few in number and seize kingship by force. They will make war with the sons of Ishmael and kill their warriors and take possession of their money and their possessions. 43. They will be ugly men, dressing in black, and they will come out of the east and they will be swift and hasty, as it is said, *the bitter and hasty nation* [Hab. 1.6]. 44. They will ascend onto the mountain height of Israel and he will decide to break into the Temple. They will tear loose its doors and Moriah will mourn.[111] 45. Four kings will arise against them. Two are princes and two are chiefs. 46. The first will be an Indian.[112] He will set up in his lifetime a king from the royal line. The [second] king who will rule over them walks in humility, his eyes are beautiful and his hair becoming, and he will die in peace and no one will call him to account in this world.[113] 47. After him a [third] king will arise amidst contention and he will station forces at the River Euphrates, but all of them will fall in one day. He will flee, but he will be captured, and there will be peace in the land all the days that he is in captivity. And his brothers will rule in all the lands. 48. The fourth king who will arise against them loves silver and gold. He will be a swarthy man and very tall, an old man and a glutton, and he will kill those who brought him out and made him king. He will make ships of bronze and fill them with silver and gold and hide

110. Or, *And it says.*

111. Jastrow (1950: 840) notes the use of the word מרות *authority, dominion*, and its Chaldean equivalent מרותא, as a wordplay for Moriah (cf. e.g. *Pes. R.* s.40; *Gen. R.* s.55).

112. I am assuming that the term קנדק is a variant of הנדקא, *Indian*, as at *2 Targ. Esth. II* 1.14, where some editions read קנדיקי and others הנדיקי.

113. Or, *and no one will exact tribute from him.*

them beneath the waters of the Euphrates to reserve them for his sons, but they are destined for Israel, as it is said, *I will give you the treasures of darkness and the hoards in secret places* [Isa. 45.3]. 49. In his day the western power will rebel and he will send many warriors there. He will kill the sons of the east and again send out many warriors and they will go and kill the sons of the west and settle in their land. 50. This will be a sign for you. When you see one week[114] it begins with rain. 51. In the second [week] half-famine is decreed. 52. In the third, great famine. 53. In the fourth, neither famine nor plenty. 54. In the fifth, great plenty. A single star springs forth from the east and at its head is a sceptre. It is the star of Messiah, as it is said, *A star goes forth from Jacob* [Num. 24.17]. 55. When it shines for Israel's prosperity then Messiah ben David will spring forth [after it]. 56. And this will be a sign for you. When you see that eastern Niron, which is in Damascus, has fallen, then the kingship of the sons of the east has fallen. Then the salvation of Israel will spring forth. Messiah ben David comes and they will ascend to Jerusalem and delight themselves over her, as it is said, *But the meek shall inherit the land and delight themselves in abundant peace* [Ps. 37.1]. 57. O that God in his mercies might send us the redeemer quickly in our days. Amen.

114.　That is, one septennate.

אגדת משיח

דרך כוכב מיעקב תאנא משום רבנן שבוע שבן דוד בא בו שנה ראשונה אין בה מזון כל צורכה. [2] שנייה חצי רעב משתלחין. [3] שלישית רעב גדול. [4] ברביעית לא רעב ולא שובע. [5] בחמישית שובע גדול. [6] ויצמח כוכב ממזרח והוא כוכבו של משיח והוא עושה במזרח ט"ו יום ואם האריך הוא לטובתן של ישראל. [7] ששית קולות ושמועות. [8] השביעית מלחמות. [9] ומוצאי שביעית יצפה למשיח ויתגאו בני מערב ויבואו ויחזיקו מלכות בלא אפים ויבאו עד מצרים וישבו כל השביה. [10] ובימים ההם יקום מלך עז פנים על עם עני ודל והוא מחזיק מלכות בחלקלקות. [11] ועל אותו הזמן אמר ישעיה לך עמי בא בחדריך וגו'. [12] אמרו חכמים רבי חייה צוה לדורו כשתשמעו שעמד מלך עז פנים לא תשבו שם שהוא גוזר כל מי שהוא אומר אחד הוא אלהי העברים יהרג. [13] והוא אומר נהיה כולנו לשון אחד ואומה אחת והוא מבטל זמנים ומועדים ושבתות וראשי חדשים ומבטל תורה מישראל שנאמר ויסבר להשנייה זמנין ודת ויתיהבון בידיה עד עידן עידנין ופלג עידן. [14] עידן שנה. [15] עידנין תרתי. [16] ופלג עידן חצי שנה. [17] אמרו לו מרי להיכן ננצל אמר להם לגליל העליון שנאמר כי בהר ציון ובירושלם תהיה פליטה. [18] ובהר ציון תהיה פליטה והיה קדש:

[19] ומחץ פאתי מואב. [20] אמר ר' הונא בשם ר' לוי מלמד שיהיו ישראל מקובצין בגליל העליון ויצפה עליהם שם משיח בן יוסף מתוך הגליל והם עולים משם וכל ישראל עמו לירושלם לקיים מה שנא' ובני פריצי עמך ינשאו להעמיד חזון ונכשלו. [21] והוא עולה ובונה את בית המקדש ומקריב קרבנות והאש יורדת מן השמים והוא מוחץ כל הכנענים. [22] ויבא על ארץ מואב והורג את חציה והשאר שובה אותה בשביה ומעלים לו מס ועושה באחרונה שלום עם מואב שנאמר ושבתי את שבות מואב וישבו ארבעים שנה לבטח אוכלים ושותים ובני נכר אכריכם וכורמיכם.

[23] וקרקר כל בני שת. [24] שהוא מקרקר כל הכנענים שנקראים בשת. [25] שנאמר כי שת לי אלהים זרע אחר. [26] ואחרי כל כל[115] זאת שומע גוג ומגוג ועולה עליהם שנאמר יתיצבו מלכי ארץ ורוזנים נסדו יחד על ה' ועל משיחו. [27] והוא נכנס והורג אותו בחוצות ירושלם שנא' והיתה עת צרה וישראל רואים כך ואומרים אבד משיח ממנו ושוב לא ישוב משיח אחר וסופדים עליו ארבע משפחות שנאמר וספדה הארץ משפחות לבד משפחת בית דוד לבד. [28] והקב"ה יוצא ונלחם עמם שנאמר ויצא ה' ונלחם בגוים ההם וההרים ימושו והגבעות תמוטנה והר הזתים יבקע מחציו. [29] והקב"ה יורד עליו וישראל נסים ונמלטים שנא' ונסתם גיא הרי. [30] וזות תהיה המגפה. [31] וישראל גולים אחרי כן למדברי

אגמות לרעות במלוחים שרשי רתמים מ"ה ימים וענני כבוד מקיפין אותם ושם
ישראל יהו נחבאים וכל מי שיש בלבו הרהור רע על הקב"ה העננים משליכין
אותו והכנענים הורגין אותו. [32] ומישראל הרבה יצאו אל הכנענים ואותם לא יהיה
להם חלק עם ישראל לעולם הבא אבל אותם העתידים להתענות במלוחים מ"ה
ימים ולקץ מ"ה ימים בת קול להם רדו לבבל שנאמר ובאת עד בבל תנצלי.
[33] ובת קול מפוצצת שנית לכו לאדום ועשו שם נקמתי שנאמר ונתתי נקמתי
באדום ביד עמי ישראל וישראל באין לרומי ובת קול יוצאה שלילית עשו בה
כאשר עשה יהושע ביריחו והם סובבים את העיר ותוקעים בשופרות ובפעם
השביעית מריעים תרועה שמע ישראל ה' אלהינו ה' אחד ונפלה חומת העיר והם
נכנסים בתוכה ומוצאין את בחוריה מתים ברחובותיה שנאמר לכן [יפלו] בחוריה
ברחובותיה וגו'. [34] ואחרי כן הם קובצין את כל שללה וישראל מבקשין את
אלהיהן ואת דוד מלכם ומיד נגלה עליהם מלך המשיח והוא אומר להם אני הוא
מלך המשיח שהייתם מחכים והוא אומר להם שאו את הכסף ואת הזהב והם
נושאים אותו ועולים שנאמר שפעת גמלים תכסך. [35] ובת קול רביעית יוצאה
ואומרת קול קורא במדבר. [36] ובת קול חמישית אומרת לא יהיה שם אריה ובת
קול ששית אומרת אתן במדבר ארז שטה והדס. [37] ובת קול שביעית מכרזת נחמו
נחמו עמי ואליהו מבשר לישראל מלך אלהיך ובת קול שמינית מכרזת ואומרת
דברו על לב ירושלים. [38] בת קול תשיעית אומרת פתחו שערים ויבוא גוי צדיק.
[39] ובת קול עשירית אומרת שאו שערים ראשיכם. [40] ויחיו המתים שנאמר יחיו
מתיך נבלתי יקומון. [41] ואז יתקבצו הגליות שנאמר והיה ביום ההוא יתקע בשופר
גדול. [42] ואז יתקיים דרך כוכב מיעקב. [43] וכן יהי רצון מלפני אבינו שבשמים
שיתקיים פסוק זה ונשא נס לגוים ואסף נדחי ישראל וגו' בימינו ובימי כל ישראל:

תם אגדת משיח

אותות המשיח

1 האות הראשון עתיד הקב"ה להעמיד שלשה מלכים וכופרים בדעתם
ומשקרים ומראים עצמם לבני אדם שהם עובדים להב"ה ואינם עובדים ומתעים
ומבלבלים כל הבריות וכופרי' אומות העולם בדיניהם ואף פושעי ישראל
המתיאשים מן הגאולה כופרים בהקב"ה ועוזבים את יראתו ועל אותו הדור נאמר
ותהי האמת נעדרת ומהו נעדרת שבעלי האמת נעשו עדרים עדרים והולכים
ובורחים ומתחבאים במערות ובמחילות עפר ונאספים כל גבורי הדור ובטלו אנשי
אמנה ונגנזין שערי חכמה והעולם עומד משנה ובאותו זמן אין מלך ולא נשיא
בישראל שנאמר כי ימים רבים ישבו ישראל אין מלך ואין שר אין זבח ואין מצבה
וגו'. [2] ולא ראשי ישיבות וגאון יעקב לא רועים נאמנים ולא חסידים ובעלי השם
וננעלי' דלתי שחקים ונסגרים שערי פרנסה וכלכלה. [3] ובזמן שמשיח יתגלה
בגבורתו דוד הולך ונופל בחייו מפני גזרות קשות ומשונות ומבוהלו' שגוזרי'

שלשה מלכים הללו. [4] ועוד שגוזרים לכפור במקדש בה׳ ובתורה והקב״ה גזר שתמלוך מלכות הרשעה ט׳ חדשים מכיפה לכיפה שנאמ׳ לכן יתנם עד עת יולדה ואין לכן אלא שבועה שנאמר לכן נשבעתי לבית עלי. [5] וגוזרים גזרו׳ קשות וכופלים מס על ישראל על אחד עשר מי שהיה נותן עשרה נותן מאה וכל מי שהיה נותן שמונה נותן שמונים וכל מי שאין לו חותכין ראשו. [6] וכל אלו תשעה חדשים מתחדשות גזרות אחר גזרות זו קשה מזו. [7] ויוצאים בני אדם מסוף העולם שהם מכוערים ביותר וכל מי שרואה אותם מת מפחדם ואינם צריכים לעשות מלחמה אלא מפחדם ממיתים הכל וכל אחד ואחד יש לו שני קדקדים ושבעה עינים והם דולקים כאש וקלים בהליכתם כצבאים. [8] באותה שעה צועקים ישראל ואומרים ווי ווי וקטנים מישראל מתבעתים והולכים ונטמנים כל אחד ואחד תחת אביו ותחת אמו ואומרים ווי ווי אבא מה נעשה ואבותיהם משיבים להם עתה אנחנו סמוכים לגאולתן של ישראל:

2 האות השני מביא הקדוש ברוך הוא חום בעולם מחמתה של חמה עם שחפת וקדחת ורבים חלאים רעים ודבר ומגפה וממיתים מאומות העולם אלף אלפים בכל יום וכל רשעים שבישראל מתים עד שיבכו אומות העולם ויצעקו אוי לנו אנה נלך ואנה נברח וחופרים כל אחד קברו בחייו ושואלין את נפשם למות. [2] ומתחבאים בצחיחין ובצריחין וחיוחין כדי לצנן את עצמם ובאים במערות ובמחילות עפר. [3] ואם תאמר איך ינצלו הצדיקים מחום החמה הקב״ה יעשה להם רפואה באותו חום שנאמר וזרחה לכם יראי שמי שמש צדקה ומרפא בכנפיה. [4] ועל אותו עדות נבא בלעם הרשע אוי מי יחיה משומו אל:

3 האות השלישי הקדוש ברוך הוא מוריד טל של דם ויראה לאומות העולם כמו מים וישתו ממנו וימותו ואף רשעי ישראל המתיאשים מן הגאולה ישתו ממנו וימותו וצדיקי׳ המחזיקי׳ באמונתו של הקדוש ברוך הוא אינם נזוקים כלל שנאמר והמשכילים יזהירו כזוהר הרקיע. [2] ויהיה כל העולם דם כל אותם השלשה ימים שנאמר כהושע ונתתי מופתים בשמים ובארץ דם ואש ותמרות עשן:

4 האות הרביעי הקדוש ברוך הוא מוריד טל של רפואה לרפאות הדם וישתו ממנה הבינוניים ויתרפאו מחלים שנאמר אהיה כטל לישראל יפרח כשושנה ויך שרשיו כלבנון:

5 האות החמישי הקדוש ברוך הוא מחזיר את השמש לחשך שלשי׳ יום שנאמר השמש יהפך לחשך והירח לדם. [2] אחר שלשים יום הקדוש ברוך הוא מחזירו לקדמותו שנאמר ואספו אסיפת אסיר על בור וסוגרו על מסגר ומרוב ימים יפקדו. [3] ומתפחדים אומות העולם ומתביישים ויודעים שבשביל ישראל כל האותות האלו ורבים מהם מתיהדי׳ בסתר שנאמר משמרים הבלי שוא חסדם יעזובו:

6 האות הששי ממליך הקדוש ברוך הוא אדום הרשעה על כל העולם כמו שאמרנו למעלה. [2] ויקם מלך אחר ברומי וימלוך על כל העולם תשעה חדשים ויחריב מדינות רבות. [3] ויחר אפו על ישראל וישליך עליהם מס גדול. [4] ויהיו ישראל באותה שעה בצרה גדולה מרוב הגזירות והמהומות שמתחדשות עליהם

בכל יום וישראל מתמעטין וכלין באותו זמן ואין עוזר לישראל ועל אותו זמן
נתנבא ישעיה ואמר וירא כי אין איש וישתומם וגומר. ⁵ לסוף תשעה חדשים יגלה
משיח בן יוסף ושמו נחמי׳ בן חושיאל עם שבט אפרים ומנשה ומקצת בני
גד. ⁶ ושומעין ישראל שבכל המדינות שבא משיח ה׳ ומתקבצים אליו מעט מכל
מדינה ומכל עיר שנאמר בירמיהו שובו בנים שובבים נאם ה׳ כי אנכי בעלתי בכם
ולקחתי אתכם אחד מעיר ושנים ממשפחה והבאתי אתכם ציון. ⁷ ויבא משיח בן
יוסף ויתגרה מלחמתו עם מלך אדום וינצח את אדום ויהרוג מהם תילי תילים
ויהרוג את מלך אדום ויחריב מדינת רומי ויוציא קצת כלי בי׳ המקדש שהם גנוזים
בבית יוליי״נוס קיסר ויבא לירושלים וישמעו ישראל ויתקבצו אליו. ⁸ ומלך מצרים
ישלים עמו ויהרוג כל אנשי המדינות אשר סביבות ירושלים עד דמשק ואשקלון
וישמעו כל אנשי העולם ויפול אימה גדולה עליהם:

7 האות השביעי הקב״ה בעל נפלאות עושה מופת בעולם. ² אמרו שיש
ברומי אבן של שיש דמות נערה יפה תואר והיא אינה עשויה ביד אדם אלא
הקב״ה בראה כן בגבורתו. ³ ובאין רשעי אומות העולם בני בליעל ומהממין אותה
ושוכבים אצלה והקדוש ב״ה משמר טפתן בתוך האבן ובורא בה בריה ויוצר בה
ולד והיא מתבקעת ויוצא ממנה דמות אדם ושמו ארמי״לוס השטן זה שהאומות
קורין אותו אנטיקרי״שטו ארכו שתים עשרה אמה ורחבו שתים עשרה ובין שתי
עיניו זרת והן עמוקות אדומות ושער ראשו כצבע זהב. ⁴ פעמי רגליו ירוקין ושתי
קדקדין יש לו. ⁵ ויבא אצל אדום הרשעה ויאמר להם משיח אני אני אלהיכם מיד
מאמינים בו וממליכים אותו עליהם ומתחברים בו כל בני עשר ובאים אצלו והולך
וכובש כל המדינות ואומר לבני עשו הביאו לי תורתי שנתתי לכם. ⁶ ומביאים לו
תפלותם ואומר להם אמת היא שנתתי לכם ואומר לאומות העולם האמינו בי כי
אני משיחכם מיד מאמינים בו. ⁷ באותה שעה משגר לנחמיה בן חושיאל ולכל
ישראל ואומר להם הביאו לי תורתכ׳ ועידו לי שאני אלוה מיד מתפחדין ויתמהו.
⁸ באותה שעה יקום נחמיה בן חושיאל ושלשים אלף גבורים מגבורי בני אפרים
ויקחו ספר תורה וקורין לפניו אנכי ה׳ אלהיך לא יהיה לך אלהים אחרים על פני.
⁹ ויאמר להם אין בתורתכם זו כלום אלא בואו והעידו לי שאני אלוה כדרך שעשו
כל האומות. ¹⁰ מיד יעמוד כנגדו נחמיה ויאמר לעבדיו תפשוהו וכפתוהו. ¹¹ מיד
יקום נחמיה בן חושיאל ושלשים אלף שעמו ויעשו עמו מלחמה ויהרגו ממנו
מאתים אלף. ¹² מיד יחרה אפו של ארמי״לוס הרשע ויקבוץ כל חילי אומות
העולם לעמק החרוץ וילחם עם ישראל ויהרגו ממנו תילי תילים וינגפו מישראל
מעט ויהרג משיח ה׳ ובאים מלאכי השרת ונוטלים אותו ומטמינים אותו עם אבות
העולם. ¹³ מיד ימס לבם של ישראל ויתש כחם וארמי״לוס הרשע לא ידע שמת
משיח שהם יודע לא היה לא היה משאיר מישראל שריד ופליט. ¹⁴ באותה שעה כל אומות
העולם טורדין את ישראל ואינם מניחים אותם לדור עמהם
במדינותיהם ואומרים ראיתם את העם בזוי ושפל שמרדו עלינו והמליכו מלך
ותהי צרה לישראל שלא היתה כמותה מימות העולם עד אותו זמן. ¹⁵ ובאותה
שעה יעמוד מיכאל לברר את הרשעים מישראל שנאמר ובעת ההיא יעמוד מיכאל
השר הגדול העומד על בני עמך והיתה צרה אשר לא נהיתה וגומר. ¹⁶ מיד יברחו

כל ישראל במדברות וכל מי שלבו מסופק בדינו חוזר על האומות העולם ואומרי׳ זו הגאולה שאנו מחכי׳ לה שהמשיח נהרג. [17] וכל מי שאינו מצפה לגאולה מתבייש ממנה וחוזר על אומות העולם. [18] באותה שעה הקב״ה בוחן את ישראל וצורפן ככסף וכזהב. [19] שנאמר בזכריה והבאתי את השלישי׳ באש וצרפתים כצרוף הכסף וכתיב ביחזקאל וברותי מכם הפושעים בי וגו׳. [20] ובדניאל כתיב יתברלו ויתלבנו ויצרפו רבים והרשיעו רשעים וגו׳ ויהיו כל שארית ישראל והקדושים והטהורים במדבר יהודה חמשה וארבעים יום ויהיו רועים ואוכלים מלוחים ועלה שיח קוטפי׳. [21] ובהם מתקיי׳ מה שנאמר בהושע לכן הנה אנכי מפתיה והולכתיה המדברה ודברתי על לבה. [22] ומנין שחמשה וארבעים יום הם שנאמר ומעת הוסר התמיד ולתת שקוץ משומ׳ אלף ומאתי׳ ותשעי׳. [23] וכתיב אשרי המחכה ויגיע לימים אלף שלש מאות שלשי׳ וחמשה. [24] נמצא בין אלו לאלו חמשה וארבעים יום. [25] באותה שעה ימותו כל רשעי ישראל שאינם ראוים לראות הגאולה. [26] ויבא ארמי״לוס וילח׳ במצרי׳ וילכדה שנאמר וארץ מצרי׳ לא תהיה לפלטה ויחזור פניו לירושלים להחריבה פעם שניה שנאמר ויטע אהלי אפדנו בין ימים להר צבי קדש ובא עד קצו ואין עוזר לו:

8 האות השמיני יעמוד מיכאל ויתקע בשופר שלשה פעמים שנא׳ והיה ביום ההוא יתקע בשופר גדול ובאו האובדי׳ וגומר וכתיב וה׳ אלהים בשופר יתקע והלך בסערות תימן. [2] תקיעה ראשונה יגלה משיח בן דוד ואליהו הנביא לאותן הצדיקים הברורים מישראל שנסו למדב׳ יהודה לסוף מ״ה ימי ויחזיקו את לבם ויחזקו את ידי׳ הרפות והברכיה׳ הכושלות יאמצו. [3] וישמעו כל ישראל הנשארי׳ בכל העולם את קול השופר וידעו כי פקד ה׳ אותם וכי באה הגאול׳ השלמה ויתקבצו ויבאו שנאמר ובאו האובדים בארץ אשור וגומר ומאותו קול יפול פחד ורתת על אומות העולם ויפלו עליה׳ חלאי׳ רעים. [4] וישראל מתאזרי׳ לצאת ויבא משיח בן דוד ואליהו הנביא עם הצדיקים ששבו ממדבר יהודה ועם כל ישראל הנקבצי׳ ויבא לירושלים ויעלה במעלות בית הנשאר׳ וישב שם וישמע ארמי״לוס שעמד מלך לישראל ויאמר עד אנה האומה הבזויה והשפלה הזאת עושין כן מיד יקברץ כל חיילי אומות העולם ויבא להלחם עם משיח ה׳ ואז הקב״ה אינו מצריכו למלחמה אלא אומר לו שב לימיני והוא אומר לישראל התיצבו וראו את ישועת ה׳ אשר יעשה לכם היום מיד הקב״ה נלחם בהם שנאמר ויצא ה׳ ונלחם בגוים ההם ביום הלחמו ביום קרב. [5] והקב״ה מוריד אש וגפרית מן השמים שנאמר ונשפטתי אתו בדבר ובדם וגש׳ שוטף ואבני אלגביש וגו׳. [6] מיד ארמי״לוס הרשע ימות הוא וכל חילו ואדום הרשעה שהחריבו בית אלהינו והגלונו מארצנו. [7] ובאותה שעה יעשו בה׳ ישראל נקמות גדולות שנאמר והיה בית יעקב אש ובית יוסף להבה ובית עשו לקש וגומר:

9 האות התשיעי יתקע מיכאל תקיעה גדולה ויבקעו מחילות המתי׳ בירושלים ויחיה אותם הקדוש ב״ה וילך משיח בן דוד ואליהו הנביא ויחיו משיח בן יוסף הנאסף בשערי ירושלם וישלחו את משיח בן דוד בשביל שארית ישראל הפזורים בכל הארצות. [2] מיד כל מלכי אומות העולם נושאים אותם על כתפותיהם ומביאים אותם לה׳ וגו׳:

10 האות העשירי תוקע מיכאל תקיעה גדולה ויוציא הקדוש ברוך הוא
מנהר גוזן ומחלח וחבור ומערי מדי כל השבטים ויבאו עם בני משה מספר
ובאין שיעור. 2 כגן עדן הארץ לפניהם ואחריהם תלהט להבה ולא ישאירו מחיה
לאומות העולם ובשעה שיצאו השבטים ענני כבוד יקיפו אותם והקב״ה הולך
לפניהם שנאמר ועלה הפורץ לפניהם והקב״ה יפתח להם מעינות של עץ חיים
וישקה אותם בדרך שנאמר בישעיה אפתח על שפיים נהרות ובתוך בקעות מעינות
אשים מדבר לאגם מים וציה למוצאי מים. 3 וכתיב לא ירעבו ולא יצמאו ולא יכם
שרב ושמש וגומר. 4 הקב״ה יזכנו לראות את הגאולה מהרה ויזכנו לראות בית
הבחירה. 5 ויקיים בנו מקרא שכתוב הנני שב את שבות אהלי יעקב ומשכנותיו
ארחם ונבנתה עיר על תלה וארמון על משפט ישב ויקיים עלינו כל נחמותיו וכל
הבטחותיו שנאמר על ידי נביאיו וכתיב בעת ההיא אביא אתכם ובעת קבצי אתכם
כי אתן אתכם לשם ולתהלה:

תמו אותות המשיח :

ספר זרובבל.

הדבר אשר היה אל זרובבל בן שאלתיל פחת יהודה (נ״א הראני שם)
המראה הזות. 2 ואני הייתי מתפלל לפני ה׳ בחזיון המראה אשר ראיתי על נהר
כבר באומרי (נ״א ואומר) ברוך אתה ה׳ מחיה המתים:
3 נהם לבבי עלי לאמר איך יהיה צורת הבית לעולמים. 4 ויענני מדלתות
השמים ויאמר לי האתה זרובבל פחת יהודה. 5 ואומר אני עבדך. 6 ויצא לי קול
(נ״א ויען לי) וידבר עמי כאשר ידבר איש אל רעהו. 7 קולו שמעתי ומראהו לא
ראיתי. 8 ואקום ואתפלל כבתחילה ואומרה (נ״א ואגמור) תפלתי ואפנה לביתי.
9 וביום אחד עשר לאדר (נ״א לחדש) היה מדבר עמי ויאמר לי בא אצלי שאל
ממני. 10 ואומר מה אשאל. 11 קטני׳ (נ״א קצרו) ימי קצי ואמלא ימי. 12 ויאמר לי
אחייך. 13 ויאמר אלי תהי חי. 14 ותשאיני רוח בין השמים ובין הארץ ויוליכני
בנינוה העיר הגדולה והיא עיר הדמים ויצר לי מאוד ואקום מצרה להתפלל
ולחלות את פני אלהי ישראל ואתודה את פשעי וחטאתי ואומר אנא ד׳ חטאתי
פשעתי ואשמתי כי נהלו כאבי. 15 אתה הוא אלהי ישראל אשר עשית הכל ברוח
פיך ובאומרך מתים יחיו. 16 ויאמר ה׳ אלי לך אל בית התורף (נ״א בית הלצות)
מקום השוק. 17 ואלך כאשר צווני. 18 ויאמר אלי פנה לך הלאה. 19 ואפנה ויגע בי
וראיתי איש נבזה ופצוע. 20 ויאמר אלי האיש הפצוע ונבזה זרובבל מה לך פה
(נ״א מלאכתך). 21 ואען ואומר רוח ה׳ נשאני באשר (נ״א בזה העיר) לא אדע
ויוליכני בזה המקום. 22 ויאמר אלי אל תירא כי למען הראותך הובאת הנה.
23 וכשמעי דבריו נחמתי ושאלתי לו מה שם המקום הזה. 24 ויאמר אלי זו הוא
רומה רבה שאני אסור בה בכלא עד בא קיצי (נ״א ואומר לו אדני אי אתה ומה

מבקש ומה תעשה הנה ויאמר אלי אני משיח השם שאני אסור פה עד עת קץ).
25 וכשמעי זאת הסתרתי פני רגע ממנו ואשוב ואביט אליו והסתרתי עוד כי יראתי.
26 ויאמר אלי אל תירא ואל תחת למה אתה מחריש. 27 ואומר שמעתי שמעך כי
משיח אלהי אתה. 28 ומיד נדמה אלי כנער מכלול יפה ונעים בחור אין כמותו.
29 ואומר אליו מתי יאיר נר ישראל. 30 ובאמרי לו הדברים והנה איש בעל כנפים
בא אלי ויאמר אלי (נ"א מוסיף עוד מה תשאל למשיח השם ועניתי ואמרתי מתי
יבא קץ הישועה ויאמר לי) כי הוא היה שר צבא ישראל שנלחם עם סנחריב ועם
מלכי כנען ועתיד הוא להלחם מלחמת ה' עם משיח ה' ועם המלך עזפני'
וארמילוס בן אבן שיצא מהאבן. 31 ויוסף מטטרון ויאמר לי המלאך אני שנהגתי
את אברהם בכל ארץ כנען ואני הוא אשר פדיתי את יצחק ונאבקתי עם יעקב
במעבר יבוק ואני שנהגתי את ישראל במדבר מ' שנה בשם ה' ואני שנגליתי
ליהושע בגלגל ואני הוא ששמי כשם רבי ושמו בקרבי. 32 ואתה זרובבל שאל
ממני ואגידה מה יקרא לעמך באחרית הימים. 33 ויאמר לי זה משיח ה' הצפון כאן
עד עת קץ (נ"א ויאמר לי משיח ה' אשר יבא בעת קץ ושמו מנחם בן עמיאל ויולד
בימי דוד מלך ישראל וישאהו רוח ויצפנהו כאן עד עת קץ) ואני שאלתי למטטרון
ויאמר אלי מטה ישועה יתן הש"י לחפצי בה אם מנחם וככב יגיה לפניה ותצא
חפצי בה ותהרוג ב' מלכים האחד נוף מתימן ושם השני אנטוכיא (נ"א אסרנו
מאנטוכיא) ואותות האלו יהיו בחג השבועות ואמת הדבר (נ"א מוסיף לכשיהרג)
וכשיבנה העיר ד' מאות ר"כ שנה יחרב שנייה ר"ו שנה לכניעת (נ"א לכשיבנה
רומא) רומה וימליכו בה שבעים מלכים וכשגמרו עשרה מלכים בה ובעשירי
יחרוב ב"ה ויוסר התמיד ומאותו יום חשוב לך ט' מאות וצ' שנה יהיה תשועת ה'
ויזכור עם קדשו לגאלם לנטלם לנשאם ולקבצם. 34 והמטה אשר יתן ה' לחפצי
בה אם מנחם משקד (נ"א מן שקדים) הוא והוא נטמן ברקת (נ"א מוסיף עיר
נפתלי). 35 והוא מטה אהרן ומשה ודוד מלך ישראל. 36 והוא המטה אשר פרח
באוהל מעד ויציץ ציץ ויגמל שקדים ואליהו בן אלעזר גנזו ברקת והיא טבריא
ושם גנזו משיח בן אפרים. 37 ויען זרובבל בן שאלתיאל (נ"א ואומר למיכאל)
ויאמר בי אדני מתי יבא נר ישראל ומה יהיה אחרי כל זאת. 38 ויאמר לי משיח בן
יוסף יבא ה' שנים אחר חפצי בה ויקבץ כל ישראל כאיש אחד ויעמדו מ' שנים
בירושלים ויקריבו קרבן ואז יעלה מלך פרס על ישראל ויהיה צרה גדולה בישראל
ותצא חפצי בה אשת נתן הנביא עם המטה אשר יתן ה' לה ויתן ה' בהם רוח
עועים ויהרגו איש את אחיו ושם ימות רשע. 39 וכשמעי דבריו נפלתי על פני
ואמרתי לו הגידה לי האמת על עם קודש. 40 וידבק בי ויראיני אבן בדמות אשה
ויאמר אלי אבן זות ישכב שטן עמה ויצא ממנה ארמילוס והוא ימלוך על כל
העולם כלו ואין מי יעמוד לפניו וכל מי שלא יאמין בו ימות בחרבו הקשה ויבא
בארץ ישראל עם עשרה המלכים לירושלים ויהרגו שם משיח בן יוסף וששה עשרה
צדיקים עמו ויגלו ישראל במדבר וחפצי בה אם מנחם עומדת שם לא יבא אותו
רשע (ולא יראה אותו רשע) ומלחמה זו תהיה בחדש אב. 41 אז ואז יהיה צרה
בישראל שלא היתה כמותה בעולם וינוסו בצריחים ומערות ובמדברות וכל א"ה

יטעו אחר אותו רשע שטן ארמילוס חוץ מישראל ויספדו כל ישראל את נחמיה בן
חושיאל שנהרג ותהיה נבלתו מושלכת לפני שערי ירושלים וחיה ועוף לא יגעו
בה. [42] וכשמעי דבריו ותצר לי מאוד (נ"א מוסיף על הריגת בן יוסף ועל כל
ישראל) ואקום להתפלל לפני ה' וישמע וישלח את מלאכו אלי ואדע כי הוא
המלאך הדובר בי ואשתחוה לפניו. [43] ויאמר אלי מה לך זרובבל. [44] ואומר אליו
הבהילוני רוח. [45] ויעמוד מטטרון ויען ויאמר זרובבל שאל ממני בטרם אלך מעמך.
[46] ואשאל לו ואומר מתי יבא נר ישראל. [47] ויען אלי ויאמר חי ה' אשר שלחני כי
אומר אליך את מעשה הש"י כי הקול הקדש שלחני אליך להגידך את כל אשר
תשאל. [48] ויאמר אלי מיכאל גשה נא אלי ושים לבך לאשר אני אומר אליך כי אמת
הדבר בשם אלהים חיים. [49] ויאמר אלי מנחם בן עמיאל יבא פתאום בחדש ניסן
ויעמד על בקעת ארבאל ויצאו אליו כל חכמי ישראל ולהם יאמר בן עמיאל אני
הוא משיח אשר שלחני ה' לבשרכם ולהצילכם מיד צורריכם ויביטו בו החכמים
ויבזוהו כמו שאתה בזית אותו (נ"א מוסיף ולא יאמינו בו) ויבער בו חמתו וילבש
בגדי נקם תלבושת ויבא בשערי ירושלים ועמו אליהו ויקיצו ויחיו את נחמיה (נ"א
בן שאלתיאל הנהרג) ויאמינו בו. [50] וכך השביעני מטטרון כי למלאות חרבות
ירושלים ט' מאות וצ' שנה יהיה תשועת ה' מנחם ואליהו יעמדו על הים הגדול
ויקראו בנביאיו ויצאו כל פגרי ישראל שהשליכו עצמם בים מפני שוביהם ואז
תעל עדת קרח ויבואו אצל משה ויחיו מתי מדבר ואסף דגל הקרחי וירד הש"י
בהר הזיתים והההר יבקע מגערתו ולוחם בגוים ההם כאיש מלחמות יעיר קנאה
ויבא משיח בן דוד ויפח באפיו של ארמילוש וימיתוהו וכל ישראל יראו את ה'
בשוב ציון עין בעין (נ"א מוסיף שנ' עין בעין יראו בשוב ה' ציון) כאיש מלחמות
וכובע ישועה בראשו ולבוש שריון וילחם בארמילוס ובחייליו ויפלו כלם פגרים
מתים בבקעת ארבאל וימלטו שרידים ויתקבצו בסלע ה' אלף חמש מאות ולבושי
שריון מאה אלף ו"ה מאות מישראל ונחמיה בראשם ויהרגום. [51] ואחרי זות יבא
מנחם בן עמיאל ונחמיהו ואליהו ויעלו לירושלים ובחדש אב ישבו חרבות
ירושלים ויהיה שמחה גדולה לישראל ויקריבו קרבניהם ויערב לה' מנחת יהודה
וישראל כבראשונה וירח ריח ניחוחינו וישמח מאד בהדר הבית הבנוי למעלה
והוסיף בה באורך וברוחב וירד מן המזרח וממדבר הגדול עד הים האחרון ועד
הנהר הגדול נהר פרת וגם ההיכל יהיה נבנה על (נ"א חמשה) ראשי הרים.
[52] ואשאל לו מה שמם ויען ויאמר לי לבנון הר המוריה ותבור וכרמל וחרמון:
[53] ואלו הם העשרה מלכים אשר יקומו על האומות ב"ז שנים האחד
סליקוס מאסמפיא. [54] השני ארממוס (נ"א ארטימוס) ממדינת הים. [55] ג' קילוס
(נ"א טליס) מגיתא. [56] ד' פלואוס (נ"א פאולס) מגליא. [57] ה' רומטרוס ממורטיא.
[58] ו' מקלנוס מזלטיא (נ"א מורקולוס מאטליא). [59] ז' הוא ארכטוניס מאדמיס
(נ"א אכטונוס מרודמא). [60] שמיני מספליסניס (נ"א אפעלסטוס) מארם נהרים.
[61] ט' פרוס מפרסי (נ"א שירון מפרש). [62] י' ארמילוס בן שפרן (נ"א מוסיף וזה
סימן דמות ארמילוס שער ראשו כזהב וכבול וידיו עד עקבי רגליו וזה עינו זרת בן
עין לעין ועיניו עקומות ושני קדקדין לו וכל רואיו יראו ממנו ועשרה מלכים

שיבראו עמו יקומו על האומות). 63 מיד אחריו והיתה לה' המלוכה. 64 ועינינו
תראנה הקריה הנסוכה אשר בגלות נמשכה בחטאנו עד הנה התוחלת נמשכה
(נ"א מיד והיתה לה' המלוכה במהרה בימינו) :

סליק ספר זרובבל :

עשרת מלכים

4 11 ואחר כל זות אם לא זכו ישראל יעמוד מלך עז פנים ויהרוג את מלך בני
מזרח בירח אב ויגזור גזרות על ישראל, ויבטל המועדים והשבתות שנאמר ויסבר
להשניה זמנין ודת ויתיהבון בידיה עד עידן ועידנין ופלג עידן (דניאל ז') עידן
שנה עידנין שנתים ופלג חצי שנה. 12 ואח"כ יעמוד מלך ושמו מושיב ומשיב כל
מי שהוא עובד ע"ז שנאמר וזעם על ברית קודש (דניאל י"א) וימלוך ט' חדשים
שנא' לכן יתנם עד עת יולדה ילדה (מיכה ה') וכמה עת יולדה ט' חדשים. 13 ואחר
כל זות ירד השטן וילך ברומי לצורת האבן ויתחבר עמה כדרך מעשה ותתעבר
האבן ותלד את ארמילוס וימלוך ארבעים יום וידיו קשים יותר מארבעים סאה
וגזור גזירות רעות על ישראל ויפסקו אנשי מעשה וירבו אנשי גזל, אם זכו ישראל
יצמח משיח בן יוסף בגליל העליון ויעלה לירושלם ויבנה ההיכל ויקריב קרבנות
ותרד אש ותאכל קרבנותיו וישבו ישראל כל ימיו לבטח. 14 ויעלה חיל גוג ויחריב
ירושלם ויהרוג את משיח בן יוסף, הדא הוא דכתיב יתיצבו מלכי ארץ וגו'
(תהלים ב'), וישראל סופדין ובוכין את משיח שנאמר והביטו אליו את אשר דקרו
וספדו עליו (זכריה י"ב) ויתחלקו לארבע כתות, ג' מהן ילכו בגולה והאחת תותר
שנאמר ויתר העם לא יכרת מן העיר (שם י"ד). 15 ואח"כ יצא הקב"ה להלחם
עמהם שנאמר ויצא ה' ונלחם בגוים ההם כיום הלחמו ביום קרב (שם) מה כתיב
תמן ועמדו רגליו ביום ההוא על הר הזיתים, ואומר וזות תהיה המגפה וגו'.
16 והקב"ה יתקע בשופר גדול ואומר לצפון תני ולתימן אל תכלאי (ישעיה מ"ג)
ואומר ופדויי ה' ישובון (שם ל"ה) ואומר לאמר לאסורים צאו ולאשר בחשך הגלו
(שם מ"ט), לאסורים צאו אלו שבנהר סמבטיון שהם באסורים, ולאשר בחשך
הגלו אלו ט' השבטים וחצי שהם יושבים [מתחת להרי חשך]. 17 והקב"ה יקבץ
אותם ויעלם לירושלם וינחם ואתם בכפלים שנאמר אנכי אנכי הוא מנחמכם (שם
נ"א). 18 אמרו ישראל לפני הקב"ה רבש"ע חטאנו לפניך על ההרים, אמר להם אני
מעבירם שנאמר כי ההרים ימושו (שם נ"ד). 19 ועוד אמרו קלקלנו בחמה ובלבנה,
אמר להם אני מעבירם שנאמר וחפרה הלבנה ובושה החמה (שם כ"ד). 20 וישלח
הקב"ה את אליהו שישמח לבם של ישראל שנאמר הנה אנכי שולח לכם את אליה
הנביא (מלאכי ג'), ומבשר להם בשורות שלום וטובות שנאמר מה נאוו על ההרים
רגלי מבשר וגו' (ישעיה נ"ב) עד שחזרה המלכות לבית דוד. 21 המלך התשיעי
זה משיח בן דוד שימלוך מסוף העולם ועד סופו שנאמר וירד מים עד ים ומנהר
עד אפסי ארץ (תהלים ע"ב), וישבו ישראל לבטח אלפים שנה ויאכלו את בהמות

ואת לויתן וזיז שדי, ולקץ אלפים שנה יתקבצו לדין שנאמר יחיינו מיומים ביום השלישי יקימנו ונחיה לפניו, זה יום הדין אשרי מי שזוכה בו [ואז ימלוך הקב״ה והוא המלך העשירי]. [22] הקב״ה יזכנו בו עם כל ישראל אמן ואמן.

[23] בריך רחמנא דסייען,
ברוך נותן ליעף כח
ולאין אונים עצמה ירבה.

פרקי משיח

5 ועתה נאמר בשבחו של מלך המשיח שעתיד לבוא עם ענני שמיא ושני שרפים מימינו ומשמאלו שנאמר וארו עם ענני שמיא כבר אנש אתי הוא. [2] דור שבן דוד בא שרפי אש נשלחים בהיכל וכוכבים נראים כאש בכל מקום ודבר שלש שנים זו אחר זו וזהו שלוחו של הקב״ה שנא׳ לפניו ילך דבר ויצא רשף לרגליו שנאמר רשפיה רשפי אש. [3] ובשנה השלישית של דבר גליות מכפרין בו ובסוף השנה המלך יהרג ובורחים במדברות והארץ תצעק ממקומה ותלמידי חכמים ימותו בוגדים בגדו ובגד בוגדים בגדו ומחזיק בה מקרא אחר ועוד בה עשירי׳ ושבה והיתה לבער. [4] ושנה חמישית בא ונתגלה בכל המלכיות המלכים כולם מתגרים זה בזה מלך פרס עם מלך ערביא ומחריבה שנאמר ונלחמו איש באחיו וגו׳ ממלכה בממלכה. [5] ובשעה שאדום נופלת מקול מפלתה ירעשו שמים וארץ וחצי העולם ילכד בשבילה שנא׳ ה׳ ממרום ישאג וממעון קדשו יתן קולו. [6] ועתיד הב״ה לקבצם המונים ולמסור אותם ביד ישראל שנאמר ונתתי נקמתי באדום ביד עמי ישראל. [7] ועתיד הקב״ה להביא שר של אדום ומלקה אותו ושר של אדום אומר היכן אברח אלך במצרים שכינה שם שנאמר הנה ה׳ רוכב על עב קל ובא מצרים. [8] אברח באדום שכינה שם שנאמר מי זה בא מאדום. [9] אברח לבבל שכינה שם שנאמר למענכם שולחתי בבלה. [10] אברח בעילם שכינה שם שנאמר ושמתי כסאי בעילם. [11] משל לשועל שאמר לה הארי תן לי מכס עמדה וברחה מהלך שלשה ימים ועוד אחזתה הארי ואמר לה תן לי המכס אף בזה המקום אמר לו אני ממך ברחתי אמר לה עדיין את במקומי עומדת. [12] כך עתיד הקב״ה לומר לשרו של אדום המפני יש לך להסתר והקב״ה נותנו בידי ישראל. [13] ועתיד הקב״ה ללבוש בגדי נקם ולהנקם משבעים אומות שנאמר לי נקם ושלם. [14] וללבוש עשרה מלבושים כנגד עשרה פעמי׳ שנקראו ישראל כלה להשם ואלו הן באתי לגני אחותי כלה. [15] אתי מלבנון כלה. [16] גן נעול אחותי כלה. [17] מה יפו דודיך אחותי כלה. [18] נפת תטפנה שפתותיך כלה. [19] לבבתני אחותי כלה. [20] קול חתן וקול כלה. [21] ותקשרם ככלה. [22] ומשוש חתן על כלה. [23] וככלה תעדה כליה. [24] ואלו הן עשרה מלבושים ה׳ מלך גאות לבש לבש ה׳ עוז התאזר ביום מתן תורה. [25] לבש ה׳ עוז התאזר ביום מתן תורה. [26] וילבש צדקה כשריון ביום שמוסר אומות העולם לישראל. [27] וילבש בגדי נקם תלבושת ביום מפלתה של אדום. [28] חמוץ בגדים

מבצרה ביום שעושה מלחמה עם אומות העולם. [29] זה הדור בלבושו ביום גוג ומגוג. [30] ויז נצחם על בגדי במלכות איטל׳. [31] ואלו שני לבושים ביום תחיית המתים שנאמר ברכי נפשי את ה׳ הוד והדר לבשת. [32] מדוע אדום ללבושך. [33] ביום שהקב״ה אוחז חרבו ועושה מלחמה שנאמר אשכיר חצי מדם וחרבי תאכל בשר. [34] ונתתי נקמתי באדום ביד עמי ישראל. [35] קודם שתפול אדום יחרבו עשרה מקומות וי׳ מקומות יהפכו וי׳ שופרות יתקעו וי׳ קולות ישמעו וט״ו מדינות יקטלו וי׳ רעות יהיו וי׳ רעות נובעות ומלך עז פנים יעמוד וגזרות רעות יגזור במלכותו. [36] ומלך גדול יצא על אלכסנדריא במחנה. [37] ורעה גדולה תהיה בעולם ושלש שנים ומחצה ימשול וימרוד. [38] ושרי אדום יפלו וי׳ מלחמות יהיו ואז יתגברו ישראל על כל האומות. [39] ונתתי נקמתי באדום. [40] ספינות מארץ ישראל עתידין לילך לאדום וישראל אומר מה לנו ולאדום שנאמר מי יובילני עיר מצור מי נחני עד אדום. [41] וישראל הולכים וחונים על צור מ׳ יום ובסוף מ׳ יום עומדים בעת קרית שמע ואומרים שמע ישראל ה׳ אלהינו ה׳ אחד. [42] וחומות המדינה נופלות והמדינה נכבשת מפניהם ובורחים בתוכה כל כסף וזהב והשאר שוסים אותה ומשם ומביאין כלי בית המקדש ומלך נחמיה המשיח יצא עמהם ובאים לירושלים. [43] וישראל אומרים למלך הערביים בית המקדש שלנו הוא קח כסף וזהב ותניח בית המקדש ומלך הערבים אומר אין לכם במקדש הזה כלום אבל אם אתם בוחרים לכם בראשונה קרבן כמו שהייתם עוסקים מקדם וגם אנחנו מקריבים ומי שנתקבל קרבנו נהיה כולנו אומה א׳. [44] וישראל מקריבין ואינן מתקבלין לפי שהשטן מקטרג לפני הקב״ה ובני קדר מקריבין ומתקבלין שנאמר כל צאן קדר יקבצו לך. [45] באותה שעה הערביים אומרים לישראל בואו ותאמינו באמונתינו וישראל משיבין אותם אם אנו הורגים ונהרגים ואין אנו כופרים בעיקר באותה שעה חרבו׳ נשלפות וקשתות נדרכות וחיצים נזרקים ומפילים חללים משער אפרים עד שער הפינה ונחמיה נהרג עמהם והנמלטים מהם יברחו למדבר מואב ולארץ בני עמון ושם עמדו פליטי ישראל ההם ויעשה השם להם שם נסים ומעין יצא להם מתהומות שנאמר בך נדחי מואב ויאכלו שם שרשי רתמים מ״ה ימים ובסוף מ״ה ימים יצמיח שם אליהו ומלך המשיח עליו ושם יבשר להם אליהו ויאמר מה לכם פה ישראל וישראל משיבין ואומרים אבדנו נחרבנו ואליהו אומר להם קומו כי אליהו אני וזה מלך המשיח ואינם מאמינים בו לפי שבא נחמיה ונהרג והוא אומר להם שמא אתם מבקשים אות כמשה והם אומרי׳ הן. [46] באותה שעה יעשה ז׳ נסים. [47] הנס הראשון מביא להם משה ודורו מן המדבר שנאמר אספו לי חסידי. [48] הנס הב׳ מעלה להם קרח וכל עדתו שנאמר תשוב תחיינו ומתהומות הארץ תשוב תעלינו. [49] הנס הג׳ מעמיד להם נחמיה שנהרג. [50] הנס הד׳ מגלה להם גניזת הארץ וצנצנת המן ושמן המשחה. [51] הנס הה׳ נותן הקב״ה מטה עוז בידו שנא׳ עזך ישראל וגו׳. [52] הו׳ טוחן כל הרי ישראל כקמה שנאמר אחריב הרים וגבעות. [53] הנס הז׳ יגלה להם הסוד שנאמר זאת אות הברית. [54] וכיון שרואים את הנסים הללו משלחים ואומרים לכל השרים הבוזזים לירושלים בואו והלחמו בהם יצאו מזומנין אחרי ישראל וישראל אומרים למלך המשיח לא טוב לנו לשבת למה באת להתגרו׳ בנו

מלחמה בראשונה והמלך המשיח אומר להם התיצבו וראו את ישועת ה׳ והוא
נופח בהם ברוח פיו וכולם יפלו חללים לפניו שנאמר וברוח שפתיו ימית רשע.
[55] צא ולמד מסנחריב שנאמר והנה כלם פגרים מתים. [56] באותה שעה יעוף אליהו
בכל העולם ויבשר לישראל שנאמר הנה אנכי שולח לכם את אליהו הנביא.
[57] ואותו יום יום אכזרי ועברה ואותו היום מפסיק בין שני עולמים ורשעים
אומרים אהא ליום כי קרוב יום ה׳ ואומ׳ הוי המתאוים יום ה׳ וירושלי׳ רחבה
ונסכה כל אותו היום שנאמר והיה יום אחד הזא יודע לה׳ כו׳. [58] גוג ומגוג יעלה
בו ביום ויחנה על ירושלם ז׳ ימים וחצי וילכד ירושלם וכנסת ישראל אומרת לפני
הקב״ה רבונו של עולם כל אומה ואומה שבזזה אותי מתביישת אני לחזור עליה
וליקח את שלי מידה והב״ה משיבה אני מכניסן כולם בתוכך שנאמר הנה יום בא
לה׳ וחולק שללך בקרבך. [59] ואספתי את כל הגוים אל ירושלי׳ למלחמה. ואלו הם
גומר אגפיה תוגרמה אפריקי גרמית גרממיה קפודקיא ברברי איטליאה כוש
אנדלוס וסבא הרמן ודולים אהרסן ססונייא גליציאה גוציא לומרדיאה קלבריאה
פנטיפולי טריפולי צור מקדונייה אינגליסי מונקך ציפרי נירו נוזן דרוניה אוסיה
טלקי אלמנייה טורסוס עילם וכל יתיריה. [60] ובני מדינתהון יוצאין ברמחים
ובחרבות ובקשתות וכל אחד מהם מחזק בדלת מוחזקת במסמרת שנאמר איש את
רעהו יעזורו ונחלקות לשלש כיתות. [61] כת ראשונה שותה כל מימי טיבריה.
[62] שנייה שותה שמרים. [63] שלישית יעברו ברגליהם ויאמרו איש לרעהו המקום
הזה של מי הוא ויחרקו אבני הרי ישראל בסוסיהם ותנתן ירושלם בידם וישבו
העיר ולא יהרגו אדם שנאמר ונלכדה העיר ונשסו הבתים והנשים תשכבנה ויענו
בתוכה שתי נשים משתי משפחות. [64] אמר רבי יוחנן תשגלנה כתיב למה הדבר
דומה למלך שנכנסו גנבים לפלטורין שלו אמר המלך אם אני תופש אותם בביתי
עכשיו הם אומרי׳ אין גבורתו של מלך אלא אלא בביתו אלא ממתין אני להם עד
שיצאו לחוץ. [65] כך הקב״ה אומר אם אני הורגן בירושלם עכשיו הן אומרים אין
כחו אלא בירושלם אלא אמתין להם עד שיצאו להר הזיתים. [66] ושם נגלה עליהם
הקב״ה בכבודו ועושה מלחמה בהם עד שלא ישתייר מהם א׳ שנאמר ויצא ה׳
ונלחם בגוים ההם כיום הלחמו ביום קרב. [67] ומכנים הקב״ה כל חיות השדה
וצפרים לאכל בשרם שנאמר אמור לצפור כל כנף. [68] ושבע שנים ישרפו ישראל
מעצי קשתם ותריסיהם ורמחיהם:

6 באותה שעה מלביש הקב״ה למשיח עטרה וישים כובע ישועה בראשו
ויתן עליו זיו והדר ויעטרהו בגדי כבוד ויעמידהו על הר גבוה לבשר
לישראל וישמיע בקולו קרבה ישועה וישראל אומרים מי אתה והוא אומר אני הוא
אפרים וישראל אומ׳ אתה הוא שקראך הקב״ה אפרים בכורי הוא הבן יקיר לי
אפרים והוא אומר להן הן וישראל אומרים לו צא ובשר לישיני מכפלה שיעמדו
תחילה. [2] באותה שעה עולה ומבשר לישיני מכפלה ואומר להם אברהם יצחק
ויעקב קומי דייכם תנומה והם משיבים ואומרים מי הוא זה שמגלה עפר מעלינו
והוא אומר להם אני משיח ה׳ קרבה ישועה קרבה השעה והם משיבים אם בודאי
כן צא ובשר לאדם הראשון שיקום תחילה. [3] באותה שעה אומרים לאדם דייך
תנומה והוא אומר מי זה שמנדד שינה מעיני והוא אומר אני משיח ה׳ מבני בניך.

⁴ מיד עומד אדם הראשון וכל דורו ואברהם יצחק ויעקב וכל הצדיקים וכל השבטים וכל הדורות מסוף העולם ועד סופו ומשמיעים קול רנה וזמרה שנאמר מה נאוו על ההרים רגלי מבשר ולמה על ההרים אלא מה נאוו משה ודורו באים מן המדבר. ⁵ ד״א מה נאוו על ההרים משל למלך שהיו לו שני בנים ומת אחד מהם ולבשו כל בני המדינת שחורים אמר המלך לבשתם שחורים עתה במיתתו של בני הראשון אני אלבישכם לבנים בשמחתו של בני השני. ⁶ כך אמר הקב״ה לכל ההרים הואיל ובכיתם על בני בשעה שגלו מארצם על ההרים אשא בכי ונהי כך אני מביא שמחתם של בני על ההרים שנאמר מה נאוו על ההרים. ⁷ נאה מלך המשיח מבשר לישראל וההרים ירקדו כעגלים לפניו ועצי השדה יהיו מכין כף אל כף בישועה של ישראל שנאמר כי בשמחה תצאו ובשלום וגומר.

⁸ מה נאים הרי ישראל מושכים חלב ודבש כנחלי מים שוטפים וגם נהרי יין שנאמר והיה ביום ההוא יטפו ההרים עסיס ומעין מבית ה׳ יצא והשקה את נחל השטים. ⁹ למה המעין דומה כשהוא יוצא מבית קודש הקדשים ועד מפתן הבית בתחילה דומה לחוט של של ההיכל דומה לחוט של ערב עד החצר דומה לקרנים וליובלאי עד המזבח דומה לקרני חגבים עד העזרה דומה לפך קטן שנאמר הנה מים מפכים ומשם יורדין כנחל שוטף וכשירין לעולה ולנדה ולחטאת.

נסתרות רב שמעון בן יוחי

אלו הן הנסתרות שנגלו לר׳ שמעון בן יוחי כשהיה חבוי במערה מפני קיסר מלך אדום ועמד בתפלה ארבעים יום וארבעים לילה והתחיל כך ה׳ אלהים עד מתי עשנת בתפלת עבדך. ² מיד נגלו אליו סתרי הקק וסתומות והתחיל לישב ולדרוש וירא את הקני. ³ כיון שראה מלכות ישמעאל שהיה בא התחיל לומר לא דיינו מה שעשה לנו מלכות אדום הרשעה אלא אף מלכות ישמעאל. ⁴ מיד ענה לו מטטרון שר הפנים ואמר לו אל תירא בן אדם שאין הב״ה מביא מלכות ישמעאל אלא כדי להושיעכם מזאת הרשעה והוא מעמיד עליהם נביא כרצונו ויכבוש להם את הארץ ובאי׳ הם ויחזירוה בגדולה ואימה גדולה תהיה ביניהם ובן בני עשו. ⁵ ענה לו רבי שמעון ואמר ומניין שהם ישועה לנו אמר לו ולא כך ישעיה הנביא אמר וראה רכב צמד פרשים וגו׳ מפני מה הוא מקדים רכב חמור רכב גמל לא היה צריך לומר אלא רכב גמל רכב חמור אלא כיון שהוא יוצא הוא רוכב על גמל צמחה מלכות בידו רוכב על חמור. ⁶ ד״א רכב חמור כיון שהוא רוכב על חמור מיכן שהם תשועה לישראל כתשועת רוכב על חמור. ⁷ ועוד היה רבי שמעון אומר ששמע מרבי ישמעאל כיון ששמע שמלכות ישמעאל בא עתידין למוד הארץ בחבלים שנאמר והארץ יחלק במחיר. ⁸ ועושים בתי קברות מרעה לצאן וכשימות אדם מהם קוברים אותו בכל מקום שהם מוצאים וחוזרין וחורשין הקבר וזורעים אותו שנאמר ככה יאכלו בני ישראל את לחמם טמא. ⁹ מפני מה שאין בית הפרס נידש. ¹⁰ עוד וירא את הקני וכי מה משל נשא אותו רשע אלא כיון שראה את בני

בניו שהם עתידים לעמוד ולשעבד את ישראל התחיל שמח ואמר איתן מושבך
רואה אני בני אדם אוכלים אלא ממצוות איתן האזרחי:
[11] המלך השני שיעמוד מישמעאל יהיה אוהב ישראל ויגדור פרצותיהם
ופרצי' ההיכל וחוצב הר המוריה ועושה אותו מישור כולו ובונה לו שם השתחויה
על אבן שתיה שנאמר ושים בסלע קנך ועושה מלחמה עם בני עשו והורג
חיילותיו וישבה שביה גדולה מהם וימות בשלום ובכבוד גדול. [12] ויעמוד מלך
גדול מחצר מות ועשה ימים מעטים ויעמדו עליו גיבורי בני קדר ויהרגוהו
ויעמידו מלך אחר ושמו מריאו ויקחהו מאחרי הצאן והאתונות ויעלוהו
למלוכה ויעמדו ממנו זרועות ארבע ויגדרו בהיכל. [13] ולקץ מלכות ארבע זרועות
יעמוד מלך אחר וימעט האיפות והמדות והמשקלות ויעשה שלש שנים בשלוה
ויהיה קטטה בעולם בימיו וישלח חיילים גדולים על אדומים ושם ימות ברעב
ויהיה עמהם מזון הרבה והוא מונע מהם אין נותן להם ויעמדו בני אדום על בני
ישמעאל ויהרגו אותם ויעמדו בני ישמעאל וישרפו המזון והנשארים יברחו ויצאו.
[14] ואחר כך יעמוד מלך הגדול וימלוך י"ט שנים. [15] ואלו הם אותותיו אדמדם
שיפן העין ויש לו שלש שומות אחת במצחו ואחת בידו הימנית ואחת בזרועו
השמאלית. [16] ונוטע נטיעות ויבנה ערים חרבות ויבקע התהומות להעלות המים
להשקות נטיעותיו ובני בני בניו מרובין לאכול וכל מי שיעמוד עליו ינתן בידו
והארץ שוקטת בימיו וימות בשלום. [17] ויעמוד מלך אחר ויבקש לכרות מימי
הירדן ויביא רחוקים מארצות נכריות לחפור ולעשות נחל ולעלות מי הירדן
להשקות הארץ ותפול עליהם חפירת הארץ ויהרגם וישמעו נשיאיהם ויעמדו על
המלך ויהרגוהו. [18] ויעמוד מלך אחר בגבורה ואיש מלחמה וקטטה בעולם בימיו
וזה לך האות כשאתה רואה שנפל גירון המערבי שבמערב השתחויה של בני
ישמעאל בדמשק נפלה מלכותו ונכנסין ויוצאין במס ואף מלכות ישמעאל חיפול
ועליהם הוא אומר שבר ה' מטה רשעים. [19] ואי זה זה מראון שער. [20] אצלו היו
גבורי בני קדר קיימים ותפשע עליו פינת מזרחים צפונית ויעלו עליו ויפלו ממנו ג'
חיילים גדולים בחידקל ובפרס והוא בורח מפניהם ונלכד ונהרג ובניו יתלו על
העץ. [21] ואח"כ יעמוד מלך עז פנים שלשה חדשים ואחר כן תמלוך מלכות
הרשעה על ישראל תשעה חדשים שנאמר לכן יתנם עד עת יולדה ילדה. [22] ויצמח
להם משיח בן יוסף ויעלה אותם לירושלם ויבנה בית המקדש ויקריב קרבנות
ותרד אש מן השמים ותאכל קרבנותיהם שנאמר ובני פריצי עמך ינשאו. [23] אם לו
זכו משיח בן אפרים בא ואם זכו יבוא משיח בן דיד ויעמוד מלך רשע ושמו
ארמילאוס הוא ימינו ועיניו קטנות ורצעת במצחו ואזנו ימנית סתומה השמאלית
פתוחה. [24] ואם ידבר לו אדם טובה יטה לו אזני סתומה אם ידבר לו אדם רעה
מטה לו אזני פתוחה. [25] והוא בריה דסטנא ודאבנא ועולה לירושלם ויעורר
מלחמה עם משיח בן אפרים בשער מזרחי שנאמר והביטו אליו את אשר דקרו
וישראל גולין למדבריי אגמים לרעות במלוחים ובשרשי רתמים מ"ה ימים ואז
נבחנים ונצרפים שנאמר והבאתי את השלישית באש וגומר. [26] וימות שם משיח
בן אפרים וישראל סופדים אותו ואחר כך יגלה להם הקב"ה משיח בן דוד וישראל
ירצו לסוקלו ואומר' לו שקר דברת שכבר נהרג משיח ואין משיח אחר עתיד

לעמוד ויבזוהו שנאמר נבזה וחדל אישים והוא חוזר לו ונכסה מהן שנאמר
וכמסתר פנים ממנו. [27] ובהצר להם לישראל הם חוזרים וצועקים מרעב וצמא
ומיד הקב״ה נגלה להם בכבודו שנאמר וראו כל בשר יחדו. [28] ומלך המשיח יצמח
שם שנאמר וארו עם ענני שמיא וכתיב בתריה וליה יהיב שלטן. [29] ויפיח באותו
ארמילוס הרשע וימיתהו שנאמר וברוח שפתיו ימית רשע. [30] והקב״ה שורק
ומקבץ כל ישראל ומעלם לירושלים שנאמר אשרקה להם ואקבצם ותרד אש מן
השמים ותאכל ירושלם עד ג׳ אמות ומפנה הזרים הערלים והטמאים מתוכה ותרד
ירושלם בנויה ומשוכללת מן השמים שיש בה שבעים ושתים מרגליות שמבהיקות
מסוף העולם ועד סופו. [31] והולכים כל האומות לנוגה שנאמר והלכו גוים לאורך.
[32] וירד היכל בנוי מן השמים שהוא קשור בזבול שכן ראה משה ע״ה ברוח
הקודש שנאמר תביאמו ותטעמו. [33] ויושבין ישראל לבטח אלפים שנה ואוכלים
בהמות ולויתן וזיז בהמות שוחטין וזיז קורע לויתן בקרסוליו ומשה יבא וישחוט
זיז שדי. [34] ולקץ אלפים שנה הקב״ה יושב על כסא דין בעמק יהושפט. [35] ומיד
השמים והארץ בלין והולכים ובלים והחמה חפרה והלבנה בושה וההרים ימוטו
והגבעות תמוטנה כדי שלא יזכירו לישראל עונותיהם ושערי גהינם נפתחות בנחל
יהושע ושערי גן עדן במזרח ביום השלישי שנאמר יחיינו מיומים אלו ימי משיח
שהם אלפים שנה. [36] וביום הג׳ זה יום הדין ואוי לו לכל מי שמת בו והקב״ה
מעביר לפניו כל אומה ואומר להם אתם שמשתחוים לאלהי כסף וזהב ראו אם
יוכלו להציל אתכם. [37] ומיד עוברים ונשרפים שנאמר ישובו רשעים לשאולה
וישראל באים אחריהם והקב״ה אומר להם למי אתם משתחוים והם אומרים כי
אתה אבינו כי אברהם לא ידענו וכו׳. [38] ואומות העולם אומרים מתוך גהינם נראה
אם ישפוט את ישראל עמו כמו ששפט אותנו. [39] מיד הקב״ה עובר עם ישראל
באמצע גהינם לפניהם ונעשה לפניהם כמים קרים שנאמר ויעבור מלכם לפניהם ואומר כי
תלך במו אש לו תכוה. [40] ובאותה שעה ננערין פושעי ישראל לגהינם י״ב חדשים
ואח״כ הקב״ה מעלה אותם ויושבים בגן עדן ומתענגים מפירותיה שנאמר ועמך
כלם צדיקים. [41] רבי שמעון אומר עתיד הקב״ה לשרוק לדבורה אשר בקצה יאורי
מצרים ובאים ועושי׳ מלחמה בתוך מצרים. [42] והמלך הראשון שמנהיג אותם
ומוציאם הוא עבד שמרד על אדונו שנאמר כה אמר ה׳ לבזה נפש למתעב גוי
אותה מתועבת שבאומות אלו בני כנען לעבד מושלים והוא מורד על אדונו
ומתקבצים אליו אנשים שמרדו על אדוניהם ויוצאים במעט ומחזיקים מלכות
בגבורה ועושים מלחמה עם בני ישמעאל והורגים גבוריהם ויורשים ממונם ואת
רכושם. [43] והם אנשים מכוערים ולובשים שחורים ויוצאים ממזרח והם מהרים
ונמהרים שנ׳ הגוי המר והנמהר. [44] ועל הר מרום ישראל יעלו ויסבר לפרוץ בהיכל
ודלתים יעקירו ומרות יבכו. [45] וארבעה מלכים יעמדו עליהם שנים נשיאים ושנים
סגנים. [46] הראשון איש קונדק וממליך מלך בחייו מזרע המלוכה והמלך שימלוך
עליהם הולך בשפלות ועיניו יפות ושערו נאה וימות בשלום ואין נפרעין ממנו בזה
העולם. [47] ואחריו יעמוד מלך במחלוקת ויעמוד חיילים על נהר פרת והוא איש שחור
ביום אחד ויברח ויאסר ויאסר וכל הימים שהוא נאסר יהיה שלום בארץ ואחיו מושלים
בכל הארצות. [48] והמלך הרביעי שיעמוד עליהם אוהב כסף וזהב והוא איש שחור

וגבה קומה זקן וגרגר והורג אותן שהוציאוהו והמליכוהו ויעשה ספינות מנחשת
רימלא אותם כסף וזהב וטומן אותם תחת מימי פרת להצניעם לבניו והם עתידים
לישראל שנאמר ונתתי לך אוצרות חשך ומטמוני מסתרים. [49] ובימיו תפשע קרן
מערבית וישלח שם גייסו' רבים והורג בני מזרח וחוזר ומשלח גייסות רבות ובאים
והורגים את בני מערב ויושבים בארצם. [50] וזה לך האות שאתה רואה שבוע אחד
תחלתו מטר. [51] ובשניה חיצי רעב משתלחין. [52] ובשלישית רעב גדול.
[53] וברביעית לא רעב ולא שובע. [54] ובחמישית שובע גדול ויצמח כוכב אחד
ממזרח ובראשו שבט והוא כוכב של ישראל שנאמר דרך כוכב מיעקב. [55] ואם
האיר לטובתן של ישראל הוא ואז יצמח משיח בן דוד. [56] וזה לך האות כשאתה
רואה שנפל נירון מזרחי שבדמשק נפלה מלכות בני מזרח ואז יצמח הישועה
לישראל ומשיח בן דוד בא ויעלו לירושלם ויתענגו עליה שנאמר ירשו ארץ
ויתענגו על רב שלום. [57] האל ברחמיו ישלח לנו הגואל במהרה בימינו אמן:

Appendix 2

TEXTS REFERRING TO INGATHERING

Below are cited the principal biblical texts referring to the ingathering movements of
the eschatological programme, which are given to support the discussion in Chapter
6 regarding the verbal roots that predominate in each stage of ingathering. They are
arranged into three groups: first, the ingathering of Israel; secondly, the ingathering
of the hostile nations to battle, and thirdly, the ingathering of the earth to worship.
Some texts might be included in more than one group, as they seem to encompass
more than one stage of ingathering. This may be because the particular writer was not
aware of a full programme, or disagreed with parts of it, or simply overlooked them,
in bringing other stages together. Such texts can only be placed where they seem
most naturally to belong. This does not invalidate the present objective, which is
simply to note the general verbal tendencies of these texts.

Following the biblical texts, passages from apocryphal and pseudepigraphal literature are cited. These show the predominance of συνάγω in all references to the pre-
deliverance stages of ingathering, as noted in Chapter 6.

1. *The Ingathering of Israel*

Deut. 30.3-4. Yhwh your God will restore your fortunes [שׁוב שׁבות]... and will
gather you [קבץ] from all peoples where Yhwh your God has scattered you. If your
outcasts are in the uttermost parts of heaven, from there Yhwh your God will gather
[קבץ] you.

Isa. 11.12. He will raise a sign for the nations, and will assemble [אסף] the outcasts of Israel from the ends of the earth, and the dispersed of Judah will he gather
[קבץ] from the four corners of heaven.

Isa. 40.11. He will shepherd his flock like a shepherd, he will gather [קבץ] the
lambs in his arms.[1]

Isa. 49.5. Yhwh... formed me... to bring Jacob back [השׁיב] to him, and that
Israel might be gathered [אסף] to him.

Isa. 49.17, 18. Your sons hasten back... Lift your eyes and look around! All of
them gather [קבץ] and come to you.

---

1.   Given the deutero-Isaianic context of return from exile in Babylon, it is probably fair to see
some allusion to the gathering of the nation in this verse.

Isa. 52.11-12. Depart, depart, go out from there... Yhwh will go before you, the God of Israel will be your ingathering [אסף].

Isa. 54.7. For a brief moment I forsook you, but with great mercies I will gather [קבץ] you.

Isa. 56.8. Lord Yhwh says, the gatherer [קבץ] of the outcasts of Israel...

Isa. 58.8. The glory of Yhwh will ingather [אסף] you.

Jer. 4.5. Sound the trumpet throughout the land! Cry aloud and say, 'Gather together [אסף]! Let us flee to the fortified cities!'

Jer. 23.3. Then I will gather [קבץ] the remnant of my flock out of all the countries where I have driven them, and I will bring them back [השׁיב] to their fold.

Jer. 29.14. 'I will gather [קבץ] you from all the nations and places where I banished you,' declares Yhwh, 'and will bring you back to the place from which I exiled you.'

Jer. 31.8. See, I will bring them from the north land and gather [קבץ] them from the ends of the earth (v. 8).

Jer. 31.10. He who scattered Israel will gather [קבץ] him, and keep him as a shepherd keeps his flock.

Jer. 32.37. I will surely gather them [קבץ] from all the lands where I banish them.

Ezek. 11.17. Therefore say, 'Thus says Lord Yhwh: "I will gather [קבץ] you from the peoples and assemble [אסף] you out of the countries where you have been scattered."'

Ezek. 20.34-36. And I will bring you out of the peoples, and gather [קבץ] you out of the lands where you have been scattered.

Ezek. 20.41. As a pleasing odour I will accept you, when I bring you out [הוצא] from the peoples and gather [קבץ] you out of the countries where you have been scattered.

Ezek. 28.25. Thus says Lord Yhwh: 'When I gather [קבץ] the house of Israel from the peoples among whom they are scattered... then they shall dwell in their own land.

Ezek. 34.12-13. I will seek out my sheep... and I will bring them out from the peoples, and gather [קבץ] them from the countries, and will bring them into their own land.

Ezek. 37.21. I... will gather [קבץ] from all sides, and bring them to their own land.

Ezek. 38.12. ... the people who were gathered [אסף] from the nations.

Ezek. 39.27. ... when I have brought them back [שׁבב] from the peoples and gathered [קבץ] them from their enemies' lands.

Hos. 2.2 [1.11]. And the sons of Judah and the sons of Israel will be gathered [קבץ] as one, and they will appoint one leader, and go up [עלה] from the earth.

Mic. 2.12. I will surely gather [אסף אאסף] all of you, Jacob. I will gather [קבץ אקבץ] the remnant of Israel; I will set them together like sheep in a fold, like a flock in its pasture.

Mic. 4.6-7. I will assemble [אסף] the lame and gather [קבץ] those who have been driven away and those whom I have injured. And I will make the lame a remnant and the ones who have strayed afar a strong nation.

Zeph. 3.19-20. I will rescue the lame and gather [קבץ] the outcast... I will bring you home at the time when I gather [קבץ] you together.

Zech. 10.8-10. I will gather [קבץ] them... Though I scattered them among the nations... I will bring them back [השיב] from the land of Egypt, and gather [קבץ] them from Assyria.

Ps. 106.47. Save us, Yhwh our God, and gather [קבץ] us from among the nations.

Ps. 107.2-3. Let the redeemed of Yhwh say so, whom he has . . . gathered in [קבץ] from the lands.

Neh. 1.8-9. Remember the word which you commanded your servant Moses, saying, '. . . even if your exiles are at the farthest horizon, I will gather [קבץ] them from there and bring them to the place which I have chosen.'

Other texts referring to the ingathering of Israel without employing the verbs אסף or קבץ are as follows.

Isa. 35.10; 51.11. The redeemed of Yhwh will return. They will enter Zion with singing, and eternal joy upon their heads. Gladness and joy will overtake them, and sorrow and sighing will flee away.

Jer. 3.12, 14, 15. 'Return, faithless Israel', declares Yhwh... 'Return, faithless people', declares Yhwh, 'for I am your husband. I will choose you—one from a town and two from a clan—and bring you to Zion. Then I will give you shepherds after my own heart...'

Jer. 12.14-15. I will uproot the house of Judah... And after I have uprooted them I will relent and have compassion on them and bring them back, each one to his inheritance and each one to his land.

Jer. 16.14-15. 'Therefore the days are coming', declares Yhwh, 'when it will no longer be said, "As Yhwh lives, who brought up the sons of Israel from the land of Egypt", but, "As Yhwh lives, who brought up [עלה] the sons of Israel from the north land and from all the lands in which he scattered them."' For I will restore them to the land I gave their fathers.

Jer. 23.7-8. 'Therefore the days are coming', declares Yhwh, 'when they will no longer say, "As Yhwh lives, who brought up the sons of Israel from the land of Egypt", but, "As Yhwh lives, who brought up [עלה] and who brought back the seed of the house of Israel from the north land and from all the lands where he scattered them."' And they will live in their own land.

Jer. 24.6. . . . the exiles from Judah, whom I sent away from this place to the land of the Chaldeans... I will bring them back to this land.

Jer. 30.3. 'The days are coming', declares Yhwh, 'when I will restore the fortunes of my people Israel and Judah, and restore them to the land I gave their fathers to possess.'

Jer. 30.10. I will surely save you out of a distant place, your descendants from the land of their exile. Jacob will again have peace and security.

Jer. 31.16-17. They will return from the land of the enemy... Your children will return to their own land.

Jer. 31.23. Again they will say these words in the land of Judah and in its cities, when I turn back their captivity: 'Yhwh bless you, righteous pasture,[2] holy hill.'

Jer. 33.26. I will restore their fortunes and have mercy on them.

Jer. 42.12. I will show you compassion so that he will have compassion on you and restore you to your land.

Jer. 50.4-7. 'In those days, at that time', declares Yhwh, 'the people of Israel and the people of Judah together will go in tears to seek Yhwh their God. They will ask the way to Zion... My people have been lost sheep; their shepherds have led them astray.'

Jer. 50.19. I will bring Israel back to his own pasture.

Ezek. 37.12. Thus says Lord Yhwh: 'Behold, I open your graves and I will bring you up from your graves, my people, and I will bring you to the land of Israel.'

Ezek. 39.25, 28. I will now bring Jacob back from captivity... Then they will know that I am Yhwh their God, for though I sent them into exile among the nations, I will gather [כנס] them to their own land, leaving none behind.

Hos. 3.5. Afterwards the sons of Israel will return and seek Yhwh their God and David their king. They will come fearfully to Yhwh and his blessings in the last days.

Hos. 11.5-11. When he roars his children will come trembling from the west. They will come trembling like birds from Egypt, like doves from Assyria. 'I will settle them in their homes', declares Yhwh.

Amos 9.14-15. I will bring back my exiled people Israel; they will rebuild the ruined cities and live in them.

Obad. 20. The exiles in Halah who are of the sons of Israel shall possess Phoenicia as far as Zarephat; and the exiles of Jerusalem who are in Sepharad shall possess the cities of the Negev.[3]

Mic. 4.10. You will go to Babylon. There you will be rescued. There Yhwh will redeem you from the hand of your foes.

Zeph. 2.1. Gather yourselves and gather [קשש], shameful nation, before the appointed time arrives...

Zech 8.7-8. Thus says Yhwh Tsebaoth: 'I will save my people from the countries of the sunrise and the sunset. I will bring them, and they will dwell in the midst of Jerusalem.'

Zech 9.12. I will free your captives from the pit with no water in it. Return to your stronghold, prisoners of hope.

Ps. 147.2. Yhwh builds up Jerusalem; the dispersed of Israel he gathers [כנס].

2. The Gathering of the Hostile Nations

Isa. 24.21-22. In that day Yhwh will punish the powers in the heavens above and the kings on the earth below. They will be gathered together [אספו אספה], prisoners in a

---

2. See the comments in Chapter 6, pp. 188-89, regarding the most frequent use of נוה as meaning *pasture*.

3. See Chapter 5, p. 162 n. 100 for a discussion of the interpretation of this verse.

pit, and locked in confinement. And after many days they will muster an army.[4]

Jer. 12.7-9. I will give the one I love into the hands of her enemies... Go and gather [אסף] all the wild beasts; bring them to devour.[5]

Ezek. 16.37, 40. I am going to gather [קבץ] all your lovers... I will gather [קבץ] them against you all around... And they will bring up [עלה] a host against you, who will stone you and hack you to pieces with their swords.

Hos. 10.10. I will punish them. Nations will be gathered [אסף] against them.

Joel 4[3].2. I will gather [קבץ] all nations and bring them down to the Valley of Jehoshaphat.

Joel 4[3].11-12. Come quickly, all nations from all around, and gather [קבץ] there. Make your warriors come down, Yhwh! Let them advance into the Valley of Jehoshaphat, for there I will sit to judge all the nations all around.

Mic 4.11-12. But now many nations are gathered [אסף] against you saying, 'Let her be defiled and our eyes will gloat on Zion!' But they do not know the thoughts of Yhwh; and they do not understand his council. For he gathers [קבץ] them like sheaves to the threshing floor.

Zeph. 3.8. I have decided to assemble [אסף] the nations, to gather [קבץ] the kingdoms, and to pour out my wrath on them.

Zech 12.3. On that day I will make Jerusalem an immovable rock for all the peoples... and all the nations of the earth will be gathered [אסף] against her.

Zech 14.2. I will gather [אסף] all the nations of the earth to fight against Jerusalem.

3. *The Gathering to Worship on Zion*

Some texts from section 1 above, which refer simply to the ingathering of Israel, might be added to this section. It is not always clear whether a particular reference is to a pre- or post-conflict ingathering. Some writers may not have known of a tradition about a conflict at the time of ingathering. However, some, particularly those of the Isaianic tradition, do appear to have considered that further Israelites were to gather along with the visiting foreign nations after a time of conflict (Isa. 66.20).

Isa. 2.2-4. In the latter days, the mountain of the house of Yhwh will be established as the chief mountain; it will be raised above the hills, and all the nations will stream to it. Many peoples will come and say, 'Come, let us go up [עלה] the mountain of Yhwh'.

Isa. 11.10. In that day the shoot of Jesse shall stand as a banner to the peoples; him shall the nations seek, and his dwellings shall be glorious.

4. The meaning *to muster an army* is attested for פקד (*BDB*: 823). For a discussion of interpretation of biblical usage of this most polysemic of verbs, see Grossfeld 1984: 83-101. He concludes that its basic range of meanings, from which the others derive, is 'to take note of, to notice, to consider, to attend to with care' (p. 92).

5. I assume here that *wild beasts* is a metaphor for the ravaging nations. This is supported not only by v. 7, cited above, but also by the animal terms, *lion, bird of prey*, describing Israel at 12.8-9.

Isa. 27.12, 13. In that day Yhwh will thresh from the grain/flood [שבלת] of Euphrates to the Wadi of Egypt, and you will be gathered [לקטו] one by one, sons of Israel. And in that day will sound a great *shofar,* and those perishing in the land of Assyria will come, and those banished in the land of Egypt, and they will worship Yhwh on the holy mountain in Jerusalem.

Isa. 43.9. All the nations gather [נקבצו] together and the peoples assemble [יאספו].

Isa. 49.17, 18. Your sons hasten back, your destroyers and desolators depart from you. Lift your eyes and look around! All of them gather [נקבצו] and come to you.

Isa. 56.6-8. And foreigners who bind themselves to Yhwh... these I will bring to my holy mountain... for my house will be called a house of prayer for all nations. Lord Yhwh declares... 'I will gather [אקבץ] yet others to them, besides the already gathered [נקבציו].'

Isa. 60.3-4. Nations will come to your light, and kings to the brightness of your rising. Lift your eyes and look around! All of them gather [נקבצו] and come to you; your sons come from afar, and your daughters are carried on the arm.

Isa. 66.18, 21, 23. 'And I, because of their deeds and their plans, am coming to gather [לקבץ] all nations and tongues, and they will come and see my glory.'... 'And I will select some of them to be priests and Levites', says Yhwh[6]... 'From one New Moon to another and from one Sabbath to another, all mankind will come and bow down before me', says Yhwh.

Jer. 3.17. At that time they will call Jerusalem 'The Throne of Yhwh', all nations will gather [קוו] to her, to the name of Yhwh in Jerusalem.

Mic 4.1-2. In the latter days, the mountain of the house of Yhwh will be established as the chief mountain; it will be raised above the hills, and peoples will stream to it. Many nations will come and say, 'Come, let us go up [עלה] the mountain of Yhwh.'

Zeph. 3.8-10. Then will I purify the lips of the peoples, that all of them may call on the name of Yhwh and serve him shoulder to shoulder. From beyond the rivers of Cush my worshippers, my scattered people, will bring me offerings.

Zech 8.20-23. Thus says Yhwh Tsebaoth: There will yet come peoples and the inhabitants of many cities. And the inhabitants of one will go to another, saying, 'Let us go now to entreat the face of Yhwh and seek Yhwh Tsebaoth. I myself am going.' And many peoples will come, and powerful nations, to seek Yhwh Tsebaoth in Jerusalem and to entreat the face of Yhwh. Thus says Yhwh Tsebaoth: In those days, ten men from all languages of nations will seize, and they will seize by the hem of his robe one man of Judah, saying, 'Let us go with you, for we have heard that God is with you.'

Zech 14.16. Then the survivors of the nations that attacked Jerusalem will go up [עלה] year after year to worship the king, Yhwh Tsebaoth, and to celebrate the Feast of Sukkoth. If any of the tribes of the earth do not go up [עלה] to Jerusalem to worship the king, Yhwh Tsebaoth, they will have no rain. If the tribe of Egypt do not go up [עלה] and enter in, then upon them shall come the plague with which Yhwh

---

6. This takes place in the aftermath of a suppressed rebellion (66.24).

smites the nations that do not go up [עלה] to the Feast of Sukkoth. This will be the penalty for Egypt and the penalty for all the nations that do not go up [עלה] to celebrate the Feast of Sukkoth.

Ps. 47.8-10 [7-9]. God has become king over the nations; God has sat down upon the throne of his holiness. The nobles of the nations assemble [אסף] as the people of the God of Abraham. For the shields of earth belong to God. He is greatly ascended.

Ps. 65.3 [2]. Hearer-of-prayer, to you all flesh will come.

Ps. 86.9. All nations that you made will come and will bow down before you, Lord, and glorify your name.

Ps. 102.22-3 [21-2]. To proclaim in Zion the name of Yhwh, and his praise in Jerusalem, when peoples are gathered together [קבץ], and kingdoms, to serve Yhwh.

2 Chron. 36.23. Thus says Cyrus, King of Persia, 'Yhwh the God of heaven has given me all the kingdoms of the earth and has appointed me to build for him a house in Jerusalem which is in Judah. Anyone of you from all his people, Yhwh his God be with him, and let him ascend [עלה].'

4. Apocryphal and Pseudepigraphal Texts

Tob. 13.5. Again he will show mercy, and will gather [συνάξει] us from all the nations among whom you (*or* we) have been scattered.

Tob. 13.13. Rejoice and be glad for the sons of the righteous; for they will be gathered together [συναχθήσονται].

Sir. 36.1, 13 [NRSV; LXX: 36.1, 10; RSV: 36.1, 11][7] Have mercy upon us, O Lord... Gather [σύναγε] all the tribes of Jacob.

Bar. 4.36-37. Look toward the east, Jerusalem, and see the joy that is coming to you from God! Behold your sons are coming, whom you sent away; they are coming gathered [συνηγμένοι] from east and west.

Bar. 5.5. Arise, Jerusalem, stand upon the height and look toward the east, and see your children gathered [συνηγμένα] from west and east.

2 Macc. 1.23-29. And the priests prayed... O Lord... Gather together [ἐπισυνάγαγε] our scattered people, deliver them that serve among the heathen, look upon them that are despised and abhorred, and let the heathen know that you are our God. Punish them that oppress us and proudly do us wrong. Plant your people again in your holy place, as Moses said.

2 Macc. 2.5, 7. And when Jeremiah came there, he found a hollow cave, in which he laid the tabernacle, and the ark, and the altar of incense, and he sealed the door... saying, 'As for that place, it shall be unknown until the time that God gather [συναγάγῃ ὁ θεὸς ἐπισυναγωγὴν] his people again together, and receive them unto mercy.'

---

7. The enumeration of the verses of this chapter varies in the different versions, due to alternative numeration and division of the hemistichs of the text.

2 Macc. 2.17-18. We hope also that God... as he promised in the law, will soon have mercy upon us and will gather [ἐπισυνάξει] us from everywhere under heaven into his holy place.

Jub. 1.15. After this they will turn to me from amongst the Gentiles with all their heart and with all their soul and with all their strength, and I shall gather them from among the Gentiles.

T. Naph. 8.3. God will appear... to save the race of Israel, and to assemble [ἐπισυνάξει] the righteous from among the nations.

T. Asher 7.7. But the Lord will gather [ἐπισυνάξει] you in faith through the hope on his compassion.

T. Ben. 10.11. All Israel will be gathered together [συναχθήσεται] unto the Lord.

Pss. Sol. 11.3. Stand up on high, Jerusalem, and behold your children gathered together [συνηγμένα] from the east and the west by the Lord.

Pss. Sol. 17.28. And he shall gather together [συνάξει] a holy people.

Pss. Sol. 17.50. Blessed are they that shall be born in those days, to behold the blessing of Israel that God shall bring to pass in the gathering [συναγωγη] of the tribes.

2 Bar. 78.7. He will not forever forget or forsake our offspring, but with much mercy will assemble again all those who were dispersed.

BIBLIOGRAPHY

Anonymous Reference Works

1960 *Talmud Yerushalmi* (Jerusalem: Torah l'Am).

1970 מקראות גדולות תורה חמש מגילות נביאים וכתובים (Torah, prophets, and writings, with rabbinic commentary) (10 vols; Jerusalem: Shiloh).

1977 *Forms of Prayer* (Oxford University Press: The Reform Synagogues of Great Britain).

Other Works by Author or Editor

Abramovitch, S., and J. Brand
1971 'Gaon', *EncJud*: VII, 315-24.

Abravanel, I.
1640 פירוש על נביאים אחרונים (Commentary on the Latter Prophets) (Amsterdam).

Achelis, H. (ed.)
1897 *Hippolyt's kleinere exegetische und homiletische Schriften*, in G.N. Bonwetsch and H. Achelis (eds.), *Hippolytus*. Bd. I. (GCS, 1; Leipzig: Hinrichs).

Ackroyd, P.R.
1962 'Zechariah', in M. Black and H.H. Rowley (eds.), *Peake's Commentary on the Bible* (Nashville: Thomas Nelson): 646-55.

Ackroyd, P.R., and C.F. Evans
1970 *The Cambridge History of the Bible* (Cambridge: Cambridge University Press).

Aland, K.
1983 *Vollständige Konkordanz zum Griechischen Neuen Testament* (2 vols.; Berlin: de Gruyter).

Albrektson, B.
1963 *Studies in the Text and Theology of the Book of Lamentations with a Critical Edition of the Peshitta Text* (STL, 21; Lund: Gleerup).

Aletti, J.-N., and J. Trublet
1983 *Approche poétique et théologique des psaumes* (Paris: Cerf).

Alexander, J.A.
1850 *The Psalms* (New York: Baker & Scribner).

Allegro, J.M.
1956a *The Dead Sea Scrolls* (Harmondsworth: Penguin Books).
1956b 'Further Light on the History of the Qumran Sect', *JBL* 75: 89-95.

Allegro, J. *et al.*
1955–82   *Discoveries in the Judaean Desert* (7 vols.; Oxford: Clarendon Press).
Allen, L.C.
1983   *Psalms 101–150* (Waco, TX: Word Books).
1986   'David as Exemplar of Spirituality: The Redactional Function of Ps 19', *Bib* 67: 544-46.
Allenbach, J. *et al.* (eds.)
1975–91   *Biblia Patristica* (Centre national de la récherche scientifique: Paris).
Alter, R.
1985   *The Art of Biblical Poetry* (New York: Basic Books).
Altmann, A. (trans. and ed.)
1946   Sa'adya Gaon, *The Book of Doctrines and Beliefs* (Philosophia Judaica Series; Oxford: Phaidon Press).
Anderson, A.A.
1972   *The Book of Psalms* (NCB; 2 vols.; London: Oliphants).
Anderson, B.W.
1983   *Out of the Depths* (Philadelphia: Westminster Press).
Arens, A.
1961   *Die Psalmen in Gottesdienst des Alten Bundes* (Trierer theologische Studien, 11; Paulinus: Trier).
1962   'Hat der Psalter seinen "Sitz im Leben" in der synagogalen Lese–ordnung des Pentateuch?', in R. de Langhe (ed.), *Le Psautier; ses origines, ses problèmes littéraires, son influence. Etudes présentées aux XIIe Journées Bibliques* (Orientalia et Biblica Lovaniensia, 4; Louvain: Publications Universitaires, 1962): 107-31.
Argyle, A.W.
1956   'Joseph the Patriarch in Patristic Teaching', *ExpTim* 67: 199-201.
Armfield, H.T.
1874   *The Gradual Psalms* (London: J.T. Hayes).
Arndt, W.F., and F.W. Gingrich
1979   *A Greek–English Lexicon of the New Testament and Other Early Christian Literature* (Chicago: University of Chicago Press).
Auffret, P.
1982   *La sagesse a bâti sa maison: Etudes de structures littéraires dans l'Ancien Testament et specialment dans les Psaumes* (Fribourg: Editions Universaires).
1986   'Complements sur la structure littéraire du Ps 2 et son rapport au Ps 1', *Biblische Notizen* 35: 7-13.
1988   ' "Allez, fils, entendez-moi": Etude structurelle du Psaume 34 et son rapport au Psaume 33', *Eglise et Théologie* 19: 5-31.
1989   'Note on the literary structure of Psalm 134', trans. D.J.A. Clines, *JSOT* 45: 87-89.
1991   'Yahve règne: Etude structurelle du Psaume 93', *ZAW* 103: 101-109.
1992   'La droite du très-haut. Etude structurelle du Psaume 77', *SJOT* 6: 92-122.
1993   *Voyez de vos yeux: Etude structurelle de vingt psaumes dont le psaume 119* (Leiden: Brill).

Augustine of Hippo
  Enarrationes in Psalmos (CCSL, 38–40; Turnhout: Brepols, 1956).
Auld, A.G.
1983 'Prophets through the Looking Glass: Between Writings and Moses',
  JSOT 27: 3-23, 41-44.
1984 'Prophets and Prophecy in Jeremiah and Kings', *ZAW* 96: 66-82.
1986 *Amos* (OTG; Sheffield: JSOT Press)
Baethgen, D.F.
1885 'Der Psalmencommentar des Theodor von Mopsuestia in syrischer
  Bearbeitung', *ZAW* 5: 53-101.
1886 'Siebzehn makkabäische Psalmen nach Theodor von Mopsuestia',
  ZAW 6: 261-88.
1897 *Die Psalmen* (HAT, 2.2; Göttingen: Vandenhoeck & Ruprecht).
Baillet, M.
1982 *Discoveries in the Judean Desert. VII. Qumran Grotte 4.III* (Oxford:
  Clarendon Press).
Barnes, W.E.
1904 *The Peshitta Psalter according to the West Syrian Text* (Cambridge:
  Cambridge University Press).
1931 *The Psalms* (Westminster Commentaries; 2 vols.; London: Methuen).
Baron, S.W.
1957–83 *A Social and Religious History of the Jews* (18 vols.; New York:
  Columbia University Press).
Barr, J.
1961 *The Semantics of Biblical Language* (London: Oxford University
  Press).
Barraclough, G. (ed.)
1979 *The Times Atlas of World History* (London: Times Books).
Barrick, W.B., and J.R. Spencer (eds.)
1984 *In the Shelter of Elyon* (JSOTSup, 31; Sheffield: JSOT Press).
Barth, C.
1976 'Concatenatio in Ersten Buch des Psalters', in B. Benzing, O. Böcher
  and G. Mayer (eds.), *Wort und Wirklichkeit: Studien zur afrikanistik
  und orientalistik* (Meisenheim am Glan: Hain): 30-40.
Barthélemy, D., and J.T. Milik
1955 *Discoveries in the Judean Desert, I* (Oxford: Clarendon Press).
Barton, J.
1986 *Oracles of God* (London: Darton, Longman, & Todd).
Bazak, Y.
1990 'The Six Chapters of the 'Hallel'—Numeralogical Ornamentation and
  Formal Structure (Psalms 113–118)', *Beth Mikra* 34: 182-91.
1991 'The Set of the Six Chapters of the 'Hallel'—Numeralogical Ornamentation and Formal Structure', *Beth Mikra* 36: 91-93.
Beaucamp, E.
1979a *Le Psautier* (2 vols.; Paris: Gabalda).
1979b 'L'unité du recueil des montées, Psaumes 120–134', *Liber Annuus
  Studii Biblici Franciscani* 29: 73-90.

Becking, B.
1992   *The Fall of Samaria: An Historical and Archaeological Study* (Leiden: Brill).
Bellinger, W.H., Jr
1984   *Psalmody and Prophecy* (JSOTSup, 27; Sheffield: JSOT Press).
Bentzen, A.
1955   *King and Messiah* (London: Lutterworth).
Berlin, A.
1983   *Poetics and Interpretation of Biblical Narrative* (Sheffield: Almond Press).
1985   *The Dynamics of Biblical Parallelism* (Bloomington: Indiana University Press).
1987   'On the Interpretation of Psalm 133', in E.R. Follis (ed.), *Directions in Biblical Hebrew Poetry* (JSOTSup, 40; Sheffield: JSOT Press): 141-47.
1989   'Lexical Cohesion and Biblical Interpretation', *Hebrew Studies* 30: 29-40.
Berlin, A., E.L. Greenstein and S.A. Geller
1982   *A Sense of Text* (Winona Lake, IN: Eisenbrauns).
Bertholdt, L.
1811   *Christologia Judaeorum* (Erlangen).
Betz, O.
1960   *Offenbarung und Schriftsforschung in der Qumrantexte* (WUNT, 6; Tübingen: Mohr).
Betz, O., and R. Riesner
1994   *Jesus, Qumran, and the Vatican* (London: SCM).
Beuken, W.A.M.
1989   'Servant and Herald of Good Tidings: Isaiah 61 as an Interpretation of Isaiah 40–55', in J. Vermeylen (ed.), *The Book of Isaiah—Le Livre d'Isaïe. Les oracles et leur relectures. Unité et complexité de l'ouvrage* (BETL, 81; Leuven: Leuven University Press): 411-42.
Beyerlin, W.
1982   *We Are Like Dreamers: Studies in Psalm 126* (trans. D. Livingstone; Edinburgh: T. & T. Clark).
Beyerlin, W., with H. Brunner *et al.*
1978   *Near Eastern Religious Texts Relating to the Old Testament* (trans. J. Bowden; London: SCM Press).
Biggs, R.D.
1967   'More Babylonian "Prophecies"', *Iraq* 29.
Black, M., and H.H. Rowley (eds.)
1962   *Peake's Commentary on the Bible* (Nashville: Thomas Nelson).
Black, M.C.
1991   *The Rejected and Slain Messiah Who Is Coming with his Angels* (Ann Arbor, MI: University Microfilms International).
Blenkinsopp, J.
1990   *Ezekiel* (Interpretation Commentary; Louisville, KY: John Knox).
Bockmuehl, M.
1991   ' "The Trumpet Shall Sound": *Shofar* Symbolism and its Reception in Early Christianity', in Horbury (ed.): 199-225.

Bodenheimer, F.S.
1960   *Animal and Man in Bible Lands* (Leiden: Brill).
de Boer, P.A.H.
1984   'Psalm 81.6a: Observations on Translation and Meaning of One
            Hebrew Line', in W.B. Barrick and J.R. Spencer (eds.), *In the Shelter
            of Elyon* (JSOTSup, 31; Sheffield: JSOT Press).
Borger, R.
1956   *Die Inschriften Asarhaddons Könige von Assyrien* (Archiv für Orient-
            forschung Beiheft, 9; Graz: E. Weidner).
Bornhaüser, K.
1928   *Das Johannesevangelium: eine Missionsschrift für Israel* (Gütersloh:
            C. Bertelsmann).
Bowman, J.
1971   'The Identity and Date of the Unnamed Feast of John 5.1', in H.
            Goedicke (ed.), *Near Eastern Studies in Honor of William Foxwell
            Albright* (Baltimore: The Johns Hopkins University Press).
Braslavi, J., and M. Avi-Yonah
            'Mount of Olives', *EncJud*: XII, 481-85.
Braude, W.G. (trans.)
1959   *The Midrash on Psalms* (Yale Judaica Series, 13; 2 vols.; New Haven:
            Yale University Press).
1968   *Pesikta Rabbati* (Yale Judaica Series, 18; 2 vols.; New Haven: Yale
            University Press).
Braude, W.G., and I.J. Kapstein
1981   *Tanna Debe Eliyyahu* (Philadelphia: Jewish Publication Society of
            America).
Brennan, J.P.
1976   'Some Hidden Harmonies in the Fifth Book of Psalms,' in R.F.
            McNamara (ed.), *Essays in Honor of Joseph P. Brennan* (Rochester,
            NY: St Bernard's Seminary).
1980   'Psalms 1–8: Some Hidden Harmonies', *BTB* 10: 25-29.
Brettler, M., and M. Fishbane (eds.)
1993   *Minhah le-Nahum* (JSOTSup, 154; Sheffield: JSOT Press).
Briggs, C.A., and E.G. Briggs
1906–1907   *The Book of Psalms* (ICC; 2 vols.; Edinburgh: T. & T. Clark).
Brock, S.P.
1967   *Testamentum Iobi* (Leiden: Brill).
Brockington, L.H.
1984   'The Syriac Apocalypse of Baruch', in H.F.D. Sparks (ed.), *The Apo-
            cryphal Old Testament* (Oxford: Clarendon Press): 835-95.
Brooke, G.J.
1988   'Christ and the Law in John 7–10,' in B. Lindars (ed.), *Law and
            Religion: Essays in the Place of the Law in Israel and Early Christ-
            ianity* (London: SPCK): 102-12.
1989–90   'Psalms 105 and 106 at Qumran', *RevQ* 14: 267-92.
1993   '4QTestament of Levi[d] (?) and the Messianic Servant High Priest', in
            P. de Boer (ed.), *From Jesus to John: Essays on Jesus and New*

Testament Christology in Honour of Marinus de Jonge (JSNTSup, 84; Sheffield: JSOT Press): 83-100.

1994   'Isa 40.3 and the Wilderness Community', in Brooke (ed.) with F.G. Martínez, *New Qumran Texts and Studies: Proceedings of the First Meeting of the International Organization for Qumran Studies, Paris 1992* (Leiden: Brill): 117-32.

Bruce, F.F.

1963   *Israel and the Nations* (Exeter: Paternoster Press).

1966   *Second Thoughts on the Dead Sea Scrolls* (Exeter: Paternoster Press).

1968   *This Is That: The New Testament Development of Old Testament Themes* (Exeter: Paternoster; Grand Rapids: Eerdmans).

1982   *1 and 2 Thessalonians* (WBC, 45; Waco, TX: Word Books).

Brueggemann, W.

1984   *The Message of the Psalms* (Minneapolis: Augsburg).

1988   *Israel's Praise* (Philadelphia: Fortress Press).

1991   'Bounded by Obedience and Praise: The Psalms as Canon', *JSOT* 50: 63-92.

1993   'Response to James L. Mays, "The Question of Context"', in McCann 1993: 29-41.

Buber, M.

1944   *Israel and Palestine* (trans. S. Godman; ET 1952; London: East and West Library).

1985   *The Legend of the Baal Shem* (ET; trans. M. Friedman; Edinburgh: T. & T. Clark).

Buber, S.

1885   *Midrash Tanhuma* (Vilnius).

1891   *Midrash Tehillim* (Vilnius: Wittwe & Gebrüder Romm).

Buchanan, G.W.

1968   'The Samaritan Origin of the Gospel of John,' 149-175 in Neusner (ed.), *Religions in Antiquity: Essays in Memory of E.R. Goodenough* (Leiden: Brill).

Bullinger, E.W.

1908   *'The Chief Musician': or Studies in the Psalms and their Titles* (London: Eyre & Spottiswoode).

Bultmann, R.

1971   *The Gospel of John* (trans. G.R. Beasley-Murray, R.W.N. Hoare and J.K. Riches; Philadelphia: Westminster Press).

Busink, Th.A.

1970–80   *Der Tempel von Jerusalem von Salomo bis Herodes* (2 vols.; Leiden: Brill).

Buss, M.J.

1963   'The Psalms of Asaph and Korah', *JBL* 82: 382-92.

Cadiou, R.

1936   *Commentaires inédits des Psaumes: Etudes sur les textes d'Origène contenus dans le ms. Vindobonensis 8* (Paris).

Caird, G.B.

1980   *The Language and Imagery of the Bible* (London: Duckworth).

Calvin, J.
1557   *Commentary on the Book of Psalms* (trans. J. Anderson; 5 vols.; Edin-
            burgh: Calvin Translation Society, 1845–49).
Caquot, A., J-M. de Tarragon and J-L. Cunchillos
1989   *Textes Ougaritiques* (Paris: Editions du Cerf).
Carley, K.W.
1974   *The Book of the Prophet Ezekiel* (CNEB; Cambridge: Cambridge
            University Press).
Carrière, J.-M.
1991   'Le Ps 72 est-il un psaume messianique?', *Bib* 72: 49-69.
Carson, D.
1987   'The Purpose of the Fourth Gospel: John 20.30-31 Reconsidered',
            JBL 108: 639-51.
Cassuto, U.
1973   'The Sequence and Arrangement of the Biblical Sections,' in *Biblical
            and Oriental Studies*, I.1-6 (2 vols.; Jerusalem: Magnes).
Castelli, D.
1874   *Il Messia Secondo gli Ebrei* (Florence: Successori le Monier).
Cathcart, K.J., and R.P. Gordon (trans. and eds.)
1989   *The Targum of the Minor Prophets* (Aramaic Bible, 14; Wilmington,
            DE: Michael Glazier).
Ceresko, A.R.
1989   'Psalm 121: A Prayer of a Warrior?', *Bib* 70: 496-510.
1990   'The Sage in the Psalms', in J.G. Gammie and L.G. Purdue (eds.), *The
            Sage in Israel and the Ancient Near East* (Winona Lake, IN: Eisen-
            brauns): 217-30.
Chance, J.B.
1988   *Jerusalem, the Temple, and the New Age in Luke–Acts* (Macon, GA:
            Mercer University).
Charles, R.H.
1908   *The Greek Versions of the Testaments of the Twelve Patriarchs* (Oxford:
            Clarendon Press).
1913   *The Apocrypha and Pseudepigrapha of the Old Testament* (Oxford:
            Clarendon Press).
1917   *The Book of Jubilees* (London: SPCK).
Charlesworth, J.H.
1983–85   *The Old Testament Pseudepigrapha* (2 vols.; London: Darton, Long-
            man & Todd).
1991   *Graphic Concordance to the Dead Sea Scrolls* (Tübingen: Mohr [Paul
            Siebeck]).
1992   *The Messiah* (Augsburg, Minneapolis: Fortress Press).
Chernoff, R.
1991   'Tehillim—the Psalms', *JBQ* 19: 191-94.
Cheyne, T.K.
1888   *The Book of Psalms* (London: Kegan Paul, Trench).
1904   *The Book of Psalms* (2 vols.; London: Kegan Paul, Trench, Trübner).

Childs, B.S.
 1960   *Myth and Reality in the Old Testament* (London: SCM, Naperville, IL: Allenson).
 1969   'Psalm 8 in the Context of the Christian Canon', *Int* 23.20-31.
 1971   'Psalm Titles and Midrashic Exegesis', *JSS* 16: 137-50.
 1976   'Reflections on the Modern Study of the Psalms', in F.M. Cross (ed.), *Magnalia Dei. The Mighty Acts of God: Essays in Memory of G. Ernest Wright* (Garden City, NY: Doubleday): 377-88.
 1979   *Introduction to the Old Testament as Scripture* (Philadelphia: Fortress Press).
 1992   *Biblical Theology of the Old and New Testaments* (London: SCM Press).

Chilton, B. (ed. and trans.)
 1987   *The Isaiah Targum* (The Aramaic Bible, 11; Edinburgh: T. & T. Clark).

Clifford, R.J.
 1979   'The Temple in the Ugaritic Myth of Baal', in F.M. Cross (ed.), *Symposia* (Cambridge, MA: ASOR): 137-45.

Cohen, A.
 1945   *The Psalms* (Soncino Books of the Bible; Hindhead, Surrey: Soncino).

Cohen, A. (ed.)
 1913   *Midrash Rabbah 'al ha-Torah* (Warsaw).

Collins, A.Y.
 1976   *The Combat Myth in the Book of Revelation* (HDR, 9; Missoula, MT: Scholars Press).

Collins, J.J.
 1987   'The Development of the Sibylline Tradition', in W. Haase (ed.), *Aufstieg und Niedergang der Römischen Welt: Geschichte und Kultur Roms im Spiegel der Neueren Forschung*, 2.20.1 (Berlin: de Gruyter): 421-59.
 1983   'Sybilline Oracles', in Charlesworth 1983–85: I, 317-472.

Collins, T.
 1987   'Decoding the Psalms: A Structural Approach to the Psalter', *JSOT* 37: 41-60.

Cook, S.L.
 1992   'Apocalypticism and the Psalter', *ZAW* 104: 82-93.

Cooke, G.A.
 1905   *A Text-Book of North Semitic Inscriptions* (Oxford: Clarendon).
 1936   *The Book of Ezekiel* (ICC; Edinburgh: T. & T. Clark).

Couroyer, B.
 1971   'Dieu ou roi? Le vocatif dans le Psaume XLV (vv. 1-9)', *RB* 78: 233-41.

Cowley, A.E., and A. Neubauer
 1897   *The Original Hebrew of Ecclesiasticus XXXIX.15 to XLIX.11* (Oxford: Clarendon Press).

Cox, S.
 1885   *The Pilgrim Psalms* (London: Dickinson).

Coxe, A.C.
  1888   *Enarrationes in Psalmos* (5 vols.; Buffalo, NY).
Craigie, P.C.
  1983a   *Ezekiel* (Daily Study Bible; Edinburgh: Saint Andrew Press).
  1983b   *Psalms 1–50* (WBC, 19; Waco, TX: Word Books).
  1984   *The Twelve Prophets* (Daily Study Bible; 2 vols.; Edinburgh: Saint
              Andrew Press).
Craigie, P.C., J.F. Drinkard, Jr. and P.H. Kelley
  1991   *Jeremiah 1–15* (WBC, 26; Waco, TX: Word Books).
Croft, S.J.L.
  1987   *The Identity of the Individual in the Psalms* (JSOTSup, 44; Sheffield:
              JSOT Press).
Cross, F.L. (ed.)
  1974   *The Oxford Dictionary of the Christian Church* (Oxford: Oxford Uni-
              versity Press).
Crown, A.D.
  1967   'Some Traces of Heterodox Theology in the Samaritan Book of
              Joshua', *Bulletin of the John Rylands Library* 50: 178-98.
  1967–68   'Dositheans, Resurrection and a Messianic Joshua', *Antichthon* 1: 70-
              85.
Cunningham, W.
  1877   *A Dissertation on the Epistle of St Barnabas* (London: Macmillan).
Dahood, M.
  1965–70   *Psalms* (AB, 16-17A; 3 vols.; Garden City, NY: Doubleday).
Dalman, G.H.
  1888   *Der leidende und der sterbende Messias der synagoge* (Berlin:
              Reuther).
  1894   *Grammatik des jüdisch-palästinischen Aramäisch* (Leipzig: Hinrichs).
Dan, J.
  1971   'Zerubbabel, Book of', *EncJud*: XVI, 1002.
Danby, H. (ed. and trans.)
  1933   *The Mishnah* (Oxford: Clarendon Press).
Daniel, S.
  1971   'Bible: Greek: Septuagint', *EncJud*: IV, 851-56.
Daube, D.
  1963   *The Exodus Pattern in the Bible* (London: Faber & Faber).
Davenport, G.L.
  1971   *Eschatology in the Book of Jubilees* (Leiden: Brill).
Davidson, A.B.
  1906   *The Book of the Prophet Ezekiel* (Cambridge Bible for Schools and
              Colleges; Cambridge: Cambridge University Press).
Davidson, R.
  1983–85   *Jeremiah & Lamentations* (Daily Study Bible; 2 vols.; Edinburgh: St
              Andrew Press).
Davies, G.H.
  1973   'Psalm 95', *ZAW* 85: 183-95.
Davies, P.R.
  1979   'Passover and the Dating of the Aqedah', *JJS* 30: 59-67.

1983	*The Damascus Covenant: An Interpretation of the 'Damascus Document'* (JSOTSup, 25; Sheffield: JSOT Press).
1985	*Daniel* (OTG, 4; Sheffield: JSOT Press).
1988	'The Teacher of Righteousness and the "End of Days"', *Mémorial Jean Carmignac, RevQ* 13: 313-17.

Davies, P.R., and B.D. Chilton
| 1978 | 'The Aqedah: A Revised Tradition History', *CBQ* 40: 514-46. |

Day, J.
| 1985 | *God's Conflict with the Dragon and the Sea* (Cambridge: Cambridge University Press). |
| 1990 | *Psalms* (Sheffield: JSOT Press). |

Dekkers, E. (ed.)
| 1995 | *Clavis patrum latinorum* (CCSL; Steenbrugge: In Abbatia Saneti Petri, 3rd edn). |

Delcor, M. (ed.)
| 1952 | 'Les sources du Deutero-Zacharie et ses procedes d'emprunt', *RB* 59: 385-411. |
| 1978 | *Qumrân. Sa piété, sa théologie, et son milieu* (BETL, 46; Gembloux, Paris: Duculot; Louvain: Louvain University Press). |

Delitzsch, F.
1846	*Symbolae ad Psalmos illustrandos isagogicæ* (Leipzig).
1887	*Biblical Commentary on the Psalms* (trans. D. Eaton; 3 vols.; London: Hodder & Stoughton).
1890	*Messianische Weissagungen in geschichtlicher Folge* (Leipzig: Faber).

Deurloo, K.
| 1992 | 'Gedächtnis des Exils—Psalm 120–134,' *TK* 55.3: 28-34. |

Dietrich, M., and O. Loretz
| 1988 | 'Von hebräisch '*m / lpny* (Ps 72:5) zu ugaritisch '*m* vor', in L. Eslinger and G. Taylor (eds.), *Ascribe to the Lord* (JSOTSup, 67; Sheffield: JSOT Press): 109-116. |

Dietrich, M., O. Loretz and J. Sanmartin
| 1976 | *Die keilalphabetischen Texte aus Ugarit einschliesslich der keilalphabetischen Texte ausserhalb Ugarits* (Neukirchen–Vluyn: Neukirchener Verlag). |

Di Lella, A.A.
| 1966 | *The Hebrew Text of Sirach* (The Hague: Mouton). |

Dodd, C.H.
| 1953 | *The Interpretation of the Fourth Gospel* (Cambridge: Cambridge University Press). |
| 1953 | *According to the Scriptures: The Substructure of New Testament Theology* (New York: Charles Scribner's Sons). |

Donner, H.
| 1988 | 'Psalm 122', in W. Claassen (ed.), *Text and Context: Old Testament and Semitic Studies for F.C. Fensham* (JSOTSup, 48; Sheffield: JSOT Press). |

Driver, S.R.
| 1906 | *The Minor Prophets* (Century Bible; Edinburgh: T.C. & E.J. Jack). |

Driver, S.R., and H.C.O. Lanchester
1915   *The Books of Joel and Amos* (Cambridge: University Press, 2nd edn).
Drummond, J.
1877   *The Jewish Messiah* (London: Longmans, Green, & Co.).
Duhm, B.
1875   *Theologie der Propheten* (Bonn: Adolph Marcus).
1899   *Psalmen* (Leipzig and Tübingen: Mohr).
1902   *Das Buch Jesaja* (Göttingen: Vandenhoeck & Ruprecht, 2nd edn).
Dupont-Sommer, A.
1961   *The Essene Writings from Qumran* (trans. G. Vermes; Oxford: Basil Blackwell).
Durham, J.I.
1987   *Exodus* (WBC, 3; Waco, TX: Word Books).
Eaton, J.H.
1967   *Psalms* (London; SCM Press).
1976   *Kingship and the Psalms* (London: SCM Press).
Ebeling, E.
1953   *Die akkadische Gebetserie 'Handerhebung'* (Literarische Keilschrifttexte aus Assur; Berlin: Akademie-Verlag).
Eben-Shmuel, J.
1954   *Midreshê Geullah* (Jerusalem).
Edersheim, A.
1885   *Prophecy and History in Relation to the Messiah* (The Warburton Lectures for 1880–84; London: Longmans, Green & Co).
1959   *The Temple* (London: James Clark).
Eichrodt, W.
1970   *Ezekiel* (2 vols.; London: SCM Press).
Eisenmann, R., and M. Wise
1992   *The Dead Sea Scrolls Uncovered* (Longmead, Dorset: Element).
Eisenstein, J.D.
1915   *Ozar Midrashim* (2 vols; New York: Eisenstein).
Elbogen, I.
1931   *Der jüdische Gottesdienst in seiner geschichtlichen Entwicklung* (Grundriss der Gesamtwissenschaft des Judentums; Frankfurt am Main).
Emerton, J.A.
1958   'The Origin of the Son of Man Imagery', *JTS* 9: 225-42.
1968   'The Syntactical Problem of Ps 45.7', *JSS* 13: 58-63.
Engnell, I.
1943   *Studies in Divine Kingship in the Ancient Near East* (Uppsala: Almqvist & Wiksells).
Epiphanius of Salamis
315–403   *Works* (ed. K. Holl; GCS; 3 vols.; Akademie-Verlag: Berlin).
Epstein, I. (ed.)
1935–52   *The Babylonian Talmud* (29 vols.; Hindhead, Surrey: Soncino).
Eshel, E., and M. Kister
1992   'A Polemical Qumran Fragment', *JJS* 43: 277-81.

Esterson, S.I.
1935   *The Commentary of Rabbi David Kimhi on Psalms (42–72)* (Baltimore: The John Hopkins University Press).
Ewald, H.
1840   *Commentary on the Prophets of the Old Testament* (trans. J.F. Smith; 5 vols.; Edinburgh: Williams & Norgate, 1875–80).
1866   *Commentary on the Psalms* (trans. E. Johnson; 2 vols.; Edinburgh and London: Williams & Norgate, 1880).
1899   *Psalmen* (Leipzig and Tübingen: Mohr).
Faulkner, R.O.
1969   *The Ancient Egyptian Pyramid Texts* (Oxford: Oxford University Press).
1985   *The Ancient Egyptian Book of the Dead* (ed. C. Andrews; London: British Museum).
Feliks, J.
1971   'Flowers', *EncJud*: VI, 1364-68.
Fillion, L.C.
1893   *Les Psaumes* (Paris: Letouzey et Ané).
Finkelstein, L. (ed.)
1969   *Sifre Debarîm* (New York: Jewish Theological Seminary of America).
Fisch, S.
1950   *Ezekiel* (Soncino Books of the Bible; Hindhead, Surrey: Soncino).
Fitzmyer, J.A.
1990   *The Dead Sea Scrolls: Major Publications and Tools for Study* (SBLRBS, 20; Atlanta: Scholars Press).
1992   *Responses to 101 Questions on the Dead Sea Scrolls* (New York: Paulist Press).
Flint, P.W.
1994   'The Psalms Scrolls from the Judaean Desert: Relationships and Textual Affiliations', in G.J. Brooke (ed.), *New Qumran Texts and Studies: Proceedings of the First Meeting of the International Organization for Qumran Studies, Paris 1992* (Leiden: Brill): 31-52.
Forbes, J.
1888   *Studies on the Book of Psalms* (Edinburgh: T. & T. Clark).
Frankel, Z.
1851   *Über den Einfluss der pal. Exegese auf die alex. Hermeneutik* (Leipzig).
Freedman, D.N.
1976   'The Twenty-third Psalm', in *Michigan Oriental Studies in Honor of George C. Cameron* (ed. Orlin; Ann Arbor: University of Michigan Press): 139-66.
Freedman, H., and M. Simon (eds.)
1939   *The Midrash (Rabbah)* (10 vols.; Hindhead, Surrey: Soncino).
Friedlander, G. (ed.)
1916   *Pirqe de Rabbi Eliezer* (London: K. Paul Trench, Trubner; New York: Bloch).
Friedlieb, J.H. (ed.)
1852   *Oracula Sibyllina* (Leipzig: Weigel).

Friedmann, M.
1880   *Pesikta Rabbati* (Vienna).
Frye, N.
1992   *The Great Code: The Bible and Literature* (London: Routledge & Kegan Paul).
Füglister, N.
1992   'Die Verwendung des Psalters zur Zeit Jesu: Der Psalter als Lehr- und Lebensbuch', *BK* 47: 200-208.
Garsiel, M.
1991a   *Biblical Names: A Literary Study of Midrashic Derivations and Puns* (Ramat Gan: Bar-Ilan University Press).
1991b   'Puns upon Names as a Literary Device in 1 Kings 1–2', *Bib* 72: 379-86.
Gaster, T.H.
1955   'Psalm 45', *JBL* 74: 239-51.
1969   *Myth, Legend, and Custom in the Old Testament* (London: Duckworth).
Geerard, M., and Glorie, F. (eds.)
1974–87   *Clavis Patrum Graecorum* (CCSG; 5 vols.; Turnhout: Brepols).
Gelston, A.
1984   'A Note on Psalm LXXIV.8', *VT* 34: 82-87.
Gese, H.
1974   *Vom Sinai zum Zion* (BEvT, 64; Munich: chr. Kaiser Verlag).
1981   *Essays on Biblical Theology* (trans. K. Crim; Minneapolis: Augsburg).
Gesenius, W.
1978   *Hebrew-Chaldee Lexicon to the Old Testament* (trans. and ed. S.P. Tregelles; Grand Rapids: Eerdmans, 13th edn).
Gibson, J.C.L.
1978   *Canaanite Myths and Legends* (Edinburgh: T. & T. Clark).
Ginsburg, C.D.
1897   *Introduction to the Massoretico-Critical Edition of the Hebrew Bible* (New York: Ktav, 1966; photolithographic copy of the London edn. of 1897).
Ginzberg, L.
1914   'Eine unbekannte jüdische Sekte', *Monatschrift für Geschichte und Wissenschaft des Judentums* 58: 159-77, 395-429.
Glück, J.J.
1970   'Paronomasia in Biblical Literature,' *Sem* 1: 50-78.
Golb, N.
1980   'The Problem of Origin and Identification of the Dead Sea Scrolls', *Proceedings of the American Philosophical Society* 124: 1-24.
Goldingay, J.E.
1989   *Daniel* (WBC, 30; Dallas, TX: Word Books).
Goldwurm, H. (ed.)
1990-   *Talmud Bavli* (Artscroll Series; Brooklyn, NY: Mesorah).
Goossens, E.
1950   'Onias le Juste, le Messie de la Nouvelle Alliance, lapidé à Jérusalem en 65 av. J.-C.', *La Nouvelle Clio* 7: 336-53.

Gordon, C.H.
1949   *Ugaritic Literature* (Rome: Pontificium Institutum Biblicum).
Goshen-Gottstein, M.H.
1966   'The Psalms Scroll (11QPsᵃ). A Problem of Canon and Text', *Textus* 5: 22-33.
Gottlieb, H.
1987   'Das kultische Leiden des Königs: Zu den Klageliedern 3,1', *SJOT* 2: 121-26.
Goulder, M.D.
1975   'The Fourth Book of the Psalter', *JTS* 26: 269-89.
1982   *The Psalms of the Sons of Korah* (JSOTSup, 20; Sheffield: JSOT Press).
1990   *The Prayers of David (Psalms 51–72)* (Sheffield: Sheffield Academic Press).
Gowan, D.E.
1986   *Eschatology in the Old Testament* (Philadelphia: Fortress Press, 1986; Edinburgh: T. & T. Clark, 1987).
Graetz, H.
1882   *Kritischer Commentar zu den Psalmen* (2 vols.; Breslau: Schottlaender).
Gray, G.B.
1913   'Psalms of Solomon', in Charles 1913: II, 625-52.
Grayson, A.H., and W.G. Lambert
1964   'Akkadian Prophecies', *JCS* 18.
Greenberg, M.
1983   *Ezekiel 1–20* (AB; Garden City, NY: Doubleday).
Greenstein, E.L., and A. Preminger
1986   *The Hebrew Bible in Literary Criticism* (New York: Ungar).
Gregory of Nyssa
            In Inscriptiones Psalmorum (ed. J. McDonough and P. Alexander; Gregorii Nysseni Opera, 5; Leiden: Brill, 1962).
Gressmann, H.
1905   *Der Ursprung der israelitisch-jüdischen Eschatologie* (Göttingen: Vandenhoeck & Ruprecht).
Griffith, L.
1968   *God in Man's Experience: The Activity of God in the Psalms* (London: Hodder & Stoughton).
Grossberg, D.
1989   *Centripetal and Centrifugal Structures in Biblical Poetry* (SBLMS, 39: Atlanta, GA: Scholars Press).
Grossfeld, B.
1984   'The Translation of Biblical Hebrew פקד in the Targum, Peshitta, Vulgate and Septuagint', *ZAW* 96: 83-101.
Guilding, A.
1952   'Some Obscured Rubrics and Lectionary Allusions in the Psalter', *JTS* NS 3: 41-55.
Guillaume, A.
1938   *Prophecy and Divination among the Hebrews and other Semites* (The Bampton Lectures for 1938; London: Hodder and Stoughton, 1938).

Gunkel, H.
1895   *Schöpfung und Chaos in Urzeit und Endzeit* (Göttingen: Vandenhoeck & Ruprecht).
1926   *Die Psalmen* (Göttingen: Vandenhoeck & Ruprecht).
1930   'The Psalms' (trans. T.H. Horner with introduction by J. Muilenberg; Philadelphia: Fortress Press, 1967).

Gunkel, H., and J. Begrich
1933   *Einleitung in die Psalmen: die Gattungen der religiösen Lyrik Israels* (Göttinger Handkommentar zum AT; Göttingen: Vandenhoeck & Ruprecht).

Habel, N.C.
1972   ' "Yahweh, Maker of Heaven and Earth": A study in tradition criticism', *JBL* 91: 321-37.

Haglund, E.
1984   *Historical Motifs in the Psalms* (Uppsala: Gleerup).

Halevi, Y. *see* Yehudah ha-Levi

Hammer, R.
1986   *Sifre: A Tannaitic Commentary on the Book of Deuteronomy* (Yale Judaica Series, 24: New Haven: Yale University Press).

Handy, L.K.
1990   'Sounds, Words and Meanings in Psalm 82', *JSOT* 47: 51-66.

Hanson, P.D.
1975   *The Dawn of Apocalyptic* (Philadelphia: Fortress Press).

Hanson, P.D. (ed).
1983   *Visionaries and their Apocalypses* (Issues in Religion and Theology 2; Philadelphia: Fortress Press; London: SPCK).

Haran, M.
1993   '11QPs[a] and the Canonical Book of Psalms', in Brettler and Fishbane 1993: 193-201.

Harden, J.M.
1922   *Psalterium Iuxta Hebraeos Hieronymi* (London: SPCK).

Hatch, E. *et al.*
1897   *A Concordance to the Septuagint* (2 vols.; Oxford: Clarendon Press).

Hay, D.
1973   *Glory at the Right Hand: Psalm 110 in Early Christianity* (SBLMS, 18; Nashville: Abingdon Press).

Hayman, A.P.
1976   'Rabbinic Judaism and the Problem of Evil', *SJT* 29: 461-76.

Heinemann, J.
1968   'The Triennial Lectionary Cycle', *JJS* 19: 41-48.
1971   'Amidah', *EncJud*: II, 838-450.
1975   'The Messiah of Ephraim and the Premature Exodus of the Tribe of Ephraim', *HTR* 68: 1-15.

Hengstenberg, E.W.
1839   *Christology of the Old Testament* (trans. R. Keith; 4 vols.; Washington: Morrison).
1845–48   *Commentary on the Psalms* (trans. P. Fairbairn and J. Thompson; Edinburgh: T. & T. Clark).

1857   *Christologie des Alten Testaments* (4 vols.; Berlin, 2nd edn).
Herbert, A.S.
1973   *Isaiah 1–39* (Cambridge New English Bible Commentary; Cambridge: Cambridge University Press).
1975   *Isaiah 40–66* (Cambridge New English Bible Commentary; Cambridge: Cambridge University Press).
Herzog, D.D.J., and D.G.I. Plitt (eds.)
1878   *Real Enzyklopädie für protestantische Theologie und Kirche* (3 vols.; Leipzig).
Hiebert, R.J.V.
1989   *The 'Syrohexaplaric' Psalter* (SBL 70; Cognate Studies, 27; Atlanta: Scholars Press).
Hirsch, S.R.
1960   *The Psalms* (2 vols.; New York: Feldheim).
Hitzig, F.
1863–65   *Die Psalmen* (Leipzig and Heidelberg: C.F. Winter'sche Verlagshandlung).
Hobbs, G.
1971   'An Introduction to the Psalms Commentary of Martin Bucer' (ThD dissertation, Strasbourg).
1984   'How Firm a Foundation: Martin Bucer's Historical Exegesis of the Psalms', *CH* 53: 477-91.
1994   'Martin Bucer and the Englishing of the Psalms: Pseudonymity in the Service of Early English Protestant Piety', in D. Wright (ed.), *Martin Bucer: Reforming Church and Community* (Cambridge: Cambridge University Press): 161-78.
Hollander, H.W., and M. de Jonge
1985   *The Testaments of the Twelve Patriarchs* (Leiden: Brill).
Hooker, M.D.
1967   *The Son of Man in Mark* (London: SPCK).
Hopkins, D.D.
1986   'New Directions in Psalms Research', *St Luke's Journal of Theology* 29: 271-83.
Hopkins, S.A.
1978   *A Miscellany of Literary Pieces from the Cambridge Genizah Collection* (Cambridge University Library Genizah Series, 3; Cambridge: Cambridge Univesity Library).
Horbury, W.
1991   *Templum Amicitiae: Essays on the Second Temple presented to Ernst Bammel* (JSOTSup, 48; Sheffield: JSOT Press).
Horbury, W., and B. McNeil
1981   *Suffering and Martyrdom in the New Testament* (Cambridge: Cambridge University Press).
Horowitz, H.S. (ed.)
1881   *Bêth 'Eqed Agadoth* (Frankfurt am Main).
1917   *Siphre D'be Rab: Fasciculus primus: Siphre ad Numeros adjecto Siphre zutta* (Leipzig).

Hossfeld, F.-L., and E. Zenger
1993   *Die Psalmen: Psalm 1–50* (DNEB, 29; Würzburg: Echter Verlag).

Hossfeld, F.-L., and E. Zenger (eds.)
1994   ' "Wer darf hinaufziehen zum Berg YHWHs?" Zur Redaktions-geschichte und Theologie der Psalmengruppe 15–24', in G. Braulik *et al.* (eds.), *Biblische Theologie und gesellschaftlicher Wandel. Für Norbert Lohfink, S.J.* (Freiburg; Herder): 166-82.

Houk, C.B.
1978   'Psalm 132, Literary Integrity, and Syllable-Word Structures', *JSOT* 6: 41-8.

Howard, D.M.
1986   *The Structure of Psalms 93–100* (Ann Arbor: University Microfilms International).
1989   'Editorial Activity in the Psalter: A State-of-the-Field Survey', *Word & World* 9: 274-85; updated repr. in McCann: 52-71.
1993   'A Contextual Reading of Psalms 90–94', in McCann 1993: 108-23.

Hultgård, A.
1980   'The Ideal "Levite", the Davidic Messiah and the Saviour Priest in the Testaments of the Twelve Patriarchs,' in G.W.E. Nickelsburg and J.J. Collins (eds.), *Ideal Figures in Ancient Judaism* (LXX and Cognate Studies, 12; Chico, CA: Scholars Press).

Humbert, P.
1946   *La 'Terou'a': Analyse d'un rite biblique* (Neuchatel: Université de Neuchatel).

Hupfeld, H.
1855   *Die Psalmen* (Gotha: Perthes).

Huwiler, E.F.
1987   'Patterns and Problems in Psalm 132', in K. Hoglund *et al.* (eds.), *The Listening Heart* (JSOTSup, 58; Sheffield: JSOT Press): 199-215.

Hyatt, J.P.
1962   'Zephaniah', in M. Black and H.H. Rowley, *Peake's Commentary on the Bible* (Wokingham, England: Von Nostrand Reinhold): 640-42.

Hyman, A.
1910   *Sefer Toledot Tana'im ve-Amora'im* (London: Hekspress).

Hyman, A.
1971   'Maimonides: Philosophy', *EncJud*: XI, 768-77.

Ibn Ezra, Abraham
1988   *Commentary on Hosea* (ed. and trans. A. Lipshitz; New York: Sepher-Hermon).

Ibn-Shmuel, Y. *see* Eben-Shmuel, J.

Illman, K.-J.
1976   *Thema und Tradition in den Asaf-Psalmen* (Meddelanden Fran Stiftelsens För Åbo Akademi Forskningsinstitut, 13; Åbo: Research Institute of the Åbo Akademi Foundation).

Irsigler, H.
1987   ' "Umsonst ist es, daß ihr früh aufsteh": Psalm 127 und die Kritik der Arbeit in Israels Weisheitsliteratur', *Biblische Notizen* 37: 48-72.

Isaac, E.
1983   'I Enoch', in Charlesworth 1983–85: I, 5-89.

Ishida, T.
1977   *The Royal Dynasties in Ancient Israel: A Study on the Formation and Development of Royal-Dynastic Ideology* (BZAW, 142; Berlin: de Gruyter).

Jacobs, L.
1991   *Structure and Form in the Babylonian Talmud* (Cambridge: University Press).

Jastrow, M.
1950   *A Dictionary of the Targumim, the Talmud Bavli and Yerushalmi, and the Midrashic Literature* (2 vols.; New York: Pardes Publishing House).

Jellinek, A.
1853–77   *Bet ha-Midrash* (6 vols.; Leipzig; Photog. repr. Jerusalem: Wahrmann, 1967).

Jeremias, J.
1965   *Theophanie. Die Geschichte einer alttestamentlichen Gattung* (Neukirchen–Vluyn: Neukirchener Verlag).

Jevons, F.B.
1914   *An Introduction to the History of Religion* (London: Methuen).

Johnson, A.R.
1942   *The One and the Many in the Israelite Conception of God* (Cardiff: University of Wales Press).
1979   *The Cultic Prophet and Israel's Psalmody* (Cardiff: University of Wales Press).

de Jonge, M.
1964   *Testamenta XII Patriarcharum* (Leiden: Brill).

de Jonge, M., and A.S. van der Woude
1966   '11QMelchizedek and the New Testament', *NTS* 12: 301-26.

Josephus, Flavius
            Works (ed. H.StJ. Thackeray, R. Marcus, A. Wikgren and L.H. Feldman; Loeb Classical Library; 9 vols.; London: Heinemann, 1963–65).

Juel, D.
1988   *Messianic Exegesis: Christological Interpretation of the Old Testament in Early Christianity* (Philadelphia: Fortress Press).

Justin Martyr
            Writings (trans. T.B. Falls; Washington, DC: The Catholic University of America in association with Consortium Books, 1948).

Kaiser, O.
1959   *Die mythische Bedeutung des Meeres in Ägypten, Ugarit und Israel* (BZAW, 78; Berlin: A. Töpelmann, 2nd edn).

Katz, M.J.
1988   *Night Tales of the Shammas* (Northvale, NJ: Aronson).

Kee, H.C.
1983   'The Testaments of the Twelve Patriarchs', in Charlesworth (ed.) 1983–85: I, 777-78.

Keel, O.
1978   *The Symbolism of the Biblical World* (London: SPCK).
Keet, C.C.
1969   *A Study of the Psalms of Ascents* (London: Mitre Press).
Kessler, W.
1889   'Die asaphitische Psalmengruppe im Beziehung auf mackabäische Lieder untersucht' (doctoral dissertation: Königlichen Universität Halle-Wittenberg; Halle an der Saale: Buchdruckerei des Waisenhauses).
Kidner, D.
1975   *Psalms 73–150* (TOTC; 2 vols.; Leicester: Inter-Varsity Press).
Kimhi, D.
1883   *Commentary on Psalms 1–41* (ed. S.M. Schiller-Szinessy; Cambridge: Deighton, Bell).
1935   *Commentary on Psalms 42–72* (ed. S.I. Esterson; Baltimore: The John Hopkins University Press).
1973   *The Commentary of Rabbi David Kimhi on Psalms CXX–CL* (ed. and trans. J. Baker and E.W. Nicholson; Cambridge: Cambridge University Press).
King, E.G.
1882   *The Yalkut on Zechariah* (Cambridge: Deighton, Bell).
1890   *The 'Asaph' Psalms in their Connexion with the Early Religion of Babylonia* (The Hulsean Lectures for 1889; Cambridge: Deighton, Bell).
1898–1905 *The Psalms* (3 vols.; Cambridge: Deighton, Bell).
Kippenberg, H.G.
1971   *Garizim und Synagoge: Traditionsgeschichtliche Untersuchungen zur samaritanischen Religion der aramäischen Periode* (Berlin: de Gruyter).
Kirkpatrick, A.F.
1892   *The Doctrines of the Prophets: The Warburtonian Lectures for 1886–90* (London: MacMillan & Co.).
1902   *The Book of Psalms* (Cambridge: Cambridge University Press).
Kissane, E.J.
1953–54   *The Book of Psalms* (Dublin: Browne & Nolan).
1954   'The Interpretation of Psalm 110', *ITQ* 21: 103-14.
Kister, M., and E. Qimron
1992   'Observations on 4QSecond Ezekiel (4Q385 2-3)' *RevQ* 15: 595-602.
Klausner, J.
1956   *The Messianic Idea in Israel* (London: Allen & Unwin).
Klijn, A.F.J.
1983   '2 Baruch', in Charlesworth (ed.) 1983–85: I, 615-52.
Kloos, C.
1986   *Yhwh's Combat with the Sea* (Leiden: Brill).
Knibb, M.
1990   'The Teacher of Righteousness—A Messianic Title?', in P.R. Davies and R.T. White (eds.), *A Tribute to Geza Vermes: Essays on Jewish and*

Christian Literature and History (JSOTSup, 100; Sheffield: JSOT Press): 51-65.

Kopfstein, M.
1881   *Die Asaph-Psalmen historisch-kritisch untersucht* (Marburg: Ehrhardt).

Krašovec, J.
1984   *Antithetic Structure in Biblical Hebrew Poetry* (Leiden: Brill).

Kraus, H.-J.
1966   *Worship in Israel* (Richmond: John Knox Press).
1978   *Psalms* (trans. H.C. Oswald; 2 vols.; Minneapolis: Augsburg, 1988).

Kselman, J.S.
1982   ' "Why Have You Abandoned Me?" A Rhetorical Study of Psalm 22', in D.J.A. Clines, D.M. Gunn and A.J. Hauser (eds.), *Art and Meaning: Rhetoric in Biblical Literature* (Sheffield: JSOT Press).

Kugel, J.L.
1981   *The Idea of Biblical Poetry, Parallelism and its History* (New Haven: Yale University Press).

Kuhn, K.G. (ed.)
1960   *Konkordanz zu den Qumrantexten* (Göttingen: Vandenhoeck & Ruprecht).

Kuhnigk, W.
1974   *Nordwestsemitische Studien zum Hoseabuch* (Rome: Biblical Institute Press).

Kuntz, J.K.
1986   'King Triumphant: A Rhetorical Study of Psalms 20–21', *HAR* 10: 157-76.

Kurfess, A-M.
1951   *Sybillinische Weissagungen* (Munich: Heimeran).

Kutscher, E. Y.
1982   *A History of the Hebrew Language* (Jerusalem: Magnes).

Laato, A.
1992   *Josiah and David Redivivus* (ConBOT, 33; Stockholm: Almqvist & Wiksell).
1992   'Psalm 132 and the Development of the Jerusalemite/Israelite Royal Ideology,' *CBQ* 54: 49-66.

Lacocque, A.
1976   *Le Livre de Daniel* (Commentaire de l'Ancien Testament, 15b; Neuchatel, Paris: Delachaux et Niestlé).

Lagarde, P.A. de
1858a   *Analecta Syriaca* (Leipzig: Teubner).
1858b   *Hippolytus Romanus* (Leipzig: Teubner; London: Williams & Norgate).
1879–80 *Orientalia* (Osnabrück: Otto Zeller Verlag, 1973).

Lamarche, P.
1961   *Zacharie IX–XIV: Structure, Litteraire, et Messianisme* (Paris: Gabalda).

Landmann, L.
1979   *Messianism in the Talmudic Era* (New York: Ktav).

Langdon, S.
1912   *Die neubabylonischen Königsinschriften* (Vorderasiatische Bibliothek,
            4; Leipzig: Hinrichs).
Larkin, K.J.A.
1994   *The Eschatology of Second Zechariah: A Study of the Formation of a
            Mantological Wisdom Anthology* (Kampen, The Netherlands: Kok
            Pharos).
Lauterbach, J.Z.
1933   *Mekilta de-Rabbi Ishamel* (3 vols.; Philadelphia: The Jewish Pub-
            lication Society of America).
Layton, S.C.
1990   'The Steward in Ancient Israel: A Study of Hebrew (*'ašer*) *'al-
            habbayit* in its Near Eastern Setting', *JBL* 109: 633-49.
Leiman, S.Z.
1968   'Abarbanel and the Censor', *JJS* 19: 49-61.
1976   *The Canonization of Hebrew Scripture* (Transactions of the American
            Academy of Arts and Sciences, 47; Hamden, CT: Anchor).
Leonitius, J.
1650   *Libellus effigiei templi Salomonis* (Amsterdam).
Levey, S.H.
1974   *The Messiah: An Aramaic Interpretation. The Messianic Exegesis of
            the Targum* (Hebrew Union College Monograph, 2; New York:
            Hebrew Union College).
Lévi, I.
1904   *The Hebrew Text of Ecclesiasticus* (Leiden: Brill).
1914-20   'L'apocalypse de Zorobabel et le roi de Perse Siroès', *REJ* 68 (1914):
            129-60; 69 (1919): 108-21; 71 (1920): 57-65.
Lewis, C.S.
1961   *Reflections on the Psalms* (Glasgow: Collins, 1979).
Liddell and Scott
1879   *Greek-English Lexicon* (abr. edn; Oxford: Clarendon Press).
Liebreich, L.J.
1955   'The Songs of Ascents and the Priestly Blessing', *JBL* 74: 33-36.
Lim, T.H.
1993   'The 'Psalms of Joshua' (4Q379 fr. 22 col. 2): A Reconsideration of
            its Text', *JJS* 44: 309-312.
Lindsey, H., and C.C. Carlson
1970   *The Late Great Planet Earth* (London: Lakeland).
Lipiński, E.
1965   *La royauté de Yahwé dans la poésie et le culte de l'ancien Israël*
            (Brussels: Paleis der Academiën).
Liver, J.
1959   'The Doctrine of the Two Messiahs in Sectarian Literature in the Time
            of the Second Commonwealth', *HTR* 52: 149-185.
Lohfink, N.
1992a   'Der Psalter und die christliche Meditation: Die Bedeutung der
            Endredaktion für das Verständnis des Psalters', *BK* 47: 195-200.

1992b   'Die Bedeutung der Endredaktion für das Verständnis des Psalters,' in
         Wafs Kanko-Kai (ed.), כי לא על לחם לבדו יחיה האדם כי על כל מוצא
         פי יהוה יחיה האדם (Festschrift Karl H. Walkenhorst; Tokyo: Lithon,
         1992): 63-84.
1992c   'Psalmengebet und Psalterredaktion', *Archiv für Liturgiewissenschaft*
         34: 1-22.

Lohse, E.
1964   *Die Texte aus Qumran* (Munich: Kösel).

Lommatzsch, C.H.E.
1831–48 *Origenis Opera Omnia* (25 vols.; Berlin).

Luther, M.
1883–1987 *Luthers Werke* (63 vols; Weimar: Böhlau).
1965   *Luther's Psalmen-Auslegung* (ed. E. Mülhaupt; 3 vols.; Göttingen:
         Vandenhoeck & Ruprecht).

McCann, J.C.
1992   'The Psalms as Instruction', *Int* 46: 117-28.
1993   'Books I–III and the Editorial Purpose of the Hebrew Psalter', in
         McCann 1993: 93-107.

McCann, J.C. (ed.)
1993   *The Shape and Shaping of the Psalter* (JSOTSup, 159; Sheffield:
         JSOT Press).

M'Caul, A.
1887   *Rabbi David Kimchi's Commentary upon the Prophecies of Zechariah*
         (London: James Duncan).

MacDonald, J.
1964   *Theology of the Samaritans* (London).

McDonald, W.J. *et al.* (eds.)
1967   *New Catholic Encyclopaedia* (18 vols.; New York: McGraw–Hill).

MacLaren, A.
1893–1904 *The Book of Psalms* (The Expositor's Bible Series; 3 vols.; London:
         Hodder & Stoughton).

MacLaurin, E.C.B
1975   'Joseph and Asaph', *VT* 25: 27-45.

Magonet, J.
1994   *A Rabbi Reads the Psalms* (London: SCM Press).

Maier, J.
1960   *Die Texte vom Toten Meer* (2 vols.; Munich: Ernst Reinhardt).

Maimonides, M.
1963   *The Guide of the Perplexed (Moreh Nevukhim)* (trans. with an intro-
         duction and notes by S. Pines; Chicago: University of Chicago Press).

Mandelbaum, B.
1962   *Pesikta de Rav Kahana* (2 vols.; New York: Jewish Theological
         Seminary of America).

Mandelkern, S.
1937   *Veteris Testamenti Concordiantiae Hebraicae atque Chaldaice* (2 vols.;
         Graz: Akademische Druck- u. Verlaganstalt, repr. 1955).

Mannati, M.
1975   'Les accusations de Psaume L.18-20', *VT* 25: 659-69.

1979   'Les psaumes graduels constituent-ils un genre littéraire distinct à
              l'interieur du psautier biblique?', *Sem* 29: 85-100.
Marmorstein, A.
1927   *The Old Rabbinic Doctrine of God* (2 vols.; Oxford: Oxford Univer-
              sity Press).
Marrs, R.R.
1987   'Psalm 122.3-4: A New Reading', *Bib* 68: 106-109.
1988   'A Cry from the Depths (Ps. 130)', *ZAW* 100: 81-90.
Mason, R.
1973   'The Use of Earlier Biblical Material in Zechariah IX–XIV: A Study
              in Inner Biblical Exegesis' (unpublished PhD thesis, University of
              London).
1977   *The Books of Haggai, Zechariah and Malachi* (CNEBC; Cambridge:
              Cambridge University Press).
Mays, J.L.
1985   'Psalm 29', *Int* 39: 60-64.
1987   'The Place of the Torah-Psalms in the Psalter', *JBL* 106: 3-12.
1991   ' "In a Vision": The Portrayal of the Messiah in the Psalms', *Ex
              Auditu* 7: 1-8.
1993   'The Question of Context in Psalm Interpretation', in McCann 1993:
              14-20.
Meeks, W.E.
1967   *The Prophet-King: Moses Traditions and the Johannine Christology*
              (Leiden: Brill).
Merx, A.
1909   *Der Messias oder Taheb der Samaritaner* (BZAW, 17; Giessen: Töpel-
              mann).
Mettinger, T.
1983   *A Farewell to the Servant Songs: A Critical Examination of an Exe-
              getical Axiom* (trans. F.H. Cryer; Scripta minora Regiae Societatis
              humaniorum litterarum Lundensis, 3; Lund: Gleerup).
Michel, A.
1954   *Le maître de justice d'après les documents de la Mer Morte, la littéra-
              ture apocryphe et rabbinique* (Avignon: Aubanel).
Migne, J.-P.
1844–55   *Patrologia Latina* (221 vols. plus indices and supplements; Paris).
1857–66   *Patrologia Graeca* (161 vols.; Paris).
Milik, J.T.
1966   'Fragment d'une source du Psautier (4QPs 89)', *RB* 73: 94-106.
1972   '*Milki-sedeq* et *Milki-reša*' dans les anciens écrits juifs et chrétiens',
              JJS 23: 95-144.
1976   *The Books of Enoch* (Oxford: Clarendon Press).
Miller, J.M.
1970   'The Korahites of Southern Judah', *CBQ* 32: 58-68.
Miller, P.D., Jr
1986   *Interpreting the Psalms* (Philadelphia: Fortress Press).
1989   'The Psalms as Praise and Poetry', *Hymn* 40: 12-16.
1993   'The Beginning of the Psalter', in McCann 1993: 83-92.

Milne, P.
 1975   'Psalm 23: Echoes of the Exodus', *SR* 4 (1974–75): 237-47.
Mitchell, H.G., J.M.P. Smith and J.A. Bewer
 1912   *A Critical and Exegetical Commentary on Haggai, Zechariah, Malachi, and Jonah* (ICC; Edinburgh: T. & T. Clark).
de Moor, Johannes C.
 1987   *An Anthology of Religious Texts from Ugarit* (Nisaba, 16; Leiden: Brill).
Moore, G.F.
 1927   *Judaism in the First Centuries of the Christian Era* (2 vols.; Cambridge, MA: Harvard University Press).
Morgenstern, J.
 1939   'The Mythological Background of Psalm 82', *HUCA* 14: 29-126.
Morrish, G.
 1897   *A Concordance of the Septuagint* (Grand Rapids: Zondervan, 1991).
Mosca, P.G.
 1986   'Once Again the Heavenly Witness of Psalm 89:38', *JBL* 105: 27-37.
Mosis, R.
 1992   'Die Mauern Jerusalems: Beobachtungen zu Psalm 51,20f.,' in J. Hausmann and H.-J. Zobel (eds.), *Alttestamentliche Glaube und biblische Theologie: Festschrift für Horst Dietrich Preuß zum 65. Geburtstag* (Stuttgart: Kohlhammer): 201-15.
Mowinckel, S.
 1921–24   *Psalmenstudien* (2 vols.; Amsterdam: Schippers, 1961; photog. repr. of Oslo edn).
 1956   *He that Cometh* (trans. G.W. Anderson; Oxford: Basil Blackwell).
 1962   *The Psalms in Israel's Worship* (2 vols.; trans. D.R. Ap-Thomas; Oxford: Basil Blackwell).
Mullen, E.T.
 1980   *The Divine Council in Canaanite and Early Hebrew Literature* (HSM, 24; Chico, CA: Scholars Press).
Murphy, R.E.
 1980   'The Faith of the Psalmist', *Int* 34: 229-39.
 1993   'Reflections on Contextual Interpretation of the Psalms,' in McCann 1993: 21-28.
Murphy-O'Connor, J.
 1985   'The Damascus Document Revisited', *RB* 92: 239-44.
Murray, R.
 1982   'Prophecy and the Cult', in R. Coggins, A. Phillips and M. Knibb (eds.), *Israel's Prophetic Tradition* (Cambridge: Cambridge University Press): 200-216.
Myers, J.
 1960   *Hosea to Jonah* (London: SCM Press).
Myers, J.M.
 1974   *I and II Esdras: Introduction, Translation and Commentary* (AB, 42; Garden City, NY).

Nasuti, H.P.
1988   *Tradition History and the Psalms of Asaph* (SBLDS, 88; Atlanta: Scholars Press).
Neale, J.M., and R.F. Littledale
1874   *A Commentary on the Psalms: From Primitive and Medieval Writers* (4 vols.; London: Joseph Masters).
Nel, P.
1988   'Psalm 132 and Covenant Theology', in W. Claassen (ed.), *Text and Context: Old Testament and Semitic Studies for F.C. Fensham* (JSOTSup, 48; Sheffield: JSOT Press).
Netanyahu, B.
1953   *Don Isaac Abravanel* (Philadelphia: Jewish Publication Society of America).
Neusner, J.
1970   *A Life of Rabban Yohanan ben Zakkai* (SPB, 6; Leiden: Brill).
1987   *Pesiqta deRab Kahana* (2 vols.; Atlanta: Scholars Press).
Newsom, C.
1988   'The "Psalms of Joshua" from Qumran Cave 4', *JJS* 39: 56-73.
Neyrey, J.H.
1989   ' "I Said: You Are Gods": Psalm 82.6 and John 10', *JBL* 108: 647-63.
Nickelsburg, G.W.E.
1975   *Studies in the Testament of Joseph* (SBLSCS, 5; Missoula, MT: Scholars Press).
Niehoff, M.
1992   *The Figure of Joseph in Post-Biblical Jewish Literature* (Leiden: Brill).
Nolland, J.
1993   *Luke 18.35–24.53* (WBC, 35c; Waco, TX: Word Books).
O'Callaghan, R.T.
1953   'A Note on the Canaanite Background of Psalm 82', *CBQ* 15: 311-14.
Oesterley, W.O.E.
1910   *The Psalms in the Jewish Church* (London: Skeffington).
1912   *Ecclesiasticus* (The Cambridge Bible; Cambridge: Cambridge University Press).
1937   *A Fresh Approach to the Psalms* (International Library of Christian Knowledge; London: Ivor Nicholson and Watson).
1939   *The Psalms* (2 vols.; London: SPCK).
Ogden, G.S., and R.R. Deutsch
1987   *Joel and Malachi: A Promise of Hope—A Call to Obedience* (International Theological Commentary; Grand Rapids: Eerdmans; Edinburgh: Handsel).
Olshausen, J.
1853   *Die Psalmen* (Leipzig: Hirzel).
O'Neill, J.
1979   'The Lamb of God in the Testaments of the Twelve Patriarchs', *JSNT* 2: 2-30.
1991a   'The Man from Heaven: SibOr 5.256-259', *JSP* 9: 87-102.

1991b	'The Desolate House and the New Kingdom of Jerusalem: Jewish Oracles of Ezra in 2 Esdras 1–2', in Horbury 1991: 226-36.
1994a	'What Is Joseph and Aseneth about?', *Henoch* 16: 189-98.
1994b	'The Question of Messianic Expectation in Pseudo-Philo's Biblical Antiquities', *Journal of Higher Criticism* 1: 85-93.

Origen

    Contra Celsum (trans. H. Chadwick; Cambridge: Cambridge University Press, 1965).

    Origenis hexaplorum quae supersunt; sive veterum interpretum graecorum in totum Vetus Testamentum fragmenta (ed. F. Field; 2 vols.; Oxford: Clarendon Press, 1875).

    Origenis Opera Omnia (ed. C.H.E. Lommatzsch; Berlin, 1831–48).

Pardee, D.

1984	'The Semantic Parallelism of Ps 89', in Barrick and Spencer 1984: 121-37.

Person, R.F.

1993	*Second Zechariah and the Deuteronomic School* (JSOTSup, 167; Sheffield: JSOT Press).

Peters, J.P.

1894	'Notes on the Pilgrim Psalter', *JBL* 13: 31-39.
1922	*The Psalms as Liturgies* (The Paddock Lectures for 1920; London: Hodder & Stoughton).

Philo Judaeus

    Works (trans. F.H. Colson *et al.*; LCL; 10 vols.; London: Heinemann, 1929–62).

Pitra, J.B. (ed.)

1876–84	*Analecta Sacra* (4 vols.; Paris: Jouby et Roger).

Pliny

    Naturalis Historia (ed. H. Rackham; 10 vols.; London: Heinemann, 1942).

Ploeg, J.P.M. van der

1965	'Le Psaume XCI dans une Recension de Qumran', *RB* 72: 210-17.
1967	'Fragments d'un manuscrit de Psaumes de Qumran (11QPs[b])', *RB* 74: 408-12 + pl. xviii.
1971	'Un petit rouleau des psaumes apocryphes (11QPsAp[a])', in G. Jeremias *et al.* (eds.), *Tradition und Glaube: Das frühe Christentum in seiner Umwelt: Festgabe für Karl Georg Kuhn zum 65. Geburtstag* (Göttingen: Vanderhoeck & Ruprecht): 128-39.
1985	'Fragments de la grotte XI', *RevQ* 12: 3-15.

Porter, J.R.

1961	'Psalm XLV.7', *JTS* 12: 51-53.
1963	'The Pentateuch and the Triennial Lectionary Cycle: An Examination of a Recent Theory', in F.F. Bruce (ed.), *Promise and Fulfillment* (Festschrift S.H. Hooke; Edinburgh: T. & T. Clark): 163-74.

Preuss, H.D.

1959	'Die Psalmenüberschriften in Targum und Midrash', *ZAW* 71: 44-54.

Prinsloo, W.S.

1985	*The Theology of the Book of Joel* (Berlin: de Gruyter).

1986 'Psalm 131: Nie my wil nie, o Here', *Skrif en Kerk* 7: 74-82.

Pritchard, J.B.

1950-74 *Ancient Near Eastern Texts* (3 vols and supp.; Princeton, NJ: Princeton University Press).

Prothero, R.E.

1903 *The Psalms in Human Life* (London: Thomas Nelson).

Provan, I.W.

1991 *Lamentations* (New Century Bible Commentary; London: Marshall Pickering; Grand Rapids: Eerdmans).

Puech, E.

1990 'Les deux derniers psaumes davidiques du rituel d'exorcisme 11QPsAp^a', in *Forty Years of Research in the Dead Sea Scrolls* (Haifa Congress, 1990).

1992a 'Fragments d'un apocryphe de Lévi et le personnage eschatologique. 4QTestLévi^{c-d}(?) et 4QAJa', in J.T. Barrera and L.V. Montaner, *The Madrid Qumran Congress* (Leiden: Brill): 449-501.

1992b 'Une apocalypse messianique (4Q521)', *RevQ* 15: 475-522.

Purvis, J.D.

1975a 'The Fourth Gospel and the Samaritans', *NovT* 17: 161-98.

1975b 'Joseph in the Samaritan Traditions', in Nickelsburg 1975: 147-53.

Qimron, E.

1992 'Observations on the Reading of "A Text about Joseph" (4Q372,1)', *RevQ* 15: 603-604.

Quasten, J., and A. di Berardino

1950-86 *Patrology* (4 vols.; Westminster, Maryland: Christian Classics).

Raabe, P.R.

1991 'Deliberate Ambiguity in the Psalter', *JBL* 110: 213-27.

Rabin, C.

1954 *The Zadokite Documents* (Oxford: Clarendon Press).

Rabinowitz, L.I.

1936 'Does Midrash Tillim Reflect the Triennial Cycle of Psalms', *JQR*, NS 26: 349-68.

1954 'A Reconsideration of "Damascus" and "390 Years" in the "Damascus" ("Zadokite") Fragments', *JBL* 73: 11-35.

1971a 'God, Name of: In the Talmud', *EncJud*: VII, 684.

1971b 'Ingathering', *EncJud*: VIII, 1373-75.

Rahlfs, A. (ed.)

1935 *Septuaginta* (Stuttgart: Württembergische Bibelanstalt).

Rashi (Rabbi Shlomo b. Isaak)

1934 *Pentateuch with Rashi's Commentary* (eds. and trans. Rosenbaum and Silbermann with Blashki and Joseph; 5 vols.; London: Shapiro, Valentine).

Rehm, M.

1968 *Der königliche Messias im Licht der Immanuel-Weissagungen des Buches Jesaja* (Eichstatter Studien neue Folge, Band 1; Kevelaer: Butzon & Bercker).

Reindl, J.
1981   'Weisheitliche Bearbeitung von Psalmen: Ein Beitrag zum Verständnis
            der Sammlung des Psalter', VTSup, 32: 333-56.
Renaud, B.
1983   'Osée II.2: *'LH MN H'RṢ*: essai d'interprétation', *VT* 33: 495-500.
Rendsburg, G.A.
1990   *Linguistic Evidence for the Northern Origin of Selected Psalms*
            (SBLMS, 43; Atlanta: Scholars Press).
Robertson-Smith, W.
1892   *The Old Testament in the Jewish Church* (London: A. & C. Black).
Robinson, J.A.T.
1960   'The Destination and Purpose of St John's Gospel', *NTS* 6: 117-31.
1976   *Redating the New Testament* (London: SCM).
Rosenthal, E.I.J.
1937   'Don Isaac Abravanel: Financier, Statesman and Scholar, 1437–1937,'
            Studia Semitica (University of Cambridge Oriental Publications, 16;
            Cambridge: Cambridge University Press, 1971): I, 21-54.
1960   'Anti-Christian Polemic in Medieval Bible Commentaries,' *JJS* 11:
            115-35.
Rowley, H.H.
1952   *The Zadokite Fragments and the Dead Sea Scrolls* (Oxford: Basil
            Blackwell).
Rudolph, W.
1976   *Haggai, Sacharja 1–8, Sacharja 9–14, Maleachi* (KAT, 13.4; Güters-
            loh: Gerd Mohn).
Russell, D.S.
1964   *The Method and Message of Jewish Apocalyptic* (OTL; London: SCM
            Press).
1992   *Divine Disclosure: An Introduction to Jewish Apocalyptic* (Minne-
            apolis: Fortress Press).
Ryle, H.E., and M.R. James
1891   *The Psalms of Solomon* (Cambridge: Cambridge University Press).
Sa'adya Gaon
c. 933   *Kitab al-'Amanat wal-I'tiqadat.* I have used two English editions.
1946   A. Altmann (trans. and abbrev.), *The Book of Doctrines and Beliefs*
            (Philosophia Judaica Series; Oxford: Phaidon Press).
1948   S. Rosenblatt (trans.), *The Book of Beliefs and Opinions* (Yale Judaica
            Series, 1; New Haven: Yale University Press).
1966   *Psalms with a Translation and Commentary of the Gaon Rabbenu
            Sa'adya b. Joseph Fayumi* (trans. into Hebrew by J. Kafiḥ; Jerusalem).
Saebo, M.
1969   *Sacharja 9–14; Untersuchungen von Text und Form* (WMANT, 34;
            Neukirchen–Vluyn: Neukirchener Verlag).
Sanders, J.A.
1965   'Pre-Masoretic Psalter Texts', *CBQ* 27: 114-23.
1966   'Variorum in the Psalms Scroll (11QPsᵃ)', *HTU* 59: 83-94.
1967   *The Dead Sea Psalms Scroll* (Ithaca, NY: Cornell University Press).
1972   *Torah and Canon* (Philadelphia: Fortress Press).

1974   'The Qumran Psalms Scroll (11QPsᵃ) Reviewed', in *On Language,
                Culture, and Religion: In Honor of Eugene A. Nida* (The Hague:
                Mouton).

Saperstein. M.
1980   *Decoding the Rabbis: A Thirteenth-Century Commentary on the Agga-
                dah* (Cambridge, MA: Harvard University Press).

Saracino, F.
1982   'Risurrezione in Ben Sira?', *Henoch* 4: 185-203.

Sarna, N.M.
1971   'Psalms, Book of', *EncJud*: XIII, 1304-22.

Sawyer, D.
1993   *Midrash Aleph Beth* (University of South Florida Studies in the
                History of Judaism, 39; Atlanta: Scholars Press).

Sawyer, J.F.A.
1973   'Hebrew Words for the Resurrection of the Dead', *VT* 23: 218-34.
1989   'Daughter of Zion and Servant of the Lord in Isaiah: A Comparison',
                JSOT 44: 89-107.

Schmidt, W.H.
1971   'Kritik am Königtum', in H.W. Wolff (ed.), *Probleme biblischer
                Theologie. G. von Rad zum 70. Geburtstag* (Munich: Kaiser Verlag).

Schökel, Alonso L.
1988   *A Manual of Hebrew Poetics* (Subsidia Biblica, 11; Rome: Pontifical
                Biblical Institute).

Schökel, Alonso L., and A. Strus
1980   'Salmo 122: Canto al nombre de Jerusalén', *Bib* 61: 234-50.

Scholem, G.
1971   'Magen David', *EncJud*: XI, 687-97.

Schreiner, S.
1977   'Psalm 110 und die Investitur des Hohenpriesters', *VT* 27: 216-22.

Schuller, E.
1990   '*4Q372* 1: A Text about Joseph', *RevQ* 14: 349-76.
1992   'The Psalm of 4Q372 1 Within the Context of Second Temple
                Prayer', *CBQ* 54: 67-79.

Schwartz, J.
1993   'Treading the Grapes of Wrath. The Wine Press in Ancient Jewish and
                Christian Tradition', *TZ* 49: 215-28, 311-24.

Scobie, C.H.H.
1966   *John the Baptist* (London: SCM).

Segal, A.F.
1977   *Two Powers in Heaven: Early Rabbinic Reports about Christianity
                and Gnosticism* (Leiden: Brill).

Segal, M.H.
1927   *A Grammar of Mishnaic Hebrew* (Oxford: Clarendon Press).

Segal, M.Z.
1972   *Sefer Ben-Sira ha-Shalem* (Jerusalem: Bialik).

Seidel, H.
1982   'Wallfahrtslieder', in H. Seidel and K. Bieritz (eds.), *Das lebendige Wort. Festgabe für G. Voigt* (Berlin: Evangelische Verlaganstalt): 26-40.

Seybold, K.
1978   *Die Wallfahrtspsalmen* (Neukirchen–Vluyn: Neukirchenei Verlag).
1979   'Die Redaktion der Wallfahrtspsalmen', *ZAW* 91: 247-68.
1990   *Introducing the Psalms* (Edinburgh: T. & T. Clark).

Seybold, K., and E. Zenger (eds.)
1994   *Neue Wege der Psalmenforschung* (Herders biblische Studien, 1: Freiburg: Herder, 1994).

Shenkel, J.D.
1965   'An interpretation of Ps. 93.5', *Bib* 46: 401-16.

Sheppard, G.T.
1980   *Wisdom as a Hermeneutical Construct: A Study in the Sapientalizing of the Old Testament* (New York: de Gruyter).
1992   'Theology and the Book of Psalms', *Int* 46: 143-55.

Shoemaker, H.S.
1988   'Psalm 131', *RevExp* 85: 89-94.

Simon, U.
1991   *Four Approaches to the Book of Psalms: From Saadiah Gaon to Abraham Ibn Ezra* (Albany, NY: State University of New York Press).

Skehan, P.W.
1978   'Qumran and Old Testament Criticism', in Delcor (ed.), 1978: 163-82.

Skehan, P.W., and A.A. Di Lella
1987   *The Wisdom of Ben Sira* (AB, 39; Garden City, NY: Doubleday).

Slotki, I.W.
1949   *Isaiah* (Soncino Books of the Bible; Hindhead, Surrey: Soncino).

Smart, J.D.
1933   'The Eschatological Interpretation of Psalm 24', *JBL* 52: 175-80.

Smith, G.A.
1898   *The Book of the Twelve Prophets* (Expositor's Bible; 2 vols.; London: Hodder & Stoughton).

Smith, L.P., and E.R. Lacheman
1950   'The Authorship of the Book of Zephaniah', *JNES* 9: 137-42.

Smith, M.S.
1992   'The Psalms as a Book for Pilgrims', *Int* 46: 156-66.

Smith, R.L.
1984   *Micah-Malachi* (Waco, TX: Word Books).

Smith, W.R.
1892   *The Old Testament in the Jewish Church* (London: A. & C. Black).

Snaith, J.G.
1974   *Ecclesiasticus* (Cambridge: Cambridge University Press).

Snaith, N.H.
1933   'The Triennial Cycle and the Psalter', *ZAW* 51 NF 10: 302-307.
1951   *Hymns of the Temple* (London: SCM Press).

Sperber, A.
1962   *The Bible in Aramaic* (Leiden: Brill).
Spittler, R.P.
1983   'Testament of Job: A New Translation and Introduction', in Charlesworth 1983–85: I: 829-68.
Sprinkle, J.M.
1989   'Literary Approaches to the Old Testament: A Survey of Recent Scholarship', *JETS* 32: 299-310.
Stankiewicz, E.
1982   'Centripetal and Centrifugal Structures in Poetry', *Semiotica* 38: 217-42.
Starcky, J.
1966   'Psaumes Apocryphes de la Grotte 4 de Qumrân', *RB* 73: 353-71.
Stauffer, E.
1956   'Der gekreuzigte Thoralehrer', in *ZRGG* 3: 250-53.
1957   *Jerusalem und Rom* (Bern: Francke Verlag).
Stemberger, G.
1972   'Das Problem der Auferstehung im Alten Testament', *Kairos* NF 14: 273-90.
Stenning, J.F.
1953   *The Targum of Isaiah* (Oxford: Oxford University Press).
Steudel, A.
1993   אחרית הימים' in the Texts from Qumran', *RevQ* 62: 225-46.
Strack, H.L., and G. Stemberger
1982–92   *Introduction to the Talmud and Midrash* (ET M. Bockmuehl; Minneapolis: Fortress Press, 1992).
Strugnell, J., and D. Dimant
1988   '4Q Second Ezekiel (4Q385)', *RevQ* 13: 45-58.
Stuart, D.
1987   *Hosea–Jonah* (WBC, 31; Waco, TX: Word Books).
Stuhlmueller, C.
1988   *Rebuilding with Hope: A Commentary on the Books of Haggai and Zechariah* (International Theological Commentary; Grand Rapids: Eerdmans).
Talmon, S.
1966   '*Pisqah Be'emsa' Pasuq* and 11QPs^a', *Textus* 5: 11-21.
1993   'Fragments of a Psalms Scroll from Masada, MPs^b (Masada 1103–1742)', in Brettler and Fishbane (eds.) 1993: 318-27.
Tate, M.E.
1990   *Psalms 51–100* (WBC, 20; Waco, TX; Word Books).
1990   'Psalm 88', *RevExp* 87: 91-95.
Telford, W.R.
1980   *The Barren Temple and the Withered Tree: A Redaction-critical Analysis of the Cursing of the Fig-tree Pericope in Mark's Gospel and its Relation to the Cleansing of the Temple Tradition* (JSNTSup, 1; Sheffield: JSOT Press).
1991   'More Fruit from the Withered Tree: Temple and Fig-Tree in Mark from a Graeco-Roman Perspective', in Horbury (ed.) 1991: 264-304.

Tertullianus, Q.S.F.
  1869–70   *The Writings of Tertullian* (ed. A. Roberts and J. Donaldson; Anti-
             Nicene Christian Library; Edinburgh: T. & T. Clark).
  1890   *Tertulliani Opera* (ed. A. Reifferscheid and G. Wissowa; Vienna:
             Tempsky).
Thirtle, J.W.
  1904   *The Titles of the Psalms* (London: Frowdie).
Tiede, D.L.
  1980   'Weeping for Jerusalem', in *Prophecy and History in Luke–Acts*
             (Philadelphia: Fortress Press): 65-96, 143-48.
Tollinton, R.B.
  1929   *Selections from the Commentaries and Homilies of Origen* (London:
             SPCK).
Torrey, C.C.
  1945   *The Apocryphal Literature* (New Haven: Yale University Press).
  1947   'The Messiah Son of Ephraim', *JBL* 66: 253-77.
Tournay, R.J.
  1960   'Le Psaume 110', *RB* 67: 5-41.
  1991   *Seeing and Hearing God with the Psalms* (trans. J.E. Crowley;
             JSOTSup, 118; Sheffield: JSOT Press).
Tov, E.
  1992   *Textual Criticism of the Hebrew Bible* (Minneapolis: Fortress Press).
  1992   'The Unpublished Qumran Texts from Caves 4 and 11', *JJS* 43: 101-
             36.
Townsend, J.T. (trans.)
  1989   *Midrash Tanhuma* (Hoboken, NJ: Ktav): I.
Trebolle Barrera, J., and L. Vegas Montaner (eds.)
  1992   *The Madrid Qumran Congress: Proceedings of the International
             Congress on the Dead Sea Scrolls, Madrid, 18–21 March, 1991*
             (STDJ, 11.1–2; 2 vols.; Leiden: Brill).
Tromp, J.
  1989   'The Text of Psalm 130: 5-6', *VT* 39: 100-103.
Tsevat, M.
  1970   'God and the Gods in Assembly: An Interpretation of Ps 82', *HUCA*
             40–41 (1969–70), 123-37.
Tylor, E.B.
  1924   *Primitive Culture* (New York: Brentano, 7th edn).
Urbach, E.E.
  1975   *The Sages: Their Concepts and Beliefs* (Jerusalem: Magnes).
Ussher, J.
  1650   *Annales Veteris Testamenti* (London).
VanderKam, J.C.
  1994   *The Dead Sea Scrolls Today* (Grand Rapids: Eerdmans; London:
             SPCK).
VanGemeren, W.A.
  1982   'Ps 131.2—*kegamul*. The Problems of Meaning and Metaphor,'
             Hebrew Studies 23: 51-57.

de Vaux, R.
1978   *The Early History of Israel* (Philadelphia: Westminster Press).
Vawter, B., and L.J. Hoppe
1991   *A New Heart: A Commentary on the Book of Ezekiel* (International Theological Commentary; Edinburgh: Handsel; Grand Rapids: Eerdmans).
Vermes, G.
1972   'Hanina ben Dosa' (in two parts), *JJS* 23: 28-50; 24: 51-64.
1973   *Jesus the Jew* (London: Fontana/Collins).
1987   *The Dead Sea Scrolls in English* (Harmondsworth: Penguin Books, 3rd edn).
1992   'The Oxford Forum for Qumran Research: Seminar on the Rule of War from Cave 4 (4Q285)', *JJS* 43: 85-94.
1992   'Qumran Forum Miscellanea I', *JJS* 43: 299-305.
Vermeylen, J.
1992   'Une prière pour le renouveau du Jérusalem. Le Psaume 51', *ETL* 68: 257-83.
Viviers, H.
1992   'Trust and Lament in the *ma'alot* Psalms (Psalms 120–134)', *OTE* 5: 64-77.
1994   'The Coherence of the *ma'ᵃlôt* Psalms (Pss 120–134)', *ZAW* 106: 275-89.
Vosté, J.-M.
1944   'Sur les titres des Psaumes dans la Pešitta,' *Bib* 25: 210-35.
Wahl, H.-M.
1992   'Psalm 67. Erwägungen zu Aufbau, Gattung und Datierung', *Bib* 73: 240-47.
Wal, A.J.O. van der
1988   'The structure of Ps 129', *VT* 38: 364-67.
Waltke, B.K., and M. O'Connor
1990   *An Introduction to Biblical Hebrew Syntax* (Winona Lake, IN: Eisenbrauns).
Walton, J.H.
1991   'Psalms: A Cantata about the Davidic Covenant', *JETS* 34: 21-31.
Wanke, G.
1966   *Die Zionstheologie der Korachiten in ihrem traditionsgeschichtlichen Zusammenhang* (BZAW, 97; Berlin: Töpelmann).
Watson, W.G.E.
1984   *Classical Hebrew Poetry: A Guide to its Techniques* (JSOTSup, 26; Sheffield: JSOT Press).
Watts, J.D.W.
1965   'YHWH-Malak Psalms', *TZ* 21: 341-48.
1975   *The Books of Joel, Obadiah, Jonah, Nahum, Habakkuk and Zephaniah* (CNEBC; Cambridge: Cambridge University Press).
1987   *Isaiah 34–66* (WBC, 25; Waco, TX; Word Books).
Weir, C.J.M.
1934   *A Lexicon of Accadian Prayers in the Rituals of Expiation* (London: Oxford University Press).

Weiser, A.
1959–62   *The Psalms* (trans. H. Hartwell; OTL; London: SCM Press.

Weitzman, M.P.
1982   'The Origin of the Peshitta Psalter', in J.A. Emerton and S.C. Reif
             (eds.), *Interpreting the Hebrew Bible: Essays in Honour of E.I.J.
             Rosenthal* (Cambridge: Cambridge University Press).
1985   'The Peshitta Psalter and its Hebrew *Vorlage*', *VT* 35: 341-54.

Welch, A.C.
1926   *The Psalter in Life, Worship and History* (Oxford: Oxford University
             Press).

Wellhausen, J.
1895   *The Book of Psalms...printed in colors* (ET J.D. Prince; *The Sacred
             Books of the Old Testament*, 14; Leipzig: Hinrichs).

Wertheimer, S.A.
1952–55   *Batei Midrashot* (2 vols.; Jerusalem: Ktab wa-Sepher).

Westermann, C.
1981   'The Formation of the Psalter', in *Praise and Lament in the Psalms*
             (trans. K.R. Crim and R.N. Soulen; Atlanta: John Knox, 1981): 250-
             58.
1989   *The Living Psalms* (trans. J.R. Porter; Edinburgh: T. & T. Clark).

de Wette W.M.L.
1811   *Commentar über die Psalmen* (ed. Gustav Baur, 1856; Heidelberg:
             Mohr, 5th edn).

Wevers, J.W.
1969   *Ezekiel* (NCB; London: Nelson).

Whitley, C.F.
1973   'Psalm 99.8', *ZAW* 85: 227-30.

Whybray, R.N.
1969   ' "Their Wrongdoings" in Psalm 99:8', *ZAW* 81: 237-39.

Widengren, G.
1977   'Yahweh's Gathering of the Dispersed', in Barrick and Spencer 1984:
             227-45.

Widyapranawa, S.H.
1990   *Isaiah 1–39: The Lord Is Saviour: Faith in National Crisis* (Inter-
             national Theological Commentary; Grand Rapids: Eerdmans; Edin-
             burgh: Handsel).

Wiesenberg, E.
1952   'The Nicanor Gate', *JJS* 3: 14-29.

Willems, G.F.
1990   'Les Psaumes dans la liturgie juive', *BTFT* 51: 397-417.

Williams, D.L.
1963   'The Date of Zephaniah', *JBL* 82: 77-88.

Willis, J.T.
1979   'Psalm 1—An Entity', *ZAW* 9: 381-401.
1990a   'A Cry of Defiance—Psalm 2', *JSOT* 47: 33-50.
1990b   'An Attempt to Decipher Psalm 121.1b', *CBQ* 52: 241-51.

Willis, T.M.
1991   '"So Great Is his Steadfast Love": A Rhetorical Analysis of Psalm
            103', *Bib* 72: 525-37.
Wilson, G.H.
1984   'Evidence of Editorial Divisions in the Hebrew Psalter', *VT* 34: 337-
            52.
1985a   *The Editing of the Hebrew Psalter* (SBLDS, 76; Chico, CA: Scholars
            Press).
1985b   'The Qumran Psalms Scroll Reconsidered: Analysis of the Debate',
            CBQ 47: 624-42.
1986   'The Use of Royal Psalms at the "Seams" of the Hebrew Psalter',
            JSOT 35: 85-94.
1992   'The Shape of the Book of Psalms', *Int* 46: 129-42.
1993a   'Shaping the Psalter: A Consideration of Editorial Linkage in the
            Book of Psalms', in McCann 1993: 72-82.
1993b   'Understanding the Purposeful Arrangement of Psalms in the Psalter:
            Pitfalls and Promise', in McCann 1993: 42-51.
Winter, J., and A. Wünsche (eds.)
1909   *Mechilta* (Leipzig: Hinrichs).
Wolff, H.W.
1942   *Jesaja 53 in Urchristentum* (Berlin: Evangelische Verlagsanstalt).
1977   *Joel and Amos* (trans. W. Janzen; Hermeneia Series; Philadelphia:
            Fortress Press).
Wolfson, H.A.
1948   *Philo: Foundations of Religious Philosophy in Judaism, Christianity
            and Islam* (2 vols.; Cambridge, MA: Harvard University Press, 2nd
            edn).
Wolkstein, D., and S.N. Kramer
1983   *Inanna Queen of Heaven and Earth* (London: Rider).
van der Woude, A.S.
1957   'Die messianischen Vorstellungen der Testamente der Zwölf Patriar-
            chen', in *Die messianischen Vorstellungen der Gemeinde von Qumran*
            (Assen: Van Gorcum).
1965   'Melchisedek als himmlische Erlösergestalt in den neugefundenen
            eschatologischen Midraschim aus Qumran Höhle XI', *OIS* 14: 354-
            73.
Wright, B.G.
1989   *No Small Difference: Sirach's Relationship to its Parent Hebrew Text*
            (SBLSCS, 26; Atlanta: Scholars Press).
Wright, R.B.
1985   'Psalms of Solomon', in Charlesworth (ed.) 1983-85: II, 639-70.
Wünsche, A.
1870   *Die Leiden des Messias* (Leipzig).
1885   *Bibliotheca Rabbinica* (3 vols.; Leipzig: Schulze).
Yadin, Y.
1965   'The Excavation of Masada—1963/4: Preliminary Report', *IEJ* 15:
            1-120.

Yehuda ha-Levi
  1947   *Kuzari: The Book of Proof and Argument,* (ed. and trans. I. Heine-
                mann; Philosophica Judaica Series, 14; Oxford: East and West).
Zimmerli, W.
  1972   'Zwillingspsalmen', in J. Schreiner (ed.), *Wort, Lied, und Gottesspruch:
                Beiträge zu Psalmen und Propheten* (Würzburg: Echter Verlag): 105-
                13.
Zimmerli, W., and J. Jeremias
  1965   *The Servant of God* (London: SCM Press).

INDEXES

INDEX OF REFERENCES

OLD TESTAMENT

OTHER ANCIENT SOURCES

INDEX OF AUTHORS

Wette, W.M.L. de 41, 43, 44, 66, 67, 69
Whybray, R.N. 290
Widengren, G. 128, 129, 133-35, 274
Widyapranawa, S.H. 157, 192
Williams, D.L. 154
Willis, J.T. 73, 245
Wilson, G.H. 61-63, 73-75, 78-82, 88,
    244, 267, 273-75, 291, 298, 301-
    303

Wise, M. 231
Wolff, H.W. 149, 207
Wolfson, H.A. 180
Woude, A.S. van der 26, 229, 259
Wyatt, N. 9

Zenger, E. 88
Zimmerli, W. 56